CURRENT ISSUES AND ENDURING QUESTIONS

Methods and Models of Argument

Second Edition

EDITED BY

SYLVAN BARNET
Professor of English, Tufts University

HUGO BEDAU
Professor of Philosophy, Tufts University

Bedford Books *of* St. Martin's Press

BOSTON

For Bedford Books

Publisher: Charles H. Christensen
Associate Publisher: Joan E. Feinberg
Managing Editor: Elizabeth M. Schaaf
Developmental Editor: Stephen A. Scipione
Production Editor: Tara L. Masih
Copyeditor: Cynthia Insolio Benn
Text and Cover Design: Sally Cole Carson
Cover Photo: © 1989 Bruce T. Martin

Manufactured in the United States of America.
4   3   2   1   0
f   e   d

For information, write: St. Martin's Press, Inc.
175 Fifth Avenue, New York, NY 10010

Editorial Offices: Bedford Books of St. Martin's Press
29 Winchester Street, Boston, MA 02116

ISBN: 0–312–02851–2

Acknowledgments

Gar Alperovitz, "The U.S. Was Wrong." *The New York Times*, August 4, 1985. Copyright © 1985 by The New York Times Company. Reprinted by permission.

Teresa Amott and Julie Matthaei, "Comparable Worth, Incomparable Pay." *Radical America* 18:5, 1984. © 1984 *Radical America*.

Benjamin Barber, "The Philosopher Despot." Copyright © 1987 by *Harper's Magazine*. All rights reserved. Reprinted from the Jan. 1988 issue by special permission.

Griffin B. Bell, et al., "For a One-Term, Six-Year Presidency." *The New York Times*, December 31, 1985. Copyright © 1985 by The New York Times Company. Reprinted by permission.

Vivian Berger, "Rolling the Dice to Decide Who Dies." Reprinted with permission, New York State Bar Association. Copyright © 1988.

Allan Bloom, "Our Listless Universities." © National Review, Inc., 150 East 35 Street, New York, NY 10016. Reprinted by permission.

Susan Brownmiller, "Let's Put Pornography Back in the Closet." Originally appeared in *Newsday*, 1979. Reprinted by permission of Susan Brownmiller.

David Bruck, "The Death Penalty." *The New Republic*, May 20, 1985. Reprinted by permission of *The New Republic*, © 1985, The New Republic, Inc.

Italo Calvino, "Why Read the Classics?" From *The Uses of Literature* by Italo Calvino, copyright © 1982, 1980 by Giulio Einaudi editore s.p.a, Torino, English translation copyright © 1986 by Harcourt Brace Jovanovich, Inc., reprinted by permission of Harcourt Brace Jovanovich, Inc. and Mrs. Esther Calvino.

Carol P. Christ, "Why Women Need the Goddess: Phenomenological, Psychological, and Political Reflections." From *Womanspirit Rising* edited by Carol P. Christ and Judith Plaskow. Copyright © 1979 by Carol P. Christ and Judith Plaskow. Reprinted by permission of Harper & Row, Publishers, Inc.

C. A. J. Coady, "Defending Human Chauvinism." From *QQ: Report from the Center for Philosophy and Public Policy*, Fall 1986, pp. 12–14. Reprinted by permission.

Acknowledgments and copyrights are continued at the back of the book on pages 742–743, which constitute an extension of the copyright page.

Preface

Myself when young did eagerly frequent
Doctor and Saint, and heard great argument
*   About it and about; but evermore*
Came out by the same door where in I went.

—*The Rubáiyát of Omar Khayyám*

We all know Omar's feeling. In a more whimsical mood we may recall the story of the divorce case in which the husband's lawyer presented his side, and the judge said, "You're right." The wife's lawyer then presented her side, and the judge said, "You're right." A third lawyer objected: "Your Honor, they can't both be right." And the judge said, "You're right, too."

One often says that every question has two sides (does the speaker really mean "your side" and "the right side"?), but in fact a question may have three, or four, or more sides. A reader of Chapters 5 and 6, in which we present ten pairs of sharply opposed views, sometimes may well sense that the truth lies neither wholly on one side nor on the other. Later chapters, with several essays on one topic, make even more abundantly clear something of the range of responses one may have to a complex problem. This is not to say, however, that there is never a right view, nor is it to say that we can always settle a disagreement by compromise. On some issues—for instance, capital punishment—one can scarcely have it both ways, but at least one can see that whichever position one opts for, the other side may still have some merit.

In Part One (Chapters 1–4) we offer a short course in methods of thinking about arguments and in methods of writing arguments. By this we do not mean gimmicks, such as the notorious note a politician stuck in the margin of the text of his speech: Argument weak; shout here. Such gimmicks, however disreputable, can, of course, be highly effective for some audiences. For a delightfully wry account of their use, we recommend that you consult "The Art of Controversy," in *The Will to Live*, by the nineteenth-century German philosopher Arthur Schopenhauer.

Schopenhauer reminds his reader that a Greek or Latin quotation (however irrelevant) can be impressive to the uninformed, and that one can win almost any argument by loftily saying, "That's all very well in theory, but it won't do in practice."

We do not offer instruction in this sort of one-upmanship. Rather, we discuss responsible ways of arguing persuasively. We know, however, that before one can write a persuasive argument one must clarify one's own ideas—and that includes arguing with oneself—in order to find out what one really thinks about a problem. Therefore we devote the first four chapters to techniques of developing ideas for oneself, as well as to ways of putting these ideas onto paper for readers. These four introductory chapters are not all lecturing: they include sixteen arguments (some by students) for analysis.

All of the essays in the book are accompanied by questions. These questions are devoted not only to what can roughly be called the "content" of the essays but also to what can (equally roughly) be called the "style"— that is, the way in which the arguments are presented. Content and style, of course, cannot really be seen apart. As Cardinal Newman said, "Thought and meaning are inseparable from each other. Matter and expression are parts of one; style is a thinking out into language." In our questions we sometimes ask the student to evaluate the effectiveness of the opening paragraph, or to explain a shift in tone from one paragraph to the next, or to characterize the persona of the author as revealed in the whole essay. In short, the book is not designed as an introduction to some powerful ideas (though in fact it is that, too); it is designed as an aid to writing thoughtful, effective arguments on important political, social, scientific, ethical, and religious issues.

Part One, then, is a preliminary (but we hope substantial) discussion of such topics as getting ideas, using sources, evaluating kinds of evidence, and organizing material. Part Two, with models of argument on current issues, begins with six short pairs of debates on such pressing issues as gun control and comparable worth. These are followed by four longer pairs of essays, again on current issues, such as the open university and affirmative action. Next come chapters addressing five issues, each discussed from several points of view. (In effect, these are mini-casebooks, suitable for controlled student research papers.) Among the topics are the value of a science requirement, abortion, and the legalization of drugs. Part Three extends the topics to "Four Enduring Questions": "Do We Have Inalienable Rights?"; "What Are the Bounds of Free Speech?"; "What Is the Ideal Society?"; and "What Are the Grounds of Religious Faith?" Here the reader encounters classical writers, such as Plato, Paul, Machiavelli, Jefferson, and Virginia Woolf, as well as such contemporary figures as B. F. Skinner, Martin Luther King, Jr., Susan Brownmiller, and Gloria Steinem.

Of the contemporary selections in the book (drawn chiefly from such sources as the *New York Times*, *The New Republic*, *Ms.*, and *Harper's*), many are very short—scarcely longer than the five-hundred word essays that students may often be asked to write.

The book ends with a four-part appendix, "Further Perspectives," which begins with a summary of the philosopher Stephen Toulmin's method for analyzing arguments. This summary will allow those interested to apply Toulmin's method to the readings in our book. The second part, a more rigorous analysis of deduction, induction, and fallacies than is usually found in textbooks designed for composition courses, reexamines, from a logician's point of view, material already treated briefly in Chapter 2. The third part, again on logic, is Max Shulman's amusing story, "Love Is a Fallacy." The fourth part, an essay by psychotherapist Carl R. Rogers, complements the discussion of audience, organization, and tone in Chapter 3.

The Instructor's Edition includes an additional appendix, "Editors' Notes," containing detailed suggestions about ways in which the essays may be approached. These notes also include many additional suggestions for writing.

New to the Second Edition · In preparing the second edition, we were greatly aided by suggestions from instructors who were using the first edition. In line with their recommendations, we have revised passages in our discussion of argumentative methods in Part One, and added a fairly detailed presentation of both the MLA and the APA systems of citation. Instructors were no less helpful in their suggestions for new readings and topics. Of the 87 selections, 36—about 40 percent—are new.

In Part One, among the six new arguments are proposals for gay marriages and for putting warning labels on alcohol, as well as essays on why four-letter words can hurt you and why we read the classics. In Part Two, eight of the fifteen current issues are new. Among them are the value of a science requirement, the legalization of drugs, and the proposal to make English the official language of the United States. In Part Three, "Enduring Questions," we have added a chapter called "Do We Have Inalienable Rights?" This chapter includes selections ranging from Plato through Martin Luther King, Jr., and extends issues and themes that have already been introduced in Part One (e.g., the argument on gay marriages) and Part Two (e.g., the arguments on abortion). Each of the four chapters in Part Three, like each of the five preceding chapters in Part Two (Chapters 7–11), consists of a topic discussed from several points of view. Instructors who have used casebooks will perhaps be especially drawn to this part of the text.

There can be no argument about the urgency of the topics that we have added, but there can be lots of arguments about the merits of the positions offered in the selections. That's where the users of this book, students and instructors alike, come in.

Acknowledgments · Finally, it is our pleasant duty to thank those who have strengthened the book by their advice: Lois Bragg, Middle Tennessee State University; Paul Brienes, Boston College; Sara Burroughs, Northwestern State University; Wendy Clein, University of Connecticut; Daniel L. Colvin, Western Illinois University; Grace C. Cooper, Ph.D., University of the District of Columbia; Corbin S. Cornell, University of Florida; Andrea C. Dragon, Rider College; Susan Eisenthal, University of Massachusetts at Boston; Lester Faigley, University of Texas at Austin; Richard Filloy, University of Oregon; Kathryn Flannery, Haverford College; Sol Gittleman, Tufts University; Rosanna Grassi, Syracuse University; M. Katherine Grimes, Louisburg College; Dr. Angela Hague, Middle Tennessee State University; Audrey Hale, Tufts University; Susan J. Hanna, Mary Washington College; Carol Hares-Stryler, University of California at Davis; Jean Harrington, Becker Junior College; Donna Hollenberg, Simmons College; Richard Hootman, University of Iowa; David Jolliffe, University of Illinois; Norman Katz, Harvard University; Misia Landau, Boston University; Zella Luria, Tufts University; Marcia Mac-Lennan, Kansas Wesleyan; Howard A. Mayer, University of Hartford; Kenneth R. McNamara, University of California, Irvine; Carolyn Miller, North Carolina State University at Raleigh; Michael G. Moran, University of Georgia; J. Karen Ray, Emporia State University; Lawrence Rice, Idaho State University; William C. Robert, Northwestern State University; Arthur M. Saltzman, Missouri Southern State College; M. Lorain Stowe, Highline Community College; Louise Strecker, University of Southern California; Gail Stygall, Indiana University; Gordon P. Symonds, Jr., Millersville University of Pennsylvania; Phillip Szenher, Roger Williams College; Mary Ann Trevathan, California Polytechnic State University; Joseph Vanderholt, Spring Hill College; Shirley D. Vatz, University of North Carolina at Greensboro; Rita Verbrugge, Grand Valley State University; Judith Weise, State University of New York, Potsdam; Don G. Wester, Oklahoma Baptist University; Arlene Wilner, Rider College; Amy Winokur, La Roche College; and Richard Young, Carnegie Mellon University. We are most grateful for their help. We are also indebted to the people at Bedford Books, especially Charles H. Christensen, Joan E. Feinberg, Elizabeth M. Schaaf, Stephen Scipione, Tara Masih, Lori Chong, Jane Betz, Chris Rutigliano, Michael Eads, and Cynthia Benn, who offered many valuable (and invaluable) suggestions. Intelligent, informed, firm yet courteous, they really know how to argue.

Contents

Part Three
MODELS OF ARGUMENT: ENDURING QUESTIONS • 431

12 Do We Have Inalienable Rights? • 433

Part One

METHODS OF ARGUMENTATIVE WRITING: A SHORT COURSE

1

Reading Arguments

Some books are to be tasted, others to be chewed, and some few to be chewed and digested.
—FRANCIS BACON

READING VERSUS SKIMMING

The arguments printed in this book need to be chewed and digested, not merely tasted. Skimming won't do. Of course you may want to run your eye rapidly over a piece, to get some idea of the topic beyond what you can get from the title, or to get a sense of the difficulty, or to ascertain the organization, or you may even look to see if a helpful summary is at the end of the essay. Fine, but the material on the whole is too complex to be absorbed by the method of reading that we use when we go through a newspaper or junk mail; this material must be chewed and digested.

To say that the material is complex is not to say that it is obscure, vague, highfalutin, pedantic, or even very difficult. To say that it is complex is to say only that it consists of interconnected or interwoven parts. These essayists, on the whole, offer beliefs that are supported by reasons. Sometimes quite a long chain of reasoning is needed to set forth the author's beliefs convincingly, and the writer may have to begin with lengthy preliminaries, such as defining terms and indicating the scope of the argument. Let's take a simple example.

First, Second, and Third Thoughts

Suppose you are reading an argument about pornographic pictures. For the present purpose, it doesn't matter whether the argument favors or opposes censorship. As you read the argument, ask yourself if "pornography" is adequately defined. Has the writer taken the trouble to make sure that the reader and the writer are thinking about the same thing? It goes

3

without saying that pornography can't be defined simply as pictures of nude figures, or even of nude figures copulating, for such a definition would include not only photographs taken for medical, sociological, and scientific purposes but also some of the world's great art. Nobody seriously thinks pornography includes such things.

Is it enough, then, to say that pornography "stirs lustful thoughts" or "appeals to prurient interests"? No, because pictures of shoes probably stir lustful thoughts in shoe fetishists, and pictures of infants in ads for diapers probably stir lustful thoughts in pedophiles. Perhaps, then, the definition must be amended to "material that stirs lustful thoughts in the average person." But will this restatement do? First, it may be hard to agree on the characteristics of "the average person." True, in other matters the law often assumes that there is such a creature as "the reasonable person," and most people would agree that in a given situation, there might be a reasonable response—for almost everyone. But we cannot be so sure that the same is true about the emotional responses of this "average person." In any case, far from stimulating sexual impulses, sadomasochistic pictures of booted men wielding whips on naked women probably turn off "the average person," yet this is the sort of material that most people would agree is pornographic.

Something must be wrong, then, with the definition that pornography is material that "stirs lustful thoughts in the average person." We began with a definition that was too broad ("pictures of nude figures"), but now we have a definition that is too narrow. We must go back to the drawing board. This is not nitpicking. The label "average person" was found to be inadequate in a case argued before the Supreme Court; because the materials in question were aimed at a homosexual audience, it was agreed that the average person would not find them sexually stimulating.

One difficulty has been that pornography is often defined according to its effect on the viewer ("genital commotion," Father Harold Gardiner, S.J., called it, in *Catholic Viewpoint on Censorship*), but different people, we know, may respond differently. In the first half of the twentieth century, in an effort to distinguish between pornography and art—after all, most people don't want to regard Botticelli's *Venus* or Michelangelo's *David* as "dirty"—it was commonly said that a true work of art does not stimulate in the spectator ideas or desires that the real object might stimulate. But in 1956 Kenneth Clark, probably the most influential English-speaking art critic of our century, changed all that; in a book called *The Nude* he announced that "no nude, however abstract, should fail to arouse in the spectator some vestige of erotic feeling."

This, Therefore That

In order to arrive at a coherent thought, or a coherent series of thoughts that will lead to a reasonable conclusion, a writer has to go through a good deal of preliminary effort; and if the writer is to convince the reader that the conclusion is sound, the reasoning that led to the conclusion must be set forth in detail, with a good deal of "This, therefore that," and "If this, then that." The arguments in this book require more comment than President Calvin Coolidge provided when his wife, who hadn't been able to go to church on a Sunday, asked him what the preacher's sermon was about. "Sin." His wife persisted: "What did the preacher say about it?" Coolidge's response: "He was against it."

But, again, our saying that most of the arguments in this book are presented at length and require careful reading does not mean that they are obscure; it means, rather, that the reader has to take the sentences one by one. And speaking of one by one, we are reminded of an episode in Lewis Carroll's *Through the Looking-Glass:*

> "Can you do Addition?" the White Queen asked. "What's one and one and one and one and one and one and one and one and one and one?"
> "I don't know," said Alice. "I lost count."
> "She can't do Addition," the Red Queen said.

It's easy enough to add one and one and one and so on, and Alice can, of course, do addition, but not at the pace that the White Queen sets. Fortunately, you can set your own pace in reading the cumulative thinking set forth in the essays. Skimming won't work, but slow reading—and thinking about what you are reading—will.

When you first pick up an essay, you may indeed want to skim it, for some of the reasons mentioned in the first paragraph on p. 3, but sooner or later you have to settle down to *read* it, and to *think* about it. The effort will be worthwhile. John Locke, the seventeenth-century English philosopher, said,

> Reading furnishes the mind with materials of knowledge; it is thinking makes what we read ours. We are of the ruminating kind, and it is not enough to cram ourselves with a great load of collections; unless we chew them over again they will not give us strength and nourishment.

SUMMARIZING

The best way to think about what you read is to take notes on your reading. If you own the book, you can jot notes in the margins or underline key terms or highlight passages with a felt pen (beware, however, of underlining or highlighting too much). Perhaps the best thing to do with a fairly difficult essay is, after reading it once, to reread it and simultaneously to take notes on a sheet of paper, perhaps summarizing each paragraph in a sentence or two.

Don't confuse a summary with a paraphrase; a **paraphrase** is a word-by-word or phrase-by-phrase rewording of a text, a sort of translation of the author's language into your own. A paraphrase is therefore as long as the original, or even longer; a **summary** is much shorter. Paraphrasing can be useful in helping you to grasp difficult passages; summarizing is useful in helping you to get the gist of the entire essay.

Summarizing each paragraph, or each group of closely related paragraphs, will help you to follow the thread of the discourse, and, when you are finished, will provide you with a useful outline of the essay. Then, when you reread the essay yet again, you may want to underline passages that you now understand are the author's key ideas—for instance, definitions, generalizations, summaries—and you may want to jot notes in the margins, questioning the logic or expressing your uncertainty or calling attention to other writers who see the matter differently.

Here is a paragraph from a 1973 decision of the Supreme Court, written by Chief Justice Warren Burger, setting forth reasons why states may censor obscene material. We follow it with a sample summary.

> If we accept the unprovable assumption that a complete education requires the reading of certain books, and the well-nigh universal belief that good books, plays, and art lift the spirit, improve the mind, enrich the human personality, and develop character, can we then say that a state legislature may not act on the corollary assumption that commerce in obscene books, or public exhibitions focused on obscene conduct, have a tendency to exert a corrupting and debasing impact leading to anti-social behavior? The sum of experience, including that of the past two decades, affords an ample basis for legislatures to conclude that a sensitive, key relationship of human existence, central to family life, community welfare, and the development of human personality, can be debased and distorted by crass commercial exploitation of sex. Nothing in the Constitution prohibits a State from reaching such a conclusion and acting on it legislatively simply because there is no conclusive empirical data.

Now for a student's summary. Notice that the summary does *not* include the reader's evaluation or any other sort of comment on the original; it is simply an attempt to condense the original. Notice too that, because its purpose was merely to assist the reader to grasp the ideas of the original by focusing on them, it is written in a sort of shorthand (not every sentence is a complete sentence), though of course if this summary were being presented in an essay it would have to be grammatical.

```
     Unprovable but acceptable assumption that good books
etc. shape character, so that legislature can assume
obscene works debase character.  Experience lets one con-
clude that exploitation of sex debases the individual,
```

```
family, and community.  Though no conclusive evidence
for this view, Constitution lets state act on it
legislatively.
```

The first sentence of the original, some eighty words, is reduced in the summary to eighteen words. Of course the summary loses much of the detail and flavor of the original: "good books etc." is not the same as "good books, plays, and art"; and "shape character" is not the same as "lift the spirit, improve the mind, enrich the human personality, and develop character." But the statement in the summary will do as a rough approximation, useful for a quick review. More important, of course, the act of writing a summary forces the reader to go slowly and to think about each sentence of the original. Such thinking may help the reader-writer to see the complexity—or the hollowness—of the original.

The sample summary in the paragraph above was just that, a summary, but when writing your summaries, it is often useful to inject your own thoughts ("seems far-fetched," "strong point," "I don't get it"), enclosing them within square brackets: [ ], or in some other way keeping these responses distinct from your summary of the writer's argument. Remember, however, that if your instructor asks you to hand in a summary, it should not contain ideas other than those found in the original piece. You can rearrange these, add transitions as needed, and so forth, but the summary should give the reader nothing but a sense of the original piece.

We don't want to nag you, but we do want to emphasize the need to read with a pencil in hand. If you read slowly, and take notes, you will find that what you read will give you the strength and nourishment that Locke spoke of.

Two Short Arguments for Analysis

Having insisted that the essays in this book need to be read slowly because the writers build one reason upon another, we will now seem to contradict ourselves by presenting two essays, the first of which is notably easy. It can *almost* be skimmed. The essay by Susan Jacoby originally appeared in the *New York Times*, a thoroughly respectable journal but not one that requires its readers to linger over every sentence. Still, compared with most of the accounts of news in the paper, Jacoby's essay requires close reading. When you read the essay you will notice that it zigs and zags, not because Jacoby is careless or wants to befuddle her readers but because she wants to build a strong case to support her point of view, and she must therefore look at some widely held views that she does *not* accept; she must set these forth, and must then give her reasons for rejecting them.

Susan Jacoby

A First Amendment Junkie

It is no news that many women are defecting from the ranks of civil libertarians on the issue of obscenity. The conviction of Larry Flynt, publisher of *Hustler* magazine—before his metamorphosis into a born-again Christian—was greeted with unabashed feminist approval. Harry Reems, the unknown actor who was convicted by a Memphis jury for conspiring to distribute the movie *Deep Throat*, has carried on his legal battles with almost no support from women who ordinarily regard themselves as supporters of the First Amendment. Feminist writers and scholars have even discussed the possibility of making common cause against pornography with adversaries of the women's movement—including opponents of the equal rights amendment and "right-to-life" forces.

All of this is deeply disturbing to a woman writer who believes, as I always have and still do, in an absolute interpretation of the First Amendment. Nothing in Larry Flynt's garbage convinces me that the late Justice Hugo L. Black was wrong in this opinion that "the Federal Government is without any power whatsoever under the Constitution to put any type of burden on free speech and expression of ideas of any kind (as distinguished from conduct)." Many women I like and respect tell me I am wrong; I cannot remember having become involved in so many heated discussions of a public issue since the end of the Vietnam War. A feminist writer described my views as those of a "First Amendment junkie."

Many feminist arguments for controls on pornography carry the implicit conviction that porn books, magazines, and movies pose a greater threat to women than similarly repulsive exercises of free speech pose to other offended groups. This conviction has, of course, been shared by everyone—regardless of race, creed, or sex—who has ever argued in favor of abridging the First Amendment. It is the argument used by some Jews who have withdrawn their support from the American Civil Liberties Union because it has defended the right of American Nazis to march

Susan Jacoby (b. 1946), a journalist since the age of 17, is well known for her feminist writings. "A First Amendment Junkie" (editor's title) appeared in a "Hers" column in the New York Times *in 1978.*

through a community inhabited by survivors of Hitler's concentration camps.

If feminists want to argue that the protection of the Constitution   4
should not be extended to *any* particularly odious or threatening form of speech, they have a reasonable argument (although I don't agree with it). But it is ridiculous to suggest that the porn shops on 42d Street are more disgusting to women than a march of neo-Nazis is to survivors of the extermination camps.

The arguments over pornography also blur the vital distinction between expression of ideas and conduct. When I say I believe unreservedly in the First Amendment, someone always comes back at me with the issue of "kiddie porn." But kiddie porn is not a First Amendment issue. It is an issue of the abuse of power—the power adults have over children—and not of obscenity. Parents and promoters have no more right to use their children to make porn movies than they do to send them to work in coal mines. The responsible adults should be prosecuted, just as adults who use children for back-breaking farm labor should be prosecuted.

Susan Brownmiller, in *Against Our Will: Men, Women and Rape*, has described pornography as "the undiluted essence of antifemale propaganda." I think this is a fair description of some types of pornography, especially of the brutish subspecies that equates sex with death and portrays women primarily as objects of violence.

The equation of sex and violence, personified by some glossy rock record album covers as well as by *Hustler*, has fed the illusion that censorship of pornography can be conducted on a more rational basis than other types of censorship. Are all pictures of naked women obsene? Clearly not, says a friend. A Renoir nude is art, she says, and *Hustler* is trash. "Any reasonable person" knows that.

But what about something between art and trash—something, say,   8
along the lines of *Playboy* or *Penthouse* magazines? I asked five women for their reactions to one picture in *Penthouse* and got responses that ranged from "lovely" and "sensuous" to "revolting" and "demeaning." Feminists, like everyone else, seldom have rational reasons for their preferences in erotica. Like members of juries, they tend to disagree when confronted with something that falls short of 100 percent vulgarity.

In any case, feminists will not be the arbiters of good taste if it becomes easier to harass, prosecute, and convict people on obscenity charges. Most of the people who want to censor girlie magazines are equally opposed to open discussion of issues that are of vital concern to women: rape, abortion, menstruation, contraception, lesbianism—in fact, the entire range of sexual experience from a women's viewpoint.

Feminist writers and editors and filmmakers have limited financial resources: Confronted by a determined prosecutor, Hugh Hefner will fare better than Susan Brownmiller. Would the Memphis jurors who convicted Harry Reems for his role in *Deep Throat* be inclined to take a more positive

view of paintings of the female genitalia done by sensitive feminist artists?
Ms. magazine has printed color reproductions of some of those art works;
Ms. is already banned from a number of high school libraries because
someone considers it threatening and/or obscene.

Feminists who want to censor what they regard as harmful pornography have essentially the same motivation as other would-be censors: They
want to use the power of the state to accomplish what they have been
unable to achieve in the marketplace of ideas and images. The impulse to
censor places no faith in the possibilities of democratic persuasion.

It isn't easy to persuade certain men that they have better uses for   12
$1.95 each month than to spend it on a copy of *Hustler?* Well, then, give
the men no choice in the matter.

I believe there is also a connection between the impulse toward censorship on the part of people who used to consider themselves civil libertarians and a more general desire to shift responsibility from individuals to
institutions. When I saw the movie *Looking for Mr. Goodbar,* I was
stunned by its series of visual images equating sex and violence, coupled
with what seems to me the mindless message (a distortion of the fine Judith
Rossner novel) that casual sex equals death. When I came out of the movie,
I was even more shocked to see parents standing in line with children
between the ages of 10 and 14.

I simply don't know why a parent would take a child to see such a
movie, any more than I understand why people feel they can't turn off a
television set their child is watching. Whenever I say that, my friends tell
me I don't know how it is because I don't have children. True, but I do
have parents. When I was a child, they did turn off the TV. They didn't
expect the Federal Communications Commission to do their job for them.

I am a First Amendment junkie. You can't OD on the First Amendment, because free speech is its own best antidote.

Suppose we want to make a rough summary, more or less paragraph
by paragraph, of Jacoby's essay. Such a summary might look something
like this. (The numbers refer to Jacoby's paragraphs.)

1. Although feminists usually support the First Amendment, when it
   comes to pornography many feminists take pretty much the position of those who oppose ERA and abortion and other causes of
   the women's movement.
2. Larry Flynt produces garbage, but I think his conviction represents an unconstitutional limitation of freedom of speech.
3, 4. Feminists who want to control (censor) pornography argue
   that it poses a greater threat to women than similar repulsive
   speech poses to other groups. If feminists want to say that all

offensive speech should be restricted they can make a case, but it is absurd to say that pornography is a "greater threat" to women than a march of neo-Nazis is to survivors of concentration camps.

5. Trust in the First Amendment is not refuted by kiddie porn; kiddie porn is not a First Amendment issue but an issue of child abuse.

6, 7, 8. Some feminists think censorship of pornography can be more "rational" than other kinds of censorship, but a picture of a nude woman strikes some women as base and others as "lovely." There is no unanimity.

9, 10. If feminists censor girlie magazines, they will find that they are unwittingly helping opponents of the women's movement to censor discussions of rape, abortion, and so on. Some of the art in the feminist magazine *Ms.* would doubtless be censored.

11, 12. Like other would-be censors, feminists want to use the power of the state to achieve what they have not achieved in "the marketplace of ideas." They display a lack of faith in "democratic persuasion."

13, 14. This attempt at censorship reveals a desire to "shift responsibility from individuals to institutions." The responsibility—for instance to keep young people from equating sex with violence—is properly the parents'.

15. We can't have too much of the First Amendment.

Jacoby's **thesis,** or major claim, or chief proposition—that any form of censorship is wrong—is clear enough, even as early as the end of her first paragraph, but it gets its life or its force from the **reasons** offered throughout the essay. If we want to reduce our outline even further, we might say that Jacoby supports her thesis by arguing several subsidiary points. We will merely assert them briefly, but Jacoby **argues** them.

a. Pornography can scarcely be thought of as more offensive than Nazism.

b. Women disagree about which pictures are pornographic.

c. Feminists who want to censor pornography will find that they help antifeminists to censor discussions of issues advocated by the women's movement.

d. Feminist advocates are in effect turning to the government to achieve what they haven't achieved in the free marketplace.

e. One sees this abdication of responsibility in the fact that parents allow their children to watch unsuitable movies and television programs.

If we want to present a brief summary in the form of a coherent paragraph—perhaps as part of our own essay, in order to show the view we are arguing in behalf of or against—we might write something like this summary. (The summary would, of course, be prefaced by a lead-in along these lines: "Susan Jacoby, writing in the *New York Times*, offered a forceful argument against censorship of pornography. Jacoby's view, briefly, is. . . .")

> When it comes to censorship of pornography, some
> feminists take a position shared by opponents of the fem-
> inist movement. They argue that pornography poses a
> greater threat to women than other forms of offensive
> speech offer to other groups, but this interpretation is
> simply a mistake. Pointing to kiddie porn is also a mis-
> take, for kiddie porn is an issue involving not the First
> Amendment but child abuse. Feminists who support censor-
> ship of pornography will inadvertently aid those who wish
> to censor discussions of abortion and rape, or art that
> is published in magazines such as Ms. The solution is
> not for individuals to turn to institutions (i.e., for
> the government to limit the First Amendment) but for in-
> dividuals to accept the responsibility for teaching young
> people not to equate sex with violence.

Whether we agree or disagree with Jacoby's thesis, we must admit that the reasons she sets forth to support it are worth thinking about. Only a reader who closely follows the reasoning with which Jacoby buttresses her thesis is in a position to accept or reject it.

Questions and Suggestions for Writing

1. What does Jacoby mean when she says she is "a First Amendment junkie"?

2. The essay is primarily an argument against the desire of some feminists to try to censor pornography of the sort that appeals to some heterosexual adult males, but the next-to-last paragraph is about television and children. Is the paragraph connected to Jacoby's overall argument? If so, how?

3. Evaluate the final paragraph as a final paragraph. (Effective final paragraphs are not, of course, all of one sort. Some, for example, round off the essay by echoing something from the opening; others politely suggest that the reader, having now seen the problem, should think further about it or even act on it. But a good final paragraph, whatever else it does, should make the reader feel that the essay has come to an end, not just broken off.)

4. This essay originally appeared in the *New York Times*. If you are unfamiliar with this newspaper, consult an issue or two in your library. Next, in a paragraph, try to characterize the readers of the paper—that is, Jacoby's audience.

5. Jacoby claims that she believes in an "absolute interpretation of the First Amendment." What does such an interpretation involve? Would it permit shouting "Fire!" in a crowded theater even though the shouter knows there is no fire? Would it permit shouting racist insults at blacks or immigrant Vietnamese? Spreading untruths about someone's past? If the "absolutist" interpretation of the First Amendment does permit these statements, does that argument show that nothing is morally wrong with uttering them? (*Does* the First Amendment, as actually interpreted by the Supreme Court today, permit any or all of these claims? Consult your reference librarian for help in answering this question.)

6. Jacoby implies that permitting prosecution of persons on obscenity charges will lead eventually to censorship of "open discussion" of important issues such as "rape, abortion, menstruation, lesbianism." Do you find her fears convincing? Does she give any evidence to support her claim?

Now let's look at a somewhat more difficult essay on a different subject, an argument about prayer. Because C. S. Lewis, a devout Christian, is addressing an audience of Christian believers, he does not have to spend time arguing on behalf of his belief in the existence of God. He knows, however, that even believers may disagree about the nature and value of prayer, and so he tries to persuade his readers to accept his view of prayer.

C. S. Lewis

Work and Prayer

"Even if I grant your point and admit that answers to prayer are theoretically possible, I shall still think they are infinitely improbable. I don't think it at all likely that God requires the ill-informed (and contradictory) advice of us humans as to how to run the world. If he is all-wise, as you say He is, doesn't He know already what is best? And if He is all-good won't He do it whether we pray or not?"

This is the case against prayer which has, in the last hundred years, intimidated thousands of people. The usual answer is that it applies only to the lowest sort of prayer, the sort that consists in asking for things to happen. The higher sort, we are told, offers no advice to God; it consists only of "communion" or intercourse with Him; and those who take this

Clive Staples Lewis (1898–1963), a professor of English literature at Oxford and later at Cambridge, wrote several important books on literature, but he is most widely known for his writings on Christianity (he converted to Christianity from atheism) and for his children's stories. This selection appeared in his book God in the Dock (1970).

line seem to suggest that the lower kind of prayer really is an absurdity and that only children or savages would use it.

I have never been satisfied with this view. The distinction between the two sorts of prayer is a sound one; and I think on the whole (I am not quite certain) that the sort which asks for nothing is the higher or more advanced. To be in the state in which you are so at one with the will of God that you wouldn't want to alter the course of events even if you could is certainly a very high or advanced condition.

But if one simply rules out the lower kind two difficulties follow. In 4 the first place, one has to say that the whole historical tradition of Christian prayer (including the Lord's Prayer itself) has been wrong; for it has always admitted prayers for our daily bread, for the recovery of the sick, for protection from enemies, for the conversion of the outside world, and the like. In the second place, though the other kind of prayer may be "higher" if you restrict yourself to it because you have got beyond the desire to use any other, there is nothing specially "high" or "spiritual" about abstaining from prayers that make requests simply because you think they're no good. It might be a very pretty thing (but, again, I'm not absolutely certain) if a little boy never asked for cake because he was so high-minded and spiritual that he didn't want any cake. But there's nothing specially pretty about a little boy who doesn't ask because he has learned that it is no use asking. I think that the whole matter needs reconsideration.

The case against prayer (I mean the "low" or old-fashioned kind) is this. The thing you ask for is either good—for you and for the world in general—or else it is not. If it is, then a good and wise God will do it anyway. If it is not, then He won't. In neither case can your prayer make any difference. But if this argument is sound, surely it is an argument not only against praying, but against doing anything whatever?

In every action, just as in every prayer, you are trying to bring about a certain result; and this result must be good or bad. Why, then, do we not argue as the opponents of prayer argue, and say that if the intended result is good God will bring it to pass without your interference, and that if it is bad He will prevent it happening whatever you do? Why wash your hands? If God intends them to be clean, they'll come clean without your washing them. If He doesn't, they'll remain dirty (as Lady Macbeth found)[1] however much soap you use. Why ask for the salt? Why put on your boots? Why do anything?

We know that we can act and that our actions produce results. Everyone who believes in God must therefore admit (quite apart from the question of prayer) that God has not chosen to write the whole of history with His own hand. Most of the events that go on in the universe are indeed out of our control, but not all. It is like a play in which the scene and the

---

[1] Shakespeare, *Macbeth*, V, i, 34–57.

general outline of the story is fixed by the author, but certain minor details are left for the actors to improvise. It may be a mystery why He should have allowed us to cause real events at all; but it is no odder that He should allow us to cause them by praying than by any other method.

Pascal says that God "instituted prayer in order to allow His creatures 8 the dignity of causality." It would perhaps be truer to say that He invented both prayer and physical action for that purpose. He gave us small creatures the dignity of being able to contribute to the course of events in two different ways. He made the matter of the universe such that we can (in those limits) do things to it; that is why we can wash our own hands and feed or murder our fellow creatures. Similarly, He made His own plan or plot of history such that it admits a certain amount of free play and can be modified in response to our prayers. If it is foolish and impudent to ask for victory in a war (on the ground that God might be expected to know best), it would be equally foolish and impudent to put on a mackintosh—does not God know best whether you ought to be wet or dry?

The two methods by which we are allowed to produce events may be called work and prayer. Both are alike in this respect—that in both we try to produce a state of affairs which God has not (or at any rate not yet) seen fit to provide "on His own." And from this point of view the old maxim *laborare est orare* (work is prayer) takes on a new meaning. What we do when we weed a field is not quite different from what we do when we pray for a good harvest. But there is an important difference all the same.

You cannot be sure of a good harvest whatever you do to a field. But you can be sure that if you pull up one weed that one weed will no longer be there. You can be sure that if you drink more than a certain amount of alcohol you will ruin your health or that if you go on for a few centuries more wasting the resources of the planet on wars and luxuries you will shorten the life of the whole human race. The kind of causality we exercise by work is, so to speak, divinely guaranteed, and therefore ruthless. By it we are free to do ourselves as much harm as we please. But the kind which we exercise by prayer is not like that; God has left Himself a discretionary power. Had He not done so, prayer would be an activity too dangerous for man and we should have the horrible state of things envisaged by Juvenal: "Enormous prayers which Heaven in anger grants."[2]

Prayers are not always—in the crude, factual sense of the word— "granted." This is not because prayer is a weaker kind of causality, but because it is a stronger kind. When it "works" at all it works unlimited by space and time. That is why God has retained a discretionary power of granting or refusing it; except on that condition prayer would destroy us. It is not unreasonable for a headmaster to say, "Such and such things you may do according to the fixed rules of this school. But such and such other things are too dangerous to be left to general rules. If you want to do them

---

[2] *Satires*, Bk. IV, Satire x, line 111.

you must come and make a request and talk over the whole matter with me in my study. And then—we'll see."

When we summarize the paragraphs of this essay, we get something like the following:

1. The opposition view: God doesn't need our advice about what to do.
2, 3. One reply is that this interpretation applies only to prayers asking God to make something happen, but not to prayers of "communion."
4. But we can't so easily dismiss the "lower" kind of prayer. First, it is an important part of the Christian tradition, used even by Christ. Second, to abstain from this sort of prayer because one thinks it is pointless is not really high-minded.
5. To repeat, the problem is this: if God is good and wise He will do what should be done, whether one prays or not, and so why pray?
6. But this argument applies not only to praying but to all other actions. Why *do* anything? Why put on shoes? Why not let God take care of everything?
7. We know that we can act and can get some results. God has chosen to let us play a role. Life is like a play in which the outline of the story is set, but the actors can improvise and fill in the details. It is a mystery why God lets us cause any events, and it is no odder that He should let us cause some events by praying.
8. God instituted action and prayer in order to let us contribute to events in two ways. By action we can influence matter (we can wash our hands, or we can murder, or we can put on a raincoat and thus keep off the rain); and by prayer we can (sometimes) modify God's plan of history.
9. Work and prayer (the two methods of causing things to happen) share this: we try to produce a state of affairs that God has not yet seen fit to provide.
10, 11. Work (for instance, weeding a field) has certain foreseeable results. But prayer, the other method of influencing history, may be so dangerous that God reserves to Himself "discretionary power." Our prayers are not always answered, because our prayers might produce evil results that we do not foresee.

There is a good deal in this brief essay, far more than scanning can take in. Lewis, like anyone who honestly seeks to argue a case, is trying to see exactly what the subject includes; in a way, he is staking out the territory. He begins with the usual view of the opposition, and then (in the second, third, and fourth paragraphs) he develops his reply by first distinguishing between two kinds of prayers. He goes on to compare prayer

, one believes that
(remember, Lewis
day do we put on
s Lewis continues,
ely arguing his case

n in which one must
advanced by a skeptic
nulate this dilemma as
oint, or not?

ing? Why? (What are
an or should do?)

t to gain the reader's

uce them? How would
xplain why they are or
s argument.

graph 10, "enormous"
anslated line puzzling,
y suited to the context.

with seeking a privilege
parison)? On what as-

50 words or so, charac-
warm or cold, stuffy or
r as space allows, sup-
quotations or (if some

2

Arguing Issues

He that wrestles with us strengthens our nerves, and sharpens our skill. Our antagonist is our helper.
—EDMUND BURKE

PERSUASION, ARGUMENT, DISPUTE

When we engage in serious argument (not name calling or mere rationalization), we not only hear ideas that may be unfamiliar, but we are also forced to examine closely our own cherished opinions, and perhaps for the first time we really come to see the strengths and weaknesses of what we believe. As John Stuart Mill put it, "He who knows only his own side of the case knows little."

It is customary, and useful, to distinguish between persuasion and argument. **Persuasion** has the broader meaning. To persuade is to win over—whether by giving reasons (that is, by argument) or by appealing to the emotions, or, for that matter, by using torture. **Argument**, one form of persuasion, relies on reason; it offers statements as reasons for other statements.

Notice that an argument, in this sense, does not require two speakers or writers representing opposed positions. The Declaration of Independence is an argument, setting forth the colonists' reasons for declaring their independence. In practice, of course, someone's argument usually advances reasons in opposition to someone else's position or belief. But even if one is writing only for oneself, trying to clarify one's thinking by setting forth reasons, the result is an argument. In a **dispute**, however, two or more people express views that are at odds.

Most of this book is about argument in the sense of the presentation of reasons, but of course reason is not the whole story. If an argument is to be effective, it must be presented persuasively. For instance, the writer's tone (attitude toward self, topic, and audience) must be appropriate if the discourse is to persuade the reader. The careful presentation of the self is not something disreputable, nor is it something that publicity agents or advertising agencies invented. Aristotle (384–322 B.C.) emphasized the importance of impressing upon the audience that the speaker is of sound sense and high moral character. We will talk at length about tone, along with other matters such as the organization of an argument, in Chapter 3, but here we deal with some of the chief devices used in reasoning.

We should note at once, however, that an argument presupposes a fixed topic. Suppose we are arguing about Jefferson's assertion, in the Declaration of Independence, that "all men are created equal." Jones subscribes to this statement, but Smith says it is nonsense, and argues that one has only to look around to see that some people are brighter than others, or healthier, or better coordinated, or whatever. Jones and Smith, if they intend to argue the point, will do well to examine what Jefferson actually wrote.

> We hold these truths to be self-evident, that all men are created equal:
> that they are endowed by their Creator with certain unalienable rights;
> and that among these are life, liberty, and the pursuit of happiness.

There is room for dispute about what Jefferson meant, and about whether he is right, but clearly he was talking about *equality of rights*, and if Smith and Jones wish to argue about Jefferson's view of equality—that is, if they wish to offer their reasons for accepting, rejecting, or modifying it—they will do well first to agree on what Jefferson said or what he probably meant to say. Jones and Smith may still hold different views; they may continue to disagree on whether Jefferson was right, and proceed to offer arguments and counterarguments to settle the point. But only if they can agree on *what* they disagree about will their dispute get somewhere.

REASON VERSUS RATIONALIZATION

Reason may not be our only way of finding the truth, but it is a way we often rely on. The subway ran yesterday at 6:00 A.M. and the day before at 6:00 A.M., and the day before, and so I infer from this evidence that it is also running today at 6:00 A.M. (a form of reasoning known as **induction**). Or: bus drivers require would-be passengers to present the exact change; I do not have the exact change; therefore I infer I cannot ride on the bus (**deduction**). (The terms *induction* and *deduction* will be discussed shortly.)

We also know that, if we set our minds to a problem, we can often find reasons (not sound ones, but reasons nevertheless) for almost anything we want to justify. Here is an entertaining example from Benjamin Franklin's *Autobiography:*

> I believe I have omitted mentioning that in my first voyage from Boston, being becalmed off Block Island, our people set about catching cod and hauled up a great many. Hitherto I had stuck to my resolution of not eating animal food, and on this occasion, I considered with my master Tryon the taking of every fish as a kind of unprovoked murder, since none of them had or ever could do us any injury that might justify the slaughter. All this seemed very reasonable. But I had formerly been a great lover of fish, and when this came hot out of the frying pan, it smelt admirably well. I balanced some time between principle and inclination, till I recollected that when the fish were opened I saw smaller fish taken out of their stomachs. Then thought I, if you eat one another, I don't see why we mayn't eat you. So I dined upon cod very heartily and continued to eat with other people, returning only now and then occasionally to a vegetable diet. So convenient a thing it is to be a *reasonable creature*, since it enables one to find or make a reason for everything one has a mind to do.

Franklin of course is being playful. He tells us that he loved fish, that this fish "smelt admirably well," and so we are prepared for him to find a reason (here one as weak as "Fish eat fish, so people may eat fish") to abandon his vegetarianism. (Fish also eat their own young. May we eat ours?) But Franklin touches on a truth: if necessary, we can find reasons to justify whatever we want. That is, instead of reasoning we may *rationalize* (devise a self-satisfying but incorrect reason), like the fox who, finding the grapes he desired were out of his reach, consoled himself with the thought they were probably sour.

THE SUBJECTS OF REASONING

Speaking broadly, we can say that the subject of an argument usually is one or more of these four issues:

1. What is *X*? One can hardly argue about the number of people sentenced to death in the United States in 1989—a glance at the appropriate reference book will give the answer—but one can argue about whether or not capital punishment as administered in the United States is discriminatory. Does the evidence, one can ask, support the view that in the United States the death penalty is unfair? Similarly, one can argue about whether a human fetus is a human being (in saying what something is, must we take account of its potentiality?), and, even if we agree that a fetus is a human being, we can further argue about whether it is a *person*. In *Roe v. Wade* the Supreme Court ruled that even the "viable" unborn human fetus is not a "person" as that term is used in the Fifth and Fourteenth Amendments. Here the question is this: Is the essential fact about the fetus that it is a person? (The topic is discussed elsewhere in this book, in several essays on abortion.)

2. What is the value of *X*? No one can argue with you if you say you prefer the plays of Tennessee Williams to those of Arthur Miller. But as soon as you say that Williams is a better playwright than Miller, you have based your preference on implicit standards, and it is incumbent on you to support your preference by giving evidence about the relative skill, insight, and accomplishments of Williams and Miller. Your argument is an evaluation. The question now at issue is the merits of the two authors and the standards appropriate for such an appraisal.

3. What are the causes (or the consequences) of *X*? Why did the rate of rape increase during a specific period? If we abolish the death penalty, will that cause the rate of murder to increase? Notice, by the way, that such problems may be complex. The phenomena that people usually argue about—say, such things as inflation, war, suicide, crime—have many causes, and it is therefore often a mistake to speak of *the* cause of *X*. A writer in *Time* mentioned that the life expectancy of an average American male is about sixty-seven years, a figure that compares unfavorably with the life expectancy of males in Japan and Israel. The *Time* writer suggested that an important cause of the relatively short life span is "the pressure to perform well in business." Perhaps. But the life expectancy of plumbers is no greater than that of managers and executives. Nutrition authority Jean Mayer, in an article in *Life*, attributed the relatively poor longevity of American males to a diet that is "rich in fat and poor in nutrients." Doubtless other authorities propose other causes, and in all likelihood no one cause accounts for the phenomenon.

4. What should (or ought or must) we do about *X*? Must we always obey the law? Should pornography be censored? Ought there to be "Good Samaritan" laws, laws making it a legal duty to intervene to save a person from death or great bodily harm, when one might do so with little or no risk to oneself? These questions involve conduct and policy; how we answer them will reveal our values and principles.

Again, an argument may take in two or more of these four issues. Someone who argues that pornography should (or should not) be censored will have to mark out the territory of the discussion by defining pornography (our first issue: What is *X*?). The argument probably will also need to examine the consequences of adopting the preferred policy (our third issue), and may even have to argue about its value—our second issue. (Some people maintain that pornography produces crime, but others maintain that it provides a harmless outlet for impulses that otherwise might vent themselves in criminal behavior.) Further, someone arguing about the wisdom of censoring pornography might have to face the objection that censorship, however desirable on account of some of its consequences, may be unconstitutional, and that even if censorship were constitutional it would (or might) have undesirable side effects, such as repressing freedom of political opinion.

SOME PROCEDURES IN ARGUMENT

Definition

We have already glanced at an argument over the proposition that "all men are created equal," and we saw that the words needed clarification. *Equal* meant, in the context, not physically or mentally equal but something like "equal in rights," equal politically and legally. Words do not always mean exactly what they seem to: Times Square is not a square but a triangle, and the Hudson River is not a river but an estuary because it is at sea level except at its upper reaches.

Definition by Synonym · Let's return, for a moment, to pornography, a word that, we saw, is not easily defined. One way to define a word is to offer a *synonym*. Thus, *pornography* can be defined, at least roughly, as "obscenity" (something indecent). But definition by synonym is usually only a start, because we find that we will have to define the synonym and anyway very few words have exact synonyms. (In fact, *pornography* and *obscenity* are not exact synonyms.)

Definition by Example · A second way to define something is to point to an example (this is often called **ostensive definition**, from the Latin *ostendere*, "to show"). This method can be very helpful, assuring that both writer and reader are looking at the same thing, but it also has its limitations. A few decades ago many people pointed to James Joyce's *Ulysses* and D.H. Lawrence's *Lady Chatterley's Lover* as examples of obscene novels, but today these books are regarded as literary masterpieces. Possibly they can be obscene and also be literary masterpieces. (Joyce's wife is reported to have said of her husband, "He may have been a great writer, but sure and he had a very dirty mind.")

One of the difficulties of using an example, however, is that the example is richer, more complex than the term it is being used to define, and this richness and complexity get in the way of achieving a clear definition. Thus, if one cites Lawrence's *Lady Chatterley's Lover* as an example of pornography, a listener may erroneously think that pornography has something to do with British novels or with heterosexual relationships outside of marriage. Yet neither of these ideas is part of the concept of pornography.

We are not trying to formulate a satisfactory definition of *pornography* here; our object is to say that an argument will be most fruitful if the participants first agree on what they are talking about, and that one way to secure such agreement is to define the topic ostensively. Choosing the right example, one that has all the central or typical characteristics, can make a topic not only clear but vivid.

Stipulative Definition · In arguing, you can legitimately **stipulate** a definition, saying, perhaps, that by *Native American* you mean any person with any Native American blood; or you can say that you mean any person who has at least one grandparent of pure Native American blood. Or you can stipulate that by *Native American* you mean someone who has at least one great-grandparent of pure Native American blood. A stipulative definition is appropriate where no fixed or standard definition is available and where some arbitrary specification is necessary in order to fix the meaning of a key term in the argument. Not everyone may be willing to accept your definition, and alternatives to your stipulations can probably be defended. In any case, when you stipulate a definition, your audience knows what *you* mean by it.

Of course it would *not* be reasonable to stipulate that by "Native American" you mean anyone with a deep interest in North American aborigines. That's just too idiosyncratic to be useful. Similarly, an essay on Jews in America will have to rely on some definition of the key idea. Perhaps the writer will stipulate the definition used in Israel: A Jew is any person with a Jewish mother, or, if not born of a Jewish mother, a person who has formally adopted the Jewish faith. Or perhaps the writer will stipulate another meaning: all people who consider themselves Jews. Some sort of reasonable definition must be offered.

To stipulate, however, that by Jews you mean persons who believe that Israel has a right to exist would hopelessly confuse matters because this definition in effect makes every Jew a Zionist, which is false. Remember the old riddle and the answer: If you call a dog's tail a leg, how many legs does a dog have? Answer: Four. Calling a tail a leg doesn't make it a leg.

Suppose someone says she means by a *Communist* "anyone who opposes the president, does not go to church, or favors a more nearly equal distribution of wealth and property." A dictionary or encyclopedia will tell us that a person is a Communist who accepts the main doctrines of Karl Marx (or perhaps of Marxism-Leninism). For many purposes, we may think of Communists as persons who belong to some Communist political party, by analogy with Democrats and Republicans. Or we may even think of a Communist as someone who supports what is common to the constitutions and governments currently in power in Russia, China, and Cuba. But what is the point of the misleading stipulative definition of *Communist* given at the beginning of this paragraph, except to cast disapproval on everyone whose views bring them within the definition?

There is no good reason for offering this definition, and there are two good reasons against it. The first is that we already have perfectly adequate definitions of *Communist,* and one should learn them and rely on them until the need to revise and improve them occurs. The second reason for refraining from using a misleading stipulative definition is that it is unfair to tar with a dirty and sticky brush nonchurchgoers and the rest by calling them derogatory names they do not deserve. Even if it is true that Communists favor more egalitarian distribution of wealth and property, the converse is *not* true: Not all egalitarians are Communists. Furthermore, if something is economically unsound or morally objectionable about such egalitarianism, the only responsible way to make that point is to argue against it.

A stipulation may be helpful and legitimate. Here is the opening paragraph of an essay by Richard B. Brandt titled "The Morality and Rationality of Suicide." Notice that the author first stipulates a definition and then, aware that the definition may strike some readers as too broad and therefore unreasonable or odd, he offers a reason on behalf of his definition:

> "Suicide" is conveniently defined, for our purposes, as doing something which results in one's death, either from the intention of ending one's life or the intention to bring about some other state of affairs (such as relief from pain) which one thinks it certain or highly probable can be achieved only by means of death or will produce death. It may seem odd to classify an act of heroic self-sacrifice on the part of a soldier as suicide. It is simpler, however, not to try to define "suicide" so that an act of suicide is always irrational or immoral in some way; if we adopt a neutral definition like the above we can still proceed to ask when an act of suicide in that sense is rational, morally justifiable, and so on, so that all evaluations anyone might wish to make can still be made.—(A *Handbook for the Study of Suicide,* ed. Seymour Perlin)

Sometimes a definition that at first seems extremely odd can be made acceptable, if strong reasons are offered in its support. Sometimes, in fact, an odd definition marks a great intellectual step forward. For instance, recently the Supreme Court recognized that "speech" includes symbolic expression such as protesting against a war by wearing armbands or by flying the flag upside down. Such actions, because they express ideas or emotions, are now protected by the First Amendment. Few people today would disagree that *speech* should include symbolic gestures. (We include a vivid example of controversy over precisely this issue, in *People v. Cohen,* one of the judicial case reports reprinted in Chapter 13.)

An example that seems notably eccentric to many readers and thus far has not gained much support is from p. 94 of *Practical Ethics,* in which Peter Singer suggests that a nonhuman being can be a *person.* He admits that "it sounds odd to call an animal a person," but says that it seems so only because of our bad habit of sharply separating ourselves from other species. For Singer, "persons" are "rational and self-conscious beings, aware of themselves as distinct entities with a past and a future." Thus, although a newborn infant is a human being, it is not a person; on the other hand, an adult chimpanzee is not a human being but probably is a person. You don't have to agree with Singer to know exactly what he means and where he stands. Moreover, if you read his essay you may even find that his reasons are plausible and that by means of his unusual definition he has enlarged your thinking.

Last Words about Definition · Since Plato's time, in the fourth century B.C., it has often been argued that the best way to give a definition is to state the *essence* of the thing being defined. Thus, the classic example defines *man* as "a rational animal." (Today, to avoid sexist implications, instead of *man* we would say *human being*.) That is, the property of *rational animality* is taken to be the essence of every human creature, and so it must be mentioned in the definition of *man*. This statement guarantees that the definition is neither too broad nor too narrow. But philosophers have long criticized this alleged ideal type of definition, on several grounds, one of which is that no one can propose such definitions without assuming that the thing being defined has an essence in the first place—an assumption that is not necessary. Thus, we may want to define *causality*, or *explanation*, or even *definition* itself, but it is doubtful whether it is sound to assume that any of these things has an essence.

A much better way to provide a definition is to offer a set of *sufficient and necessary conditions*. Suppose we want to define the word *circle* and are conscious of the need to keep circles distinct from other geometrical figures such as rectangles and spheres. We might express our definition by citing sufficient and necessary conditions as follows: "Anything is a circle if and only if it is a closed plane figure, all points on the circumference of which are equidistant from the center." Using the connective "if and only" between the definition and the thing being defined helps to force into our consciousness the need to make the definition neither too exclusive (too narrow) nor too inclusive (too broad). Of course, for most ordinary purposes we don't require such a formally precise and explicit definition. Nevertheless, perhaps the best criterion to keep in mind when assessing a proposed definition is whether it can be stated in the "if and only if" form, and whether, if it is so stated, it is true; that is, if it truly specifies *all and only* the things covered by the word being defined.

Assumptions

We have already said that in the form of discourse known as argument, certain statements are offered as reasons for other statements. But even the longest and most complex chain of reasoning or proof is fastened to an **assumption**, *an unexamined belief*. (Even if such a belief is shared by writer and reader, it is no less an assumption.) Benjamin Franklin argued against paying salaries to the holders of executive offices in the federal government on the grounds that men are moved by ambition and by avarice (love of power and of money), and that powerful positions that also confer wealth incite men to do their worst. These assumptions he stated, though he felt no need to argue them at length because he assumed that his readers shared them.

An assumption may be unstated. The writer, painstakingly arguing specific points, may choose to keep one or more of the assumptions tacit. Or the writer may be as unaware of some underlying assumption as of the surrounding air. For example, Franklin didn't even bother to state another assumption. He assumed that persons of wealth who accept an unpaying job (after all, only persons of wealth could afford to hold unpaid government jobs) will have at heart the interests of all classes of people, not only the interests of their own class. Few people today hold this view, and surely one reason we pay our legislators is to make certain that the legislature does not consist only of people whose incomes may give them an inadequate view of the needs of others.

An Example: Assumptions in the Argument about Abortion

1. Ours is a pluralistic society, in which we believe that the religious beliefs of one group should not be imposed on others.
2. Personal privacy is a right, and a woman's body is hers, not to be violated by laws that tell her she cannot do certain things to her body.

But these (and other) arguments *assume* that a fetus is not a human being, and therefore is not entitled to protection against assaults. Virtually all of us assume that it is usually wrong to kill a human being. Granted, we may find instances in which we believe it is acceptable to take a human life, such as self-defense against a would-be murderer, but even here we find a shared assumption, that human beings are ordinarily entitled not to be killed.

The argument on abortion, then, usually depends on opposed assumptions: for one group, the fetus is a human being, and for the other group it is not. Persons arguing one side or the other of the abortion issue ought to be aware that opponents may not share their assumptions.

Premises and Syllogisms

Premises are stated assumptions used as reasons in an argument. The joining of two premises—two statements or propositions taken to be true—to produce a conclusion, a third statement, is called a **syllogism** (Greek, for "a reckoning together"). The classic example is this:

Major Premise: All human beings are mortal.

Minor Premise: Socrates is a human being.

Conclusion: Socrates is mortal.

Deduction

The process of moving from one statement ("All human beings are mortal") through another ("Socrates is a human being") to yet a further statement ("Socrates is mortal") is called **deduction,** from Latin "lead down from." In this sense, deductive reasoning does not give us any new knowledge, although it is easy to construct examples that have so many premises, or premises that are so complex that the conclusion really does come as news to most who examine the argument. Thus, the great detective Sherlock Holmes was credited by his admiring colleague, Dr. Watson, with unusual powers of deduction. Watson meant in part that Holmes could see the logical consequences of apparently disconnected reasons, the number and complexity of which left others at a loss. What is common in all cases of deduction is that the reasons or premises offered are supposed to contain within themselves, so to speak, the conclusion extracted from them.

Often a syllogism is abbreviated. Martin Luther King, Jr., defending a protest march, wrote, in "Letter from Birmingham Jail" (p. 498):

> You assert that our actions, even though peaceful, must be condemned because they precipitate violence.

Fully expressed, the argument that King attributes to his critics would be stated thus:

> We must condemn actions (even if peaceful) that precipitate violence.
>
> This action (though peaceful) will precipitate violence.
>
> Therefore we must condemn this action.

An incomplete or abbreviated syllogism, in which one of the premises is left unstated, of the sort found in King's original quotation, is called an **enthymeme** (Greek: "in the mind").

Here is another, more whimsical example of an enthymeme, in which both a premise and the conclusion are left implicit. Thoreau is said to have remarked that "Circumstantial evidence can be very strong, as when you find a trout in the milk." The joke, perhaps intelligible only to people born before 1930 or so, depends on the fact that milk used to be sold "in bulk"; that is, ladled out of a big can directly to the customer by the farmer or grocer. This practice was finally prohibited in the 1930s because for centuries the sellers, in order to increase their profit, were known to dilute the milk with water. Thoreau's enthymeme can be fully expressed thus:

Trout live only in water.

This milk has a trout in it.

Therefore this milk has water in it.

Sound Arguments

The purpose of a syllogism is to *prove* its conclusion from its premises. This is done by making sure that the argument satisfies both of two independent criteria:

First, all of the premises must be *true*.

Second, the syllogism must be *valid*.

Once these criteria are satisfied, the conclusion of the syllogism is guaranteed. Any such argument is said to prove its conclusion, or, to use another term, is said to be **sound**. Here's an example of a sound argument, a syllogism that proves its conclusion:

No city in Nevada has a population over 200,000.

Denver has a population over 200,000.

Therefore Denver is not a city in Nevada.

Each premise is true, and the syllogism is valid, so it proves its conclusion.

But how do we tell in any given case that an argument is sound? We perform two different tests, one for the truth of each of the premises and another for the validity of the argument.

The basic test for the truth of a premise is to determine whether what it asserts corresponds with reality; if it does, then it is true, and if it doesn't then it is false. Everything depends on the content of the premise—what it asserts—and the evidence for it. (In the syllogism above, we tested the truth of the premises by relying on information in a recent almanac.)

The test for validity is quite different. We define a valid argument as one in which the conclusion follows from the premises, so that if all the premises are true then the conclusion *must* be true, too. The general test for validity, then, is this: If one grants the premises, one must also grant the conclusion. Or to put it another way, if one grants the premises but denies the conclusion, is one caught in a self-contradiction? If so, the argument is valid; if not, the argument is invalid.

The syllogism above obviously passes this test. If you grant the population information given in the premises but deny the conclusion, you have contradicted yourself. Even if the population information were in error, the conclusion in this syllogism would still follow from the premises—the hallmark of a valid argument! This is because validity of an argument is a purely formal matter concerning the *relation* between premises and conclusion given what they mean.

One can see this more clearly by examining an argument that is valid but that does *not* prove its conclusion. Here is an example of such a syllogism:

> Every elephant lives in Africa.
>
> Whatever lives in Africa breathes fire.
>
> Therefore every elephant breathes fire.

We know that the premises and the conclusion are false: Some elephants are native to India (while others live in the Portland Zoo), and no elephant is a fire-breather. But the truth of the premises and the conclusion is beside the point. Just a little reflection assures us that *if* both of these premises were true, then the conclusion would have to be true as well. That is, anyone who grants the premises of this syllogism and yet denies the conclusion has contradicted herself. So the validity of an argument does not in any way depend on the truth of the premises or the conclusion.

A sound argument, as we said, is an argument that passes both the test of true premises and the test of valid inference. To put it another way, a sound argument is one that passes the test of *content* (the premises are true, as a matter of fact) and the test of *form* (its premises and conclusion, by virtue of their very meanings, are so related that it is impossible for the premises to be true and the conclusion false).

Accordingly, an unsound argument, an argument that fails to prove its conclusion, suffers from one or both of two defects. First, not all of the premises are true. Second, the argument is invalid. Usually it is one or both of these defects that we have in mind when we object to someone's argument as "illogical." In evaluating someone's deductive argument, therefore, you must always ask: Is it vulnerable to criticism on the ground that one (or more) of its premises is false? Or is the inference itself vulnerable, because whether or not all the premises are all true, even if they were the conclusion still wouldn't follow?

A Word about False Premises · Suppose that one or more of the premises of a syllogism is false, but the syllogism itself is valid. What does that tell us about the truth of the conclusion? Consider this example:

> All Americans prefer vanilla ice cream to other flavors.
>
> George Bush is an American.
>
> Therefore George Bush prefers vanilla ice cream to other flavors.

The first (or major) premise in this syllogism is false. Yet the argument passes our formal test for validity; it is clear that if one grants both premises, one must accept the conclusion. So we can say that the conclusion *follows from* its premises, even though the premises *do not prove* the conclusion. This is not as paradoxical as it may sound. For all we know, the conclusion of this argument may in fact be true; George Bush may indeed prefer vanilla ice cream, and the odds are that he does, since consumption statistics show that most Americans prefer vanilla. Nevertheless, if the conclusion in this syllogism is true, it is not because this argument proved it.

A Word about Invalid Syllogisms · Usually, one can detect a false premise in an argument, especially when the suspect premise appears in some else's argument. A trickier business is the invalid syllogism. Consider this argument:

All crows are black.

This bird is black.

Therefore this bird is a crow.

Let's assume that both of the premises are true. What does this tell us about the truth of the conclusion? Nothing, because the argument is invalid. The *form* of the reasoning, the structure of the argument, is such that its premises (whether true or false) do not guarantee the conclusion. Even if both the premises were true, the conclusion might still be false.

In the syllogism above, the conclusion may well be true. It could be that the bird referred to in the second (minor) premise is a crow. But the conclusion might be false, because not only crows are black; ravens and blackbirds are also black. If the minor premise is asserted on the strength of observing a blackbird, then the conclusion surely is false: *This* bird is *not* a crow. So the argument is invalid, since as it stands it would lead us from true premises to a false conclusion.

How do we tell, in general and in particular cases, whether a syllogism is valid? As you know, chemists use litmus paper to enable them to tell instantly whether the liquid in a test tube is an acid or a base. Unfortunately, logic has no litmus test to tell us instantly whether an argument is valid or invalid. Logicians beginning with Aristotle have developed techniques that enable them to test any given argument, no matter how complex or subtle, to determine its validity. But the results of their labors cannot be expressed in a paragraph or even a few pages; not for nothing are semester-long courses devoted to teaching formal deductive logic. Apart from advising you to consult the appendix on these matters ("A Logician's View," p. 699), all we can do here is repeat two basic points.

First, validity of deductive arguments is a matter of their *form* or *structure*. Even syllogisms come in a large variety of forms (256 different ones, to be precise), and only some of these forms are valid. Second, all valid deductive arguments (and only such arguments) pass this test: If one accepts all the premises, then one must accept the conclusion as well.

Hence, if it is possible to accept the premises but reject the conclusion (without self-contradiction, of course), then the argument is invalid.

Let us exit from further discussion of this important but difficult subject on a lighter note. Many illogical arguments masquerade as logical. Consider this example: If it takes a horse and carriage four hours to go from Pinsk to Chelm, does it follow that if you have a carriage with two horses you will get there in two hours? In an appendix to this book we discuss at some length other kinds of deductive arguments, as well as **fallacies**, which are kinds of invalid reasoning.

Induction

Whereas the purpose of deduction is to extract the hidden consequences of our beliefs and assumptions, the purpose of **induction** is to use information about observed cases in order to reach a conclusion about unobserved cases. (The word comes from Latin *in ducere*, "to lead into," or "to lead up to.") If we observe that the bite of a certain snake is poisonous, we may conclude on this evidence that another snake of the same general type is also poisonous. Our inference might be even broader. If we observe that snake after snake of a certain type has a poisonous bite, and that these snakes are all rattlesnakes, we are tempted to **generalize** that all rattlesnakes are poisonous.

Unlike deduction, induction gives us conclusions that go beyond the information contained in the premises used in their support. Not surprisingly, the conclusions of inductive reasoning are not always true, even when all the premises are true. Earlier we gave as an example the conclusion that the subway runs at 6:00 A.M. every day because on previous days we observed that it ran at 6:00 A.M. Suppose, following this reasoning, one arrives at the subway platform just before 6:00 A.M. on a given day only to discover after an hour of waiting that there still is no train. Possibly today is Sunday, and the subway doesn't run before 7:00 A.M. Or possibly there was a breakdown earlier this morning. Whatever the explanation, we relied on a sample that was not large enough (a larger sample might have included some early morning breakdowns), or not representative enough (a more representative sample would have included the later starts on holidays).

A Word about Samples · When we reason inductively, much depends on the size and the quality of the sample. We may interview five members of Alpha Tau Omega and find that all five are Republicans, yet we cannot legitimately conclude that all members of ATO are Republicans. The problem is not always one of failing to interview large numbers. A poll of ten thousand college students tells us very little about "college students" if all ten thousand are white males at the University of Texas.

In short: An argument that uses samples ought to tell the reader how the samples were chosen. If it does not provide this information, it may rightly be treated with suspicion.

Evidence

Induction is obviously of use in arguing. If, for example, one is arguing that handguns should be controlled, one will point to specific cases in which handguns caused accidents, or were used to commit crimes. If one is arguing that abortion has a traumatic effect on women, one will point to women who testify to that effect. Each instance constitutes **evidence** for the relevant generalization.

In a courtroom, evidence bearing on the guilt of the accused is introduced by the prosecution, and evidence to the contrary is introduced by the defense. Not all evidence is admissible (hearsay, for one, is not, even if it is true), and the law of evidence is a highly developed subject in jurisprudence. In the forum of daily life, the sources of evidence are less disciplined. Daily experience, a particularly memorable observation, an unusual event we witnessed—any or all of these may be used as evidence for (or against) some belief, theory, hypothesis, or explanation. The systematic study of what experience can yield is what science does, and one of the most distinctive features of the evidence that scientists can marshal on behalf of their claims is that it is the result of **experimentation**. Experiments are deliberately contrived situations, often quite complex in their technology, designed to yield particular observations. What the ordinary person does with unaided eye and ear, the scientist does, much more carefully and thoroughly, with the help of laboratory instruments.

The variety, extent, and reliability of the evidence obtained in daily life and in the laboratory are quite different. It is hardly a surprise that in our civilization, much more weight is attached to the "findings" of scientists than to the corroborative (much less the contrary) experiences of the ordinary person. No one today would seriously argue that the sun really does go around the earth, just because it looks that way; nor would we argue that because viruses are invisible to the naked eye they cannot cause symptoms such as swellings and fevers, which are quite plainly visible.

Examples

One form of evidence is the **example**. Suppose that we argue that a candidate is untrustworthy and should not be elected to public office. We point to episodes in his career—his misuse of funds in 1984, and the false charges he made against an opponent in 1988—as examples of his untrustworthiness. Or, if we are arguing that Truman dropped the atom bomb in order to save American (and, for that matter, Japanese) lives that otherwise would have been lost in a hard-fought invasion of Japan, we point to the stubbornness of the Japanese defenders in battles on Saipan, Iwo Jima, and Okinawa, where the Japanese fought to the death rather than surrender.

These examples, we say, show us that the Japanese defenders of the main islands would have fought to the end, even though they knew they would be defeated. Or, if we take a different view of Truman's action, and argue that the war in effect was already won and that Truman had no excuse for dropping the bomb, we can cite examples of the Japanese willingness to end the war, such as secret negotiations in which they sent out peace feelers.

An example is a sample; the two words come from the same Old French word, *essample*, from the Latin *exemplum*, which means "something taken out"; that is, a selection from the group. A Yiddish proverb shrewdly says that "'For example' is no proof," but the evidence of well-chosen examples can go a long way toward helping a writer to convince an audience.

In arguments, three sorts of examples are especially common:

1. real events,
2. invented instances (artificial or hypothetical cases),
3. analogies.

We will treat each of these briefly.

Real Events · In referring to Truman's decision to drop the atom bomb, we have already touched on examples drawn from real events, the battles at Saipan and elsewhere. And we have also seen Ben Franklin pointing to an allegedly real happening, a fish that had consumed a smaller fish. The advantage of an example drawn from real life, whether a great historical event or a local incident, is that its reality lends weight to it. It can't simply be brushed off.

On the other hand, an example drawn from reality may not provide as clear-cut an instance as could be wished for. Thus, to cite the Japanese behavior at Saipan and at Iwo Jima as evidence that the Japanese later would have fought to the death in an American invasion of Japan, and would therefore have inflicted terrible losses on themselves and on the Americans, is to open the argument to the response that in August 1945, when Truman dropped the bomb, the situation was different. In June and July 1945, Japanese diplomats had already sent out secret peace feelers; Emperor Hirohito probably wanted peace by then; and so on.

Similarly, in support of the argument that nations will not resort to atomic weapons, some people have offered as evidence the fact that since World War I the great powers have not used poison gas. But the argument needs more support than this fact provides. Poison gas was not decisive or even highly effective in World War I. Moreover, the invention of gas masks made it obsolete.

In short, any *real* event is, so to speak, so entangled in its historical circumstances that one may question whether indeed it is adequate, or even relevant evidence in the case being argued. In using a real event as an example (and real events certainly can be used), the writer ordinarily must demonstrate that the event can be taken out of its historical context so to speak, and used in the new context of argument. Thus, in an argument against any further use in warfare of atomic weapons, one might point to the example of the many deaths and horrible injuries inflicted on the Japanese at Hiroshima and Nagasaki, in the confident belief that these effects of nuclear weapons will invariably occur and did not depend on any special circumstances of their use in Japan in 1945.

Invented Instances · Artificial or hypothetical cases, **invented instances**, have the great advantage of being protected from objections of the sort just given. Recall Thoreau's trout in the milk; that was a colorful hypothetical case that nicely illustrated his point. An invented instance ("Let's assume that a burglar promises not to shoot a householder if the householder swears not to identify him. Is the householder bound by the oath?") is something like a drawing of a flower in a botany textbook, or a diagram of the folds of a mountain in a geology textbook. It is admittedly false, but by virtue of its simplifications it sets forth the relevant details very clearly. Thus, in a discussion of rights, Charles Frankel says:

> Strictly speaking, when we assert a right for X, we assert that Y has a duty. Strictly speaking, the assertion that Y has such a duty presupposes that Y has the capacity to perform this duty. It would be nonsense to say, for example, that a non-swimmer has a moral duty to swim to the help of a drowning man.

This invented example is admirably clear, and it is immune to charges that might muddy the issue if Frankel, instead of referring to a wholly abstract person, Y, talked about some real person, Jones, who did not rescue a drowning man. For then he would get bogged down over arguing about whether Jones *really* couldn't swim well enough to help, and so on.

Yet invented cases have their drawbacks. First and foremost, they cannot be used as evidence. A purely hypothetical example can illustrate a point or provoke reconsideration of a generalization, but it cannot substitute for actual events as evidence supporting an inductive inference. Sometimes such examples are so fanciful, so remote from life that they fail to carry conviction with the reader. Thus Judith Jarvis Thomson asks us (p. 337) to imagine that we wake up one day and find that against our will a celebrated violinist whose body is not adequately functioning has been hooked up into our body, for life-support. Do we have the right to unplug the violinist? Readers of the essays in this book will have to decide for themselves whether such invented cases proposed by various authors are helpful or whether they are so remote that they hinder thought. Readers will have to decide, too, about when they can use invented cases to advance their own arguments.

But we add one point: Even a highly fanciful invented case can have the valuable effect of forcing us to see where we stand. We may say that we are, in all circumstances, against vivisection. But what would we say if we thought that an experiment on one mouse would save the life of someone whom we love? Or, conversely, if one approves of vivisection, would one also approve of sacrificing the last giant panda in order to save the life of a senile stranger, a person who in any case probably would not live longer than another year? Artificial cases of this sort can help us to see that, well, no, we don't really mean to say such-and-such when we said so-and-so.

Analogies · The third sort of example, **analogy**, is a kind of comparison. Strictly, an analogy is an extended comparison in which unlike things are shown to be similar in several ways. Thus, if one wants to argue that a head of state should have extraordinary power during wartime, one can argue that the state at such a time is like a ship in a storm: the crew is needed to lend its help, but the decisions are best left to the captain. (Notice that an analogy compares things that are relatively *un*like. Comparing the plight of one ship to another, or of one government to another, is not an analogy; it is an inductive inference from one case of the same sort to another such case.) Or take another analogy: We have already glanced at Judith Thomson's hypothetical case in which the reader wakes up to find himself or herself hooked up to a violinist. Thomson uses this situation as an analogy in an argument about abortion. The reader stands for the mother, the violinist for the unwanted fetus. Whether this analogy is close enough to pregnancy to help illuminate our thinking about abortion is something we leave for readers of Thomson's essay to decide.

The problem with argument by analogy is this: Two admittedly different things are agreed to be similar in several ways, and the arguer goes on to assert or imply that they are also similar in the point that is being argued. (That is why Thomson argues that if something is true of the reader-hooked-up-to-a-violinist, it is also true of the pregnant mother-hooked-up-to-a-fetus.) But of course despite some similarities, the two things which are said to be analogous and which are indeed similar in characteristics A, B, and C, are also different, let's say in characteristics D and E. As Bishop Butler said, about two hundred and fifty years ago, "Everything is what it is, and not another thing."

Analogies can be convincing, especially because they can make complex issues simple ("Don't change horses in midstream" of course is not a statement about riding horses across a river, but about choosing leaders in critical times). Still, in the end, analogies can prove nothing. What may be true about riding horses across a stream need not be true about choosing leaders in troubled times, or not true about a given change of leadership. Riding horses across a stream and choosing leaders are, at bottom, different things, and however much these activities may be said to resemble one another, they remain different, and what is true for one need not be true for the other.

Analogies can be helpful in developing our thoughts. It is sometimes argued, for instance—on the analogy of the doctor-patient or the lawyer-client or the priest-penitent relationship—that newspaper and television reporters should not be required to reveal their confidential sources. That is worth thinking about: Do the similarities run deep enough, or are there fundamental differences? Or take another example: Some writers who support abortion argue that the fetus is not a person any more than the acorn is an oak. That is also worth thinking about. But one should also think about this response: A fetus is not a person, just as an acorn is not an oak, but an acorn is a potential oak, and a fetus is a potential person, a potential adult human being. Children, even newborn infants, have rights, and one way to explain this claim is to call attention to their potentiality to become mature adults. And so some people argue that the fetus, by analogy, has the rights of an infant, for the fetus, like the infant, is a potential adult.

While we're on this subject let's consider a very brief comparison made by Jill Knight, a member of the British Parliament, whose speech opposing abortion is reprinted on p. 50:

> Babies are not like bad teeth, to be jerked out because they cause suffering.

Her point is effectively put; it remains for the reader to decide whether or not fetuses are *babies*; and, second, if a fetus is not a baby, *why* it can or can't be treated like a bad tooth. And yet a further bit of analogical reasoning, again about abortion: Thomas Sowell, an economist at the Hoover Institute, grants that women have a legal right to abortion, but he objects to the government's paying for abortions:

> Because the courts have ruled that women have a legal right to an abortion, some people have jumped to the conclusion that the government has to pay for it. You have a constitutional right to privacy, but the government has no obligation to pay for your window shades.—(*Pink and Brown People*, p. 57)

We leave it to the reader to decide if the analogy is compelling—that is, if the points of resemblance are sufficiently significant to allow one to conclude that what is true of people wanting window shades should be true of people wanting abortions.

Authoritative Testimony

Another form of evidence is **testimony**, the citation or quotation of authorities. In daily life we rely heavily on authorities of all sorts: We get a doctor's opinion about our health, we read a book because an intelligent friend recommends it, we see a movie because a critic gave it a good review, and we pay at least a little attention to the weather forecaster.

In setting forth an argument, one often tries to show that one's view is supported by notable figures, perhaps Jefferson, Washington, and Lincoln, or scientists who won the Nobel Prize. You may recall that in the first chapter, in talking about definitions of pornography, we referred to Kenneth Clark. To make certain that you were impressed by his testimony even if you had never heard of him, we described him as "probably the most influential English-speaking art critic of the twentieth century." But heed some words of caution:

1. Be sure that the authority, however notable, is an authority on the topic in question. A well-known biologist on vitamins, yes, but not on the justice of a war.
2. Be sure the authority is not biased. A chemist employed by the tobacco industry isn't likely to admit that smoking may be harmful, and a "director of publications" (that means a press agent) for a hockey team isn't likely to admit that ice hockey stimulates violence.
3. Beware of nameless authorities: "a thousand doctors," "leading educators," "researchers at a major medical school."
4. Be careful in using authorities who indeed were great authorities in their day but who now may be out of date (Adam Smith on economics, Julius Caesar on the art of war, Pasteur on medicine).
5. Cite authorities whose opinions your readers will value. William Buckley's opinion means a good deal to readers of *The National Review* but not to most feminists. Gloria Steinem's opinion carries weight with many feminists but not much with persons who oppose abortion. If you are writing for the general reader, your usual audience, cite authorities who are likely to be accepted by the general reader.

Statistics

The last sort of evidence we will discuss here is quantitative or statistical. The maxim, More is Better, captures a basic idea of quantitative evidence. Because we know that 90 percent is greater than 75 percent, we are usually ready to grant that any claim supported by experience in 90 percent of the cases is more likely to be true than an alternative claim supported by experience only 75 percent of the time. The greater the difference, the greater our confidence. Consider an example. Honors at graduation from college are often computed on a student's cumulative grade-point average (GPA). The undisputed assumption is that the nearer a student's GPA is to a perfect record (4.0), the better scholar he or she is, and therefore the more deserving of highest honors. Consequently, a student with a GPA of 3.9 at the end of her senior year is a stronger candidate for graduation summa cum laude than another student with a GPA of 3.6. When faculty members on the Honors Committee argue over the relative academic merits of graduating seniors, we know that these quantitative, statistical differences in student GPAs will be the basic (even if not the only) kind of evidence under discussion.

Three Ways of Using "Average": Mean, Mode, and Median · Statistical data can serve as the premises for many kinds of arguments, deductive as well as inductive. Deductive use of statistics, at least in simple cases, is not very interesting: If the average height of thousand-year-old redwood trees is more than 300 feet, then the actual height of some of these trees must be more than 300 feet. But how do we arrive at an average in the first place? An inductive use of statistical information is needed. Indeed, one of the most important ways to use the basic tools of all statistics—observation and counting—is to infer the average of something. The concept of an average is essential to the expression of true generalizations about the usual, typical, and normal, and their opposites—the unusual, atypical, abnormal, in short, the deviant. But the idea of the average, as statisticians have shown, is complex and ambiguous. We have several equally intelligible ways of defining the idea of an average. Three of them are of particular importance and need to be kept distinct.

Suppose you read in the newspaper that the average number of cars each day that pass an intersection is 132. How should such a claim be understood? On what evidence does it rest? The evidence for it probably was obtained by having someone (or a machine) posted at the intersection count the cars on, say, a dozen days, distributed randomly through a two- or three-week period, then adding up the number observed and dividing this sum by the number of days. The resulting average is called by statisticians the **mean** (or arithmetic mean). How reliable is this average? That will depend on a number of factors, such as seasonal variation in traffic patterns (when schools or offices in the neighborhood are on vacation, less traffic in the area would be expected). Even if reliable today and tomorrow, the computed average may rapidly prove false within a year or two because of other factors, such as redesign of a nearby highway, major construction in the area near the intersection, and so forth.

Now consider a different example. Suppose you read in the newspaper that the average American family has 2.1 children. Because this number was probably arrived at by totaling the children currently alive who are living with their parents and then dividing by the number of families, the number 2.1 represents the mean of children per family household. But if instead the statistic reported was that "the average American family has 2 children," this number might not be the average in the sense of the mean at all. Instead, it might be the number that the statistician would call the **mode**. That is, among American households with children, more have two children than have any other number. Such a conclusion would be reached by tallying all the one-child families, the two-child families, the three-child families, and so on, and then inspecting the totals for each size of family to determine which is the greatest. The idea, then, of the average number of children in the American family can be given either of two completely different statistical interpretations, each of which has been correctly inferred from the data.

Suppose, however, taking a third example, that on your freshman biology midyear examination, you received a grade of C. This grade comes as a disappointment, because you scored 81 of a possible 100 and thought this result ought to give you at least a low B. In other words, you received an average grade (in the sense that a C is midway between an A and an F) for what you thought was above-average work. When asked, your instructor explains that the midterm examination was graded on the curve, and that the average for the class was indeed a C, and your performance was no better than average. She reached this conclusion after she had corrected the examination and found that lots of students scored in the 70s and 80s, the test in fact being easier than she had expected, and the rank-order distribution of the class's grades showed that the midpoint of the distribution was an 80. Because examination grades were assigned on the curve, 80 turned out to be the class average; this was the score that divided the rank-order distribution into equal parts, one half above and the other half below that point. This midpoint is the average that statisticians call the **median.**

Every distribution can be analyzed using these three kinds of averages (the mean, the mode, the median), and which is best depends entirely on one's purpose. If you want to assert that some one thing occurs most frequently in an array, then you need to examine your data to find out the mode. Or perhaps someone claims that the midpoint between the two extremes in the whole distribution is what matters. Then the task becomes one of inferring the median. Is it instead the fraction or portion of the whole that each entity would have if the whole were parceled out equally? That is the mean.

Graphs, Tables, Numbers · Statistical information can be marshaled and presented in many forms, but it tends to fall into two main types: the graphic and the numerical. Graphs, tables, and pie charts are familiar ways of presenting quantitative data in an eye-catching manner. To prepare the graphics, however, one first has to get the numbers themselves under control, and for many purposes (such as writing argumentative essays) it is probably more convenient simply to stick with the numbers themselves.

But should the numbers be presented in percentages, or in fractions? Should one report, say, that the federal budget underwent a twofold increase over the decade, or that it increased by 100 percent, or that it doubled, or that the budget at the beginning of the decade was one-half what it was at the end? Taken strictly, these are equivalent ways of saying the same thing. Choice among them, therefore, in an example like this, perhaps will rest on whether one's aim is to dramatize the increase (a 100 percent increase looks larger than a doubling) or to play down the size of the increase.

Evaluating Statistical Evidence · Statistics often get a bad name because it is so easy to misuse them, unintentionally or not, and so difficult to be sure that they have been correctly gathered in the first place. (We remind you of the old saw, "There are lies, damned lies, and statistics.") Every branch of social science and natural science needs statistical information, and countless decisions in public and private life are based on quantitative data in statistical form. It is extremely important, therefore, to be sensitive to the sources and reliability of the statistics, and to develop a healthy skepticism when confronted with statistics whose parentage is not fully explained.

Even if one has accurate figures, it may be hard to know what to make of them. Take the figures for violent crime, which increased in the 1960s and early 1970s, then leveled off, and began to decline in 1981. Did America become more violent for a while, and then become more law-abiding? Bruce Jackson in *Law and Disorder* suggests that much of the rise in the 1960s was due to the baby boom of 1948 to 1952. Whereas in 1960 the United States had only about eleven million people aged 20 to 24, by 1972 it had almost eighteen million of them, and it is people in this age group who are most likely to commit violent crimes. The decline in the rate of violent crime in the 1980s was accompanied by a decline in the proportion of the population in this age group—though of course some politicians and law-enforcement officers took credit for the reduction in violent crime.

Regard statistical evidence (like all other evidence) cautiously and don't accept it until you have thought about these questions:

1. Was it compiled by a disinterested source?
2. Is it based on an adequate sample? (A study pointed out that criminals have an average IQ of 91–93, whereas the general population has an IQ of 100. The conclusion drawn was that criminals have a lower IQ than the general population. This reading may be accurate, but some doubts have been expressed. For instance, because the entire sample of criminals consisted only of *convicted* criminals, this sample may be biased; possibly the criminals with higher IQs have enough intelligence not to get caught. Or, if they are caught, they are smart enough to hire better lawyers.)
3. Is the statistical evidence recent enough to be relevant?
4. How many of the factors likely to be relevant were identified and measured?

5. Are the figures open to a different and equally plausible interpretation? (Remember the decline in violent crime, for which law-enforcement officers took credit.)

We are not suggesting, of course, that everyone who uses statistics is trying to deceive, or even that many who use statistics are unconsciously deceived by them. We mean only to suggest that statistics are open to widely different interpretations and that often those columns of numbers, so precise with their decimal points, are in fact imprecise and possibly even worthless because they may be based on insufficient or biased samples.

SATIRE, IRONY, SARCASM

In talking about definition, deduction, and evidence, we have been talking about means of rational persuasion. But, as we mentioned earlier, there arc also other means of persuasion. Take force, for example. If X kicks Y, threatens to destroy Y's means of livelihood, or threatens Y's life, X may persuade Y to cooperate. As Al Capone noted, "You can get more out of people with a gun and a kind word than with just a kind word." Another form of persuasion, irrational but sometimes highly effective, is **satire**, which works by witty ridicule. A cartoonist may persuade viewers that a politician's views are unsound by caricaturing (and thus ridiculing) the politician's appearance, or by presenting a grotesquely distorted (funny, but unfair) picture of the issue.

Satiric artists often use caricature; satiric writers, also seeking to persuade by means of ridicule, often use **verbal irony.** In irony of this sort there is a contrast between what is said and what is meant. For instance, words of praise may be meant to imply blame (when Cassius says, "Brutus is an honorable man," he means his hearers to think that Brutus is dishonorable), and words of modesty may be meant to imply superiority ("Of course I'm too simple to understand this problem"). Such language, when heavy-handed, is called **sarcasm** ("You're a great guy," said to someone who will not lend the speaker ten dollars). If it is witty—if the jeering is in some degree clever—it is called irony rather than sarcasm.

Although ridicule is not a form of argument (because it is not a form of reasoning), passages of ridicule, especially verbal irony, sometimes appear in essays that are arguments. These passages, like reasons, or for that matter like appeals to the emotions, are efforts to persuade the hearer to accept the speaker's point of view. For example, in Judy Syfers's essay "I Want a Wife" (p. 56), the writer, a woman, cannot really mean that she wants a wife. The pretense that she wants a wife gives the essay a playful, joking quality; her words must mean something other than what they seem to mean. But that she is not merely joking (satire has been defined as "joking in earnest") is evident; she is seeking to persuade. She has a point, and she could argue it straight, but that would produce a very different sort of essay.

SIX ARGUMENTS FOR ANALYSIS

Patricia Taylor

It's Time to Put Warning Labels on Alcohol

Spuds MacKenzie is tending goal. It's the last shot of the game, and Spuds makes an incredible save. The skillful maneuver by Anheuser-Busch's mascot is part of an Olympian effort to convince Americans that drinking is harmless and all-American. But during the next Olympiad, the ads may have a new twist. The bottle of Bud hoisted by the Spudettes may carry a message about the risks of alcohol.

Since 1977, when the Food and Drug Administration commissioner, Donald Kennedy, first recommended warning labels on alcoholic beverages, more than one million people have died from alcohol-related problems, one-fourth due to drinking and driving. The costs have been equally staggering—over one trillion dollars.

Congress is now considering a bill, that would require health warning labels on all alcoholic beverages, much as cigarettes are now labeled. Drinkers would be alerted to the risks of alcohol, just as consumers of bubble bath, over-the-counter drugs, and other products are told about the health risks of those products.[1]

While industry opponents deride the usefulness of warning labels, the   4 United States Public Health Service says, "Studies which have examined the impact of health warning labels in 'real world' situations have concluded that the labels did have an impact on consumer behavior."

Five different proposed labels would cover proven risks related to alcoholic beverages, ranging from birth defects to auto crashes. In 1981 the Surgeon General of the United States first advised women who are pregnant or considering pregnancy not to drink. Last year the National Institute on Alcohol Abuse and Alcoholism concluded that alcohol is the leading cause of mental retardation caused by known teratogenic agents (those that produce birth defects).

Alcohol is still involved in more than 50 percent of traffic fatalities. For those between the ages of 16 and 24, alcohol-related traffic deaths are

---

[1] This bill was later approved. Manufacturers of beer, wine, and liquor are now required to put labels on their containers warning that alcohol can cause birth defects and other health problems. [Editors' note]

Patricia Taylor (b. 1948) is director of the Alcohol Policies Project of the Center for Science in the Public Interest, in Washington. This article first appeared in the Op Ed section of the New York Times, *1988.*

the No. 1 killer. Warning labels would reinforce programs to reduce drinking and driving.

Another label, this one warning that alcohol is a potentially addictive drug, would dispel any notion that some alcoholic beverages are as harmless as soft drinks. New "cooler" products barely taste of alcohol but contain more than beer. In many states, you can walk into your local grocery store and purchase alcoholic beverages off the fruit juice shelf with names that give no hint that the product contains alcohol.

And on beer labels there isn't a single word to indicate that the contents are alcoholic. Many beer drinkers, especially teen-agers, think a can of beer is "safer" than a rum and Coke, even though the two contain equal amounts of alcohol. 8

Other labels would inform consumers about alcohol's contribution to liver disease, hypertension and cancer, and about the risk of drinking while taking prescription and over-the-counter drugs.

Alcoholic beverage producers certainly don't want consumers to associate drinking with mental retardation, alcoholism, cirrhosis of the liver, and death on the highways. So instead of informing drinkers about health and safety risks, they bombard us with $2 billion worth of slick promotional campaigns annually. According to Neil Postman, professor of media ecology at New York University, and his colleagues, children see more than 100,000 beer commercials on television before they are old enough to legally drink and drive. The ads do more than sell particular brands; they sell the assumption that drinking is not just safe, but essential to a happy, successful life.

Some companies do sponsor occasional ads to remind us to drink "moderately." Unfortunately, those ads are designed more to undercut prevention-oriented legislative initiatives than to educate drinkers about health risks. The fact is, the $70 billion-a-year booze industry simply can't afford moderate drinking. Its best customers are heavy drinkers, who account for half of all sales. If those drinkers drank less, sales—and profits—would plummet.

Industry officials often argue that warnings on their products would ultimately lead to warnings on everything from eggs to underwear. It's a cute argument, but it just doesn't wash. Only two products—alcohol and tobacco—are potentially addictive and sold legally directly to consumers despite their destructive impact on our nation's health. 12

With some luck, Congress will see through the anti-warning propaganda and respond to their constituents' concerns about alcohol.

Of course, health warnings alone won't eliminate alcohol problems. We really need a comprehensive strategy that would include expanded educational programs, mass media campaigns to neutralize industry's huge ad campaigns, and sharply higher Federal alcohol excise taxes. But passage of the pending bill with its clear, concise label notices, is an important place to start.

Questions and Suggestions for Writing

1. What devices or techniques does Patricia Taylor use in an effort to make her argument convincing?

2. In paragraph 11 Taylor speaks of "the . . . booze industry." Why do you suppose she uses this term—and why only at this late point rather than earlier in the essay?

3. Evaluate Taylor's final paragraph as a final paragraph.

4. In paragraph 12 Taylor pairs alcohol with tobacco as "potentially addictive," implying that since labels are put on tobacco they ought also to be put on alcohol. Is it relevant to object that before putting warning labels on tobacco the government had decided that tobacco *in any amount* could be hazardous, whereas there is some evidence (at least according to persons in the alcohol industry) that moderate consumption of alcohol may be a benefit?

5. Do you believe our society is hypocritical in tolerating the sale and consumption of intoxicating beverages and prohibiting the sale and consumption of marijuana, cocaine, opium, heroin, and other drugs? Explain your position in an essay of 500 words.

6. If consumption of alcohol is as harmful as Taylor claims (see paras. 5–6, 9–10), why shouldn't the manufacture, sale, and use of alcohol be made illegal? Write an essay of 500 words defending your position.

7. In paragraph 12 Taylor reports a so-called slippery slope objection, and she replies to it: "It just doesn't wash." Write a 250-word essay explaining this objection, her reply, and whether you agree with her reply.

8. A spokesman for the Beer Institute, arguing that warning labels may actually be harmful, said that they would obscure "the difference between moderate and abusive consumption." Further, he said, warning labels would encourage youngsters to drink by making alcohol a "forbidden fruit." The label, he said, "will act as a challenge, taunting adolescents to prove they can handle drinking no matter what the older generation says." How much merit do you find in these arguments against warning labels?

Thomas B. Stoddard

Gay Marriages: Make Them Legal

"In sickness and in health, 'til death do us part." With those familiar words, millions of people each year are married, a public affirmation of a private bond that both society and the newlyweds hope will endure. Yet for nearly four years, Karen Thompson was denied the company of the one person to whom she had pledged lifelong devotion. Her partner is a woman, Sharon Kowalski, and their home state of Minnesota, like every other jurisdiction in the United States, refuses to permit two individuals of the same sex to marry.

Karen Thompson and Sharon Kowalski are spouses in every respect except the legal. They exchanged vows and rings; they lived together until November 13, 1983—when Ms. Kowalski was severely injured when her car was struck by a drunk driver. She lost the capacity to walk or to speak more than several words at a time, and needed constant care.

Ms. Thompson sought a court ruling granting her guardianship over her partner, but Ms. Kowalski's parents opposed the petition and obtained sole guardianship. They moved Ms. Kowalski to a nursing home 300 miles away from Ms. Thompson and forbade all visits between the two women. Last month, as part of a reevaluation of Ms. Kowalski's mental competency, Ms. Thompson was permitted to visit her partner again. But the prolonged injustice and anguish inflicted on both women hold a moral for everyone.

Marriage, the Supreme Court declared in 1967, is "one of the basic 4 civil rights of man" (and, presumably, of woman as well). The freedom to marry, said the Court, is "essential to the orderly pursuit of happiness."

Marriage is not just a symbolic state. It can be the key to survival, emotional and financial. Marriage triggers a universe of rights, privileges, and presumptions. A married person can share in a spouse's estate even when there is no will. She is typically entitled to the group insurance and pension programs offered by the spouse's employer, and she enjoys tax advantages. She cannot be compelled to testify against her spouse in legal proceedings.

The decision whether or not to marry belongs properly to individuals—not the government. Yet at present, all 50 states deny that choice to millions of gay and lesbian Americans. While marriage has historically required a male partner and a female partner, history alone cannot sanc-

---

Thomas. B. Stoddard (b. 1948), a lawyer, is executive director of the Lambda Legal Defense and Education fund, a gay rights organization. This article is from the Op Ed section of the New York Times, *1988.*

tify injustice. If tradition were the only measure, most states would still limit matrimony to partners of the same race.

As recently as 1967, before the Supreme Court declared miscegenation statutes unconstitutional, sixteen states still prohibited marriages between a white person and a black person. When all the excuses were stripped away, it was clear that the only purpose of those laws was, in the words of the Supreme Court, "to maintain white supremacy."

Those who argue against reforming the marriage statutes because they 8 believe that same sex marriage would be "antifamily" overlook the obvious: marriage creates families and promotes social stability. In an increasingly loveless world, those who wish to commit themselves to a relationship founded upon devotion should be encouraged, not scorned. Government has no legitimate interest in how that love is expressed.

And it can no longer be argued—if it ever could—that marriage is fundamentally a procreative unit. Otherwise, states would forbid marriage between those who, by reason of age or infertility, cannot have children, as well as those who elect not to.

As the case of Sharon Kowalski and Karen Thompson demonstrates, sanctimonious illusions lead directly to the suffering of others. Denied the right to marry, these two women are left subject to the whims and prejudices of others, and of the law.

Depriving millions of gay American adults the marriages of their choice, and the rights that flow from marriage, denies equal protection of the law. They, their families and friends, together with fair-minded people everywhere, should demand an end to this monstrous injustice.

Questions and Suggestions for Writing

1. Study the essay as an example of ways to argue. What sorts of arguments does Stoddard offer? Obviously he does not offer statistics, or cite authorities, but what *does* he do in an effort to convince the reader?

2. Stoddard draws an analogy between laws that used to prohibit marriage between persons of different races and laws that still prohibit marriage between persons of the same sex. Evaluate this analogy in an essay of 100 words.

3. Stoddard cites Karen Thompson and Sharon Kowalski. Presumably he could have found, if he had wished, a comparable example using two men rather than two women. Do you think the effect of his essay would be better, worse, or the same if his example used men rather than women? Why?

4. Do you find adequate Stoddard's response to the charge that "same sex marriage would be 'antifamily'"? Why?

5. One widespread assumption is that the family exists in order to produce children. Stoddard mentions this, but he does not mention that although gay couples cannot produce children they can (where legally permitted to do so) rear children, and thus fulfill a social need. (Further, if the couple is lesbian,

one of the women can even be the natural mother.) Do you think he was wise to omit this argument in behalf of same-sex marriages? Why?

6. Think about what principal claims one might make to contradict Stoddard's claims, and then write a 500-word essay defending this proposition: Lawful marriage should be limited to heterosexual couples. Or, if you believe that gay marriages should be legitimized, write an essay offering additional support to Stoddard's essay.

7. Stoddard's whole purpose is to break down the prejudice against same-sex marriages, but he seems to take for granted the appropriateness of monogamy. Yet one might argue against Stoddard that if society opened the door to same-sex marriages, it would be hard to keep the door closed to polygamy or polyandry. Write a 500-word essay exploring this question.

Alan M. Dershowitz

Shouting "Fire!"

Justice Oliver Wendell Holmes' classic example of unprotected speech—falsely shouting "Fire!" in a crowded theater—has been invoked so often, by so many people, in such diverse contexts, that it has become part of our national folk language.

But in spite of its hallowed position in both the jurisprudence of the First Amendment and the arsenal of political discourse, it is and was an inapt analogy, even in the context in which it was originally offered. It has lately become—despite, perhaps even because of, the frequency and promiscuousness of its invocation—little more than a caricature of logical argumentation.

The case that gave rise to the "Fire!"-in-a-crowded-theater analogy— *Schenck v. United States*, involved the prosecution of Charles Schenck, who was the general secretary of the Socialist party in Philadelphia, and Elizabeth Baer, who was its recording secretary. In 1917 a jury found Schenck and Baer guilty of attempting to cause insubordination among soldiers who had been drafted to fight in the first World War. They and other party members had circulated leaflets urging draftees not to "submit to intimidation" by fighting in a war being conducted on behalf of "Wall Street's chosen few." Schenck admitted, and the Court found, that the intent of the pamphlet's "impassioned language" was to "influence" draftees to resist the draft. Interestingly, however, Justice Holmes noted that

Alan M. Dershowitz (b. 1938) is a professor of law at Harvard Law School and the author of Taking Liberties (1989). *This essay appeared in the* Harvard Law Bulletin, *1989.*

nothing in the pamphlet suggested that the draftees should use unlawful or violent means to oppose conscription.

Justice Holmes acknowledged that "in many places and in ordinary times the defendants, in saying all that was said in the circular, would have been within their constitutional rights." "But," he added, "the character of every act depends upon the circumstances in which it is done." And to illustrate that truism he went on to say,

> The most stringent protection of free speech would not protect a man in falsely shouting fire in a theater, and causing a panic. It does not even protect a man from an injunction against uttering words that may have all the effect of force.

The example of shouting "Fire!" obviously bore little relationship to the facts of the Schenck case. The Schenck pamphlet contained a substantive political message. It urged its draftee readers to *think* about the message and then—if they so chose—to act on it in a lawful and nonviolent way. The man who shouts "Fire!" in a crowded theater is neither sending a political message nor inviting his listener to think about what he has said and decide what to do in a rational, calculated manner. On the contrary, the message is designed to force action *without* contemplation. The message "Fire!" is directed not to the mind and the conscience of the listener but, rather, to his adrenaline and his feet. It is a stimulus to immediate *action*, not thoughtful reflection. It is—as Justice Holmes recognized in his follow-up sentence—the functional equivalent of "uttering words that may have all the effect of force."

Indeed, in that respect the shout of "Fire!" is not even speech, in any meaningful sense of that term. It is a *clang* sound, the equivalent of setting off a nonverbal alarm. Had Justice Holmes been more honest about his example, he would have said that freedom of speech does not protect a kid who pulls a fire alarm in the absence of a fire. But that obviously would have been irrelevant to the case at hand. The proposition that pulling an alarm is not protected speech certainly leads to the conclusion that shouting the word *fire* is also not protected. But the core analogy is the nonverbal alarm, and the derivative example is the verbal shout. By cleverly substituting the derivative shout for the core alarm, Holmes made it possible to analogize one set of words to another—as he could not have done if he had begun with the self-evident proposition that setting off an alarm bell is not free speech.

The analogy is thus not only inapt but also insulting. Most Americans do not respond to political rhetoric with the same kind of automatic acceptance expected of schoolchildren responding to a fire drill. Not a single recipient of the Schenck pamphlet is known to have changed his mind after reading it. Indeed, one draftee, who appeared as a prosecution witness, was asked whether reading a pamphlet asserting that the draft law was unjust would make him "immediately decide that you must erase that law." Not surprisingly, he replied, "I do my own thinking." A theatergoer would probably not respond similarly if asked how he would react to a shout of "Fire!"

Another important reason why the analogy is inapt is that Holmes emphasizes the factual falsity of the shout "Fire!" The Schenck pamphlet, however, was not factually false. It contained political opinions and ideas about the causes of the war and about appropriate and lawful responses to the draft. As the Supreme Court recently reaffirmed (in *Falwell v. Hustler*), "The First Amendment recognizes no such thing as a 'false' idea." Nor does it recognize false opinions about the causes or cures for war.

A closer analogy to the facts of the Schenck case might have been provided by a person's standing outside a theater, offering the patrons a leaflet advising them that in his opinion the theater was structurally unsafe, and urging them not to enter but to complain to the building inspectors. That analogy, however, would not have served Holmes's argument for punishing Schenck. Holmes needed an analogy that would appear relevant to Schenck's political speech, but one that would invite the conclusion that censorship was appropriate.

Analogies are, by their nature, matters of degree. Some are closer to the core example than others. But any attempt to analogize political ideas in a pamphlet, ugly parody in a magazine, offensive movies in a theater, or controversial newspaper articles to the very different act of shouting "Fire!" in a crowded theater is either self-deceptive or self-serving.

The government does, of course, have some arguable legitimate bases for suppressing speech that bear no relationship to shouting "Fire!" It may ban the publication of nuclear-weapon codes, information about troop movements, and the identity of undercover agents. It may criminalize extortion threats and conspiratorial agreements. These expressions may lead directly to serious harm, but the mechanisms of causation are very different from that at work when an alarm is sounded. One may also argue—less persuasively, in my view—against protecting certain forms of public obscenity and defamatory statements. Here, too, the mechanisms of causation are very different. None of these exceptions to the First Amendment's exhortation that the government "shall make no law . . . abridging the freedom of speech, or of the press" is anything like falsely shouting "Fire!" in a crowded theater; they all must be justified on other grounds.

A comedian once told his audience, during a stand-up routine, about the time he was standing around a fire with a crowd of people and got in trouble for yelling "Theater, theater!" That, I think, is about as clever and productive a use as anyone has ever made of Holmes's flawed analogy.

Questions and Suggestions for Writing

1. Consider Holmes's analogy (para. 4). Would he have thought it an unconstitutional abuse of free speech for someone to shout "Fire!" in a crowded theater,

believing erroneously that there was a fire? Would it matter, do you think, in such a case if the shouter caused a panic in which several people were injured or trampled to death? Why, or why not?

2. Do you think that it matters to Dershowitz's argument whether the political speech being repressed by the government is true or false? Why, or why not?

3. In paragraph 9 Dershowitz offers his own alternative analogy for the Schenck case. Suppose you believed that America's entry into the First World War was justified, and that the draft was also, and so was the conviction of Schenck. How would you defend Holmes's analogy against Dershowitz's criticisms? Could you think of a better analogy than Holmes's for this purpose? How would you attack Dershowitz's analogy?

4. In making a point in paragraph 7, Dershowitz quotes the testimony of a draftee. Do you think the point needs support, or is it self-evident? If it is not self-evident, does the draftee's testimony convince you of the truth of Dershowitz's point?

5. Read the *Cohen* case (p. 530) and ask yourself: Would Justice Holmes have argued that Cohen's conviction should stand? Would Dershowitz agree? Write a 250-word essay explaining your understanding of the position of both these thinkers on this case.

Jill Knight

Now Why Not Ask a Woman?

I am not a member of Women's Liberation, nor do I seek to escalate the battle between the sexes, but I must say at the outset that, to my mind, abortion is really a *woman's* subject. How can any man guess what it is like to start a pregnancy when one doesn't know how on earth one is going to be able to care for the baby: the anguish or fear or worry when the first signs are unmistakable? The male of the species doesn't vomit all the time, or get cumbersome, or have to figure out how he is going to keep on working in the later months, or plan how he is going to earn *and* look after the baby at the same time.

There are other factors. Take my case: my children are almost grown up; I have succeeded, after years of work and preparation, in a fascinating job which I enjoy thoroughly. If I were to start another baby, that would go, and my whole life would have to alter drastically.

Jill Knight (b. 1923), a Conservative member of the British Parliament since 1966, delivered this speech before the House of Commons in 1970.

So let's say I do understand, perhaps more basically than my respected and erudite male colleagues, why pressure has grown up for abortion to be legalized.

On the other hand, fully understanding all this, I am 100 percent against abortion—unless there are incontrovertible medical reasons why it must be done. If the terrible choice has to be made between the *life* of the mother and the life of the child, I think the mother should be saved because she probably has a husband, perhaps other children, and possibly parents, too, who love her and rely upon her. But abortion because the baby is inconvenient, or the mother doesn't happen to want one—never.

I used not to feel so strongly; like most people, I had never really examined the subject. But I did oppose the Abortion Bill, when it was first introduced in the British House of Commons, and my opposition led me to study the ramifications of this intensely complicated matter. The more I studied it, the more against abortion I became.

A lot of well-meaning people join the pro-abortion lobby because they have been revolted by horrendous tales of backstreet abortions. Grisly talk about unsavory operators, grubby kitchen tables, coat-hangers, hooks or knitting needles used as instruments on terrified girls, leads the kindly listener to vehement opposition—and the entirely wrong assumption that all this will be brought to an end if abortion is legalized. In point of fact, as we in Britain have discovered, backstreet operations continue however many legal abortions go on. This is because the cost of an abortion in a private clinic is generally high, and because in a National Health Service (free) hospital, the woman will have to give her name and address, which she is often reluctant to do; after all, there is no operation for which a woman wants to have greater anonymity than abortion.

Nevertheless, there is less social conscience about having the operation than there used to be. After all, even Parliament doesn't appear to think there is anything very wrong in having an abortion, and this attitude has certainly contributed to the astronomical rise in the number of abortions in Britain. Before the Act, we had about 10,000 per year—now the figure is 138,000 per year, and still rising.

As any doctor knows, depression and rejection of the child is quite a normal phenomenon of early pregnancy. Perhaps the mother-to-be feels sick, perhaps she regrets spoiled holiday plans, perhaps she did not intend to start a baby just then. However, before the Abortion Act it would never have entered her head to go along to her G.P. and ask to have the pregnancy ended. Within a few weeks she would not only accept her condition, but usually begin to look forward with pleasure to her baby. Now, with the possibility of abortion firmly before her, the knowledge that the highest authority in the land has sanctioned it, and the fact that her temporary period of rejection coincides with the "best" time to have an abortion, medically speaking, off she goes.

This huge rise in the number of abortions has meant that the gynecological units in our hospitals are grossly overworked, and women who need obstetrical care, other than an abortion, are finding that they are pushed to the bottom of the queue endlessly, because "abortion patients cannot wait." The recent concern expressed in a report from the Royal College of Gynaecologists and Obstetricians on this matter went on to state that two of the women who had been constantly relegated to the bottom of the list for entry to hospital were found, when finally admitted, to have been suffering from early cancer of the cervix.

Many women suffer from varying forms of gynecological disorder which are distressing and/or painful. How can it be right that they should have their suffering doubled or trebled because the beds they need are constantly occupied by abortion patients?

Any country or State which is contemplating making abortion available on demand had better ask itself whether it has the medical facilities, and the medical staff, to take on what is going to be a very heavy case-load indeed. Pro-abortionists say, "But if a woman is going to have a baby, she will have to go into hospital anyway, so why should there be any more pressure on hospital services if she goes in for an abortion instead?" But maternity cases are almost always straightforward: the doctors and nurses have usually looked after hundreds, and the process goes smoothly. Abortion cases are different—in the *time* at which the operation is being carried out (just how pregnant a woman is makes a lot of difference), in the circumstances surrounding the case, and in the psychological state of the patient. Reputable doctors take far longer in assessing abortion patients than they do in dealing with normal pregnancies. Besides, as we have found in Britain, it is possible to go into hospital two or three times for an abortion in the time it takes to have one baby.

Another thing about the situation which has arisen in Britain is the 12 way in which, all too often, a woman who is in hospital because she either wants a baby very much, and is being given treatment which may bring this about, *or* because she has just lost a baby through miscarriage, is put in the next bed to an abortion patient. Sometimes she is sandwiched between two. The Royal College of Nursing, in the week in which I write this chapter, has made a statement deploring this, and the heartbreak it causes. Because of the pressure under which gynecological wards are working, it is administratively impossible to avoid this happening.

Our nurses are clearly very distressed—or the vast majority are—at several other angles, too. There is no limit to the time after which an abortion may be performed in Britain. In the first three years after the Abortion Act went through, 528 babies were aborted at over 24 weeks gestation. Remember, many babies born prematurely at six months have been reared successfully—I have a very good friend who boasts of being a "six-month baby."

We had one case in Britain where a baby who had been aborted cried pitifully as it was about to be put into an incinerator by a hospital orderly. That baby was a seven-month baby. The figures show that there must have been many, many other babies killed or left to die after abortion, for when they are as late as that, I understand the abortion takes the form of a caesarean section.

A nurse came to see me recently to tell me that her experiences since the Abortion Act had now driven her to give up nursing. She told me that she had been ordered to dispose of a six-month baby boy, after an abortion. In the premature baby unit in her ward, they had a six-month baby boy, born too early. "We are doing everything we can for him," she said. "He is a lovely little chap, and I think he is going to make it. But how can I square it with my conscience that I do all in my power to save one baby, and kill off the other—*for no better reason than that the mother of the first wants him, and the mother of the second does not.*"

Women's Lib, which strongly supports abortion on demand, says a woman has a right to do what she wants with her body. So she does; what she has no right to do is to destroy *another* body. Pro-abortionists hate to admit there is any question of a baby being destroyed in an abortion. "Why do you make such a fuss?" they cry "It's only a blob." Yet, by the time a woman knows beyond all doubt that she is pregnant, she has a quite recognizable baby inside her. 16

The less the woman knows about the actual abortion, the better the pro-abortionists are pleased. After all, it takes a pretty strong stomach to accept the fact that many abortions are carried out by the insertion of an instrument into the womb, and the pulling out of separate bits of the baby at each insertion. Not nice, really: first an arm, then a leg, then a bit of head or shoulder, lying in a sterile dish in the operating theater.

But the point that Women's Lib misses is that freely available abortion can make women *more* enslaved, not less.

Parents, husbands, doctors more anxious to make money than to give their patient time and care—all these groups, in their separate ways, can and do exert pressure on a frightened or bewildered girl to have an abortion. I will quote from just two of the letters I have in my file, to illustrate my point.

The first is from a married woman in the London area who writes: 20

I had an abortion last July, and did so under pressure from my husband. It was emotional pressure, I suppose, for I had just become pregnant quite accidentally when my third baby was just two and a half months old. I feel so mixed-up and find it hard to understand how such a thing could ever have happened. The simple truth is that I signed the form, and therefore it is perhaps my fault for not having the strength of character to do what I know to be the right thing. The abortion itself was obtained very easily. I saw the doctor alone for less than five minutes; I gave him no reasons whatsoever that could possibly have justified him in granting the abortion so readily. He did in fact send me to see the medical social worker who told me that I had been sent to her because the doctor did not feel I had sufficient reason for an abortion. But during my conversation with her the telephone rang and it was the doctor, who had reread my notes and discovered that my husband was quite prepared to pay for it.

It all seems so complicated and difficult to put on paper. I had the abortion and feel that much of the blame must lie with me. Since it happened I have been depressed and no one seems to care. I am supposed to forget and forgive but I feel nothing but bitterness and hatred toward those people who allowed it to happen. If this letter will help in any way, I shall feel I have done something to protect unborn babies from being conveniently disposed of.

The second letter is from a young girl of eighteen who is not married:

I am about to complete a Sixth Form course at Grammar School. I have been going steady with a boy for two years, and he attends the same school. I have just discovered that I am five weeks pregnant and I feel I am in a desperate situation. My boyfriend, and his parents, want me to have an abortion. My father and mother have told me I must get an abortion and they will not allow me in the house otherwise. My father has heart trouble and my mother and sister say I am slowly killing him and if I keep the baby they say he will probably die of a heart attack.

I feel very selfish about the whole situation and I would hate to see my mother and father unhappy. I want to discuss the whole situation with someone, but my mother will not allow me out of the house. They take and collect me from school.

I understand how my parents feel, but to me to get an abortion would be the end of the world. I could never forget the fact that I had once been pregnant. I desperately want to keep the baby, but I am constantly being reminded that at the moment it is only a cell. This cell is the living nucleus of a potential human being and already I love it and feel it is part of me. I would do all in my power to keep the baby. I know it would mean great sacrifices on my part, but to me it would be worth every penny and every ounce of effort. I know I would love the baby and do everything possible to make it happy. I have weighed up both sides of the argument for and against an abortion, but I feel an abortion would be a disaster for me. I am a healthy eighteen-year-old; I feel an abortion would be heartbreaking and unnecessary.

We tried to help that girl, but her parents, his parents, and the boy himself, won. I have not heard from her since.

Some of the worst letters I have had have come from women who had had an abortion many years previously, but have never been able to forget it. Particularly if she is not able to have a baby when she *does* want one (and this is frequently what happens) the woman tends to feel ashamed and guilty. "God has paid me back," wrote one woman.

Of course, many women who have abortions do not feel like this at all. 24 The harder a woman is, the less an abortion bothers her; but the sensitive ones experience anguish of which no one warned them—no one asked them to stop and think.

I am not a Catholic, but my Catholic friends usually share my view that responsible family planning, not abortion, is the answer. The tragedy is that the overwhelming majority of women who seek abortions in Britain today admit that they were following no form of contraception when they became pregnant. This seems to me quite appalling. In my book of rules there is all the difference in the world between not starting a baby, and getting rid of the one you have started.

Before the Abortion Act went through in Britain, all the public communications media, and thus public opinion, was vociferously in favor of making abortion easily available. Now, after four years, the reverse is generally true. We have seen what a tiger we have by the tail. We now know the many evils of abortion-on-demand. The soaring abortion figures; the lack of care for the patient in the mushrooming abortion clinics where cash takes inevitable priority over care; the strain on hospitals, nurses, and reputable doctors; the people who tout for some of the private clinics, getting money for each patient they bring; the effect on women who want other hospital care; the psychological kick-back of abortion; the lack of babies for adoption.

A Labour government spokesman congratulated that government about two years after the Abortion Act went through because there were 120,000 fewer illegitimate babies than there would have been. I think he was wrong—that no congratulations were in order at all. I think one should work toward removing the stigma of illegitimacy, not kill the babies off. Many people want babies who cannot have them: once they could adopt a baby, but now there are none in Britain to adopt.

Abortion is a complex subject. Those who take the trouble to investi- 28 gate it thoroughly hardly ever campaign for it. Those who have learned what it means to a country when abortion legislation gets into the statute book are sadder and wiser people.

Questions and Suggestions for Writing ══════════════

1. Evaluate the title of the essay.

2. Knight says that "abortion is really a *woman's* subject." Would the reasoning she uses to support this view show, in parallel manner, that (a) the political behavior of the state of Israel is really a Jewish subject, or (b) the content of courses in Afro-American culture programs is really for blacks to decide, or (c) policies dealing with excessive drinking are really an alcoholic's subject?

3. Which side in the abortion controversy would be more likely to make the point that Knight makes in her first paragraph? What is Knight up to?

4. What is Knight doing in her second paragraph?

5. Evaluate the argument in the eighth paragraph, beginning "As any doctor knows . . ."

6. Evaluate Knight's use of testimony, calling attention to strengths and weaknesses.

7. Set forth Knight's arguments against abortion, summarizing each argument in a sentence or two.

8. Whatever your own position on abortion, write two paragraphs, one on what you think is her strongest argument, and another on what you think is her weakest argument, explaining why the one argument is comparatively strong and the other comparatively weak.

9. Do you find in this essay any generalizations that, on reflection, you think are wrong or perhaps unprovable? If so, list them.

10. Knight favors "removing the stigma of illegitimacy" and arranging for adoption of unwanted babies as a better alternative to unwanted pregnancy than abortion. What objections might be raised to the adequacy of this alternative?

11. Write a paragraph describing Knight's personality, as you perceive it through this essay. (Is she judicious, or bigoted, or zealous, or what? Which passages provide evidence for your opinion?)

Judy Syfers

I Want a Wife

I belong to that classification of people known as wives. I am A Wife. And, not altogether incidentally, I am a mother.

Not too long ago a male friend of mine appeared on the scene fresh from a recent divorce. He had one child, who is, of course, with his ex-wife. He is looking for another wife. As I thought about him while I was ironing one evening, it suddenly occurred to me that I, too, would like to have a wife. Why do I want a wife?

I would like to go back to school so that I can become economically independent, support myself, and, if need be, support those dependent

---

Born in San Francisco in 1937, Judy Syfers married in 1960, and two years later earned a bachelor's degree in painting at the University of Iowa. Active in the women's movement and in other political causes, she has worked as an author, an editor, and a secretary. The essay reprinted here, written before she and her husband separated, appeared originally in the first issue of Ms. *in 1972.*

upon me. I want a wife who will work and send me to school. And while I am going to school I want a wife to take care of my children. I want a wife to keep track of the children's doctor and dentist appointments. And to keep track of mine, too. I want a wife to make sure my children eat properly and are kept clean. I want a wife who will wash the children's clothes and keep them mended. I want a wife who is a good nurturant attendant to my children, who arranges for their schooling, makes sure that they have an adequate social life with their peers, takes them to the park, the zoo, etc. I want a wife who takes care of the children when they are sick, a wife who arranges to be around when the children need special care, because, of course, I cannot miss classes at school. My wife must arrange to lose time at work and not lose the job. It may mean a small cut in my wife's income from time to time, but I guess I can tolerate that. Needless to say, my wife will arrange and pay for the care of the children while my wife is working.

I want a wife who will take care of *my* physical needs. I want a wife 4 who will keep my house clean. A wife who will pick up after my children, a wife who will pick up after me. I want a wife who will keep my clothes clean, ironed, mended, replaced when need be, and who will see to it that my personal things are kept in their proper place so that I can find what I need the minute I need it. I want a wife who cooks the meals, a wife who is a *good* cook. I want a wife who will plan the menus, do the necessary grocery shopping, prepare the meals, serve them pleasantly, and then do the cleaning up while I do my studying. I want a wife who will care for me when I am sick and sympathize with my pain and loss of time from school. I want a wife to go along when our family takes a vacation so that someone can continue to care for me and my children when I need a rest and change of scene.

I want a wife who will not bother me with rambling complaints about a wife's duties. But I want a wife who will listen to me when I feel the need to explain a rather difficult point I have come across in my course of studies. And I want a wife who will type my papers for me when I have written them.

I want a wife who will take care of the details of my social life. When my wife and I are invited out by my friends, I want a wife who will take care of the babysitting arrangements. When I meet people at school that I like and want to entertain, I want a wife who will have the house clean, will prepare a special meal, serve it to me and my friends, and not interrupt when I talk about things that interest me and my friends. I want a wife who will have arranged that the children are fed and ready for bed before my guests arrive so that the children do not bother us. I want a wife who takes care of the needs of my guests so that they feel comfortable, who makes sure that they have an ashtray, that they are passed the hors d'oeuvres, that they are offered a second helping of the food, that their wine glasses are replenished when necessary, that their coffee is served to them as they like it. And I want a wife who knows that sometimes I need a night out by myself.

I want a wife who is sensitive to my sexual needs, a wife who makes love passionately and eagerly when I feel like it, a wife who makes sure that I am satisfied. And, of course, I want a wife who will not demand sexual attention when I am not in the mood for it. I want a wife who assumes the complete responsibility for birth control, because I do not want more children. I want a wife who will remain sexually faithful to me so that I do not have to clutter up my intellectual life with jealousies. And I want a wife who understands that *my* sexual needs may entail more than strict adherence to monogamy. I must, after all, be able to relate to people as fully as possible.

If, by chance, I find another person more suitable as a wife than the wife I already have, I want the liberty to replace my present wife with another one. Naturally, I will expect a fresh, new life; my wife will take the children and be solely responsible for them so that I am left free.   8

When I am through with school and have a job, I want my wife to quit working and remain at home so that my wife can more fully and completely take care of a wife's duties.

My God, who *wouldn't* want a wife?

Questions and Suggestions for Writing

1. If one were to summarize Syfers's first paragraph, one might say it adds up to "I am a wife and a mother." But analyze it closely. Exactly what does the second sentence add to the first? And what does "not altogether incidentally" add to the third sentence?

2. Syfers uses the word "wife" in sentences where one ordinarily would use "she" or "her." Why? And why does she begin paragraphs 4,5,6, and 7 with the same words, "I want a wife"?

3. In her second paragraph Syfers says that the child of her divorced male friend "is, of course, with his ex-wife." In the context of the entire essay, what does this sentence mean?

4. Complete the following sentence by offering a definition: "According to Judy Syfers, a wife is. . . ."

5. Try to state the essential argument of Syfers's essay in a simple syllogism. (*Hint:* Start by identifying the thesis or conclusion you think she is trying to establish, and then try to formulate two premises, based on what she has written, which would establish the conclusion.)

6. Drawing on your experience as observer of the world around you (and perhaps as husband, wife, or ex-spouse), do you think Syfers's picture of a wife's role is grossly exaggerated? Or is it (allowing for some serious playfulness) fairly accurate, even though it was written in 1971? If grossly exaggerated, is the essay

therefore meaningless? If fairly accurate, what attitudes and practices does it encourage you to support? Explain.

7. Whether or not you agree with Syfers's vision of marriage in our society, write an essay (500 words) titled "I Want a Husband," imitating her style and approach. Write the best possible essay, and then decide which of the two essays makes a fairer comment on current society. Or, if you believe Syfers is utterly misleading, write an essay titled "I Want a Wife," seeing the matter in a different light.

8. If you feel that you have been pressed into an unappreciated, unreasonable role—built-in babysitter, listening post, or girl (or boy or man or woman) Friday—write an essay of 500 words that will help the reader to see both your plight and the injustice of the system. (*Hint:* A little humor will help to keep your essay from seeming to be a prolonged whine.)

Italo Calvino

Why Read the Classics?

Let us begin with a few suggested definitions.

(1) The classics are the books of which we usually hear people say, "I am rereading . . ." and never "I am reading . . ."

This happens at least among those who consider themselves "very well read." It does not hold good for young people at the age when they first encounter the world, and the classics as a part of that world.

The reiterative prefix before the verb "read" may be a small hypocrisy on the part of people ashamed to admit they have not read a famous book. To reassure them, we need only observe that, however vast any person's basic reading may be, there still remain an enormous number of fundamental works that he has not read.

Hands up, anyone who has read the whole of Herodotus and the whole of Thucydides! And Saint-Simon? And Cardinal de Retz? But even the great nineteenth-century cycles of novels are more often talked about than read. In France they begin to read Balzac in school, and, judging by the number of copies in circulation, one may suppose that they go on 4

Italo Calvino (1923–1985) was of Italian descent but he was born in Cuba, where his father was engaged in agricultural research. Soon after his birth, the family returned to Italy, where Calvino was educated. During World War II he was a member of the anti-Fascist resistance; later he edited an intellectual journal and wrote stories, novels, and essays. This is a translation of an essay that originally appeared in L'Espresso, Rome, 1981.

reading him even after that, but if a Gallup poll were taken in Italy, I'm afraid that Balzac would come in practically last. Dickens fans in Italy form a tiny elite; as soon as its members meet, they begin to chatter about characters and episodes as if they were discussing people and things of their own acquaintance. Years ago, while teaching in America, Michel Butor got fed up with being asked about Emile Zola, whom he had never read, so he made up his mind to read the entire Rougon–Macquart cycle. He found it was completely different from what he had thought: a fabulous mythological and cosmogonical family tree, which he went on to describe in a wonderful essay.

In other words, to read a great book for the first time in one's maturity is an extraordinary pleasure, different from (though one cannot say greater or lesser than) the pleasure of having read it in one's youth. Youth brings to reading, as to any other experience, a particular flavor and a particular sense of importance, whereas in maturity one appreciates (or ought to appreciate) many more details and levels and meanings. We may therefore attempt the next definition:

(2) We use the word "classics" for books that are treasured by those who have read and loved them; but they are treasured no less by those who have the luck to read them for the first time in the best conditions to enjoy them.

In fact, reading in youth can be rather unfruitful, due to impatience, distraction, inexperience with the product's "instructions for use," and inexperience in life itself. Books read then can be (possibly at one and the same time) formative, in the sense that they give a form to future experiences, providing models, terms of comparison, schemes for classification, scales of value, exemplars of beauty—all things that continue to operate even if a book read in one's youth is almost or totally forgotten. If we reread the book at a mature age, we are likely to rediscover these constants, which by this time are part of our inner mechanisms, but whose origins we have long forgotten. A literary work can succeed in making us forget it as such, but it leaves its seed in us. The definition we can give is therefore this:

(3) The classics are books that exert a peculiar influence, both when they refuse to be eradicated from the mind and when they conceal themselves in the folds of memory, camouflaging themselves as the collective or individual unconscious.

There should therefore be a time in adult life devoted to revisiting the most important books of our youth. Even if the books have remained the same (though they do change, in the light of an altered historical perspective), we have most certainly changed, and our encounter will be an entirely new thing.

Hence, whether we use the verb "read" or the verb "reread" is of little   8 importance. Indeed, we may say:

(4) Every rereading of a classic is as much a voyage of discovery as the first reading.

(5) Every reading of a classic is in fact a rereading.

Definition 4 may be considered a corollary of this next one:

(6) A classic is a book that has never finished saying what it has to say.

Whereas definition 5 depends on a more specific formula, such as this:

(7) The classics are the books that come down to us bearing the traces of readings previous to ours, and bringing in their wake the traces they themselves have left on the culture or cultures they have passed through (or, more simply, on language and customs).

All this is true both of the ancient and of the modern classics. If I read the *Odyssey* I read Homer's text, but I cannot forget all that the adventures of Ulysses have come to mean in the course of the centuries, and I cannot help wondering if these meanings were implicit in the text, or whether they are incrustations or distortions or expansions. When reading Kafka, I cannot avoid approving or rejecting the legitimacy of the adjective "Kafkaesque," which one is likely to hear every quarter of an hour, applied indiscriminately. If I read Turgenev's *Fathers and Sons* or Dostoyevsky's *The Possessed*, I cannot help thinking how the characters have continued to be reincarnated right down to our own day.

The reading of a classic ought to give us a surprise or two vis-à-vis the notion that we had of it. For this reason, I can never sufficiently highly recommend the direct reading of the text itself, leaving aside the critical biography, commentaries, and interpretations as much as possible. Schools and universities ought to help us understand that no book that talks *about* a book says more than the book in question, but instead they do their level best to make us think the opposite. There is a very widespread topsy-turviness of values whereby the introduction, critical apparatus, and bibliography are used as a smokescreen to hide what the text has to say and, indeed, can say only if left to speak for itself without intermediaries who claim to know more than the text does. We may conclude that:

(8) A classic does not necessarily teach us anything we did not know before. In a classic we sometimes discover something we have always known (or thought we knew), but without knowing that this author said it first, or at least is associated with it in a special way. And this, too, is a surprise that gives a lot of pleasure, such as we always gain from the discovery of an origin, a relationship, an affinity. From all this we may derive a definition of this type:

(9) The classics are books which, upon reading, we find even fresher, more unexpected, and more marvelous than we had thought from hearing about them.

Naturally, this only happens when a classic really works as such—that is, when it establishes a personal rapport with the reader. If the spark doesn't come, that's a pity; but we do not read the classics out of duty or respect, only out of love. Except at school. And school should enable you to know, either well or badly, a certain number of classics among which—or in reference to which—you can then choose *your* classics. School is obliged to give you the instruments needed to make a choice, but the choices that count are those that occur outside and after school.

It is only by reading without bias that you might possibly come across 12 the book that becomes *your* book. I know an excellent art historian, an extraordinarily well-read man, who out of all the books there are has focused his special love on *Pickwick Papers;* at every opportunity he comes up with some quip from Dickens's book, and connects each and every event in life with some Pickwickian episode. Little by little he himself, and true philosophy, and the universe, have taken on the shape and form of the *Pickwick Papers* by a process of complete identification. In this way we arrive at a very lofty and demanding notion of what a classic is:

(10) We use the word "classic" of a book that takes the form of an equivalent to the universe, on a level with the ancient talisman. With this definition we are approaching the idea of the "total book," as Mallarmé conceived of it.

But a classic can establish an equally strong rapport in terms of opposition and antithesis. Everything that Jean-Jacques Rousseau thinks and does is very dear to my heart, yet everything fills me with an irrepressible desire to contradict him, to criticize him, to quarrel with him. It is a question of personal antipathy on a temperamental level, on account of which I ought to have no choice but not to read him; and yet I cannot help numbering him among *my* authors. I will therefore say:

(11) *Your* classic author is the one you cannot feel indifferent to, who helps you to define yourself in relation to him, even in dispute with him.

I think I have no need to justify myself for using the word "classic" without making distinctions as to age, style, or authority. What distinguishes the classic, in the argument I am making, may be only an echo effect that holds good both for an ancient work and for a modern one that has already achieved its place in a cultural continuum. We might say:

(12) A classic is a book that comes before other classics; but anyone who has read the others first, and then reads this one, instantly recognizes its place in the family tree.

At this point I can no longer put off the vital problem of how to relate the reading of the classics to the reading of all the other books that are anything but classics. It is a problem connected with such questions as "Why read the classics rather than concentrate on books that enable us to understand our own times more deeply?" or "Where shall we find the time and peace of mind to read the classics, overwhelmed as we are by the avalanche of current events?"

We can, of course, imagine some blessed soul who devotes his reading 16 time exclusively to Lucretius, Lucian, Montaigne, Erasmus, Quevedo, Marlowe, the *Discourse on Method, Wilhelm Meister,* Coleridge, Ruskin, Proust, and Valéry, with a few forays in the direction of Murasaki or the Icelandic Sagas. And all this without having to write reviews of the latest publications, or papers to compete for a university chair, or articles for

magazines on tight deadlines. To keep up such a diet without any con-
tamination, this blessed soul would have to abstain from reading the
newspapers, and never be tempted by the latest novel or sociological
investigation. But we have to see how far such rigor would be either
justified or profitable. The latest news may well be banal or mortifying,
but it nonetheless remains a point at which to stand and look both backward and forward. To be able to read the classics, you have to know "from
where" you are reading them; otherwise both the book and the reader will
be lost in a timeless cloud. This, then, is the reason why the greatest "yield"
from reading the classics will be obtained by someone who knows how to
alternate them with the proper dose of current affairs. And this does not
necessarily imply a state of imperturbable inner calm. It can also be the
fruit of nervous impatience, of a huffing-and-puffing discontent of mind.

Maybe the ideal thing would be to hearken to current events as we do
to the din outside the window that informs us about traffic jams and
sudden changes in the weather, while we listen to the voice of the classics
sounding clear and articulate inside the room. But it is already a lot for
most people if the presence of the classics is perceived as a distant rumble
far outside a room that is swamped by the trivia of the moment, as by a
television at full blast. Let us therefore add:

(13) A classic is something that tends to relegate the concerns of the
moment to the status of background noise, but at the same time this
background noise is something we cannot do without.

(14) A classic is something that persists as a background noise even
when the most incompatible momentary concerns are in control of the
situation.

There remains the fact that reading the classics appears to clash with
our rhythm of life, which no longer affords long periods of time or the
spaciousness of humanistic leisure. It also conflicts with the eclecticism of
our culture, which would never be capable of compiling a catalogue of
things classical such as would suit our needs.

These latter conditions were fully realized in the case of Leopardi,
given his solitary life in his father's house (his "*paterno ostello*"), his cult of
Greek and Latin antiquity, and the formidable library put at his disposal
by his father, Monaldo. To which we may add the entire body of Italian
literature and French literature, with the exception of novels and the
"latest hits" in general, which were left to beguile the leisure of his sister
Paolina ("*your* Stendhal," he wrote her once). Even with his intense
interest in science and history, he was often willing to rely on texts that
were not entirely up-to-date, taking the habits of birds from Buffon, the
mummies of Fredrik Ruysch from Fontanelle, the voyage of Columbus
from Robertson.

In these days a classical education like the young Leopardi's is unthinkable; above all, Count Monaldo's library has multiplied explosively.
The ranks of the old titles have been decimated, while new ones have

20

proliferated in all modern literatures and cultures. There is nothing for it but for all of us to invent our own ideal libraries of classics. I would say that such a library ought to be composed half of books we have read and that have really counted for us, and half of books we propose to read and presume will come to count—leaving a section of empty shelves for surprises and occasional discoveries.

I realize that Leopardi is the only name I have cited from Italian literature—a result of the explosion of the library. Now I ought to rewrite the whole article to make it perfectly clear that the classics help us to understand who we are and where we stand, a purpose for which it is indispensable to compare Italians with foreigners and foreigners with Italians. Then I ought to rewrite it yet again, lest anyone believe that the classics ought to be read because they "serve any purpose" whatever. The only reason one can possibly adduce is that to read the classics is better than not to read the classics.

And if anyone objects that it is not worth taking so much trouble, then I will quote Cioran (who is not yet a classic but will become one): "While they were preparing the hemlock, Socrates was learning a tune on the flute. 'What good will it do you,' they asked, 'to know this tune before you die?'"

Questions and Suggestions for Writing

1. By the end of the fourth paragraph, what is your impression of Calvino? What sort of person does he seem to be? Would you have liked to take a course in literature with him? Why, or why not?

2. Calvino suggests, in paragraph 8, that his fourth definition is a corollary of his sixth definition. What does he mean by "corollary" in this context? Would he say of his fifth definition that it is a corollary of his seventh? (See para. 8.) Why, or why not?

3. In paragraph 10 Calvino says that "The reading of a classic ought to give us a surprise or two, vis-à-vis the notion that we had of it." Does your experience of a classic—perhaps a play by Shakespeare, or Mary Shelley's *Frankenstein*, or Mark Twain's *Huckleberry Finn*—confirm Calvino's assertion? If so, how?

4. In paragraph 10 Calvino says that we can get "a lot of pleasure" from a classic that does not "teach us anything we did not know before." Does your experience confirm this assertion? If so, amplify the point, with reference to a particular classic.

5. In paragraph 13 Calvino says that a classic can provoke a reader's desire to contradict the author. He goes so far as to say that a "classic author is the one you cannot feel indifferent to, who helps you to define yourself—even in dispute with him." If you know, from your experience, what he is talking about, explain this point with reference to some work (a book, or perhaps a film, or even a song) that you treasure partly because you disagree with it.

6. Calvino seems to allow for the possibility that *my* list of classics might not be identical with *your* list, and yet that both lists are correct. Would he go so far as to allow that our two lists might have no common items? Explain your answer.

7. How do you think Calvino would have wanted Socrates to reply to the question put to him by his friends just before his death (para. 22)?

8. In paragraph 21 Calvino says that we read a classic to "help us to understand who we are and where we stand." Having announced this "purpose," he immediately says he ought to rewrite the essay "lest anyone believe that the classics ought to be read because they 'serve any purpose.'" Has he hopelessly contradicted himself? Or is his contradiction interesting? Is there some explanation for the apparent contradiction?

9. A good definition is supposed to cover all and only the items referred to by the terms being defined. Measured by this criterion, which is the best and which is the worst of the many definitions Calvino discusses, and why?

3

Writing an Argument, and Writing an Analysis of an Argument

When the Lord finished the world, He pronounced it good. That is what I said about my first work, too. But Time, I tell you, Time takes the confidence out of these incautious early opinions.
—MARK TWAIN

WRITING AN ARGUMENT

Any sort of writing is, Joan Didion says, an "act of saying," specifically an act of saying "See it my way." Even the humblest writer is in effect saying with Martin Luther, "Here I stand; I can do no other. God help me. Amen."

That may sound rather grand, but it is true; when we write we are putting ourselves on the line. Teachers know it, and students know it too; that's one reason all of us, teachers and students, have trouble writing. In a conversation we can cover ourselves with such expressions as "Well, I don't know, but I sort of think that . . . ," and we can always revise our position ("Oh, well, I didn't mean it that way") but once we have handed in the final version of our writing we are helpless. We are (putting it strongly) naked to our enemies.

Getting Ideas

As indicated in the previous paragraph, we often improve our thoughts when we try to explain them to someone else. Partly, of course, we are responding to questions or objections raised by our companion in the conversation, but partly we are responding to ourselves; almost as soon as we hear what we have to say, we may find that it won't do, and, if we are lucky, we may find a better idea surfacing. One of the best ways of getting ideas is to talk things over.

The process of talking things over usually begins with the text that you are reading; your marginal notes, your summary, and your queries parenthetically incorporated within your summary are a kind of dialogue between you and the author you are reading. More obviously, when you talk with friends about your topic you are trying out and developing ideas. Finally, after reading, taking notes, and talking, you may feel that you now have clear ideas and you need only put them into writing. And so you take a sheet of blank paper, and perhaps a paralyzing thought suddenly strikes: "I have ideas but just can't put them into words."

Despite what many people believe, writing is not only a matter of putting one's ideas into words. Just as talking with others is a way of getting ideas, *writing is a way of getting and developing ideas.* If fear of putting ourselves on record is one big reason we have trouble writing, another big reason is our fear that we have no ideas worth putting down. But by writing a draft, however weak, we can help ourselves to get ideas. One puts something down on paper, and almost immediately sees that it needs improvement, not simply a little polishing but a substantial overhaul. One writes, "Truman was justified in dropping the atom bomb for two reasons," and as soon as one writes these words, a third reason comes to mind. Or perhaps one of those "two reasons" no longer seems very good. As the little girl shrewdly replied when an adult told her to think before she spoke, "How do I know what I think before I hear what I say?" We have to see what we say, we have to get something down on paper, before we realize that we need to make it better.

Writing, then, is really rewriting; that is, revising, and a revision is a *re-vision*, a second look. The paper that you hand in should be clear and may even seem effortless, but in all likelihood the clarity and apparent ease are the result of a struggle with yourself, a struggle during which you greatly improved your first thoughts. One begins by putting down one's ideas, such as they are, perhaps even in the random order in which they occurred, but sooner or later comes the job of looking at them critically, developing what is useful in them and chucking out what is not. If you follow this procedure you will be in the company of Picasso, who said that he "advanced by means of destruction."

Whether you advance bit by bit (writing a sentence, revising it, writing the next, and so on) or whether you write an entire first draft and then revise it and revise it again and again is mostly a matter of temperament. Probably most people combine both approaches, backing up occasionally but trying to get to the end fairly soon so that they can see rather quickly what they know, or think they know, and can then start the real work of thinking, of converting their initial ideas into something substantial.

Getting Ideas by Asking Questions · Getting ideas is mostly a matter of asking (and then thinking about) questions. We append questions to the end of each argument in this book, not in order to torment you but in order to help you to think about the arguments, for instance to turn your attention to especially important matters. If your instructor asks you to write an answer to one of these questions, you are lucky: Examining the question will stimulate your mind to work in a definite direction. But if a topic is not assigned, and you are asked to write an argument, you will find that some ideas (possibly poor ones, at this stage, but that doesn't matter because you will soon revise) will come to mind if you ask yourself questions. Earlier, on pages 20–21, we listed some basic questions:

1. What is X?
2. What is the value of X?
3. What are the causes (or the consequences) of X?
4. What should (or ought or must) we do about X?

One or more of these questions may get you going. Thinking about the first question, for example, will require you to try to produce a definition, and as you work at producing a satisfactory definition, you may find new ideas arising. If a question seems relevant, start writing, even if you write only a fragmentary sentence. You'll probably find that one word leads to another and that ideas begin to appear. Even if these ideas seem weak as you write them, don't be discouraged; you have something on paper, and returning to these lines, perhaps in five minutes or perhaps the next day, you will probably find that some are not at all bad, and that others will stimulate you to better ones.

It may be useful to record your ideas in a special notebook reserved for the purpose. Such a **journal** can be a valuable resource when it comes time to write your paper. Many students find it easier to focus their thoughts on writing if during the period of gestation they have been jotting down relevant ideas on something more substantial than slips of paper or loose sheets. The very act of designating a notebook as your journal for a course can be the first step in focusing your attention on the eventual need to write a paper.

If what we have just said does not sound convincing, and you know from experience that you often have trouble getting started with your writing, don't despair; first aid is at hand in a sure-fire method that we will now talk about.

Imagining an Audience

Of course the questions that you ask yourself, in order to stimulate your thoughts, will depend primarily on what you are writing about, but five additional questions are always relevant:

1. Who are my readers?
2. What do they believe?
3. How much common ground do we share?
4. What do I want my readers to believe?
5. What do they need to know?

These questions require a little comment. The literal answer to the first probably is "the teacher," but (unless you are given instructions to the contrary) you should not write specifically for the teacher; instead, you should write for an audience that is, generally speaking, like your classmates. In short, your imagined audience is literate, intelligent, and moderately well informed, but it does not know everything that you know, and it does not know your response to the problem that you are addressing.

The essays in this book are from many different sources, each with its own audience. An essay from the *New York Times* is addressed to the educated general reader; an essay from *Ms.* is addressed to readers sympathetic to the feminist movement. An essay from *Commonweal*, a Roman Catholic publication addressed to the nonspecialist, is likely to differ in point of view or tone from one in *Time*, even though both articles may advance approximately the same position. The writer of the article in *Commonweal* may, for example, effectively cite church fathers and distinguished Roman Catholic writers as authorities, whereas the writer of an article addressed largely to non-Catholic readers probably will cite few or even none of these figures because the audience might be unfamiliar with them and therefore unimpressed by their views.

The tone as well as the gist of the argument is in some degree shaped by the audience. For instance, popular journals, such as *The National Review* and *Ms.* are more likely to use ridicule than are journals chiefly addressed at, say, an academic audience.

The Audience as Collaborator

If you imagine an audience, and keep asking yourself what this audience needs to be told and what it doesn't need to be told, you will find that material comes to mind, just as it comes to mind when a friend asks you what a film was about, and who was in it, and how you liked it. Your readers do not have to be told that Thomas Jefferson was an American statesman in the early years of this country's history, but they do have to be told that Thomas Huxley was a late nineteenth-century English advocate of Darwinism. You would identify Huxley because it's your hunch that your classmates never heard of him, or even if they may have heard the name, they can't quite identify it. But what if your class has been assigned an essay by Huxley? Because your imagined reader knows Huxley's name and knows at least a little about him, you don't have to identify Huxley as an Englishman of the nineteenth century, but you do still have to remind your reader about aspects of his essay, and you do have to tell your reader about your responses to it.

After all, even if the class has read an essay by Huxley, you cannot assume that your classmates know the essay inside out. Obviously you can't say, "Huxley's third reason is also unconvincing," without reminding the reader, by means of a brief summary, of his third reason. Again, think of your classmates as your imagined readers; put yourself in their shoes, and be sure that your essay does not make unreasonable demands. If you ask yourself, "What do my readers need to know?" (and "What do I want them to believe?") you will find some answers arising, and you will start writing.

We have said that you should imagine your audience as your classmates. But this is not the whole truth. In a sense, your argument is addressed not simply to your classmates but to the world interested in ideas. Even though you can reasonably assume that your classmates have read only one work by Huxley, you will not begin your essay by writing "Huxley's essay is deceptively easy." You will have to name the work; it is possible that a reader has read some other work by Huxley. And by precisely identifying your subject you help to ease the reader into your essay. Similarly, you won't begin by writing.

> The majority opinion in *Walker v. City of Birmingham* was that. . . .

Rather, you'll write something like this:

> In *Walker v. City of Birmingham*, the Supreme Court ruled in 1966 that city authorities acted lawfully when they jailed Martin Luther King, Jr., and other clergymen in 1963 for marching in Birmingham without a permit. Justice Potter Stewart delivered the majority opinion, which held that. . . .

By the way, if you think you suffer from a writing block, the mere act of writing out such obvious truths will help you to get started. You will find that putting a few words down on paper, perhaps merely copying the essay's title or an interesting quotation from the essay, will stimulate you to jot down thoughts that you didn't know you had in you.

Thinking about your audience can help you to put some words on paper; even more important, it can help you to get ideas. Our second and third questions about the audience, you recall, were

What do they believe?

and

How much common ground do we share?

Presumably your imagined audience does not share your views, or at least does not fully share them. But why? How can these readers hold a position that to you seems unreasonable? If you try to put yourself into your readers' shoes, and if you think about what your audience knows or thinks it knows, you will find yourself getting ideas. You do not believe (let's assume) that people should be allowed to smoke in enclosed public places, but you know that some people hold a different view. Why do they hold it? Try to state their view *in a way that would be satisfactory to them*. Having done so, you may come to perceive that your conclusions and theirs differ because they are based on different premises, perhaps different ideas about human rights. Examine the opposition's premises carefully, and explain, first to yourself and ultimately to your readers, *why* you find some premises unsound.

Possibly some facts are in dispute, such as whether nonsmokers may be harmed by exposure to tobacco. The thing to do, then, is to check the facts. If you find that harm to nonsmokers has not been proved, but you nevertheless believe that smoking should be prohibited in enclosed public places, of course you can't premise your argument on the wrongfulness of harming the innocent (in this case, the nonsmokers). You will have to develop arguments that take account of the facts, whatever they are.

Among the relevant facts there surely are some that your audience or your opponent will not dispute. The same is true of the values relevant to the discussion; the two of you are very likely to agree, if only you stop to think about it, that you share belief in some of the same values (such as the principle mentioned above, that it is wrong to harm the innocent). These areas of shared agreement are crucial to effective persuasion in argument. If you wish to persuade, you'll have to begin by finding *premises you can share with your audience*. Try to identify and isolate these areas of agreement. There are two good reasons for doing so:

1. There is no point in disputing facts or values on which you really agree, and
2. it usually helps to establish goodwill between you and your opponent when you can point to beliefs, assumptions, facts, values that the two of you share.

In a few moments we will return to the need to share some of the opposition's ideas.

The Thesis

Let's assume that you are writing an argumentative essay—perhaps an evaluation of an argument in this book—and you have what seems to be a pretty good draft, or at least a bunch of notes that are the result of hard thinking. You really do have ideas now, and you want to present them effectively. How will you organize your essay? No one formula works best for every essayist and for every essay, but it is usually advisable to formulate a basic **thesis**, a central point, a chief position, and to state it early. Every essay that is any good, even a book-length one, has a thesis, a main point, which can be stated briefly. Remember Coolidge's remark on the preacher's sermon on sin: "He was against it." Don't confuse the **topic** (here it is sin) with the thesis (opposition to sin). The thesis is the argumentative theme, the author's primary claim or contention, the proposition that the rest of the essay will explain and defend. Of course the thesis may sound like a commonplace, but the book or essay or sermon ought to develop it interestingly and convincingly.

Here are some sample theses:

Smoking should be prohibited in all enclosed public places.

Smoking should be limited to specific parts of enclosed public places, and entirely prohibited in small spaces, such as elevators.

Proprietors of public places such as restaurants and sports arenas should be free to determine whether they wish to prohibit, limit, or impose no limitations on smokers.

The Audience—Once Again—As Collaborator

Recall that in writing college papers it is usually best to write for a general audience, an audience rather like your classmates but without the specific knowledge that they all share as students enrolled in one course. If the topic is smoking in public places, the audience presumably consists of smokers and nonsmokers. Thinking about our second question, What do the readers need to know?, may prompt you to give statistics about the harmful effects of smoking. Or, if you are arguing on behalf of smokers, it may prompt you to cite studies claiming that no evidence conclusively demonstrates that cigarette smoking is harmful to nonsmokers. If indeed you are writing for a general audience, and you are not advancing a highly unfamiliar view, our third question (What does the audience believe?) is less important here, but if the audience is specialized, such as an antismoking group, or a group of restaurant owners who fear that antismoking regulations will interfere with their business, or a group of civil libertarians, obviously an effective essay will have to address their special beliefs.

In addressing their beliefs (let's assume that you do not share them, or do not share them fully), you must try to establish some common ground. If you advocate requiring restaurants to provide nonsmoking areas, you should at least recognize the possibility that this arrangement will result in inconvenience for the proprietor. But perhaps (the good news) it will regain some lost customers or will attract some new customers. This thought should prompt you to think of kinds of evidence, perhaps testimony or statistics.

When one formulates a thesis and asks questions about it, of the type just given, one begins to get ideas about how to organize the material, or at least one begins to see that some sort of organization will have to be worked out. The thesis may be clear and simple, but the reasons (the argument) may take 500 pages. The thesis is the point; the argument sets forth the evidence that is offered to support the thesis.

The Title

It's not a bad idea to announce your thesis in your title. If you scan the table of contents of this book, you will notice that a fair number of essayists use the title to let the readers know, at least in a very general way, what position will be advocated. Here are a few examples:

Gay Marriages: Make Them Legal

Smokers Get a Raw Deal

Why Handguns Must Be Outlawed

True, these titles are not especially engaging, but the reader welcomes them because they give some information about the writer's thesis.

Some titles do not announce the thesis but effectively announce the topic:

Work and Prayer

Is All Discrimination Unfair?

The Death Penalty

Although not clever or witty, these titles are informative.

Some titles seek to attract attention or to stimulate the imagination:

A First Amendment Junkie

I Have a Dream

Now Why Not Ask a Woman?

Viva Bilingualism

All of these are effective, but a word of caution is appropriate here. In your effort to engage your readers' attention, be careful not to sound like a wise guy. You want to engage your readers, not turn them off.

The Opening Paragraphs

You may not wish to announce your thesis in your title, but if you don't announce it there, you should set it forth very early in the argument, in your introductory paragraph or paragraphs. In her title, "Human Rights and Foreign Policy," Jeane J. Kirkpatrick merely announces her topic (subject) as opposed to her thesis (point), but she begins to hint at the thesis in her first paragraph, by deprecating President Jimmy Carter's policy:

> In this paper I deal with three broad subjects: first, the content and consequences of the Carter administration's human rights policy; second, the prerequisites of a more adequate theory of human rights; and third, some characteristics of a more successful human rights policy.

Or consider this opening paragraph from Peter Singer's "Animal Liberation":

> We are familiar with Black Liberation, Gay Liberation, and a variety of other movements. With Women's Liberation some thought we had

come to the end of the road. Discrimination on the basis of sex, it has been said, is the last form of discrimination that is universally accepted and practiced without pretense, even in those liberal circles which have long prided themselves on their freedom from racial discrimination. But one should always be wary of talking of "the last remaining form of discrimination." If we have learned anything from the liberation movements, we should have learned how difficult it is to be aware of the ways in which we discriminate until they are forcefully pointed out to us. A liberation movement demands an expansion of our moral horizons, so that practices that were previously regarded as natural and inevitable are now seen as intolerable.

Although Singer's introductory paragraph nowhere mentions animal liberation, in conjunction with its title it gives us a good idea of what Singer is up to and where he is going. Singer knows that his audience will be skeptical, so he reminds them that many of us in previous years were skeptical of causes that we now take for granted. He adopts a strategy used fairly often by writers who advance highly unconventional theses: rather than beginning with a bold announcement of a thesis that may turn off readers because it sounds offensive or absurd, Singer warms his readers up, gaining their interest by cautioning them politely that although they may at first be skeptical of animal liberation, if they stay with his essay they may come to feel that they have expanded their horizons.

Notice, too, that Singer begins by establishing common ground with his readers; he assumes, probably correctly, that his readers share his view that other forms of discrimination (now seen to be unjust) were once widely practiced and were assumed to be acceptable and natural. In this paragraph, then, Singer is not only showing himself to be fair-minded but is also letting us know that he will advance a daring idea. His opening wins our attention and our goodwill. A writer can hardly hope to do more. In a few pages we will talk a little more about winning the audience.

In your introductory paragraphs you may have to give some background informing or reminding your readers of material that they will have to be familiar with if they are to follow your essay. In writing, or at least in revising these paragraphs, remember to keep in mind this question: What do my readers need to know? Much, of course, depends on who your audience is, but unless your teacher offers other instructions, assume that you are writing for people who are pretty much like your classmates.

After announcing the topic, giving the necessary background, and stating your position (and perhaps the opposition's) in as engaging a manner as possible, it is usually a good idea to give the reader an idea of how you will proceed. Look on the preceding page at Kirkpatrick's opening paragraph, for an obvious though not entirely ingratiating illustration. She tells us she will deal with three subjects, and she names them. Her approach in the paragraph is concise, obvious, and effective.

Similarly, you may, for instance, want to announce fairly early that there are four common objections to your thesis, and that you will take them up one by one, in an announced order, beginning with the weakest (or most widely held, or whatever) and moving to the strongest (or least familiar), after which you will advance your own view in greater detail. Of course not every argument begins with refuting the other side, though many arguments do. The point to remember is that you usually ought to tell your readers where you will be taking them and by what route.

Opening paragraphs, then, usually do at least one (and often all) of these:

1. attract the reader's interest;
2. give an idea of the topic, and often of the thesis;
3. engage the reader's goodwill, usually by recognizing that the opposing view may be held by responsible people, and indeed has some merit in it;
4. give an idea of how the writer will organize the argument.

Organizing and Revising the Body of the Essay

Most arguments more or less follow this organization:

1. **Statement of the problem.** Whether the problem is stated briefly or at length depends on the nature of the problem and the writer's audience.
2. **Statement of the structure of the essay.** After stating the problem at the appropriate length, the writer often briefly indicates the structure of the rest of the essay. The commonest structure is suggested below, in points 3 and 4.
3. **Survey of alternative solutions.** In addition to stating the alternatives, the writer probably conveys willingness to recognize not only the integrity of the proposers but also the (partial) merit of at least some of the alternative solutions.

The next stage, which constitutes most of the body of the essay, usually is this:

4. **Arguments in support of the proposed solution.** The evidence offered will, of course, depend on the nature of the problem. Statistics, authorities, analogies may or may not be relevant. This part of the essay often also includes arguments answering possible objections, especially objections that (a) the proposal won't work (perhaps it is alleged to be too expensive, or to make unrealistic demands on human nature, or to fail to get to the heart of the problem), and objections that (b) the proposed solution will create problems greater than the present difficulty.

Of course not every essay will follow this pattern, but let's assume that in the introductory paragraphs you have sketched the topic, and have fairly and courteously set forth the opposition's view, recognizing its merits and indicating the degree to which you can share part of that view. You now want to set forth your arguments explaining why you differ on some essentials.

In setting forth your own position, you can begin either with your strongest reasons or your weakest. Each method of organization has advantages and disadvantages. If you begin with your strongest, the essay may seem to peter out; if you begin with the weakest, you build to a climax but your readers may not still be with you because they may have felt at the start that the essay was frivolous. The solution to this last possibility is to make sure that even your weakest argument is an argument of some strength. You can, moreover, assure your readers that stronger points will soon be offered and you offer this point first only because you want to show that you are aware of it, and that, slight though it is, it deserves some attention. The body of the essay, then, is devoted to arguing a position, which means not only offering supporting reasons but also offering refutations of possible objections to these reasons.

Doubtless you will sometimes be uncertain, as you draft your essay, whether to present a point before or after another point. Try to put yourself into your reader's shoes: Which point do you think the reader needs to know first? Which point *leads to* which further point? Your argument should not be a mere list of points, of course; rather, it should clearly integrate one point with another in order to develop an idea. But in all likelihood you won't have a strong sense of the best organization until you have written a draft and have reread it. You are likely to find that the organization needs some revising in order to make your argument clear to a reader.

Checking Paragraphs · When you revise your draft, watch out also for short paragraphs. Although a paragraph of only two or three sentences (like some in this chapter) may occasionally be helpful as a transition between complicated points, most short paragraphs are undeveloped paragraphs. (Newspaper editors favor very short paragraphs because they can be read rapidly when printed in the narrow columns typical of newspapers. There is no reason for you to imitate this style in the argumentative essays you will be writing.) In revising, when you find a paragraph of only a sentence or two or three, check first to see if it should be joined to the paragraph that precedes or follows. Second, if on rereading you are certain that a given paragraph should not be tied to what comes before or after, think about amplifying the paragraph with supporting detail (this is not the same as mere padding).

Checking Transitions · Make sure, too, in revising, that the reader can move easily from the beginning of a paragraph to the end, and from one paragraph to the next. Transitions help the reader to perceive the connections between the units of the argument. For example (that's a transition, of course), they may

> **illustrate:** *for example, for instance, consider this case;*
>
> **connect logically:** *thus, as a result, therefore, so, it follows;*
>
> **compare:** *similarly, in like manner, just as, analogously;*
>
> **contrast:** *on the other hand, in contrast, however, but;*
>
> **summarize:** *in short, briefly.*

Expressions such as these serve as guideposts that enable your reader to move easily through your essay.

When writers revise an early draft they chiefly

1. **unify** the essay by eliminating irrelevancies;
2. **organize** the essay by keeping in mind an imagined audience;
3. **clarify** the essay by fleshing out thin paragraphs, by making certain that the transitions are adequate, and by making certain that generalizations are adequately supported by concrete details and examples.

We are not talking about polish or elegance; we are talking about the most fundamental matters.

The Ending

What about concluding paragraphs, in which you try to summarize the main points and reaffirm your position? If you can look back over your essay and can add something that enriches it and at the same time wraps it up, fine, but don't feel compelled to say, "Thus, in conclusion, I have argued X, Y, and Z, and I have refuted Jones." After all, *conclusion* can have two meanings: (1) ending, or finish, as the ending of a joke or a novel; (2) judgment or decision reached after deliberation. Your essay should finish effectively (the first sense), but it need not announce a judgment (the second).

If the essay is fairly short, so that a reader can more or less keep the whole thing in mind, you may not need to restate your view. Just make sure that you have covered the ground, and that your last sentence is a good one. Notice that neither of the essays printed later in this chapter ends with a formal conclusion, though each ends conclusively, with a note of finality.

The Uses of an Outline

Some writers find it useful to sketch an **outline** as soon as they think they know what they want to say, even before they write a first draft; others write an outline after a draft that has given them additional ideas. These procedures can be helpful in planning a tentative organization, but remember that in revising a draft new ideas will arise, and the outline may have to be modified. A preliminary outline is chiefly useful as a means of getting going, not as a guide to the final essay.

The Outline as a Way of Checking a Draft · Whether or not you use a preliminary outline, we suggest that after you have written what you hope is your last draft, you make an outline of it; there is no better way of finding out if the essay is well organized. Go through the draft and jot down the chief points, in the order in which you make them, and then examine your jottings to see if they indeed form a reasonable sequence. If no structure or sequence clearly appears in the outline, then your argument probably doesn't have any, either. Therefore, produce another draft, moving things around, adding or subtracting paragraphs—cutting and pasting into a new sequence, with transitions as needed—and then make another outline to see if the sequence now is satisfactory.

Tone and the Writer's Persona

Although this book is chiefly about argument in the sense of rational discourse—the presentation of reasons—the appeal to reason is only one form of persuasion. Another form is the appeal to emotion—to pity, for example. Aristotle saw, in addition to the appeal to reason and the appeal to emotion, a third form of persuasion, the appeal to the character of the speaker. He called it the *ethical appeal*. The idea is that effective speakers convey the suggestion that they are persons of good sense, benevolence, and honesty. Their discourse, accordingly, inspires confidence in their listeners. It is, of course, a fact that when we read an argument we are often aware of the "person" or "voice" behind the words, and our assent to the argument depends partly on the extent to which we can share the speaker's assumptions, look at the matter from the speaker's point of view—in short *identify* with this speaker.

How can a writer inspire the confidence that lets readers identify themselves with the writer? To begin with, the writer should possess the virtues Aristotle specified: intelligence or good sense, honesty, and benevolence or goodwill. As the Roman proverb puts it, "No one gives what he does not have." But because you are reading this book, you have reason to believe that you are intelligent, and the authors will assume that you are honest and well intentioned. Still, possession of these qualities is not a guarantee that you will convey them in your writing. Like all other writers, you will have to revise your drafts so that these qualities become apparent, or, stated more moderately, you will have to revise so that nothing in the essay causes a reader to doubt your intelligence, honesty, and goodwill. A blunder in logic, a misleading quotation, a snide remark—all such slips can cause readers to withdraw their sympathy from the writer.

But of course all good argumentative essays do not sound exactly alike; they do not all reveal the same speaker. Each writer develops his or her own voice or (as literary critics and teachers call it) persona. In fact, one writer will have several voices or personae, depending on the topic and the audience. President George Bush delivering an address on the State of the Union has one persona; chatting with a reporter at his summer home he has another. This change is not a matter of hypocrisy. Different circumstances call for different language. As a French writer put it, there is a time to speak of "Paris," and a time to speak of "the capital of the nation." When Lincoln spoke at Gettysburg, he didn't say "Eighty-seven years ago," but "Four score and seven years ago." We might say that just as some occasions required him to be the folksy Honest Abe, the occasion of the dedication of hallowed ground required him to be formal and solemn, and so the president of the United States appropriately used biblical language. The election campaigns called for one persona, and this occasion called for a different persona.

When we talk about a writer's persona, we mean the way in which the writer presents his or her attitudes:

the attitude toward *the self*,

toward *the audience*, and

toward *the subject*.

Thus, if a writer says,

I have thought long and hard about this subject, and I can say with assurance that . . .

we may feel that we are listening to a self-satisfied ass who probably is simply mouthing other people's opinions. Certainly he is mouthing other people's clichés: "long and hard," "say with assurance."

Let's look at a slightly subtler example of an utterance that reveals an attitude. When we read that

President Nixon was hounded out of office by journalists

we hear a respectful attitude toward Nixon ("President Nixon") and a hostile attitude toward the press ("hounded"). If the writer's attitudes were reversed, she might have said something like this:

The press turned the searchlight on Tricky Dick's criminal shenanigans.

"Tricky Dick" and "criminal" are obvious enough, but notice that "shenanigans" also implies the writer's contempt for Nixon, and of course "turned the searchlight" suggests that the press is a source of illumination, a source of truth. The original version and the revision both say that the press was responsible for Nixon's resignation, but the original version ("President Nixon was hounded") conveys indignation toward journalists, whereas the revision conveys contempt for Nixon.

These two versions suggest two speakers who differ not only in their view of Nixon but also in their manner, including the seriousness with which they take themselves. Although the passage is very short, it seems to us that the first speaker conveys righteous indignation ("hounded"), whereas the second conveys amused contempt ("shenanigans"). To our ears the tone, as well as the point, differs in the two versions.

We are talking about **loaded words**, words that convey the writer's attitude and which by their connotations are meant to win the reader to the writer's side. Compare "freedom fighter" with "terrorist," "pro-choice" with "pro-abortion," or "pro-life" with "anti-abortion." "Freedom fighter," "pro-choice," and "pro-life" sound like good things; speakers who use these words are seeking to establish themselves as virtuous people who are supporting worthy causes.

Tone is not a matter only of the choice of individual words ("hounded out of office," versus, let's say, "compelled to resign," or "pro-choice" versus "pro-abortion"); it is also a matter of such things as the selection and type of examples. A writer who offers many examples, especially ones drawn from ordinary life, conveys a persona different from that of a writer who offers no examples, or only an occasional invented instance. The first of these probably is, one might say, friendlier, more down-to-earth.

Last Words on Tone · On the whole, in writing an argument it is advisable to be courteous, respectful of your topic, of your audience, and even of your opposition. It is rarely effective to regard as villains or fools persons who hold views different from yours, especially if some of them are in your audience. Keep in mind the story of the two strangers on a train who, striking up a conversation, found that both were clergymen, though of different faiths. Then one said to the other, "Well, why shouldn't we be friends? After all, we both serve God, you in your way and I in His."

Complacency is all right when engaging in jokes but not in arguments. Recognize the opposition, assume that the views are held in good faith, state the views fairly (if you don't, you do a disservice not only to the opposition but to your own position, because the perceptive reader will not take you seriously), and be temperate in arguing your own position: "If I understand their view correctly . . ."; "It seems reasonable to conclude that . . ."; "Perhaps, then, we can agree that. . . ."

"We," "One," or "I"?

The use of "we" in the last sentence brings us to another point: May the first-person pronouns "I" and "we" be used? In this book, because two of us are writing, we often use "we" to mean the two authors. And we sometimes use "we" to mean the authors and the readers, as in sentences like the one that ends the previous paragraph. This shifting use of one word can be troublesome, but we hope (clearly the "we" here refers only to the authors) that we have avoided any ambiguity. But can, or should, or must, an individual use "we" instead of "I"? The short answer is no.

If you are simply speaking for yourself, use "I." Attempts to avoid the first person singular by saying things like "This writer thinks . . . ," and "It is thought that . . . ," and "One thinks that . . . ," are far more irritating (and wordy) than the use of "I." The so-called editorial "we" is as odd-sounding in a student's argument as is the royal "we." Mark Twain said that the only ones who can appropriately say "we" are kings, editors, and people with a tapeworm. And because one "one" leads to another, making the sentence sound (James Thurber's words) "like a trombone solo," it's best to admit that you are the author, and to use "I." But of course there is no need to preface every sentence with "I think." The reader knows that the essay is yours; just write it, using "I" when you must, but not needlessly.

A Checklist for Written Arguments

After you have written a couple of drafts and feel you may be getting near your final version, you may want to consult this checklist:

1. Topic sufficiently narrowed?
2. Thesis (to be advanced or refuted) stated early and clearly, perhaps even in the title?
3. Audience kept in mind? Opposing views stated fairly and as sympathetically as possible? Controversial terms defined?
4. Assumptions likely to be shared by readers? If not, are they argued rather than merely asserted?
5. Focus clear (for example, evaluation, or recommendation of policy)?
6. Evidence (examples, testimony, statistics) adequate and sound?
7. Inferences valid?
8. Organization clear? (Effective opening, coherent sequence of arguments, unpretentious ending?)
9. All worthy opposition faced?
10. Tone appropriate?

ANALYZING SOMEONE ELSE'S ARGUMENT

Examining the Author's Thesis

Most of your writing in other courses will require you to write an analysis of someone else's writing. In a course in political science you may have to analyze, say, an essay published in *Foreign Affairs*, perhaps reprinted in a textbook, that argues that nuclear weapons preserve peace; or a course in sociology may require you to analyze a report on the correlation between fatal accidents and drunk drivers under the age of twenty-one.

Much of your writing, in short, will set forth reasoned responses to your reading, as preparation for making an argument of your own.

Obviously you must understand an essay before you can analyze it thoughtfully. You must read it several times—not just skim it—and (the hard part) you must think about it. Again, you'll find that your thinking is stimulated if you take notes and if you ask yourself questions about the material. Notes will help you to keep track of the writer's thoughts and also of your own responses to the writer's thesis. The writer probably *does* have a thesis, a point, an argument, and if so, you must try to locate it. Perhaps the thesis is explicitly stated in the title or in a sentence or two near the beginning of the essay or in a concluding paragraph, but perhaps you will have to infer it from the essay as a whole.

Notice that we said the writer *probably* has a thesis. Much of what you read will indeed be primarily an argument; the writer explicitly or implicitly is trying to support some thesis and to convince you to agree with it. But some of what you read will be relatively neutral, with the argument just faintly discernible. A work may, for instance, chiefly be a report: Here are the data, or here is what X, Y, and Z said; make of it what you will. A report might simply state how various ethnic groups voted in an election. In a report of this sort, of course the writer hopes to persuade readers that the facts are correct, but no thesis is advanced, at least not explicitly or perhaps even consciously; the writer is not evidently arguing a point and trying to change our minds. Such a document differs greatly from an essay by a political analyst who presents similar findings in order to persuade a candidate to sacrifice the votes of this ethnic bloc in order to get more votes from other blocs.

Examining the Author's Purpose

Before writing your analysis, try to form a clear idea of the author's purpose. Judging from the essay or the book, was the purpose to persuade, or was it to report? An analysis of a pure report (a work apparently without a thesis or argumentative angle) on ethnic voting will deal chiefly with the accuracy of the report. It will, for example, consider whether the sample poll was representative.

Much material that poses as a report really has a thesis built into it, consciously or unconsciously. The best evidence that the prose you are reading is argumentative prose is the presence of two kinds of key terms:

> **transitions that imply the drawing of a conclusion:** *therefore, because, for the reason that, consequently;*
>
> **verbs that imply proof:** *confirms, accounts for, proves, disproves, refutes.*

Keep your eye out for such terms and scrutinize their precise role whenever they appear. If the essay does not advance a thesis, think of a thesis (a hypothesis) that it might support or some conventional belief that it might undermine.

Examining the Author's Methods

If the essay advances a thesis, you will want to analyze the strategies or methods of argument that allegedly support the thesis.

Does the writer quote authorities? Are these authorities really competent in this field? Are equally competent authorities who take a different view ignored?

If statistics are used, are they appropriate to the point being argued? Can they be interpreted differently?

Are the assumptions acceptable?

Are all relevant factors considered?

In writing your analysis, you will want to tell your reader something about the author's purpose and something about the author's methods. It is usually a good idea at the start of your analysis—if not in the first paragraph then in the second or third—to let the reader know the purpose (and thesis, if there is one) of the work you are analyzing, and then to summarize the work briefly.

Next you will probably find it useful (your reader will certainly find it helpful) to write out *your* thesis (your evaluation or judgment). You might say, for instance, that the essay is impressive but not conclusive, or is undermined by convincing contrary evidence, or relies too much on unsupported generalizations, or is wholly admirable, or whatever. Remember, because your paper is itself an argument, it needs its own thesis.

And then, of course, comes the job of setting forth your analysis and the support for your thesis. There is no one way of going about this work. If, say, your author gives four arguments (for example: an appeal to common sense, the testimony of authorities, the evidence of comparisons, an appeal to self-interest), you may want to take these four arguments up in sequence. Or you may want to begin by discussing the simplest of the four, and then go on to the more difficult ones. Or you may want first to discuss the author's two arguments that you think are sound and then turn to the two that you think are not. And, as you warm to your thesis, you may want to clinch your case by constructing a fifth argument, absent from the work under scrutiny but in your view highly important. In short, the organization of your analysis may or may not follow the organization of the work you are analyzing.

Examining the Author's Persona

You will probably also want to analyze something a bit more elusive than the author's explicit arguments: the author's self-presentation. Does the author seek to persuade us partly by presenting himself or herself as conscientious, friendly, self-effacing, authoritative, tentative, or in some other light? Most writers do two things: they present evidence, and they present themselves (or, more precisely, they present the image of themselves that they wish us to behold). In some persuasive writing this persona or voice or presentation of the self may be no less important than the presentation of evidence.

In establishing a persona, writers adopt various rhetorical strategies, ranging from the use of characteristic words to the use of a particular form of organization. For instance, the writer who speaks of an opponent's "gimmicks" instead of "strategy" is trying to downgrade the opponent and also to convey the self-image of a streetwise person. On a larger scale, consider the way in which evidence is presented and the kind of evidence offered. One writer may first bombard the reader with facts and then spend relatively little time drawing conclusions. Another may rely chiefly on generalizations, waiting until the end of the essay to bring the thesis home with a few details. Another may begin with a few facts and spend most of the space reflecting on these. One writer may seem professorial or pedantic, offering examples of an academic sort; another, whose examples are drawn from ordinary life, may seem like a regular guy. All such devices deserve comment in your analysis.

The writer's persona, then, may color the thesis and develop it in a distinctive way. If we accept the thesis, it is partly because the writer has won our goodwill.

The author of an essay may, for example, seem fair minded and open minded, treating the opposition with great courtesy and expressing interest in hearing other views. Such a tactic is, of course, itself a persuasive device. Or take an author who appears to rely on hard evidence such as statistics. This reliance on seemingly objective truths is itself a way of seeking to persuade.

Especially in analyzing a work in which the author's persona and ideas are blended, you will want to spend some time commenting on the persona. Whether you discuss it near the beginning of your analysis or near the end will depend on your own sense of how you want to construct your essay, and this decision will partly depend on the work you are analyzing. For example, if the persona is kept in the background, and is thus relatively invisible, you may want to make that point fairly early, to get it out of the way, and then concentrate on more interesting matters. If, however, the persona is interesting—and perhaps seductive, whether because it seems so scrupulously objective or so engagingly subjective—you may want to hint at this quality early in your essay, and then develop the point while you consider the arguments.

Summary

In the last few pages we have tried to persuade you that, in writing an analysis of your reading, you must do the following:

1. Read and reread thoughtfully. Taking notes will help you to think about what you are reading;
2. Be aware of the purpose of the material to which you are responding.

We have also tried to point out these facts:

3. Most of the nonliterary material that you will read is designed to argue, or to report, or to do both.
4. Most of this material also presents the writer's personality, or voice, and this voice usually merits attention in an analysis. An essay on, say, nuclear war, in a journal devoted to political science, may include a voice that moves from an objective tone to a mildly ironic tone to a hortatory tone, and this voice is worth commenting on.

Possibly all this explanation is obvious. There is yet another point, though, equally obvious but often neglected by students who begin by writing an analysis and end up by writing only a summary, a shortened version of the work they have read:

5. Although your essay is an analysis of someone else's writing, and you may have to include a summary of the work you are writing about, your essay is *your* essay. The thesis, the organization, and the tone are yours. Your thesis, for example, may be that although the author is convinced she has presented a strong case, her case is far from proved. Your organization may be deeply indebted to the work you are analyzing, but it need not be. The author may have begun with specific examples and then gone on to make generalizations and to draw conclusions, but you may begin with the conclusions. Similarly, your tone may resemble your subject's (let's say the voice is Courteous Academic), but it will nevertheless have its own ring, its own tone of (say) urgency, or caution, or coolness.

An Argument, and a Student's Analysis of the Argument

Stanley S. Scott

Smokers Get a Raw Deal

The civil rights act, the voting rights act and a host of antidiscrimination laws notwithstanding, millions of Americans are still forced to sit in the back of planes, trains and buses. Many more are subject to segregation in public places. Some are even denied housing and employment: victims of an alarming—yet socially acceptable—public hostility.

This new form of discrimination is based on smoking behavior.

If you happen to enjoy a cigarette, you are the potential target of violent antismokers and overzealous public enforcers determined to force their beliefs on the rest of society.

Ever since people began smoking, smokers and nonsmokers have been   4 able to live with one another using common courtesy and common sense. Not anymore. Today, smokers must put up with virtually unenforceable laws regulating when and where they can smoke—laws intended as much to discourage smoking itself as to protect the rights of nonsmokers. Much worse, supposedly responsible organizations devoted to the "public interest" are encouraging the harassment of those who smoke.

This year, for example, the American Cancer Society is promoting programs that encourage people to attack smokers with canisters of gas, to blast them with horns, to squirt them with oversized water guns and burn them in effigy.

Harmless fun? Not quite. Consider the incidents that are appearing on police blotters across America:

> In a New York restaurant, a young man celebrating with friends was zapped in the face by a man with an aerosol spray can. His offense: lighting a cigarette. The aggressor was the head of a militant anti-smoker organization whose goal is to mobilize an army of two million zealots to spray smokers in the face.

> In a suburban Seattle drugstore, a man puffing on a cigarette while he waited for a prescription to be filled was ordered to stop by an elderly customer who pulled a gun on him.

Here is a very short essay, from the Op Ed page of the New York Times, *followed by a student's analysis of it. Stanley S. Scott (b. 1933) is vice president and director of corporate affairs of Philip Morris Companies Inc.*

A 23-year-old lit up a cigarette on a Los Angeles bus. A passenger objected. When the smoker objected to the objection, he was fatally stabbed.

A transit policeman, using his reserve gun, shot and fatally wounded a man on a subway train in the Bronx in a shootout over smoking a cigarette.

The basic freedoms of more than 50 million American smokers are at risk today. Tomorrow, who knows what personal behavior will become socially unacceptable, subject to restrictive laws and public ridicule? Could travel by private car make the social engineers' hit list because it is less safe than public transit? Could ice cream, cake, and cookies become socially unacceptable because their consumption causes obesity? What about sky diving, mountain climbing, skiing, and contact sports? How far will we allow this to spread?

The question all Americans must ask themselves is: can a nation that 8 has struggled so valiantly to eliminate bias based on race, religion, and sex afford to allow a fresh set of categories to encourage new forms of hostility between large groups of citizens?

After all, discrimination is discrimination, no matter what it is based on.

Now for the student's analysis of Scott's essay—and then our analysis of the student's analysis, on pp. 88–91.

Tom Wu
English 2B
Professor McCabe
March 13, 1989

Is All Discrimination Unfair?

Stanley S. Scott's "Smokers Get a Raw Deal," though a poor
argument, is an extremely clever piece of writing. Scott writes
clearly and he holds a reader's attention. Take his opening
paragraph, which evokes the bad old days of Jim Crow segregation, when blacks were forced to ride at the back of the bus.
Scott tells us, to our surprise, that there still are Americans
who are forced to ride at the back of the bus. Who, we wonder,
are the people who are treated so unfairly--or we would wonder,
if the title of the essay hadn't let us make an easy guess.
They are smokers. Of course most Americans detest segregation,
and Scott thus hopes to tap our feelings of decency and fair
play, so that we will recognize that smokers are people too, and
they ought not to be subjected to the same evil that blacks were
subjected to. He returns to this motif at the end of his essay,
when he says, "After all, discrimination is discrimination, no
matter what you call it." Scott is, so it seems, on the side of
fair play.

But "discrimination" has two meanings. One is the ability
to make accurate distinctions, as in "She can discriminate between instant coffee and freshly ground coffee." The second
meaning is quite different: an act based on prejudice, as in
"She does not discriminate against the handicapped," and of
course this is Scott's meaning. Blacks were the victims of discrimination in this second sense when they were forced to sit at
the back of the bus simply because they were black, not because
they engaged in any action that might reasonably be perceived as
offensive or harmful to others. That sort of segregation was
the result of prejudice; it held people accountable for something (their color) over which they had no control. But smokers
voluntarily engage in an action which can be annoying to others
(like playing loud music on a radio at midnight, with the win-

dows open) and which may have effects that can injure others. In pursuing their "right," smokers thus can interfere with the rights of others. In short, the "segregation" and "discrimination" against smokers is in no way comparable to the earlier treatment of blacks. Scott illegitimately--one might say outrageously--suggests that segregating smokers is as unjust, and as blindly prejudiced, as was the segregating of blacks.

Between his opening and his closing paragraphs, which present smokers as victims of "discrimination," he cites several instances of smokers who were subjected to violence, including two smokers who were killed. His point is, again, to show that smokers are being treated as blacks once were, and are in effect subjected to lynch law. The instances of violence that he cites are deplorable, but they scarcely prove that it is wrong to insist that people do not have the unrestricted right to smoke in public places. It is clearly wrong to assault smokers, but surely these assaults do not therefore make it right for smokers to subject others to smoke that annoys and may harm.

Scott's third chief argument, set forth in the third paragraph from the end, is to claim that if today we infringe on "the basic freedoms of more than 50 million American smokers" we will perhaps tomorrow infringe on the freedom of yet other Americans. Here Scott makes an appeal to patriotism ("basic freedoms," "American") and at the same time warns the reader that the reader's innocent pleasures, such as eating ice cream or cake, are threatened. But this extension is preposterous: smoking undoubtedly is greatly bothersome to many nonsmokers, and may even be unhealthy for them; eating ice cream cannot affect onlookers. If it was deceptive to class smokers with blacks, it is equally deceptive to classify smoking with eating ice cream. Scott is trying to tell us that if we allow smokers to be isolated, we will wake up and find that _we_ are the next who will be isolated by those who don't happen to like our habits, however innocent. The nation, he says, in his next-to-last paragraph, has "struggled valiantly [we are to pat ourselves on the back] to eliminate bias based on race, religion,

and sex." Can we, he asks, afford to let a new bias divide us?
The answer, of course, is that indeed we should discriminate,
not in Scott's sense, but in the sense of making distinctions.
We discriminate, entirely properly, between the selling of pure
food and of tainted food, between law-abiding citizens and criminals, between licensed doctors and unlicensed ones, and so on.
If smokers are a serious nuisance and a potential health hazard,
it is scarcely un-American to protect the innocent from them.
That's not discrimination (in Scott's sense) but is simply fair
play.

AN ANALYSIS OF THE STUDENT'S ANALYSIS

Tom Wu's essay seems to us to be excellent, doubtless the product of a
good deal of thoughtful revision. What makes the essay effective? We can
enumerate the chief reasons:

1. The essay has a title that is of at least a little interest, giving a hint
   of what is to follow. A title such as "An Analysis of an Argument"
   or "Scott on Smoking" would be acceptable, certainly better than
   no title at all, but in general it is a good idea to try to construct a
   more informative or a more interesting title that (like this one)
   arouses interest, perhaps by stirring the reader's curiosity.
2. The author identifies his subject (he names the writer and the title
   of his essay) early.
3. He reveals his thesis early. His topic is Scott's essay; his thesis or
   point is that it is clever but wrongheaded. Notice, by the way, that
   he looks closely at Scott's use of the word "discrimination," and
   that he defines this word carefully. Defining terms is essential in
   argumentative essays. Of course Scott did *not* define the word,
   probably because he hoped his misuse of it would be overlooked.
4. He takes up all of Scott's main points.
5. He uses a few brief quotations, to let us hear Scott's voice and to
   assure us that he is staying close to Scott, but he does not pad his
   essay with long quotations.
6. The essay has a sensible organization. The student begins with the
   beginning of Scott's essay, and then, because Scott uses the opening motif again at the end, touches on the end. The writer is not
   skipping around; he is taking a single point (a "new discrimination" is upon us) and following it through.

7. He next turns to Scott's next argument, that smokers are subjected to violence. He doesn't try to touch on each of Scott's four examples—he hasn't room, in an essay of 500 to 600 words—but he treats their gist fairly.

8. He touches on Scott's next point, that no one will be safe from other forms of discrimination, and shows that it is both a gross exaggeration and, because it equates utterly unlike forms of behavior, a piece of faulty thinking.

9. He concludes (without the stiffness of saying "in conclusion") with some general comments on discrimination, thus picking up a motif he introduced early in his essay. His essay, like Scott's, uses a sort of frame, or, changing the figure, it finishes off by tying a knot that was begun at the start. He even repeats the words "fair play," which he used at the end of his first paragraph, and neatly turns them to his advantage.

10. Notice, finally, that he sticks closely to Scott's essay. He does not go off on a tangent and talk about the harm that smokers do to themselves. Because the assignment was to analyze Scott's essay (rather than to offer his own views on smoking) he confines himself to analyzing the essay.

FIVE ARGUMENTS FOR ANALYSIS

Caldwell Titcomb

Star-Spangled Earache: What So Loudly We Wail

Not long ago Representative Andrew Jacobs, Jr., of Indiana filed a bill to replace "The Star-Spangled Banner" with "America the Beautiful" as our national anthem. Many people have long advocated just such a change, and for a number of reasons the bill deserves wide support.

"The Star-Spangled Banner" has been the official national anthem only since March 3, 1931. Most people assume that it has been the anthem virtually from time immemorial and that it is thus now sacrosanct. But

---

Caldwell Titcomb (b. 1926), a professor of music at Brandeis University, has composed stage and film music scores. This essay first appeared in The New Republic, *1985.*

clearly there is nothing wrong with supplanting something that has been in effect for only fifty-odd years.

The music is by an Englishman, John Stafford Smith (1750–1836), who wrote it as a drinking song for a London social club, the Anacreontic Society. Is our nation so poverty-stricken that we must rule out homegrown music?

The tune is a constant stumbling block. Technically, it covers a span of   4 a twelfth—that is, an octave plus a perfect fifth. Not only is it difficult for the general public to sing, but it has repeatedly caused trouble even for professional opera singers. Some people assert that this problem could be solved by selecting the right key for performance. But the point is that *all* twelve possible keys are poor. No matter what the key, the tune goes either too high or too low (and both, for some people). What's more, the tune is irregular in its phrasing, and does not always fit the text well. In "Whose broad stripes," for instance, assigning "broad" to a tiny sixteenth note is bad.

Finally, Francis Scott Key's poem (1814) is not suitable. It is of low quality as poetry, and its subject matter is too specific and too militaristic, dealing with a one-day incident in a war. Are glaring rockets and bursting bombs the essence of the nation? I wonder how many people have really read through all four stanzas and thought about the words. The third stanza is particularly offensive: "Their blood has wash'd out their foul footsteps' pollution. / No refuge could save the hireling and slave / From the terror of flight or the gloom of the grave." When a bank celebrated the last Independence Day by buying a full page in the *New York Times* to print the tune and text of the anthem, not surprisingly the dreadful third stanza was entirely omitted. The poem has little to recommend it except for the single line, "The land of the free and the home of the brave."

Why choose "America the Beautiful" in its place?

Both the text and music are by citizens of the United States. And now that we have overcome the notion that this is mainly a man's world, it is additionally fitting that the poem was written by a woman, Katharine Lee Bates (1859–1929), and the music by a man, Samuel Augustus Ward (1848–1903).

The music (composed in 1882) is simple and dignified, and exhibits   8 balanced phrasing. The tune has a range of only a ninth—that is, an octave plus one step—which means that almost anyone, trained or untrained, can sing it. For the musically sophisticated, there is also a neat touch in the four-voice harmonization that has been standard since its first publication in 1888: the soprano tune of the first line becomes the bass part of the third line.

The poem—originally written in 1893, and by a happy coincidence first printed in the Fourth of July issue of a periodical in 1895 (and twice somewhat revised by its author)—is in its final form an admirable text of broad scope. It is not bellicose or geographically restricted, and all four stanzas can be sung without embarrassment. It was inspired by a trip taken by an Easterner through the Midwest (with a visit to the Chicago World's Columbian Exposition: "alabaster cities gleam") and on across "the fruited plain" and "amber waves of grain" to the Rocky Mountains (Pikes Peak in Colorado: "purple mountain majesties").

It acknowledges both urban and rural life. It pays homage to our nation's past and to those who have sacrificed themselves for their country (without glorifying war), it points to present virtues, and it voices a goal that our nation should aspire to ("brotherhood / From sea to shining sea"). Even a celebrated foreign historian was impelled to comment: "Few patriotic songs breathe such broad, humane idealism as this."

This joining of words and music has stood the test of time. The piece is taught and learned in school throughout the country, and is known and loved by the populace at large, which can sing it effectively, confidently, and with pride.

There has long been widespread advocacy for making it our national 12 anthem. When the selection of an anthem was before Congress in 1931, several organizations, acting independently, took a strong stand in favor of "America the Beautiful" and against "The Star-Spangled Banner," including the National Federation of Music Clubs, the National Hymn Society, the Music Supervisors National Conference, and education experts at Columbia Teachers College.

When the controversy resurfaced in Boston in 1977 (as it periodically does here and there), a poll of *Boston Globe* readers revealed that they favored "America the Beautiful" over "The Star-Spangled Banner" by a vote of 493 to 220. And it has already been adopted as the official song of the National Federation of Women's Clubs.

From time to time people have expressed a preference for other choices, but these can easily be shown unsuitable. "The Battle Hymn of the Republic" (1861), like "The Star-Spangled Banner," is too warlike, and its tune belongs to "John Brown's Body Lies A-Mould'ring in the Grave." The music of Irving Berlin's "God Bless America" (1918) is insufficiently dignified, and the text setting is faulty. "My Country 'Tis of Thee" uses the music of the British national anthem, and thus cannot be seriously considered. John Philip Sousa's "The Stars and Stripes Forever" (1897) is as great a march as anyone has ever composed, but it lacks a text and only its refrain would lend itself to singing. The idea of having a nationwide contest for a new anthem has been tried, without success. If tried again, there would surely be no agreement.

When one takes all factors into account, "America the Beautiful" is by far the outstanding candidate. It would indeed be fortunate if the entire country could sing "America the Beautiful" as the official national anthem when it celebrates the 200th anniversary of the Constitution on September 17, 1987. We have less than two years to accomplish this worthy task.

Questions and Suggestions for Writing

1. Evaluate Titcomb's title and first paragraph. How effective do you think they are? How would you defend (or criticize) them?

2. List, in order, Titcomb's arguments for replacing the anthem. Do you think the sequence is reasonable and effective? Why, or why not?

3. Suppose someone were to argue, by analogy, that since the national bird is the bald eagle, not exactly a gentle creature, it is appropriate that the national anthem be similarly vigorous and even warlike. Write a 100-word essay supporting or attacking the analogy.

4. Titcomb asserts in paragraph 5 that "the poem has little to recommend it except for the single line, 'The land of the free and the home of the brave.'" Do you agree with his evaluation? And, whether you agree or not, do you think he should have *argued* that Key's poem is weak rather than merely asserted that it is?

5. The second half of the essay, arguing that "America the Beautiful" is the best substitute, rejects "The Battle Hymn of the Republic," "God Bless America," "My Country 'Tis of Thee," and "The Stars and Stripes Forever." Can you make a case for any of these in preference to "America the Beautiful"? Or for a song he does not mention, "Born in the U.S.A."?

6. As the final paragraph indicates, Titcomb wrote the essay in 1985, two years before the two-hundredth anniversary of the Constitution. We have now passed that landmark, and so his final paragraph is no longer appropriate. Regardless of the merits of Titcomb's position, write a new concluding paragraph for his essay.

Tina Bakka

Locking Students Out

Let's begin by defining "bilingual education." As commonly used today, the term does *not* mean teaching students a language other than English (almost everyone would agree that foreign-language instruction should be available, and that it is desirable for Americans to be fluent not only in English but also in some other language); nor does "bilingual education" mean offering courses in English as a Second Language to students whose native language is, for example, Chinese or Spanish or Navajo or Aleut. (Again, almost everyone would agree that such instruc-

---

Born in Chicago in 1952 and educated in Arizona, Bakka has taught English as a second language in secondary school.

tion should be offered where economically possible.) Rather, it means offering instruction in such courses as mathematics, history, and science *in the student's native language*, while also offering courses in English as a Second Language. Programs vary in details, but the idea is that the non-native speaker should be spared the trauma of total immersion in English until he or she has completed several years of studying English as a second language. During this period, instruction in other subjects is given in the student's native language.

Proponents of bilingual education usually offer two not entirely consistent arguments: (1) it eases the youngster's transition into American culture, and (2) it preserves the youngster's cultural heritage. In the brief space available, I will argue against both of these positions.

First, despite the statistics commonly offered by proponents of bilingual education, there is no impartial evidence that such education in fact improves the academic work of students. Impartial investigators have consistently found that the results of the studies are uncertain. For example, Iris Rothberg, writing in *Harvard Educational Review*, May 1982, says that the research findings are contradictory and inconclusive. Keith A. Baker and Adriane A. de Kanter, in "Effectiveness of Bilingual Education: A Review of the Literature" (an unpaginated document issued by the United States Department of Education in 1981), find that "The case for the effectiveness of transitional bilingual education is so weak that exclusive reliance on this instruction method is not justified. Too little is known about the problems of educating language minorities to prescribe a specific remedy at the Federal level."

Why has the bilingual approach recently been invented, and why does   4 it get so much attention? Part of the answer, of course, is that the U.S. Census for 1980 found that more than 10 percent of the United States population spoke a language other than English at home. Of this 10 percent, half spoke Spanish. And since it is agreed that Hispanics were undercounted in the census, the actual figure of Spanish-speaking children is even higher than the official estimate. Although bilingual programs exist in many languages, Spanish is by far the most prominent, accounting for about 80 percent, and bilingual programs have been advocated most often, and most vigorously, for Spanish-speaking children. I will return to this point later, but first I want to speak more generally.

The two extreme solutions to the question of how to educate non-native speakers of English are these: (1) "immersion," in which the students hear and speak only English in school, and (2) bilingualism, in which students study major subjects in their native language and study English as a second language. The first approach, until recently the only approach, is based on the idea that America is a "melting pot" in which Russians, Germans, Italians, Chinese, and all others who come here should become "Americans." The method is sink or swim; the failure of the method cannot be calculated—we can hardly measure the psychological pain that some people endured—but the success can be. The history of the United States is, on the whole, a history of the success of immigrants. One has only to look at the names in a newspaper, or at the names in Congress, or at the names of teachers in any large school, to see a wide variety of ethnic backgrounds. Again, we cannot calculate the cost—the traumatic feelings undergone by countless non-native speakers of English who were baffled by what to them was an unintelligible language—but we do know that in the past the overwhelming majority coped and succeeded. This at least can be said for the total-immersion approach. (At this point perhaps I should mention that although I favor immersion, in most cases it should be complemented with instruction in English as a second language to assist students to do good work in their other courses.)

The second approach, bilingualism, usually requires a minimum of three years of instruction in English before instruction in other subjects is offered in English. (Many advocates argue for six years, and some even argue for twelve years.) Proponents base their view on two arguments: (1) total immersion is traumatic, and (2) the "melting pot," in which ethnic identity is dissolved, has been discredited; the "salad bowl" or the "mosaic," in which ethnic identity is preserved, is said to be a much better outcome to aim for. The first of these arguments, about the psychological well-being of the child, is supported by claiming that a non-native speaker "can't learn English all day." But this is simply wrong; the child does not spend most of his or her day in school. There is plenty of time away from school for the child to speak the native language with friends and families, and even during school hours the child will inevitably speak the native language outside of the classroom, for instance in the hallways, the cafeteria, and at play. Further, young children are highly adaptive; they learn foreign languages relatively easily, and to postpone their entry into the English-speaking world is to make more difficult, ultimately, their learning of English. Bilingual programs, though originally intended to assist the student's transition into American culture, now for the most part impede the move by maintaining the child's home culture.

Moreover, although immersion may have adverse psychological effects on some children (again, these cannot be measured, and proponents of bilingualism have sometimes simply resorted to scare tactics), bilingual programs themselves may have adverse psychological effects, for they segregate children and make them feel that they are not part of mainstream America. Children in a bilingual program may come to believe that because they are in some sort of special program, they are judged unable to participate in the "regular" program. And the "Anglo" children may come to hold a similar view, seeing the Spanish-speaking child as an inferior who needs special help not only in learning English but in learning anything.

This brings us to the second argument advanced in favor of programs 8 in bilingual education: they preserve ethnic identity. I have just suggested that this method, intended to preserve ethnic identity, can in fact lead to a sense of inferiority; the non-native speakers of English think they must have special help, and the native speakers think that the others can't cope. Both thoughts are destructive. And both are utterly false. Ethnic identity can be preserved even in a system of total immersion. If one looks around, one easily sees that even third and fourth generation Americans still value aspects of the culture of their ancestors. This is evident in countless ways, for instance in the religions they believe in, the foods they eat, the holidays they celebrate, and the jokes they tell. To some extent it is also evident in the jobs they enter.

But this gets to another, extremely important point. In America, jobs largely determine "class," since "class" is almost entirely a matter of money. Money largely depends on the kind of job one holds. It is a fact that most native speakers of Spanish in the United States belong to an economically disadvantaged class. Their disadvantage can be overcome only when they enter gringo society. I am speaking broadly, of course. There are many prosperous native speakers of Spanish, some active chiefly in Spanish-speaking communities; but on the whole, the better paying jobs are in the gringo world, and the only way to get these jobs is to be at home in that world. To be at ease in that world requires fluency in the language, and an acceptance of the fact that English is the dominant language in this country.

In the past, severe discrimination operated against immigrants with certain cultural backgrounds, including Hispanics. This discrimination has not disappeared, but it is fading, and legal measures have been taken to reduce what remains. Discrimination, which in part meant keeping Hispanics out of better paying jobs, surely was largely responsible for the lack of interest in becoming American citizens that many Mexican immigrants displayed. The statistics are sad. John R. Garcia points out, in *International Migration Review*, Winter 1981, that since 1920 the annual rates for naturalization of eligible Mexican-origin migrants vary between 3.89 and 5.88 percent. How does this figure compare with figures for other groups? "The average rate of naturalization is one-tenth that of other immigrants' naturalization rates, and this pattern has not changed significantly over the years." Why? Apparently because in most communities these persons of Mexican origin were not led to feel they were part of America. In Garcia's words, they do not feel much "social identity with being American" (p. 620). Because they were taught minimal English their options were severely limited. Segregating them reinforced their belief that they were outsiders, and prevented them from participating fully in the politics and economy (and prosperity) of America.

I am arguing, then, that the proponents of bilingual education are short-sighted; they talk of preserving ethnic culture, but they do not see that their sort of preservation leads to a perpetuation of an economic disadvantage and to a sense of alienation. This in turn leads to a lack of full participation in the public life of America. Proponents of bilingualism see and value ethnic identity, but they do not see that non-native speakers need *two* identities if they are to thrive, a private (ethnic) identity and also a public (economic, political) identity. All people living in this country must be able not only to cherish their particular or private tradition but also to claim a portion of the dominant culture—a portion of money and of political power. To do this, they must be at ease in the public (Anglo) as well as in the private world. That may not be simple, but immersion (supplemented with instruction in English as a second language) is far more likely to bring this about than is a pedagogical program that keeps young students from studying social sciences and physical and biological sciences in English. Only when youngsters feel that these subjects are to be mastered in English, however difficult the task, will we have youngsters who can confidently aim at careers in those fields, and can confidently claim a place (with the accompanying economic advantages) in society as a whole. Most of the others will find themselves locked out.

Questions and Suggestions for Writing

1. Before you read Bakka's essay did you have a clear idea of what "bilingual education" is? Why does Bakka go to some pains to define the topic early?

2. Do you find Bakka's definition clear and adequate? If so, write a paragraph to account for the success of her definition (analyze her method of defining). If you don't find it clear and adequate, call attention to the weaknesses.

3. In paragraph 3, Bakka casts doubt on the statistical data collected so far. Do you think that statistical data can or should provide a decisive answer to the question of how non-native speakers should be educated?

4. Bakka argues that bilingual programs may make the students feel inferior, and may cause other students to regard those students as inferior. If you have any first-hand experience (on either side of the fence), write an essay of 250–500 words, supporting or countering her view on this matter.

5. In her ninth and tenth paragraphs Bakka argues that bilingual programs help to keep students in an economically disadvantaged class. In a paragraph indicate whether you think they do, and in a second paragraph indicate whether you think economical considerations are relevant in solving the problem.

Barbara Lawrence

Four-Letter Words Can Hurt You

Why should any words be called obscene? Don't they all describe natural human functions? Am I trying to tell them, my students demand, that the "strong, earthy, gut-honest"—or, if they are fans of Norman Mailer, the "rich, liberating, existential"—language they use to describe sexual activity isn't preferable to "phony-sounding, middle-class words like 'intercourse' and 'copulate'?" "Cop You Late!" they say with fancy inflections and gagging grimaces. "Now, what is *that* supposed to mean?"

Well, what is it supposed to mean? And why indeed should one group of words describing human functions and human organs be acceptable in ordinary conversation and another, describing presumably the same organs and functions, be tabooed—so much so, in fact, that some of these words still cannot appear in print in many parts of the English-speaking world?

The argument that these taboos exist only because of "sexual hangups" (middle-class, middle-age, feminist), or even that they are a result of class oppression (the contempt of the Norman conquerors for the language of their Anglo-Saxon serfs), ignores a much more likely explanation, it seems to me, and that is the sources and functions of the words themselves.

The best known of the tabooed sexual verbs, for example, comes from the German *ficken*, meaning "to strike"; combined, according to Partridge's etymological dictionary *Origins*, with the Latin sexual verb *futuere;* associated in turn with the Latin *fustis*, "a staff or cudgel"; the Celtic *buc*, "a point, hence to pierce"; the Irish *bot*, "the male member"; the Latin *battuere*, "to beat"; the Gaelic *batair*, "a cudgeller"; the Early Irish *bualaim*, "I strike"; and so forth. It is one of what etymologists sometimes call "the sadistic group of words for the man's part in copulation." 4

The brutality of this word, then, and its equivalents ("screw," "bang," etc.), is not an illusion of the middle class or a crotchet of Women's Liberation. In their origins and imagery these words carry undeniably painful, if not sadistic, implications, the object of which is almost always female. Consider, for example, what a "screw" actually does to the wood it penetrates; what a painful, even mutilating, activity this kind of analogy suggests. "Screw" is particularly interesting in this context, since the noun, according to Partridge, comes from words meaning "groove," "nut," "ditch," "breeding sow," "scrofula" and "swelling," while the verb, besides

Barbara Lawrence teaches at the State University of New York at Old Westbury.
This essay first appeared in 1973 as an Op Ed piece in the New York Times.

its explicit imagery, has antecedent associations to "write on," "scratch," "scarify," and so forth—a revealing fusion of a mechanical or painful action with an obviously denigrated object.

Not all obscene words, of course, are as implicitly sadistic or denigrating to women as these, but all that I know seem to serve a similar purpose: to reduce the human organism (especially the female organism) and human functions (especially sexual and procreative) to their least organic, most mechanical dimension; to substitute a trivializing or deforming resemblance for the complex human reality of what is being described.

Tabooed male descriptives, when they are not openly denigrating to women, often serve to divorce a male organ or function from any significant interaction with the female. Take the word "testes," for example, suggesting "witnesses" (from the Latin *testis*) to the sexual and procreative strengths of the male organ; and the obscene counterpart of this word, which suggests little more than a mechanical shape. Or compare almost any of the "rich," "liberating" sexual verbs, so fashionable today among male writers, with that much-derided Latin word "copulate" ("to bind or join together") or even that Anglo-Saxon phrase (which seems to have had no trouble surviving the Norman Conquest) "make love."

How arrogantly self-involved the tabooed words seem in comparison   8
to either of the other terms, and how contemptuous of the female partner. Understandably so, of course, if she is only a "skirt," a "broad," a "chick," a "pussycat" or a "piece." If she is, in other words, no more than her skirt, or what her skirt conceals; no more than a breeder, or the broadest part of her; no more than a piece of a human being or a "piece of tail."

The most severely tabooed of all the female descriptives incidentally, are those like a "piece of tail," which suggest (either explicitly or through antecedents) that there is no significant difference between the female channel through which we are all conceived and born and the anal outlet common to both sexes—a distinction that pornographers have always enjoyed obscuring.

This effort to deny women their biological identity, their individuality, their humanness, is such an important aspect of obscene language that one can only marvel at how seldom, in an era preoccupied with definitions of obscenity, this fact is brought to our attention. One problem, of course, is that many of the people in the best position to do this (critics, teachers, writers) are so reluctant today to admit that they are angered or shocked by obscenity. Bored, maybe, unimpressed, aesthetically displeased, but—no matter how brutal or denigrating the material—never angered, never shocked.

And yet how eloquently angered, how piously shocked many of these same people become if denigrating language is used about any minority group other than women; if the obscenities are racial or ethnic, that is, rather than sexual. Words like "coon," "kike," "spic," "wop," after all, deform identity, deny individuality and humanness in almost exactly the same way that sexual vulgarisms and obscenities do.

No one that I know, least of all my students, would fail to question the   12
values of a society whose literature and entertainment rested heavily on
racial or ethnic pejoratives. Are the values of a society whose literature and
entertainment rest as heavily as ours on sexual pejoratives any less questionable?

Questions and Suggestions for Writing

1. In addition to giving evidence to support her view, what persuasive device(s)
   does Lawrence use?

2. Lawrence dismisses without much argument (para. 3) two alternative explanations for the presence of taboo words in our language. Do either of these
   explanations strike you as more plausible than the one she prefers? Explain.

3. Lawrence uses but does not define the terms *obscene* and *obscenity*. Complete
   the following definition:

   A word or expression is obscene (or used obscenely) if and only if. . . .

   Would such words as *kike, nigger,* and *shit* be obscene under your proposed
   definition? Why, or why not?

4. Suppose one were to argue against Lawrence that the taboo words men (especially young men) in our culture use to refer to the act of sexual intercourse
   and to young women really do reflect the prevailing male view of the sex act and
   of the opposite sex, and therefore it does little good to denounce these terms as
   obscene or to point out the fact that women are offended by their use. What
   might your response be?

George Orwell

Killing Civilians

Miss Vera Brittain's pamphlet, *Seed of Chaos,* is an eloquent attack on
indiscriminate or "obliteration" bombing. "Owing to the RAF raids," she
says, "thousands of helpless and innocent people in German, Italian and
German-occupied cities are being subjected to agonising forms of death

---

*George Orwell (1903–1950) is the pen name adopted in 1934 by Eric Blair,
British essayist, novelist, and satirist. Orwell was born in India but educated at
Eton in England. He served as a police officer in Burma from 1922 to 1927,
returned to England and Paris, where he taught school and then began to write.
He next went to Spain, where he fought on the side of the Loyalists in the Spanish
Civil War. Back in England, he worked for the British Broadcasting Corporation
during World War II and continued to write. Considering the immense fame of his*

and injury comparable to the worst tortures of the Middle Ages." Various well-known opponents of bombing, such as General Franco and Major-General Fuller, are brought out in support of this. Miss Brittain is not, however, taking the pacifist standpoint. She is willing and anxious to win the war, apparently. She merely wishes us to stick to "legitimate" methods of war and abandon civilian bombing, which she fears will blacken our reputation in the eyes of posterity. Her pamphlet is issued by the Bombing Restriction Committee, which has issued others with similar titles.

Now, no one in his senses regards bombing, or any other operation of war, with anything but disgust. On the other hand, no decent person cares tuppence for the opinion of posterity. And there is something very distasteful in accepting war as an instrument and at the same time wanting to dodge responsibility for its more obviously barbarous features. Pacifism is a tenable position, provided that you are willing to take the consequences. But all talk of "limiting" or "humanising" war is sheer humbug, based on the fact that the average human being never bothers to examine catchwords.

The catchwords used in this connection are "killing civilians," "massacre of women and children" and "destruction of our cultural heritage." It is tacitly assumed that air bombing does more of this kind of thing than ground warfare.

When you look a bit closer, the first question that strikes you is: Why is it worse to kill civilians than soldiers? Obviously one must not kill children if it is in any way avoidable, but it is only in propaganda pamphlets that every bomb drops on a school or an orphanage. A bomb kills a cross section of the population; but not quite a representative selection, because the children and expectant mothers are usually the first to be evacuated, and some of the young men will be away in the army. Probably a disproportionately large number of bomb victims will be middle-aged. (Up to date, German bombs have killed between six and seven thousand children in this country. This is, I believe, less than the number killed in road accidents in the same period.) On the other hand, "normal" or "legitimate" warfare picks out and slaughters all the healthiest and bravest of the young male population. Every time a German submarine goes to the bottom about fifty young men of fine physique and good nerve are suffocated. Yet people who would hold up their hands at the very words "civilian bombing" will repeat with satisfaction such phrases as "We are winning the Battle of the Atlantic." Heaven knows how many people our blitz on Germany and the

work, notably Animal Farm (1945) and Nineteen Eighty-Four (1948), it is surprising to realize that he was a writer for fewer than twenty years and achieved little recognition until a few years before his death. He died at the age of forty-seven, of a lung ailment contracted as a child.

From December 3, 1943 to February 16, 1945, Orwell wrote a regular column for Tribune, a London weekly. This column, titled "As I Please," was often devoted to several topics; we reprint part of one of these columns, with our own title.

occupied countries has killed and will kill, but you can be quite certain it will never come anywhere near the slaughter that has happened on the Russian front.

War is not avoidable at this stage of history, and since it has to happen it does not seem to me a bad thing that others should be killed besides young men. I wrote in 1937: "Sometimes it is a comfort to me to think that the aeroplane is altering the conditions of war. Perhaps when the next great war comes we may see that sight unprecedented in all history, a jingo with a bullet hole in him." We haven't yet seen that (it is perhaps a contradiction in terms), but at any rate the suffering of this war has been shared out more evenly than the last one was. The immunity of the civilian, one of the things that have made war possible, has been shattered. Unlike Miss Brittain, I don't regret that. I can't feel that war is "humanised" by being confined to the slaughter of the young and becomes "barbarous" when the old get killed as well.

As to international agreements to "limit" war, they are never kept when it pays to break them. Long before the last war the nations had agreed not to use gas, but they used it all the same. This time they have refrained, merely because gas is comparatively ineffective in a war of movement, while its use against civilian populations would be sure to provoke reprisals in kind. Against an enemy who can't hit back, e.g. the Abyssinians, it is used readily enough. War is of its nature barbarous, it is better to admit that. If we see ourselves as the savages we are, some improvement is possible, or at least thinkable.

Questions and Suggestions for Writing

1. Formulate a thesis sentence for Orwell's essay.

2. Nowhere in his first paragraph does Orwell explicitly say whether he approves or disapproves of Vera Brittain's views, but by the end of the paragraph one knows that he disapproves. How does one know? What signals does Orwell send?

3. Orwell says, in his second paragraph, that "no decent person cares tuppence for the opinion of posterity." What does he mean? Do you think the statement is, at least generally speaking, true? On what basis do you arrive at your opinion?

4. Taking issue with the traditional view that civilians should not be targets of warfare, Orwell writes: "Why is it worse to kill civilians than soldiers? Obviously one must not kill children if it is in any way avoidable. . . ." But if killing civilians is as acceptable as killing soldiers, why is killing children less acceptable than killing adults? What possible arguments might be offered on behalf of sparing children that would not apply as well to adult civilians? (Children are younger, of course, but is this difference relevant?)

5. Orwell's evident approval of killing German civilians, given that England and Germany were at war and killing each other's soldiers, does *not* ostensibly rest

on his view that (1) Germany started the war, or that (2) German civilians cannot be spared the destructive side effects of legitimate air raids on military targets, or that (3) German civilians support the Nazi government in its aggressive war effort. Do you think it rests, nevertheless, implicitly on one or more of these assumptions? If not, then on what does it rest?

6. Suppose it were argued that, in fact, the sinking of German U-boats actually did help bring the war nearer to victory for the Allies, but the "obliteration bombing" of German cities did not. Would this result, do you think, cause Orwell to abandon his toleration of air raids?

7. Suppose someone, after reading Orwell's essay, said that the author expresses a cynical view of humanitarian efforts to limit the cruelty of warfare. In an essay of 500 words indicate whether you agree with this judgment. Cite evidence from Orwell's essay to support your view.

8. Do you think the moral objections to the killing of civilians in air raids are considerable when a warring nation's munitions factories and military forces are completely separated geographically from its civilian population, and the soldiers are all volunteers, but that these objections diminish in importance when there are no front lines and it is virtually impossible to distinguish the civilians from the military (as in South Vietnam in the 1960s)? Write your answer in an essay of 500 words.

Jonathan Swift

A Modest Proposal

**For Preventing the Children of Poor People in Ireland
from Being a Burden to Their Parents or Country,
and for Making Them Beneficial to the Public**

It is a melancholy object to those who walk through this great town or travel in the country, when they see the streets, the roads, and cabin doors, crowded with beggars of the female sex, followed by three, four, or six children, all in rags and importuning every passenger for an alms. These mothers, instead of being able to work for their honest livelihood, are forced to employ all their time in strolling to beg sustenance for their

---

Swift (1667–1745) was born in Ireland of English stock. An Anglican clergyman, he became Dean of St. Patrick's in Dublin in 1723, but the post he really wanted, that of high office in England, was never given to him. A prolific pamphleteer on religious and political issues, Swift today is known not as a churchman but as a satirist. His best-known works are Gulliver's Travels *(1726, a serious satire but now popularly thought of as a children's book) and "A Modest Proposal" (1729). In "A Modest Proposal," which was published anonymously, Swift addresses the great suffering that the Irish endured under the British.*

helpless infants: who as they grow up either turn thieves for want of work, or leave their dear native country to fight for the pretender in Spain, or sell themselves to the Barbadoes.

I think it is agreed by all parties that this prodigious number of children in the arms, or on the backs, or at the heels of their mothers, and frequently of their fathers, is in the present deplorable state of the kingdom a very great additional grievance; and, therefore, whoever could find out a fair, cheap, and easy method of making these children sound, useful members of the commonwealth, would deserve so well of the public as to have his statue set up for a preserver of the nation.

But my intention is very far from being confined to provide only for the children of professed beggars; it is of a much greater extent, and shall take in the whole number of infants at a certain age who are born of parents in effect as little able to support them as those who demand our charity in the streets.

As to my own part, having turned my thoughts for many years upon this important subject, and maturely weighed the several schemes of our projectors,[1] I have always found them grossly mistaken in their computation. It is true, a child just dropped from its dam may be supported by her milk for a solar year, with little other nourishment; at most not above the value of 2s.,[2] which the mother may certainly get, or the value in scraps, by her lawful occupation of begging; and it is exactly at one year old that I propose to provide for them in such a manner as instead of being a charge upon their parents or the parish, or wanting food and raiment for the rest of their lives, they shall on the contrary contribute to the feeding, and partly to the clothing, of many thousands.

There is likewise another great advantage in my scheme, that it will prevent those voluntary abortions, and that horrid practice of women murdering their bastard children, alas! too frequent among us! sacrificing the poor innocent babes I doubt more to avoid the expense than the shame, which would move tears and pity in the most savage and inhuman breast.

The number of souls in this kingdom being usually reckoned one million and a half, of these I calculate there may be about 200,000 couple whose wives are breeders; from which number I subtract 30,000 couple who are able to maintain their own children (although I apprehend there cannot be so many, under the present distress of the kingdom); but this being granted, there will remain 170,000 breeders. I again subtract 50,000 for those women who miscarry, or whose children die by accident or disease within the year. There only remain 120,000 children of poor parents annually born. The question therefore is, how this number shall be reared and provided for? which, as I have already said, under the present situation of affairs, is utterly impossible by all the methods hitherto pro-

---

[1] **projectors** Persons who devise plans. [All notes are by the editors.]
[2] **2s.** Two shillings. Later "£" is an abbreviation for pounds sterling and "d" for pence.

posed. For we can neither employ them in handicraft or agriculture; we neither build houses (I mean in the country) nor cultivate land; they can very seldom pick up a livelihood by stealing, till they arrive at six years old, except where they are of towardly parts; although I confess they learn the rudiments much earlier; during which time they can, however, be properly looked upon only as probationers; as I have been informed by a principal gentleman in the county of Cavan, who protested to me that he never knew above one or two instances under the age of six, even in a part of the kingdom so renowned for the quickest proficiency in that art.

I am assured by our merchants, that a boy or a girl before twelve years old is no salable commodity; and even when they come to this age they will not yield above 3£. or 3£. 2s. 6d. at most on the exchange; which cannot turn to account either to the parents or kingdom, the charge of nutriment and rags having been at least four times that value.

I shall now therefore humbly propose my own thoughts, which I hope 8 will not be liable to the least objection.

I have been assured by a very knowing American of my acquaintance in London, that a young healthy child well nursed is at a year old a most delicious, nourishing, and wholesome food, whether stewed, roasted, baked, or broiled; and I make no doubt that it will equally serve in a fricassee or a ragout.

I do therefore humbly offer it to public consideration that of the 120,000 children already computed, 20,000 may be reserved for breed, whereof only one-fourth part to be males; which is more than we allow to sheep, black cattle, or swine; and my reason is, that these children are seldom the fruits of marriage, a circumstance not much regarded by our savages; therefore one male will be sufficient to serve four females. That the remaining 100,000 may, at a year old, be offered in sale to the persons of quality and fortune through the kindgom; always advising the mother to let them suck plentifully in the last month, so as to render them plump and fat for a good table. A child will make two dishes at an entertainment for friends; and when the family dines alone, the fore or hind quarter will make a reasonable dish, and seasoned with a little pepper or salt will be very good boiled on the fourth day, especially in winter.

I have reckoned upon a medium that a child just born will weigh 12 pounds, and in a solar year, if tolerably nursed, will increase to 28 pounds.

I grant this food will be somewhat dear, and therefore very proper for 12 landlords, who, as they have already devoured most of the parents, seem to have the best title to the children.

Infant's flesh will be in season throughout the year, but more plentiful in March, and a little before and after: for we are told by a grave author, an eminent French physician, that fish being a prolific diet, there are more children born in Roman Catholic countries about nine months after Lent than at any other season; therefore, reckoning a year after Lent, the markets will be more glutted than usual, because the number of popish infants is at least three to one in this kingdom: and therefore it will have one other collateral advantage, by lessening the number of papists among us.

I have already computed the charge of nursing a beggar's child (in which list I reckon all cottagers, laborers, and four-fifths of the farmers) to be about 2s. per annum, rags included; and I believe no gentleman would repine to give 10s. for the carcass of a good fat child, which, as I have said, will make four dishes of excellent nutritive meat, when he has only some particular friend or his own family to dine with him. Thus the squire will learn to be a good landlord, and grow popular among the tenants; the mother will have 8s. net profit, and be fit for work till she produces another child.

Those who are more thrifty (as I must confess the times require) may flay the carcass; the skin of which artificially dressed will make admirable gloves for ladies, and summer boots for fine gentlemen.

As to our city of Dublin, shambles[3] may be appointed for this purpose   16 in the most convenient parts of it, and butchers we may be assured will not be wanting: although I rather recommend buying the children alive, and dressing them hot from the knife as we do roasting pigs.

A very worthy person, a true lover of his country, and whose virtues I highly esteem, was lately pleased in discoursing on this matter to offer a refinement upon my scheme. He said that many gentlemen of this kingdom, having of late destroyed their deer, he conceived that the want of venison might be well supplied by the bodies of young lads and maidens, not exceeding fourteen years of age nor under twelve; so great a number of both sexes in every country being now ready to starve for want of work and service; and these to be disposed of by their parents, if alive, or otherwise by their nearest relations. But with due deference to so excellent a friend and so deserving a patriot, I cannot be altogether in his sentiments; for as to the males, my American acquaintance assured me from frequent experience that their flesh was generally tough and lean, like that of our school-boys by continual exercise, and their taste disagreeable; and to fatten them would not answer the charge. Then as to the females, it would, I think, with humble submission be a loss to the public, because they soon would become breeders themselves: and besides, it is not improbable that some scrupulous people might be apt to censure such a practice (although indeed very unjustly), as a little bordering upon cruelty; which, I confess, has always been with me the strongest objection against any project, how well soever intended.

But in order to justify my friend, he confessed that this expedient was put into his head by the famous Psalmanazar[4] a native of the island

---

[3] **shambles** Slaughterhouses.

[4] **Psalmanazar** George Psalmanazar (c. 1679–1763), a Frenchman who claimed to be from Formosa (now Taiwan); wrote *An Historical and Geographical Description of Formosa* (1704). The hoax was exposed soon after publication.

Formosa, who came from thence to London about twenty years ago: and in conversation told my friend, that in his country when any young person happened to be put to death, the executioner sold the carcass to persons of quality as a prime dainty; and that in his time the body of a plump girl of fifteen, who was crucified for an attempt to poison the emperor, was sold to his imperial majesty's prime minister of state, and other great mandarins of the court, in joints from the gibbet, at 400 crowns. Neither indeed can I deny, that if the same use were made of several plump young girls in this town, who without one single groat to their fortunes cannot stir abroad without a chair, and appear at the playhouse and assemblies in foreign fineries which they never will pay for, the kingdom would not be the worse.

Some persons of a desponding spirit are in great concern about the vast number of poor people, who are aged, diseased, or maimed, and I have been desired to employ my thoughts what course may be taken to ease the nation of so grievous an encumbrance. But I am not in the least pain upon that matter, because it is very well known that they are every day dying and rotting by cold and famine, and filth and vermin, as fast as can be reasonably expected. And as to the young laborers, they are now in as hopeful a condition: They cannot get work, and consequently pine away for want of nourishment, to a degree that if at any time they are accidentally hired to common labor, they have not strength to perform it; and thus the country and themselves are happily delivered from the evils to come.

I have too long digressed, and therefore shall return to my subject. I   20 think the advantages by the proposal which I have made are obvious and many, as well as of the highest importance.

For first, as I have already observed, it would greatly lessen the number of papists, with whom we are yearly overrun, being the principal breeders of the nation as well as our most dangerous enemies; and who stay at home on purpose to deliver the kingdom to the Pretender, hoping to take their advantage by the absence of so many good Protestants, who have chosen rather to leave their country than stay at home and pay tithes against their conscience to an Episcopal curate.

Secondly, The poor tenants will have something valuable of their own, which by law may be made liable to distress and help to pay their landlord's rent, their corn and cattle being already seized, and money a thing unknown.

Thirdly, Whereas the maintenance of 100,000 children from two years old and upward, cannot be computed at less than 10s. a-piece per annum, the nation's stock will be thereby increased £50,000 per annum, beside the profit of a new dish introduced to the tables of all gentlemen of fortune in the kingdom who have any refinement in taste. And the money will circulate among ourselves, the goods being entirely of our own growth and manufacture.

Fourthly, The constant breeders beside the gain of 8s. sterling per 24
annum by the sale of their children, will be rid of the charge of maintaining them after the first year.

Fifthly, This food would likewise bring great custom to taverns, where the vintners will certainly be so prudent as to procure the best receipts for dressing it to perfection, and consequently have their houses frequented by all the fine gentlemen, who justly value themselves upon their knowledge in good eating; and a skilful cook who understands how to oblige his guests, will contrive to make it as expensive as they please.

Sixthly, This would be a great inducement to marriage, which all wise nations have either encouraged by rewards or enforced by laws and penalties. It would increase the care and tenderness of mothers toward their children, when they were sure of a settlement for life to the poor babes, provided in some sort by the public, to their annual profit instead of expense. We should see an honest emulation among the married women, which of them would bring the fattest child to the market. Men would become as fond of their wives during the time of their pregnancy as they are now of their mares in foal, their cows in calf, their sows when they are ready to farrow; nor offer to beat or kick them (as is too frequent a practice) for fear of a miscarriage.

Many other advantages might be enumerated. For instance, the addition of some thousand carcasses in our exportation of barreled beef, the propagation of swine's flesh, and improvement in the art of making good bacon, so much wanted among us by the great destruction of pigs, too frequent at our table; which are no way comparable in taste or magnificence to a well-grown, fat, yearling child, which roasted whole will make a considerable figure at a lord mayor's feast or any other public entertainment. But this and many others I omit, being studious of brevity.

Supposing that 1,000 families in this city would be constant customers 28
for infants' flesh, besides others who might have it at merry-meetings, particularly at weddings and christenings, I compute that Dublin would take off annually about 20,000 carcasses; and the rest of the kingdom (where probably they will be sold somewhat cheaper) the remaining 80,000.

I can think of no one objection that will possibly be raised against this proposal, unless it should be urged that the number of people will be thereby much lessened in the kingdom. This I freely own, and it was indeed one principal design in offering it to the world. I desire the reader will observe, that I calculate my remedy for this one individual kingdom of Ireland and for no other that ever was, is, or I think ever can be upon earth. Therefore let no man talk to me of other expedients: of taxing our absentees at 5s. a pound: of using neither clothes nor household furniture except what is of our own growth and manufacture: of utterly rejecting the materials and instruments that promote foreign luxury: of curing the expensiveness of pride, vanity, idleness, and gaming in our women: of introducing a vein of parsimony, prudence, and temperance: of learning to love our country, in the want of which we differ even from Laplanders and the inhabitants of Topinamboo: of quitting our animosities and factions, nor acting any longer like the Jews, who were murdering one another at the very moment their city was taken: of being a little cautious not to sell our country and conscience for nothing: of teaching landlords to have at least one degree of mercy toward their tenants: lastly, of putting a spirit of honesty, industry, and skill into our shopkeepers; who, if a resolution could now be taken to buy only our native goods, would immediately unite to cheat and exact upon us in the price the measure, and the goodness, nor could ever yet be brought to make one fair proposal of just dealing, though often and earnestly invited to it.

Therefore I repeat, let no man talk to me of these and the like expedients, till he has at least some glimpse of hope that there will be ever some hearty and sincere attempt to put them in practice.

But as to myself, having been wearied out for many years with offering vain, idle, visionary thoughts, and at length utterly despairing of success, I fortunately fell upon this proposal; which, as it is wholly new, so it has something solid and real, of no expense and little trouble, full in our own power, and whereby we can incur no danger in disobliging England. For this kind of commodity will not bear exportation, the flesh being of too tender a consistence to admit a long continuance in salt, although perhaps I could name a country which would be glad to eat up our whole nation without it.

After all, I am not so violently bent upon my own opinion as to reject 32 any offer proposed by wise men, which shall be found equally innocent, cheap, easy, and effectual. But before something of that kind shall be advanced in contradiction to my scheme, and offering a better, I desire the author or authors will be pleased maturely to consider two points. First, as things now stand, how they will be able to find food and raiment for 100,000 useless mouths and backs. And secondly, there being a round million of creatures in human figure throughout this kingdom, whose subsistence put into a common stock would leave them in debt 2,000,000£. sterling, adding those who are beggars by profession to the bulk of farmers, cottagers, and laborers, with the wives and children who are beggars in effect; I desire those politicians who dislike my overture, and may perhaps be so bold as to attempt an answer, that they will first ask the parents of these mortals, whether they would not at this day think it a great happiness to have been sold for food at a year old in the manner I prescribe, and thereby have avoided such a perpetual scene of misfortunes as they have since gone through by the oppression of landlords, the impossibility of paying rent without money or trade, the want of common sustenance, with neither house nor clothes to cover them from the inclemencies of the weather, and the most inevitable prospect of entailing the like or greater miseries upon their breed for ever.

I profess, in the sincerity of my heart, that I have not the least personal interest in endeavoring to promote this necessary work, having no other motive than the public good of my country, by advancing our trade, providing for infants, relieving the poor, and giving some pleasure to the rich. I have no children by which I can propose to get a single penny; the youngest being nine years old, and my wife past childbearing.

Questions and Suggestions For Writing

1. In paragraph 4 the speaker of the essay mentions proposals set forth by "projectors"; that is, by advocates of other proposals or projects. On the basis of the first two paragraphs of "A Modest Proposal," how would you characterize *this* projector, the speaker of the essay? Write your characterization in one paragraph. Then, in a second paragraph, characterize the projector as you understand him, having read the entire essay. In your second paragraph, indicate what *he thinks he is*, and also what the reader sees he really is.

2. The speaker or persona of "A Modest Proposal" is confident that selling children "for a good table" is a better idea than any of the then current methods of disposing of unwanted children, including abortion and infanticide. Can you think of any argument that might favor abortion or infanticide for parents in dire straits, rather than the projector's scheme?

3. In paragraph 29 the speaker considers, but dismisses out of hand, several other solutions to the wretched plight of the Irish poor. Write a 500-word essay in which you explain each of these ideas and their combined merits as an alternative solution to the one he favors.

4. What does the projector imply are the causes of the Irish poverty he deplores? Are there possible causes he has omitted? (If so, what are they?)

5. Imagine yourself as one of the poor parents to whom Swift refers, and write a 250-word essay explaining why you prefer not to sell your infant to the local butcher.

6. The modern version of the problem to which the proposal is addressed is called "population policy." How would you describe our nation's current population policy? Do we have a population policy, in fact? If not, what would you propose? If we do have one, would you propose any changes in it? Why, or why not?

7. It is sometimes suggested that just as persons need to get a license to drive a car, to hunt with a gun, or to marry, a husband and wife ought to be required to get a license to have a child. Would you favor this idea, assuming that it applied to you as a possible parent? Would Swift? Explain your answers in an essay of 500 words.

8. Consider the six arguments advanced in paragraphs 21–26, and write a 1,000-word essay criticizing all of them. Or, if you find that one or more of the arguments is really unanswerable, explain why you find it so compelling.

4

Using Sources

WHY USE SOURCES?

At the beginning of Chapter 3, we mentioned that many people fear to write because they fear they have no ideas. We pointed out that one *gets* ideas by writing; in the exercise of writing a draft, ideas begin to form, and these ideas stimulate further ideas, especially when one questions what one has written. But of course in writing about complex, serious questions, nobody is expected to invent all the answers. On the contrary, a writer is expected to be familiar with the chief answers already produced by others, and to make use of them through selective incorporation and criticism. In short, writers are not expected to reinvent the wheel; rather, they are expected to make good use of it, and perhaps round it off a bit or replace a defective spoke. In order to think out your own views in writing, you are expected to do some preliminary research into the views of others.

We use the word *research* broadly. It need not require taking copious notes on everything written on your topic; rather, it can involve no more than familiarizing yourself with at least some of the chief responses to your topic. In one way or another, almost everyone does some research. If we are going to buy a car, we may read an issue or two of a magazine that rates cars, or we may talk to a few people who own models that we are thinking of buying, and then we visit a couple of dealers to find out who is offering the best price.

Research, in short, is not an activity conducted only by college professors or by students who visit the library in order to write research papers. It is an activity that all of us engage in to some degree. In writing a research paper, you will engage in it to a great degree. But doing research is not the whole of a research paper. The reader expects the writer to have *thought* about the research, and to develop an argument based on the findings. Most businesses today devote an entire section to research and development. That's what is needed in writing, too. The reader wants not only a lot of facts but also a developed idea, a point to which the facts lead. Don't let your reader say of your paper what Gertrude Stein said of Oakland, California: "When you get there, there isn't any there there."

Some topics, of course, require more research than others, and some people are expected to spend more time doing research than others. A professional historian writing about President Eisenhower's dealings with Senator Joe McCarthy may have to read, or at least scan, thousands of unpublished documents in search of the necessary information. But even a professional has only so much time, and, having to draw the line somewhere, will assume (perhaps falsely) that the big pile of documents in the closet over there—apparently on an irrelevant subject—can be ignored.

A college student, writing a paper in a course, works under severely limited time, and can be excused for neglecting vast quantities of unpublished material, or even published material. For such a student, it is probably enough to consult Eisenhower's published correspondence, several good books on Eisenhower and on McCarthy, and some newspaper and magazine articles written during the years of McCarthy's misbehavior. On the basis of such evidence a thoughtful student can come to reasonably informed conclusions of what Eisenhower did and did not do, and can argue the thesis that Eisenhower's method of dealing with McCarthy was (or was not) effective.

Even an argument on a topic on which we all may think we already have opinions, such as whether the Olympics should be open to professional athletes, will benefit from research. By reading books and articles, a writer can learn such relevant things as: (1) even in ancient Greece the athletes were subsidized, so that in effect they were professionals; (2) eligibility today varies from sport to sport. For instance, in tennis, professionals under age twenty-one can compete; in basketball, players who have played in National Basketball Association games are ineligible, but anyone else can compete, including European professionals—or even an American such as Antoine Carr, who had played in the Italian Basketball League and was reported to have earned $200,000. Soccer professionals can compete, except those who have played in World Cup matches for European or South American countries. Track events bar professionals—even if they have professionally competed only in some other sport. Thus, Ron Brown, a sprinter, was barred from the track events in 1984 because he had signed a professional football contract. Football is not an Olympic event, and Brown in fact had not played professional football—he had merely signed a contract—but he nevertheless was barred. Of course a writer can argue that professionals in any sport should (or should not) be allowed to compete in the Olympics, but the argument will scarcely compel assent if it takes no account of what is already being done, and why it is being done.

To take a related matter, consider arguments about whether athletes should be permitted to take anabolic steroids, drugs that supposedly build up muscle, restore energy, and enhance aggressiveness. A thoughtful argument on this subject will have to take account of information that the writer can gather only by reading. Do steroids really have the effects commonly attributed to them? And are they dangerous? If they are dangerous, how dangerous are they? (After all, competitive sports are inherently dangerous, some of them highly so. Many boxers, jockeys, and football players have suffered severe injury, even death, from competing. Does anyone believe that anabolic steroids are more dangerous than the contests themselves?) Obviously, again, a respectable argument about steroids will have to show awareness of what is known about them.

Or take this question: Why did President Truman order that atomic bombs be dropped on Hiroshima and Nagasaki? The most obvious answer is, to end the war, but some historians believe he had a very different purpose. In their view, Japan's defeat was ensured before the bombs were dropped, and the Japanese were ready to surrender; the bombs were dropped not to save American (or Japanese) lives, but to show Russia that we were not to be pushed around. Scholars who hold this view, such as Gar Alperovitz in *Atomic Diplomacy*, argue that Japanese civilians in Hiroshima and Nagasaki were incinerated not to save the lives of American soldiers who otherwise would have died in an invasion of Japan, but to teach Stalin a lesson. Dropping the bombs, it is argued, marked not the end of the Pacific War but the beginning of the Cold War.

One must ask: What evidence supports this argument or claim or thesis, which assumes that Truman could not have thought the bomb was needed to defeat the Japanese because the Japanese knew they were defeated and would soon surrender without a hard-fought defense that would cost hundreds of thousands of lives? Moreover, what about the momentum that had built up to use the bomb? After all, years of effort and two billion dollars had been expended to produce a weapon with the intention of using it to end the war. If the argument we are considering is correct, all this background counted for little or nothing in Truman's decision, a decision purely diplomatic and coolly indifferent to human life. The task for the writer is to evaluate the evidence available, and then to argue for or against the view that Truman's purpose in dropping the bomb was to impress the Soviet government.

A student writing on the topic (whether arguing one view or the other), will certainly want to read the chief books on the subject (Alperovitz's, cited above, Martin Sherwin's *A World Destroyed*, and John Toland's *The Rising Sun*), and perhaps reviews of them, especially the reviews in journals devoted to political science. (Reading a searching review of a serious scholarly book is a good way quickly to identify some of the book's main contributions and controversial claims.) Truman's letters and statements, and books and articles about Truman, are also clearly relevant, and doubtless important articles are to be found in recent issues of scholarly journals. In fact, even an essay on such a topic as whether Truman was morally justified in using the atomic bomb for *any* purpose will be a stronger essay if it is well informed about such matters as the estimated loss of life that an invasion would have cost, the international rules governing weapons, and Truman's own statements about the issue.

How does one go about finding the material needed to write a well-informed argument? We will provide help, but first we want to offer a few words about choosing a topic.

CHOOSING A TOPIC

We will be brief. If a topic is not assigned, choose one that

1. interests you, and that
2. can be researched with reasonable thoroughness in the allotted time.

Topics such as registration for the draft, affirmative action, abortion, and bilingual education obviously impinge on our lives, and it may well be that one such topic is of especial interest to you.

As for the second point—a compassable topic—if the chief evidence for your tentative topic consists of a thousand unpublished letters a thousand miles away, or is in German and you don't read German, you will have to find something else to write on. Similarly, a topic such as the causes of World War II can hardly be mastered in a few weeks or argued in a ten-page paper. It is simply too big.

You can, however, write a solid paper analyzing, evaluating, and arguing for or against General Eisenhower's views on atomic warfare. What were they—and when did he hold them? (In books in 1948 and 1963 Eisenhower says that he opposed the use of the bomb before Hiroshima, and that he argued with Secretary of War Henry Stimson against dropping it, but what evidence supports these claims? Was Eisenhower in his books rewriting history?) Eisenhower's own writings, and books on Eisenhower, will of course be the major sources, but you will also want to look at books and articles about Stimson, and at publications that contain information about the views of other generals, so that, for instance, you can compare Eisenhower's view with Marshall's or MacArthur's.

Your instructor understands that you are not going to spend a year writing a 200-page book, but you should understand that you must do more than consult the article on Eisenhower in one encyclopedia and the article on atomic energy in another encyclopedia.

FINDING MATERIAL

The sources that you use will of course depend on your topic. For some topics, interviews that you conduct may be the chief source material, but most topics will require research in the library.

Notice that we have spoken of a topic, not of a thesis or even of a hypothesis (tentative thesis). Advanced students, because they have been wondering about some problem for a while, usually have not only a topic but also a hypothesis or even a thesis in mind. Less experienced students are not always in this happy position: before they can offer a hypothesis, they have to find a problem. Some instructors assign topics; others rely on students to find their own topics, based on readings in the course or in other courses.

When you have a *topic* ("Eisenhower and the atomic bomb"), and perhaps a *thesis* (an attitude toward the topic, a claim that you want to argue, such as "Eisenhower's disapproval of the bomb was the product of the gentleman-soldier code that he had learned at West Point"), it is often useful to scan a relevant book. You may already know of a relevant book, and it is likely in turn to cite others. If, however, you don't know of any book, you can find one by consulting the card catalog in the library, which lists books not only by author and by title but also by subject.

Of course if you are writing about Eisenhower, in the card catalog you will find cards for books by him and about him listed under his name. But what if you are writing about the controversy over the use of steroids by athletes? If you look up "steroids" in the catalog, you will find a card labeled "steroids," and behind this card will be cards for books the library has on this topic. Equally important, on the card will be the direction to "see also" several other specified topics, some of which will doubtless be relevant to your topic.

In fact, to learn what headings are included in the catalog, you don't even have to go to the catalog. You have only to look at a tome called *Subject Headings Used in the Dictionary Catalogs of the Library of Congress*, where you will find headings with cross-references indicated by *sa* ("see also"). Let's assume that you want to write about athletes' use of steroids. If you check *Subject Headings* for "steroids," you'll find an entry, and you'll also find a cross-reference to "anabolic steroids." If you look up "athletes" you'll find several cross-references; not all of these will, of course, be relevant, but you'll certainly want to follow up on the cross-references to "Athletic ability" and to "Medical examinations," and probably to "Sports medicine." After you have jotted down the headings that seem relevant, go to the card catalog, look for the headings you have located, and you will find cards for books the library has on the topic.

If there are many books on the topic, how do you choose just one? Choose first a fairly thin one, of fairly recent date, published by a reputable publisher. You may even want to jot down two or three titles and then check reviews of these books before choosing one book to skim. Five indexes enable you easily to locate book reviews in newspapers and periodicals:

Book Review Digest (1905–)

Book Review Index (1965–)

Index to Book Reviews in the Humanities (1960–)

Humanities Index (1974–)

Social Sciences Index (1974–)

Book Review Digest includes brief extracts from the reviews, and so look there first, but its coverage is not as broad as the other indexes.

Scanning a recent book that has been favorably reviewed will give you an overview of your topic, from which you can formulate or reformulate a tentative thesis.

A very recent book may include notes or a bibliography that will put you on to most of the chief discussions of the problem, but unless the book came out yesterday, it is bound to be dated. And even if it came out yesterday it was probably written a year ago (it takes from six months to a year to turn a manuscript into a book), and so you will want to look for recent material, probably articles published in recent periodicals. The indexes with broadest coverage of periodicals are:

Readers' Guide to Periodical Literature (1900–)

Humanities Index (1974–)

Social Sciences Index (1974–)

Readers' Guide is an index to more than a hundred serials, chiefly popular or semipopular publications such as the *Atlantic, Sports Illustrated,* and *Newsweek.* These publications have their uses, especially for papers dealing with current controversies, but for most topics one needs extended scholarly discussions published in learned journals, and for help in finding them one turns to the other two indexes.

The indexes just mentioned, along with the *New York Times Index* (1851–), which lets you find articles published in the newspaper, are the ones most commonly used, but here are some valuable specialized indexes:

Applied Science and Technology Index (1958–)

Art Index (1929–)

Biological and Agricultural Index (1964–)

Biography Index (1947–)

Business Periodicals Index (1958–)

Chemical Abstracts (1907–)

Dramatic Index (1909–49)

Education Index (1929–)

Engineering Index Monthly and Author Index (1906–)

Film Literature Index (1973–)

Index to Legal Periodicals (1908–)

International Index to Film Periodicals (1972–)

MLA International Bibliography (1921–); an annual listing of books and articles on linguistics and on literature in modern languages

Monthly Catalog of United States Government Publications (1895–)

Music Index (1949–)

Philosopher's Index (1967–)

Poole's Index for Periodical Literature (1802–1907)

Public Affairs Information Service Bulletin (1915–)

United Nations Document Index (1950–)

Ordinarily it makes sense to begin with the most recent year, and to work one's way backward, collecting citations for material of the last four or five years. The recent material usually incorporates older findings, but occasionally you will have to consult an early piece, especially if the recent material suggests that it is still vital.

An enormous amount of computerized information, much of it updated daily, is also available through databases such as ERIC and DIALOG. Your reference librarian can tell you what services are available (and at what cost) at your institution.

READING AND TAKING NOTES

Most readers and writers have idiosyncratic ways of going about the business of doing research. Some can read only when their feet are on the desk, and some can take notes only when their feet are planted on the floor. The suggestions that follow are simply our way of doing research; we recommend it, but we know that others are quite successful using other methods.

When we have jotted down the citations to books and articles, and have actually obtained a work from the library, we usually scan it rather than read it, to get an idea of whether it is worth reading carefully, and, even more important, whether it is worth the labor of taking notes. For an article, look especially at the beginning. Sometimes an abstract gives the gist of the whole piece, but even if there is no abstract, the opening paragraph may announce the topic, the thesis, and the approach. And look at the end of the essay, where you may find a summary. If the article still seems worth reading, read it, perhaps without taking notes, and then (having got the sense of it) read it again, taking notes. For a book, scan the table of contents and the preface to see if it really is as relevant as the title suggests. If the book has an index, you may want to check the page references to some essential topic or term, to see how much relevant material really is in the book.

When it comes to taking notes, all researchers have their own habits that they swear by, and they can't imagine any other way of working. Possibly you already are fixed in your habits, but if not, you may want to borrow ours. We use 4-by-6-inch index cards. Smaller cards don't have space for enough notes, and larger cards have space for too much. We recommend the following techniques.

1. Write in ink (pencil gets smudgy).
2. Put only one idea on each card (though an idea may include several facts).
3. Write on only one side of the card (notes on the back usually get lost).
4. Summarize, for the most part, rather than quote at length.
5. Quote only passages in which the writing is especially effective, or which are in some way crucial.
6. Make sure that all quotations are exact. Enclose quoted words within quotation marks, indicate omissions by ellipses (three spaced periods), and enclose within square brackets ([ ]) any additions you make.
7. *Never* copy a passage, changing an occasional word. Either copy it word for word, with punctuation intact, and enclose it within quotation marks, or summarize it drastically. If you copy a passage but change a word here and there, you may later make the mistake of using your note verbatim in your essay, and you will be guilty of plagiarism.
8. Give the page number of your source, whether you summarize or quote. If a quotation you have copied runs in the original from the bottom of page 210 to the top of page 211, in your notes put a diagonal line (/) after the last word on page 210, so that later, if in your paper you quote only the material from page 210, you will know that you must cite 210 and not 210–11.
9. Indicate the source. The author's last name is enough if you have consulted only one work by the author; but if you consult more than one work by an author, you need further identification, such as the author's name and a short title.
10. Don't hesitate to add your own comments about the substance of what you are recording. Such comments as "but contrast with Sherwin" or "seems illogical" or "evidence?" will ensure that you are thinking as well as writing, and will be of value when you come to transform your notes into a draft. Be sure, however, to enclose such notes within double diagonals (//), or to mark them in some other way, so that later you will know they are yours and not your source's.

11. Put a brief heading on the card, such as "Truman's last words on A-bomb."
12. Write a bibliographic card for each source, copying the author's name as it appears on the work (but last name first), the name of the translator if there is one, and (for a book) the title (taken from the title page, not from the cover), place of publication, publisher, and date. For a journal, note (in addition to the author's name, which you record with the author's last name first) the title of the article, the title of the journal, the volume and year for scholarly journals, and the day, week, or month and the year for popular works such as *Time*, and the pages that the article encompasses.

A WORD ABOUT PLAGIARISM

Plagiarism is the unacknowledged use of someone else's work. The word comes from a Latin word for "kidnapping," and plagiarism is indeed the stealing of something engendered by someone else. We won't deliver a sermon on the dishonesty (and folly) of plagiarism; we intend only to help you understand exactly what plagiarism is, and the first thing to say is that plagiarism is not limited to the unacknowledged quotation of words.

Even if you change every third word in your source, and you do not give the author credit, you are plagiarizing. Here is an example of this sort of plagiarism, based on the previous sentence:

> Even if you alter every third or fourth word from your source, and you fail to give credit to the author, you will be guilty of plagiarism.

Even if the writer of this paraphrase had cited a source after it, the writer would still be guilty of plagiarism, because the passage borrows not only the idea but the shape of the presentation, the sentence structure. The writer of this passage hasn't really written anything; he or she has only adapted something. What the writer needs to do is to write something like this:

> Changing an occasional word does not free the writer from the obligation to cite a source.

And the source would still need to be cited, if the central idea were not a commonplace one.

You are plagiarizing if without giving credit you use someone else's ideas—even if you put these ideas entirely into your own words. When you use another's ideas, you must indicate your indebtedness by saying something like "Alperovitz points out that . . ." or "Secretary of War Stimson, as Martin Sherwin notes, never expressed himself on this point." Alperovitz and Sherwin pointed out something that you had not thought of, and so you must give them credit if you want to use their findings.

Again, even if after a paraphrase you cite your source, you are plagiarizing. How, you may wonder, can you be guilty of plagiarism if you cite a source? Easy. A reader assumes that the citation refers to information or an opinion, *not* to the presentation or development of the idea; and of course in a paraphrase you are not presenting or developing the material in your own way. What you must do is take the idea and put it entirely into your own words, perhaps reducing a paragraph of a hundred words to a sentence of ten words, and you must still give credit for the idea. If you believe that the original hundred words are so perfectly put that they cannot be transformed without great loss, you'll have to quote them, and cite your source. But clearly there is no point in paraphrasing the author's hundred words into a hundred of your own. Either quote or summarize, but cite the source.

Keep in mind, too, that almost all generalizations about human nature, no matter how common and familiar (e.g., males are innately more aggressive than females) are not indisputable facts; they are at best hypotheses on which people differ and therefore should either not be asserted at all or should be supported by some cited source or authority. Similarly, because nearly all statistics (whether on the intelligence of criminals or the accuracy of lie detectors) are the result of some particular research and may well have been superseded or challenged by other investigators, it is advisable to cite a source for any statistics you use unless you are convinced they are indisputable, such as the number of registered voters in Memphis in 1988.

On the other hand, there is something called **common knowledge**, and the sources for such information need not be cited. The term does not, however, mean exactly what it seems to. It is common knowledge, of course, that Ronald Reagan was an American president (so you don't cite a source when you make that statement), and under the conventional interpretation of this doctrine, it is also common knowledge that he was born in 1911. In fact, of course, few people other than Reagan's wife and children know this date. Still, material that can be found in many places and that is indisputable belongs to all of us; therefore a writer need not cite her source when she says that Reagan was born in 1911. Probably she checked a dictionary or an encyclopedia for the date, but the source doesn't matter. Dozens of sources will give exactly the same information and, in fact, no reader wants to be bothered with a citation on such a point.

Some students have a little trouble developing a sense of what is and what is not common knowledge. Although, as we have just said, readers don't want to hear about the sources for information that is indisputable and can be documented in many places, if you are in doubt about whether to cite a source, cite it. Better risk boring the reader a bit than risk being accused of plagiarism.

WRITING THE PAPER

Organizing One's Notes

If you have read thoughtfully and taken careful (and, again, thought-ful) notes on your reading, and then (yet again) have thought about these notes, you are well on the way to writing a good paper. You have, in fact, already written some of it, in your notes. By now you should clearly have in mind the thesis you intend to argue. But of course you still have to organize the material, and, doubtless, even as you set about organizing it you will find points that will require you to do some additional research and much additional thinking.

Sort the index cards into packets, each packet devoted to one theme or point (for instance, one packet on the extent of use of steroids, another on evidence that steroids are harmful, yet another on arguments that even if harmful they should be permitted). Put aside all notes that—however interesting—you now see are irrelevant to your paper.

Next, arrange the packets into a tentative sequence. In effect, you are preparing a working outline. At its simplest, say, you will give three arguments on behalf of X, and then three counterarguments. (Or you might decide that it is better to alternate material from the two sets of three packets each, following each argument with an objection. At this stage, you can't be sure of the organization you will finally use, but make a tentative decision.)

The First Draft

Draft the essay, without worrying much about an elegant opening paragraph. Just write some sort of adequate opening that states the topic and your thesis. When you revise the whole later, you can put some effort into developing an effective opening. (Most experienced writers find that the opening paragraph in the final version is almost the last thing they write.)

If you handwrite or typewrite your draft, leave wide margins all around, so that later, when you reread it, you can add material. And try to use a separate sheet for each separable topic, such as each argument. This procedure lets you avoid cutting and pasting or recopying if you find, at a later stage, that you need to reorganize the essay. Even better is to compose on a word processor, which will let you effortlessly make additions anywhere.

In writing your draft, carefully copy into the draft all quotations that you plan to use. The mere act of copying the quotations will make you think about them. If you are faced with a long quotation, resist the temptation to write "see card" in your draft; copy the entire quotation, or paste the card (or a photocopy of it) on the page of your draft. (In the next section of this chapter we will talk briefly about leading into quotations, and about the form of quotations.) Include the citations, perhaps within double diagonals (//) in the draft, so that later if you need to check references in the library you don't have to go hunting through your index cards.

Later Drafts

Give the draft, and yourself, a rest, perhaps for a day or two, and then go back to it, read it over, make necessary revisions, and then outline it. That is, on a sheet of paper chart the organization and development, perhaps by jotting down a sentence summarizing each paragraph or each group of closely related paragraphs. Your outline or map may now show you that the paper obviously suffers from poor organization. For instance, it may reveal that you neglected to respond to one argument, or that one point is needlessly treated in two places. It may also help you to see that if you gave three arguments and then three counterarguments, you probably should instead have followed each argument with its rebuttal. Or, on the other hand, if you alternated arguments and objections, it may now seem better to use two main groups, all the arguments and then all the criticisms.

No one formula is always right. Much will depend on the complexity of the material. If the arguments are highly complex, it is better to respond to them one by one than to expect a reader to hold three complex arguments in mind before you get around to responding. If, however, the arguments can be stated briefly and clearly, it is effective to state all three, and then to go on to the responses. If you write on a word processor you will find it easy, even fun, to move passages of text around. If you write by hand, or on a typewriter, unless you put only one topic on each sheet you will have to use scissors and paste or transparent tape to produce your next draft—and your next. Allow enough time to produce several drafts.

A few more words about organization:

a. There is a difference between a paper that *has* an organization and

b. a paper that *shows* what the organization is.

Write papers of the second sort, but (there is always a "but") take care not to belabor the obvious. Inexperienced writers sometimes either hide the organization so thoroughly that a reader cannot find it, or, on the other hand, they so ploddingly lay out the structure ("Eighth, I will show . . .") that the reader becomes impatient. Yet it is better to be overly explicit than to be obscure.

The ideal, of course, is the middle route. Make the overall strategy of your organization evident by occasional explicit signs at the beginning of a paragraph ("We have seen . . . ," "It is time to consider the objections . . . ," "By far the most important . . . "); elsewhere make certain that the implicit structure is evident to the reader. When you reread your draft, if you try to imagine that you are one of your classmates, you will probably be able to sense exactly where explicit signs are needed, and where they are not needed.

Choosing a Tentative Title

By now a couple of tentative titles for your essay should have crossed your mind. If possible, choose a title that is both interesting and informative. Consider these three titles:

```
Are Steroids Harmful?
The Fuss over Steroids
Steroids: A Dangerous Game
```

"Are Steroids Harmful?" is faintly interesting, and it lets the reader know the gist of the subject, but it gives no clue about the writer's thesis, the writer's contention or argument. "The Fuss over Steroids" is somewhat better, for it gives information about the writer's position. "Steroids: A Dangerous Game" is still better; it announces the subject ("steroids") and the thesis ("dangerous"), and it also displays a touch of wit, because "game" glances at the world of athletics.

Don't try too hard, however; better a simple, direct, informative title than a strained, puzzling, or overly cute one. And remember to make sure that everything in your essay is relevant to your title. In fact, your title should help you to organize the essay and to delete irrelevant material.

The Final Draft

When at last you have a draft that is for the most part satisfactory, check to make sure that transitions from sentence to sentence and from paragraph to paragraph are clear ("Further evidence," "On the other hand," "A weakness, however, is apparent"), and then worry about your opening and your closing paragraphs. Your opening should be clear, interesting, and focused; if neither the title nor the first paragraph announces your thesis, the second paragraph probably should do so.

The final paragraph need not say, "In conclusion, I have shown that. . . ." It should effectively end the essay, but it need not summarize your conclusions. We have already offered a few words about final paragraphs (p. 77), but the best way to learn how to write such paragraphs is to study the endings of some of the essays in this book, and to adopt the strategies that appeal to you.

Be sure that all indebtedness is properly acknowledged. We have talked about plagiarism; now we will turn to the business of introducing quotations effectively.

QUOTING FROM SOURCES

The Use and Abuse of Quotations

When is it necessary, or appropriate, to quote? Sometimes the reader must see the exact words of your source; the gist won't do. If you are arguing that X's definition of "rights" is too inclusive, your readers have to know exactly how X defined "rights." Your brief summary of the definition may be unfair to X; in fact, you want to convince your readers that you are being fair, and so you quote X's definition, word for word. Moreover, if the passage is only a sentence or two long, or even if it runs to a paragraph, it may be so compactly stated that it defies summary. And to attempt to paraphrase it—substituting "natural" for "inalienable," and so forth— saves no space and only introduces imprecision. There is nothing to do but to quote it, word for word.

Second, you may want to quote a passage which could be summarized but which is so effectively stated that you want your readers to have the pleasure of reading the original. Of course readers will not give you credit for writing these words, but they will give you credit for your taste, and for your effort to make especially pleasant the business of reading your paper.

In short, use (but don't overuse) quotations. Speaking roughly, quotations should occupy no more than 10 or 15 percent of your paper, and they may occupy much less. Most of your paper should set forth your ideas, not other people's ideas.

How to Quote

Long and Short Quotations · **Long** quotations (five or more lines of typed prose, or three or more lines of poetry) are set off from your text. To set off material on a new line, indent ten spaces from the left margin and type the quotation double-spaced. (Some style manuals call for triple-spacing before and after a long quotation, and for typing it single-spaced. Ask your instructors if they have a preference.) Quotations that are set off are *not* enclosed within quotation marks.

Short quotations are treated differently. They are embedded within the text; they are enclosed within quotation marks but otherwise they do not stand out.

All quotations, whether set off or embedded, must be exact. If you omit any words, you must indicate the ellipsis by substituting three spaced periods for the omission; if you insert any words or punctuation, you must indicate the addition by enclosing it within square brackets, not to be confused with parentheses.

Leading into a Quotation · Now for a less mechanical matter, the way in which a quotation is introduced. To say that it is "introduced" implies that one leads into it, though on rare occasions a quotation appears without an introduction, perhaps immediately after the title. Normally one leads into a quotation by giving the name of the author and (no less important) clues about purpose and about the content of the quotation. For example:

```
William James provides a clear answer to Huxley when he
says that ". . ."
```

The writer has been writing about Huxley, and now is signaling readers that they will be getting James's reply. The writer is also signaling (in "a clear answer") that the reply is satisfactory. If the writer believed that James's answer was not really acceptable, the lead-in might have run thus:

```
William James attempts to answer Huxley, but his response
does not really meet the difficulty Huxley calls atten-
tion to.  James writes, ". . ."
```

Or:

```
William James provided what he took to be an answer to
Huxley, when he said that ". . ."
```

In this last example, clearly the words "what he took to be an answer" imply that the essayist will show, after the quotation from James, that the answer is in some degree inadequate. Or the essayist may wish to suggest the inadequacy even more strongly:

```
William James provided what he took to be an answer to
Huxley, but he used the word "religion" in a way that
Huxley would not have allowed.  James argues that ". . ."
```

If after reading something by Huxley we had merely been given "William James says . . . ," we wouldn't know whether we would be getting confirmation, refutation, or something else. The essayist would have put a needless burden on the readers. Generally speaking, the more difficult the quotation, the more important is the introductory or explanatory lead-in, but even the simplest quotation profits from some sort of brief lead-in, such as "James reaffirms this point when he says. . . ."

DOCUMENTATION

In the course of your essay, you will probably quote or summarize material derived from a source. You must give credit, and although there is no one form of documentation to which all scholarly fields subscribe, two forms are widely followed. One, established by the Modern Language

Association (MLA), is used chiefly in the humanities; the other, established by the American Psychological Association (APA), is used chiefly in the social sciences.

We include two papers that use sources. The first, "Support for the A.M.A. Anti-Smoking Campaign" (p. 147), uses the MLA format; the second, "Why Handguns Must Be Outlawed" (p. 196), uses the APA format. (You may notice that various styles are illustrated in other selections we have included.)

A Note on Footnotes

Before discussing these two formats a few words about footnotes are in order. Before the MLA and the APA developed their rules of style, citations commonly were given in footnotes. Although today footnotes are not so frequently used to give citations, they still may be useful for another purpose. If you want to include some material that may seem intrusive in the body of the paper, you may relegate it to a footnote. For example, in a footnote you might translate a quotation given in a foreign language, or you might demote from text to footnote a paragraph explaining why you are not taking account of such-and-such a point. By putting the matter in a footnote you are signaling the reader that it is dispensable; it is something relevant but not essential, something extra that you are, so to speak, tossing in. Don't make a habit of writing this sort of note, but there are times when it is appropriate.

To indicate in the body of the text that you are adding a footnote, type a raised arabic numeral. Do *not* first hit the space bar; do *not* type a period after the numeral; do *not* enclose the numeral within parentheses. Usually the superior numeral is placed at the end of the sentence, but place it earlier if clarity requires. If the numeral is at the end of a sentence, hit the space bar twice before beginning the next sentence. If the numeral is within the sentence, hit the space bar once, and continue the sentence.

The note itself will go at the bottom of the page of text on which the footnote number appears. After the last line of text on the page, double-space twice, then indent five spaces, elevate the carriage half a line, type the numeral (again, without a period and without enclosing it within parentheses), lower the carriage, then hit the space bar once and type the note. If the note runs more than one line, type it double-spaced (unless your instructor tells you to the contrary), flush with the left margin. Double-space between notes, and begin each note with an indented raised numeral and then a capital letter. End each note with a period or, if the sentence calls for one, a question mark.

MLA Format

This discussion is divided into two parts, a discussion of citations within the text of the essay, and a discussion of the list of references, called Works Cited, that is given at the end of the essay.

Citations within the Text · Brief citations within the body of the essay give credit, in a highly abbreviated way, to the sources for material you quote, summarize, or make use of in any other way. These citations are made clear by a list of sources, entitled Works Cited, appended to the essay. Thus, in your essay you may say something like this:

```
Commenting on the relative costs of capital punishment
and life imprisonment, Ernest van den Haag says that he
doubts "that capital punishment really is more expen-
sive" (33).
```

The **citation,** the number 33 in parentheses, means that the quoted words come from page 33 of a source (listed in Works Cited) written by van den Haag. Without Works Cited, a reader would have no way of knowing that you are quoting from page 33 of an article that appeared in the February 8, 1985 issue of *National Review.*

Usually the parenthetic citation appears at the end of a sentence, as in the example just given, but it can appear elsewhere; its position will depend chiefly on your ear, your eye, and the context. You might, for example, write the sentence thus:

```
Ernest van den Haag doubts that "capital punishment
really is more expensive" than life imprisonment (33),
but other writers have presented figures that contra-
dict him.
```

Five points must be made about these examples:

1. **Quotation marks.** The closing quotation mark appears after the last word of the quotation, *not* after the parenthetic citation. Since the citation is not part of the quotation, the citation is not included within the quotation marks.

2. **Omission of words (ellipsis).** If you are quoting only a phrase, as in the examples given, you do not need to indicate (by three spaced periods) that you are omitting material before or after the quotation. But if for some reason you want to omit a part of the quotation you must indicate the omission, by inserting **ellipsis.** To take a simple example, if you omit the word "really" from van den Haag's phrase, you must alert the reader to the omission:

```
Ernest van den Haag doubts that "capital punishment . . .
is more expensive" than life imprisonment (33).
```

Suppose you are quoting a sentence but wish to omit material from the end of the sentence. Suppose, also, that the quotation forms the end of your sentence. Write a lead-in phrase, then quote as much from your source as you need, then type three spaced periods for the omission, close the quotation, give the parenthetic citation, and finally type a fourth period to indicate the end of your sentence.

Here's an example. Suppose you want to quote the first part of a sentence that runs, "We could insist that the cost of capital punishment be reduced so as to diminish the differences." Your sentence would incorporate the desired extract as follows:

> Van den Haag says, "We could insist that the cost of cap-
> ital punishment be reduced . . ." (33).

3. **Punctuation with parenthetic citations.** In the examples, the punctuation (a period or a comma in the examples) *follows* the citation. If, however, the quotation ends with a question mark, include the question mark *within* the quotation, since it is part of the quotation.

> Van den Haag asks, "Isn't it better—more just and
> more useful--that criminals, if they do not have the cer-
> tainty of punishment, at least run the risk of suffering
> it?" (35)

But if the question mark is your own, and not in the source, put it after the citation, thus:

> What answer can be given to van den Haag's doubt that
> "capital punishment really is more expensive" (33)?

4. **Two or more works by an author.** If your list of Works Cited includes two or more works by an author, you cannot, in your essay, simply cite a page number, since the reader will not know which of the works you are referring to. You must give additional information. You can give it in your lead-in, thus:

> In "New Arguments Against Capital Punishment," van den
> Haag expresses doubt "that capital punishment really is
> more expensive" than life imprisonment (33).

Or you can give the title, in a shortened form, within the citation:

> Van den Haag expresses doubt that "capital punishment
> really is more expensive" than life imprisonment ("New
> Arguments" 33).

5. **Citing even when you do not quote.** Even if you don't quote a source directly, but use its point in a paraphrase or a summary, you will give a citation:

```
Van den Haag thinks that life imprisonment costs more
than capital punishment (33).
```

Notice that in all of the previous examples, the author's name is given in the text (rather than within the parenthetic citation). But there are several other ways of giving the citation, and we shall look at them now. (We have already seen, in the example given under paragraph 4, that the title and the page number can be given within the citation.)

AUTHOR AND PAGE NUMBER IN PARENTHESES

```
It has been argued that life imprisonment is more costly
than capital punishment (van den Haag 33).
```

AUTHOR, TITLE, AND PAGE NUMBER IN PARENTHESES

We have seen that if Works Cited includes two or more works by an author, you will have to give the title of the work on which you are drawing, either in your lead-in phrase or within the parenthetic citation. Similarly, if you are citing someone who is listed more than once in Works Cited, and for some reason you do not mention the name of the author or the work in your lead-in, you must add the information in your citation:

```
Doubt has been expressed that capital punishment is as
costly as life imprisonment (van den Haag, "New Argu-
ments" 33).
```

A GOVERNMENT DOCUMENT OR A WORK OF CORPORATE AUTHORSHIP

Treat the issuing body as the author. Thus, you will probably write something like this:

```
The Commission on Food Control, in Food Resources Today,
concludes that there is no danger (37-38).
```

A WORK BY TWO OR MORE AUTHORS

If a work is by *two* authors, give the names of both, either in the parenthetic citation (the first example below) or in a lead-in (the second example below):

```
There is not a single example of the phenomenon (Smith
and Dale 182-83).
```

```
Smith and Dale insist there is not a single example of
the phenomenon (182-83).
```

If there are *three or more authors*, give the last name of the first author, followed by "et al." (an abbreviation for *et alii*, Latin for "and others"), thus:

```
Gittleman et al. argue (43) that. . . .
```

Or:

```
On average, the cost is even higher (Gittleman
et al. 43).
```

Parenthetic Citation of an Indirect Source (Citation of Material that Itself Was Quoted or Summarized in Your Source)

Suppose you are reading a book by Jones, in which she quotes Smith, and you wish to use Smith's material. Your citation must refer the reader to Jones—the source you are using—but of course you cannot attribute the words to Jones. You will have to make it clear that you are quoting Smith, and so, after a lead-in phrase like "Smith says," followed by the quotation, you will give a parenthetic citation along these lines:

```
(qtd. in Jones 324-25).
```

Parenthetic Citation of Two or More Works

```
The costs are simply too high (Smith 301; Jones 28).
```

Notice that a semicolon, followed by a space, separates the two sources.

A Work in More Than One Volume

This is a bit tricky.

If you have used only one volume, in Works Cited you will specify the volume, and so in the parenthetic in-text citation you will not need to specify the volume. All that you need to include in the citation is a page number, as illustrated by most of the examples that we have given.

If you have used more than one volume, your parenthetic citation will have to specify the volume as well as the page, thus:

```
Jackson points out that fewer than one hundred fifty peo-
ple fit this description (2: 351).
```

The reference is to page 351 in volume 2 of a work by Jackson.

If, however, you are citing not a page but an entire volume—let's say volume 2—your parenthetic citation will look like this:

Jackson exhaustively studies this problem (vol. 2).

Or:

Jackson (vol. 2) exhaustively studies this problem.

Notice the following points:

1. In citing a volume and page, the volume number, like the page number, is given in arabic (not roman) numerals, even if the original used roman numerals.
2. The volume number is followed by a colon, then a space, then the page number.
3. If you cite a volume number without a page number, as in the last example quoted, the abbreviation is "vol." Otherwise do *not* use such abbreviations as "vol." and "p." and "pg."

An Anonymous Work

For an anonymous work, give the title in your lead-in, or give it in a shortened form in your parenthetic citation:

A Prisoner's View of Killing includes a poll taken of the inmates on Death Row (32).

Or:

A poll is available (Prisoner's View 32).

An Interview

Probably you won't need a parenthetic citation, because you'll say something like

Vivian Berger, in an interview, said. . . .

or

According to Vivian Berger, in an interview, . . .

and when your reader turns to Works Cited, he or she will see that Berger is listed, along with the date of the interview. But if you do not mention the source's name in the lead-in, you will have to give it in the parentheses, thus:

```
Contrary to popular belief, the death penalty is not
reserved for serial killers and depraved murderers
(Berger).
```

The List of Works Cited (MLA Format)

As the previous pages explain, parenthetic documentation consists of references that become clear when the reader consults the list titled Works Cited, given at the end of an essay.

The list of Works Cited continues the pagination of the essay; if the last page of text is 10, then Works Cited begins on page 11. Type the page number in the upper right corner, a half inch from the top of the sheet. Next, type "Works Cited" (*not* enclosed within quotation marks), centered, one inch from the top, then double-space and type the first entry.

An Overview · Here are some general guidelines.

FORM ON THE PAGE

1. Begin each entry flush with the left margin, but if an entry runs to more than one line, indent five spaces for each succeeding line of the entry.
2. Double-space each entry, and double-space between entries.
3. Underline titles of works published independently, for instance books, pamphlets, and journals. Enclose within quotation marks a work not published independently, for instance an article in a journal, or a short story.
4. If you are citing a book that includes the title of another book, underline the main title but do *not* underline the title mentioned. Example:

```
A Study of Mill's On Liberty
```

5. In the sample entries below, pay attention to the use of commas, colons, and spaces after punctuation.

ALPHABETIC ORDER

1. Arrange the list alphabetically by author, with the author's last name first.
2. For information about anonymous works, works with more than one author, and two or more works by one author, see below.

A Closer Look · Here is more detailed advice.

THE AUTHOR'S NAME · Notice that the last name is given first, but otherwise the name is given as on the title page. Do not substitute initials for names written out on the title page.

If your list includes two or more works by an author the author's name is not repeated for the second title, but is represented by three hyphens followed by a period and two spaces. The sequence of the works is determined by the alphabetic order of the titles. Thus, Smith's book called *Poverty* would be listed ahead of her book called *Welfare*. See the example below, listing two works by Roger Brown.

For a book by more than one author, see page 135.

Anonymous works are listed under the first word of the title, or the second word if the first is *A*, *An*, or *The*, or a foreign equivalent. In a few moments we will discuss books by more than one author, government documents, and works of corporate authorship.

THE TITLE

Take the title from the title page, not from the cover or the spine, but disregard any unusual typography such as the use of all capital letters or the use of the ampersand (&) for *and*. Underline the title and subtitle (separate them by a colon) with one continuous underline, to indicate italics, but do not underline the period that concludes this part of the entry. Example:

```
The Death Penalty: A New View.
```

PLACE OF PUBLICATION, PUBLISHER, AND DATE

For the place of publication, provide the name of the city; you can usually find it either on the title page or on the reverse of the title page. If a number of cities are listed, provide only the first. If the city is not likely to be known, or if it may be confused with another city of the same name (as is Cambridge, Massachusetts, with Cambridge, England) add the name of the state.

The name of the publisher is abbreviated. Usually the first word is enough (Random House becomes Random), but if the first word is a first name, such as in Alfred A. Knopf, the surname (Knopf) is used instead. University presses are abbreviated thus: Yale UP, U of Chicago P, State U of New York P.

The date of publication of a book is given when known; if no date appears on the book, write n.d. to indicate "no date."

SAMPLE ENTRIES · Here are some examples, illustrating the points we have covered thus far:

```
Douglas, Ann.  The Feminization of American Culture.  New
     York: Knopf, 1977.
Brown, Roger.  Social Psychology.  New York: Free, 1965.
---.  Words and Things.  Glencoe, Ill.: Free, 1958.
```

Hartman, Chester. The Transformation of San Francisco.
Totowa, N.J.: Rowan, 1984.

Kellerman, Barbara. The Political Presidency: Practice of
Leadership from Kennedy through Reagan. New York:
Oxford UP, 1984.

Notice that a period follows the author's name, and another period follows the title. If a subtitle is given, as it is for Kellerman's book, it is separated from the title by a colon and a space. A colon follows the place of publication, a comma follows the publisher, and a period follows the date.

A BOOK BY MORE THAN ONE AUTHOR

The book is alphabetized under the last name of the first author named on the title page. If there are *two or three authors*, the names of these are given (after the first author's name) in the normal order, *first name first*.

Gilbert, Sandra M., and Susan Gubar. The Madwoman in the
Attic: The Woman Writer and the Nineteenth-Century
Literary Imagination. New Haven, Conn.: Yale UP,
1979.

Notice, again, that although the first author's name is given *last name first*, the second author's name is given in the normal order, first name first. Notice, too, that a comma is put after the first name of the first author, separating the authors.

If there are *more than three authors*, give the name of only the first, and then add (but *not* enclosed within quotation marks) "et al." (Latin for "and others").

Altshuler, Alan, et al. The Future of the Automobile.
Cambridge, Mass.: MIT P, 1984.

GOVERNMENT DOCUMENTS

If the writer is not known, treat the government and the agency as the author. Most federal documents are issued by the Government Printing Office (abbreviated to GPO) in Washington, D.C.

United States Congress. Office of Technology Assessment. Computerized Manufacturing Automation: Employment, Education, and the Workplace. Washington:
GPO, 1984.

WORKS OF CORPORATE AUTHORSHIP

Begin the citation with the corporate author, even if the same body is also the publisher, as in the first example:

```
American Psychiatric Association.  Psychiatric Glossary.
     Washington: American Psychiatric Association.  1984.
Carnegie Council on Policy Studies in Higher Education.
     Giving Youth a Better Chance: Options for Education,
     Work, and Service.  San Francisco: Jossey, 1980.
```

A REPRINT, FOR INSTANCE A PAPERBACK VERSION OF AN OLDER CLOTHBOUND BOOK

```
Gray, Francine du Plessix.  Divine Disobedience: Profiles
     in Catholic Radicalism.  1970.  New York: Vintage,
     1971.
```

After the title, give the date of original publication (it can usually be found on the reverse of the title page of the reprint you are using), then a period, and then the place, publisher, and date of the edition you are using. The example indicates that Gray's book was originally published in 1970 and that the student is using the Vintage reprint of 1971.

A BOOK IN SEVERAL VOLUMES

If you have used more than one volume, in a citation within your essay you will (as explained on pp. 131–132) indicate a reference to, say, page 250 of volume 3 thus: (3: 250).

If, however, you have used only one volume of the set—let's say volume 3—in your entry in Works Cited specify which volume you used, as in the next example:

```
Friedel, Frank.  Franklin D. Roosevelt.  4 vols.  Boston:
     Little, 1973.  Vol. 3.
```

With such an entry in Works Cited, the parenthetic citation within your essay would be to the page only, not to the volume and page, since a reader who consults Works Cited will understand that you used only volume 3. But notice that in Works Cited, although you specify volume 3, you also give the total number of volumes.

ONE BOOK WITH A SEPARATE TITLE IN A SET OF VOLUMES

Sometimes a set with a title makes use also of a separate title for each book in the set. If you are listing such a book, use the following form:

Churchill, Winston. The Age of Revolution. Vol. 3 of
A History of the English-Speaking Peoples.
New York: Dodd, 1957.

A Book with an Author and an Editor

Kant, Immanuel. The Philosophy of Kant: Immanuel Kant's
Moral and Political Writings. Ed. Carl J.
Friedrich. New York: Modern, 1949.
Churchill, Winston, and Franklin D. Roosevelt. The Com-
plete Correspondence. 3 vols. Ed. Warren F.
Kimball. Princeton UP, 1985.

If the book has one editor, the abbreviation is "ed."; if two or more editors,
"eds."

If you are making use of the editor's introduction or other editorial
material rather than of the author's work, list the book under the name of
the editor rather than of the author, as shown below under "An Introduction, Foreword, or Afterword."

A Revised Edition of a Book

Arendt, Hannah. Eichmann in Jerusalem. Revised and enlarged ed. New York: Viking, 1965.
Honour, Hugh, and John Fleming. The Visual Arts: A
History. 2nd ed. Englewood Cliffs, N.J.: Pren-
tice, 1986.

A Translated Book

Franqui, Carlos. Family Portrait with Fidel: A Memoir.
Trans. Alfred MacAdam. New York: Random, 1984.

An Introduction, Foreword, or Afterword

Goldberg, Arthur J. Foreword. An Eye for an Eye? The
Morality of Punishing by Death. By Stephen
Nathanson. Totowa, N.J.: Rowman, 1987.

Usually a book with an introduction or some such comparable material is
listed under the name of the author of the book (here Nathanson) rather
than under the name of the writer of the introduction (here Goldberg), but
if you are referring to the apparatus rather than to the book itself, use the

form just given. The words "Introduction," "Preface," "Foreword," and "Afterword" are neither enclosed within quotation marks nor underlined.

A BOOK WITH AN EDITOR BUT NO AUTHOR

Let's assume that you have used a book of essays written by various people but collected by an editor (or editors), whose name appears on the collection.

> LaValley, Albert J., ed. Focus on Hitchcock. Englewood
>   Cliffs, N.J.: Prentice, 1972.

A WORK WITHIN A VOLUME OF WORKS BY ONE AUTHOR

The following entry indicates that a short work by Susan Sontag, an essay called "The Aesthetics of Silence," appears in a book by Sontag titled *Styles of Radical Will*. Notice that the inclusive page numbers of the short work are cited, not merely page numbers that you may happen to refer to but the page numbers of the entire piece.

> Susan Sontag. "The Aesthetics of Silence." In Styles
>   of Radical Will. New York: Farrar, 1969. 3-34.

A BOOK REVIEW

Here is an example, citing Gerstein's review of Walker's book. Gerstein's review was published in a journal called *Ethics*.

> Gerstein, Robert S. Rev. of Punishment, Danger and
>   Stigma: The Morality of Criminal Justice, by Nigel
>   Walker. Ethics 93 (1983): 408-10.

If the review has a title, give the title between the period following the reviewer's name and "Rev."

If a review is anonymous, list it under the first word of the title, or under the second word if the first word is *A*, *An*, or *The*. If an anonymous review has no title, begin the entry with "Rev. of" and then give the title of the work reviewed; alphabetize the entry under the title of the work reviewed.

AN ARTICLE OR ESSAY—NOT A REPRINT—IN A COLLECTION

A book may consist of a collection (edited by one or more persons) of new essays by several authors. Here is a reference to one essay in such a book. (The essay, by Balmforth, occupies pages 19–35 in a collection edited by Bevan.)

Balmforth, Henry. "Science and Religion." Steps to
    Christian Understanding. Ed. R. J. W. Bevan.
    London: Oxford UP, 1958. 19-35.

AN ARTICLE OR ESSAY REPRINTED IN A COLLECTION

The previous example (Balmforth's essay in Bevan's collection) was for
an essay written for a collection. But some collections reprint earlier
material, such as essays from journals or chapters from books. The following example cites an essay that was originally printed in a book called *The
Cinema of Alfred Hitchcock*. This essay has been reprinted in a later
collection of essays on Hitchcock, edited by Arthur J. LaValley, and it was
LaValley's collection that the student used.

Bogdanovich, Peter. "Interviews with Alfred Hitchcock."
    The Cinema of Alfred Hitchcock. New York: Museum of
    Modern Art, 1963. 15-18. Rpt. in Focus on Hitch-
    cock. Ed. Albert J. LaValley. Englewood Cliffs,
    N.J.: Prentice, 1972. 28-31.

The student has read Bogdanovitch's essay or chapter, but not in Bogdanovich's book, where it occupied pages 15–18. The material was actually read on pages 28–31 in a collection of writings on Hitchcock, edited by
LaValley. Details of the original publication—title, date, page numbers,
and so forth—were found in LaValley's collection. Almost all editors will
include this information, either on the copyright page or at the foot of the
reprinted essay, but sometimes they do not give the original page numbers.
In such a case, you need not include the original numbers in your entry.

Notice that the entry begins with the author and the title of the work
you are citing (here, Bogdanovich's interviews), not with the name of the
editor of the collection or the title of the collection.

AN ENCYCLOPEDIA OR OTHER ALPHABETICALLY ARRANGED REFERENCE WORK

The publisher, place of publication, volume number, and page number do *not* have to be given. For such works, list only the edition (if it is
given) and the date.

For a *signed* article, begin with the author's last name. (If the article is
signed with initials, check elsewhere in the volume for a list of abbreviations, which will inform you what the initials stand for, and use the
following form.)

Williams, Donald C. "Free Will and Determinism." Ency-
    clopedia Americana. 1987 ed.

For an *unsigned article,* begin with the title of the article:

```
"Tobacco."  Encyclopaedia Britannica: Macropaedia.
     1988 ed.
"Automation."  The Business Reference Book.  1977 ed.
```

A TELEVISION OR RADIO PROGRAM

```
Sixty Minutes.  CBS.  26 Feb. 1989.
```

AN ARTICLE IN A SCHOLARLY JOURNAL · The title of the article is enclosed within quotation marks, and the title of the journal is underlined to indicate italics.

Some journals are paginated consecutively; the pagination of the second issue begins where the first issue leaves off. Other journals begin each issue with page 1. The forms of the citations differ slightly. First, an article in

A JOURNAL THAT IS PAGINATED CONSECUTIVELY

```
Vilas, Carlos M.  "Popular Insurgency and Social Revolu-
     tion in Central America," Latin American Perspec-
     tives 15 (1988): 55-77.
```

Vilas's article occupies pages 55–77 in volume 15, which was published in 1988. (Notice that the volume number is followed by a space, and then by the year, in parentheses, and then by a colon, a space, and the page numbers of the entire article.) Because the journal is paginated consecutively, the issue number does *not* need to be specified.

A JOURNAL THAT BEGINS EACH ISSUE WITH PAGE 1

If the journal is, for instance, a quarterly, there will be four page 1's each year, so the issue number must be given. After the volume number, type a period and (without hitting the space bar) the issue number, as in the next example:

```
Greenberg, Jack.  "Civil Rights Enforcement Activity of
     the Department of Justice."  The Black Law Journal
     8.1 (1983): 60-67.
```

Greenberg's article appeared in the first issue of volume 8 of *The Black Law Journal.*

AN ARTICLE IN A WEEKLY, BIWEEKLY, OR MONTHLY PUBLICATION

```
Lamar, Jacob V.  "The Immigration Mess."  Time 27 Febru-
     ary 1989: 14-15.
```

AN ARTICLE IN A NEWSPAPER

Because a newspaper usually consists of several sections, a section number or a capital letter may precede the page number. The example indicates that an article begins on page 1 of section 2 and is continued on a later page.

```
Chu, Harry.  "Art Thief Defends Action."  New York
     Times 8 Feb. 1989,  sec. 2: 1+.
```

A DATABASE SOURCE

Treat material obtained from a computer service, such as Bibliographies Retrieval Service (BRS), like other printed material, but at the end of the entry add the name of the service and the identification number of the item.

```
Jackson, Morton.  "A Look at Profits."  Harvard Business
     Review 40 (1962): 106-13.  Bibliographies Retrieval
     Service, 1984.  Accession No. 621081.
```

Caution: Although we have covered the most usual kinds of sources, it is entirely possible that you will come across a source that does not fit any of the categories that we have discussed. For two hundred pages of explanations of these matters, covering the proper way to cite all sorts of troublesome and unbelievable (but real) sources, see Joseph Gibaldi and Walter S. Achtert, *MLA Handbook for Writers of Research Papers*, 3rd ed. (New York: Modern Language Association of America, 1988).

APA Format

Your paper will conclude with a page headed "References," in which you list all of your sources. If the last page of your essay is numbered 10, number the first page of references 11.

Citations within the Text · The APA style emphasizes the date of publication; the date appears not only in the list of references at the end of the paper, but also in the paper itself, when you give a brief parenthetic citation of a source that you have quoted or summarized or in any other way used. Here is an example:

```
Statistics are readily available (Smith, 1989, p. 20).
```

The title of Smith's book or article will be given at the end of your paper, in the list titled "References." We will discuss the form of the material listed in References in a moment, but first we will look at some typical citations within the text of a student's essay.

A SUMMARY OF AN ENTIRE WORK

Smith (1988) holds the same view.

Or

Similar views are held widely (Smith, 1988; Jones & Metz, 1990).

A REFERENCE TO A PAGE OR TO PAGES

Smith (1988, p. 17) argues that "the death penalty is a lottery, and blacks usually are the losers."

A REFERENCE TO AN AUTHOR WHO IN THE LIST OF REFERENCES IS REPRESENTED BY MORE THAN ONE WORK

If in References you list two or more works that an author published in the same year, the works are listed in alphabetic order, by the first letter of the title. The first work is labeled *a*, the second *b*, and so on. Here is a reference to the second work that Smith published in 1989:

Florida presents "a fair example" of how the death penalty is administered (Smith, 1989b).

References · Your brief parenthetic citations are made clear when the reader consults the list you give in References. Type this list on a separate page, continuing the pagination of your essay.

An Overview · Here are some general guidelines.

FORM ON THE PAGE
1. Begin each entry flush with the left margin, but if an entry runs to more than one line, indent three spaces for each succeeding line of the entry.
2. Double-space each entry, and double-space between entries.

ALPHABETIC ORDER
1. Arrange the list alphabetically by author.
2. Give the author's last name first, then the initial of the first and of the middle name (if any).
3. If there is more than one author, name all of the authors, again inverting the name (last name first) and giving only initials for first and middle names. (But do not invert the editor's name when the entry begins with the name of an author who has written an article in an edited book.) When there are two or more authors, use an ampersand (&) before the name of the last author. Example (here,

of an article in the tenth volume of a journal called *Developmental Psychology*):

Drabman, R. S. & Thomas, M. H. (1974). Does media violence increase children's tolerance of real-life aggression? Developmental Psychology, 10, 418-421.

4. If you list more than one work by an author, do so in the order of
   publication, the earliest first. If two works by an author were
   published in the same year, give them in alphabetic order by the
   first letter of the title, disregarding *A*, *An*, or *The*, and their
   foreign equivalent. Designate the first work as "a," the second as
   "b." Repeat the author's name at the start of each entry.

Donnerstein, E. (1980a). Aggressive erotica and violence
   against women. Journal of Personality and Social Psy-
   chology, 39, 269-77.
Donnerstein, E. (1980b). Pornography and violence
   against women. Annals of the New York Academy of Sci-
   ences, 347, 227-288.
Donnerstein, E. (1983). Erotica and human aggression.
   In R. Green and E. Donnerstein (Eds.). Aggression:
   Theoretical and empirical reviews (pp. 87-103). New
   York: Academic Press.

FORM OF TITLE

1. In references to books, capitalize only the first letter of the first
   word of the title (and of the subtitle, if any) and capitalize proper
   nouns. Underline the complete title.
2. In references to articles in periodicals or in edited books, capitalize
   only the first letter of the first word of the article's title (and
   subtitle, if any), and all proper nouns. Do not put the title within
   quotation marks. Type a period after the title of the article. For the
   title of the journal, and the volume and page numbers, see the next
   instruction.
3. In references to periodicals, give the volume number in arabic
   numerals, and underline it. Do *not* use *vol.* before the number, and
   do not use *p.* or *pg.* before the page numbers.

Sample References · Here are some samples to follow.

A BOOK BY ONE AUTHOR

Pavlov, I. P. (1927). Conditioned reflexes. G. V.
   Anrep, trans. London: Oxford University Press.

A BOOK BY MORE THAN ONE AUTHOR

Belenky, M. F., Clinchy, B. M., Goldberger, N. R., &
    Torule, J. M. (1986). Women's ways of knowing: The
    development of self, voice, and mind. New York: Basic
    Books.

A COLLECTION OF ESSAYS

Christ, C. P. & Plaskow, J. (Eds.). (1979). Womanspirit
    rising: A feminist reader in religion. New York:
    Harper & Row.

A WORK IN A COLLECTION OF ESSAYS

Fiorenza, E. (1979). Women in the early Christian move-
    ment. In C. P. Christ and J. Plaskow (Eds.).
    Womanspirit rising: A feminist reader in religion
    (pp. 84-92). New York: Harper & Row, 1979.

GOVERNMENT DOCUMENTS

If the writer is not known, treat the government and the agency as the
author. Most federal documents are issued by the Government Printing
Office in Washington, D.C.

United States Congress. Office of Technology Assessment.
    (1984). Computerized manufacturing automation:
    Employment, education, and the workplace. Washington,
    D.C.: U.S. Government Printing Office.

AN ARTICLE IN A JOURNAL WITH CONTINUOUS PAGINATION

Tversky, A., & Kahneman, D. (1981). The framing of deci-
    sions and the psychology of choice. Science, 211,
    453-458.

AN ARTICLE IN A JOURNAL THAT PAGINATES
EACH ISSUE SEPARATELY

Foot, R. J. (1988-89). Nuclear coercion and the ending
    of the Korean conflict. International Security,
    13(4), 92-112.

The reference informs us that the article appeared in issue number 4 of
volume 13.

An Article from a Monthly or Weekly Magazine

Maran, S. P. (1988, April). In our backyard, a star ex-
    plodes. Smithsonian, pp. 46-57.
Greenwald, J. (1989, February 27). Gimme shelter. Time,
    pp. 50-51.

An Article in a Newspaper

Connell, R. (1989, February 6). Career concerns at
    heart of 1980s' campus protests. Los Angeles Times,
    pp. 1, 3.

(*Note:* If no author is given, simply begin with the date, in parentheses.)

A Book Review

Daniels, Norman. (1984). Understanding physician power
    [Review of Paul Starr, The social transformation of
    American medicine]. Philosophy and Public Affairs, 13,
    347-56.

Daniels is the reviewer, not the author of the book. The book under review is called *The Social Transformation of American Medicine,* but the review, published in volume 13 of *Philosophy and Public Affairs,* had its own title, "Understanding Physician Power."

If the review does not have a title, after the date (in parentheses) of the review type a period, two spaces, and then a square bracket, and proceed as in the example just given.

For a full account of the APA method of dealing with all sorts of unusual citations, see the third edition (1983) of the APA manual, *Publication Manual of the American Psychological Association.*

A FINAL CHECKLIST FOR PAPERS USING SOURCES

Early in this book, on page 81, is a checklist with ten points to think about when revising an argumentative essay. Here it is again, with four additional points especially relevant to papers that draw upon sources.

1. Topic sufficiently narrowed?
2. Thesis (to be advanced or refuted) stated early and clearly, perhaps even in title?
3. Audience kept in mind? Opposing views stated fairly and as sympathetically as possible? Controversial terms defined?

4. Assumptions likely to be shared by readers? If not, are they argued rather than merely asserted?
5. Focus clear (for example, evaluation, or recommendation of policy)?
6. Evidence (examples, testimony, statistics) adequate and sound?
7. Inferences valid?
8. Organization clear? (Effective opening, coherent sequence of arguments, unpretentious ending?)
9. All worthy opposition faced?
10. Tone appropriate?
11. All borrowed words and ideas credited?
12. Quotations and summaries not excessively long? Quotations accurate? Quotations provided with helpful lead-ins?
13. Documentation in proper form?
14. All irrelevancies deleted?

A SHORT DOCUMENTED STUDENT PAPER

Although the following argument is not a full-scale research paper, it does make good use of sources. Early in the semester the students were asked to choose one topic from a list of ten, and to write a documented argument of 750 to 1250 words (three to five pages of double-spaced typing). The completed paper was due two weeks after the topics were distributed. The assignment, a prelude to working on a research paper of 2,500 to 3,000 words, was in part designed to give students practice in finding and in using sources.

The topic selected by this student was, as given in the list, "Write an argument about the American Medical Association's recent decision to lobby for legislation banning cigarette advertisements."

Citations are given in the MLA form. For an example of an essay using the APA form, see Nan Desuka, "Why Handguns Must Be Outlawed" (p. 196).

Santiago 1

Josephine Santiago
Professor Hume
Eng 002
Feb. 11, 1989

                Support for the A.M.A. Anti-Smoking Campaign
     The American Medical Association's announcement, in Decem-
ber 1985, that it will lobby Congress to pass legislation preventing cigarette manufacturers from advertising in newspapers
and magazines--and, for that matter, on billboards and in the
sky--has met a mixed reaction. Some people hail it, spokesper-
sons for the tobacco and the advertising industries oppose it,
and some impartial people fear it may be a step toward censorship. I am convinced, however, that it cannot reasonably be
thought of as censorship of ideas, and I therefore want to argue
that the proposed legislation is not only necessary but is also
an acceptable limitation on freedom of expression.
     Let's begin with three assumptions. First, let's assume
smoking is indeed harmful. Few people doubt the Surgeon General's report of 1982, titled The Health Consequences of Smoking.
In the report Dr. C. Everett Koop stated that "Cigarette smoking
. . . is the chief, single, avoidable cause of death in our society and the most important public health issue of our time"
(xi). More recently Surgeon General Koop has said that there
are 350,000 deaths annually in the United States, from lung cancer, heart disease, and chronic lung disease (Molotsky 20).
These facts must be accepted. Second, let's assume that smoking
is so widespread and (for some people) so addictive that prohibition is not a real possibility. Third, let's assume that
government has the right, perhaps even the duty, to interfere
with liberty if the public interest is seriously threatened.
The last assumption needs amplification.
     We are so used to thinking that we are a free society that
we may forget that the government puts many limitations on us.
James Fallows gives some obvious examples:
               If you're a motorcyclist, you can't ride without a
          helmet; if you're a kid, you can't buy dirty books; if

>you're overweight, you can't use cyclamates; if you're
>depressed, there are fences to keep you from jumping
>off the Golden Gate bridge, and police to arrest you
>if you survive. (22)

Of course the government prohibits us from engaging in criminal
activities, but as Fallows points out, it also prevents us from
engaging in certain activities that are harmful to ourselves.

Limitations of the sort just mentioned are acceptable because they are in the interest of society. We recognize, for
example, that drivers should be licensed. If inexperienced or
drunk drivers are on the road, none of us is safe. But of
course prohibiting advertising is different from prohibiting
drunks from driving; it sounds like an abridgment of the First
Amendment's guarantee of freedom of speech. I admit that prohibiting cigarette companies is, in the broadest view of the
term, an abridgment of freedom of speech, but I think it is an
abridgment that the public interest requires. Second, I think
it is not comparable to the abridgment of freedom to express
ideas. Let's look at some facts.

According to Richard Lacayo (56), the tobacco industry
spends each year about $872,000,000 on advertising. It spends
this money because advertising sells cigarettes; the most heavily advertised brands (for instance Marlboro) are the brands
that sell most. A study by Joseph Califano, when he was Secretary of Health, Education, and Welfare, found that four million
children and teenagers were regular smokers (195), and Marlboro
was the most popular cigarette with this group.

The cigarette companies regularly claim that advertisements
do not recruit new smokers but are designed to induce smokers to
shift from one brand to another (Lacayo 50). The companies
point out that they do not use sports stars or entertainment
stars, and they do not use any models under age twenty-five.
But children and teenagers are not attracted only by sports and
entertainment figures, or by people under twenty-five. The fact
that so many young people smoke Marlboro cigarettes suggests
that the Marlboro ads are convincing to them. These ads, with

Santiago 3

the famous Marlboro man, and with their suggestions of independence and open spaces, probably appeal to the fantasies
of youngsters who, it can be safely said, feel that they are not
granted enough independence.

Peter Taylor provides some evidence to demonstrate that advertising does induce young people to smoke (304-05). In 1977
Sweden restricted ads in newspapers and magazines, allowing only
a cigarette pack--with no background--to be shown. No youthful
lovers, no refreshing streams, no sandy beaches, nothing seductive. At the time of the new law, 9 percent of the thirteen-
year-old boys smoked, and 11 percent of the thirteen-year-old
girls smoked. Two years later, only 5 percent of the thirteen-
year-old boys smoked, and only 6 percent of the girls. That is
a reduction of almost half. The statistics for older children
are not so impressive, but they are encouraging nevertheless.
In 1977, 25 percent of the boys of sixteen smoked, and 40 percent of the girls of sixteen smoked. In 1979, the 25 percent
had dropped to 21 percent, and the 40 percent had dropped to 33
percent. The point, then, is to keep young people from starting, and that is why advertising should be prohibited. Of
course, some young people, imitating their elders, will take up
smoking even without advertising. But the results in Sweden,
and the Califano study, strongly suggest that advertisements induce young people to smoke. Moreover, people who start young
are the most likely prospects for serious medical problems.
Fallows points out that "smokers are 5 times as likely to develop cancer if they begin at 15 than at 25" (24).

Now for the second problem, that the A.M.A.'s proposal may
introduce other forms of censorship. Three convincing replies
can be made. First, the public interest sometimes requires
limits on freedom, and surely a thousand deaths a day due to
cigarettes is a serious threat to the public interest. Second,
although those who oppose the prohibition of advertisements for
cigarettes say that such legislation would lead to bans on advertisements for alcohol, junk food, sports cars, or whatever
product some self-appointed group finds dangerous, one can say,

yes, if these things do indeed cause the massive destruction
that tobacco does, they too should not be advertised. But so
far, of course, no serious studies suggest that these products
come anywhere near equaling tobacco as a killer. Consequently,
so long as these products are not proved to be massive dangers
to the public interest, there is no reason for legislation banning them.

A third argument against prohibiting ads for tobacco is
that this limitation on freedom of speech may lead to limitations on open political discussion. But surely it is clear that
there is a distinction between advertising consumer goods and
(so to speak) advertising ideas. That is, no one can reasonably
put into the same category an ad for cigarettes and an ad for a
political or social issue, or a picture of the Marlboro man and
a picture of a political candidate. In fact, the Supreme Court
has long recognized that advertising is not protected to the
same degree that political debate and artistic expression are.
Lacayo cites the Supreme Court's 1971 decision upholding the ban
on cigarette ads on television (56).

The issue comes down to this: Do we agree that 350,000
deaths a year from cigarette-related illnesses are intolerable,
and that we must make a vigorous effort to reduce the number of
people who take up smoking? We know that ads do in fact persuade many people to smoke. We know also that the Supreme Court
distinguishes between advertising and the exchange of ideas, and
that the Court recognizes limits on advertising. To claim that
banishing the advertising of cigarettes is a step toward banishing freedom of political or artistic expression is, then, to
fill the air with smoke.

Santiago 5

Works Cited

Califano, Joseph A., Jr. Governing America: An Insider's Report
    from the White House and the Cabinet. New York: Simon,
    1981.

Fallows, James. "Ashtray Libertarians." New Republic 21 Oct.
    1978: 22-25.

Koop, C. Everett. The Health Consequences of Smoking: The
    Changing Cigarette. Washington: Department of Health and
    Human Services, 1981.

Lacayo, Richard. "Setting Off the Smoke Alarm." Time 23 Dec.
    1985: 56.

Molotsky, Irvin. "U.S. Cites Broad Smoking Health Risks." New
    York Times 22 Dec. 1985, natl. ed.: A20.

Taylor, Peter. The Smoke Ring: Tobacco, Money and Politics.
    Rev. ed. New York: NAL, 1985.

There may be some soft spots in this essay on the A.M.A. proposal. For instance, the decline in the percentage of Swedish youngsters who smoke may be due to factors other than the limits on advertising, such as an educational campaign, or an increase in the price of tobacco. On the whole, though, the essay seems strong, especially as a study preliminary to a longer paper.

In rereading the essay, notice these strengths:

1. The title, though not especially attractive, is focused. It gives the reader an idea of what is to come.
2. The opening paragraph provides necessary background and (at the end) announces the thesis.
3. Quotations are adequately introduced, and they are fairly brief. For the most part the writer summarizes rather than quotes her sources at length.
4. The writer guides her readers by announcing (in the paragraph beginning "Limitations") that she will treat two topics, and she then goes on to treat these two topics in the announced order.
5. The final paragraph is a brief summary, but without the stiffness of "Thus we have seen," and the final sentence has an engaging bit of wordplay in it, ending the essay on a forceful but genial note.

Part Two

MODELS OF ARGUMENT: CURRENT ISSUES

5

Pro and Con: Short Debates

SHOULD WE ADOPT A SIX-YEAR PRESIDENCY?

Griffin B. Bell, Herbert Brownell, William E. Simon, and Cyrus R. Vance

For a One-Term, Six-Year Presidency

Once again, thanks to President Reagan's observations about the 22nd Amendment, the nation is turning its attention to the presidential term. How long can—or should—a chief executive run the country? Does reelection enhance or diminish a president's ability to govern effectively?

Mr. Reagan has advocated repeal of the 22nd Amendment so that presidents may again run for an unlimited number of four-year terms. We

---

The four writers of this essay have all held high public office. Bell (b. 1918) was Attorney General from 1977 to 1979; Brownell (b. 1904), Attorney General, 1953 to 1957; Simon (b. 1927), Secretary of the Treasury, 1974 to 1977; Vance (b. 1917), Secretary of State, 1977 to 1980. They serve as national cochairmen of the Committee for a Single Six-Year Presidential Term. Their essay (like the response by Arthur Schlesinger, Jr., printed afterward) originally appeared in the New York Times *in 1985.*

agree that it is time to repeal the 22nd Amendment: However, we believe a new amendment should replace it. It is our belief—a belief shared by many Americans—that the national interest would be better served by a constitutional amendment providing for a single six-year term.

The idea of a single term is older than the Republic. The length and number of presidential terms was debated at the Constitutional Convention, and the decision was left to the discretion of George Washington. Once in office, he ran for a second term—but reluctantly—because he believed that service in official capacities should be limited. Sixteen presidents since Washington, beginning with Andrew Jackson and continuing through Jimmy Carter, have endorsed a single six-year term as a preferable alternative to multiple terms. The six-year term proposal was a part of the Democratic platform in 1913 and passed the Senate that year.

The single six-year term has received renewed attention in recent years 4 because of widespread bipartisan concern that, under the two-term system, reelection pressures lie at the heart of our inability to manage complex, long-term national problems, domestic and foreign. Opponents of the idea declare that the potential hazards facing "lame duck" presidents under a single term outweigh the damage now caused by delays in decision-making during a reelection campaign. Historical evidence contradicts that view.

According to Kenneth P. O'Donnell, President John F. Kennedy's appointments secretary, in early 1963 Mr. Kennedy told Senator Mike Mansfield that although he knew there was no future for us in Vietnam, he could not expect to be reelected, given the mood of the country, if he withdrew American forces before the election.

Richard M. Nixon acknowledged in his book *The Real War* that he exaggerated the potential of détente in 1972 because he wanted "political credit" in the coming election. The break-in at the Watergate Hotel and subsequent upheaval were directly attributable to the Nixon administration's obsession with reelection.

Gerald R. Ford did not press to a conclusion the strategic arms agreements reached at the Vladivostok summit meeting when those agreements were opposed by his challenger in the presidential primaries, Ronald Reagan.

In 1980, the Middle East autonomy negotiations were not pushed by 8 President Jimmy Carter as vigorously as they might have been in a nonelection year.

In the 1984 election, if President Reagan did not have to face the federal deficit as a campaign issue, he would likely have acknowledged its importance earlier and begun addressing it as early as 1982 and 1983, rather than now.

These examples indicate that important policy decisions are often deferred because of the enormous pressures a reelection campaign places on presidents. The result is that long-term foreign and domestic policies often lack steadiness, continuity, and predictability.

Regardless of party affiliation or popularity, all presidents have delayed some of the hardest and most important decisions until a second term. Lyndon B. Johnson summed it up when he said, after leaving office: "If a fellow knew from the beginning that he had a definite limitation and the bell is going to ring at a certain time, he might be able to tackle some of the problems he's inclined to postpone."

What of being a "lame duck" president? That factor is largely a myth. 12 If it now appears more difficult for presidents to get the job done at the beginning of the second term, it is because there is a strong temptation built into the two-term system to defer the hard, unpopular decisions until the second term.

Dwight D. Eisenhower, as the only president to have served two full terms under the 22nd Amendment, provides a test case of the "lame duck" theory. Despite Democratic control of Congress in both terms, he won passage of more constructive legislation in his second term than in his first. The time spent on reelection activity was minimized, permitting the president to function more effectively as a political leader. In 1959, he declared he would veto major spending bills and, if overridden, would increase taxes. That decision would have been very unpopular in a first-term election period, but it helped contribute to low inflation and unemployment in his second term.

Ronald Reagan now has the opportunity to dispel the "lame duck" notion that clouds perceptions of his second term. We're already talking about who will be the next president. Yet the responsibility for managing this nation is in the hands of today's, not tomorrow's, chief executive. That responsibility begins the moment a president takes office and remains until the moment his term ends.

President Eisenhower entered his second term opposing the 22nd Amendment for the same reason as President Reagan. He left office a vigorous proponent of a single six-year term because of his strong belief that he was able to function more effectively once the pressures of reelection were removed. Perhaps experience will also lead Mr. Reagan to this view.

As the nation approaches 1987, the 200th anniversary of the drafting 16 of the Constitution, it is appropriate to respond to Thomas Jefferson's plea that each generation reexamine it in light of contemporary needs. Dr. Milton Eisenhower, founder of the current national movement for the single six-year presidential term, spoke for many Americans when he wrote that he favored a single six-year term so that a president would "have no incentive to propose and fight for measures conceived mainly to enhance his chances for reelection or merely to confound the opposition."

Rather than relegate Mr. Reagan prematurely to a "lame duck" status, we would more profitably spend our time determining how we can enable a modern president to manage government more effectively during his whole term. The single six-year term is the right place to start, and congressional hearings are the first essential step to put the issue squarely before the American people.

Questions and Suggestions for Writing

1. Think about the effect, in the first paragraph, of putting "or should" within dashes, and of putting "should" after (rather than before) "can." Write a paragraph in which you analyze the differences between the original version and these two variations:

   a. "How long can, or should, a chief executive run the country?"
   b. "How long should—or can—a chief executive run the country?"

2. What is the function of the third paragraph? Is it meant to offer evidence on behalf of a single term, or is it merely to show that the idea is far from new? Evaluate the paragraph under each interpretation of its purpose.

3. Positions attributed to Presidents Kennedy, Nixon, Ford, Carter, and Reagan are offered as evidence. How weighty do you find their testimony? Why?

4. Evaluate the authors' reply to the "lame-duck" objection.

5. Complete this sentence: "The heart of the authors' argument is that one six-year presidential term is preferable to the present system because. . . ."

Arthur Schlesinger, Jr.

Against a One-Term, Six-Year Presidency

The proposal of a single six-year presidential term has been around for a long time. High-minded men have urged it from the beginning of the Republic. The Constitutional Convention turned it down in 1787, and recurrent efforts to put it in the Constitution have regularly failed in the

---

A professor at the City University of New York and a writer of books on American history, Arthur Schlesinger (b. 1917) is also an active member of the Democratic party. In 1961 President Kennedy appointed him special assistant for Latin American affairs. His book on Kennedy's White House years, A Thousand Days *(1965), won the Pulitzer Prize for biography.*

The essay reprinted here is from the New York Times, *written in response to the preceding essay by Griffin Bell et al.*

two centuries since. Quite right: It is a terrible idea for a number of reasons, among them that it is at war with the philosophy of democracy.

The basic argument for the one-term, six-year presidency is that the quest for reelection is at the heart of our problems with self-government. The desire for reelection, it is claimed, drives presidents to do things they would not otherwise do. It leads them to make easy promises and to postpone hard decisions. A single six-year term would liberate presidents from the pressures and temptations of politics. Instead of worrying about reelection, they would be free to do only what was best for the country.

The argument is superficially attractive. But when you think about it, it is profoundly antidemocratic in its implications. It assumes presidents know better than anyone else what is best for the country and that the people are so wrongheaded and ignorant that presidents should be encouraged to disregard their wishes. It assumes that the less responsive a president is to popular desires and needs, the better president he will be. It assumes that the democratic process is the obstacle to wise decisions.

The theory of American democracy is quite the opposite. It is that the give-and-take of the democratic process is the best source of wise decisions. It is that the president's duty is not to ignore and override popular concerns but to acknowledge and heed them. It is that the president's accountability to the popular will is the best guarantee that he will do a good job.   4

The one-term limitation, as Gouverneur Morris, final draftsman of the Constitution, persuaded the convention, would "destroy the great motive to good behavior," which is the hope of reelection. A president, said Oliver Ellsworth, another founding father, "should be reelected if his conduct prove worthy of it. And he will be more likely to render himself worthy of it if he be rewardable with it."

Few things have a more tonic effect on a president's sensitivity to public needs and hopes than the desire for reelection. "A president immunized from political considerations," Clark Clifford told the Senate Judiciary Committee when it was considering the proposal some years ago, "is a president who need not listen to the people, respond to majority sentiment, or pay attention to views that may be diverse, intense, and perhaps at variance with his own. . . . Concern for one's own political future can be a powerful stimulus to responsible and responsive performance in office."

We all saw the tempering effect of the desire for reelection on Ronald Reagan in 1984. He dropped his earlier talk about the "evil empire," announced a concealed passion for arms control, slowed down the movement toward intervention in Central America, affirmed his loyalty to social security and the "safety net," and in other ways moderated his hard ideological positions. A single six-year term would have given Reaganite ideology full, uninhibited sway.

The ban on reelection has other perverse consequences. Forbidding a president to run again, Gouverneur Morris said, is "as much as to say that   8 we should give him the benefit of experience, and then deprive ourselves of the use of it." George Washington stoutly opposed the idea. "I can see no propriety," he wrote, "in precluding ourselves from the service of any man, who on some great emergency shall be deemed universally most capable of serving the public."

Jefferson, after initially favoring a single seven-year term, thought more carefully and changed his mind. Seven years, he concluded, were "too long to be irremovable"; "service for eight years with a power to remove at the end of the first four" was the way to do it. Woodrow Wilson agreed, observing that a six-year term is too long for a poor president and too short for a good one and that the decision belongs to the people. "By seeking to determine by fixed constitutional provision what the people are perfectly competent to determine by themselves," Wilson said in 1913, "we cast a doubt upon the whole theory of popular government."

A single six-year term would release presidents from the test of submitting their records to the voters. It would enshrine the "president-knows-best" myth, which has already got us into sufficient trouble as a nation. It would be a mighty blow against presidential accountability. It would be a mighty reinforcement of the imperial presidency. It would be an impeachment of the democratic process itself. The founding fathers were everlastingly right when they turned down this well-intentioned but ill-considered proposal 200 years ago.

Questions and Suggestions for Writing

1. Schlesinger opposes the idea of one six-year term; why does he begin by seeming to suggest its merits?

2. Taking into account the preceding essay by Bell, Brownell, Simon, and Vance, do you think that Schlesinger fairly summarizes his opposition in his second paragraph?

3. In his final paragraph Schlesinger begins four consecutive sentences with "It would." Why? Why does he *not* use this formula in his final sentence?

4. If Schlesinger's arguments against a single six-year presidential term are so good, why doesn't he extend them to favor repeal of the 22nd Amendment, which limits the president to two terms?

5. Schlesinger repeatedly cites the views of distinguished American statesmen and political observers in favor of his position. Is this an illegitimate appeal to authority? How can you tell?

6. Review both essays on the single six-year presidential term and specify the issues of factual controversy that, in your mind, are still unsettled. Do the merits of the case for or against the proposed six-year term turn on these facts, or on something else? Explain in an essay of 500 words.

WOULD HIGHER EDUCATION BE BETTER OR WORSE WITHOUT TENURED PROFESSORS?

R. Keith Miller

Tenure: A Cause of Intellectual Cowardice

Society likes to harbor the illusion that teachers are some special breed—noble, self-sacrificing souls who are dedicated to their jobs and who find within those jobs a spiritual satisfaction that is its own reward. The truth of the matter is that teachers are people, too, and there are precious few who would continue to teach—simply for the joy of it—if they were financially independent.

Having a healthy respect for the value of leisure, I'd be the last to blame anyone for that. But when we begin to look at academics more realistically, we must recognize that one of the principal features of our educational establishment, the tenure system, leaves much to be desired. Tenure amounts to virtually unlimited job security, and I can think of no reason why teachers should have special protection regardless of productivity.

The standard defense for tenure is that it works as a safeguard for academic freedom. According to such reasoning, teachers are custodians of the truth, and as such, they must be allowed to teach unpopular ideas. Regardless of the uninspired performance of most academics in the early 1950s—when ideas were challenged more militantly than at any other time in our century—we are encouraged to believe that, thanks to tenure, several divisions of elderly professors will be able to man the barricades of intellectual truth when the Philistines next attack.

But that isn't the way it works at all. The great irony of tenure is that the system which was purportedly designed to insure academic freedom actually works against it. It has created within our colleges and universities a rigid and carefully defined class structure. There are the tenured and the untenured—the powerful and the secure who can do pretty much as they choose, and the young supplicants who, regardless of abilities, find themselves circumscribed at almost every turn. Rather than safeguarding academic freedom, the tenure system is one of the chief causes of intellectual cowardice in our schools.

R. Keith Miller (b. 1949), now a professor of English at the University of Wisconsin at Stevens Point, wrote this article when he was an assistant professor at that institution. This essay and the following essay by Margaret Edwards were published in 1979 in the Chronicle of Higher Education.

For up to seven long years, the promise of "getting tenure" is held over instructors' heads until they are encouraged to believe that it is the whole point of their careers. During that time, they are painfully aware that their success is dependent upon the goodwill of their superiors. If they are to stand any hope of academic consecration, then they must be careful not to offend. In all too many cases, they learn that it can be foolish to decline an invitation and suicidal to vote their conscience. They must conform to the political and social norm or perish.

Under such a system, intelligence is seldom its own reward. Tenure is often given for reasons that have nothing to do with the instructor's ability in the classroom.

It would be much better to abolish tenure, and force all instructors to be subject to comparable demands. To do so would be to make our universities more democratic and, very possibly, more responsive to new ideas. And it would bring an end to the way in which schools are often forced to lose valued instructors after a few years, only because there are no tenured positions available.

It does not follow that academic life would become more ruthless than 8 ever, every instructor being caught in a perpetual struggle to maintain his position. Contracts could still be designed so that teachers would be guaranteed a very considerable—if no longer absolute—degree of job security. Following an initial probationary period of two years, instructors could be offered renewable three-year contracts, protecting them against arbitrary dismissal, and including the provision that at least one year's notice be given in the case of an appointment that was not being renewed.

Such a system would give less security than tenure, but it would still be generous by the standards of the marketplace. The corporate vice-president who, after thirty years of service, is asked to vacate his office by the end of the week, might well envy the professor who knows that he is assured at least a full year should he ever find it necessary to look for another job.

As it is now, tenure is little more than a trap. It traps the untenured into a world of anxious political machinations, and it traps the tenured into jobs they cannot afford to leave, no matter how unhappy they have become within them.

If we were to abolish tenure, we would gain in flexibility what we lose in security. And it is worth remembering that maximum security is found only in prisons.

Questions and Suggestions for Writing

1. In the first paragraph, which assertions are, in your opinion, facts, and which are conjectures or opinions? Does Miller distinguish, in this paragraph, between matters of fact and matters of opinion?

2. Miller attacks the tenure system in part because it awards job security without regard to a teacher's "productivity" (para. 2). How would you propose to define this term? How do you think a teacher's productivity should be measured, so that a department chairperson or dean, say, could give objective meaning to such judgments as "Smith is twice as productive a teacher as Brown"?

3. How would you characterize the tone of the third paragraph? Cite some phrases that you think give the paragraph its tone. Do you think the tone helps to persuade the reader? Why, or why not?

4. Paragraphs 8 and 9 suggest that professors be offered three-year renewable contracts. Miller does not, however, indicate who will decide whether a contract is to be renewed, and on what basis. Assume that tenure does not exist in your institution, and that an instructor who has already served through six three-year contracts is up for renewal. Who should make the decision? Colleagues (junior and senior) in the department? Administrators? Students? Some combination? Be as precise as possible, and then weigh this system against a system of tenure.

5. Miller claims that "tenure is often given for reasons that have nothing to do with the instructor's ability in the classroom" (para. 6). What evidence does he give to support this judgment? Arrange to interview six faculty members of your college, three tenured and three nontenured, and write a 500-word essay evaluating Miller's claim in the light of your findings.

Margaret Edwards

Tenure: A Fitting Reward for a Long Apprenticeship

A case against tenure for professors sometimes rests on the premise that competent young teachers deserve the spaces occupied by the incompetent tenured professors. Under the present system, the argument goes, well-qualified graduates are being excluded while "deadwood" remains.

That is true enough, yet if the case were no more complicated than that, tenure would have been abolished some time ago. College administrators could decide to change policies and tenure could be suspended or eliminated, but what would take its place might not be nearly so flexible. Since the college teaching profession is no longer expanding, inevitably its "new blood" is being lost. This hemorrhage of personnel who might be

Margaret Edwards (b. 1945) is an associate professor of English at the University of Vermont. The following article is reprinted from the Chronicle of Higher Education, *1979.*

better, more creative, and more lively is a tragedy brought on by a shrinking market, not by tenure per se.

Often the college professor is compared to other professionals who don't have tenure and presumably don't need it, who keep refreshed and vigorous in a free-for-all of switching their jobs and proving their merits. But the academic world is not like the "real" world, as its critics often point out, and even its defenders agree. The job of a college or university professor is utterly dependent upon and defined by the institution. You can't be a professor without a college or a university in which to "profess."

No tenure exists for journalists, lawyers, doctors, or industrial re-   4
searchers, say the critics. However, the journalist can write as a freelancer, the industrial researcher can apply for patents, the lawyer and doctor need only their professional degrees and equipped offices to set themselves up in business. In contrast, the college professor cannot quit the university, go out and rent an auditorium, buy a blackboard and a box of chalk, then advertise as someone willing and able to bestow a B.S. or B.A. There is no such thing as freelance professoring.

To some who criticize tenure, corporate executives are the equivalent of professors of the business world and therefore seem to provide an analogy. Turnover is expected in their jobs. True; yet I can hardly equate my business friends, who make $35,000 and more, with my professor friends, who make salaries pitiful by comparison. If the executive faces a world of "up or out," surely what makes him face it is a salary commensurate with his anxiety.

When a college or university refuses to grant a professor tenure, it doesn't just shunt him from one job to another; it puts him out on the street. I used to sit through lectures delivered by a tenured professor so boring that visions of his starving in rags did not make me squeamish. Conversely, I have known excellent colleagues to lose tenure and be denied access to classrooms where their skills were deeply appreciated.

However, if tenure did not exist, would good professors flourish and bad ones wither away? Probably not. What would keep an institution from firing the majority of its staff the moment they became "too expensive"— say, reached a certain salary at age forty or so? Young blood is not only hot; it's also cheaper.

College professors are not like executives, journalists, etc., as much as   8
they are like other educators. It is not remarkable that elementary- and high-school teachers belong to unions. College professors, in a world without tenure, would join them. "Academic freedom" is no longer an issue. After all, a union could preserve "academic" as well as other freedoms and privileges. It is rare that a trade union dumps someone for radical views or for a deviance from traditional mores. Actually, tenure review is far more rigorous than what unions require for membership.

Unions recruit jobholders; they don't exclude them. When you pay your dues, you get your card. Getting tenure is much harder.

I think that our present system, in spite of its gross inequities, may be more responsive to student, professional, and institutional needs than the alternative. A union of professors would not bring more young teachers into the fold; it would merely dig much deeper what's already entrenched.

All professions harbor incompetents. Bad teachers happen to be exposed in their inadequacy more ruthlessly than bad doctors, bad lawyers, or bad car mechanics. "What you see is what you get" in the classroom. Yet the wrong diagnosis, the case misfiled in court, the shoddy work on an engine—aren't these mishaps more difficult to judge and more sinister in their results? Given the possibility of errors and dire consequences, it is astonishing how few doctors are suspended from practice, how few lawyers are disbarred, how few auto-repair shops are shut down. The academic profession is not more rife than others with shysters and dullards.

Positions in the academic world have been attractive to intelligent graduates not because such positions offer high salaries or plush facilities, but because they offer free time for the writing and research necessary in making a contribution to a specialized field, they offer the chance to belong to an intellectual community of students and colleagues interested in related subjects, and they offer the security of tenure.

Tenure is one of the few benefits that make a very long apprenticeship 12 seem worth the effort. Doctors of medicine, whose course of professional training is usually considered the most difficult, spend four years in medical school, one year in internship, three years in residency, a total of eight years, then begin to practice. However, most professors who have doctoral degrees have spent at least three years in graduate classes, at least one year in writing a dissertation, and a minimum of six years in an untenured faculty role, a total of *ten* years, before being granted what is, in effect, simply a license to practice. In this context, it does not seem to me that tenure is an outrageous privilege.

Questions and Suggestions for Writing

1. Study Edwards's argument in paragraphs 3–4. Is she trying to establish the proposition (a) that tenure *doesn't* exist for journalists and other professionals because they can set themselves up in business without fitting into any complex institution or (b) that tenure *shouldn't* exist for journalists and others because they can set themselves up? Or is she arguing for both (a) and (b)? Explain your interpretation.

2. Paragraphs 3–6 are largely devoted to arguing that college professors are not, in an essential respect, comparable to other professionals. (The article was written in 1979, so the figure given for the salary of a business executive, and the

unspecified but implied salary for a professor, must be modified, but the disparity between the two still exists.) Do you accept Edwards's argument in these paragraphs? If not, why not?

3. Reread Edwards's sixth paragraph, and explain its role in her overall argument.

4. Reread paragraphs 8 and 9, and explain why Edwards draws a parallel between trade unions and the tenure system for professors. In favoring the tenure system over a professors' union, is it important to her argument that she is right in claiming that "Getting tenure is much harder" than getting a union card?

5. Although Edwards prefers a tenure system to a professors' union, some colleges and universities have both, and only a few have neither. Write a 500-word essay arguing for or against a professors' union for your college's faculty.

Is Comparable Worth Fair and Workable?

Teresa Amott and Julie Matthaei

Comparable Worth, Incomparable Pay

The Emergence of the Comparable-Worth Strategy

When the Equal Pay Act of 1963 prohibited unequal pay for equal work and the broader Civil Rights Act of 1964 set affirmative action into motion, many assumed that the gap between men and women's wages would close. Instead, the average salary for a woman working full-time year-round remained roughly 60 percent of the salary earned by a man. The constancy of the wage gap in the face of antidiscrimination legislation drew attention to the fact that women and men rarely hold the same jobs. Traditional sex roles and outright sex discrimination by employers and

Teresa Amott (b. 1951) and Julie Matthaei (b. 1951) both teach economics at Wellesley College and work for the Economic Literacy Project of Women for Economic Justice, a Boston-based educational resource. Matthaei is the author of An Economic History of Women in America *(1982); Amott has written on militarism and poverty in* Socialist Review, The Women's Review of Books, *and* New Political Science. *The essay reprinted here originally appeared in 1984, in a journal titled* Radical America.

workers have had the result of excluding women from most occupations other than homemaking and its labor market extensions. Those paid occupations open to women shared low pay, few opportunities for advancement, and often centered around nurturing and serving others. Throughout the decade of the 1970s, over 40 percent of all women workers were concentrated in ten occupations, most of which were over 70 percent female—for example, nursing, secretarial and clerical work, teaching, and food service. In contrast, men, especially white men, had more job options and more opportunity for high pay and promotion. For instance, stock clerks, predominantly male, earn more than bank tellers, who are predominantly female, and registered nurses earn less than mail carriers. As a result of this occupational segregation, legislation prohibiting unequal pay for equal jobs failed to address the heart of pay inequity between the sexes: men and women earning unequal pay for different jobs.

The idea of comparable worth was devised to raise women's wages in female-dominated occupations up to the level paid in male occupations of "comparable worth." Also known as pay equity, comparable worth means that jobs deemed to be of "equal value to the employer" should pay the same, regardless of their sex or race-typing. The first wage comparability case before the courts was based on race.[1] However, subsequent attempts to apply the Civil Rights Act to nonidentical jobs have focused on wage differences origins from gender-based job segregation.

Some of the first attempts to broaden the concept of equal pay emerged during World War II, when unions such as the UAW and the IUE fought differential pay for men and women workers in order to prevent an overall reduction in pay scales and to generate greater unity between men and women workers.[2] Since then, the ranks of pay equity advocates have grown and a more feminist construction has been placed on the concept. Women's rights groups, working women's organizations, and unions representing women workers are currently pursuing three strategies for achieving comparable worth corrections to pay inequities based on sex or color: litigation, collective bargaining, and legislation. Often a combination of these strategies is utilized by pay equity advocates.

Litigation. Prior to a 1981 Supreme Court decision, the courts were uniformly unfriendly to charges of sex discrimination in pay across different jobs. In Denver, where nurses charged discrimination because the city paid them less than tree trimmers and sign painters, the judge ruled against the nurses, arguing that the doctrine of comparable worth was   4

---

[1] The case was Quarles v. Phillip Morris. For more information, see Judy Scales-Trent, "Comparable Worth: Is This a Theory for Black Workers?" unpublished paper, State University of New York at Buffalo Law School, 1984.

[2] Ruth Milkman, "The Reproduction of Job Segregation by Sex: A Study of the Sexual Division in the Auto and Electrical Manufacturing Industries in the 1960s." Ph.D. Dissertation, University of California at Berkeley, 1981.

"pregnant with the possibility of disrupting the entire economic system."[3] In 1981, however, the Supreme Court ruled that Title VII of the 1964 Civil Rights Act could be applied to prohibit wage differences in similar, but not identical, jobs.[4] Since then, there have been lower court decisions, such as one in the state of Washington, which have awarded back pay to women whose jobs have been systematically undervalued.

Collective Bargaining. A variety of unions, including AFSCME, CWA, IUE, SEIU, UAW, UE and others, have adopted pay equity as a goal in bargaining, as well as in membership education and lobbying. Most efforts have focused on public employees, largely because information on pay scales is more accessible, and state agencies may be more vulnerable to public pressure brought through community–labor alliances. Local 101 of AFSCME in San Jose, California, is one of the public sector success stories. These city employees struck to win a substantial pay increase and "special adjustments" to upgrade jobs held predominantly by women.[5] Unions often combine litigation with bargaining, as in the case of an IUE local which won pay equity raises for women workers employed at a Massachusetts General Electric plant.

Legislation. Many states have adopted legislation calling for a pay equity study of state employment, and others, including California, Minnesota, and Washington, have passed statutes which require public sector wages to be set on the basis of comparable worth.[6] In Idaho, a law which assigns pay in state positions on the basis of skill and responsibility has produced a 16 percent increase in pay for female clerical workers. Other states have begun to raise wages in predominantly women's jobs without explicit recourse to comparable worth. In New Mexico, for instance, over $3 million was appropriated in 1983 to raise the wages of the lowest paid state employees, over 80 percent of them women, even though a job evaluation study has not yet been completed.

[3] League of Women Voters Education Fund, "Women and Work: Pay Equity," Publication No. 110, 1982.

[4] Ibid. The decision was County of Washington, Oregon v. Gunther, and involved female jail matrons who were paid 70 percent of the salary for male guards.

[5] Ibid.

[6] A good source of information on state and local government pay equity initiatives is "Who's Working for Working Women," published by the Comparable Worth Project, the National Committee on Pay Equity and the National Women's Political Caucus in 1984. The pamphlet contains an excellent bibliography and a list of resource groups in each state. To order, write the National Committee on Pay Equity, 1201 16th Street, N.W., Suite 422, Washington, D.C., 20036.

IMPLEMENTING COMPARABLE WORTH

The primary mechanism for implementing comparable worth in wage structures is the job-analysis/job-evaluation study, and efforts for pay equity usually involve ridding an existing study of inherent sex bias and/or demanding a formal job evaluation study where one does not exist.

Job evaluation studies were in use long before pay equity advocates recognized their potential in comparable worth struggles. Generally speaking, most large, bureaucratic firms and state agencies do not negotiate a wage directly with each employee, but rather assign an employee to a particular rung of a job ladder. The worker's position on the job ladder determines his or her wages. Workers in the same job would thus receive the same salary, while workers in different jobs would be paid differently. To determine pay scales, large firms use fairly systematic job analysis/ evaluation schemes, often prepared by outside consultants. The first step of the study analyzes jobs through examination of job descriptions and, sometimes, discussions with workers. In the most common type of evaluation, known as a point-factor system, points are assigned to each job on the basis of criteria (factors) such as skills, effort, responsibility, and working conditions. In the final stage of the process, dollar values are assigned to the points in each category. The same procedures, and often the same consultants, are used for job evaluations in pay equity cases. In smaller firms, the process is much more informal, but rankings of jobs are still undertaken.

Despite the aura of objectivity surrounding these studies, there is no objective way to determine the relative productivity of jobs. Due to the division of labor, a myriad of different workers contribute to the output of any product, and it is impossible to distinguish their different contributions. How can one technically measure the relative importance of dieticians, nurses, or pharmacological staff to a hospital? Normally, hospital administrators pay market wages—the amount needed to attract workers—and infer the relative worth of these different workers from their wage rates. Job evaluation studies, on the other hand, attempt to determine relative productivity of jobs apart from the market. To do this, they must subjectively choose a set of factors and weights. There are many ways in which sex, race, and class bias can enter into the calculations.

One critical area is the selection and definition of factors to be evaluated. For example, it is common to define responsibility as supervisory responsibility over other workers, machines, or money. In this case, child care workers would receive low points for "responsibility" even though their jobs entail enormous responsibility for children under their care. Similarly, skilled activities such as nurturing and guidance are rarely counted, causing traditional women's jobs to receive lower points than men's jobs. Boredom from routinized work is not commonly considered worthy of points as an adverse working condition, although outdoor work and heavy lifting are.

Another critical area is the weighting of different factors, accomplished either through the number of points allocated to each factor or by the method which assigns dollars to points. This has the effect of determining the relative worth of different factors, and generally involves sophisticated statistical techniques such as multiple regression analysis. In effect, consulting firms specializing in job evaluations rely on previous correlations between existing pay scales and measured factor points to predict for new clients what a job's salary should be. From the perspective of the employer, the best point rankings are those which duplicate the existing pay hierarchy as closely as possible, since this seemingly "objective" technique can then be used to legitimize pay differentials. This means that job evaluation schemes usually embody existing pay practices, complete with sex, race, or gender bias. For example, the maximum number of points assigned for responsibility may be 2,000, while adverse working conditions are awarded only a maximum of 200 points; this would ensure that managerial jobs pay more than service or operative jobs.

Despite these biased methods, current methods of evaluating jobs can still be used to win pay raises for those in "undervalued" work. For example, most studies have found that male and female jobs with equal point evaluations are paid differently because of the weighing of different factors mentioned above or because firms use different ranking schemes for different types of jobs. In these cases, legislation or bargaining agreements mandating equal pay for jobs of equal point value (under the same ranking scheme) can achieve somewhere between 5 and 25 percent pay increases.[7]

Much more can be won by eliminating bias from the technique. This requires wide access to information about existing or contemplated job evaluation studies. We need to disseminate information on how consulting firms such as Hay Associates, which serves approximately 40 percent of the Fortune 500 companies,[8] conduct their studies, and we need to bargain for input at all stages of the evaluation process. The more we involve ourselves in the technique, taking power from the technocrats, the more success we will have. Progress has already been achieved in this area. Most unions have staff members who are experts on the technique and feminist proponents of comparable worth are currently at work expanding the definitions of factors so as to recognize the value of women's traditional work skills. (One of the most important redefinitions has been the inclusion of respon-

---

[7] For more information on the uses and limitations of job evaluation schemes, see Helen Remick, ed., *Comparable Worth and Wage Discrimination: Technical Possibilities and Political Realities*, Temple University Press, 1984, and Donald Treiman and Heidi Hartman, *Women Work and Wages: Equal Pay for Jobs of Equal Value;* National Academy of Sciences, 1981.

[8] Ronnie Steinberg, "A Want of Harmony: Perspectives on Wage Discrimination," in Remick, op. cit.

sibility for children as a compensable factor.) More work needs to be done to rid the method of race and class bias.

How Radical Is Comparable Worth?

While comparable worth directly challenges sexual inequality in the labor market, it may also have the potential for other radical change.

Comparable worth promises to undermine male supremacy outside the labor market as well. Feminists have long noted the way in which the lower wages of women have reinforced the traditional nuclear family and women's responsibility for unpaid work in the home.

As long as women are denied access to men's jobs, and few women's jobs pay a living wage, women are under strong economic pressure to marry. Married women's financial dependence upon their husbands contributes to sexual inequality within marriage. The economic costs of leaving or being left by one's husband are illustrated by the high percentage of women heading families on their own who live in poverty. The risk of poverty is highest for women of color; in 1982, 56.2 percent of black and 55.4 percent of Latino families headed by women were poor. 16

In addition, comparable worth subjects the pay structure to scrutiny it rarely receives. Conventional economic wisdom argues that in the "perfectly competitive market economy," workers are paid according to their "marginal product," that is, according to their contributions to the production process. (In graduate school, one of our teachers built models which assumed that women were 60 percent as productive as men, justifying this with the fact that full-time women workers earned on average, 60 percent as much as men!) Comparable worth debunks such convenient rationalizations of the pay structure, and the sexist assumptions they both reflect and create, by showing that the force behind pay differences has not been productivity differences but rather power and discrimination. Thus, it presents a radical critique of our system of income distribution through the "free market," and presents an alternative way of achieving what the market had promised: the distribution of income to workers according to their contributions in a manner which is fair and incentive-creating at the same time.

Finally, while comparable worth does not directly attack occupational segregation by sex, it may do so indirectly. On the one hand, by making traditionally feminine jobs palatable to women, comparable worth may reduce the incentives for women to seek entrance into male-dominated, more privileged jobs. On the other hand, as traditionally feminine jobs begin to offer wages comparable to those of masculine jobs, more men will find them attractive. Also, as women begin to fight for and expect working conditions comparable to those of men, they may find men's jobs more desirable, and be more willing to fight to get them.

Broadening the Comparable-Worth Agenda

Comparable worth gains effectiveness and constituency when combined with other progressive demands.

Conservative economists have warned that raising wages for women's work would create uncontrollable inflation. While firms will try to increase their prices (and state agencies, their tax revenues), the inflationary impact would depend upon the magnitude and speed of the pay equity adjustment, as well as the ability of firms and governments to pass on the costs. (This, in turn, depends upon the degree of monopoly power and citizen resistance to tax increases.) Finally, inflation is not the worst of all evils, and can be limited by the use of wage-price controls, long a demand of progressives.

What is more worrisome are the other possible reactions of firms and state agencies to an increase in the price of women's labor: automation, elimination of state programs, and runaway shops to countries in which women still provide a superexploitable labor force. Already, computerization is threatening clerical workers and job flight has created massive structural unemployment in the United States. In order for comparable worth struggles not to exacerbate these problems, they must be pursued in conjunction with demands for job security, retraining, and plant-closing legislation.

So as to aid all undervalued workers, pay equity must also be extended to include comparisons between comparable but racially segregated jobs. Even this extension will not solve all workers' problems. Workers without jobs will not benefit, nor will workers in those jobs calculated to have the least worth. Since these are the main job problems faced by men of color, comparable worth offers little to them. Raising pay for women in certain jobs reduces inequality between women and men on the same level of the job hierarchy, but increases the relative poverty of those at the bottom of the hierarchy. Their problems can only be solved by a more comprehensive restructuring of work and by a deeper and more radical discussion of the worth of work.

As currently practiced, the doctrine of comparable worth accepts the idea of a hierarchy of workers, more or less "worthy" on the basis of some objective criteria. However, as radicals become involved in decisions about what factors should merit higher pay, we may well begin to question the rationale for the hierarchy itself. If the discussion of what makes work worthy is extended to the grass roots, we may well determine that all jobs are equally worthy. We may decide that workers in unskilled, routinized jobs may be doing the hardest work of all, for such work saps and denies their very humanity. Why should those whose jobs give them the most opportunity to develop and use their abilities also be paid the most? The traditional argument—that higher pay must be offered as an incentive for workers to gain skills and training—is contradicted by the fact that our highly paid jobs attract many more workers than employers demand. And given unequal access to education and training, a hierarchical pay scheme becomes a mechanism for the intergenerational transmission of wealth privilege, with its historically linked racism, sexism, and classism.

We see comparable worth as one of the most innovative and promising 24 approaches to redressing sexual inequality. In fact, given the present reactionary climate, it is one of the few struggles in which tangible progress against injustice is being achieved. Furthermore, as we have pointed out, it raises larger questions about the fairness of the "free market" system, questions which may even undermine the rationale for income inequality.

Questions and Suggestions for Writing

1. In their second paragraph the authors define *comparable worth* and state that the term is a synonym for *pay equity*. What kind of information do the authors think is needed to establish that two jobs—say, being a stock clerk and driving a truck—are or are not of "equal value to the employer"?

2. In paragraph 3 the authors refer to "three strategies" currently being pursued to secure pay equity. Explain each of the strategies. Do the authors seem to prefer one to the others? Why, or why not?

3. What do the authors mean when they say, in paragraph 9, that "there is no objective way to determine the relative productivity of jobs"? If they are right, how is it possible to construct equitable pay scales among different jobs—or are such scales inherently "arbitrary," as Charles Krauthammer argues in the next essay?

4. What is the point-factor system (para. 11) of job evaluation? Construct a hypothetical point-factor system for a part-time or summer job you have held.

5. In paragraph 11, the authors call attention to the fact that "responsibility" can win 2,000 points, but "adverse working conditions" can win only 200 points. In the next paragraph this system of evaluation is called "biased." Do you agree that it is biased, and therefore unfair? Why?

6. In paragraphs 14–18, how do the authors answer their own question, "How radical is comparable worth?" What makes a program or policy radical, or more radical than the status quo?

7. The authors begin their essay with references to two acts, the Equal Pay Act of 1963, which prohibits unequal pay for equal work, and the Civil Rights Act of 1964, which authorized affirmative action. Yet paragraph 16 begins thus: "As long as women are denied access to men's jobs. . . ." With these two acts on the books, *are* women still denied "access to men's jobs"? If so, why? If not, does this condition undermine the authors' plea for comparable worth? (By the way, what exactly *is* "affirmative action," as required by law?)

8. In the first paragraph Amott and Matthaei call attention to the fact that full-time women workers earn, on the average, only about 60 percent as much as

full-time male workers earn. They attribute the discrepancy to sex discrimination. George Gilder, in *Wealth and Poverty*, explains the discrepancy by arguing that women are emotionally more attuned to taking care of their families and that therefore they put less effort into their jobs. Lester Thurow, in the *New York Times*, 8 March 1981, offers a third explanation. He argues that the decade between age twenty-five and age thirty-five is crucial (one can predict with considerable accuracy which men, now at age thirty-five, later will be economically successful), and that this period is "precisely the decade when women are most apt to leave the labor force or become part-time workers to have children." Of the three explanations for the discrepancy in pay, which seems to you to be the most accurate? Why?

9. The last section of the essay (paras. 19–24) is titled "Broadening the Comparable Worth Agenda." Reread the section, and then explain in a paragraph why the authors put this point in their last section rather than (say) in their first.

10. In this final section the authors suggest that "workers in unskilled, routinized jobs may be doing the hardest work of all." If you have ever worked at such a job (perhaps pumping gas, or serving hamburgers, or making change), write a 500-word essay describing your experience, including its effects on you, and evaluating the Amott–Matthaei thesis.

Charles Krauthammer

The Just Wage: From Bad to Worth

The latest entry on the list of sacred democratic causes is comparable worth. According to that doctrine, it is demonstrable that low-paying female-dominated jobs, like nursing, are worth as much (to employers or society) as "comparable" male-dominated jobs, like plumbing, and that therefore by right and by law they should be paid the same. Comparable worth has become not only *the* women's issue of the 1980s, but also the most prominent civil rights issue not specifically directed at blacks. The Democratic party has warmly embraced it. Every one of its presidential candidates has endorsed it. In the 1984 platform, that sea of well-intended

Charles Krauthammer (b. 1950) holds a medical degree and has served as Chief Resident in Psychiatry at Harvard Medical School. In 1978, after he went to Washington to assist in planning psychiatric research for the Carter administration, he began to contribute articles to The New Republic, *a liberal weekly. During the 1980 campaign he served as a speechwriter for the Democratic vice-presidential candidate, Walter Mondale, and then joined the staff of* The New Republic, *in which this essay originally appeared in 1984.*

ambiguity and evasion, there are few islands of certainty. Comparable worth is one of them.

Comparable worth is advancing in the courts, too. In 1981 the Supreme Court opened the door a crack by ruling that female prison guards could sue for violation of the equal-pay provisions of the 1964 Civil Rights Act, even though they did not do precisely the same work as the better paid male prison guards. That narrow ruling was broken open in December 1983 in a sweeping victory for comparable worth in Washington State. A federal district judge found the state guilty of massive discrimination because its female-dominated jobs were paying less than "comparable" male-dominated jobs. He ordered an immediate increase in the women's wages and restitution for past injury. The back pay alone will run into the hundreds of millions of dollars.

Comparable worth may indeed be an idea whose time has come. Where does it come from? When the plumber makes a house call and charges forty dollars an hour to fix a leak, the instinct of most people is to suspect that the plumber is overpaid—the beneficiary of some combination of scarce skills, powerful unions, and dumb luck. The instinct of comparable worth advocates is to see the plumber's wage as a standard of fairness, to conclude that the rest of us (meaning: women) are underpaid, and to identify discrimination as the source of that underpayment. But since overt discrimination on the basis of sex has been legally forbidden for twenty years, to make that charge stick nowadays requires a bit of subtlety.

One claim is that women's wages are depressed today because of a   4 legacy of past discrimination: namely, the "crowding" of women into certain fields (like nursing, teaching, secretarial work), thus artificially depressing their wages. Did sexual stereotyping really "crowd" women into their jobs? Sexual stereotyping worked both ways: it kept women in, but it also kept men out, thus artifically excluding potential wage competition from half the population, and, more important, from about two-thirds to three-quarters of the labor force (because of the higher participation rate of men). Sex segregation is obviously unfair, but it is hard to see how it caused downward pressure on women's wages when, at the same time, through the socially enforced exclusion of men, it sheltered "women's work" from a vast pool of competitors. Moreover, as the social barriers that kept men and women from entering each other's traditional fields have fallen during the last twenty years, there has been much more movement of women into men's fields than vice versa. "Women's work" is less crowded than ever.

If the crowding argument is weak, then one is forced to resort to the "grand conspiracy" theory. "The system of wages was set up by a grand conspiracy, so to speak, that has held down the wages of women to minimize labor costs," explained the business agent of the union that in 1981 struck for and won a famous comparable worth settlement in San Jose. But since to minimize labor costs employers try to hold down the wages of everyone, the thrust of the argument must be that there is a particular desire to do so additionally in the case of women. In other words, the market is inherently discriminatory. Women nurses are paid less than they deserve, simply because they are women. How to prove it? Comparing their wages to that of male nurses won't do, since their pay is, by law, equal. So one must compare nurses' wages to that of, say, plumbers, show that nurses make less, and claim that nurses are discriminated against because they deserve—they are worth—the same.

What is the basis of that claim? In San Jose, Washington State, and other comparable worth cases, the basis is a "study." A consultant is called in to set up a committee to rank every job according to certain criteria. In Washington State, the Willis scale gives marks for "knowledge and skills," "mental demands," "accountability," and "working conditions." The committee then awards points in each category to every job, tallies them up, and declares those with equal totals to have—*voilà!*—comparable worth.

There is no need to belabor the absurdity of this system, so I'll stick to the high points. It is, above all, a mandate for arbitrariness: every subjective determination, no matter how whimsically arrived at, is first enshrined in a number to give it an entirely specious solidity, then added to another number no less insubstantial, to yield a total entirely meaningless. (An exercise: Compare, with numbers, the "mental demands" on a truck driver and a secretary.) Everything is arbitrary: the categories, the rankings, even the choice of judges. And even if none of this were true, even if every category were ontologically self-evident, every ranking mathematically precise, every judge Solomonic, there remains one factor wholly unaccounted for which permits the system to be skewed in any direction one wishes: the *weight* assigned to each category. In the Willis scale, points for "knowledge and skills" are worth as much as points for "working conditions." But does ten points in knowledge and skills make up for ten points in hazardous working conditions? Who is to say that a secretary's two years of college are equal in worth to—and not half or double the worth of—the trucker's risk of getting killed on the highways? Mr. Willis, that's who.

Conclusions based on such "studies" are not a whit less capricious than 8 the simple assertion, "Secretaries are worth as much as truck drivers." Trotting out Willis, of course, allows you to dress up a feeling in scientific trappings. It allows H.R. 4599, Representative Mary Rose Oakar's bill legislating comparable worth in federal employment, to dispose of the arbitrariness problem in the *definitions*. "Job evaluation technique" is defined as "an objective method of determining the comparable value of different jobs." Next problem.

Some advocates of comparable worth, aware of this objectivity conundrum and perhaps less confident that it can be defined out of existence, propose an alternate solution. Instead of ranking the intrinsic worth of the job (by admittedly arbitrary criteria), they propose ranking the worth of the worker. Barbara Bergmann, an economist at the University of Maryland, believes that people with similar qualifications, training, and experience should be receiving the same return on their "human capital." Breaking new ground in discrimination theory, she claims that "in a nondiscriminatory setup, identical people should be paid identically." And what makes people identical? Their credentials: qualifications, training, experience. This is not just credentialism gone wild, and highly disadvantageous to non-yuppy workers with poor résumés, who need the help of the women's movement the most; it leads to the logical absurdity that people should be paid not for the actual work they do, but for the work they *could* do. We've gone from equal pay for equal work to equal pay for comparable work, to equal pay for potential work. Summarizing the Bergmann position, the Center for Philosophy in Public Policy at the University of Maryland explains helpfully that "if a nursing supervisor could do the work of a higher paid hospital purchasing agent, then her wages should be the same as his." But why stop there? What if her credentials arc the same as those of the hospital administrator, or her city councillor, or her U.S. senator? And what about the starving actress, waiting on tables for a living? If she can act as well as Bo Derek (to set a standard anyone can meet), shouldn't she be getting a million dollars a year—that is, if the "setup" is to deserve the adjective "nondiscriminatory"?

Now, even if there were a shred of merit in any of these systems for determining comparable worth, we should be wary of implementing them if only because of the sheer social chaos they would create. The only sure consequence of comparable worth one can foresee was described by the winning attorney in the Washington State case: "This decision . . . should stimulate an avalanche of private litigation on behalf of the victims of discrimination." The judicial and bureaucratic monster comparable worth will call into being—a whole new layer of judges, court-appointed "masters" (there already is one in the Washington State suit), lawyers, and consultants—will not just sit once to fix wages and then retire. The process will be endless. Fairness will require constant readjustment. There will still exist such a thing as supply and demand. Even if comparable worth advocates succeed in abolishing it for women's work (remember, Washington State was found to have broken the law for paying women market wages rather than comparable worth wages), it will still operate for men's wages, the standard by which women's (comparable worth) wages will be set. Now, what if nurses are awarded plumbers' pay, and there develops a housing slowdown and a plumber surplus, and plumbers' wages fall? Will nurses' salaries have to be ratcheted down? And if not, what is to prevent the plumbers from suing, alleging they are underpaid relative to comparably equal nurses?

Which brings us to the equity problem. Almost everyone feels he or she is underpaid. Moreover, even a plumber can point to at least one person or group of persons who are getting more than they are "worth." Why can't he claim that class of people as the equitable standard, and march to court demanding restitution? If comparable worth is simple justice, as its advocates claim, why should only women be entitled to it? Why not comparable worth for everyone?

The whole search for the "just wage," which is what comparable 12 worth is all about, is, like the search for the "just price," inherently elusive in a capitalist system. It is not that justice has nothing to say about wages and prices in a market economy, but that what it does say it says negatively. For example, it declares that whatever the wage, it must be the same for people regardless of sex, race, or other characteristics; but it doesn't say what the wage should be. Even the minimum-wage law says merely that a wage may not be below a certain floor. (Even capitalism has a notion of exploitative labor.) Beyond that, the law is silent. The reason it is silent, the reason we decide to let the market decide, is no great mystery. It was first elaborated by Adam Smith, and amplified by the experience of the Soviet Union and other command economies. Market economies are agnostic on the question of a just wage or a just price not simply because of a philosophical belief that the question, if it is a question, is unanswerable, but also because of the belief, and the experience, that attempts to answer it have a habit of leaving everyone worse off than before.

Finally, even granting that women in traditionally female jobs are underpaid, it is not as if we live in a fixed economy which blocks off all avenues of redress. If secretaries are indeed paid less than they are "worth," they have several options. One is suggested by Coleman Young, the mayor of Detroit, a former labor leader and no conservative: "If a painter makes more than a secretary, then let more women be painters. Equal opportunity and affirmative action is how you do that." A woman entering the labor force today has no claim that she has been crowded into low-paying professions because of discrimination. She has choices.

Older women, of course, who have already invested much in their professions, are more constrained. But they have the same avenues open to them—such as organizing—as other similarly constrained (predominantly male) workers who struggle for higher wages in other settings. In Denver, for example, nurses sought comparable-worth wage gains in court and lost; they then went on strike and won. True, in some occupations, even strong unions can't raise wages very much. But as the president of the International Ladies Garment Workers Union (85 percent female) explained in objecting to a highfalutin AFL-CIO endorsement of comparable worth, the problem is not discrimination but the market. His workers have low wages because they compete with workers overseas who are paid thirty cents an hour. Comparable-worth doctrine may declare that garment workers ought to be making as much as truck drivers. But if the theory ever became practice, garment workers would be free of more than discrimination. They would be free of their jobs.

Why is the obvious about comparable worth so rarely heard? Why is it for Democrats the ultimate motherhood issue? Because here again the party of the big heart identifies a class of people who feel they aren't getting their just due, blames that condition on a single cause (discrimination), then offers a "rational" solution, on whose messy details it prefers not to dwell. But those details add up to a swamp of mindless arbitrariness and bureaucratic inefficiency, shrouded in a fine mist of pseudoscientific objectivity. And the surest results will be unending litigation and an entirely new generation of inequities. These inequities, moreover, will be frozen in place by force of law, and thus that much more difficult to dislodge.

Comparable worth asks the question: How many nurses would it take 16 to screw in a lightbulb? The joke is that, having not the faintest idea, it demands that a committee invent an answer, that the answer become law, and that the law supplant the market. Even Karl Marx, who also had legitimate complaints about the equity of wages set by the market, had a more plausible alternative.

Questions and Suggestions for Writing

1. Suppose you had read nothing of this essay except the opening and closing paragraphs. What position on the merits of comparable worth would you expect the author to take? In a paragraph or two explain, by citing evidence and commenting on it, how you came to your conclusion.

2. In paragraph 6 Krauthammer briefly explains the method of scoring. Look at the last sentence in the paragraph. How does Krauthammer convey his contempt for the system without explicitly denouncing it? Now suppose a writer supported the system. Rewrite that sentence in such a way as to suggest a favorable attitude.

3. Krauthammer distinguishes (paras. 4 and 5) two arguments for comparable worth—the "crowding" argument and the "conspiracy" argument—and rejects both. Read the essay preceding this one, by Teresa Amott and Julie Matthaei, and decide whether they use either of these arguments. If so, which do you find more convincing, the argument or Krauthammer's criticism of it? Why?

4. Krauthammer suggests (para. 7) that it is impossible to assign meaningful numerical values to the categories established by the Willis scale: "knowledge and skills," "mental demands," "accountability," and "working conditions." If you have ever held two rather different jobs, or if you are at least fairly familiar with two different jobs, write a paragraph explaining whether these jobs might be reasonably evaluated along Willis's lines.

5. Krauthammer believes that "everything is arbitrary" (paragraph 7) in evaluating the comparable worth of different jobs. Yet he advocates (paragraph 12) that we should "let the market decide" the pay scales of different jobs. Is this any less "arbitrary"? Has he implicitly contradicted himself? Why, or why not?

6. Make a rough outline of Krauthammer's essay, and then in a paragraph evaluate the strategy of his presentation of his arguments.

7. Krauthammer begins paragraph 10, "Now, even if there were a shred of merit in any of these systems for determining comparable worth, we should be wary of implementing them if only because of the sheer social chaos they would create." How good a reason is this? Could one have said the same thing about the American bid for independence in 1776, or about the abolition of slavery, or later of child labor? Is Krauthammer in effect saying that even if our present system is unjust, it's better to live with it than to risk "chaos"? Do you find terribly alarming the consequences he foresees? Write an essay of 500 words arguing some aspect of Krauthammer's argument that the issue should be dropped because it would, if implemented, introduce chaos. (You may, of course, either agree or disagree with him.) Or consider this idea: In the 1930s it was predicted that the proposed minimum-wage law would lead to chaos. In an essay of 500 words explain why Krauthammer probably would argue that the two cases are not comparable.

Should English Be Our Official Language?

Walter Darlington Huddleston

Speech on Behalf of a Constitutional Amendment to Make English the Official Language of the United States

Mr. President, the remarks I am about to make will be readily understood by my distinguished colleagues in the Congress. They will be understood by my constituents in Kentucky. They will be understood by the journalists in the press gallery, and by most of their readers across the country.

No simultaneous interpreters will be needed for those in this chamber, and no translators will be needed for most of those who will be reading these words in the *Congressional Record*.

Walter Darlington Huddleston (b. 1926) served in the United States Senate as a senator from Kentucky from 1973 to 1985. He made this speech in 1983.

In order to guarantee that this current state of affairs endures, as it has for over two hundred years. I am introducing today a constitutional amendment to make English the official language of the United States.

The amendment addresses something so basic, so very fundamental to   4
our sense of identity as Americans, that some, who are in full agreement with the objectives of this amendment, will nevertheless question the necessity for it. So widely held is the assumption that English already is our national language, that the notion of stating this in our national charter may seem like restating the obvious. However, I can assure my colleagues that this is not the case and that the need for a constitutional amendment grows stronger every day.

Almost alone among the world's very large and populous nations, the United States enjoys the blessings of one primary language, spoken and understood by most of its citizens. The previously unquestioned acceptance of this language by immigrants from every linguistic and cultural background has enabled us to come together as one people. It has allowed us to discuss our differences, to argue about our problems and to compromise on solutions. It has allowed us to develop a stable and cohesive society that is the envy of many fractured ones, without imposing any strict standards of homogeneity, or even bothering to designate the language, which is ours by custom, as the Nation's official one.

As a nation of immigrants, our great strength has been drawn from our ability to assimilate vast numbers of people from many different cultures and ethnic groups into a nation of people that can work together with cooperation and understanding. This process was often referred to as the melting pot and in the past it has been seen as an almost magical concept that helped to make the United States the greatest nation on Earth.

But for the last fifteen years, we have experienced a growing resistance to the acceptance of our historic language, an antagonistic questioning of the melting pot philosophy that has traditionally helped speed newcomers into the American mainstream.

Initially, the demands to make things easier for the newcomers seemed   8
modest enough; and a generous people, appreciative of cultural diversity, was willing to make some allowances. For example, the English language requirements for naturalization were removed for elderly immigrants living here for twenty years who were still unable to meet them; and the use of a child's home language in the school setting was encouraged, in a well-intentioned attempt to soften the pain of adjustment from the home to the English-speaking society that school represents.

However, the demands have sharply escalated, and so has the tone in which they are presented. Bilingual education has gradually lost its role as a transitional way of teaching English, and now mandates a bicultural component. This mandate has been primarily shaped and promoted by the federal government. The unfortunate result is that thousands of immigrant

and nonimmigrant children are languishing in near-permanent bilingual/
bicultural programs, kept in a state of prolonged confusion suspended
between two worlds, and not understanding what is expected of them.
They and their parents are given false hopes that their cultural traditions
can be fully maintained in this country, and that the mastery of English is
not so important, after all.

This change in attitude was aptly described by Theodore H. White in
his book *America in Search of Itself* wherein he stated:

> Some Hispanics have, however, made a demand never voiced by
> immigrants before: that the United States, in effect, officially recognize
> itself as a bicultural, bilingual nation. . . . [They] demand that the
> United States become a bilingual country, with all children entitled to be
> taught in the language of their heritage, at public expense. No better
> hymn to the American tradition has ever been written than *The Educa-*
> *tion of Hyman Kaplan*, by Leo Rosten, which describes with tears and
> laughter the efforts of the earlier immigrants . . . to learn the language
> of the country in which they wished to live. In New York today, forty
> years later, Hispanic entitlement has created a college, Hostos Com-
> munity College—supported by public taxes—which is officially bi-
> lingual; half its students receive instruction primarily in Spanish, as they
> strive to escape from the subculture of the Spanish ghetto. Bilingualism is
> an awkward word—but it has torn apart communities from Canada to
> Brittany, from Belgium to India. It expresses not a sense of tolerance but
> a demand for divisions.

This misdirected public policy of bilingualism has been created primarily by the federal government, at the insistence of special interest
groups, and it continues today because elected officials do not want to run
the risk of taking a position that could, in some way, offend these groups.
An example of how far this special interest influence reaches can be seen by
President Reagan's reversal on the issue. At the beginning of his administration he attempted to kill the bilingual program; now he is embracing
the concept.

Over the last few years the federal government has spent approx-   12
imately $1 billion on the bilingual education program and this year alone
it cost $139 million. What we have bought with this money is a program
that strives to keep separate cultural identities rather than a program that
strives to teach English. It is a program which ignores the basic fact that in
order to learn another language the student must talk, read and use that
language on a regular basis.

The failure of bilingual education programs to teach children how to
speak English in the shortest time has been documented by a study done at
the U.S. Department of Education and by the recent report of the Twentieth Century Fund Task Force on Federal Elementary and Secondary
Education Policy. The latter report stated unequivocally that:

> The Task Force recommends that the federal government clearly state that the most important objective of elementary and secondary education in the United States is the development of literacy in the English language. . . .
>
> The Task Force recommends that federal funds now going to the bilingual program be used to teach non-English-speaking children how to speak, read, and write English.

Even though the bilingual education program has received failing marks by many reputable educators, it still survives because it is a political issue rather than an educational issue. What this means is that we will continue to finance an expensive bilingual program that does more to preserve cultural identities than it does to teach children to speak English.

In the area of voting rights we have also formulated a national policy that encourages voting citizens not to learn to speak English. The Voting Rights Act, which was reauthorized in 1982, requires bilingual ballots if more than 5 percent of the citizens of voting age in a jurisdiction are members of specified language minority groups and the illiteracy rate is higher than the national rate. As a result bilingual ballots are required by federal law to be provided in 30 states—even if there is no demand for them.

In essence, we have gone far beyond providing a necessary service on a temporary basis; and, we are now engaged in actively encouraging the use of bilingual ballots, even though in many cases they may not be needed. The wisdom of this policy is clearly lacking when you consider that the vast bulk of political debate, whether it is in the printed press or the electronic media, is conducted in English. By failing to provide a positive incentive for voting citizens to learn English, we are actually denying them full participation in the political process. Instead, we are making them dependent upon a few interpreters or go-betweens for information as to how they should vote. Although this process helps to preserve minority voting blocks, it seriously undercuts the democratic concept that every voting individual should be as fully informed as possible about the issues and the candidates. 16

In many parts of the country foreign language ballots are under attack. In San Francisco, a local initiative petition has been filed urging that local governments be allowed to print ballots in English only. In that area ballots are now printed in English, Spanish, Chinese, and because of the new census figures, Tagalog ballots will probably be printed in the future.

There are other less prominent provisions of federal law which now require the use of foreign languages. For example, 28 U.S.C. 1827 requires the Director of the Administrative Office of the U.S. courts to establish a program for the use of foreign language interpreters in federal civil and criminal proceedings for parties whose primary language is other than

English; 42 U.S.C. 254 requires the use of foreign language personnel in connection with federally funded migrant and community health centers; and 42 U.S.C. 4577 requires the use of foreign language personnel in the alcohol abuse and treatment programs. Although I can understand that this kind of assistance is helpful, the fact that it must be legislated strongly indicates that we are failing miserably in our efforts to teach immigrants and many of our native born how to speak, read and write English.

The federal laws requiring the use of interpreters and foreign languages are merely the tip of the iceberg. I recently sent a request to all of the state governors and the major federal agencies asking for information regarding non-English forms and publications that their offices produce, which are intended for use in this country. Although my staff is still in the process of reviewing the data, and I have not yet received responses to all of my letters, we know that hundreds of different non-English forms and publications are now being printed and distributed on a wide scale throughout the United States. These publications cover a broad spectrum and range from White House press releases in Spanish to National Labor Relations Board notices in thirty-two different languages. The non-English materials which I have received are in a stack that is about 3 feet high, and we are adding to it almost daily. However, even when all the responses are in we still will not have a complete picture of the use of official, non-English publications. Many of the states are only sending a few samples of what they produce, and I am told that if copies of all bilingual educational materials were sent we could fill a large room. While distribution of these materials may be seen as providing just another government service, it can also be seen as reducing the incentive to learn English and demonstrates a growing nationwide problem.

At the nongovernment level there is a great deal of emphasis being placed on the use of non-English languages. In some major metropolitan areas English is the second language; minorities, who speak only English, are being told that they must learn a foreign language in order to be eligible for a job in parts of this country; and, in many stores non-English languages are the only ones used to conduct business. It is not uncommon to find areas in this country where an individual can live all of his or her life having all of his social, commercial, and intellectual needs met without the use of English.

Statistics show a disconcerting trend away from the common use of English. In 1975 the Bureau of the Census reported that about 8 million people in this country used a language other than English in their households. When the census was conducted in 1980 the number of people who spoke a language other than English at home was found to be over 22 million. Although these numbers are subject to many interpretations, to me they indicate—very strongly—that the melting pot is not working as it once did.

My assumption is confirmed by a recent population bulletin, "U.S. Hispanics; Changing the Face of America," which concluded that because of their common language and large numbers, Hispanics will take longer than other immigrant groups to assimilate into the American society.

If this situation were static and merely a reflection of the large scale legal and illegal immigration the United States has been experiencing over the last few years—in 1980 more immigrants entered the United States than at any time other than the peak years at the turn of the century—there would not be cause for concern. However, what we are seeing is a decrease in the use of English and a widely accepted attitude that it is not necessary to learn English.

There is a new philosophy taking hold, and it is gaining more and more acceptance. In the June 13, 1983, *Time* magazine an article stated in regard to this new philosophy, that: 24

> Now, however, a new bilingualism and biculturalism is being promulgated that would deliberately fragment the Nation into separate, unassimilated groups . . . The new metaphor is not the melting pot but the salad bowl, with each element distinct. The biculturalists seek to use public services, particularly schools, not to Americanize the young but to heighten their consciousness of belonging to another heritage.

The United States is presently at a crucial juncture. We can either continue down the same path we have walked for the last two hundred years, using the melting pot philosophy to forge a strong and united nation or, we can take the new path that leads in the direction of another Tower of Babel.

There are many nations in the world today that would give a great deal to have the kind of internal social and political stability that a single primary language (English) has afforded us. For us to consciously make the decision to throw away this stabilizing force would be seen as foolish and stupid in countries that have paid a high price for not having a universally accepted language.

We have to look no further than the nation which is closest to us geographically and culturally—Canada. They have had a long-running experience with bilingualism and biculturalism, and it is an experience that still generates divisiveness and still threatens to shatter the nation's unity. The key cause of Canada's internal conflict is language. According to the Annual Report, 1981, of the Commissioner of Official Languages, the total cost so far in implementing the Canadian Official Languages Act "is on the order of $4 billion spread over the 12 years. The question of cost-effectiveness is more problematical. Measured against the goals of relieving English-French tensions and fostering a common pride in the value of our national languages, the results may be more questionable."

Belgium is another nation that has suffered severe internal dissent, 28
much of which has been caused by language differences. In the last thirty-
nine years the political coalitions that are necessary to govern that country
have been broken apart over thirty times by the fights between the French-
speaking Walloons and the Dutch-speaking Flemish. This political squab-
bling has had serious consequences for Belgium, and it is not the kind of
situation to which any nation should voluntarily subject itself.

This type of political instability has been repeated throughout history,
and is still occurring in many countries today. In countless places, differences in language have either caused or contributed significantly to
political, social, and economic instability. While the absence of language
differences does not guarantee that these problems will not occur, I believe
that it does significantly reduce the chances that they will occur.

The constitutional amendment which I am proposing is not unusual,
and in fact, many nations have one official language. According to the
Library of Congress these include, but are not limited to, Austria, Bul-
garia, Denmark, France, the German Democratic Republic, the Federal
Republic of Germany, Greece, Hungary, Italy, the Netherlands, Norway,
Poland, Romania, and Sweden.

Within the United States there is ample tradition and legislation to
justify this approach. According to the Library of Congress:

> Several Federal statutes and numerous State laws do require the use of
> English in a variety of areas.
> Thus, the Nationality Act of 1940 (8 U.S.C. 423) requires that—
> "No person . . . shall be naturalized as a citizen of the United States
> upon his own petition who cannot demonstrate—
> "(1) an understanding of the English language, including an ability to
> read, write and speak words in ordinary usage in the English language"
> (with provisos).
> Secondly, 28 U.S.C. 865 requires that in determining whether a
> person is qualified for jury service, the chief judge of a district court
> "shall deem any person qualified to serve on grand and petit juries in the
> district court unless he (the prospective juror)—
> "(2) is unable to read, write, and understand the English language
> with a degree of proficiency sufficient to fill out satisfactorily the juror
> qualification form;
> "(3) is unable to speak the English language. . . ."
> At the state level, most states have statutes requiring the use of
> English as the language of instruction in the public schools. Some states
> also statutorily require English as the language of legal proceedings and
> legal notices, of business regulation, etc.

More recently, the U.S. Senate has spoken out very strongly in favor of 32
establishing English as the official language. On August 13, 1982, Senator
Hayakawa introduced an amendment to the Immigration Reform and
Control Act declaring that "the English language is the official language of

the United States." On a rollcall vote seventy-eight senators voted for this amendment and it was included in the bill. When this same bill was again reported out of the Judiciary Committee on April 21, 1983 it again contained this language, and the report of the full committee stated:

> If immigration is continued at a high level, yet a substantial portion of these new persons and their descendants do not assimilate into the society, they have the potential to create in America a measure of the same social, political, and economic problems which exist in the countries from which they have chosen to depart. Furthermore, if language and cultural separatism rise above a certain level, the unity and political stability of the nation will—in time—be seriously diminished. Pluralism, within a united American nation, has been the single greatest strength of this country. This unity comes from a common language and a core public culture of certain shared values, beliefs, and customs which make us distinctly "Americans."

The concerns that were expressed by the Senate Judiciary Committee are reflected in the concerns of thousands of citizens throughout this country. In fact, a new national organization has recently been created called U.S. English. The honorary chairman of this organization is former U.S. Senator S. I. Hayakawa, who speaks with a great deal of authority on this issue because he is an immigrant and distinguished scholar of semantics and languages.

U.S. English refers to itself as "a national, non-profit, non-partisan organization . . . founded to defend the public interest in the growing debate on bilingualism and biculturalism."

If we continue along the path we now follow, I believe that we will do irreparable damage to the fragile unity that our common language has helped us preserve for over two hundred years. Cultural pluralism is an established value in our national life, and one which we greatly cherish. Paradoxically, cultural pluralism can only continue if we retain our common meeting ground; namely, the English language. If we allow this bond to erode, we will no longer enjoy the benefits of cultural diversity, but rather, we will suffer the bitterness of ethnic confrontations and cultural separatism.

The constitutional language I am proposing is simple and straightforward: It would serve to establish a principle that would strengthen us as a nation. However, I am aware that adding to the Constitution takes us into uncharted waters, and that there will be many misleading allegations about the extent of the problem and the proposed remedy. This is one of the reasons I have chosen to propose a constitutional amendment in order to address this issue. It will focus national attention on the problem, and subject it to the type of thorough national debate which is necessary.

During this constitutional process, all parties, sides, and interests will have the opportunity to present their respective points of view. This will guarantee that the final version submitted to the states for ratification will accomplish only what is needed to be accomplished and that basic individual rights are not interfered with.

Even though I believe that the constitutional language I am proposing will work, I am open to all recommendations and I will carefully consider any proposed improvements or modifications. However, regardless of the final language, to a large extent it is the legislative history which determines how the language will be interpreted.

Accordingly, it is my intent that the amendment I am proposing would not do a number of things.

First. It would not prohibit or discourage the use of foreign languages 40 and cultures in private contexts, such as in homes, churches, communities, private organizations, commerce, and private schools. The United States is rich in ethnic cultures and they would continue to survive as they have in the past.

Second. It would not prohibit the teaching of foreign languages in the Nation's public schools or colleges, nor will it prohibit foreign language requirements in academic institutions.

Third. It will not prevent the use of second languages for the purpose of public convenience and safety in limited circumstances.

On the other hand the amendment would accomplish a number of objectives.

First. It would bring national recognition to the proposition that a 44 common language is necessary to preserve the basic internal unity that is required for a stable and growing nation.

Second. It would establish English as the official language of federal, state, and local governments throughout the United States.

Third. Since voting by citizens is the method of choosing the representatives of these governments and is the first step in the official process of governing, it would prevent the printing of ballots in foreign languages.

Fourth. It would permit bilingual education where it could be clearly demonstrated that the primary objective and practical result is the teaching of English to students as rapidly as possible, and not cultural maintenance. It would not affect the use of total immersion in English, which is a proven method of teaching English.

Fifth. It would discourage discrimination and exploitation by making 48 it clear to immigrant parents and children that learning English is indispensable for full participation in the American society and economy and by speeding them into the mainstream of our society and economy as rapidly as possible.

Sixth. It would reaffirm that we are truly "one Nation . . . indivisible. . . ."

Mr. President, national unity is not a subject to be taken lightly, for without it we would lose much of the strength which sets us apart as a great nation. I believe that history has taught us that one of the vital ingredients for obtaining national unity is a commonly accepted language.

This has been confirmed by our own past experience in this country, and it has been proven by other countries that have been divided and weakened by their internal arguments centering around language differences.

National unity does not require that each person think and act like everyone else. However, it does require that there be some common threads that run throughout our society and hold us together. One of these threads is our common belief and support of a democratic form of government, and the right of every person to fully participate in it. Unfortunately, this right of full participation means very little if each individual does not possess the means of exercising it. This participation requires the ability to obtain information and to communicate our beliefs and concerns to others. Undoubtedly this process is greatly hindered without the existence of a commonly accepted and used language.

In essence, what a policy of bilingualism/biculturalism does is to 52 segregate minorities from the mainstream of our politics, economy, and society because we are not making it possible for them to freely enter into that mainstream. We are pushing them aside into their own communities, and denying them the tools with which to break out. I have always been against segregation of any kind, and by not assuring that every person in this country can speak and understand English we are still practicing segregation. It was wrong when we segregated blacks because of color and it is just as wrong when we create a system which segregates any group of people by language.

As Americans we are a unique people and one of the things that makes us uniquely American is our common language—English. My proposed constitutional amendment would assure that anyone in this country can fully take part in the American dream and that future generations also will have this privilege.

Mr. President, I ask unanimous consent that the joint resolution be printed in the *Record*.

There being no objection, the joint resolution was ordered to be printed in the *Record*, as follows:

S.J. Res. 167

Resolved by the Senate and House of Representatives of the United States of America in Congress assembled, (two-thirds of each House concurring therein), That the following article is proposed as an amendment to the Constitution of the United States, which shall be valid to all intents and purposes as part of the Constitution if ratified by the legislatures of three-fourths of the several States within seven years after its submission to the States for ratification:

ARTICLE

"Sec. 1. The English language shall be the official language of the United States.

"Sec. 2. The Congress shall have the power to enforce this article by appropriate legislation."

Questions and Suggestions for Writing

1. Paragraph 9 claims that programs in bilingual education (a) keep many children "in a state of prolonged confusion," (b) give the children and their parents "false hopes that their cultural traditions can be fully maintained in this country," and (c) imply "that the mastery of English is not so important, after all." If you have participated in a bilingual education program, or have some familiarity with persons who have participated, do you agree with all or any of these assertions? Explain.

2. In paragraph 10 Huddleston quotes Theodore White: "Bilingualism . . . has torn apart communities from Canada to Brittany, from Belgium to India." (Paras. 27 and 28 also refer to Canada and Belgium.) Do some research on the alleged destructive effects of bilingualism in one of these countries, and then consider if the conditions in that country are sufficiently close to conditions in the United States for a lesson to be drawn.

3. Paragraph 14 asserts that "the bilingual education program . . . is a political issue." What does that mean?

4. In paragraph 20 Huddleston says that "in some major metropolitan areas" persons who speak only English "are being told that they must learn a foreign language in order to be eligible for a job." No example is given, but Miami may be such an example. Because Miami is a banking center for many Latin American countries and much of this business is conducted in Spanish, certain positions in effect call for fluency in Spanish. Do you think it is unjust, or unwise, to require fluency in Spanish for these positions?

5. Paragraph 21 admits that the statistics showing an increase in the number of people who commonly use a language other than English in their households "are subject to many interpretations." What might some of these interpretations be? Paragraph 23 provides a clue. Is this explanation distressing to you? Why?

6. *Time* magazine (quoted in para. 24) argues that the traditional image of the melting pot has been replaced with a new image, the salad bowl. Putting aside, at least for the moment, the truth of the assertion, consider the two images. What are their implications? (Notice Huddleston's use of the melting pot in para. 25.) Do you find one image more powerful than the other? In paragraph 25 Huddleston introduces yet another image, the Tower of Babel. What was the original Tower of Babel, to which he refers? Do you agree with him that our current bilingual policies have us headed in that direction?

7. In paragraph 33 Huddleston says that "the concerns that were expressed by the Senate Judiciary Committee are reflected in the concerns of thousands of citizens throughout this country." Given the size of the population of the United States (by the way, about how large is it?), is "thousands" a large number? Is it larger than the number of citizens who may well hold a contrary view?

8. Paragraph 35 calls attention to a *paradox* (an apparent contradiction). Do you agree that "cultural pluralism can only continue if we retain our common meeting ground; namely the English language"?

9. Reread paragraph 42, and then consider the following questions. In neighborhoods where there are many recent immigrants, or large numbers of persons not fluent in English, should the community provide highway signs in foreign languages as well as English? Should courts provide interpreters? Should emergency rooms in hospitals provide interpreters? Should police 911 numbers be staffed by bilingual persons?

10. Paragraph 52 asserts that "we are pushing . . . aside" non-English speakers, thereby creating a new form of "segregation" comparable to the earlier segregation of blacks. Evaluate the comparison.

James Fallows

Viva Bilingualism

In his classic work of crackpot anthropology, *The Japanese Brain*, Dr. Tadanobu Tsunoda told his Japanese readers not to feel bad about their difficulties learning other languages, especially English. "Isn't it remarkable," he said (I am paraphrasing), "that whenever you meet someone who speaks English really well, he turns out to be a drip?"

The Japanese have their own reasons for seeking such reassurance. Their students learn English exactly the way Americans (used to) learn Latin: through long, boring analyses of antique written passages. Not surprisingly, most of them feel about as comfortable making English conversation as I would if Julius Caesar strolled up for a chat. The few Japanese who do speak good English have generally lived overseas—and to that extent have become less Japanese and, by local standards, more like drips.

Still, for all the peculiar Japaneseness of his sentiment, the spirit of Dr. Tsunoda is alive in America today. It is reflected in the general disdain for bilingualism and bilingual education, and in campaigns like the one on California's ballot last week, sponsored by the group called U.S. English, to declare that English is America's "official" language.

Yes, yes, everyone needs to learn English. America doesn't want to become Quebec. We have enough other forces pulling us apart that we don't want linguistic divisions too. But is there any reason to get so worked up about today's Spanish-speaking immigrants, even if they keep learning Spanish while in school? I will confess that I once shared U.S. English–type fears about Spanish language separatism. But having spent a long

4

James Fallows (b. 1949), the Washington editor of the Atlantic, *wrote this article while based in Asia. It appeared in* The New Republic *in 1986.*

time reporting among immigrants and seeing how much their children wanted to learn English, I'm not worried anymore. And, having been out of the country most of this year, I've come to think that the whole American language scare rests on two bogus and amazingly parochial assumptions.

The first is a view of bilingualism as a kind of polygamy. That is, according to Western standards it just doesn't work to have two wives. The partners in a marriage require a certain exclusive commitment from each other. If a man gives it to one wife, there's not enough left over to give to someone else. Similarly with language: there's only so much room in a person's brain, and if he speaks one language—let us say Spanish—really well, he'll be all filled up and won't learn English. And if his brain were not a problem, his heart would be, since he can be truly loyal to only one language. I'm burlesquing the argument a little, but not much. Why would anyone worry about students taking "maintenance" courses in Spanish, if not for the fear that Spanish would somehow use up the mental and emotional space English should fill?

In the American context, it's easy to see why people might feel this way. Ninety-nine percent of all Americans can happily live their lives speaking and thinking about no language but English. Foreign-language education has been falling off, and except in unusual circumstances— wars, mainly—it has never had much practical reinforcement anyway. When we come across people in the United States who obviously know a foreign language, the main signal is usually that their English is so poor.

But suppose that mastering a second language is less like having two wives than like having two children. Maybe there's not really a limit in the brain or heart, and spreading attention among several languages—like spreading love among several children—may actually enrich everyone involved. Without going through all the linguistic arguments showing that bilingualism is possible and natural (one impressive recent summary was *Mirror of Language* by Kenji Hakuta, published this year) I will merely say that after about five seconds of talking with someone who really is bilingual, the two-child, rather than two-wife, view comes to make much more sense.

Everyone has heard about the Scandinavians and Swiss, who grow up   8 in a big swirl of languages and can talk easily to anyone they meet. Their example may seem too high-toned to be persuasive in connection with today's Spanish-speaking immigrants, so consider the more down-to-earth illustrations of multilingualism to be found all over Asia.

Seven years ago, the government of Singapore launched a "Speak Mandarin!" campaign, designed to supplant various southern Chinese dialects with Mandarin. (This is roughly similar to a "Speak Like Prince Charles!" campaign being launched in West Virginia.) Since then, competence in Mandarin has gone up—and so has mastery of English. At the beginning of the Speak Mandarin campaign, the pass rate for O-level (high school) exams in English was 41 percent. Now it's 61 percent. During the same period, the O-level pass rate for Mandarin went from 84 percent to 92 percent. The children managed to get better at both languages at once.

Just north of Singapore is Malaysia, another one-time British colony whose main political problem is managing relations among three distinct ethnic groups: Malays, Chinese, and Indians. Each of the groups speaks a different language at home—Malay for the Malays, Cantonese or Hokkien for the Chinese, Tamil for the Indians. But if you put any two Malaysians together in a room, it's almost certain that they'll be able to speak to each other, in either Malay or English, since most people are bilingual and many speak three or more languages. (The Chinese generally speak one or two Chinese dialects, plus English and/or Malay. The Indians speak English or Malay on top of Tamil, and many or most Malays speak English.) Neither Tamil nor the Chinese dialects travel well outside the ethnic group, and Malay doesn't travel anywhere else but Indonesia, so most Malaysians have a strong incentive to learn another language.

I should emphasize that I'm talking about people who in no way fit modern America's idea of a rarefied intellectual elite. They are wizened Chinese shopkeepers, unschooled Indian night guards, grubby Malay food hawkers, in addition to more polished characters who've traveled around the world. Yet somehow they all find room in their brains for more than one language at a time. Is it so implausible that Americans can do the same?

The second antibilingual assumption, rarely stated but clearly there, 12 is that English is some kind of fragile blossom, about to be blown apart by harsh blasts from the Spanish-speaking world. Come on! Never before in world history has a language been as dominant as English is now. In every corner of the world, people realize that their chances to play on the big stage—to make money, have choices, travel—depend on learning English. They don't always succeed, but more and more of them try. In Malaysia, in South China, even in linguophobic Japan, my family's main problem as we travel has been coping with people who spring from behind every lamppost and tofu stand, eager to practice the English they've picked up from the shortwave radio. Malaysia ships out tens of thousands of young people each year for studies in the United States, Australia, and England. Guess what language they have to learn before they go.

It may seem that modern America shamelessly coddles its immigrants, with all those Spanish-language street signs and TV broadcasts and "maintenance" courses, which together reduce the incentive to learn English. Well, I've spent most of this year in a position similar to the immigrants', and it's not as comfortable or satisfactory as it may look. Japan makes many more accommodations to the English language than America does to Spanish. Tokyo has four English-language daily newspapers—more than most American cities—plus several magazines. The major train and sub-way routes have English signs, most big-city restaurants have English menus, all major hotels have English-speaking staff. Students applying for university admission must pass tests in (written) English. Most shop-keepers, policemen, and passersby can make sense of written-down English messages. Even the Shinkansen, or bullet train, makes its announce-ments in both Japanese and English—which is comparable to the Eastern shuttle giving each "Please have your fares ready" message in Spanish as well as English. The nighttime TV news broadcasts now come in a bi-lingual version—you push a button on your set to switch from Japanese to English. It is as if the "CBS Evening News" could be simultaneously heard in Spanish.

Does all of this reduce the incentive to learn Japanese, or the feeling of being left out if you don't? Hah! Even though Japanese society is vastly more permeated by English than American society is by Spanish, each day brings ten thousand reminders of what you're missing if you don't know the language. You can't read the mainstream newspapers, can't follow most shows on TV, can't communicate above the "please-give-me-a-ticket-to-Kyoto" level. Without learning the language, you could never hope to win a place as anything but a fringe figure. Some adults nonetheless live out a ghettoized, English-only existence, because Japanese is no cinch, but for-eign children raised in Japan pick up the language as the only way to participate.

The incentives for America's newcomers to learn English are even stronger. How are an immigrant's children going to go to any college, get any kind of white-collar job, live anything but a straitened, ghetto exis-tence unless they speak English? When are the SATs, Bruce Springsteen songs, and the David Letterman show going to be in Spanish—or Korean, or Tagalog? If Malaysians and rural Chinese can see that English is their route to a wider world, are Guatemalans and Cubans who've made it to America so much more obtuse? And if they keep up their Spanish at the same time, even through the dreaded "maintenance" courses, why don't we count that as a good thing? It's good for them, in making their lives richer and their minds more flexible, and it's good for the country, in enlarging its ability to deal with the rest of the world.

The adult immigrants themselves don't usually succeed in learning 16 English, any more than my wife and I have become fluent in Japanese. But that has been true of America's immigrants for two hundred years. (The main exception were the Eastern European Jewish immigrants of the early twentieth century, who moved into English faster than Italians, Germans, Poles, or today's Latin Americans.) The Cubans' and Mexicans' children are the ones who learn, as previous immigrants' children have. When someone can find large numbers of children who are being raised in America but don't see English as a necessity, then I'll start to worry.

We don't want to become Quebec—and we're not about to. Quebec, Belgium, Sri Lanka, and other places with language problems have old, settled groups who've lived alongside each other, in mutual dislike, for many years—not new groups of immigrants continually being absorbed. We don't need to declare English our official language, because it already is that—as no one knows better than the immigrants and their children. Anywhere else in the world, people would laugh at the idea that English is in any way imperiled. Let's calm down and enjoy the joke too.

Questions and Suggestions for Writing

1. Which of Fallows's arguments are based on his own rather unusual experience? How much weight do you give to the conclusions he draws from this experience? That is, why do you trust, or not trust, these arguments?

2. Fallows insists (para. 4) that most Spanish-speaking immigrants to the United States want their children to learn English. If true, and if true of other immigrants as well, do you think this would persuade advocates of official English to abandon their efforts to amend the constitution? Why, or why not?

3. Evaluate Fallows's argument (paras. 5–7) that bilingualism is more like having two children than like having two wives (or husbands). Can you think of a better analogy?

4. In paragraph 11 Fallows summarizes his point: ordinary people can "find room in their brains for more than one language at a time." First, are you convinced of this point? Second, is the point relevant to the U.S. English movement?

5. In paragraph 13 Fallows argues that "Japan makes many more accommodations to the English language than America does to Spanish." He cites the presence, in Japan, of English-language newspapers and magazines, subway signs, etc. He does not mention, however, that Japan offers no aid whatsoever to a schoolchild who does not speak Japanese. In a Japanese school, so far as the non-Japanese child is concerned, it's sink or swim. Given this fact, do you think it is fair to say that "Japan makes many more accommodations to the English language than America does to Spanish"?

6. Why do you suppose Japan offers the aid that it does to persons who don't speak Japanese? Put it this way: To whom is the aid offered, and why? Are the persons in Japan who don't speak Japanese closely comparable to the persons in the United States who don't speak English? If not, is the difference relevant to the argument? Why, or why not?

7. Early in his essay, in paragraph 4, Fallows mentions Quebec, and he mentions it again in his final paragraph when he says that Quebec is irrelevant to the argument. Do you agree that it is irrelevant? Why, or why not?

8. Can you think of any significant counterarguments that Fallows does not face? If so, what are they?

9. Fallows doesn't point to any harms or costs (monetary, or of any other sort) that would accrue if English were made our official language. Is this a weakness in his argument? Why, or why not? Can you think of any harms or costs?

Would Gun Control Really Help?

Nan Desuka

Why Handguns Must Be Outlawed

"Guns don't kill people—criminals do." That's a powerful slogan, much more powerful than its alternate version, "Guns don't kill people—people kill people." But this second version, though less effective, is much nearer to the whole truth. Although accurate statistics are hard to come by, and even harder to interpret, it seems indisputable that large numbers of people, not just criminals, kill, with a handgun, other people. Scarcely a day goes by without a newspaper in any large city reporting that a child has found a gun, kept by the child's parents for self-protection, and has, in playing with this new-found toy, killed himself or a playmate. Or we read of a storekeeper, trying to protect himself during a robbery, who inadvertently shoots an innocent customer. These killers are not, in any reasonable sense of the word, criminals. They are just people who happen to kill people. No wonder the gun lobby prefers the first version of the slogan, "Guns don't kill people—criminals do." This version suggests that the only problem is criminals, not you or me, or our children, and certainly not the members of the National Rifle Association.

Those of us who want strict control of handguns—for me that means the outlawing of handguns, except to the police and related service units—have not been able to come up with a slogan equal in power to "Guns don't kill people—criminals do." The best we have been able to come up with is a mildly amusing bumper sticker showing a teddy bear, with the words "Defend your right to arm bears." Humor can be a powerful weapon (even in writing *on behalf* of gun control, one slips into using the imagery of force), and our playful bumper sticker somehow deflates the self-righteousness of the gun lobby, but doesn't equal the power (again the imagery of force) of "Guns don't kill people—criminals do." For one thing, the effective alliteration of "criminals" and "kill" binds the two words, making everything so terribly simple. Criminals kill; when there are no criminals, there will be no deaths from guns.

But this notion won't do. Despite the uncertainty of some statistical evidence, everyone knows, or should know, that only about 30 percent of murders are committed by robbers or rapists (Kates, 1978). For the most

---

Nan Desuka (1957–1985) was born in Japan but at age two was brought by her parents to Los Angeles, where she was educated. Although she most often wrote about ecology, she occasionally wrote about other controversial topics.

part the victims of handguns know their assailants well. These victims are women killed by jealous husbands, or they are the women's lovers; or they are drinking buddies who get into a violent argument; or they are innocent people who get shot by disgruntled (and probably demented) employees or fellow workers who have (or imagine) a grudge. Or they are, as I've already said, bystanders at a robbery, killed by a storekeeper. Or they are children playing with their father's gun.

Of course this is not the whole story. Hardened criminals also have 4 guns, and they use them. The murders committed by robbers and rapists are what give credence to Barry Goldwater's quip, "We have a crime problem in this country, not a gun problem" (1975, p. 186). But here again the half-truth of a slogan is used to mislead, used to direct attention away from a national tragedy. Different sources issue different statistics, but a conservative estimate is that handguns annually murder at least 15,000 Americans, accidentally kill at least another 3,000, and wound at least another 100,000. Handguns are easily available, both to criminals and to decent people who believe they need a gun in order to protect themselves from criminals. The decent people, unfortunately, have good cause to believe they need protection. Many parts of many cities are utterly unsafe, and even the tiniest village may harbor a murderer. Senator Goldwater is right in saying there is a crime problem (that's the truth of his half-truth), but he is wrong in saying there is not also a gun problem.

Surely the homicide rate would markedly decrease if handguns were outlawed. The FBI reports (*Uniform Crime Reports*, 1985) that more than 60 percent of all murders are caused by guns, and handguns are involved in more than 70 percent of these. Surely many, even most, of these handgun killings would not occur if the killer had to use a rifle, club, or knife. Of course violent lovers, angry drunks, and deranged employees would still flail out with knives or baseball bats, but some of their victims would be able to run away, with few or no injuries, and most of those who could not run away would nevertheless survive, badly injured but at least alive. But if handguns are outlawed, we are told, responsible citizens will have no way to protect themselves from criminals. First, one should remember that at least 90 percent of America's burglaries are committed when no one is at home. The householder's gun, if he or she has one, is in a drawer of the bedside table, and the gun gets lifted along with the jewelry, adding one more gun to the estimated 100,000 handguns annually stolen from law-abiding citizens (Shields, 1981). Second, if the householder is at home, and attempts to use the gun, he or she is more likely to get killed or wounded than to kill or deter the intruder. Another way of looking at this last point is to recall that for every burglar who is halted by the sight of a handgun, four innocent people are killed by handgun accidents.

Because handguns are not accurate beyond ten or fifteen feet, they are not the weapons of sportsmen. Their sole purpose is to kill or at least to disable a person at close range. But only a minority of persons killed with these weapons are criminals. Since handguns chiefly destroy the innocent, they must be outlawed—not simply controlled more strictly, but outlawed—to all except to law-enforcement officials. Attempts to control handguns are costly and ineffective, but even if they were cheap and effective stricter controls would not take handguns out of circulation among criminals, because licensed guns are stolen from homeowners and shopkeepers, and thus fall into criminal hands. According to Wright, Rossi, and Daly (1983, p. 181), about 40 percent of the handguns used in crimes are stolen, chiefly from homes that the guns were supposed to protect.

The National Rifle Association is fond of quoting a University of Wisconsin study that says, "gun control laws have no individual or collective effect in reducing the rate of violent crime" (cited in Smith, 1981, p. 17). Agreed—but what if handguns were not available? What if the manufacturer of handguns is severely regulated, and if the guns may be sold only to police officers? True, even if handguns are outlawed, some criminals will manage to get them, but surely fewer petty criminals will have guns. It is simply untrue for the gun lobby to assert that all criminals—since they are by definition lawbreakers—will find ways to get handguns. For the most part, if the sale of handguns is outlawed, guns won't be available, and fewer criminals will have guns. And if fewer criminals have guns, there is every reason to believe that violent crime will decline. A youth armed only with a knife is less likely to try to rob a store than if he is armed with a gun. This commonsense reasoning does not imply that if handguns are outlawed crime will suddenly disappear, or even that an especially repulsive crime such as rape will decrease markedly. A rapist armed with a knife probably has a sufficient weapon. But *some* violent crime will almost surely decrease. And the decrease will probably be significant if in addition to outlawing handguns, severe mandatory punishments are imposed on a person who is found to possess one, and even severer mandatory punishments are imposed on a person who uses one while committing a crime. Again, none of this activity will solve "the crime problem," but neither will anything else, including the "get tough with criminals" attitude of Senator Goldwater. And of course any attempt to reduce crime (one cannot realistically talk of "solving" the crime problem) will have to pay attention to our systems of bail, plea bargaining, and parole, but outlawing handguns will help.

What will the cost be? First, to take "cost" in its most literal sense, 8 there will be the cost of reimbursing gun owners for the weapons they surrender. Every owner of a handgun ought to be paid the fair market value of the weapon. Since the number of handguns is estimated to be between fifty million and ninety million, the cost will be considerable, but it will be far less than the costs—both in money and in sorrow—that result from deaths due to handguns.

Second, one may well ask if there is another sort of cost, a cost to our liberty, to our constitutional rights. The issue is important, and persons who advocate abolition of handguns are blind or thoughtless if they simply brush it off. On the other hand, opponents of gun control do all of us a disservice by insisting over and over that the Constitution guarantees "the right to bear arms." The Second Amendment in the Bill of Rights says this: "A well-regulated militia being necessary to the security of a free State, the right of the people to keep and bear arms shall not be infringed." It is true that the founding fathers, mindful of the British attempt to disarm the colonists, viewed the presence of "a well-regulated militia" as a safeguard of democracy. Their intention is quite clear, even to one who has not read Stephen P. Halbrook's *That Every Man Be Armed*, an exhaustive argument in favor of the right to bear arms. There can be no doubt that the framers of the Constitution and the Bill of Rights believed that armed insurrection was a justifiable means of countering oppression and tyranny. The Second Amendment may be fairly paraphrased thus: *"Because* an organized militia is necessary to the security of the State, the people have the right to possess weapons." But the owners of handguns are not members of a well-regulated militia. Furthermore, nothing in the proposal to ban handguns would deprive citizens of their rifles or other long-arm guns. All handguns, however, even large ones, should be banned. "Let's face it," Guenther W. Bachmann (a vice president of Smith and Wesson) admits, "they are all concealable" (Kennedy, 1981, p. 6). In any case, it is a fact that when gun control laws have been tested in the courts, they have been found to be constitutional. The constitutional argument was worth making, but the question must now be regarded as settled, not only by the courts but by anyone who reads the Second Amendment.

Still, is it not true that "If guns are outlawed, only outlaws will have guns"? This is yet another powerful slogan, but it is simply not true. First, we are talking not about "guns" but about handguns. Second, the police will have guns—handguns and others—and these trained professionals are the ones on whom we must rely for protection against criminals. Of course the police have not eradicated crime; and of course we must hope that in the future they will be more successful in protecting all citizens. But we must also recognize that the efforts of private citizens to protect themselves with handguns has chiefly taken the lives not of criminals but of innocent people.

References

Goldwater, B. (1975, December). Why gun control laws don't work. *Reader's Digest*, 183–188.

Halbrook, S. P. (1985). *That every man be armed: The evolution of a constitutional right.* Albuquerque: University of New Mexico Press.

Kates, D. B., Jr. (1978, September) Against civil disarming. *Harper's,* pp. 28–33.

Kennedy, E. (1981, October 5). Handguns: Preferred instruments of criminals. *Congressional Record,* 1–9.

Shields, P. (1981). *Guns don't die—people do.* New York: Arbor House.

Smith, A. (1981, April). Fifty million handguns. *Esquire,* 16–18.

Uniform crime reports for the United States (1985). Washington, DC: U.S. Department of Justice.

Wright, J. D., Rossi, P. H., & Daly, K. (1983). *Under the gun.* New York: Aldine.

Questions and Suggestions for Writing

1. Reread the first and last paragraphs, and then in a sentence or two comment on the writer's strategy for opening and closing her essay.

2. On the whole, does the writer strike you as a person who is fair, or who at least is trying to be fair? Support your answer by citing specific passages that lead you to your opinion.

3. Many opponents of gun control argue that control of handguns will be only a first move down the slippery slope that leads to laws prohibiting private ownership of any sort of gun. Even if you hold this view, state as best you can the arguments that one might offer against it. (Notice that you are asked to offer arguments, not merely an assertion that it won't happen.)

4. Do you agree with Desuka that a reasonable reading of the Second Amendment reveals that individuals do not have a constitutional right to own handguns, even though the founding fathers said that "the right of the people to keep and bear arms shall not be infringed"?

5. Write a 500-word analysis of Desuka's essay (for a sample analysis see p. 88), or write a 500-word reply to her essay, responding to her main points.

6. Do you think the prohibition of handguns is feasible? Could it be enforced? Would the effort to enforce it result in worse problems than we already have? Write a 500-word essay defending or attacking the feasibility of Desuka's proposal.

Henry A. Selib

The Case against More Laws

Not long ago, Detroit enacted severely restricting antigun laws. Within a year, antigun forces all over the country were trumpeting that crimes of violence in which guns had been used showed a marked reduction in that city.

Unfortunately, the antigun crowd conveniently forgot to tell us that at the time the new laws were enacted, the Detroit police force was augmented by about 14 percent with most of the added officers assigned to the city's high crime areas. It was the police, of course, that lowered the crime rate, not the new laws, for all kinds of crime in Detroit showed reduction.

The fact is that the growing incidence of crime—especially violent crime—in our country cannot be traced to so simple a cause as the number of guns in private hands or the lack of various gun laws.

The evidence that one can connect gun ownership with crimes of   4
violence simply doesn't exist, and this forces the antigun crowd to manufacture evidence or to distort and misinterpret whatever can be used to their advantage.

They indicate, for example, that in states with strong gun laws, the crime rate is lower than in states with little restrictive legislation. Like many half truths, this too is terribly misleading. In states like New Hampshire, Iowa, Vermont, and many others where gun laws are "weaker," the per capita homicide rate is actually much lower than it is in many states where the laws are tough. Thus, we might just as well argue that the stronger the gun laws, the higher the homicide rate.

The facts are that homicide rates are high in the south (weak laws); moderately high in the big industrial states (stronger laws); and low through the north, northwest and upper New England (weak laws). There simply is no connection between a community's gun laws or lack thereof and the incidence of gun crimes.

Or take this oft-quoted canard: "Since 1900, 750,000 Americans have been killed by privately owned guns." This assertion, taken from Carl Bakal's *The Right to Bear Arms*, is based upon incomplete records and estimates, and its obvious implication is [that all of these killings are] homicides. But Bakal's figures include at least 140,000 accidents and 340,000 suicides.

The long-standing controversy between the advocates of strict gun   8
controls and those opposed has proven only that a mass of "facts" and

---

The Boston Globe *invited Henry A. Selib (1924–1989), a member of the National Rifle Association and the Massachusetts State Rifle and Pistol Association, to contribute this essay to a 1973 debate on gun control.*

statistics are easily available to those on both sides to use selectively. Indeed, sometimes the same facts are used to support both sides.

Let me show you how this can be. The antigun group asks us to note that in England, where severe, restrictive legislation against pistol ownership has existed since the turn of the century, there is little gun homicide and little crime committed with guns. This is supposed to be a compelling argument in favor of stricter gun controls here.

But in the decade from 1960 to 1970, gun crimes in England increased some 750 percent—this in a country where there aren't supposed to be any pistols in private hands. What is demonstrated forcefully in England is that in a place where guns are outlawed, only outlaws have guns.

There is a terrible irony here. Whenever some community succeeds in enacting tough gun laws, the happiest people are the criminals. They know that the law-abiding citizen will obey the new law, however much he may believe it ineffective. The criminal, of course, doesn't give up or register his guns and he knows that he can now rob or steal with the likelihood that no one will have the means to resist him.

The gun owner, the sportsman, the competition shooter, the firearms 12 collector would be willing, even anxious, to give up his hobby if someone, somewhere, could demonstrate that his community would be safer, and sharp inroads would be made in the fight against crime. Gun owners have as much respect and reverence for life as the antigunners and are just as appalled at the rate at which violent crime seems to be growing in some parts of our country.

There is no question but that some people should not—must not—have guns. Because of this, some sort of regulation is obviously necessary. Most everyone would agree that felons, addicts, morons, juveniles, alcoholics, the mentally incompetent and others in whose hands even an icepick or baseball bat becomes a deadly weapon, should be denied guns.

But unless it can be demonstrated that an individual should not have a gun, he should be issued a license and should be counseled in the proper and safe use of the weapon. Punishment for crimes committed with guns must be specially severe, but let not the average gun owner suffer because a few people cannot be trusted.

If we want to eliminate violence in our society, whether guns are involved or not, let us attack the problem as the socioeconomist problem that it is.

The nuts and the misguided will continue to kill one way or another, 16 and the criminal will continue his nefarious ways. But these are all reflections that violence and crime are abroad in the land, not that guns are the cause. Indeed, magazines like *The American Rifleman*, official publication of the National Rifle Association (NRA), often devote considerable space to stories of crimes that never happened because somebody had a gun to prevent them. The NRA has, for more than 100 years, been in the forefront of advocating strict penalties for wrongdoers who use guns; for educating citizens young and old in the proper use of guns.

Crime and violence are immense problems, and their elimination should be a major concern for all of us.

Let's not hamstring our police, and let's allocate the necessary state funds to do the job.

But don't make the gun owner a patsy for a problem he didn't create and can't control alone.

That's like reducing traffic deaths by enacting laws prohibiting 20 drinking.

Questions and Suggestions for Writing

1. Of course Selib's title tells us where he stands, but putting this aside, what word(s) in his first paragraph also indicate his position? What word in his second paragraph especially conveys his hostility to proponents of gun control?

2. Are you satisfied that Selib's argument in the second paragraph, buttressed by statistics, refutes the position of advocates of gun control? Why?

3. In paragraph 6, the author in his first sentence offers evidence, and in the second sentence draws a conclusion. Can one draw the further conclusion that *therefore* gun control is useless? Explain.

4. Assuming that the statistics in paragraph 7 are correct, do they lead you to conclude that gun control is either useless or improper? Explain.

5. Selib agrees that several categories of persons should be denied guns, and surely Desuka (p. 196) would agree. Imagine you are a legislator who supports such restrictions. Write a proposed law to achieve this end, and then write a rationale, of some 500 words, for its enactment. Do not propose anything that Selib would oppose.

DOES EVOLUTION REFUTE CREATIONISM?

Stephen Jay Gould

Evolution as Fact and Theory

Kirtley Mather, who died last year at age eighty-nine, was a pillar of both science and the Christian religion in America and one of my dearest friends. The difference of half a century in our ages evaporated before our common interests. The most curious thing we shared was a battle we each fought at the same age. For Kirtley had gone to Tennessee with Clarence Darrow to testify for evolution at the Scopes trial of 1925.[1] When I think that we are enmeshed again in the same struggle for one of the best documented, most compelling and exciting concepts in all of science, I don't know whether to laugh or cry.

According to idealized principles of scientific discourse, the arousal of dormant issues should reflect fresh data that give renewed life to abandoned notions. Those outside the current debate may therefore be excused for suspecting that creationists have come up with something new, or that evolutionists have generated some serious internal trouble. But nothing has changed; the creationists have not a single new fact or argument. Darrow and Bryan were at least more entertaining than we lesser antagonists today. The rise of creationism is politics, pure and simple; it represents one issue (and by no means the major concern) of the resurgent evangelical right. Arguments that seemed kooky just a decade ago have reentered the mainstream.

CREATIONISM IS NOT SCIENCE

The basic attack of the creationists falls apart on two general counts before we even reach the supposed factual details of their complaints

---

[1] In 1925 Tennessee made it a crime to teach evolution. In the "Monkey Trial," John Scopes was accused of teaching evolution in high school. He was defended by Clarence Darrow; the prosecution attorney was William Jennings Bryan. Scopes was convicted, and the law remained on the books until 1967, but the evolutionists considered that they had won a moral victory. [All notes are by the editors.]

A professor of geology at Harvard University, Gould (b. 1941) teaches paleontology, biology, and the history of science. Many of his essays have been collected in four highly readable books, one of which is Evolution as Fact and Theory *(1981). This essay originally appeared in* Discover Magazine, *1981.*

against evolution. First, they play upon a vernacular misunderstanding of the word "theory" to convey the false impression that we evolutionists are covering up the rotten core of our edifice. Second, they misuse a popular philosophy of science to argue that they are behaving scientifically in attacking evolution. Yet the same philosophy demonstrates that their own belief is not science, and that "scientific creationism" is therefore meaningless and self-contradictory, a superb example of what Orwell[2] called "newspeak."

In the American vernacular, "theory" often means "imperfect fact"— 4 part of a hierarchy of confidence running downhill from fact to theory to hypothesis to guess. Thus the power of the creationist argument: Evolution is "only" a theory, and intense debate now rages about many aspects of the theory. If evolution is less than a fact, and scientists can't even make up their minds about the theory, then what confidence can we have in it? Indeed, President Reagan echoed this argument before an evangelical group in Dallas when he said (in what I devoutly hope was campaign rhetoric): "Well, it is a theory. It is a scientific theory only, and it has in recent years been challenged in the world of science—that is, not believed in the scientific community to be as infallible as it once was."

Well, evolution *is* a theory. It is also a fact. And facts and theories are different things, not rungs in a hierarchy of increasing certainty. Facts are the world's data. Theories are structures of ideas that explain and interpret facts. Facts do not go away when scientists debate rival theories to explain them. Einstein's theory of gravitation replaced Newton's, but apples did not suspend themselves in midair pending the outcome. And human beings evolved from apelike ancestors whether they did so by Darwin's proposed mechanism or by some other, yet to be discovered.

Moreover, "fact" does not mean "absolute certainty." The final proofs of logic and mathematics flow deductively from stated premises and achieve certainty only because they are *not* about the empirical world. Evolutionists make no claim for perpetual truth, though creationists often do (and then attack us for a style of argument that they themselves favor). In science, "fact" can only mean "confirmed to such a degree that it would be perverse to withhold provisional assent." I suppose that apples might start to rise tomorrow, but the possibility does not merit equal time in physics classrooms.

Evolutionists have been clear about this distinction between fact and theory from the very beginning, if only because we have always acknowledged how far we are from completely understanding the mechanisms (theory) by which evolution (fact) occurred. Darwin continually emphasized the difference between his two great and separate accomplishments:

---

[2] **Orwell** George Orwell (1903–1950), English essayist and novelist. In Orwell's *1984* the rulers have designed a language called *newspeak*, in which it is impossible to think independently.

establishing the fact of evolution, and proposing a theory—natural selection—to explain the mechanism of evolution. He wrote in *The Descent of Man:* "I had two distinct objects in view; firstly, to show that species had not been separately created, and secondly, that natural selection had been the chief agent of change. . . . Hence if I have erred in . . . having exaggerated its natural selection's power. . . . I have at least, as I hope, done good service in aiding to overthrow the dogma of separate creations."

Thus Darwin acknowledged the provisional nature of natural selection while affirming the fact of evolution. The fruitful theoretical debate that Darwin initiated has never ceased. From the 1940s through the 1960s, Darwin's own theory of natural selection did achieve a temporary hegemony that it never enjoyed in his lifetime. But renewed debate characterizes our decade, and, while no biologist questions the importance of natural selection, many now doubt its ubiquity. In particular, many evolutionists argue that substantial amounts of genetic change may not be subject to natural selection and may spread through populations at random. Others are challenging Darwin's linking of natural selection with gradual, imperceptible change through all intermediary degrees; they are arguing that most evolutionary events may occur far more rapidly than Darwin envisioned.

Scientists regard debates on fundamental issues of theory as a sign of intellectual health and a source of excitement. Science is—and how else can I say it?—most fun when it plays with interesting ideas, examines their implications, and recognizes that old information may be explained in surprisingly new ways. Evolutionary theory is now enjoying this uncommon vigor. Yet amidst all this turmoil no biologist has been led to doubt the fact that evolution occurred; we are debating *how* it happened. We are all trying to explain the same thing: the tree of evolutionary descent linking all organisms by ties of genealogy. Creationists pervert and caricature this debate by conveniently neglecting the common conviction that underlies it, and by falsely suggesting that we now doubt the very phenomenon we are struggling to understand.

Using another invalid argument, creationists claim that "the dogma of separate creations," as Darwin characterized it a century ago, is a scientific theory meriting equal time with evolution in high school biology curricula. But a prevailing viewpoint among philosophers of science belies this creationist argument. Philosopher Karl Popper has argued for decades that the primary criterion of science is the falsifiability of its theories. We can never prove absolutely, but we can falsify. A set of ideas that cannot, in principle, be falsified is not science.

The entire creationist argument involves little more than a rhetorical attempt to falsify evolution by presenting supposed contradictions among its supporters. Their brand of creationism, they claim, is "scientific" because it follows the Popperian model in trying to demolish evolution. Yet Popper's argument must apply in both directions. One does not become a scientist by the simple act of trying to falsify another scientific system; one has to present an alternative system that also meets Popper's criterion—it too must be falsifiable in principle.

"Scientific creationism" is a self-contradictory, nonsense phrase precisely because it cannot be falsified. I can envision observations and experiments that would disprove any evolutionary theory I know, but I cannot imagine what potential data could lead creationists to abandon their beliefs. Unbeatable systems are dogma, not science. Lest I seem harsh or rhetorical, I quote creationism's leading intellectual, Duane Gish, Ph.D., from his recent (1978) book *Evolution? The Fossils Say No!* "By creation we mean the bringing into being by a supernatural Creator of the basic kinds of plants and animals by the process of sudden, or fiat, creation. We do not know how the Creator created, what processes He used, *for He used processes which are not now operating anywhere in the natural universe* [Gish's italics]. This is why we refer to creation as special creation. We cannot discover by scientific investigations anything about the creative processes used by the Creator." Pray tell, Dr. Gish, in the light of your last sentence, what then is "scientific" creationism?

THE FACT OF EVOLUTION

Our confidence that evolution occurred centers upon three general arguments. First, we have abundant, direct, observational evidence of evolution in action, from both the field and the laboratory. It ranges from countless experiments on change in nearly everything about fruit flies subjected to artificial selection in the laboratory to the famous British moths that turned black when industrial soot darkened the trees upon which they rest. (The moths gain protection from sharp-sighted bird predators by blending into the background.) Creationists do not deny these observations; how could they? Creationists have tightened their act. They now argue that God only created "basic kinds," and allowed for limited evolutionary meandering within them. Thus toy poodles and Great Danes come from the dog kind and moths can change color, but nature cannot convert a dog to a cat or a monkey to a man.

The second and third arguments for evolution—the case for major changes—do not involve direct observation of evolution in action. They rest upon inference, but are no less secure for that reason. Major evolutionary change requires too much time for direct observation on the scale of recorded human history. All historical sciences rest upon inference, and evolution is no different from geology, cosmology, or human history in this respect. In principle, we cannot observe processes that operated in the past. We must infer them from results that still survive: living and fossil organisms for evolution, documents and artifacts for human history, strata and topography for geology.

The second argument—that the imperfection of nature reveals evolution—strikes many people as ironic, for they feel that evolution should be most elegantly displayed in the nearly perfect adaptation expressed by some organisms—the chamber of a gull's wing, or butterflies that cannot be seen in ground litter because they mimic leaves so precisely. But perfection could be imposed by a wise creator or evolved by natural selection. Perfection covers the tracks of past history. And past history—the evidence of descent—is our mark of evolution.

Evolution lies exposed in the *imperfections* that record a history of descent. Why should a rat run, a bat fly, a porpoise swim, and I type this essay with structures built of the same bones unless we all inherited them from a common ancestor? An engineer, starting from scratch, could design better limbs in each case. Why should all the large native mammals of Australia be marsupials, unless they descended from a common ancestor isolated on this island continent? Marsupials are not "better," or ideally suited for Australia; many have been wiped out by placental mammals imported by man from other continents. This principle of imperfection extends to all historical sciences. When we recognize the etymology of September, October, November, and December (seventh, eighth, ninth, and tenth, from the Latin), we know that two additional items (January and February) must have been added to an original calendar of ten months.

The third argument is more direct: Transitions are often found in the fossil record. Preserved transitions are not common—and should not be, according to our understanding of evolution (see next section)—but they are not entirely wanting, as creationists often claim. The lower jaw of reptiles contains several bones, that of mammals only one. The nonmammalian jawbones are reduced, step by step, in mammalian ancestors until they become tiny nubbins located at the back of the jaw. The "hammer" and "anvil" bones of the mammalian ear are descendants of these nubbins. How could such a transition be accomplished? the creationists ask. Surely a bone is either entirely in the jaw or in the ear. Yet paleontologists have discovered two transitional lineages or therapsids (the so-called mammal-like reptiles) with a double jaw joint—one composed of the old quadrate and articular bones (soon to become the hammer and anvil), the other of the squamosal and dentary bones (as in modern mammals). For that matter, what better transitional form could we desire than the oldest human, *Australopithecus afarensis*, with its apelike palate, its human upright stance, and a cranial capacity larger than any ape's of the same body size but a full 1,000 cubic centimeters below ours? If God made each of the half dozen human species discovered in ancient rocks, why did he create in an unbroken temporal sequence of progressively more modern features—increasing cranial capacity, reduced face and teeth, larger body size? Did he create to mimic evolution and test our faith thereby?

AN EXAMPLE OF CREATIONIST ARGUMENT

Faced with these facts of evolution and the philosophical bankruptcy of their own position, creationists rely upon distortion and innuendo to buttress their rhetorical claim. If I sound sharp or bitter, indeed I am—for I have become a major target of these practices.

I count myself among the evolutionists who argue for a jerky, or episodic, rather than a smoothly gradual, pace of change. In 1972 my colleague Niles Eldredge and I developed the theory of punctuated equilibrium [*Discover*, October]. We argued that two outstanding facts of the fossil record—geologically "sudden" origin of new species and failure to change thereafter (stasis)—reflect the predictions of evolutionary theory, not the imperfections of the fossil record. In most theories, small isolated populations are the source of new species, and the process of speciation takes thousands or tens of thousands of years. This amount of time, so long when measured against our lives, is a geological microsecond. It represents much less than 1 percent of the average life span for a fossil invertebrate species—more than 10 million years. Large, widespread, and well-established species, on the other hand, are not expected to change very much. We believe that the inertia of large populations explains the stasis of most fossil species over millions of years.

We proposed the theory of punctuated equilibrium largely to provide 20 a different explanation for pervasive trends in the fossil record. Trends, we argued, cannot be attributed to gradual transformation within lineages, but must arise from the differential success of certain kinds of species. A trend, we argued, is more like climbing a flight of stairs (punctuations and stasis) than rolling up an inclined plane.

Since we proposed punctuated equilibria to explain trends, it is infuriating to be quoted again and again by creationists—whether through design or stupidity, I do not know—as admitting that the fossil record includes no transitional forms. Transitional forms are generally lacking at the species level, but are abundant between larger groups. The evolution from reptiles to mammals, as mentioned earlier, is well documented. Yet a pamphlet entitled "Harvard Scientists Agree Evolution Is a Hoax" states: "The facts of punctuated equilibrium which Gould and Eldredge . . . are forcing Darwinists to swallow fit the picture that Bryan insisted on, and which God has revealed to us in the Bible."

Continuing the distortion, several creationists have equated the theory of punctuated equilibrium with a caricature of the beliefs of Richard Goldschmidt, a great early geneticist. Goldschmidt argued, in a famous book published in 1940, that new groups can arise all at once through major mutations. He referred to these suddenly transformed creatures as "hopeful monsters." (I am attracted to some aspects of the noncaricatured version, but Goldschmidt's theory still has nothing to do with punctuated equilibrium.) Creationist Luther Sunderland talks of the "punctuated equilibrium hopeful monster theory" and tells his hopeful readers that "it amounts to tacit admission that antievolutionists are correct in asserting there is no fossil evidence supporting the theory that all life is connected to a common ancestor." Duane Gish writes, "According to Goldschmidt, and now apparently according to Gould, a reptile laid an egg from which the first bird, feathers and all, was produced." Any evolutionist who believed such nonsense would rightly be laughed off the intellectual stage; yet the only theory that could ever envision such a scenario for the evolution of birds is creationism—God acts in the egg.

CONCLUSION

I am both angry at and amused by the creationists; but mostly I am deeply sad. Sad for many reasons. Sad because so many people who respond to creationist appeals are troubled for the right reason, but venting their anger at the wrong target. It is true that scientists have often been dogmatic and elitist. It is true that we have often allowed the white-coated, advertising image to represent us—"Scientists say that Brand X cures bunions ten times faster than. . . ." We have not fought it adequately because we derive benefits from appearing as a new priesthood. It is also true that faceless bureaucratic state power intrudes more and more into our lives and removes choices that should belong to individuals and communities. I can understand that requiring that evolution be taught in the schools might be seen as one more insult on all these grounds. But the culprit is not, and cannot be, evolution or any other fact of the natural world. Identify and fight your legitimate enemies by all means, but we are not among them.

I am sad because the practical result of this brouhaha will not be 24 expanded coverage to include creationism (that would also make me sad), but the reduction or excision of evolution from high school curricula. Evolution is one of the half dozen "great ideas" developed by science. It speaks to the profound issues of genealogy that fascinate all of us—the "roots" phenomenon writ large. Where did we come from? Where did life arise? How did it develop? How are organisms related? It forces us to think, ponder, and wonder. Shall we deprive millions of this knowledge and once again teach biology as a set of dull and unconnected facts, without the thread that weaves diverse material into a supple unity?

But most of all I am saddened by a trend I am just beginning to discern among my colleagues. I sense that some now wish to mute the healthy debate about theory that has brought new life to evolutionary biology. It provides grist for creationist mills, they say, even if only by distortion. Perhaps we should lie low and rally round the flag of strict Darwinism, at least for the moment—a kind of old-time religion on our part.

But we should borrow another metaphor and recognize that we too have to tread a straight and narrow path, surrounded by roads to perdition. For if we ever begin to suppress our search to understand nature, to quench our own intellectual excitement in a misguided effort to present a united front where it does not and should not exist, then we are truly lost.

Questions and Suggestions for Writing

1. What is the point of Gould's first sentence? Of his first paragraph? That is, what is he seeking to do in this paragraph?

2. In his second paragraph Gould says that "the rise of creationism is politics, pure and simple." When you first came across this sentence, did you believe it? By the end of the essay has Gould convinced you of its truth?

3. In paragraph 5 Gould says that evolution "is also a fact," and he goes on to say that "facts do not go away when scientists debate rival theories to explain them." He cites falling apples, and concludes the paragraph by saying, "And human beings evolved from apelike ancestors whether they did so by Darwin's proposed mechanism or by some other, yet to be discovered." Do you find his evidence compelling? Why?

4. Gould says that evolution is a "theory" and is also a "fact," and he defines both words. Now, Gould is a "teacher" and he is also a "writer"; one thing can of course have two (or more) attributes. But does Gould's discussion make it entirely clear to you that something can be both a fact and a theory? If so, write a paragraph explaining the point to someone who finds Gould a bit unclear. If not, write a paragraph explaining why the matter is confusing.

5. Gould begins paragraph 12 by saying, "'Scientific creationism' is a self-contradictory, nonsense phrase." A phrase or doctrine is self-contradictory if and only if it can be put into the form: p and not -p (where p is some sentence expressing the phrase or doctrine, and not -p denies p. For example: "This is a cat and is not a cat.") Can you restate the position of scientific creationism in this form? Do you believe that Gish (below) would assert both parts of this contradiction, or not?

6. The first of Gould's three arguments for evolution is, he says, based on "abundant, direct, observational evidence of evolution." Read the reply to Gould's essay by Gish (below) and answer these questions: Does Gish concede that these pieces of evidence do indeed exist? How does Gish think they bear on the controversy between the creationist and the evolutionist?

7. In his second argument Gould mentions "imperfections." What are they, exactly? In a paragraph explain why Gould concedes that this argument does not

involve "direct observation of evolution in action" but instead "rest[s] upon inference."

8. Gould's third argument involves "transitional forms." Does he give any examples of such forms? Why are they important in the controversy over evolution? How does Gould apparently use his "theory of punctuated equilibrium" to account for the rarity of such forms?

9. In a paragraph analyze Gould's final paragraph. What makes it effective (or ineffective) as a final paragraph?

Duane T. Gish

A Reply to Gould

To the Editors:

In his essay "Evolution as Fact and Theory" [May 1981], Stephen Jay Gould states that creationists claim creation is a scientific theory. This is a false accusation. Creationists have repeatedly stated that neither creation nor evolution is a scientific theory (and each is equally religious). Gould in fact quotes from my book, *Evolution? The Fossils Say No!*, in which I state that both concepts of origins fail the criteria of a scientific theory.

Gould uses the argument of Sir Karl Popper that the primary criterion of a scientific theory is its potential falsifiability, and then uses this sword to strike down creation as a scientific theory, Fine. Gould surely realizes, however, that this is a two-edged sword. Sir Karl has used it to strike down evolution as a scientific theory, stating that Darwinism is not a testable scientific theory, but a metaphysical research program (*Unended Quest*, 1976).

Another criterion that must apply to a scientific theory is the ability to repeatedly observe the events, processes, or properties used to support the theory. There were obviously no human witnesses to the origin of the universe, the origin of life, or in fact to the origin of a single living thing, and even if evolution were occurring today, the process would require far

---

Duane T. Gish (b. 1921) holds a Ph.D. in biochemistry from the University of California, Berkeley. He has carried out biochemical and biomedical research at Cornell University and at Berkeley, and now is Associate Director of the Institute for Creation Research and Professor of Natural Science at Christian Heritage College in San Diego. An active lecturer and writer, his book titled Evolution: The Fossils Say No! *is widely regarded as a standard presentation of creationism.*

Reprinted here is a letter he wrote to the magazine Discover, *responding to an article by Stephen Jay Gould published in an earlier issue. (Gould's article precedes Gish's on p. 204.) The title of Gish's letter is ours.*

in excess of all recorded history to produce sufficient change to document evolution. Evolution has not and cannot be observed any more than creation.

Gould states, "Theories are structures of ideas that explain and interpret facts." Certainly, creation and evolution can both be used as theories in that sense. Furthermore, one or the other must be true, since ultimately they are the only two alternatives we have to explain origins.

Gould charges creationists with dogma. Please note, however, Gould's own dogmatism. His use of the term "fact of evolution" appears throughout his paper. Furthermore, Gould seems to have a strange view of the relationship of fact and theory. He says, "Facts do not go away when scientists debate rival theories to explain them. Einstein's theory of gravitation replaced Newton's, but apples did not suspend themselves in midair pending the outcome. And human beings evolved from apelike ancestors whether they did so by Darwin's proposed mechanism or by some other, yet to be discovered." Well, evolutionists believe indeed that both apes and hydrogen evolved into people (the latter just took longer), but neither has ever been observed. All of us, however, have seen apples fall off trees.

Gould's "fact of evolution" immediately deteriorates into "three general arguments," two of which quickly deteriorate further into mere inferences. Gould's only direct observational evidence for evolution (his first argument) is experiments on fruit flies and observations on peppered moths in Britain. Neither, of course, offers evidence for evolution, for from beginning to end fruit flies remain fruit flies and peppered moths remain peppered moths. The task of the evolutionist is to answer the question how moths came to be moths, tigers came to be tigers, and people came to be people. In fact, this type of evidence is what Gould himself has sought in recent years to discredit as an explanation for the origin of higher categories.

Gould's second argument is an inference based on *imperfections*. He mentions homologous structures as evidence for evolution from a common ancestor. Gould should know first that many, if not most, homologous structures are not even possessed by the assumed common ancestor and secondly that the actual evidence (particularly that from genetics) is so contradictory to what is predicted by evolution that Sir Gavin de Beer titled his Oxford biology reader (1971) on that subject *Homology, an Unsolved Problem*. Sir Gavin, along with S. C. Harland, felt compelled to suggest that organs, such as the eye, remain unchanged while the genes governing these structures become wholly altered during the evolutionary process! The whole Darwinian edifice collapses if that is true.

Gould's third argument is based on inferences drawn from the fossil record. The fossil record, with its "explosive appearance" (the term often used by geologists) of the highly complex creatures found in Cambrian rocks, for which no ancestors have been found, and the systematic absence of transitional forms between all higher categories of plants and animals, has proven an embarrassment to evolutionists ever since Darwin. Gould's argument, however, is that "transitions are often found in the fossil record." That is surprising indeed, since he seems intent in other publications to convey just the opposite opinion.

For example, in his 1977 *Natural History* essay "The Return of Hopeful Monsters," after recounting the derision meted out to Richard Goldschmidt for his hopeful-monster mechanism of evolution, Gould says, "I do, however, predict that during the next decade Goldschmidt will be largely vindicated in the world of evolutionary biology." Why? Among others, "The fossil record with its abrupt transitions offers no support for gradual change." A bit later: "All paleontologists know that the fossil record contains precious little in the way of intermediate forms; transitions between major groups are characteristically abrupt." Many similar statements by Gould and others could be cited.

Finally, Gould assails Sunderland and me for linking him to a hopeful-monster mechanism whereby a reptile laid an egg and a bird was hatched. He says an evolutionist who believed such nonsense would rightly be laughed off the intellectual stage. Let's see, then, what Goldschmidt really did say. In *The Material Basis of Evolution*, Goldschmidt says, "I need only quote Schindewolf (1936), the most progressive investigator known to me. He shows by examples from fossil material that the major evolutionary advances must have taken place in single large steps. . . . He shows that the many missing links in the paleontological record are sought for in vain because they have never existed: 'The first bird hatched from a reptilian egg.'" By Gould's own testimony, then, Goldschmidt, Gould's hero of the next decade, should be laughed off the intellectual stage.

Along with thousands of other creation scientists, in view of a wealth of evidence from thermodynamics, probability relationships, biology, molecular biology, paleontology, and cosmology, I have become convinced that evolution theory is scientifically untenable and that the concept of direct, special creation is a far more credible explanation.

Duane T. Gish
Vice President
Institute for Creation Research
El Cajon, California

Questions and Suggestions for Writing

1. In his opening paragraph, Gish claims that evolution is "religion." What do you think he means by this judgment? Do you agree with it? What evidence do you think Gish might cite to defend this claim? (Read the preceding essay by Gould before trying to answer this question.)

2. Gish describes Gould's explanation of evolution as an account that "immediately deteriorates" from "facts" to "arguments." What impression is this

language intended to create in the reader's mind? Is it a fair impression of Gould's actual essay?

3. Both Gish and Gould appeal to "the criterion of demarcation" proposed by the philosopher Sir Karl Popper. According to this criterion, any theory, doctrine, or hypothesis is scientific (as opposed to nonscientific) if and only if it is possible that some experiment or other observational evidence could *dis*confirm or falsify the theory. Reexamine Gould's three arguments for evolution. Can you imagine any experiences or experiments that might disconfirm or falsify evolution as Gould presents it?

4. In his third paragraph Gish says, "Evolution has not and cannot be observed any more than creation." Judging from Gould's essay (p. 204), would Gould agree? Support your answer with evidence from Gould's essay.

5. In paragraph 4 Gish asserts that either evolution or creation "must be true." Why does he assert this judgment? Is he right?

6. In paragraph 8 Gish expresses surprise at Gould's assertion that "'transitions are often found in the fossil record,'" because in some of Gould's other publications he emphasizes the enormous gaps in the fossil record. In his next paragraph Gish quotes Gould. Do the quotations seem to you hopelessly at odds with the opinions Gould expresses in the essay that we reprint? Why?

7. Reread Gish's closing paragraph. What effect is it intended to have on the reader?

8. We have called attention to Gish's statement, in his first paragraph, that creationists do not claim creationism is a scientific theory. Yet in his final paragraph Gish speaks of himself as one among "thousands" of "creation scientists." Is there a contradiction here?

6

Pro and Con: Longer Debates

Allan Bloom

Our Listless Universities

I

    I begin with my conclusion: students in our best universities do not believe in anything, and those universities are doing nothing about it, nor can they. An easygoing American kind of nihilism has descended upon us, a nihilism without terror of the abyss. The great questions—God, freedom, and immortality, according to Kant—hardly touch the young. And

---

Allan Bloom (b. 1930) is a professor of the Committee on Social Thought and the College at the University of Chicago. He has translated Plato's Republic *and Rousseau's* Émile, *and is the author of* Shakespeare's Politics. *He later amplified these remarks in* The Closing of the American Mind *(1988), a book that for many months was a best-seller. The article reprinted here is from the* National Review, *1982.*

the universities, which should encourage the quest for the clarification of such questions, are the very source of the doctrine which makes that quest appear futile.

The heads of the young are stuffed with a jargon derived from the despair of European thinkers, gaily repackaged for American consumption and presented as the foundation for a pluralistic society. That jargon becomes a substitute for real experiences and instinct; one suspects that modern thought has produced an artificial soul to replace the old one supplied by nature, which was full of dangerous longings, loves, hates, and awes. The new soul's language consists of terms like *value, ideology, self, commitment, identity*—every word derived from recent German philosophy, and each carrying a heavy baggage of dubious theoretical interpretation of which its users are blissfully unaware. They take such language to be as unproblematic and immediate as night and day. It now constitutes our peculiar common sense.

The new language subtly injects into our system the perspective of "do your own thing" as the only plausible way of life. I know that sounds vaguely passé, a remnant leftover from the sixties. But it is precisely the routinization of the passions of the sixties that is the core of what is going on now, just as the sixties were merely a radicalization of earlier tendencies.

The American regime has always attempted to palliate extreme beliefs 4
that lead to civil strife, particularly religious beliefs. The members of sects had to obey the laws and be loyal to the Constitution; if they did so, others had to leave them alone. To make things work, it was thought helpful that men's beliefs be moderated. There was a conscious, if covert, effort to weaken religious fervor by assigning religion to the realm of opinion as opposed to knowledge. But everyone had to have an intense belief in the right of freedom of religion; the existence of that natural right was not to be treated as a matter of opinion.

The insatiable appetite for freedom to live as one pleases thrives on this aspect of modern democratic thought. The expansion of the area exempt from legitimate regulation is effected by contracting the claims to moral and political knowledge. It appears that full freedom can be attained only when there is no such knowledge. The effective way to defang oppressors is to persuade them that they are ignorant of the good. There are no absolutes: freedom is absolute.

A doctrine that gives equal rights to any way of life whatsoever has the double advantage of licensing one's own way of life and of giving one a democratic good conscience. The very lack of morality is a morality and permits what Saul Bellow has called "easy virtue," a mixture of egotism and high-mindedness. Now, in feeling as well as in speech, a large segment of our young are open, open to every "lifestyle." But the fatal consequence of this openness has been the withering of their belief in their own way of life and of their capacity to generate goals. The palliation of beliefs culminates in pallid belief. A soul which esteems indiscriminately must be an artificial soul, and that, to repeat, is what we are coming near to constituting, not by some inevitable historical process but by a conscious educational project. This project masquerades as the essential democratic theory without which we would collapse into tyranny or the war of all prejudices against all. Its premise is that truth itself must be prejudice or at least treated as such.

The tendency toward indiscriminateness—the currently negative connotation of the word *discrimination* tells us much—is apparently perennial in democracy. The need to subordinate the more refined sensibilities to a common denominator and the unwillingness to order the soul's desires according to their rank conduce to easygoingness. The democratic ethos obscures the reason for the desirability of such self-mastery. This is the moral problem of democracy and why fortuitous external necessities like war or poverty seem to bring out the best in us. Plato describes the natural bent of the democratic man thus:

> He . . . also lives along day by day, gratifying the desire that occurs to him, at one time drinking and listening to the flute, at another downing water and reducing; now practicing gymnastics, and again idling and neglecting everything; and sometimes spending his time as though he were occupied with philosophy. Often he engages in politics and, jumping up, says and does whatever chances to come to him; and if he ever admires any soldiers, he turns in that direction; and if it's moneymakers, in that one. And there is neither order nor necessity in his life, but calling this life sweet, free, and blessed he follows it throughout.

This account is easily recognizable when applied to the middle-class 8 youth who attend America's top colleges and universities. But Plato's description omits a more sinister element in our situation. Plato's young man believes that each of the lives he follows is really good, at least when he follows it. His problem is that he cannot keep his mind made up. Our young person, by contrast, is always plagued by a gnawing doubt as to whether the activity he undertakes is worth anything, whether this end is not just another "value," an illusion that men once believed in but which our "historical consciousness" reveals as only a cultural phenomenon. There are a thousand and one such goals; they are not believed in because they exist, they exist because one believes in them. Since we now know this, we can no longer believe. The veil of illusion has been torn away forever. The trendy language for this alleged experience is *demystification* or *demythologization*. This teaching now has the status of dogma. It leads to a loss of immediacy in all experience and a suspicion that every way of life is a "role." The substitution of the expression "lifestyle," which we can change at will, for the good life, the rational quest for which is the origin of philosophy, tells the story. That is what I mean by nihilism, and this nihilism has resulted from a questionable doctrine that we seem no longer able to question.

All of us who are under sixty know something about this doctrine and its transmission, for since the thirties it is what the schools have been teaching. For fifty years the only spiritual substance they have been trying to convey is openness, the disdain for the ethnocentric. Of course, they have also been teaching the three Rs, but their moral and intellectual energy has been turned almost exclusively in this direction. Schools once produced citizens, or gentlemen, or believers; now they produce the unprejudiced. A university professor confronting entering freshmen can be almost certain that most of them will know that there are no absolutes and that one cannot say that one culture is superior to another. They can scarcely believe that someone might seriously argue the contrary; the attempt to do so meets either self-satisfied smiles at something so old-fashioned or outbursts of anger at a threat to decent respect for other human beings. In the thirties this teaching was actually warring against some real prejudices of race, religion, or nation; but what remains now is mostly the means for weakening conviction when convictions have disappeared.

The doctrine of cultural relativism did not emerge from the study of cultures. It was a philosophic doctrine that gave a special interpretation of the meaning of culture and had a special political attractiveness. It could appeal to the taste for diversity as opposed to our principled homogeneity. All kinds of people climbed aboard—disaffected Southern snobs who had never accepted the Declaration and the Constitution anyhow, Stalinists who wanted us to love Soviet tyranny without being too explicit about it, and similar types. No choices would have to be made. We could have the charms of old cultures, of what one now calls roots, along with democratic liberties. All that was required was an education making other ways attractive and disenchanting one's own. It is not so much the knowledge of other cultures that is important, but the consciousness that one loves one's own way because it is one's own, not because it is good. People must understand that they are what they are and what they believe only because of accidents of time and place.

The equality of values seemed to be a decisive step in the march of equality. So sure were our social scientists of the truth and vigor of democracy that they did not even dimly perceive what Weber knew, that his view undermined democracy, which stands or falls with reason. Only democracy traces all its authority to reason; other kinds of regimes can more or less explicitly appeal to other sources. When we talk about the West's lack of conviction or lack of will, we show that we are beginning to recognize what has happened to us. Exhortations to believe, however, are useless. It is only by thinking ideas through again that we can determine whether our reason can any longer give assent to our principles.

But this serious reconsideration is not taking place in the universities.   12

II

Today a young person does not generally go off to the university with the expectation of having an intellectual adventure, of discovering strange new worlds, of finding out what the comprehensive truth about man is. This is partly because he thinks he already knows, partly because he thinks such truth unavailable. And the university does not try to persuade him that he is coming to it for the purpose of being liberally educated, at least in any meaningful sense of the term—to study how to be free, to be able to think for himself. The university has no vision, no view of what a human being must know in order to be considered educated. Its general purpose is lost amid the incoherent variety of special purposes that have accreted within it. Such a general purpose may be vague and undemonstrable, but for just this reason it requires the most study. The meaning of life is unclear, but that is why we must spend our lives clarifying it rather than letting the question go. The university's function is to remind students of the importance and urgency of the question and give them the means to pursue it. Universities do have other responsibilities, but this should be their highest priority.

They have, however, been so battered by modern doctrines, social demands, the requirements of the emancipated specialties, that they have tacitly agreed not to open Pandora's box and start a civil war. They provide a general framework that keeps the peace but they lack a goal of their own.

When the arriving student surveys the scene, he sees a bewildering variety of choices. The professional schools beckon him by providing him with an immediate motive: a lucrative and prestigious livelihood guaranteed by simply staying in the university to the conclusion of training. Medicine and law were always such possibilities; with the recent addition of the MBA, the temptation has radically increased. If the student decides to take this route, liberal education is practically over for him.

If he first turns his eye to what was traditionally thought to be the center of the university, he will confront—aside from a few hot programs like black studies, native studies, women's studies, which are largely exercises in consciousness-raising—the natural sciences, the social sciences, and the humanities. 16

The natural sciences thrive, full of good conscience and good works. But they are ever more specialized and ever more separate from the rest of the university; they have no need of it. They don't object to liberal education, if it doesn't get in the way of their research and training. And they have nothing to say, even about themselves or their role in the whole human picture, let alone about the kinds of questions that agitated Descartes, Newton, and Leibniz. Their results speak for themselves, but they do not say quite enough.

The social sciences are the source of much useful research and information, but they are long past the first effervescence of their Marxist-

Freudian-Weberian period. Then they expected to find a new and more scientific way to answer the old questions of philosophy. Such hopes and claims quietly disappeared from the scene during the past fifteen years. Their solid reasons for existence are in specialized study of interest rates, Iranian politics, or urban trends. Practically no economist conceives of doing what Adam Smith did, and the few who try produce petty and trivial stuff. The case is pretty much the same for the other social sciences. They are theoretically barren, and the literature read and used by them is mostly ephemera of the last fifty years.

The remainder is to be found in the humanities, the smallest, least funded, most dispirited part of the university. The humanities are the repository of the books that are at the foundation of our religion, our philosophy, our politics, our science, as well as our art. Here, if anywhere, one ought to find the means to doubt what seems most certain. Only here are the questions about knowledge, about the good life, about God and love and death, at home in the university. If, however, one looks at the humanistic side of the campus, one finds a hodgepodge of disciplines, not integrally related with one another and without much sense of common purpose. The books are divided up among language departments, according to the largely accidental fact of the language in which they were written. Such departments have as their primary responsibility the teaching of the language in question (a very depressing responsibility now that languages have fallen into particular disfavor with students).

Humanists in general are the guardians of great books, but rarely take 20 seriously the naive notion that these books might contain the truth which has escaped us. Yet without the belief that from Plato one might learn how to live or that from Shakespeare one might get the deepest insight into the passions and the virtues, no one who is not professionally obligated will take them seriously. Try as they may, the humanities will fail to interest if they do not teach *the truth*, even as natural and social science are supposed to do. To present the great writers and artists as representatives of cultures or examples of the way thought is related to society, or in any of the other modes common today, is to render them uninteresting to the healthy intellect. The comprehensive questions have their natural home in the humanities, but it is there that the historical-cultural doubt about the possibility of answering them is most acute. Professors of humanities more than any others wonder whether they have a truth to tell.

Philosophy should, of course, provide the focus for the most needful study. But it is just one department among many and, in the democracy of the specialists, it no longer has the will to insist that it is the queen of the sciences. Moreover, in most philosophy departments the study of the classic texts is not central. Professors "do" their own philosophy and do not try to pose the questions as they were posed by the old writers. This is especially the case for the dominant school of thought in the United States, the Oxford school.

Of all university members, humanists have the least self-confidence. The students are abandoning them, and they have difficulty speaking to the concerns of the age. They fear they may have to huckster—if they are not already doing so—in order to keep afloat. In their heart of hearts many doubt that they have much to say. After all, most of the writers they promote can be convicted of elitism and sexism, the paramount sins of the day.

There are, to be sure, many dedicated individuals in the humanities who know what needs to be done and can draw students' attention to the impoverished state of their experience and show them that great texts address their concerns. But the endeavor of these professors is a lonely one with little corporate resonance. The students are not reading the same books and addressing the same questions, so that their common social life cannot be affected by a common intellectual life.

It should be added that the humanities are also the center of some of the fastest selling intellectual items of the day—structuralism, deconstructionism, and Marxist humanism. The members of these schools— particularly rampant in comparative literature—do read books and talk big ideas. In that sense they are the closest thing to what the university should be about. The problem with them, and all of them are alike in this respect, is that the books are not taken seriously on their own grounds but are used as vile bodies for the sake of demonstrating theses brought to them by the interpreters. They know what they are looking for before they begin. Their approaches are ultimately derived from Marx or Nietzsche, whose teachings are tacitly taken to be true.

It is small wonder that the student is bewildered about what it means to be educated. The new liberal education requirements some universities are instituting are little more than tours of what is being done in the various workshops. To be sure, they always add on a course requirement, in a non-Western civilization or culture, but that is just another bit of demagogy serving the indoctrination of openness. Serious physicists would never require a course in non-Western physics. Culture and civilization are irrelevant to the truth. One finds it where one can. Only if truth is relative to culture does this make sense. But, once again, this is our dogma, accepted for covert political reasons. This dogma is the greatest enemy of liberal education. It undermines the unity of man, our common humanity in the intellect, which makes the university possible and permits it to treat man as simply without distinction.

III

Three conclusions have forced themselves on me about students, their characters and ways, conclusions that have to do with their education and their educability. They are not scientific generalizations based on survey research, but they are the result of long observation of, and careful listening to, young people in our better universities by one who is intensely interested in their real openness, their openness to higher learning.

1. **Books.** They are no longer an important part of the lives of students. "Information" is important, but profound and beautiful books are not where they go for it. They have no books that are companions and friends to which they look for counsel, companionship, inspiration, or pleasure. They do not expect to find in them sympathy for, or clarification of, their inmost desires and experiences. The link between the classic books and the young, which persisted for so long and in so many circumstances, and is the only means of connecting the here and the now with the always, this link has been broken. The Bible and Plutarch have ceased to be a part of the soul's furniture, an incalculable loss of fullness and awareness of which the victims are unaware.

The loss of the taste for reading has been blamed on television, the 28 universal villain of social critics. But lack of reverence for antiquity and contempt for tradition are democratic tendencies. It should be the university's business to provide a corrective to these tendencies; however, I believe that the universities are most to blame for them. After all, they taught the schoolteachers. For a very long time now the universities have been preoccupied with abstract modern schools of thought that were understood to have surpassed all earlier thought and rendered it obsolete. And their primary concern has been to indoctrinate social attitudes, to "socialize," rather than to educate. The old books are still around, but one "knows" that they contain mere opinions, no better than any others. The result is true philistinism, a withering of taste and a conformity to what is prevalent in the present. It means the young have no heroes, no objects of aspiration. It is all both relaxing and boring, a soft imprisonment.

2. **Music.** While I am not certain about the effects of television, I am quite certain about those of music. Many students do not watch much television while in college, but they do listen to music. From the time of puberty, and earlier, music has been the food of their souls. This is the audio generation. And classical music is dead, at least as a common taste. Rock is all there is.

There is now one culture for everyone, in music as in language. It is a music that moves the young powerfully and immediately. Its beat goes to the depth of their souls and inarticulately expresses their inarticulate longings. Those longings are sexual, and the beat appeals almost exclusively to that. It caters to kiddy sexuality, at best to puppy love. The first untutored feelings of adolescents are taken over by this music and given a form and a satisfaction. The words make little difference; they may be explicitly sexual, or sermons in favor of nuclear disarmament, or even religious—the motor of it all is eroticism. The youngsters know this perfectly well, even if their parents do not.

Rock music caused a great evolution in the relations between parents and children. Its success was the result of an amazing cooperation among lust, art, and commercial shrewdness. Without parents realizing it, their children were liberated from them. The children had money to spend. The record companies recognized as much and sold them music appealing to their secret desires. Never before was a form of art (however questionable) directed to so young an audience. This art gave children's feelings public respectability. The education of children had escaped their parents, no matter how hard they tried to prevent it. The most powerful formative influence on children between twelve and eighteen is not the school, not the church, not the home, but rock music and all that goes with it. It is not an elevating but a leveling influence. The children have as their heroes banal, drug- and sex-ridden guttersnipes who foment rebellion not only against parents but against all noble sentiments. This is the emotional nourishment they ingest in these precious years. It is the real junk food.

One thing I have no difficulty teaching students today is the passage in 32 the *Republic* where Socrates explains that control over music is control over character and that the rhythm and the melody are more powerful than the words. They do not especially like Socrates' views on music, but they understand perfectly what he is about and the importance of the issue.

3. **Sex.** No change has been so rapid, so great, and so surprising as the change in the last twenty years concerning sex and the relations between the sexes. Young people of college age are very much affected by the sexual passion and preoccupied with love, marriage, and the family (to use an old formula that is now painfully inadequate to what is really meant). It is an age of excitement and uncertainty, and much of the motivation for study and reflection of a broader sort comes from the will to adorn and clarify erotic longings.

It is, however, in this domain that the listless, nihilistic mood has its practical expression and most affects the life of the students. The prevailing atmosphere deprives sex of seriousness as well as of charm. And, what is more, it makes it very difficult to think about sex. In a permissive era, when it is almost respectable to think and even do the deeds of Oedipus, shame and guilt have taken refuge in a new redoubt and made certain things unthinkable. Terror grips man at the thought he might be sexist. For all other tastes there is sympathy and support in universities. Sexism, whatever it may mean, is unpardonable.

The great change in sexual behavior has taken place in two stages. The first is what was called the sexual revolution. This meant simply that pre- and extramarital sex became much more common, and the various penalties for promiscuity were either much reduced or disappeared. In the middle sixties I noticed that very nice students who previously would have hidden their affairs abandoned all pretense. They would invite their professors to dine in apartments where they lived together and not hesitate to give expression to physical intimacy in a way that even married couples would rarely do before their peers.

This kind of change, of course, implied a very different way of thinking about things. Desire always existed, but it used to war with conscience, shame, and modesty. These now had to be deprecated as prejudices, as pointing to nothing beyond themselves. Religious and philosophic moral teachings that supported such sentiments became old hat, and a certain materialism which justified bodily satisfaction seemed more plausible.

The world looks very different than it once did to young people entering college. The kinds of questions they ask, and the sensitivities they bring to these fresh circumstances, are vastly altered. The tension of high expectation has been relaxed; there is much they no longer have to find out. A significant minority of students couple off very early and live together throughout college with full awareness that they intend to go their separate ways afterward. They are just taking care of certain needs in a sensible way. There is, for a member of an older generation, an incomprehensible slackness of soul in all this. Certainly the adventurousness of such people, who are half-married but without the moral benefits of responsibility, is lamed. There is nothing wild, Dionysian, searching, in our promiscuity. It has a dull, sterilized, scientific character.

One must add that an increasing number of students come from divorced families and include in their calculation the possibility or the likelihood of divorce in their own future. The possibility of separation is not a neutral fact, allowing people to stay or go; it encourages separation because it establishes a psychology of separateness.

The result is inevitably egotism, not because the individuals are evil or naturally more prone to selfishness than those of another era. If there is no other thing to be attached to, the desires concerning ourselves are ever present. This tendency is particularly pronounced in an age when political ties are weak. People can hardly be blamed for not being attached when there is nothing that calls forth attachment. There can be no doubt that the sexual revolution plays a great role in dissolving the bonds founded on sexual relationships. What is not sufficiently understood is that in modern society there is little else that can be the basis for moral association. There is a repulsive lack of self-knowledge in those who attack the "nuclear family" and are rhapsodic about the "extended family" and real "community." Looseness is thus made into an ethical critique of our society. The "extended family" is no more possible in our time or consonant with our principles than is feudalism, while the "nuclear family" is still a viable alternative, but one that needs support in theory and practice. It provides a natural basis for connectedness. One can give it up, but one has to know the price. There is simply nothing else that is generally operative in society at large.

But even more powerful than all of the above changes are the effects of feminism, which is still early in its career of reform and is the second stage of the great change of which I am speaking. The theme is too vast to treat properly, but one can say that it, much more than the sexual revolution, takes place on the level of thought rather than that of instinct. Consciousness must be altered. Women have been exploited and misused throughout the entire past, and only now can one find out their real potential. We are on the threshold of a whole new world and a whole new understanding. And Right and Left are in large measure united on the issue. There is an almost universal agreement, among those who count for university students, that feminism is simply justified as is.

The degree of common agreement comes home to me when I teach the Socrates fantasy in the *Republic* about the abolition of the difference between the sexes. Twenty years ago it was an occasion of laughter, and my problem was to get students to take it seriously. Today it seems perfectly commonplace, and students take it all too seriously, failing to catch the irony. They do not note the degree to which Socrates acts as though men and women have no bodies and lightly give up all the things that are one's own, particularly those one loves—parents, spouses, children. All of them are connected with the bisexuality of the species. In doing this, Socrates shows the ambiguity of our nature and the degree of tension between our common humanity and our sexual separateness. The balance between the two is always fraught with difficulties. One must decide which has primacy; and this decision must be made in full awareness of the loss entailed by it. Our students no longer understand this.

It is here that a great difference between the situation of women and that of men comes to light. Women today have, to use our new talk, an agenda. They want to have the opportunity to pursue careers, and they want to find ways to reconcile this goal with having families. Also, it is their movement, so they are involved and excited, have much to talk about. The men, on the other hand, are waiting to be told what is on the agenda and ready to conform to its demands. There is little inclination to resist. All the principles have been accepted; it only remains to see how to live by them. Women are to have careers just as do men and, if there is to be marriage, the wife's career is not to be sacrificed to the man's; home and children are a shared responsibility; when and if there are to be children is up to the woman, and the decision to terminate or complete a pregnancy is a woman's right. Above all, women are not to have a "role" imposed on them. They have a right of self-definition. The women were the victims and must be the leaders in their recovery from victimization. The men, as they themselves see it, have to be understanding and flexible. There are no guidelines; each case is individual. One can't know what to expect. Openness, again, is the virtue.

The result is a desexualization of life, all the while that a lot of sexual activity is going on, and a reduction of the differences between the sexes. Anger and spiritedness are definitely out. Men and women in universities frequently share common dwellings and common facilities. Sex is all right, but it creates a problem. There are no forms in which it is to express itself, and it is a reminder of differentiation where there is supposed to be none. It is difficult to shift from the mode of sameness into that of romance. Therefore advances are tentative, nobody is quite sure where they are to begin, and men's fear of stereotyping women is ever-present. It is love that is being sacrificed, for it makes woman into an object to be possessed. Dating is almost a thing of the past. Men and women are together in what is supposed to be an easy camaraderie. If coupling takes place, it must not disturb the smooth surface of common human endeavor. Above all: no courtship or courtliness. Now there is friendship, mutual respect, communication; realism without foolish fabulation or hopes. One wonders what primal feelings and desires are pushed down beneath the pat uniformity of the speech they almost all use, a self-congratulatory speech which affirms that they are the first to have discovered how to relate to other people.

This conviction has as its first consequence that all old books are no longer relevant, because their authors were sexists (if they happened to be women, they were maimed by living in sexist society). There is little need of the commissars who are popping up all over the place to make the point that Eve, Cleopatra, Emma Bovary, and Anna Karenina are parts of male chauvinist propaganda. The students have gotten the point. These figures can't move their imaginations because their situations have nothing to do with situations in which students expect to find themselves. They need no inquisition to root out sexist heresies—although they will get one. And in the absence (temporary, of course) of a literature produced by feminism to rival the literature of Sophocles, Shakespeare, Racine, and Stendhal, students are without literary inspiration. Teaching romantic novels to university students (in spite of the healthy perseverance of this genre, as indicated by the success of the Harlequin romances—I find one free in every box of Hefty garbage bags I buy these days) is a quasi-impossibility. Students are either not interested or use it as grist for their ideological mill. Such books do not cause them to wonder whether they are missing something. All that passion seems pointless.

Notwithstanding all our relativism, there are certain things we know and which cannot be doubted. These are the tenets of the egalitarian creed, and today its primary tenet is that the past was sexist. This means that all the doubts which tradition should inspire in us in order to liberate us from the prejudices of our time are in principle closed to us. This is the source of the contentless certainty that is the hallmark of the young. This is what a teacher faces today. I do not say that the situation is impossible or worse than it ever was. The human condition is always beset by problems. But these are *our* problems, and we must face them clearly. They constitute a crisis for humane learning but also reaffirm the need for it. The bleak picture is often relieved by the rays of natural curiosity about a better way: it can happen any time a student confronts a great book.

Questions and Suggestions for Writing

1. In paragraph 9 Bloom writes, "Schools once produced citizens, or gentlemen, or believers; now they produce the unprejudiced." In the context of his earlier paragraphs, what does Bloom mean by "unprejudiced"?

2. Reread the first twelve paragraphs (section I), and formulate a view of Bloom. Is he thinking carefully, or is he striking out intemperately, or what? On what do you base your view?

3. Is it fair to say that in Bloom's remarks about earlier days he simply ignores the fact that the universities which "once produced citizens, or gentlemen, or believers" tolerated and indeed endorsed slavery and the disenfranchisement of women? If so, is this criticism fatal to his argument? Why, or why not?

4. In paragraph 13 Bloom says, "Today a young person does not generally go off to the university with the expectation of having an intellectual adventure, of discovering strange new worlds, of finding out what the comprehensive truth about man is. This is partly because he thinks such truth is unavailable." Putting aside the sexism in the use of "he" for men and women, do you think his charge here is true? To what degree, if any, does Bloom describe your expectations when you entered college? Or the expectations of most of your friends?

5. In paragraph 23 Bloom complains that "The students are not reading the same books and addressing the same questions, so that their common social life cannot be affected by a common intellectual life." Assuming the truth of the assertion that the students are not reading the same books—that is, assuming that there is no common core of required texts—what can be said against Bloom's assertion? For instance, do you think it can be argued that when students read "the same books," they may be lulled into thinking that there are not other books that challenge the views of the common core? (In the next paragraph Bloom complains that the humanists share approaches, derived from Marx and Nietzsche, which they believe to be true. Is this assertion itself an attack on Bloom's belief that students should be "reading the same books"?)

6. In paragraph 25, objecting to the requirement of a course "in a non-Western civilization or culture," Bloom says, "Serious physicists would never require a course in non-Western physics. Culture and civilization are irrelevant to truth. One finds it where one can." Can you think of valid answers for not requiring a course in non-Western physics but for nevertheless requiring a course in non-Western civilization or culture? By the way, how does a course in traditional Chinese medicine, or traditional African methods of healing, strike you? Why?

7. In paragraph 30, talking about rock music, Bloom says that young people know "perfectly well" that (whatever the words) "the motor of it all is eroticism." Do you agree? If not, why not? And do you agree with Bloom's assertion, in the next paragraph, that rock heroes "foment rebellion against all noble sentiments"?

8. In paragraph 37 Bloom complains that unmarried students "couple off very early and live together throughout college with full awareness that they intend

to go their separate ways afterward." He concludes the paragraph by saying, "There is nothing wild, Dionysian, searching, in our promiscuity. It has a dull, sterilized, scientific character." Judging from your own experience in college, is he right? And even if he is right, can a defense nevertheless be made of behavior he criticizes?

9. Bloom embraces the apparent paradox that we live in an era of "desexualization of life, all the while that a lot of sexual activity is going on" (para. 43). Is this paradox genuine or not? Write a 250-word essay exploring both sides of Bloom's position as quoted above.

10. In paragraph 44 Bloom says that romantic novels "do not cause [students] to wonder whether they are missing something. All that passion seems pointless." If you have read any romantic fiction—Bloom cites Harlequin novels—do you agree with his characterization of the reader's response? Why, or why not?

11. In his last paragraph, Bloom says that "tradition" should inspire us to "doubts," in order "to liberate us from the prejudices of our time." If you have read some classic work—say *Hamlet* or *Pride and Prejudice* or *Huckleberry Finn*— has it inspired in you any doubt of "the prejudices of our time"? Explain.

12. Bloom dismisses "black studies, native studies, women's studies" as "largely exercises in consciousness-raising" (para. 16). Why does he imply that this is not equally true of such traditional subjects as, say, philosophy or history? Write a 500-word essay supporting or attacking the proposition that these traditional subjects, too, are merely exercises in consciousness-raising.

13. After reading Bloom's essay to the end, prepare a list of a half dozen specific proposals that Bloom apparently thinks might remedy the situation that he deplores. Do you think some or all of these remedies are feasible? Write a 500-word essay arguing the point.

Benjamin Barber

The Philosopher Despot

Allan Bloom's *The Closing of the American Mind* is not a book, it is a phenomenon: one of those mega-literary comets that dazzles without being clearly seen, and thus mesmerizes its critics as it speeds across America's celebrity firmament. The perplexities are staggering. How does an obscure academician known chiefly for his translations of Plato and Rousseau

Benjamin Barber (b. 1939), a professor of political science at Rutgers University, is the author of The Conquest of Politics. *Here we print his response (originally published in* Harper's) *to* The Closing of the American Mind, *the book in which Allan Bloom amplified his ideas set forth earlier in the preceding selection, "Our Listless Universities."*

become a national celebrity? How can a book about the decadence of esoteric European philosophers such as Heidegger climb to the top of the best-seller list for over six months and sell nearly a half-million copies in hardback? Why are Americans so anxious to welcome a book that claims they can't read, so willing to accept a polemic that excoriates their literary intelligence? Why are liberal critics and egalitarian educators beside themselves with admiration for what can only be called a raging assault on liberal tolerance and democratic education?

From its publication last spring, *The Closing of the American Mind* took the country as much by surprise as by storm. The publisher printed only 10,000 copies of a book that at least one major publisher had turned down in a preliminary version. Bloom's beatification began mildly enough with a *New York Times* daily review calling his treatise a "remarkable" exercise in "electric-shock therapy" for complacent teachers; the Sunday *Book Review* picked up steam by lauding it as "an extraordinary meditation on the fate of liberal education in this country." Unqualified raves from many other critics followed, culminating in major spreads in weeklies such as *Newsweek*.

By late last summer, still a best-seller, the book had become a touch-stone for every imaginable contemporary debate on education, as well as a totem for the neoconservative assault on higher education, affirmative action, equal opportunity, rock music, the sixties, the young, and sex. In September George Will paid homage to Bloom in a *Newsweek* column titled "Learning from the Giants." George Levine ran a controversial national colloquium on Bloom at Rutgers University, and *Reader's Digest* took a full-page ad in the *New York Times* to reprint their editor's version of what was called Allan Bloom's decisive "answer" to the question "What's wrong with American education?" Typical of the hyperbolic hoopla was a three-part cover story in *Insight* that referred to Bloom's argument as "the most penetrating analysis of the United States to appear in many years." The book is now descending from its apogee, but its extraordinary trajectory suggests a phenomenon that has yet to be explained.

What on earth is going on here? It certainly is not the old literary love   4 story, for the affection America seems to feel for Bloom is anything but reciprocated. It is as if the professor and the country have met on a blind date and the country, though found sorely wanting by the professor, nevertheless insists on finding the professor irresistible. He charges Americans with flat-souled philistinism, and they buy almost a half-million copies of his scathing denunciation. He claims the country has deserted the university and blames democracy for the debacle, so the country adopts him as its favorite democratic educator.

Can the mystery be unraveled? We know well enough how this peculiar land of paradox—ambivalent land of the free—can make paradoxical heroes out of freedom's severest critics. How it offers popular success to those who contemn its popular virtues; and how, to those who disdain its materialism, it offers riches. *The Other America, The Making of a Counter Culture*, and *The Greening of America* had similar receptions. Yet those books were written in the spirit of progress and reform; they saw American reality as out of tune with the promise of the American soul, and they called for progress not reaction. In *The Closing of the American Mind* we confront a different phenomenon: a most enticing, a most subtle, a most learned, a most dangerous tract. What we have here is an extraordinary and adept exercise in the Noble Lie aimed at persuading Americans that philosophy is superior to ordinary American life and philosophers superior to ordinary American citizens; and consequently this nation's higher education ought to be organized around the edification of the *few* who embody philosophy rather than the *many* who embody America.

Bloom's book is as artful and painless a piece of subversion as we are likely to encounter from a critic of democracy. For it is written by a philosopher for whom rhetoric is "a gentle art of deception," a polemicist who believes political writing in a democratic society is necessarily an act of concealment. If Americans have failed fully to understand what Bloom means, it may be because Bloom has not said exactly what he means—or does not mean exactly what he has said. In its overt hostility to all the "leading notions of modern democratic thought" such as "equality, freedom, peace, [and] cosmopolitanism," *The Closing of the American Mind* would seem to qualify as one of the most profoundly antidemocratic books ever written for a popular audience. That, however, is not how Bloom puts it. Ever the prudent educator, Bloom believes that to say exactly what you mean about liberty and equality when you live in a liberal democratic state is to court the fate of Socrates, who was tried and executed by the Athenians for thinking little of their liberty and less of their democracy. Not one of the critics raving about the nobility of Bloom's philosophical project for the reconstruction of the American soul seems to have noticed that his philosopher "loves the truth" but "he does not love to tell the truth." The leading characteristic of this ostensible paean to the virtues of open discourse is in reality a commitment to closed communication—to esoteric meaning and rhetorical ambivalence.

Bloom's celebrants have accepted his intent as stated in his preface:

> This essay—a meditation on the state of our souls, particularly those of the young, and their education—is written from the perspective of a teacher. . . . [who is] dedicated to liberal education. . . . Attention to the young, knowing what their hungers are and what they can digest, is the essence of the craft.

Commentators have treated his book as a racy companion volume to 8
E. D. Hirsch's *Cultural Literacy*, with which it seems to share a yearning

for a more civilized culture and an affection for the so-called Great Books. Typical of this interpretation is the *Reader's Digest* review:

> [Bloom] tells us the closing of the American mind has resulted directly from "openness"—that perverse new virtue which urges us to be nonjudgmental and prevents us from "talking with any conviction about good and evil." Yet Americans long for something lost—the great moral truths upon which civilization rests. . . . Education is not merely about facts—it is about *truth* and the "state of our souls" . . . If there is a reassertion of moral truth rather than relativistic values, this book will be remembered as a catalyst.

The Allan Bloom honored by the critics is the philosophical moralist, doing battle with the forces of philistinism, relativism, and nihilism that beset a civilization living in the valley of the shadow of death—that is to say, in the shadow of the death of God. He appears in their encomiums as liberal humanist and concerned teacher, making war on students who fail to live up to the Socratic ideal.

With the artful and worshipful interlocutors of Socrates perching as archetypes in his imagination, Bloom can hardly be other than appalled by the average American eighteen-year-old, who is more than a little artless and never very reverent, particularly toward teachers. Bloom rails with indignation at the young and what the corruptions of democratic education (the sixties) have done to them. He is repelled by their tastes, their pastimes, their sexual practices, their "niceness," their music, their reading habits, their lack of "prejudices," and their "flat-souled" lack of nobility. No wonder he complains that "Harvard, Yale, and Princeton are not what they used to be—the last resorts of aristocratic sentiment within the democracy." At times Bloom's unrelenting sixties-bashing sounds like the screeching of an aging parent wrapped in a Roman toga—ranting about the nobility of the ancients because he cannot comprehend his daughter's purple hair. When he tells us that an American university which pledges itself to serve democracy's needs is indistinguishable from a German university which dedicates itself to the service of Nazism, or that Woodstock is the American Nuremberg (flower children listening to Jimi Hendrix are to be regarded as clones of black-shirted fascists organizing a new era of genocide), we may wonder what has happened to the philosopher in search of great souls.

Yet underlying Bloom's hostility to the sixties is a more profound anger. Like the champions of the new conservatism, Bloom is hostile not only to the moral decline of the university and its students but to much of what democrats and progressives have accomplished in the last fifty years. He does not simply oppose feminism or the abolition of the double standard in the abstract, he condemns them because they destroy the old sexual arrangements whereby a man could "think he was doing a wonderful thing for a woman, and expect to be admired for what he brought." Feminists are not merely the destroyers of the family, they are "the latest enemy of the vitality of classic texts," and since classic texts are the touchstones of a philosophical society, of civilization itself.

Bloom is aghast at modern value-relativism—that the young have neither values nor even prejudices—but he is also censorious about the values they choose to embrace. Thus, to him a concern for nuclear survival is bogus posturing; a belief in tolerance is a sign of moral flabbiness; to be "nice" and "without prejudices" merely underscores shallowness. Bloom condemns not just equality and the struggle for rights (which he believes have in any case been "won"), but the notion of rights itself, which for him means dedication to "life, liberty, and the pursuit of property and sex." The true villains are then neither Betty Friedan nor Abbie Hoffman but Erich Fromm and John Dewey—not the armed prophets of the Weather Underground but the far more dangerous unarmed prophets of therapeutic salvation and the brotherhood of man.

Bloom opposes democratic values not only as a conservative ideologue [12] but as a philosopher wedded to reason. It is not really the last twenty or even the last fifty years that disturb Allan Bloom: it is the last two hundred years. The problems go back at least to the French Revolution and to those aspects of the philosophy of Enlightenment that led to the Revolution, since, as always for Bloom, history proceeds out of ideas rather than the other way around. In fact, nothing has been quite the same since a court composed of distrustful Athenian freemen put noble Socrates to death for the crime of being a truth-speaking philosopher in an opinion-governed society. The great divide is less between modern conservatives and modern democrats than between ancients and moderns—the central theme of Bloom's mentor and teacher, the great University of Chicago political philosopher Leo Strauss.

The German philosopher Friedrich Nietzsche signals the final eclipse of the ancient world for Bloom. Bloom's ambivalence about Nietzsche is one of the more impenetrable puzzles of *The Closing of the American Mind*, a puzzle that makes its profoundly antidemocratic argument difficult for critics to apprehend. Bloom is simultaneously full of praise for Nietzsche's analysis of modernity (he is "an unparalleled diagnostician of the ills of modernity") and full of indignation at what he considers to be the American trivialization of Nietzschean philosophy. This he regards as the primary cause of the closing of the American mind.

Nietzsche is at once hero and villian, astute cultural critic of bourgeois culture in the abstract, but nefarious corrupter of American youth in practice. Bloom's ambivalence about him is rooted in his distrust of democracy. Like Voltaire, who urges gentlemen to send their servants out of the room before debating whether God actually exists, Bloom worries not about Nietzsche's nihilistic announcement of the death of God, but about what philistine Americans may make of this unhappy news. The danger is not philosophical relativism, but pop relativism; not Nietzsche, but the "doctrinaire Woody Allen" whose way of looking at things "has immediate roots in the most profound German philosophy." If Woody Allen as a pop Nietzsche seems farfetched, Bloom himself often seems like a slightly paranoid Tocqueville who, burdened by an aristocratic background and Continental manners, finds himself inexplicably residing in the state of Illinois among barbarians he both worships and despises.

As a modern, Bloom cannot really deny that the credentials for both absolute Truth and a Supreme Being have become philosophically suspect: Nietzsche was merely the messenger for the news of their delegitimation by science and the Enlightenment. The trouble lies neither in the messenger nor in the message, but in the hungry masses that, equipped with a democratic education, beg to receive the grim tidings. These tidings only strip them of their myths and their religious comfort. Because the masses are constitutionally unfit for philosophy, the Truth leaves them defenseless and renders them dangerous. Faced with the news of God's death and Truth's uncertainty, mass man in America has simply put his soulless self in God's place, to the peril of learning, philosophy, and civilization. The demise of Authority engenders the Revolt of the Masses, whose trivialized mass culture is at war with everything noble and good. Virtue gives way to utility, reason to passion, the good to self-interest.

But how to tell such things to mass man himself? Men possessed of the idea that each of them is God must be handled carefully. To remind them of their own mortality and to tell them of the death of God may work terrible pain upon them. To avenge their suffering the messenger might be executed! The solution Bloom can only hint at (the philosopher cannot speak honestly) is certainly not to inundate the masses with books they cannot understand and are likely to misconstrue. Rather, it is to send them—like Voltaire's servants—out of the room. Bloom notes and his admirers delight in the great irony by which "openness" (which produces relativism and then nihilism) has led to the closing of the American mind. They might do well to note the still greater irony that reopening the American mind may for Bloom depend on the closing of the American university—since open minds seem to function best in highly selective, closed schools. To the educable, an education; to the rest, protection from fearsome half-truths, and a diet of noble lies such as may be required to insulate the university from mediocrity and democratic taste. Affirmative action puts into the classroom young men who can learn from Hobbes and Nietzsche only the lesson of the rightfulness of their appetites; feminism puts into the classroom young women who can learn from Dewey and Freud only the lesson of their equality with, or perhaps even their sexual superiority to, men. Philosophy is not finally to be saved by handing out Great Books to small minds, but by locking the library doors.

Bloom is remarkably candid about the nature of "the real community of man," which "is the community of those who seek the truth, of the potential knowers." To be sure, this community "in principle" includes all men "to the extent they desire to know. *But in fact this includes only a few, the true friends, as Plato was to Aristotle . . .*" (emphasis added). Bloom's rhetorical journey finally begins and ends with the ancients—with Socrates. How much misery mankind might have been spared; what revolutions, what prejudices, what myths, what armed braggarts might have vanished from the historical landscape, had the Athenians loved and followed Socrates instead of executing him.

Bloom's democratic admirers overlook his belief that democracy for the many (those not like him) and education for the few (those like him) proceed from radically incompatible premises. According to Bloom, society ought ideally to be arranged to achieve the latter even if it means undermining the former. "Never did I think," he writes, "that the university was properly ministerial to the society around it. Rather I thought and think that society is ministerial to the university . . ." Without the university thus understood, the theoretical life collapses "back into the primal slime" (presumably democratic society) from which it "cannot re-emerge."

The citizen of a democracy who understands what Bloom intends in the honor he pays Socrates will be wary in the face of Bloom's modern pedagogical claims. The citizen has every reason to mistrust the philosopher who mistrusts him. After all, it was the tyranny of "Truth" politicized that justified the divine right of kings, the Inquisition, the Reign of Terror, and such modern orthodoxies as totalitarianism.

Bloom may not be arguing that "the old [forms] were good or that we should go back to them," but he has two crucial quarrels to pick with America: the quarrel of the philosopher with democracy and equality; and the quarrel of the ambivalent cosmopolitan both with the European decadence he fears and the American philistinism he despises. The quarrel between philosophy and democracy is the quarrel between Socrates and Athens, and we have seen how deeply that struggle affects Bloom. The quarrel between America and Europe is more complex, and Bloom is torn between the two.

Champion of an innocent America corrupted by the tainting cynicism of Europe's antiphilosophies, Bloom sees himself as a loyal but knowing son of the Republic anxious to protect its less-sophisticated citizens from the Old World's newfangled nihilisms. If it is true that God has died (and there are times when Nietzsche's bad news seems also to be Bloom's bad news), don't tell the Americans! They already have a penchant for the vulgar, the novel, and the experimental, and will seize on God's withdrawal from the cosmos as a reason to try to master it themselves. In place of the tragic acceptance that characterized the ancients, the Americans will deploy ideologies of reform, growth, progress, and revolution. With their hands clasping computers and spliced genes, and their heads bursting with progressive ideologies from Marxism to welfarism, they will set out to replace their vanished Creator and improve upon his handiwork.

Nonetheless, even as Bloom cherishes America's insularity from the contagion of European cultural relativism, he cherishes Europe. As an American he may be suspicious of Europe's cynical intellectuals, but as a partisan of Europe, he is even more suspicious of America's self-righteously innocent anti-intellectuals. With innocence comes a simpleminded disdain for ideas that, as the historian Richard Hofstadter has noticed, inures us to books and debases our souls. We are finally much too practical a people for Bloom's taste: philosophy enjoins reflection, but the "hidden premise of the realm of freedom [America] is that action has primacy over thought." Bloom's aristocratic hostility to America's spirited practicality, to its optimism about change (America as the New World), to its belief in the second chance, blinds him to certain strengths of the American polity, as well as to the relationship of ordinary human beings to books.

America's true philosophers are not bookmen or academicians or theorists. They are poets such as Emily Dickinson and Walt Whitman, essayists such as Henry Adams and Ralph Waldo Emerson, lawyers such as James Madison and Hugo Black, and moral leaders such as John Brown, Susan B. Anthony, and Martin Luther King, Jr. Bloom can argue with Dewey while Leo Strauss argues with Nietzsche, but America's true educators dwell elsewhere; their podiums are found in the open air rather than the library, the town hall rather than the seminar hall.

We continue to learn more from our doers than from our talkers, from 24 Jefferson and Franklin, Eugene Debs and Robert Taft, Harry Hopkins, and, yes, even David Stockman. Bloom yearns for heroes and condemns us for having none worthy of the name, but what democrats aspire to is, as Brecht has written, not a country that has no heroes but a country that needs no heroes. At their best, Americans have been their own heroes, their nation a creation of anonymous settlers, cattlemen, garment workers, grade-school teachers, factory laborers, entrepreneurs, farmers, longshoremen, inventors, and just plain folks. Bloom simply gets America wrong. If Americans lack confidence in those who claim to possess Truth, it is because they are the descendants of immigrants who fled such Truthsayers. Disguised as inquisitors, prosecutors, and king's counselors, such dogmatists impressed their Truths on the illiterate "rabble" in the form of chains. Bloom (it is almost as if he misses the chains) longs for the days in which Protestants and Catholics, hating each other, demonstrated they were "taking their beliefs seriously." Is the average American to be faulted for preferring the frivolous shallows of religious tolerance to the seriousness of the Salem witch-hunts?

The lugubrious lesson Americans may wish to draw from both Socrates and Bloom is that the philosopher's ideal of the open mind seems to flourish best in a closed society where, if philosophers do not rule, those who do rule must defer to philosophy. We ought to remember that benevolent autocrats like Frederick the Great made comfortable homes for philosophers such as Voltaire, even as those philosophers conceived rational blueprints in which there would be no room for kings. The king can at least pretend to be philosophical, whereas the self-governing common man will disdain the superior airs of both philosophers and kings. Tyrants may indeed be better friends to Truth than citizens who must learn how to live with uncertainty and difference. We citizens can understand why a philosopher of noble intentions may be aghast at a society moved by the suspicion that one man is as good as the next; but, still, we might be expected to meet the philosopher's subtle arguments with something more than a weak and self-nullifying cheer. For we are being asked implicitly to choose between the open mind and the open society, being asked to close the university to the many in order to secure it for the few, being asked to make reflection and its requisites the master of action and its requisites, being asked finally to turn the democratic culture that ought to be the university's finest product into the servant of universities that produce something called Truth. And how we answer such questions will not only affect what kind of education we will have, but whether we will remain a free and egalitarian society devoted to justice, or become a nation of deferential tutees who have been talked out of our freedom by a critic of all that has transpired since the ancient world gave way to the modern.

A great many Americans have come to sympathize with Bloom, anxious about the loss of fixed points, wishing for simpler, more orderly times. President Reagan's longing for a court filled with somber purists, his attorney general's belief in a doctrine of original intentions that turns the flexible genius of the Constitution into a Rosetta stone by which every modern conflict might be resolved, the secretary of education's campaign against the educational reforms of the sixties, the Moral Majority's demand that the whole nation be subjected to drug testing—these are so many cries to be delivered from the twentieth century. These are the voices not of mere conservatives but of zealots, the anxious ones who see in the victories of liberty only the specter of anarchy; in equality, the victory of mediocrity; in social justice, a warrant for envy and disorder. Allan Bloom's book offers certainty to the confused and comfort to the fearful. It is a new Book of Truth for an era after God. Its only rival is democracy, which Bloom, with those he comforts, can only despise.

Nevertheless, the ideology of democracy is a sound, one might even say noble, response to the dilemmas of modernity: it permits us to live with our uncertainty, our agnosticism, our doubt, our sense of abandonment, our isolation, without murdering one another; it even promises a modicum of justice made up of equal parts of compassion and tolerance. It does not rescue us from our era, but it helps us live with its perils. The most apt response to Bloom's attempt to teach us how to be noble might be for us to teach him how to be democratic. It might even be that he would get the better of the exchange.

Questions and Suggestions for Writing

1. Barber regards Bloom as an enemy of democracy, and especially of democracy in education. Do you agree in this judgment? What evidence can you cite from Bloom's own remarks (p. 216) in support of, or in opposition to, this view?

2. Barber mentions three books critical of American culture (para. 5) which he evidently holds in higher esteem than Bloom's book. Check out one of these books from the college library, read it, and write a 500- to 750-word essay setting forth its main themes, arguments, and conclusions.

3. Barber mentions "the so-called Great Books" (para. 8). Do some research in the library and prepare a list of two dozen such books, including (if possible) at least one that you have read. Why do you suppose they are called "Great Books"— that is, what do you think the criteria are, and what is the evidence that these two dozen satisfy the criteria? In a 500-word essay explain the role that you think the study of such books should have in a liberal education. Do you think Barber would agree with you?

4. Barber mentions "the death of God" (paras. 15–17). Do some research in the library and write a 250-word essay on the theme: the Evidence that God is Dead in Our Society. (*Note:* Your thesis of course may be that little or no evidence supports the proposition.)

5. Barber reminds his readers of the historic "tyranny of 'Truth' politicized" (paras. 19 and 24), whereas Bloom insists that the task of the humanities is to "teach *the truth*" (para. 20). Can these two views be reconciled? What "truths" does Bloom think the humanities can teach? Would Barber disagree? Write a 500-word essay answering these questions.

6. In para. 5 Barber says, of the popularity of Bloom's attack on his presumed readers, "Can the mystery be unraveled?" Do you think Barber does unravel the mystery? If so, summarize Barber's explanation.

Is Affirmative Action Unfair?

William Bradford Reynolds

Equal Opportunity, Not Equal Results

No one disputes that "affirmative action" is a subject of vital significance for our society. The character of our country is determined in large measure by the manner in which we treat our individual citizens—whether we treat them fairly or unfairly, whether we ensure equal opportunity to all individuals, or guarantee equal results to selected groups. As assistant attorney general, I am faced daily with what seem to have emerged on the civil rights horizon as the two predominant competing values that drive the debate on this issue—that is, the value of equal opportunity and the value of equal results. I have devoted a great deal of time and attention to the very different meanings these concepts lend to the phrase "affirmative action."

Typically, to the understandable confusion of almost everyone, "affirmative action" is the term used to refer to both of these contrasting values. There is, however, a world of difference between "affirmative action" as a measure for ensuring equality of opportunity and "affirmative action" as a tool for achieving equality of results.

In the former instance, affirmative steps are taken so that all individuals (whatever their race, color, sex, or national origin) will be given the chance to compete with all others on equal terms; each is to be given his or her place at the starting line without advantage or disadvantage. In the latter, by contrast, the promise of affirmative action is that those who participate will arrive at the finish line in prearranged places—places allocated by race or sex.

I have expressed on a number of occasions my conviction that the   4 promise of equal results is a false one. We can never assure equal results in a world in which individuals differ greatly in motivation and ability; nor, in my view, is such a promise morally or constitutionally acceptable. In fact, this was well understood at the time that the concept of "affirmative action" was first introduced as a remedial technique in the civil rights arena. In its original formulation, that concept embraced only non-preferential affirmative efforts, such as training programs and enhanced recruitment activities, aimed at opening wide the doors of opportunity to

William Bradford Reynolds (b. 1942) was Assistant Attorney General for Civil Rights in the Department of Justice during the Reagan administration. This essay is reprinted from The Moral Foundations of Civil Rights *(1986).*

all Americans who cared to enter. Thus, President Kennedy's Executive Order 10925, one of the earliest to speak to the subject, stated that federal contractors should "take affirmative action to ensure that the applicants are employed, and that employees are treated during employment, without regard to their race, creed, color, or national origin."

This principle was understood by all at that time to mean simply that individuals previously neglected in the search for talent must be allowed to apply and be considered along with all others for available jobs or contracting opportunities, but that the hiring and selection decisions would be made from the pool of applicants without regard to race, creed, color, or national origin—and later sex. No one was to be afforded a preference, or special treatment, because of group membership; rather, all were to be treated equally as individuals based on personal ability and worth.

This administration's commitment is to what Vice Chairman of the Civil Rights Commission Morris Abram calls the "original and undefiled meaning" of "affirmative action." Where unlawful discrimination exists, we see that it is brought to an abrupt and uncompromising halt; where that discrimination has harmed any individual, we ensure that every victim of the wrongdoing receives "make-whole" relief; and, where affirmative steps in the nature of training programs and enhanced recruitment efforts are needed, we require such steps to be taken to force open the doors of opportunity that have too long remained closed to far too many.

The criticism, of course, is that we do not go far enough. The remedial use of goals and timetables, quotas, or other such numerical devices, designed to achieve a particular balance in race or sex in the work force, has been accepted by the lower federal courts as an available instrument of relief, and therefore, it is argued, such an approach should not be abandoned. There are several responses to this sort of argumentation.

The first is a strictly legal one and rests on the Supreme Court's recent   8 decision in *Firefighters Local Union No. 1784 v. Stotts*, 104 S. Ct. 2576 (1984). The Supreme Court in *Stotts* did not merely hold that federal courts are prohibited from ordering racially preferential layoffs to maintain a certain racial percentage, or that courts cannot disrupt bona fide seniority systems. To be sure, it did so rule, but the Court said much more, and in unmistakably forceful terms. As Justice Stevens remarked during his August 4, 1984, commencement address at Northwestern University, the decision represents "a far-reaching pronouncement concerning the limits on a court's power to prescribe affirmative action as a remedy for proven violations of Title VII of the Civil Rights Act." For the *Stotts* majority grounded the decision, at bottom, on the holding that federal courts are without *any* authority under Section 706(g)—the remedial provision of Title VII—to order a remedy, either by consent decree or after full litigation, that goes beyond enjoining the unlawful conduct and awarding "make-whole" relief for actual victims of the discrimination. Thus, quotas or other preferential techniques that, by design, benefit nonvictims because of race or sex cannot be a part of Title VII relief ordered in a court case, whether the context is hiring, promotion, or layoffs.

A brief review of the opinion's language is particularly useful to understanding the sweep of the decision. At issue in *Stotts* was a district court injunction ordering that certain white firefighters with greater seniority be laid off before blacks with less seniority in order to preserve a certain percentage of black representation in the fire department's work force. The Supreme Court held that this order was improper because "there was no finding that any of the blacks protected from layoff had been a victim of discrimination."[1] Relying explicitly on Section 706(g) of Title VII, the Court held that Congress intended to "provide make-whole relief only to those who have been actual victims of illegal discrimination."[2]

Specific portions of the legislative history of the act were cited in support of this interpretation. For example, Hubert Humphrey, the principal force behind passage of Title VII in the Senate, had assured his colleagues during consideration of the statute that:

> [t]here is nothing in [the proposed bill] that will give any power to the Commission *or to any court* to require hiring, firing or promotion of employees in order to meet a racial "quota" or to achieve a certain racial balance. That bugaboo has been brought up a dozen times; but it is nonexistent.[3]

Moreover, the Court recognized that the interpretive memorandum of the bill entered into the Congressional Record by Senators Clark and Case stated unambiguously that "Title VII does not permit the ordering of racial quotas in business or unions."[4]

After *Stotts*, it is, I think, abundantly clear that Section 706(g) of Title VII does not tolerate remedial action by courts that would grant to nonvictims of discrimination—at the expense of wholly innocent employees or potential employees—an employment preference based solely on the fact that they are members of a particular race or gender. Quotas, or any other numerical device based on color or sex, are by definition victim-blind: they embrace without distinction, and accord preferential treatment to, persons having no claim to "make-whole" relief. Accordingly, whether such formulas are employed for hiring, promotion, or layoffs, they must fail under any reading of the statute's remedial provision.

There are equally strong policy reasons for coming to this conclusion. The remedial use of preferences had been justified by the courts primarily on the theory that they are necessary to cure "the effects of past discrimina-

12

---

[1]Firefighters Local Union No. 1784 v. Stotts, 104 S.Ct. 2576, 2588 (1984).
[2]Ibid., at 2589.
[3]110 Congressional Record 6549 (1964) (emphasis added).
[4]Ibid., at 6566 (emphasis added by the Court).

tion" and thus, in the words of one Supreme Court Justice, to "get beyond racism."[5] This reasoning is twice-flawed.

First, it is premised on the proposition that any racial imbalance in the employer's work force is explainable only as a lingering effect of past racial discrimination. The analysis is no different where gender-based discrimination is involved. Yet, in either instance, equating "underrepresentation" of certain groups with discrimination against those groups ignores the fact that occupation selection in a free society is determined by a host of factors, principally individual interest, industry, and ability. It simply is not the case that applicants for any given job come proportionally qualified by race, gender, and ethnic origin in accordance with U.S. population statistics. Nor do the career interests of individuals break down proportionally among racial or gender groups. Accordingly, a selection process free of discrimination is no more likely to produce "proportional representation" along race or sex lines than it is to ensure proportionality among persons grouped according to hair color, shoe size, or any other irrelevant personal characteristic. No human endeavor, since the beginning of time, has attracted persons sharing a common physical characteristic in numbers proportional to the representation of such persons in the community. "Affirmative action" assumptions that one might expect otherwise in the absence of race or gender discrimination are ill-conceived.

Second, and more important, there is nothing *remedial*—let alone *equitable*—about a court order that *requires* the hiring, promotion, or retention of a person who has not suffered discrimination solely because that person is a member of the same racial or gender group as other persons who were victimized by the discriminatory employment practices. The rights protected under Title VII belong to individuals, not to groups. The Supreme Court made clear some years ago that "the basic policy of Title VII requires that courts focus on fairness to individuals rather than fairness to classes."[6] The same message was again delivered in *Stotts*. As indicated, remedying a violation of Title VII requires that the individual victimized by the unlawful discrimination be restored to his or her "rightful place." It almost goes without saying, however, that a person who is *not* victimized by the employer's discriminatory practices has no claim to a "rightful place" in the employer's work force. And according preferential treatment to *nonvictims* in no way remedies the injury suffered by persons who have in fact been discriminated against in violation of Title VII.

Moreover, racial quotas and other forms of preferential treatment unjustifiably infringe on the legitimate employment interests and expectations of third parties, such as incumbent employees, who are free of any involvement in the employer's wrongdoing. To be sure, awarding retroac-

---

[5]University of California Regents v. Bakke, 438 U.S. 265, 407 (1978) (Justice Blackmun, concurring).

[6]Los Angeles Department of Water & Power v. Manhart, 435 U.S. 702, 708 (1978).

tive seniority and other forms of "rightful place" relief to individual victims of discrimination also unavoidably infringes upon the employment interests and expectations of innocent third parties. Indeed, this fact has compelled some, including Chief Justice Burger, to charge that granting rightful place relief to victims of racial discrimination is on the order of "robbing Peter to pay Paul."[7]

The legitimate "rightful place" claims of identifiable victims of dis- 16 crimination, however, warrant imposition of a remedy that calls for a sharing of the burden by those innocent incumbent employees whose "places" in the work force are the product of, or at least enhanced by, the employer's unlawful discrimination. Restoring the victim of discrimination to the position he or she would have occupied but for the discrimination merely requires incumbent employees to surrender some of the largesse discriminatorily conferred upon them. In other words, there is justice in requiring Peter, as a kind of third-party beneficiary of the employer's discriminatory conduct, to share in the burden of making good on the debt to Paul created by that conduct. But an incumbent employee should not be called upon as well to sacrifice or otherwise compromise his legitimate employment interests in order to accommodate persons *never wronged* by the employer's unlawful conduct. An order directing Peter to pay Paul in the absence of any proof of a debt owing to Paul is without remedial justification and cannot be squared with basic notions of fairness.

Proponents of the so-called remedial use of class-based preferences often counter this point with a twofold response. First, they note that the effort to identify and make whole all victims of the employer's discriminatory practices will never be 100 percent successful. While no one can dispute the validity of this unfortunate point, race- and gender-conscious preferences simply do not answer this problem. The injury suffered by a discriminatee who cannot be located is in no way ameliorated—much less remedied—by conferring preferential treatment on other randomly selected members of his or her race or sex. A person suffering from an appendicitis is not relieved of the pain by an appendectomy performed on the patient in the next room.

Second, proponents of judicially imposed numerical preferences argue that preferences are necessary to ensure that the employer does not return to his or her discriminatory ways. The fallacy in this reasoning is self-evident. Far from *preventing* future discrimination, imposition of such remedial devices *guarantees* future discrimination. Only the color or gender of the ox being gored is changed.

It is against this backdrop that the Court's decision in *Stotts* assumes so much significance in the "affirmative action" debate. The inescapable consequence of *Stotts* is to move government at the federal, state, and local

[7]Franks v. Bowman Transportation Co., 424 U.S. 747, 781 (1976) (Justice Burger, dissenting).

levels noticeably closer to the overriding objective of providing all citizens with a truly equal opportunity to compete on merit for the benefits that our society has to offer—an opportunity that allows an individual to go as far as the person's energy, ability, enthusiasm, imagination, and effort will allow—and not be hemmed in by the artificial allotment given to his or her group in the form of a numerical preference. The promise is that we might now be able to bring an end to that stifling process by which government and society view their citizens as possessors of racial or gender characteristics, not as the unique individuals they are; where advancements are viewed not as hard-won achievements, but as conferred "benefits."

The use of race or sex, in an effort to restructure society along lines 20 that better represent someone's preconceived notions of how our limited educational and economic resources should be allocated among the many groups in our pluralistic society, necessarily forecloses opportunities to those having the misfortune—solely by reason of gender or skin color—to be members of a group whose allotment has already been filled. Those so denied, such as the more senior white Memphis firefighters laid off to achieve a more perfect racial balance in the fire department, are discriminated against every bit as much as the black Memphis firefighters excluded from employment. In our zeal to eradicate discrimination from society, we must be ever vigilant not to allow considerations of race or sex to intrude upon the decisional process of government. That was precisely the directive handed down by Congress in the Civil Rights Act of 1964 and, as *Stotts* made clear, the command has full application to the courts. Plainly, "affirmative action" remedies must be guided by no different principle. For the simple fact remains that wherever it occurs, and however explained, "no discrimination based on race [or sex] is benign. . . . no action disadvantaging a person because of color [or gender] is affirmative."[8]

Questions and Suggestions for Writing

1. "Affirmative action" apparently means different things (paras. 1–6). Which do you think is the most important meaning, and why? Complete the following definition: Affirmative action on behalf of a certain group of persons consists in. . . .

2. Some students have found the structure of Reynolds's second sentence in paragraph 1 obscure, though clarified by his third sentence. Rewrite the second sentence to make his meaning crystal clear.

3. Does Executive Order 10925 include what Morris Abrams calls "'make-whole' relief" (see paras. 4, 6)? Explain your answer.

---

[8]United Steelworkers of America, AFL-CIO v. Weber, 443 U.S. 193, 254 (1979) (Justice Rehnquist, dissenting).

4. Study carefully paragraphs 6–11, and explain the difference between affirmative action programs that provide remedies confined to "make-whole relief" and programs not so limited.

5. According to Reynolds, the Supreme Court in its decision in the *Stott* case ruled against the use of Section 706(g) to grant remedies for past discrimination except to "actual victims of discrimination" (para. 8). Reynolds obviously supports this ruling. Write a 250-word essay explaining his reasons.

6. Thomas Nagel (the following essay) defends affirmative action. What arguments of Reynolds, if any, does Nagel criticize?

7. Suppose Peter and Paul work for the same employer, doing comparable jobs, and that Peter has greater seniority than Paul. Suppose also that Peter is white, Paul black. Suppose further that a reduction in work force is required for general economic reasons, so Paul is laid off (under the seniority principle, "Last hired first fired"). Paul, however, argues that Peter should have been laid off instead, because had it not been for racial discrimination in hiring years ago, he and Peter would have had equal seniority—or perhaps he would have had even more seniority than Peter. Would the Supreme Court's ruling in *Stott*, as explained by Reynolds, support Paul's claim, or not? In any case, what do you think of Paul's argument, and why?

Thomas Nagel

A Defense of Affirmative Action

The term *affirmative action* has changed in meaning since it was first introduced. Originally it referred only to special efforts to ensure equal opportunity for members of groups that had been subject to discrimination. These efforts included public advertisement of positions to be filled, active recruitment of qualified applicants from the formerly excluded groups, and special training programs to help them meet the standards for admission or appointment. There was also close attention to procedures of appointment, and sometimes to the results, with a view to detecting continued discrimination, conscious or unconscious.

More recently the term has come to refer also to some degree of definite preference for members of these groups in determining access to positions from which they were formerly excluded. Such preference might be allowed to influence decisions only between candidates who are otherwise equally qualified, but usually it involves the selection of women or

Thomas Nagel (b. 1937), professor of philosophy at New York University, is the author of several books, including The View from Nowhere (1986). *This essay appeared in* QQ, *1981.*

minority members over other candidates who are better qualified for the position.

Let me call the first sort of policy "weak affirmative action" and the second "strong affirmative action." It is important to distinguish them, because the distinction is sometimes blurred in practice. It is strong affirmative action—the policy of preference—that arouses controversy. Most people would agree that weak or precautionary affirmative action is a good thing, and worth its cost in time and energy. But this does not imply that strong affirmative action is also justified.

I shall claim that in the present state of things it is justified, most clearly with respect to blacks. But I also believe that a defender of the practice must acknowledge that there are serious arguments against it, and that it is defensible only because the arguments for it have great weight. Moral opinion in this country is sharply divided over the issue because significant values are involved on both sides. My own view is that while strong affirmative action is intrinsically undesirable, it is a legitimate and perhaps indispensable method of pursuing a goal so important to the national welfare that it can be justified as a temporary, though not short-term, policy for both public and private institutions. In this respect it is like other policies that impose burdens on some for the public good.

Three Objections

I shall begin with the argument against. There are three objections to strong affirmative action: that it is inefficient; that it is unfair; and that it damages self-esteem.

The degree of inefficiency depends on how strong a role racial or sexual preference plays in the process of selection. Among candidates meeting the basic qualifications for a position, those better qualified will on the average perform better, whether they are doctors, policemen, teachers, or electricians. There may be some cases, as in preferential college admissions, where the immediate usefulness of making educational resources available to an individual is thought to be greater because of the use to which the education will be put or because of the internal effects on the institution itself. But by and large, policies of strong affirmative action must reckon with the costs of some lowering in performance level: the stronger the preference, the larger the cost to be justified. Since both the costs and the value of the results will vary from case to case, this suggests that no one policy of affirmative action is likely to be correct in all cases, and that the cost in performance level should be taken into account in the design of a legitimate policy.

The charge of unfairness arouses the deepest disagreements. To be passed over because of membership in a group one was born into, where this has nothing to do with one's individual qualifications for a position, can arouse strong feelings of resentment. It is a departure from the ideal—one of the values finally recognized in our society—that people should be judged so far as possible on the basis of individual characteristics rather than involuntary group membership.

This does not mean that strong affirmative action is morally repugnant in the manner of racial or sexual discrimination. It is nothing like those practices, for though like them it employs race and sex as criteria of selection, it does so for entirely different reasons. Racial and sexual discrimination are based on contempt or even loathing for the excluded group, a feeling that certain contacts with them are degrading to members of the dominant group, that they are fit only for subordinate positions or menial work. Strong affirmative action involves none of this: it is simply a means of increasing the social and economic strength of formerly victimized groups, and does not stigmatize others. 8

There is an element of individual unfairness here, but it is more like the unfairness of conscription in wartime, or of property condemnation under the right of eminent domain. Those who benefit or lose out because of their race or sex cannot be said to deserve their good or bad fortune.

It might be said on the other side that the beneficiaries of affirmative action deserve it as compensation for past discrimination, and that compensation is rightly exacted from the group that has benefited from discrimination in the past. But this is a bad argument, because as the practice usually works, no effort is made to give preference to those who have suffered most from discrimination, or to prefer them especially to those who have benefited most from it, or been guilty of it. Only candidates who in other qualifications fall on one or other side of the margin of decision will directly benefit or lose from the policy, and these are not necessarily, or even probably, the ones who especially deserve it. Women or blacks who don't have the qualifications even to be considered are likely to have been handicapped more by the effects of discrimination than those who receive preference. And the marginal white male candidate who is turned down can evoke our sympathy if he asks, "Why me?" (A policy of explicitly *compensatory* preference, which took into account each individual's background of poverty and discrimination, would escape some of these objections, and it has its defenders, but it is not the policy I want to defend. Whatever its merits, it will not serve the same purpose as direct affirmative action.)

The third objection concerns self-esteem, and is particularly serious. While strong affirmative action is in effect, and generally known to be so, no one in an affirmative action category who gets a desirable job or is admitted to a selective university can be sure that he or she has not benefited from the policy. Even those who would have made it anyway fall under suspicion, from themselves and from others: it comes to be widely felt that success does not mean the same thing for women and minorities. This painful damage to esteem cannot be avoided. It should make any defender of strong affirmative action want the practice to end as soon as it has achieved its basic purpose.

Justifying Affirmative Action

I have examined these three objections and tried to assess their weight,   12 in order to decide how strong a countervailing reason is needed to justify such a policy. In my view, taken together they imply that strong affirmative action involving significant preference should be undertaken only if it will substantially further a social goal of the first importance. While this condition is not met by all programs of affirmative action now in effect, it is met by those which address the most deep-seated, stubborn, and radically unhealthy divisions in the society, divisions whose removal is a condition of basic justice and social cohesion.

The situation of black people in our country is unique in this respect. For almost a century after the abolition of slavery we had a rigid racial caste system of the ugliest kind, and it only began to break up twenty-five years ago. In the South it was enforced by law, and in the North, in a somewhat less severe form, by social convention. Whites were thought to be defiled by social or residential proximity to blacks, intermarriage was taboo, blacks were denied the same level of public goods—education and legal protection—as whites, were restricted to the most menial occupations, and were barred from any positions of authority over whites. The visceral feelings of black inferiority and untouchability that this system expressed were deeply ingrained in the members of both races, and they continue, not surprisingly, to have their effect. Blacks still form, to a considerable extent, a hereditary social and economic community characterized by widespread poverty, unemployment, and social alienation.

When this society finally got around to moving against the caste system, it might have done no more than to enforce straight equality of opportunity, perhaps with the help of weak affirmative action, and then wait a few hundred years while things gradually got better. Fortunately it decided instead to accelerate the process by both public and private institutional action, because there was wide recognition of the intractable character of the problem posed by this insular minority and its place in the nation's history and collective consciousness. This has not been going on very long, but the results are already impressive, especially in speeding the advancement of blacks into the middle class. Affirmative action has not done much to improve the position of poor and unskilled blacks. That is the most serious part of the problem, and it requires a more direct economic attack. But increased access to higher education and upper-level jobs is an essential part of what must be achieved to break the structure of drastic separation that was left largely undisturbed by the legal abolition of the caste system.

Changes of this kind require a generation or two. My guess is that strong affirmative action for blacks will continue to be justified into the early decades of the next century, but that by then it will have accomplished what it can and will no longer be worth the costs. One point deserves special emphasis. The goal to be pursued is the reduction of a great social injustice, not proportional representation of the races in all institutions and professions. Proportional racial representation is of no value in itself. It is not a legitimate social goal, and it should certainly not be the aim of strong affirmative action, whose drawbacks make it worth adopting only against a serious and intractable social evil.

This implies that the justification for strong affirmative action is 16 much weaker in the case of other racial and ethnic groups, and in the case of women. At least, the practice will be justified in a narrower range of circumstances and for a shorter span of time than it is for blacks. No other group has been treated quite like this, and no other group is in a comparable status. Hispanic-Americans occupy an intermediate position, but it seems to me frankly absurd to include persons of oriental descent as beneficiaries of affirmative action, strong or weak. They are not a severely deprived and excluded minority, and their eligibility serves only to swell the numbers that can be included on affirmative action reports. It also suggests that there is a drift in the policy toward adopting the goal of racial proportional representation for its own sake. This is a foolish mistake, and should be resisted. The only legitimate goal of the policy is to reduce egregious racial stratification.

With respect to women, I believe that except over the short term, and in professions or institutions from which their absence is particularly marked, strong affirmative action is not warranted and weak affirmative action is enough. This is based simply on the expectation that the social and economic situation of women will improve quite rapidly under conditions of full equality of opportunity. Recent progress provides some evidence for this. Women do not form a separate hereditary community, characteristically poor and uneducated, and their position is not likely to be self-perpetuating in the same way as that of an outcast race. The process requires less artificial acceleration, and any need for strong affirmative action for women can be expected to end sooner than it ends for blacks.

I said at the outset that there was a tendency to blur the distinction between weak and strong affirmative action. This occurs especially in the use of numerical quotas, a topic on which I want to comment briefly.

A quota may be a method of either weak or strong affirmative action, depending on the circumstances. It amounts to weak affirmative action—a safeguard against discrimination—if, and only if, there is independent evidence that average qualifications for the positions being filled are no lower in the group to which a minimum quota is being assigned than in the applicant group as a whole. This can be presumed true of unskilled jobs that most people can do, but it becomes less likely, and harder to establish, the greater the skill and education required for the position. At these levels, a quota proportional to population, or even to representation of the group in the applicant pool, is almost certain to amount to strong affirmative action. Moreover it is strong affirmative action of a particularly crude and indiscriminate kind, because it permits no variation in the degree of preference on the basis of costs in efficiency, depending on the qualification gap. For this reason I should defend quotas only where they serve the purpose of weak affirmative action. On the whole, strong affirmative action is better implemented by including group preference as one factor in appointment or admission decisions, and letting the results depend on its interaction with other factors.

I have tried to show that the arguments against strong affirmative 20 action are clearly outweighed at present by the need for exceptional measures to remove the stubborn residues of racial caste. But advocates of the policy should acknowledge the reasons against it, which will ensure its termination when it is no longer necessary. Affirmative action is not an end in itself, but a means of dealing with a social situation that should be intolerable to us all.

Questions and Suggestions for Writing

1. Nagel distinguishes between "weak" and "strong" affirmative action (paras. 1–3). He does not bother to defend the weak variety. Do you think this kind of affirmative action is justified? Why, or why not? Read the article by Reynolds (p. 239) and decide whether he would agree.

2. Nagel's concept of "strong" affirmative action (para. 2) includes two different ideas: (a) breaking ties among equally qualified candidates by choosing non-whites or women over white males, and (b) preferring candidates who are nonwhite or women over white males regardless of their relative qualifications. Do you think it is easier to defend (a) rather than (b)? Why, or why not?

3. Nagel identifies three arguments against "strong" affirmative action. Read the essay by Reynolds (p. 239) and explain whether he advances any of these arguments. If he does, who—Nagel or Reynolds—has the better of the dispute? If he doesn't advance any of these three arguments, how do you think Nagel would respond to the arguments Reynolds does propose?

4. Nagel argues (paras. 7–10) against the claim that "strong" affirmative action is unfair. Does his argument try to show (a) that it is not unfair at all, or (b) that it is not as unfair as the discrimination it is intended to replace, or (c) does he advance some completely different argument? Write a 250-word essay explaining your answers.

5. In light of Nagel's thesis (para. 12) concerning when "strong" affirmative action is justified, would he agree or disagree with the Supreme Court's decision in *Stott?* (See the essay by Reynolds, pp. 240–41.)

6. Nagel thinks that even "strong" affirmative action will not remedy the plight of poor blacks, and so he advocates "a more direct economic attack" (para. 14). What sorts of programs do you think he has in mind? Write a 500-word essay identifying three such policies or programs, and explain why you think they would help.

7. Nagel mentions Hispanics and Asians but explicitly excludes the latter as undeserving of "strong" affirmative action programs (para. 16). What about American Indians? Do you think Native Americans' claims on such programs is comparable to that of blacks? of Hispanics? of Asians? Explain your view in an essay of 250 words.

8. Presumably your college has some sort of affirmative action admissions program. Is it of the "weak" or "strong" variety, as Nagel defines those terms? Does it involve numerical quotas? Would Nagel defend them if it does? Would he advocate them if it doesn't? Write a 500-word essay on the topic, explaining your college program and defending or criticizing it.

Is a Human-Centered Ethics Just Another Prejudice?

Peter Singer

Animal Liberation

I

We are familiar with Black Liberation, Gay Liberation, and a variety of other movements. With Women's Liberation some thought we had come to the end of the road. Discrimination on the basis of sex, it has been said, is the last form of discrimination that is universally accepted and practiced without pretense, even in those liberal circles which have long prided

---

Educated at the University of Melbourne and at Oxford, Singer (b. 1946) has taught at Oxford and now teaches at Monash University in Australia. He has written on a variety of ethical issues, but he is especially known for caring about the rights of animals.

This essay originally appeared in the New York Review of Books *(1973), as a review of* Animals, Men and Morals, *edited by Stanley and Roslind Godlovitch and John Harris.*

themselves on their freedom from racial discrimination. But one should always be wary of talking of "the last remaining form of discrimination." If we have learned anything from the liberation movements, we should have learned how difficult it is to be aware of the ways in which we discriminate until they are forcefully pointed out to us. A liberation movement demands an expansion of our moral horizons, so that practices that were previously regarded as natural and inevitable are now seen as intolerable.

Animals, Men and Morals is a manifesto for an Animal Liberation movement. The contributors to the book may not all see the issue this way. They are a varied group. Philosophers, ranging from professors to graduate students, make up the largest contingent. There are five of them, including the three editors, and there is also an extract from the unjustly neglected German philosopher with an English name, Leonard Nelson, who died in 1927. There are essays by two novelist/critics, Brigid Brophy and Maureen Duffy, and another by Muriel the Lady Dowding, widow of Dowding of Battle of Britain fame and the founder of "Beauty without Cruelty," a movement that campaigns against the use of animals for furs and cosmetics. The other pieces are by a psychologist, a botanist, a sociologist, and Ruth Harrison, who is probably best described as a professional campaigner for animal welfare.

Whether or not these people, as individuals, would all agree that they are launching a liberation movement for animals, the book as a whole amounts to no less. It is a demand for a complete change in our attitudes to nonhumans. It is a demand that we cease to regard the exploitation of other species as natural and inevitable, and that, instead, we see it as a continuing moral outrage. Patrick Corbett, Professor of Philosophy at Sussex University, captures the spirit of the book in his closing words:

> We require now to extend the great principles of liberty, equality and fraternity over the lives of animals. Let animal slavery join human slavery in the graveyard of the past.

The reader is likely to be skeptical. "Animal Liberation" sounds more   4
like a parody of liberation movements than a serious objective. The reader may think: We support the claims of blacks and women for equality because blacks and women really are equal to whites and males—equal in intelligence and in abilities, capacity for leadership, rationality, and so on. Humans and nonhumans obviously are not equal in these respects. Since justice demands only that we treat equals equally, unequal treatment of humans and nonhumans cannot be an injustice.

This is a tempting reply, but a dangerous one. It commits the nonracist and nonsexist to a dogmatic belief that blacks and women really are just as intelligent, able, etc., as whites and males—and no more. Quite possibly this happens to be the case. Certainly attempts to prove that racial or sexual differences in these respects have a genetic origin have not been conclusive. But do we really want to stake our demand for equality on the assumption that there are no genetic differences of this kind between the different races or sexes? Surely the appropriate response to those who claim to have found evidence for such genetic differences is not to stick to the belief that there are no differences, whatever the evidence to the contrary; rather one should be clear that the claim to equality does not depend on IQ. Moral equality is distinct from factual equality. Otherwise it would be nonsense to talk of the equality of human beings, since humans, as individuals, obviously differ in intelligence and almost any ability one cares to name. If possessing greater intelligence does not entitle one human to exploit another, why should it entitle humans to exploit nonhumans?

Jeremy Bentham expressed the essential basis of equality in his famous formula: "Each to count for one and none for more than one." In other words, the interests of every being that has interests are to be taken into account and treated equally with the like interests of any other being. Other moral philosophers, before and after Bentham, have made the same point in different ways. Our concern for others must not depend on whether they possess certain characteristics, though just what that concern involves may, of course, vary according to such characteristics.

Bentham, incidentally, was well aware that the logic of the demand for racial equality did not stop at the equality of humans. He wrote:

> The day *may* come when the rest of the animal creation may acquire those rights which never could have been withholden from them but by the hand of tyranny. The French have already discovered that the blackness of the skin is no reason why a human being should be abandoned without redress to the caprice of a tormentor. It may one day come to be recognized that the number of the legs, the villosity of the skin, or the termination of the *os sacrum*, are reasons equally insufficient for abandoning a sensitive being to the same fate. What else is it that should trace the insuperable line? Is it the faculty of reason, or perhaps the faculty of discourse? But a full-grown horse or dog is beyond comparison a more rational, as well as a more conversable animal, than an infant of a day, or a week, or even a month, old. But suppose they were otherwise, what would it avail? The question is not, Can they *reason?* nor Can they *talk?* but, Can they *suffer?*[1]

Surely Bentham was right. If a being suffers, there can be no moral justification for refusing to take that suffering into consideration, and, indeed, to count it equally with the like suffering (if rough comparisons can be made) of any other being.

So the only question is: Do animals other than man suffer? Most people agree unhesitatingly that animals like cats and dogs can and do

[1] *The Principles of Morals and Legislation.* ch. XVII, sec. I, footnote to paragraph 4.

suffer, and this seems also to be assumed by those laws that prohibit wanton cruelty to such animals. Personally, I have no doubt at all about this and find it hard to take seriously the doubts that a few people apparently do have. The editors and contributors of *Animals, Men and Morals* seem to feel the same way, for although the question is raised more than once, doubts are quickly dismissed each time. Nevertheless, because this is such a fundamental point, it is worth asking what grounds we have for attributing suffering to other animals.

It is best to begin by asking what grounds any individual human has for supposing that other humans feel pain. Since pain is a state of consciousness, a "mental event," it can never be directly observed. No observations, whether behavioral signs such as writhing or screaming or physiological or neurological recordings, are observations of pain itself. Pain is something one feels, and one can only infer that others are feeling it from various external indications. The fact that only philosophers are ever skeptical about whether other humans feel pain shows that we regard such inference as justifiable in the case of humans.

Is there any reason why the same inference should be unjustifiable for other animals? Nearly all the external signs which lead us to infer pain in other humans can be seen in other species, especially "higher" animals such as mammals and birds. Behavioral signs—writhing, yelping, or other forms of calling, attempts to avoid the source of pain, and many others—are present. We know, too, that these animals are biologically similar in the relevant respects, having nervous systems like ours which can be observed to function as ours do.

So the grounds for inferring that these animals can feel pain are nearly as good as the grounds for inferring other humans do. Only nearly, for there is one behavioral sign that humans have but nonhumans, with the exception of one or two specially raised chimpanzees, do not have. This, of course, is a developed language. As the quotation from Bentham indicates, this has long been regarded as an important distinction between man and other animals. Other animals may communicate with each other, but not in the way we do. Following Chomsky,[2] many people now mark this distinction by saying that only humans communicate in a form that is governed by rules of syntax. (For the purposes of this argument, linguists allow those chimpanzees who have learned a syntactic sign language to rank as honorary humans.) Nevertheless, as Bentham pointed out, this distinction is not relevant to the question of how animals ought to be treated, unless it can be linked to the issue of whether animals suffer.

This link may be attempted in two ways. First, there is a hazy line of   12
philosophical thought, stemming perhaps from some doctrines associated with Wittgenstein, which maintains that we cannot meaningfully at-

[2]**Chomsky** Noam Chomsky (b. 1928), a professor of linguistics and the author of (among other books) *Language and Mind* (1972). [Editors' note]

tribute states of consciousness to beings without language. I have not seen this argument made explicit in print, though I have come across it in conversation. This position seems to me very implausible, and I doubt that it would be held at all if it were not thought to be a consequence of a broader view of the significance of language. It may be that the use of a public, rule-governed language is a precondition of conceptual thought. It may even be, although personally I doubt it, that we cannot meaningfully speak of a creature having an intention unless that creature can use a language. But states like pain, surely, are more primitive than either of these, and seem to have nothing to do with language.

Indeed, as Jane Goodall points out in her study of chimpanzees, when it comes to the expression of feelings and emotions, humans tend to fall back on nonlinguistic modes of communication which are often found among apes, such as a cheering pat on the back, an exuberant embrace, a clasp of hands, and so on.[3] Michael Peters makes a similar point in his contribution to *Animals, Men and Morals* when he notes that the basic signals we use to convey pain, fear, sexual arousal, and so on are not specific to our species. So there seems to be no reason at all to believe that a creature without language cannot suffer.

The second, and more easily appreciated way of linking language and the existence of pain is to say that the best evidence that we can have that another creature is in pain is when he tells us that he is. This is a distinct line of argument, for it is not being denied that a non-language-user conceivably could suffer, but only that we could know that he is suffering. Still, this line of argument seems to me to fail, and for reasons similar to those just given. "I am in pain" is not the best possible evidence that the speaker is in pain (he might be lying) and it is certainly not the only possible evidence. Behavioral signs and knowledge of the animal's biological similarity to ourselves together provide adequate evidence that animals do suffer. After all, we would not accept linguistic evidence if it contradicted the rest of the evidence. If a man was severely burned, and behaved as if he were in pain, writhing, groaning, being very careful not to let his burned skin touch anything, and so on, but later said he had not been in pain at all, we would be more likely to conclude that he was lying or suffering from amnesia than that he had not been in pain.

Even if there were stronger grounds for refusing to attribute pain to those who do not have a language, the consequences of this refusal might lead us to examine these grounds unusually critically. Human infants, as well as some adults, are unable to use language. Are we to deny that a year-old infant can suffer? If not, how can language be crucial? Of course, most parents can understand the responses of even very young infants better than they understand the responses of other animals, and sometimes infant responses can be understood in the light of later development.

---

[3]Jane van Lawick-Goodall, *In the Shadow of Man* (Houghton Mifflin, 1971), p. 225.

This, however, is just a fact about the relative knowledge we have of 16
our own species and other species, and most of this knowledge is simply
derived from closer contact. Those who have studied the behavior of other
animals soon learn to understand their responses at least as well as we
understand those of an infant. (I am not referring to Jane Goodall's and
other well-known studies of apes. Consider, for example, the degree of
understanding achieved by Tinbergen from watching herring gulls.)[4] Just
as we can understand infant human behavior in the light of adult human
behavior, so we can understand the behavior of other species in the light of
our own behavior (and sometimes we can understand our own behavior
better in the light of the behavior of other species).

The grounds we have for believing that other mammals and birds
suffer are, then, closely analogous to the grounds we have for believing that
other humans suffer. It remains to consider how far down the evolutionary
scale this analogy holds. Obviously it becomes poorer when we get further
away from man. To be more precise would require a detailed examination
of all that we know about other forms of life. With fish, reptiles, and other
vertebrates the analogy still seems strong, with molluscs like oysters it is
much weaker. Insects are more difficult, and it may be that in our present
state of knowledge we must be agnostic about whether they are capable of
suffering.

If there is no moral justification for ignoring suffering when it occurs,
and it does occur in other species, what are we to say of our attitudes
toward these other species? Richard Ryder, one of the contributors to
Animals, Men and Morals, uses the term "speciesism" to describe the belief
that we are entitled to treat members of other species in a way in which it
would be wrong to treat members of our own species. The term is not
euphonious, but it neatly makes the analogy with racism. The nonracist
would do well to bear the analogy in mind when he is inclined to defend
human behavior toward nonhumans. "Shouldn't we worry about improving the lot of our own species before we concern ourselves with other
species?" he may ask. If we substitute "race" for "species" we shall see that
the question is better not asked. "Is a vegetarian diet nutritionally adequate?" resembles the slaveowner's claim that he and the whole economy
of the South would be ruined without slave labor. There is even a parallel
with skeptical doubts about whether animals suffer, for some defenders of slavery professed to doubt whether blacks really suffer in the way
whites do.

I do not want to give the impression, however, that the case for Animal
Liberation is based on the analogy with racism and no more. On the
contrary, *Animals, Men and Morals* describes the various ways in which
humans exploit nonhumans, and several contributors consider the defenses
that have been offered, including the defense of meat-eating mentioned in

---

[4] N. Tinbergen, *The Herring Gull's World* (Basic Books, 1961).

the last paragraph. Sometimes the rebuttals are scornfully dismissive, rather than carefully designed to convince the detached critic. This may be a fault, but it is a fault that is inevitable, given the kind of book this is. The issue is not one on which one can remain detached. As the editors state in their Introduction:

> Once the full force of moral assessment has been made explicit there can be no rational excuse left for killing animals, be they killed for food, science, or sheer personal indulgence. We have not assembled this book to provide the reader with yet another manual on how to make brutalities less brutal. Compromise, in the traditional sense of the term, is simple unthinking weakness when one considers the actual reasons for our crude relationships with the other animals.

The point is that on this issue there are few critics who are genuinely 20 detached. People who eat pieces of slaughtered nonhumans every day find it hard to believe that they are doing wrong; and they also find it hard to imagine what else they could eat. So for those who do not place nonhumans beyond the pale of morality, there comes a stage when further argument seems pointless, a stage at which one can only accuse one's opponent of hypocrisy and reach for the sort of sociological account of our practices and the way we defend them that is attempted by David Wood in his contribution to this book. On the other hand, to those unconvinced by the arguments, and unable to accept that they are merely rationalizing their dietary preferences and their fear of being thought peculiar, such sociological explanations can only seem insultingly arrogant.

II

The logic of speciesism is most apparent in the practice of experimenting on nonhumans in order to benefit humans. This is because the issue is rarely obscured by allegations that nonhumans are so different from humans that we cannot know anything about whether they suffer. The defender of vivisection cannot use this argument because he needs to stress the similarities between man and other animals in order to justify the usefulness to the former of experiments on the latter. The researcher who makes rats choose between starvation and electric shocks to see if they develop ulcers (they do) does so because he knows that the rat has a nervous system very similar to man's, and presumably feels an electric shock in a similar way.

Richard Ryder's restrained account of experiments on animals made me angrier with my fellow men than anything else in this book. Ryder, a clinical psychologist by profession, himself experimented on animals before he came to hold the view he puts forward in his essay. Experimenting on animals is now a large industry, both academic and commercial. In

1969, more than 5 million experiments were performed in Britain, the vast majority without anesthetic (though how many of these involved pain is not known). There are no accurate U.S. figures, since there is no federal law on the subject, and in many cases no state law either. Estimates vary from 20 million to 200 million. Ryder suggests that 80 million may be the best guess. We tend to think that this is all for vital medical research, but of course it is not. Huge numbers of animals are used in university departments from Forestry to Psychology, and even more are used for commercial purposes, to test whether cosmetics can cause skin damage, or shampoos eye damage, or to test food additives or laxatives or sleeping pills or anything else.

A standard test for foodstuffs is the "LD50." The object of this test is to find the dosage level at which 50 percent of the test animals will die. This means that nearly all of them will become very sick before finally succumbing or surviving. When the substance is a harmless one, it may be necessary to force huge doses down the animals, until in some cases sheer volume or concentration causes death.

Ryder gives a selection of experiments, taken from recent scientific journals. I will quote two, not for the sake of indulging in gory details, but in order to give an idea of what normal researchers think they may legitimately do to other species. The point is not that the individual researchers are cruel men, but that they are behaving in a way that is allowed by our speciesist attitudes. As Ryder points out, even if only 1 percent of the experiments involve severe pain, that is 50,000 experiments in Britain each year, or nearly 150 every day (and about fifteen times as many in the United States, if Ryder's guess is right). Here then are two experiments:

> O.S. Ray and R.J. Barrett of Pittsburgh gave electric shocks to the feet of 1,042 mice. They then caused convulsions by giving more intense shocks through cup-shaped electrodes applied to the animals' eyes or through pressure spring clips attached to their ears. Unfortunately some of the mice who "successfully completed Day One training were found sick or dead prior to testing on Day Two." [*Journal of Comparative and Physiological Psychology*, 1969, vol. 67, pp. 110–116]
>
> At the National Institute for Medical Research, Mill Hill, London, W. Feldberg and S. L. Sherwood injected chemicals into the brains of cats— "with a number of widely different substances, recurrent patterns of reaction were obtained. Retching, vomiting, defecation, increased salivation and greatly accelerated respiration leading to panting were common features." . . .
>
> The injection into the brain of a large dose of Tubocuraine caused the cat to jump "from the table to the floor and then straight into its cage, where it started calling more and more noisily whilst moving about restlessly and jerkily . . . finally the cat fell with legs and neck flexed, jerking in rapid clonic movements, the condition being that of a major

24

[epileptic] convulsion . . . within a few seconds the cat got up, ran for a few yards at high speed and fell in another fit. The whole process was repeated several times within the next ten minutes, during which the cat lost faeces and foamed at the mouth."

This animal finally died thirty-five minutes after the brain injection. [*Journal of Physiology*, 1954, vol. 123, pp. 148–167]

There is nothing secret about these experiments. One has only to open any recent volume of a learned journal, such as the *Journal of Comparative and Physiological Psychology*, to find full descriptions of experiments of this sort, together with the results obtained—results that are frequently trivial and obvious. The experiments are often supported by public funds.

It is a significant indication of the level of acceptability of these practices that, although these experiments are taking place at this moment on university campuses throughout the country, there has, so far as I know, not been the slightest protest from the student movement. Students have been rightly concerned that their universities should not discriminate on grounds of race or sex, and that they should not serve the purposes of the military or big business. Speciesism continues undisturbed, and many students participate in it. There may be a few qualms at first, but since everyone regards it as normal, and it may even be a required part of a course, the student soon becomes hardened and, dismissing his earlier feelings as "mere sentiment," comes to regard animals as statistics rather than sentient beings with interests that warrant consideration.

Argument about vivisection has often missed the point because it has been put in absolutist terms: Would the abolitionist be prepared to let thousands die if they could be saved by experimenting on a single animal? The way to reply to this purely hypothetical question is to pose another: Would the experimenter be prepared to experiment on a human orphan under six months old, if it were the only way to save many lives? (I say "orphan" to avoid the complication of parental feelings, although in doing so I am being overfair to the experimenter, since the nonhuman subjects of experiments are not orphans.) A negative answer to this question indicates that the experimenter's readiness to use nonhumans is simple discrimination, for adult apes, cats, mice, and other mammals are more conscious of what is happening to them, more self-directing, and, so far as we can tell, just as sensitive to pain as a human infant. There is no characteristic that human infants possess that adult mammals do not have to the same or a higher degree.

(It might be possible to hold that what makes it wrong to experiment 28 on a human infant is that the infant will in time develop into more than the nonhuman, but one would then, to be consistent, have to oppose abortion, and perhaps contraception, too, for the fetus and the egg and sperm have the same potential as the infant. Moreover, one would still have no reason for experimenting on a nonhuman rather than a human with brain damage severe enough to make it impossible for him to rise above infant level.)

The experimenter, then, shows a bias for his own species whenever he carries out an experiment on a nonhuman for a purpose that he would not think justified him in using a human being at an equal or lower level of sentience, awareness, ability to be self-directing, etc. No one familiar with the kind of results yielded by these experiments can have the slightest doubt that if this bias were eliminated the number of experiments performed would be zero or very close to it.

III

If it is vivisection that shows the logic of speciesism most clearly, it is the use of other species for food that is at the heart of our attitudes toward them. Most of *Animals, Men and Morals* is an attack on meat eating—an attack which is based solely on concern for nonhumans, without reference to arguments derived from considerations of ecology, macrobiotics, health, or religion.

The idea that nonhumans are utilities, means to our ends, pervades our thought. Even conservationists who are concerned about the slaughter of wildfowl but not about the vastly greater slaughter of chickens for our tables are thinking in this way—they are worried about what we would lose if there were less wildlife. Stanley Godlovitch, pursuing the Marxist idea that our thinking is formed by the activities we undertake in satisfying our needs, suggests that man's first classification of his environment was into Edibles and Inedibles. Most animals came into the first category, and there they have remained.

Man may always have killed other species for food, but he has never 32 exploited them so ruthlessly as he does today. Farming has succumbed to business methods, the objective being to get the highest possible ratio of output (meat, eggs, milk) to input (fodder, labor costs, etc.). Ruth Harrison's essay "On Factory Farming" gives an account of some aspects of modern methods, and of the unsuccessful British campaign for effective controls, a campaign which was sparked off by her *Animal Machines* (London: Stuart, 1964).

Her article is in no way a substitute for her earlier book. This is a pity since, as she says, "Farm produce is still associated with mental pictures of animals browsing in the fields . . . of hens having a last forage before going to roost. . . ." Yet neither in her article nor elsewhere in *Animals, Men and Morals* is this false image replaced by a clear idea of the nature and extent of factory farming. We learn of this only indirectly, when we hear of the code of reform proposed by an advisory committee set up by the British government.

Among the proposals, which the government refused to implement on the grounds that they were too idealistic, were: *"Any animal should at least have room to turn around freely."*

Factory farm animals need liberation in the most literal sense. Veal calves are kept in stalls five feet by two feet. They are usually slaughtered when about four months old, and have been too big to turn in their stalls for at least a month. Intensive beef herds, kept in stalls only proportionately larger for much longer periods, account for a growing percentage of beef production. Sows are often similarly confined when pregnant, which, because of artificial methods of increasing fertility, can be most of the time. Animals confined in this way do not waste food by exercising, nor do they develop unpalatable muscle.

"A dry bedded area should be provided for all stock." Intensively kept 36 animals usually have to stand and sleep on slatted floors without straw, because this makes cleaning easier.

"Palatable roughage must be readily available to all calves after one week of age." In order to produce the pale veal housewives are said to prefer, calves are fed on an all-liquid diet until slaughter, even though they are long past the age at which they would normally eat grass. They develop a craving for roughage, evidenced by attempts to gnaw wood from their stalls. (For the same reason, their diet is deficient in iron.)

"Battery cages for poultry should be large enough for a bird to be able to stretch one wing at a time." Under current British practice, a cage for four or five laying hens has a floor area of twenty inches by eighteen inches, scarcely larger than a double page of the *New York Review of Books*. In this space, on a sloping wire floor (sloping so the eggs roll down, wire so the dung drops through) the birds live for a year or eighteen months while artificial lighting and temperature conditions combine with drugs in their food to squeeze the maximum number of eggs out of them. Table birds are also sometimes kept in cages. More often they are reared in sheds, no less crowded. Under these conditions all the birds' natural activities are frustrated, and they develop "vices" such as pecking each other to death. To prevent this, beaks are often cut off, and the sheds kept dark.

How many of those who support factory farming by buying its produce know anything about the way it is produced? How many have heard something about it, but are reluctant to check up for fear that it will make them uncomfortable? To nonspeciesists, the typical consumer's mixture of ignorance, reluctance to find out the truth, and vague belief that nothing really bad could be allowed seems analogous to the attitudes of "decent Germans" to the death camps.

There are, of course, some defenders of factory farming. Their argu- 40 ments are considered, though again rather sketchily, by John Harris. Among the most common: "Since they have never known anything else, they don't suffer." This argument will not be put by anyone who knows anything about animal behavior, since he will know that not all behavior has to be learned. Chickens attempt to stretch wings, walk around, scratch, and even dustbathe or build a nest, even though they have never lived under conditions that allowed these activities. Calves can suffer from maternal deprivation no matter at what age they were taken from their mothers. "We need these intensive methods to provide protein for a growing population." As ecologists and famine relief organizations know, we can produce far more protein per acre if we grow the right vegetable crop, soy beans for instance, than if we use the land to grow crops to be converted into protein by animals who use nearly 90 percent of the protein themselves, even when unable to exercise.

There will be many readers of this book who will agree that factory farming involves an unjustifiable degree of exploitation of sentient creatures, and yet will want to say that there is nothing wrong with rearing animals for food, provided it is done "humanely." These people are saying, in effect, that although we should not cause animals to suffer, there is nothing wrong with killing them.

There are two possible replies to this view. One is to attempt to show that this combination of attitudes is absurd. Roslind Godlovitch takes this course in her essay, which is an examination of some common attitudes to animals. She argues that from the combination of "animal suffering is to be avoided" and "there is nothing wrong with killing animals" it follows that all animal life ought to be exterminated (since all sentient creatures will suffer to some degree at some point in their lives). Euthanasia is a contentious issue only because we place some value on living. If we did not, the least amount of suffering would justify it. Accordingly, if we deny that we have a duty to exterminate all animal life, we must concede that we are placing some value on animal life.

This argument seems to me valid, although one could still reply that the value of animal life is to be derived from the pleasures that life can have for them, so that, provided their lives have a balance of pleasure over pain, we are justified in rearing them. But this would imply that we ought to produce animals and let them live as pleasantly as possible, without suffering.

At this point, one can make the second of the two possible replies to the view that rearing and killing animals for food is all right so long as it is done humanely. This second reply is that so long as we think that a nonhuman may be killed simply so that a human can satisfy his taste for meat, we are still thinking of nonhumans as means rather than as ends in themselves. The factory farm is nothing more than the application of technology to this concept. Even traditional methods involve castration, the separation of mothers and their young, the breaking up of herds, branding or earpunching, and of course transportation to the abattoirs and the final moments of terror when the animal smells blood and senses danger. If we were to try rearing animals so that they lived and died without suffering, we should find that to do so on anything like the scale of today's meat industry would be a sheer impossibility. Meat would become the prerogative of the rich.

I have been able to discuss only some of the contributions to this book, saying nothing about, for instance, the essays on killing for furs and for sport. Nor have I considered all the detailed questions that need to be asked once we start thinking about other species in the radically different way presented by this book. What, for instance, are we to do about genuine conflicts of interest like rats biting slum children? I am not sure of the answer, but the essential point is just that we *do* see this as a conflict of interests, that we recognize that rats have interests too. Then we may begin to think about other ways of resolving the conflict—perhaps by leaving out rat baits that sterilize the rats instead of killing them.

I have not discussed such problems because they are side issues compared with the exploitation of other species for food and for experimental purposes. On these central matters, I hope that I have said enough to show that this book, despite its flaws, is a challenge to every human to recognize his attitudes to nonhumans as a form of prejudice no less objectionable than racism or sexism. It is a challenge that demands not just a change of attitudes, but a change in our way of life, for it requires us to become vegetarians.

Can a purely moral demand of this kind succeed? The odds are certainly against it. The book holds out no inducements. It does not tell us that we will become healthier, or enjoy life more, if we cease exploiting animals. Animal Liberation will require greater altruism on the part of mankind than any other liberation movement, since animals are incapable of demanding it for themselves, or of protesting against their exploitation by votes, demonstrations, or bombs. Is man capable of such genuine altruism? Who knows? If this book does have a significant effect, however, it will be a vindication of all those who have believed that man has within himself the potential for more than cruelty and selfishness.

Questions and Suggestions for Writing

1. In his fourth paragraph Singer formulates an argument on behalf of the skeptical reader. Examine that argument closely, restate it in your own words, and evaluate it. Which of its premises are most vulnerable to criticism? Why?

2. Singer quotes with approval (para. 7) Bentham's comment, "The question is not, Can they *reason?* nor Can they *talk?* but, Can they *suffer?*" Do you find this argument persuasive? Can you think of any effective challenge to it?

3. Singer allows that although developed linguistic capacity is not necessary for a creature to have pain, perhaps such a capacity is necessary for "having an intention" (para. 12). Do you think this concession is correct? Have you ever seen animal behavior that you would be willing to describe or explain as

evidence that the animal has an intention to do something, despite knowing that the animal cannot talk?

4. Singer thinks that the readiness to experiment on animals cuts out the ground for believing that animals don't suffer pain (see para. 21). Do you agree with this reasoning?

5. Singer confesses (para. 22) to being made especially angry "with my fellow men" after reading the accounts of animal experimentation. What is it that aroused his anger? Do such feelings, and the acknowledgment that one has them, have any place in a sober discussion about the merits of animal experimentation? Why, or why not?

6. What is "factory farming" (paras. 32–40)? Why is Singer opposed to it?

7. To the claim that "there is nothing wrong with rearing animals for food, provided it is done 'humanely,'" Singer offers two replies (paras. 42–44). In an essay of 250 words summarize them briefly and then indicate whether either persuades you, and why or why not.

8. Suppose someone were to say to Singer: "You claim that capacity to suffer is the relevant factor in deciding whether a creature deserves to be treated as my moral equal. But you're wrong—the relevant factor is whether the creature is *alive*. Being alive is what matters, not being capable of feeling pain." In one or two paragraphs declare what you think would be Singer's reply.

9. Do you think it is worse to kill an animal for its fur than to kill, cook, and eat an animal? Is it worse to kill an animal for sport than to kill it for medical experimentation? What is Singer's view? Explain your view, making use of Singer's if you wish, in an essay of 500 words.

10. Are there any arguments, in your opinion, which show the immorality of eating human flesh (cannibalism) but which do not show a similar objection to eating animal flesh? Write a 500-word essay in which you discuss the issue.

C. A. J. Coady

Defending Human Chauvinism

My title is a little misleading. Although I shall be offering certain thoughts in defense of a position that some would regard as "human chauvinism" or "speciesism" I am really more concerned with getting clear about just what is being said by those who use those terms in clamorous denunciation and what value their supporting arguments have.

C. A. J. Coady (b. 1936) is Reader in Philosophy at the University of Melbourne, Australia. This article appeared in QQ, 1986.

The locus of my comments will be the moral concerns and outlooks that have fathered (or mothered?) two political movements—animal liberation and environmentalism. Despite points of tension between the animal and nature liberationists, both have in common that they may be plausibly viewed as calling for a new ethic. The characteristic move of the new ethicists is to declare that the traditional ethic is defective in its emphasis on the importance of human beings. This is speciesism or human chauvinism. The old ethic was human centered, the new will be . . . well, it will have some other center.

ONE BAD ARGUMENT

One bad argument against speciesism consists in drawing attention to the fact that just as we come to realize that moral concern cannot be restricted to the members of our own race ("racism") or of our own sex ("sexism"), so by a sort of analogical extension we come to see that it cannot be restricted to our own species ("speciesism"). But this argument gets things the wrong way round. It is clearly possible for someone who puts special moral importance upon humankind to object to racist policies precisely because they treat their victims as being not human or, in Hitler's classic phrase, subhuman. When we consider that a common element in the usual moral criticism of racism and sexism is precisely that such outlooks ignore the fact that the members of the maltreated class are members of the human species like ourselves, then the condemnation of speciesism can hardly seem a simple extension of those other condemnations.

JUSTIFYING HUMAN SUPERIORITY

Yet, at this point, it will be said that the idea that there is something   4
specially morally important about human beings needs justification. I am of two minds about this demand for justification. I think it can be met but I'm not sure that it has to be. There are various ground floor considerations in ethics as in any other enterprise—for an animal liberationist such things as the "intrinsic good" of pleasure and the "intrinsic evil" of pain are usually ground floor. No further justification is given for them, or needed. It is not clear to me that membership in the human species does not function in a similarly fundamental way in ethics so that there is as much absurdity, if not more, in asking "Why does it matter morally that she is human?" as in asking "Why does it matter morally that she is in pain?" Nonetheless, since justification is preferable to intuition where it can be given let me try to do so.

Before trying to provide such a justification let us be clear what it involves. We need some characterization, not necessarily a very precise one, of what it is about humankind that makes it worthy of more moral consideration than other known kinds such as ants, dogs, pine trees, a strain of flu virus, or a type of rock. What we would thereby show, if successful, is that what environmentalists, such as the Routleys, call "the greater value assumption"—the assumption that human beings are of greater value, morally, than individuals of other species—is no mere assumption. We would also perhaps then vindicate a "human-centered ethic" in some sense of that confusing phrase.

A further caution is in order about what the task involves. We are trying to exhibit features of humankind that show that the human species is morally distinctive, but these need not be such as to show that no moral respect or even duty is owed to other species. The assumption to be vindicated is a greater value assumption, not an exclusive value assumption. An exclusive value assumption would entail an attitude to nature that sees no value at all in either the animate or inanimate environment except insofar as it subserves rather narrowly conceived human interests.

INTRINSIC VALUES IN NATURE?

The issue of whether there are intrinsic values in the nonanimate world has become a point of serious division between the environmentalists and the animalists because the former object to the latter's emphasis on pain, pleasure, and associated interests as the sole or primary deposit of value. The environmentalists object either that sentience is not a precondition for having interests or that it is not a precondition for having value. They accuse animal liberationists like Peter Singer of the dastardly sin of "sentiencism." The Routleys and others are fond of producing examples our responses to which are supposed to show that there are intrinsic values to nonanimate nature. Let me cite just a few.

(1) The last man example. This concerns the last man on earth, sole [8] survivor of the collapse of the world system, who sets to work eliminating (painlessly) every living thing, animal or plant, and perhaps defacing mountains as well. If we think he has acted wrongly, presumably we are recognizing intrinsic value in nonhuman and even in nonanimate entities.

(2) The river example. This is to illustrate the idea that natural phenomena can be damaged independently of any human or animal related damage in a way that calls for compensation. The idea is that pollution of a river involves more than damage to the humans affected by it so that compensation requires restoration of the river to its unpolluted state and not merely monetary compensation to any people affected.

(3) The noise in the forest example. This concerns an objection to "making unnecessary and excessive noise" in a forest. It is held that the

believer in the new ethic's intrinsic values will avoid such noise even if no other humans are around to hear and he will so act "out of respect for the forest and its nonhuman inhabitants." Adherents of the traditional ethic will feel free to shout and howl as the mood takes them.

Before I leave these examples for your judgment let me comment briefly on (2) and (3) because I have certain dissatisfactions with them. The river example is defective, as it stands, in placing so much weight on monetary compensation, since the people affected may need to have an unpolluted river in the future so that they do not suffer further damage and they may in any case prefer the appearance of a beautiful, clear, unpolluted stream in which they can catch healthy fish. If we remove these features by paying the people so much that they can move to the banks of another, clean river and then so arrange things (noncoercively) that no humans or even animals are affected by the state of the river, is it so obvious that some moral wrong has been done by continuing to pollute the stream in a good (human) cause? In the forest example we must, I think, exclude noise that might actually cause damage to a wild animal by, say, bursting its eardrums, but if we set that aside can it seriously be claimed that a moral issue about the noise arises?

Speciesism Vindicated

Let me now return to my defense of the greater value assumption. 12 Insofar as the Routleys and other advocates of a new ethic rely upon the deliverances of intuition about the morality of shouting in the forest, the last man on earth, and so on, it seems to me that man's greater moral importance over animals, ecosystems, trees, or whatever is far more obvious than any of the intuitions of the new ethic. Consider a small child being attacked by a rat. It is perfectly obvious to anyone not unbalanced by theory that it is morally right to injure or kill the rat if that is necessary to save the child. It makes no difference that the rat may be very smart (for a rat) and the child backward or that the child provoked the attack. Anyone who hesitated to act because of such considerations would be a moral idiot. Normally, at the level of intuition, serious human welfare clearly outweighs that of animals. I do not know how much we can rely on appeals to intuition, but they seem inescapable in these debates and I think one should be wary of being bluffed out of one's pro-human intuitions. One should be particularly suspicious when marginal intuitions are used to construct an argument which is supposed to disenfranchise more robust intuitions.

As for a characterization of the superiority of the human species, my view is that we should not seek to uncover just *one* characteristic such as rationality (though plainly rationality is important) but rather highlight a cluster of interconnected characteristics. So one could cite, in addition to rationality, the capacity for artistic creation, the capacity for theoretical knowledge of the universe and of oneself, the capacity for love including love of one's enemies, and very centrally the capacity for moral goodness. This last provides a crucial distinction between the inanimate, plant, and brute creation on the one side and humanity on the other and makes talk of a moral community among humans, mountains, trees, lakes, fish, and kangaroos a bit one-sided. I should add that I do not here propose a particularly optimistic view of the human species since I recognize that it is an essential concomitant of the capacities listed that they can be abused and that they imply the capacity for irrationality and wickedness. This is what human freedom, which is involved in all these characteristics, typically allows. Nonetheless, that man has this complex of features makes him as a species more morally significant than the nonhuman world as we know it.

OBJECTIONS ANSWERED

There is a strategy employed by the Routleys and also by Peter Singer against claims of the form mine has taken. For any quality that is suggested as giving humans moral superiority the strategy is to declare: (a) that some nonhuman object or process or creature has it, too; (b) that not all humans have it; or (c) that some humans have it in different degrees to others. So in the case of rationality, for instance, we are told that some animals have it, that some defective or immature humans lack it, and that Einstein has more of it than others. In the case of the cluster of properties I have proposed, however, it seems clear that our species is marked by these qualities, and being marked by them is deserving of moral respect, and it is merely delusional to suppose that the cluster is exhibited by any species in the nonhuman world as we know it. The wildest claims on behalf of Washoe, the talking chimpanzee, do not really establish him as an even moderately boring dinner guest. The passion to denigrate the human world has led to very extravagant and ill-founded claims for the linguistic and related achievements of chimpanzees and dolphins. Washoe's exploits have recently been subjected to much more sober and critical scientific assessment than they received at the hands of the original investigators with alarmingly deflationary results.

As to the second and third parts of the strategy, it is of course true that there are immature, senile, and defective members of the species, but only an inordinately individualistic ideology can hold that such members should be given treatment that takes no account of their species membership. We have a vital interest in the immature, the retarded, and the defective of our kind since, apart from anything else, we normal adults have been immature and may become damaged or handicapped. The focus of moral concern upon isolated individuals and their present attributes rather than upon species, groups, kinds, and types is not the only or, one might think, the sanest stance possible for moral theory. As to those members of the species who possess the featured capacities to an outstanding degree, several responses are possible. One is to note that it is very unlikely that many will possess the *complex* to a degree that raises problems of differential respect; a second is to distinguish issues to do with law, politics, and generally civil justice from those that concern other areas of morality—there are well-known reasons for not having legal and political inequalities, but these reasons do not necessarily apply in other areas of moral interest. Perhaps the saint is worthy of special moral respect and even more.

A final point about chauvinism. I wonder whether it wouldn't be 16 appropriate to say something here on behalf of artifacts and machines. Are the new ethicists in danger of sliding into a form of nature chauvinism?

Questions and Suggestions for Writing

1. Coady indicates (para. 1) some reservations about his choice of title. After reading his essay, propose a more accurate but equally provocative title.

2. Read the preceding essay, by Peter Singer, and decide whether he does or does not advocate what Coady calls "one bad argument" (para. 2).

3. Coady admits to doubts (para. 4) over whether acts can be defended by the retort "Because she's human" any better or worse than by the retort "Because she's in pain." Do you think either of these reasons has the edge over the other? Explain.

4. Evaluate Coady's replies to the river and forest noise arguments (paras. 9–11).

5. Coady ignores the last man argument (para. 8). Do you think it proves its point, or fails to do so? Explain.

6. Given what Coady says about the life of a child versus the life of a rat (para. 12), what do you think he would say about forcing people to stop buying and selling ivory to save the last elephants or refusing to create a life-saving drug for humans if it could be obtained only by fatal experimentation on the last porpoise?

7. Suppose someone were to object to Coady's final reasoning (paras. 14–15) by arguing that it is one thing to point to the "cluster of attributes" that human beings typically possess, and quite another to insist, as he does, that this constitutes a "moral"—or morally relevant—difference between us and other species that lack these attributes. How do you think Coady could or should reply?

WAS FREUD RIGHT ABOUT WOMEN?

Sigmund Freud

Femininity

Today's lecture . . . may serve to give you an example of a detailed piece of analytic work, and I can say two things to recommend it. It brings forward nothing but observed facts, almost without any speculative additions, and it deals with a subject which has a claim on your interest second almost to no other. Throughout history people have knocked their heads against the riddle of the nature of femininity—

> Häupter in Hieroglyphenmützen,
> Häupter in Turban und schwarzem Barett,
> Perückenhäupter und tausend andre
> Arme, schwitzende Menschenhäupter. . . .[1]

Nor will *you* have escaped worrying over this problem—those of you who are men; to those of you who are women this will not apply—you are yourselves the problem. When you meet a human being, the first distinction you make is "male or female?" and you are accustomed to make the distinction with unhesitating certainty. Anatomical science shares your certainty at one point and not much further. The male sexual product, the spermatozoon, and its vehicle are male; the ovum and the organism that harbors it are female. In both sexes organs have been formed which serve exclusively for the sexual functions; they were probably developed from the same [innate] disposition into two different forms. Besides this, in both sexes the other organs, the bodily shapes and tissues, show the influence of the individual's sex, but this is inconstant and its amount variable; these are what are known as the secondary sexual characters. Science next tells

---

[1]Heads in hieroglyphic bonnets,
  Heads in turbans and black birettas,
  Heads in wigs and thousand other
  Wretched, sweating heads of humans. . . .
        (Heine, *Nordsee* [Second Cycle, VII, "Fragen"].)
                    [Translator's note]

Sigmund Freud (1856–1939), trained in Vienna and Paris as a doctor, was the founder of psychoanalysis. Before moving to London as a refugee from the Nazis and nearing the end of his long life, he imagined himself once again in the lecture halls speaking to students. The result was his little book, New Introductory Lectures on Psychoanalysis *(1933), from which this chapter is taken.*

you something that runs counter to your expectations and is probably calculated to confuse your feelings. It draws your attention to the fact that portions of the male sexual apparatus also appear in women's bodies, though in an atrophied state, and vice versa in the alternative case. It regards their occurrence as indications of *bisexuality*, as though an individual is not a man or a woman but always both—merely a certain amount more the one than the other. You will then be asked to make yourselves familiar with the idea that the proportion in which masculine and feminine are mixed in an individual is subject to quite considerable fluctuations. Since, however, apart from the very rarest cases, only one kind of sexual product—ova or semen—is nevertheless present in one person, you are bound to have doubts as to the decisive significance of those elements and must conclude that what constitutes masculinity or femininity is an unknown characteristic which anatomy cannot lay hold of.

Can psychology do so perhaps? We are accustomed to employ "masculine" and "feminine" as mental qualities as well, and have in the same way transferred the notion of bisexuality to mental life. Thus we speak of a person, whether male or female, as behaving in a masculine way in one connection and in a feminine way in another. But you will soon perceive that this is only giving way to anatomy or to convention. You cannot give the concepts of "masculine" and "feminine" *any* new connotation. The distinction is not a psychological one; when you say "masculine," you usually mean "active," and when you say "feminine," you usually mean "passive." Now it is true that a relation of the kind exists. The male sex-cell is actively mobile and searches out the female one, and the latter, the ovum, is immobile and waits passively. This behavior of the elementary sexual organisms is indeed a model for the conduct of sexual individuals during intercourse. The male pursues the female for the purpose of sexual union, seizes hold of her, and penetrates into her. But by this you have precisely reduced the characteristic of masculinity to the factor of aggressiveness so far as psychology is concerned. You may well doubt whether you have gained any real advantage from this when you reflect that in some classes of animals the females are the stronger and more aggressive and the male is active only in the single act of sexual union. This is so, for instance, with the spiders. Even the functions of rearing and caring for the young, which strike us as feminine par excellence, are not invariably attached to the female sex in animals. In quite high species we find that the sexes share the task of caring for the young between them or even that the male alone devotes himself to it. Even in the sphere of human sexual life you soon see how inadequate it is to make masculine behavior coincide with activity and feminine with passivity. A mother is active in every sense toward her child; the act of lactation itself may equally be described as the mother suckling the baby or as her being sucked by it. The further you go from the narrow sexual sphere the more obvious will the "error of superimposition"[2] become. Women can display great activity in various directions, men are not able to live in company with their own kind unless they develop a large amount of passive adaptability. If you now tell me that these facts go to prove precisely that both men and women are bisexual in the psychological sense, I shall conclude that you have decided in your own minds to make "active" coincide with "masculine" and "passive" with "feminine." But I advise you against it. It seems to me to serve no useful purpose and adds nothing to our knowledge.

One might consider characterizing femininity psychologically as giv-   4
ing preference to passive aims. This is not, of course, the same thing as passivity; to achieve a passive aim may call for a large amount of activity. It is perhaps the case that in a woman, on the basis of her share in the sexual function, a preference for passive behavior and passive aims is carried over into her life to greater or lesser extent, in proportion to the limits, restricted or far-reaching, within which her sexual life thus serves as a model. But we must beware in this of underestimating the influence of social customs, which similarly force women into passive situations. All this is still far from being cleared up. There is one particularly constant relation between femininity and instinctual life which we do not want to overlook. The suppression of women's aggressiveness which is prescribed for them constitutionally and imposed on them socially favors the develop-ment of powerful masochistic impulses, which succeed, as we know, in binding erotically the destructive trends which have been diverted inward. Thus masochism, as people say, is truly feminine. But if, as happens so often, you meet with masochism in men, what is left to you but to say that these men exhibit very plain feminine traits?

And now you are already prepared to hear that psychology too is unable to solve the riddle of femininity. The explanation must no doubt come from elsewhere, and cannot come till we have learned how in general the differentiation of living organisms into two sexes came about. We know nothing about it, yet the existence of two sexes is a most striking charac-teristic of organic life which distinguishes it sharply from inanimate na-ture. However, we find enough to study in those human individuals who, through the possession of female genitals, are characterized as manifestly or predominantly feminine. In conformity with its peculiar nature, psy-choanalysis does not try to describe what a woman is—that would be a task it could scarcely perform—but sets about inquiring how she comes into being, how a woman develops out of a child with a bisexual disposi-tion. In recent times we have begun to learn a little about this, thanks to the circumstance that several of our excellent women colleagues in analysis have begun to work at the question. The discussion of this has gained special attractiveness from the distinction between the sexes. For the

---

[2][I.e., mistaking two different things for a single one. The term was explained in *Introductory Lectures*, XX.]

ladies, whenever some comparison seemed to turn out unfavorable to their sex, were able to utter a suspicion that we, the male analysts, had been unable to overcome certain deeply rooted prejudices against what was feminine, and that this was being paid for in the partiality of our researches. We, on the other hand, standing on the ground of bisexuality, had no difficulty in avoiding impoliteness. We had only to say: "This doesn't apply to *you*. You're the exception; on this point you're more masculine than feminine."

We approach the investigation of the sexual development of women with two expectations. The first is that here once more the constitution will not adapt itself to its function without a struggle. The second is that the decisive turning-points will already have been prepared for or completed before puberty. Both expectations are promptly confirmed. Furthermore, a comparison with what happens with boys tells us that the development of a little girl into a normal woman is more difficult and more complicated, since it includes two extra tasks, to which there is nothing corresponding in the development of a man. Let us follow the parallel lines from their beginning. Undoubtedly the material is different to start with in boys and girls: it did not need psychoanalysis to establish that. The difference in the structure of the genitals is accompanied by other bodily differences which are too well known to call for mention. Differences emerge too in the instinctual disposition which give a glimpse of the later nature of women. A little girl is as a rule less aggressive, defiant, and self-sufficient; she seems to have a greater need for being shown affection and on that account to be more dependent and pliant. It is probably only as a result of this pliancy that she can be taught more easily and quicker to control her excretions: urine and feces are the first gifts that children make to those who look after them, and controlling them is the first concession to which the instinctual life of children can be induced. One gets an impression, too, that little girls are more intelligent and livelier than boys of the same age; they go out more to meet the external world and at the same time form stronger object-cathexes. I cannot say whether this lead in development has been confirmed by exact observations, but in any case there is no question that girls cannot be described as intellectually backward. These sexual differences are not, however, of great consequence: they can be outweighed by individual variations. For our immediate purposes they can be disregarded.

Both sexes seem to pass through the early phases of libidinal development in the same manner. It might have been expected that in girls there would already have been some lag in aggressiveness in the sadistic-anal phase, but such is not the case. Analysis of children's play has shown our women analysts that the aggressive impulses of little girls leave nothing to be desired in the way of abundance and violence. With their entry into the phallic phase the differences between the sexes are completely eclipsed by their agreements. We are now obliged to recognize that the little girl is a little man. In boys, as we know, this phase is marked by the fact that they have learned how to derive pleasurable sensations from their small penis and connect its excited state with their ideas of sexual intercourse. Little girls do the same thing with their still smaller clitoris. It seems that with them all their masturbatory acts are carried out on this penis-equivalent, and that the truly feminine vagina is still undiscovered by both sexes. It is true that there are a few isolated reports of early vaginal sensations as well, but it could not be easy to distinguish these from sensations in the anus or vestibulum; in any case they cannot play a great part. We are entitled to keep to our view that in the phallic phase of girls the clitoris is the leading erotogenic zone. But it is not, of course, going to remain so. With the change to femininity the clitoris should wholly or in part hand over its sensitivity, and at the same time its importance, to the vagina. This would be one of the two tasks which a woman has to perform in the course of her development, whereas the more fortunate man has only to continue at the time of his sexual maturity the activity that he has previously carried out at the period of the early efflorescence of his sexuality.

We shall return to the part played by the clitoris; let us now turn to the second task with which a girl's development is burdened. A boy's mother is the first object of his love, and she remains so too during the formation of his Oedipus complex and, in essence, all through his life. For a girl too her first object must be her mother (and the figures of wet-nurses and foster-mothers that merge into her). The first object-cathexes occur in attachment to the satisfaction of the major and simple vital needs, and the circumstances of the care of children are the same for both sexes. But in the Oedipus situation the girl's father has become her love-object, and we expect that in the normal course of development she will find her way from this paternal object to her final choice of an object. In the course of time, therefore, a girl has to change her erotogenic zone and her object—both of which a boy retains. The question then arises of how this happens: in particular, how does a girl pass from her mother to an attachment to her father? Or, in other words, how does she pass from her masculine phase to the feminine one to which she is biologically destined?

It would be a solution of ideal simplicity if we could suppose that from a particular age onward the elementary influence of the mutual attraction between the sexes makes itself felt and impels the small woman toward men, while the same law allows the boy to continue with his mother. We might suppose in addition that in this the children are following the pointer given them by the sexual preference of their parents. But we are not going to find things so easy; we scarcely know whether we are to believe seriously in the power of which poets talk so much and with such enthusiasm but which cannot be further dissected analytically. We have found an answer of quite another sort by means of laborious investigations, the material for which at least was easy to arrive at. For you must know that the number of women who remain till a late age tenderly dependent on a paternal object, or indeed on their real fathers, is very great. We have established some surprising facts about these women with an intense attachment of long duration to their fathers. We knew, of course, that there had been a preliminary stage of attachment to the mother, but we did not know that it could be so rich in content and so long-lasting, and could leave behind so many opportunities for fixations and dispositions. During this time the girl's father is only a troublesome rival; in some cases the attachment to her mother lasts beyond the fourth year of life. Almost everything that we find later in her relation to her father was already present in this earlier attachment and has been transferred subsequently on to her father. In short, we get an impression that we cannot understand women unless we appreciate this phase of their pre-Oedipus attachment to their mother.

We shall be glad, then, to know the nature of the girl's libidinal relations to her mother. The answer is that they are of very many different kinds. Since they persist through all three phases of infantile sexuality, they also take on the characteristics of the different phases and express themselves by oral, sadistic-anal, and phallic wishes. These wishes represent active as well as passive impulses; if we relate them to the differentiation of the sexes which is to appear later—though we should avoid doing so as far as possible—we may call them masculine and feminine. Besides this, they are completely ambivalent, both affectionate and of a hostile and aggressive nature. The latter often only come to light after being changed into anxiety ideas. It is not always easy to point to a formulation of these early sexual wishes; what is most clearly expressed is a wish to get the mother with child and the corresponding wish to bear her a child—both belonging to the phallic period and sufficiently surprising, but established beyond doubt by analytic observation. The attractiveness of these investigations lies in the surprising detailed findings which they bring us. Thus, for instance, we discover the fear of being murdered or poisoned, which may later form the core of a paranoic illness, already present in this pre-Oedipus period, in relation to the mother. Or another case: You will recall an interesting episode in the history of analytic research which caused me many distressing hours. In the period in which the main interest was directed to discovering infantile sexual traumas, almost all my women patients told me that they had been seduced by their fathers. I was driven to recognize in the end that these reports were untrue and so came to understand that hysterical symptoms are derived from fantasies and not from real occurrences. It was only later that I was able to recognize in this fantasy of being seduced by the father the expression of the typical Oedipus complex in women. And now we find the fantasy of seduction once more in the pre-Oedipus prehistory of girls; but the seducer is regularly the mother. Here, however, the fantasy touches the ground of reality, for it was really the mother who by her activities over the child's bodily hygiene inevitably stimulated, and perhaps even roused for the first time, pleasurable sensations in her genitals.

I have no doubt you are ready to suspect that this portrayal of the abundance and strength of a little girl's sexual relations with her mother is very much overdrawn. After all, one has opportunities of seeing little girls and notices nothing of the sort. But the objection is not to the point. Enough can be seen in the children if one knows how to look. And besides, you should consider how little of its sexual wishes a child can bring to preconscious expression or communicate at all. Accordingly we are only within our rights if we study the residues and consequences of this emotional world in retrospect, in people in whom these processes of development had attained a specially clear and even excessive degree of expansion. Pathology has always done us the service of making discernible by isolation and exaggeration conditions which would remain concealed in a normal state. And since our investigations have been carried out on people who were by no means seriously abnormal, I think we should regard their outcome as deserving belief.

We will now turn our interest on to the single question of what it is 12 that brings this powerful attachment of the girl to her mother to an end. This, as we know, is its usual fate: it is destined to make room for an attachment to her father. Here we come upon a fact which is a pointer to our further advance. This step in development does not involve only a simple change of object. The turning away from the mother is accompanied by hostility; the attachment to the mother ends in hate. A hate of that kind may become very striking and last all through life; it may be carefully overcompensated later on; as a rule one part of it is overcome while another part persists. Events of later years naturally influence this greatly. We will restrict ourselves, however, to studying it at the time at which the girl turns to her father and to inquiring into the motives for it. We are then given a long list of accusations and grievances against the mother which are supposed to justify the child's hostile feelings; they are of varying validity which we shall not fail to examine. A number of them are obvious rationalizations and the true sources of enmity remain to be found. I hope you will be interested if on this occasion I take you through all the details of a psychoanalytic investigation.

The reproach against the mother which goes back furthest is that she gave the child too little milk—which is construed against her as lack of love. Now there is some justification for this reproach in our families. Mothers often have insufficient nourishment to give their children and are content to suckle them for a few months, for half or three-quarters of a year. Among primitive peoples children are fed at their mother's breast for two or three years. The figure of the wet-nurse who suckles the child is as a rule merged into the mother; when this has not happened, the reproach is turned into another one—that the nurse, who fed the child so willingly, was sent away by the mother too early. But whatever the true state of affairs may have been, it is impossible that the child's reproach can be justified as often as it is met with. It seems, rather, that the child's avidity for its earliest nourishment is altogether insatiable, that it never gets over the pain of losing its mother's breast. I should not be surprised if the analysis of a primitive child, who could still suck at its mother's breast when it was already able to run about and talk, were to bring the same reproach to light. The fear of being poisoned is also probably connected with the withdrawal of the breast. Poison is nourishment that makes one ill. Perhaps children trace back their early illnesses too to this frustration. A fair amount of intellectual education is a prerequisite for believing in chance; primitive people and uneducated ones, and no doubt children as well, are able to assign a ground for everything that happens. Perhaps originally it was a reason on animistic lines. Even today in some strata of our population no one can die without having been killed by someone else—preferably by the doctor. And the regular reaction of a neurotic to the death of someone closely connected with him is to put the blame on himself for having caused the death.

The next accusation against the child's mother flares up when the next baby appears in the nursery. If possible the connection with oral frustration is preserved: the mother could not or would not give the child any more milk because she needed the nourishment for the new arrival. In cases in which the two children are so close in age that lactation is prejudiced by the second pregnancy, this reproach acquires a real basis, and it is a remarkable fact that a child, even with an age difference of only eleven months, is not too young to take notice of what is happening. But what the child grudges the unwanted intruder and rival is not only the suckling but all the other signs of maternal care. It feels that it has been dethroned, despoiled, prejudiced in its rights; it casts a jealous hatred upon the new baby and develops a grievance against the faithless mother which often finds expression in a disagreeable change in its behavior. It becomes "naughty," perhaps, irritable and disobedient and goes back on the advances it has made toward controlling its excretions. All of this has been very long familiar and is accepted as self-evident; but we rarely form a correct idea of the strength of these jealous impulses, of the tenacity with which they persist and of the magnitude of their influence on later development. Especially as this jealousy is constantly receiving fresh nourishment in the later years of childhood and the whole shock is repeated with the birth of each new brother or sister. Nor does it make much difference if the child happens to remain the mother's preferred favorite. A child's demands for love are immoderate, they make exclusive claims and tolerate no sharing.

An abundant source of a child's hostility to its mother is provided by its multifarious sexual wishes, which alter according to the phase of the libido and which cannot for the most part be satisfied. The strongest of

these frustrations occur at the phallic period, if the mother forbids pleasurable activity with the genitals—often with severe threats and every sign of
displeasure—activity to which, after all, she herself had introduced the
child. One would think these were reasons enough to account for a girl's
turning away from her mother. One would judge, if so, that the estrangement follows inevitably from the nature of children's sexuality, from the
immoderate character of their demand for love and the impossibility of
fulfilling their sexual wishes. It might be thought indeed that this first love-
relation of the child's is doomed to dissolution for the very reason that it is
the first, for these early object-cathexes are regularly ambivalent to a high
degree. A powerful tendency to aggressiveness is always present beside a
powerful love, and the more passionately a child loves its object the more
sensitive does it become to disappointments and frustrations from that
object; and in the end the love must succumb to the accumulated hostility.
Or the idea that there is an original ambivalence such as this in erotic
cathexes may be rejected, and it may be pointed out that it is the special
nature of the mother-child relation that leads, with equal inevitability, to
the destruction of the child's love; for even the mildest upbringing cannot
avoid using compulsion and introducing restrictions, and any such intervention in the child's liberty must provoke as a reaction an inclination to
rebelliousness and aggressiveness. A discussion of these possibilities might,
I think, be most interesting; but an objection suddenly emerges which
forces our interest in another direction. All these factors—the slights, the
disappointments in love, the jealousy, the seduction followed by
prohibition—are, after all, also in operation in the relation of a *boy* to his
mother and are yet unable to alienate him from the maternal object.
Unless we can find something that is specific for girls and is not present or
not in the same way present in boys, we shall not have explained the
termination of the attachment of girls to their mother.

    I believe we have found this specific factor, and indeed where we   16
expected to find it, even though in a surprising form. Where we expected
to find it, I say, for it lies in the castration complex. After all, the
anatomical distinction [between the sexes] must express itself in psychical
consequences. It was, however, a surprise to learn from analyses that girls
hold their mother responsible for their lack of a penis and do not forgive
her for their being thus put at a disadvantage.

    As you hear, then, we ascribe a castration complex to women as well.
And for good reasons, though its content cannot be the same as with boys.
In the latter the castration complex arises after they have learned from the
sight of the female genitals that the organ which they value so highly need
not necessarily accompany the body. At this the boy recalls to mind the
threats he brought on himself by his doings with that organ, he begins to
give credence to them and falls under the influence of fear of castration,
which will be the most powerful motive force in his subsequent development. The castration complex of girls is also started by the sight of the

genitals of the other sex. They at once notice the difference and, it must be admitted, its significance too. They feel seriously wronged, often declare that they want to "have something like it too," and fall a victim to "envy for the penis," which will leave ineradicable traces on their development and the formation of their character and which will not be surmounted in even the most favorable cases without a severe expenditure of psychical energy. The girl's recognition of the fact of her being without a penis does not by any means imply that she submits to the fact easily. On the contrary, she continues to hold on for a long time to the wish to get something like it herself and she believes in that possibility for improbably long years; and analysis can show that, at a period when knowledge of reality has long since rejected the fulfillment of the wish as unattainable, it persists in the unconscious and retains a considerable cathexis of energy. The wish to get the longed-for penis eventually in spite of everything may contribute to the motives that drive a mature woman to analysis, and what she may reasonably expect from analysis—a capacity, for instance, to carry on an intellectual profession—may often be recognized as a sublimated modification of this repressed wish.

One cannot very well doubt the importance of envy for the penis. You may take it as an instance of male injustice if I assert that envy and jealousy play an even greater part in the mental life of women than of men. It is not that I think these characteristics are absent in men or that I think they have no other roots in women than envy for the penis; but I am inclined to attribute their greater amount in women to this latter influence. Some analysts, however, have shown an inclination to depreciate the importance of this first installment of penis-envy in the phallic phase. They are of opinion that what we find of this attitude in women is in the main a secondary structure which has come about on the occasion of later conflicts by regression to this early infantile impulse. This, however, is a general problem of depth psychology. In many pathological—or even unusual—instinctual attitudes (for instance, in all sexual perversions) the question arises of how much of their strength is to be attributed to early infantile fixations and how much to the influence of later experiences and developments. In such cases it is almost always a matter of complemental series such as we put forward in our discussion of the aetiology of the neuroses. Both factors play a part in varying amounts in the causation; a less on the one side is balanced by a more on the other. The infantile factor sets the pattern in all cases but does not always determine the issue, though it often does. Precisely in the case of penis-envy I should argue decidedly in favor of the preponderance of the infantile factor.

The discovery that she is castrated is a turning-point in a girl's growth. Three possible lines of development start from it: one leads to sexual inhibition or to neurosis, the second to change of character in the sense of a masculinity complex, the third, finally, to normal femininity. We have learned a fair amount, though not everything, about all three.

The essential content of the first is as follows: The little girl has 20 hitherto lived in a masculine way, has been able to get pleasure by the excitation of her clitoris, and has brought this activity into relation with her sexual wishes directed toward her mother, which are often active ones; now, owing to the influence of her penis-envy, she loses her enjoyment in her phallic sexuality. Her self-love is mortified by the comparison with the boy's far superior equipment and in consequence she renounces her masturbatory satisfaction from her clitoris, repudiates her love for her mother, and at the same time not infrequently represses a good part of her sexual trends in general. No doubt her turning away from her mother does not occur all at once, for to begin with the girl regards her castration as an individual misfortune, and only gradually extends it to other females and finally to her mother as well. Her love was directed to her *phallic* mother; with the discovery that her mother is castrated it becomes possible to drop her as an object, so that the motives for hostility, which have long been accumulating, gain the upper hand. This means, therefore, that as a result of the discovery of women's lack of a penis they are debased in value for girls just as they are for boys and later perhaps for men.

You all know the immense etiological importance attributed by our neurotic patients to their masturbation. They make it responsible for all their troubles and we have the greatest difficulty in persuading them that they are mistaken. In fact, however, we ought to admit to them that they are right, for masturbation is the executive agent of infantile sexuality, from the faulty development of which they are indeed suffering. But what neurotics mostly blame is the masturbation of the period of puberty; they have mostly forgotten that of early infancy, which is what is really in question. I wish I might have an opportunity some time of explaining to you at length how important all the factual details of early masturbation become for the individual's subsequent neurosis or character: whether or not it was discovered, how the parents struggled against it or permitted it, or whether he succeeded in suppressing it himself. All of this leaves permanent traces on his development. But I am on the whole glad that I need not do this. It would be a hard and tedious task and at the end of it you would put me in an embarrassing situation by quite certainly asking me to give you some practical advice as to how a parent or educator should deal with the masturbation of small children. From the development of girls, which is what my present lecture is concerned with, I can give you the example of a child herself trying to get free from masturbating. She does not always succeed in this. If envy for the penis has provoked a powerful impulse against clitoridal masturbation but this nevertheless refuses to give way, a violent struggle for liberation ensues in which the girl, as it were, herself takes over the role of her deposed mother and gives expression to her entire dissatisfaction with her inferior clitoris in her efforts against obtaining satisfaction from it. Many years later, when her masturbatory activity has long since been suppressed, an interest still persists which we must interpret as a defense against a temptation that is still dreaded. It manifests itself in the emergence of sympathy for those to whom similar difficulties are attributed, it plays a part as a motive in contracting a marriage and, indeed, it may determine the choice of a husband or lover. Disposing of early infantile masturbation is truly no easy or indifferent business.

Along with the abandonment of clitoridal masturbation a certain amount of activity is renounced. Passivity now has the upper hand, and the girl's turning to her father is accomplished principally with the help of passive instinctual impulses. You can see that a wave of development like this, which clears the phallic activity out of the way, smooths the ground for femininity. If too much is not lost in the course of it through repression, this femininity may turn out to be normal. The wish with which the girl turns to her father is no doubt originally the wish for the penis which her mother has refused her and which she now expects from her father. The feminine situation is only established, however, if the wish for a penis is replaced by one for a baby, if, that is, a baby takes the place of a penis in accordance with an ancient symbolic equivalence. It has not escaped us that the girl has wished for a baby earlier, in the undisturbed phallic phase: that, of course, was the meaning of her playing with dolls. But that play was not in fact an expression of her femininity; it served as an identification with her mother with the intention of substituting activity for passivity. *She* was playing the part of her mother and the doll was herself: now she could do with the baby everything that her mother used to do with her. Not until the emergence of the wish for a penis does the doll-baby become a baby from the girl's father, and thereafter the aim of the most powerful feminine wish. Her happiness is great if later on this wish for a baby finds fulfillment in reality, and quite especially so if the baby is a little boy who brings the longed-for penis with him. Often enough in her combined picture of "a baby from her father" the emphasis is laid on the baby and her father left unstressed. In this way the ancient masculine wish for the possession of a penis is still faintly visible through the femininity now achieved. But perhaps we ought rather to recognize this wish for a penis as being par excellence a feminine one.

With the transference of the wish for a penis-baby on to her father, the girl has entered the situation of the Oedipus complex. Her hostility to her mother, which did not need to be freshly created, is now greatly intensified, for she becomes the girl's rival, who receives from her father everything that she desires from him. For a long time the girl's Oedipus complex concealed her pre-Oedipus attachment to her mother from our view, though it is nevertheless so important and leaves such lasting fixations behind it. For girls the Oedipus situation is the outcome of a long and difficult development; it is a kind of preliminary solution, a position of rest which is not soon abandoned, especially as the beginning of the latency period is not far distant. And we are now struck by a difference between the two sexes, which is probably momentous, in regard to the relation of the Oedipus complex to the castration complex. In a boy the Oedipus complex, in which he desires his mother and would like to get rid of his father as being a rival, develops naturally from the phase of his phallic sexuality. The threat of castration compels him, however, to give up that attitude. Under the impression of the danger of losing his penis, the Oedipus complex is abandoned, repressed and, in the most normal cases, entirely destroyed, and a severe super-ego is set up as its heir. What happens with a girl is almost the opposite. The castration complex prepares for the Oedipus complex instead of destroying it; the girl is driven out of her attachment to her mother through the influence of her envy for the penis and she enters the Oedipus situation as though into a haven of refuge. In the absence of fear of castration the chief motive is lacking which leads boys to surmount the Oedipus complex. Girls remain in it for an indeterminate length of time; they demolish it late and, even so, incompletely. In these circumstances the formation of the super-ego must suffer; it cannot attain the strength and independence which give it its cultural significance, and feminists are not pleased when we point out to them the effects of this factor upon the average feminine character.

To go back a little. We mentioned as the second possible reaction to 24 the discovery of female castration the development of a powerful masculinity complex. By this we mean that the girl refuses, as it were, to recognize the unwelcome fact and, defiantly rebellious, even exaggerates her previous masculinity, clings to her clitoridal activity and takes refuge in an identification with her phallic mother or her father. What can it be that decides in favor of this outcome? We can only suppose that it is a constitutional factor, a greater amount of activity, such as is ordinarily characteristic of a male. However that may be, the essence of this process is that at this point in development the wave of passivity is avoided which opens the way to the turn toward femininity. The extreme achievement of such a masculinity complex would appear to be the influencing of the choice of an object in the sense of manifest homosexuality. Analytic experience teaches us, to be sure, that female homosexuality is seldom or never a direct continuation of infantile masculinity. Even for a girl of this kind it seems necessary that she should take her father as an object for some time and enter the Oedipus situation. But afterward, as a result of her inevitable disappointments from her father, she is driven to regress into her early masculinity complex. The significance of these disappointments must not be exaggerated; a girl who is destined to become feminine is not spared them, though they do not have the same effect. The predominance of the constitutional factor seems indisputable; but the two phases in the development of female homosexuality are well mirrored in the practices of homosexuals, who play the parts of mother and baby with each other as often and as clearly as those of husband and wife.

What I have been telling you here may be described as the prehistory of women. It is a product of the very last few years and may have been of interest to you as an example of detailed analytic work. Since its subject is woman, I will venture on this occasion to mention by name a few of the women who have made valuable contributions to this investigation. Dr. Ruth Mack Brunswick was the first to describe a case of neurosis which went back to a fixation in the pre-Oedipus stage and had never reached the Oedipus situation at all. The case took the form of jealous paranoia and proved accessible to therapy. Dr. Jeanne Lampl-de Groot has established the incredible phallic activity of girls toward their mothers by some assured observations, and Dr. Helene Deutsch has shown that the erotic actions of homosexual women reproduce the relations between mother and baby.

It is not my intention to pursue the further behavior of femininity through puberty to the period of maturity. Our knowledge, moreover, would be insufficient for the purpose. But I will bring a few features together in what follows. Taking its prehistory as a starting-point, I will only emphasize here that the development of femininity remains exposed to disturbance by the residual phenomena of the early masculine period. Regressions to the fixations of the pre-Oedipus phases very frequently occur; in the course of some women's lives there is a repeated alternation between periods in which masculinity or femininity gains the upper hand. Some portion of what we men call "the enigma of women" may perhaps be derived from this expression of bisexuality in women's lives. But another question seems to have become ripe for judgment in the course of these researches. We have called the motive force of sexual life "the libido." Sexual life is dominated by the polarity of masculine–feminine; thus the notion suggests itself of considering the relation of the libido to this antithesis. It would not be surprising if it were to turn out that each sexuality had its own special libido appropriated to it, so that one sort of libido would pursue the aims of a masculine sexual life and another sort those of a feminine one. But nothing of the kind is true. There is only one libido, which serves both the masculine and the feminine sexual functions. To it itself we cannot assign any sex; if, following the conventional equation of activity and masculinity, we are inclined to describe it as masculine, we must not forget that it also covers trends with a passive aim. Nevertheless the juxtaposition "feminine libido" is without any justification. Furthermore, it is our impression that more constraint has been applied to the libido when it is pressed into the service of the feminine function, and that—to speak teleologically—Nature takes less careful account of its [that function's] demands than in the case of masculinity. And the reason for this may lie—thinking once again teleologically—in the fact that the accomplishment of the aim of biology has been entrusted to the aggressiveness of men and has been made to some extent independent of women's consent.

The sexual frigidity of women, the frequency of which appears to confirm this disregard, is a phenomenon that is still insufficiently understood. Sometimes it is psychogenic and in that case accessible to influence; but in other cases it suggests the hypothesis of its being constitutionally determined and even of there being a contributory anatomical factor.

I have promised to tell you of a few more psychical peculiarities of mature femininity, as we come across them in analytic observation. We do not lay claim to more than an average validity for these assertions; nor is it always easy to distinguish what should be ascribed to the influence of the sexual function and what to social breeding. Thus, we attribute a larger amount of narcissism to femininity, which also affects women's choice of object, so that to be loved is a stronger need for them than to love. The effect of penis-envy has a share, further, in the physical vanity of women, since they are bound to value their charms more highly as a late compensation for their original sexual inferiority. Shame, which is considered to be a feminine characteristic par excellence but is far more a matter of convention than might be supposed, has as its purpose, we believe, concealment of genital deficiency. We are not forgetting that at a later time shame takes on other functions. It seems that women have made few contributions to the discoveries and inventions in the history of civilization; there is, however, one technique which they may have invented—that of plaiting and weaving. If that is so, we should be tempted to guess the unconscious motive for the achievement. Nature herself would seem to have given the model which this achievement imitates by causing the growth at maturity of the pubic hair that conceals the genitals. The step that remained to be taken lay in making the threads adhere to one another, while on the body they stick into the skin and are only matted together. If you reject this idea as fantastic and regard my belief in the influence of lack of a penis on the configuration of femininity as an *idée fixe*, I am of course defenseless.

The determinants of women's choice of an object are often made unrecognizable by social conditions. Where the choice is able to show itself freely, it is often made in accordance with the narcissistic ideal of the man whom the girl had wished to become. If the girl has remained in her attachment to her father—that is, in the Oedipus complex—her choice is made according to the paternal type. Since, when she turned from her mother to her father, the hostility of her ambivalent relation remained with her mother, a choice of this kind should guarantee a happy marriage. But very often the outcome is of a kind that presents a general threat to such a settlement of the conflict due to ambivalence. The hostility that has been left behind follows in the train of the positive attachment and spreads over on the new object. The woman's husband, who to begin with inherited from her father, becomes after a time her mother's heir as well. So it may easily happen that the second half of a woman's life may be filled by the struggle against her husband, just as the shorter first half was filled by her rebellion against her mother. When this reaction has been lived through, a second marriage may easily turn out very much more satisfying. Another alteration in a woman's nature, for which lovers are unprepared, may occur in a marriage after the first child is born. Under the influence of a woman's becoming a mother herself, an identification with her own mother may be revived, against which she had striven up till the time of her marriage, and this may attract all the available libido to itself, so that the compulsion to repeat reproduces an unhappy marriage between her parents. The difference in a mother's reaction to the birth of a son or a daughter shows that the old factor of lack of a penis has even now not lost its strength. A mother is only brought unlimited satisfaction by her relation to a son; this is altogether the most perfect, the most free from ambivalence of all human relationships. A mother can transfer to her son the ambition which she has been obliged to suppress in herself, and she can expect from him the satisfaction of all that has been left over in her of her masculinity complex. Even a marriage is not made secure until the wife has succeeded in making her husband her child as well and in acting as a mother to him.

A woman's identification with her mother allows us to distinguish two strata: the pre-Oedipus one which rests on her affectionate attachment to her mother and takes her as a model, and the later one from the Oedipus complex which seeks to get rid of her mother and take her place with her father. We are no doubt justified in saying that much of both of them is left over for the future and that neither of them is adequately surmounted in the course of development. But the phase of the affectionate pre-Oedipus attachment is the decisive one for a woman's future: during it preparations are made for the acquisition of the characteristics with which she will later fulfill her role in the sexual function and perform her invaluable social tasks. It is in this identification too that she acquires her attractiveness to a man, whose Oedipus attachment to his mother it kindles into passion. How often it happens, however, that it is only his son who obtains what he himself aspired to! One gets an impression that a man's love and a woman's are a phase apart psychologically.

The fact that women must be regarded as having little sense of justice is no doubt related to the predominance of envy in their mental life; for the demand for justice is a modification of envy and lays down the condition subject to which one can put envy aside. We also regard women as weaker in their social interests and as having less capacity for sublimating their instincts than men. The former is no doubt derived from the dissocial quality which unquestionably characterizes all sexual relations. Lovers find sufficiency in each other, and families too resist inclusion in more comprehensive associations. The aptitude for sublimation is subject to the greatest individual variations. On the other hand I cannot help mentioning an impression that we are constantly receiving during analytic practice. A man of about thirty strikes us as a youthful, somewhat unformed individual, whom we expect to make powerful use of the possibilities for development opened up to him by analysis. A woman of the same age, however, oftens frightens us by her psychical rigidity and unchangeability. Her libido has taken up final positions and seems incapable of exchanging them for others. There are no paths open to further development; it is as though the whole process had already run its course and remains thenceforward insusceptible to influence—as though, indeed, the difficult development to femininity had exhausted the possibilities of the person concerned. As therapists we lament this state of things, even if we succeed in putting an end to our patient's ailment by doing away with her neurotic conflict.

That is all I had to say to you about femininity. It is certainly 32 incomplete and fragmentary and does not always sound friendly. But do not forget that I have only been describing women in so far as their nature is determined by their sexual function. It is true that that influence extends very far; but we do not overlook the fact that an individual woman may be a human being in other respects as well. If you want to know more about femininity, inquire from your own experiences of life, or turn to the poets, or wait until science can give you deeper and more coherent information.

Questions and Suggestions for Writing

1. Freud claims (para. 1) that his ensuing discussion "brings forward nothing but observed facts, almost without any speculative additions." Cite a clear example in his essay of "observed fact" and another example of "speculative addition." Do you agree that the former are far more frequent than the latter? Write a 250-word essay on the theme, The Observational Basis for Freud's Claims about Femininity.

2. Suppose someone were to argue: Given Freud's criticism of the moral qualities of women (paras. 18, 31), he really should argue that women are morally inferior to men and so do not deserve legal, political, and social equality with men. Do you think Freud would have agreed? If not, how might he have rejected such an argument?

3. Near the end of his essay (para. 25) Freud cites the empirical research of three female (and no male) psychoanalysts. Does the fact that the source of the data he relies on for his portrait of the psychosexual inferiority of women derives in part from research by women tend to give added credibility to his views or not? Explain.

4. Freud remarks that during "the phallic phase" of development, "the little girl is a little man" (para. 7). Why doesn't he say, instead, "the little boy is a little woman"? What reason, if any, does he give for using the psychosexual development of the male as his focus, rather than the female? Can you think of plausible reasons of your own?

5. In light of contemporary evidence that many children are sexually abused by their fathers, do you think we should regard Freud's insistence (para. 10) that women patients who reported to him seduction by their fathers were manifesting "hysterical symptoms derived from fantasies?"

6. Freud attaches great significance to the "castration complex" in women. How should this term be defined in light of his remarks?

7. Freud frequently mentions the "Oedipus complex" as it affects boys and girls. Who was Oedipus and how should this term be defined? By the way, if you have read the play, do you think that Oedipus had an Oedipus complex? Why?

8. Freud refers to "the aggressiveness of men," which he claims "the aim of biology" has made manifest in behavior "to some extent independent of woman's consent" (para. 26). Do you think that this remark of Freud's suggests that he would be tolerant of "date rape" or other forms of sexual assault on women, or at least more tolerant than feminists would be? Explain.

9. It is difficult, Freud points out (para. 28), to distinguish with confidence those differences between men and women that "should be ascribed to the influence of the sexual function" and, on the other hand, those that should be ascribed to the influence of "social breeding." Are there any characteristics of women that Freud ascribes to the former that you think should be ascribed to the latter? Are there characteristics he does not mention that you would ascribe to "social breeding"? Write a 500-word essay on the theme, The Nature of Women: Sexual Function vs. Social Breeding.

Kate Millett

A Critique of Freud

I

In reconsidering Freud's theories on women we must ask ourselves not only what conclusions he drew from the evidence at hand but also upon what assumptions he drew them. Freud did not accept his patients' symptoms as evidence of a justified dissatisfaction with the limiting circumstances imposed on them by society, but as symptomatic of an independent and universal feminine tendency.[1] He named this tendency "penis envy," traced its origin to childhood experience and based his theory of the psychology of women upon it, aligning what he took to be the three corollaries of feminine psychology, passivity, masochism, and narcissism, so that each was dependent upon, or related to, penis envy.

As the Freudian understanding of female personality is based upon the idea of penis envy, it requires an elaborate, and often repetitious, exposi-

---

[1] Here Freud's procedure was very different from the liberal and humane attitude he adopted toward patients suffering from sexual inhibition.

Kate Millett (b. 1934) is a professor of English, a sculptor, and a filmwriter. The following excerpt, from a chapter titled "Freud and the Influence of Psychoanalytic Thought," comes from her best-known book, Sexual Politics *(1970).*

tion.[2] Beginning with the theory of penis envy, the definition of the female is negative—what she is is the result of the fact that she is not a male and "lacks" a penis. Freud assumed that the female's discovery of her sex is, in and of itself, a catastrophe of such vast proportions that it haunts a woman all through life and accounts for most aspects of her temperament. His entire psychology of women, from which all modern psychology and psychoanalysis derives heavily, is built upon an original tragic experience—born female. Purportedly, Freud is here only relaying the information supplied by women themselves, the patients who furnished his clinical data, the basis of his later generalities about all women. It was in this way, Freud believed, he had been permitted to see how women accepted the idea that to be born female is to be born "castrated":

> As we learn from psycho-analytic work, women regard themselves as wronged from infancy, as undeservedly cut short and set back; and the embitterment of so many daughters against their mothers derives, in the last analysis, from the reproach against her of having brought them into the world as women instead of as men.[3]

Assuming that this were true, the crucial question, manifestly, is to ask why this might be so. Either maleness is indeed an *inherently* superior phenomenon, and in which case its "betterness" could be empirically proved and demonstrated, or the female misapprehends and reasons erroneously that she is inferior. And again, one must ask why. What forces in her experience, her society and socialization have led her to see herself as an inferior being? The answer would seem to lie in the conditions of patriarchal society and the inferior position of women within this society. But Freud did not choose to pursue such a line of reasoning, preferring instead an etiology of childhood experience based upon the biological fact of anatomical differences.

While it is supremely unfortunate that Freud should prefer to bypass the more likely social hypothesis to concentrate upon the distortions of infantile subjectivity, his analysis might yet have made considerable sense were he sufficiently objective to acknowledge that woman is born female in a masculine-dominated culture which is bent upon extending its values

---

[2]See especially "Femininity." After making use of such patently invidious terms as "the boy's far superior equipment" (p. 126), "her inferior clitoris" (p. 127), "genital deficiency" (p. 132), and "original sexual inferiority" (p. 132), Freud proposes to his audience that penis envy is the foundation of his whole theory of female psychology, warning them that should they demur before his hypothesis, they would sabotage the entire construct: "If you reject the idea as fantastic and regard my belief in the influence of lack of a penis on the configuration of femininity as an *idée fixe*, I am of course defenseless" (p. 132). My critique of Freud's notions of women is indebted to an unpublished summary by Frances Kamm.

[3]Freud, "Some Character Types Met with in Psycho-Analysis Work" (1915) *Collected Papers of Sigmund Freud*, edited by Joan Riviere (New York, Basic Books, 1959), Vol. IV, p. 323.

even to anatomy and is therefore capable of investing biological phenomena with symbolic force. In much the same manner we perceive that
the traumatizing circumstance of being born black in a white racist society
invests skin color with symbolic value while telling us nothing about racial
traits as such.

In dismissing the wider cultural context of feminine dissatisfaction
and isolating it in early childhood experience, Freud again ignored the
social context of childhood by locating a literal feminine "castration"
complex in the child's discovery of the anatomical differentiation between
the sexes. Freud believed he had found the key to feminine experience—in
that moment when girls discover they are "castrated"—a "momentous
discovery which little girls are destined to make":

> They notice the penis of a brother or playmate, strikingly visible and of
> large proportions, at once recognize it as the superior counterpart of
> their own small and inconspicuous organ, and from that time forward
> fall a victim to envy for the penis.[4]

There are several unexplained assumptions here: why is the girl instantly
struck by the proposition that bigger is better? Might she just as easily,
reasoning from the naïveté of childish narcissism imagine the penis is an
excrescence and take her own body as norm? Boys clearly do, as Freud
makes clear, and in doing so respond to sexual enlightenment not with the
reflection that their own bodies are peculiar, but, far otherwise, with a
"horror of the mutilated creature or triumphant contempt for her."[5] Secondly, the superiority of this "superior counterpart," which the girl is said
to "recognize at once" in the penis, is assumed to relate to the autoerotic
satisfactions of childhood; but here again the child's experience provides
no support for such an assumption.

Much of Freudian theory rests upon this moment of discovery and one
is struck how, in the case of the female, to recapitulate the peculiar drama
of penis envy is to rehearse again the fable of the Fall, a Fall that is Eve's
alone.[6] As children, male and female first inhabit a paradisiacal playground where roles are interchangeable, active and passive, masculine and
feminine. Until the awesome lapsarian moment when the female discovers
her inferiority, her castration, we are asked to believe that she had assumed
her clitoris a penis. One wonders why. Freud believes it is because she

---

[4]Freud, "Some Psychological Consequences of the Anatomical Distinctions between the
Sexes" (1925) *Collected Papers*, Vol. V, p. 190.

[5]Ibid., p. 191.

[6]Not only has Adam grace within his loins to assure him he belongs to a superior species, but
even his later fears of castration which come to him after a glimpse of the "mutilated
creature" causes him to repress his Oedipal desires (out of fear of a castrating father's revenge)
and in the process develop the strong super-ego which Freud believes accounts for what he
took to be the male's inevitable and transcendent moral and cultural superiority.

masturbated with it, and he assumes that she will conclude that what is best for such purposes must be a penis.[7] Freud insists upon calling the period of clitoral autoeroticism "phallic" in girls.

Moreover, the revelation which Freud imagined would poison female life is probably, in most cases, a glimpse of a male playmate urinating or having a bath. It is never explained how the girl child makes the logical jump from the sight of bathing or urination of knowledge that the boy masturbates with this novel article. Even should her first sight of the penis occur in masturbatory games, Freud's supposition that she could judge this foreign item to be more conducive to autoerotic pleasure than her own clitoris (she having no possible experience of penile autoeroticism as males have none of clitoral) such an assumption is groundless. Yet Freud believed that female autoeroticism declines as a result of enlightenment, finding in this "yet another surprising effect of penis-envy, or of the discovery of the inferiority of the clitoris."[8] Here, as is so often the case, one cannot separate Freud's account of how a child reasons from how Freud himself reasons, and his own language, invariably pejorative, tends to confuse the issue irremediably. Indeed, since he has no objective proof of any consequence to offer in support of his notion of penis envy or of a female castration complex,[9] one is struck by how thoroughly the subjectivity in which all these events are cast tends to be Freud's own, or that of a strong masculine bias, even of a rather gross male-supremacist bias.[10]

This habitual masculine bias of Freud's own terms and diction, and the attitude it implies, is increased and further emphasized by his followers: Deutsch refers to the clitoris as an "inadequate substitute" for the

[7]Because she feels free, equal, and active then, Freud says "the little girl is a little man." "Femininity," p. 118. So strong is Freud's masculine bias here that it has obliterated linguistic integrity: the autoerotic state might as well, in both cases, be called "clitoral" for all the light shed by these terms. Freud's usage is predicated on the belief that masturbation is the active pursuit of pleasure, and activity masculine per se, "We are entitled to keep to our view that in the phallic phase of girls the clitoris is the leading erotogenic zone." Ibid.

[8]"Some Psychological Consequences of the Anatomical Distinctions between the Sexes," p. 193.

[9]The entirety of Freud's clinical data always consists of his analysis of patients and his own self-analysis. In the case of penis envy he has remarkably little evidence from patients and his description of masculine contempt and feminine grief upon the discovery of sexual differences are extraordinarily autobiographical. Little Hans (Freud's own grandson) a five-year-old boy with an obsessive concern for his "widdler" furnishes the rest of the masculine data. Though an admirable topic of precise clinical research, it was and is, remarkably difficult for Freud, or anyone else, to make generalizations about how children first come to sexual knowledge, family and cultural patterns being so diverse, further complicated by the host of variable factors within individual experience, such as the number, age, and sex of siblings, the strength and consistency of the nakedness taboo, etc.

[10]Ernest Jones aptly described Freud's attitude here as "phallocentric." There is something behind Freud's assumptions reminiscent of the ancient misogynist postulate that females are but incomplete or imperfect males—e.g., deformed humans, the male being accepted as the norm—a view shared by Augustine, Aquinas, etc.

penis; Karl Abraham refers to a "poverty in external genitals" in the female, and all conclude that even bearing children can be but a poor substitute for a constitutional inadequacy.[11] As Klein observes in her critique of Freud, it is a curious hypothesis that "one half of humanity should have biological reasons to feel at a disadvantage for not having what the other half possess (but not vice versa)."[12] It is especially curious to imagine that half the race should attribute their clear and obvious social-status inferiority to the crudest biological reasons when so many more promising social factors are involved.

It would seem that Freud has managed by this highly unlikely hypothesis to assume that young females negate the validity, and even, to some extent, the existence, of female sexual characteristics altogether. Surely the first thing all children must notice is that mother has breasts, while father has none. What is possibly the rather impressive effect of childbirth on young minds is here overlooked, together with the girl's knowledge not only of her clitoris, but her vagina as well.

In formulating the theory of penis envy, Freud not only neglected the possibility of a social explanation for feminine dissatisfaction but precluded it by postulating a literal jealousy of the organ whereby the male is distinguished. As it would appear absurd to charge adult women with these values, the child, and a drastic experience situated far back in childhood, are invoked. Nearly the entirety of feminine development, adjusted or maladjusted, is now to be seen in terms of the cataclysmic moment of discovered castration.

So far, Freud has merely pursued a line of reasoning he attributes, rightly or wrongly, to the subjectivity of female youth. Right or wrong, his account purports to be little more than description of what girls erroneously believe. But there is prescription as well in the Freudian account. For while the discovery of her castration is purported to be a universal experience in the female, her response to this fate is the criterion by which her health, her maturity, and her future are determined through a rather elaborate series of stages: "After a woman has become aware of the wound to her narcissism, she develops, like a scar, a sense of inferiority. When she has passed beyond her first attempt at explaining her lack of a penis as being a punishment personal to herself and has realized that that sexual character is a universal one, she begins to share the contempt felt by men for a sex which is the lesser in so important a respect."[13] The female first blames her mother, "who sent her into the world so insufficiently

---

[11]Karl Abraham, "Manifestations of the Female Castration Complex," *International Journal of Psychoanalysis*, Vol. 3, March 1922.

[12]Viola Klein, *The Feminine Character* (London: Kegan Paul, 1946), pp. 83–84.

[13]"Some Psychological Consequences of the Anatomical Distinction Between the Sexes," p. 192.

equipped" and who is "almost always held responsible for her lack of a penis."[14] Again, Freud's own language makes no distinction here between fact and feminine fantasy. It is not enough the girl reject her own sex however; if she is to mature, she must redirect her self positively toward a masculine object. This is designated as the beginning of the Oedipal stage in the female. We are told that the girl now gives up the hope of impregnating her mother, an ambition Freud attributes to her. (One wonders how youth has discovered conception, an elaborate and subtle process which children do not discover by themselves, and not all primitive adults can fathom.) The girl is said to assume her female parent has mutilated her as a judgment on her general unworthiness, or possibly for the crime of masturbation, and now turns her anxious attention to her father.[15]

At this stage of her childhood the little girl at first expects her father to prove magnanimous and award her a penis. Later, disappointed in this hope, she learns to content herself with the aspiration of bearing his baby. The baby is given out as a curious item; it is actually a penis, not a baby at all: "the girl's libido slips into position by means—there is really no other way to put it—of the equation 'penis-child.'"[16] Although she will never relinquish some hope of acquiring a penis ("we ought to recognize this wish for a penis as being par excellence a feminine one")[17] a baby is as close to a penis as the girl shall get. The new penis wish is metamorphosed into a baby, a quaint feminine-coated penis, which has the added merit of being a respectable ambition. (It is interesting that Freud should imagine the young female's fears center about castration rather than rape—a phenomenon which girls are in fact, and with reason, in dread of, since it happens to them and castration does not.) Girls, he informs us, now relinquish some of their anxiety over their castration, but never cease to envy and resent penises[18] and so while "impotent" they remain in the world a constant hazard to the well-provided male. There are overtones here of a faintly capitalist antagonism between the haves and the have nots. This seems to account for the considerable fear of women inherent in Freudian ideology and the force of an accusation of penis envy when leveled at mature women.

The Freudian "family romance," domestic psychodrama more horrific than a soap opera, continues. The archetypal girl is now flung into the Oedipal stage of desire for her father, having been persuaded of the total inadequacy of her clitoris, and therefore of her sex and her self. The boy,   12

[14]Ibid., p. 193.

[15]The description of female psychological development is from Freud's *Three Contributions to the Theory of Sex*, "Femininity," "Some Psychological Consequences of the Anatomical Distinction between the Sexes," and "Female Sexuality."

[16]"Some Psychological Consequences of the Anatomical Distinctions between the Sexes," p. 195.

[17]"Femininity," p. 128.

[18]See "Female Sexuality" (1931), *Collected Works*, Vol. V, pp. 252–72.

meanwhile is so aghast by the implications of sexual enlightenment that he at first represses the information. Later, he can absorb it only by accompanying the discovery of sexual differentiation with an overpowering contempt for the female. It is difficult to understand how, setting aside the social context, as Freud's theory does so firmly, a boy could ever become this convinced of the superiority of the penis. Yet Freud assures us that "as a result of the discovery of women's lack of a penis they [females] are debased in value for girls just as they are for boys and later perhaps for men."[19]

Conflict with the father warns the boy that the castration catastrophe might occur to him as well. He grows wary for his own emblem and surrenders his sexual desires for his mother out of fear.[20] Freud's exegesis of the neurotic excitements of nuclear family life might constitute, in itself, considerable evidence of the damaging effects of this institution, since through the parents, it presents to the very young a set of primary sexual objects who are a pair of adults with whom intercourse would be incestuous were it even physically possible.

While Freud strongly prescribes that all lingering hopes of acquiring a penis be abandoned and sublimated in maternity, what he recommends is merely a displacement, since even maternal desires rest upon the last vestige of penile aspiration. For, as she continues to mature, we are told, the female never gives up the hope of a penis, now always properly equated with a baby. Thus men grow to love women, or better yet, their idea of women, whereas women grow to love babies.[21] It is said that the female doggedly continues her sad phallic quest in childbirth, never outgrowing her Oedipal circumstance of wanting a penis by having a baby. "Her happiness is great if later on this wish for a baby finds fulfillment in reality, and quite especially so if the baby is a little boy who brings the longed-for penis with him."[22] Freudian logic has succeeded in converting childbirth, an impressive female accomplishment, and the only function its rationale permits her, into nothing more than a hunt for a male organ. It somehow becomes the male prerogative even to give birth, as babies are but surrogate penises. The female is bested at the only function Freudian theory recommends for her, reproduction. Furthermore, her libido is actually said to be too small to qualify her as a constructive agent here, since Freud repeatedly states she has less sexual drive than the male. Woman is thus granted very little validity even within her limited existence and second-rate biological equipment: were she to deliver an entire orphanage of progeny, they would only be so many dildoes.

---

[19]"Femininity," p. 127.

[20]"Some Psychological Consequences of the Anatomical Distinction between the Sexes" and elsewhere in connection with the Oedipus complex in males.

[21]"Femininity," p. 134.

[22]Ibid., p. 128.

Until active "phallic" autoeroticism ceases, with the acceptance of clitoral inferiority, correct maturation cannot proceed. Here Freud is particularly prescriptive: "masturbation, at all events of the clitoris, is a masculine activity and the elimination of the clitoral sexuality is a necessary precondition for the development of femininity."[23] (Femininity is prescribed as both normal and healthy. Later we shall investigate what it consists of more thoroughly.) Adolescent autoeroticism is outlawed; abstinence is essential to correct female development. In a girl whose development is fortunate so far, there are still obstacles: "she acknowledges the fact of her castration, the consequent superiority of the male and her own inferiority, but she also rebels against these unpleasant facts."[24] Freud finds it typical of nature that "the constitution will not adapt itself to its function without a struggle."[25] And so it is that while the regenerate female seeks fulfillment in a life devoted to reproduction, others persist in the error of aspiring to an existence beyond the biological level of confinement to maternity and reproduction—falling into the error Freud calls "the masculinity complex."[26] This is how one is to account for the many deviant women, both those who renounce sexuality or divert it to members of their own sex, as well as those who pursue "masculine aims." The latter group do not seek the penis openly and honestly in maternity, but instead desire to enter universities, pursue an autonomous or independent course in life, take up with feminism, or grow restless and require treatment as "neurotics." Freud's method was to castigate such "immature" women as "regressive" or incomplete persons, clinical cases of "arrested development."[27]

How penis envy, repressed but never overcome, becomes the primary   16
source of health or pathology; good or evil in female life is left to a mysterious deciding force called the "constitutional factor."[28] Consequently, if a woman takes her fate gracefully, though still a member of an obviously inferior species, she may at least acknowledge her plight and confine herself to maternity. But should she grow insubordinate, she will invade the larger world which Freud is unthinkingly convinced is, of itself, male "territory" and seek to "compete," thereby threatening men. She may then be convicted of "masculinity complex" or "masculine protest."

In such cases Freud and his school after him will do all in their power to convince her of the error of her ways: by gentle persuasion, harsh

[23]"Some Psychological Consequences of the Anatomical Distinctions between the Sexes," p. 194.

[24]"Female Sexuality," p. 257.

[25]"Femininity," p. 117.

[26]"And if the defense against femininity is so vigorous, from what other source can it derive its strength than from that striving for masculinity which found its earlier expression in the child's penis-envy and might well take its name from this." "Female Sexuality," p. 272.

[27]See "Femininity," p. 130, and elsewhere, also "Analysis Terminable and Interminable," Collected Works, Vol. V.

[28]"Femininity," p. 130.

ridicule, and when vulgar Freudianism has come to power, by the actual mental policing of "pop psych." The renegade must adjust or succumb. One is never enlightened as to what proof exists that all human (as distinct from biological or reproductive) pursuits, interesting or uninteresting, designated male "territory," are in fact intrinsically so, or on what biological grounds it can be proven that literacy, the university, or the professions are really inherently male. It would be easy to say that Freud mistakes custom for inherency, the male's domination of cultural modes for nature, but his hypothesis is so weighted with expedient interest that to do this would be to call him naïve.

A philosophy which assumes that "the demand for justice is a modification of envy,"[29] and informs the dispossessed that the circumstances of their deprivation are organic, therefore unalterable, is capable of condoning a great deal of injustice. One can predict the advice such a philosophy would have in store for other disadvantaged groups displeased with the status quo, and as the social and political effects of such lines of reasoning are fairly clear, it is not difficult to see why Freud finally became so popular a thinker in conservative societies.

Freud had spurned an excellent opportunity to open the door to hundreds of enlightening studies on the effect of male-supremacist culture on the ego development of the young female, preferring instead to sanctify her oppression in terms of the inevitable law of "biology." The theory of penis envy has so effectively obfuscated understanding that all psychology has done since has not yet unraveled this matter of social causation. If, as seems unlikely, penis envy can mean anything at all, it is productive only within the total cultural context of sex. And here it would seem that girls are fully cognizant of male supremacy long before they see their brother's penis. It is so much a part of their culture, so entirely present in the favoritism of school and family, in the image of each sex presented to them by all media, religion, and in every model of the adult world they perceive, that to associate it with a boy's distinguishing genital would, since they have learned a thousand other distinguishing sexual marks by now, be either redundant or irrelevant. Confronted with so much concrete evidence of the male's superior status, sensing on all sides the depreciation in which they are held, girls envy not the penis, but only what the penis gives one social pretensions to. Freud appears to have made a major and rather foolish confusion between biology and culture, anatomy and status. It is still more apparent that his audience found such a confusion serviceable.

However complacent he may appear, the feminist movement appears [20] to have posed a considerable threat to Freud. His statements on women are often punctuated with barbs against the feminist point of view. The charge of penis envy against all rebels is reiterated again and again, an incantation to disarm the specter of emancipated or intellectual women, oddities who are putting themselves to unnecessary trouble in a futile effort to

[29]Ibid., p. 134.

compensate for their organic inferiority by stabs at cultural achievement, for which Freud assumes the possession of a penis is a sine qua non. He even complains that the women who consult him in psychoanalysis do so to obtain a penis.[30] Since this is obscure, it is necessary to translate: Female patients consulted him in the hope of becoming more productive in their work; in return for their fees Freud did what he could to cause them to abandon their vocations as unnatural aberrations.[31] Convinced that the connection between the penis and intellectual ability is unquestionably organic, Freud protests with a genial shrug "in the psychic field the biological factor is really the rock bottom."[32] The intellectual superiority of the male, constitutionally linked with the penis, is close to an ascertainable fact for Freud, a rock bottom of remarkable comfort.

Freud believed that two aspects of woman's character are directly related to penis envy: modesty and jealousy. It is her self-despair over the "defect" of her "castration," we are told, which gives rise to the well-known shame of women. One is struck at how much kinder Victorian chivalry could be with its rigamarole about "purity." Freud designated shame as a feminine characteristic "par excellence."[33] Its purpose, in his view, is simply the concealment of her hapless defect. As among the primitives, so today, the woman hides her parts to hide her wound. When Freud suggests that modesty in women was originally designed "for concealment of genital deficiency" he is even willing to describe pubic hair as the response of "nature herself" to cover the female fault.[34]

Although it is one of Freud's favorite notions that women have not, and for constitutional reasons cannot, contribute to civilization (Otto Weininger, a misogynist thinker to whom Freud was often indebted, thought genius itself masculine and a female genius a contradiction in

[30]"The wish to get the longed-for penis eventually, in spite of everything, may contribute to the motives that drive a mature woman to analysis . . . a capacity, for instance, to carry on an intellectual profession—may often be recognized as a sublimated modification of this repressed wish." ("Femininity," p. 125.) What should happen however, is this: "the unsatisfied wish for a penis should be converted into a wish for a child and for a man who possesses a penis." ("Analysis Terminable and Interminable," p. 355.) Intellectual striving or an urge for human fulfillment beyond this confining recipe is castigated as unrepressed bisexuality or "masculine striving" where "the wish for masculinity persists in the unconscious, and . . . exercises a disturbing influence." (Ibid.)

[31]It is difficult work, and Freud confesses that "at no point in one's analytic work does one suffer more from the oppressive feeling that one is 'talking to the winds' than when one is trying to persuade a female patient to abandon her wish for a penis on the ground of its being unrealizable." "Analysis Terminable and Interminable," p. 356.

[32]"We often feel that when we have reached the penis wish and the masculine protest we have penetrated all the psychological strata and reached 'bedrock' and that our task is accomplished. And this is probably correct, for in the psychic field the biological factor is really the rock bottom. The repudiation of femininity must surely be biological fact, part of the great riddle of sex." Ibid., p. 356–57.

[33]"Femininity," p. 132.

[34]Ibid.

terms) Freud does allow that women might have invented weaving and plaiting—discoveries that spring from an identical impulse—the need to hide their deformity.[35]

A folklike accusation of female jealousy is also part of Freud's program and he assures us this vice springs from penis envy as well.[36] He is of the opinion that males are less prone to sexual jealousy (on many occasions Freud puts in a good word for the double standard which makes men's lives richer in sexual opportunity) and he sees in the vigilance of husbands, fathers, and brothers, only the watchful care of property owners. Monogamous marriage is an institution with which he found much fault, but mainly on the grounds that it hampers masculine freedom. The attribution of moral jealousy and a low moral sense to women inspires Freud to remarks of this kind—"the fact that women must be regarded as having little sense of justice, is no doubt related to the predominance of envy in their mental life."[37] In view of the social position of women this is a remarkably damaging accusation, for to accuse a deprived group of spitefulness and no sense of fairness, is to discredit or deprive its members of the moral position which is their only claim for just treatment.

Coming as it did, at the peak of the sexual revolution, Freud's doctrine of penis envy is in fact a superbly timed accusation, enabling masculine sentiment to take the offensive again as it had not since the disappearance of overt misogyny when the pose of chivalry became fashionable. The whole weight of responsibility, and even of guilt, is now placed upon any woman unwilling to "stay in her place." The theory of penis envy shifts the blame of her suffering to the female for daring to aspire to a biologically impossible state. Any hankering for a less humiliating and circumscribed existence is immediately ascribed to unnatural and unrealistic deviation from her genetic identity and therefore her fate. A woman who resists "femininity," e.g., feminine temperament, status, and role, is thought to court neurosis, for femininity is her fate as "anatomy is destiny." In so evading the only destiny nature has granted her, she courts nothingness.

Freud's circular method in formulating penis envy begins by reporting children's distorted impressions, gradually comes to accept them as the correct reaction, goes on to present its own irresponsible version of the sociosexual context, and then, through a nearly imperceptible series of transitions, slides from description to a form of prescription which insures the continuance of the patriarchal status quo, under the guise of health and normality. Apart from ridicule, the counterrevolutionary period never employed a more withering or destructive weapon against feminist insurgence than the Freudian accusation of penis envy.

[35]Ibid.

[36]Ibid., p. 134. The charge is made in "Female Sexuality" and a number of other places as well.

[37]Ibid.

Questions and Suggestions for Writing

1. Millet suggests (para. 3) a similarity between being born female in a male-dominated society, and being born black in a white racist society. Can you suggest any differences? Which do you think are the more important, the similarities or the differences? Explain.

2. Millet challenges Freud (para. 4) with several questions that she does not herself try to answer. How do you think Freud might reply? Is this an effective tactic in her critique of Freud? Why, or why not?

3. Freud is attacked for his failure to present "objective proof" for the alleged ubiquity of "penis envy" among women (para. 6). Reread Freud's essay and explain in an essay of 250 words whether you think her criticism is fair.

4. Millett contrasts Freud's "descriptions" with his "prescriptions" regarding the female "castration complex" (para. 10). State precisely what his descriptions and prescriptions are. Do the prescriptions rest on the descriptions, or on something else? Explain.

5. In paragraphs 10–11, Millett uses parenthetical comments to criticize Freud's views in the course of her paraphrase of them. Is this style effective? Is it fair to Freud? Explain.

6. Throughout her essay (for instance, in para. 12) Millett refers to Freud's neglect of "the social context" in which men and women, boys and girls, find themselves. Describe this social context as she sees it. Why does Millett think that failure to take it into account undermines much, perhaps most, of Freud's teachings about femininity?

7

Does a Science Requirement Make Sense?

Morris Shamos

The Lesson Every Child Need Not Learn

Last year, Edward D. Hirsch, Jr., a professor of English at the University of Virginia, published a list of several thousand terms that, in his view, should be familiar to every thinking citizen in the United States. The list was appended to Hirsch's book, *Cultural Literacy: What Every American Needs to Know,* in which he sought to show that a grasp of such background information is the key to effective communication and, hence, to full participation in our society. It included names, ideas, and objects, literary terms, historical events, and geographical references, ranging in scope from such standard grade school fare as Galileo, 1492, Moscow, and the Second World War to such often forgotten, but not entirely unfamiliar, items as James Clerk Maxwell, 1066, Harper's Ferry, and French Impressionism. Hirsch's approach was useful, not only because it confronted the question of what constitutes a core of factual knowledge, which should be of value to educators generally, but, more important, because it forced the issue of the level of understanding one must have of these terms to share in our culture.

Morris Shamos (b. 1917) is a professor emeritus of physics at New York University and a past president of both the National Science Teachers Association and the New York Academy of Sciences. This article first appeared in The Sciences, *1988.*

One quality that sets apart Hirsch's list from a list that might have been drawn up, say, three centuries ago is the inclusion of a large number of science-related terms; they make up somewhat more than 15 percent of the total, and include, for example, *entropy, natural selection,* and *the periodic table of the elements.* This, of course, reflects the growing impact of science on Western culture during the past three hundred years. Indeed, so important has science become that we now speak of scientific literacy as an indispensable element in, if not an actual partner to, cultural literacy as a whole.

The current movement toward scientific literacy actually dates back to the period immediately after the Second World War, when the drive for bigger and better science curricula in the nation's schools began to gain momentum. In 1954, the National Science Foundation, an independent federal agency whose principal function is to support basic and applied research, began funding education programs designed to increase the pool from which science and engineering professionals are drawn.

Then, in October of 1957, the Soviets launched Sputnik, the first man-made satellite to orbit Earth. Determined not to allow the Soviet Union to surpass the United States in scientific and technological achievement, Congress increased NSF's education budget, from $3.5 million to $19 million, and eventually to $61 million, and enlarged the agency's statutory authority, permitting it to support science, mathematics, and engineering education at all levels, including the elementary grades. At the same time, the National Defense Education Act of 1958 authorized the Office of Education, then part of the Department of Health, Education and Welfare, to make funds available to schools for remodeling laboratory facilities and for acquiring equipment and teaching aids. Several billion dollars was poured into these programs over the next two decades. What had begun as an attempt to train more scientists and engineers soon expanded, at least in the minds of many educators, into an effort to provide all students, and the public generally, with a broad understanding of science and technology.

Science, as a result, became a major feature of the general precollege curriculum in the United States and other highly industrialized nations. Where some state education departments failed to make science courses mandatory for high school graduation, colleges usually accomplished the same end by requiring a minimum scientific background for admission. And the colleges, in turn, perpetuated the notion that science should be part of the lore of educated adults by insisting that most graduates at least be exposed to it.

Notwithstanding the sincerity and efforts of teachers and administrators, these education reforms have proved ineffective. Granted, the public may be more sensitive today than it was forty years ago to some science-based issues—nuclear weapons, the war on cancer, computers—but its current understanding of the facts and principles that underlie such issues is no better than it was just after the war. As measured by any reasonable

4

benchmark, even by Hirsch's vocabulary test, we are still a nation of scientific illiterates, which has led some educators to suggest that shortages of professional scientists and engineers are in store. An even greater threat, say the critics, is the prospect that, unless all citizens become scientifically literate, they will be unable to participate intelligently in a technological society and to perform competently in the workplace, with the result that the United States might soon become a second-rate nation.

During the past several decades, the American education system has been the target of a great deal of criticism, some of it deserved, but in this instance the critics are wrong. For, heretical though it may seem, requiring science courses, no matter how thoughtfully designed, of everyone in grade school, secondary school, and college will not produce a scientifically literate society. What's worse, the rationale for seeking such literacy is ill-conceived: widespread scientific literacy is *not* essential to develop an intelligent electorate, to maintain a science and engineering work force, or to prepare people for life in an increasingly technological society. Science, of course, should be taught in schools, and taught with the best methods and facilities at our disposal, but for reasons other than these.

What, in fact, do we mean by scientific literacy? While there exists no clear, widely accepted definition, it is fair to say that the scientifically literate individual falls somewhere between two extremes. At one extreme is the man or woman who understands the foundations, current status, and most of the important problems of at least several of the life and the physical sciences. This understanding need not be operational; that is, to be scientifically literate, one does not have to be able to conduct research or to solve problems in the field. But one should be able to read knowingly (including some of the technical literature), and engage intelligently in discussions, on topics relating to such disciplines. Judged according to this standard, few of us, even among scientists and engineers, could be considered literates, which means only that the criterion is too demanding, not that such literacy is undesirable. At the other extreme is the sort of person envisioned by Hirsch—the individual who has acquired a large glossary of technical terms, perhaps by rote, and a brief definition of each. Here the notion of literacy tends to become somewhat fuzzy. It is one thing to nod in recognition of technical terms when reading or listening to accounts of scientific matters and perhaps in this way feel less estranged from science. But it is quite another to appreciate the significance of such terms and be able to employ them in meaningful discourse. Recognition alone cannot be equated with understanding.

Consider, as an example of how difficult it is to define scientific literacy, the one so often cited as a criterion of such literacy—namely, the second law of thermodynamics. Three decades ago, the physicist C. P. Snow suggested that familiarity with the second law should be equivalent to having read a work of Shakespeare. Using Snow's standard, a scientifically literate person might be expected to know not only that the second law is one of the most important concepts in science but also that it asserts that heat cannot pass unaided from a cool body to a warm body and that one can conclude from this that, because the universe is not reversible, its entropy must be increasing. It is safe to say that such understanding more than satisfies Hirsch's definition of scientific literacy, but it raises more questions than it answers.

What, after all, are thermodynamics, heat, entropy, and reversible processes? Why is the second law considered more important than the first law, which asserts that the total energy of the universe always remains constant? And what of the consequences of the second law: Shouldn't a literate individual understand that entropy is a measure of the orderliness of a system and that an ever increasing entropy means the universe is tending toward greater disorder, or running down, that the concept of entropy provides an arrow of time, so to speak, which permits us to record the past but not the future (probably a silly observation to most people, but one that has profound philosophical implications)?

Where shall we stop? Should we expect a scientific literate to know that living organisms appear to defy the principle of increasing entropy because they seemingly tend toward greater order? But that on more careful analysis the entropy of the overall system that supports the organism, including its food supply and environment, actually increases? Even at this point, there is much more that the truly literate individual might be expected to know—why the scientific community has confidence in the laws of thermodynamics; how the laws apply to practical problems in virtually all the natural and engineering sciences (cell metabolism, heat loss in engines, the corrosion of metals); and why they leave us with a pragmatic warning: Beware of anyone trying to sell you what appears to be a perpetual motion machine. The point is that in science there is much more to most ideas than can be conveyed by a simple definition. Concepts such as the second law cannot be treated in isolation; knowing how they interrelate with other facts and principles is essential if one is to achieve true literacy.

But in a sense, all this is beside the point, since, even by Hirsch's 12 standard, few people can be considered scientifically literate. An upper bound can be placed on the number of people who fit this category by assuming that the group includes scientists and engineers; physicians and dentists; science teachers, writers, and editors; and dedicated readers of popular-science literature. According to the most recent census, these groups total only about four or four and a half million people, roughly 2.4 to 2.7 percent of the country's population. Thus, even by the most generous criterion, fewer than 3 percent of American citizens *might* qualify as scientific literates. It matters little that a much larger number were exposed to science in school; even if such learning was effective at the time, for most it was soon forgotten.

Remember, too, that this estimate assumes that *all* scientists, engineers, and science teachers fit the definition. Yet we know that most scientists and engineers confine their technical interests to narrow fields, and some science teachers do not even understand what constitutes scientific knowledge. Incredible as it may seem, a recent survey of high school biology teachers in Ohio showed that a quarter of the respondents believe that creationism should be taught along with evolution as a *scientific* theory of the origin of life. Hence, if anything, this estimate probably errs on the high side. A discouraging conclusion, to be sure, but, given the nature of twentieth-century science, we can hardly expect it to be otherwise.

One of the intrinsic properties that make science difficult to master is its cumulative nature. Indeed, in the view of many scientists and educators, it is this property that most distinguishes science from other forms of intellectual activity. Progress is not a characteristic of the humanities; one would never claim that Michelangelo was less advanced than Picasso. Contrast this with Isaac Newton's declaration that he saw farther by "standing on the shoulders of giants," or consider the increase in scientific publications since Newton's time. Whereas three hundred years ago only a handful of scientific works were published each year, now at least forty thousand journals, representing about a million scientific papers, are published annually.

Merely deciding what portion of this information is worth knowing is no small task. As an illustration of the disagreements that arise, compare Hirsch's list of science-related terms with a list compiled by Charles L. Koelsche and Ashley G. Morgan, Jr., and included in their 1964 book, *Scientific Literacy in the Sixties.* Koelsche and Morgan gathered information needed by readers to understand popular-science articles, yielding a vocabulary list only slightly longer than Hirsch's. Yet fewer than a third of the terms on the two lists are identical. Since the central precepts of science did not change significantly during the intervening two decades, the sizable difference between the lists suggests a discrepancy between what some members of the scientific community perceive as important and what appears in the public press. And there is no reason to believe that this discrepancy has diminished.

Even if agreement could be reached about vocabulary, other, less 16 tractable obstacles stand in the way of achieving scientific literacy. For one thing, the borders that once sharply separated the sciences are crumbling. No longer can the life sciences be completely understood apart from physics and chemistry: biophysics, biochemistry, and biotechnology were virtually unheard of a century ago; today, they are but a few reminders that the sciences have become more and more interdependent.

What's more, an ever widening chasm has opened between scientific and commonsense world views. Aristotle had no difficulty communicating the kind of teleological explanations of phenomena that were in vogue during the fourth century B.C. To explain the acceleration of a falling body, for example, he needed only to observe that "the traveler hastens as he approaches his destination." Or he might account for a variety of pneumatic phenomena by invoking the idea summed up in the aphorism "Nature abhors a vacuum." This mode of explanation not only appealed to early Greek and Roman scholars but also set a pattern of hopeless confusion in science that persisted until the Renaissance.

Only a hundred years ago, when American colleges and universities came to accept science subjects as appropriate prerequisites for admission, it was possible to speak of the universe as a well-behaved, deterministic mechanism made up of billiard-ball-like atoms. But science has since elaborated this commonsense view, as the English astronomer Arthur S. Eddington pointed out in the introduction to his series of Gifford lectures at the University of Edinburgh in 1927.

Eddington spoke of the "two tables" that stood before him. One was the familiar, commonplace object of the real world: it had dimension, color, substance, and some degree of permanence. The second table—the scientific one—was a total stranger to the real world. According to modern physics, it consisted mostly of empty space (the regions between the nuclei of the atoms of which it was composed) and a staggering number of electric charges (electrons) that moved about with great speed and whose combined bulk amounted to much less than one billionth of the real table's bulk. Yet, despite this strange construction, the table supported such things as books and elbows—because the electric charges within its atoms continually collided with similar electric charges in the objects placed on it, preventing them from "falling through" the empty spaces.

And physics is not alone in becoming obscure; chemistry, molecular 20 biology, and other fields have moved in that direction, as well. Though scientific inquiry usually begins with observations of the everyday world and concludes by returning to that world in the form of technology, the steps between these two extremes, where the real scientific work is done, are largely unfathomable to all but specialists. We have no commonsense counterparts for photons, genes, novas, or black holes; when scientists talk about these things, they reason by means of models—abstractions that agree with what is known about certain phenomena (or, more often, about their effects) but that are not necessarily meant to be pictures of those phenomena. The most extreme form of such reasoning, and thus the most radical departure from everyday discourse, is mathematics.

As far as most students are concerned, mathematics was invented to complicate, rather than facilitate, the study of science. Granted, some come to appreciate equations as tools for applying scientific laws to particular situations—Newton's laws of motion to the trajectory of a rocket, for instance. But in fact, the primary function of mathematics is not computation; it is discovery. Mathematics is the only language by which statements about nature can be made in symbolic form and then combined according to logical rules to lead to new knowledge of the universe. Classic examples are Galileo's definitions of velocity and acceleration, which, when stated in mathematical form and combined algebraically, enabled him to derive the entire science of uniformly accelerated motion, including the laws of falling bodies and the motion of a projectile. Avoiding mathematics, which seems to be the principal attraction offered by some science courses these days, may be a way of drawing students; but by ignoring the theoretical structure of science, this strategy conveys a false impression of the overall scientific enterprise.

Taken together, the cumulative nature of science and its reliance on descriptions that run counter to common sense, especially on mathematics, make it necessary to devote extraordinary effort to the task of becoming scientifically literate. Most of us, certainly the 90 percent of high school students who do not become scientists, appear to be unwilling to make this effort.

Even if widespread scientific literacy were possible to achieve, it is not nearly as essential to success in the twentieth century as is commonly believed. Consider the argument cited most frequently: We live in a scientific age, a time in which we all are touched by the discoveries of science, if not directly, then at least by the technologies that result from them. Many issues and problems facing society—dwindling world food supplies, pollution, nuclear testing, genetic engineering, the Strategic Defense Initiative (Star Wars)—have technological bases. An informed electorate, one that is scientifically literate, would be best able to deal with such issues—to reach independent judgments and elect officials who properly reflect those judgments.

One cannot easily quarrel with such a rationale; it is an ideal devoutly 24 to be wished. In fact, though, no reasonable amount of scientific training could possibly prepare one to form credible judgments on the wide variety of issues the country faces. What's more, being scientifically informed is no guarantee of certainty. Even professional scientists frequently disagree on science-based public policy issues, and for reasons that can be equally convincing. Take the Strategic Defense Initiative: physicists and engineers have lined up on both sides of the fence regarding the feasibility of almost every aspect of the system, including the target-locating systems, the laser beams that would be used to destroy enemy warheads, and the software that would direct the entire operation.

Another popular argument in favor of scientific literacy is that it better prepares a nonscientist to function in business or professional life. If there is any truth to this, students fail to perceive it, and small wonder: they need only look at their own professional family members and friends, at wealthy businessmen and powerful public officials, at people in the arts and professors of humanities—all successful and respected members of society and most, if not all, illiterate in science. After all, what bearing does a lawyer's understanding of the double helix have on the success of his practice? How many times does a banker call on the uncertainty principle to make an investment decision? Is it necessary that the mayor of New York be versed in plate tectonics to run city hall? Would a knowledge of chaos theory have boosted the careers of Luciano Pavarotti or Laurence Olivier? The same questions could be asked of all educated adults in the work force.

The need to increase the nation's scientific manpower pool to avoid future shortages is a third argument often made in behalf of scientific literacy. Many educators and employers feel that students must decide to go into science before graduating from high school, since few choose to do so afterward. Hence the rationale for developing scientific literacy among all students: the expectation that more will then choose careers in science and engineering. This argument fails on two counts.

First, roughly 10 percent of the country's high school freshmen profess a desire to become scientists or engineers, and about half of these actually go on to fulfill that desire. The other 90 percent are not science-bound, nor are they likely to have any direct involvement with science after their formal schooling. Requiring science of all students in the hope that one in twenty or thirty will choose it as a career is hardly an efficient means to this end. Moreover, it has never been demonstrated that a compulsory science curriculum produces more professional scientists than a voluntary course of study. Surely there are more effective and less costly ways of attracting students into the sciences, should this be necessary.

Second, there is no hard evidence of impending manpower shortages. 28 The number of students graduating with science or engineering degrees increased after 1955 at an average annual rate of about 5 percent, then leveled off during the 1980s owing to a decrease both in demand and in the high school population. Besides being irresponsible, turning out more scientists than the marketplace demands, purely on speculation, is a poor argument for scientific literacy for all. If shortages were certain—say, in technical areas in which the United States might be falling behind such countries as Japan—improving the precollege education of *only* science-bound students would be a far easier and more appropriate goal.

The fourth argument for scientific literacy, the only one with a ring of truth to it, relates to America's technology-oriented economy. Will office workers who can handle computers be in greater demand than those who cannot? Will manufacturers be looking for factory workers who can operate the robots that will displace much of the human labor force? The answer to each question, of course, is yes. But does this mean that general literacy in science will be required? Probably not, as the history of technology clearly shows. We learned to use electronic typewriters, office copiers, video equipment, electronic machine tools, and many other devices through specific on-the-job training or simple written instructions, without knowledge of the machines' inner workings, largely because such devices are specifically designed for use by nonexperts. So it is specious to contend that achieving scientific (or even technological) literacy will better prepare students for tomorrow's job market. Granted, the workplace may come to demand a higher degree of technical sophistication from nonscientists than is now required; the way to meet that demand, however, is not to attempt to make all students technically proficient but to enhance technical-education programs for students who choose them.

If widespread scientific literacy is not necessary for responsible citizenship, economic success, maintaining a pool of scientists, or using machines, is there *anything* that can be said in its favor? There is, and it can be traced to ideas espoused by such nineteenth-century scientists as the biologist Thomas Huxley and the mathematician Jules-Henri Poincaré. Students have the most to gain, said Huxley and Poincaré, if they study science chiefly for the aesthetic and intellectual values it bestows. "The scientist does not study nature because it is useful," wrote Poincaré, in *The Value of Science*, published in 1907. "He studies it because he delights in it, and he delights in it because it is beautiful." Not widely accepted when first proposed, Poincaré's idea may be one whose time has finally come.

During early encounters with science—observing fire, light, magnetism, chemical changes, small animals—students nearly always are fascinated and curious. Then, as time goes by, and as science courses increasingly stress memorization, facts, and the study of subjects for which the student has no personal interest, the magic wears off and is replaced by boredom or, worse, outright rejection. Evidence of this inevitable alienation can be found in every high school science classroom in the United States.

Perhaps there is a lesson here. If the dream of scientific literacy for all 32 now lies shattered, it is because it was an impossible dream to begin with. Acknowledging this might allow us to pursue a goal that appears less ambitious but, in the long run, is more promising. Is it not more desirable to nurture an *appreciation* of science and thereby keep open the possibility of full literacy for some individual than to force-feed facts and formulas and thereby instill a distaste for science that probably guarantees life-long ignorance?

Questions and Suggestions for Writing

1. Shamos's first six paragraphs are largely devoted to arguing that, despite required science courses, "we are still a nation of scientific illiterates." In the middle of paragraph 7 he introduces a new point: "scientific literacy is *not* essential. . . ." Has Shamos wasted the first six paragraphs, or do those paragraphs serve a useful function in his essay?

2. In paragraphs 8–11 Shamos discusses definitions of scientific literacy. How would you define the term? Would you agree with Shamos, given your defini-

tion, that it is neither possible nor necessary that most Americans become scientifically literate?

3. The beginning of the first sentence of paragraph 23 ("Even if widespread scientific literacy were possible to achieve") assumes that the preceding twenty-two paragraphs have demonstrated that scientific literacy probably cannot be achieved. Has Shamos in fact convinced you of the improbability or even impossibility? Why, or why not?

4. Consider the following reply to Shamos's objection (para. 23) to what he regards as the most popular argument for promoting scientific literacy: Whatever may be true about the "Star Wars" (SDI) controversy, a more scientifically literate society would grasp the dangers of ozone depletion, or of acid rain, and the necessity of recycling waste and increasing the use of renewable energy sources. Do you agree? If so, how would you support your position?

5. In paragraphs 23–29 Shamos summarizes four arguments commonly offered in behalf of requiring courses in science. Do you think his summaries are fair? Are his refutations fair? Can you think of any further arguments in favor of requiring science courses that Shamos omits?

6. Suppose one were to object to Shamos's final position (para. 50) that he makes a tacit plea to keep scientific knowledge confined to an intellectual elite (of whom he is one), and an elite, moreover, that has no concern for practical applications of scientific knowledge to practical problems. How much merit do you find in this objection?

7. Reread Shamos's last two paragraphs, thinking about them as an argument, and especially about their place in his overall argument. Why do you suppose he ends—rather than begins—with these paragraphs? Second, think about the paragraphs as writing, especially about their tone. How would you characterize Shamo's tone? Is it courteous, wishy-washy, something else?

8. Shamos refers to scientific disagreement over SDI. After researching the matter in your library, write a 500-word essay on the theme: Controversial Scientific Questions Regarding SDI.

RESPONSES TO SHAMOS

Readers of Shamos's article sent the following replies, which *The Sciences* (the magazine in which the article first appeared) published in a later issue along with a response by Shamos.

While Morris Shamos makes a strong case for abandoning the goal of achieving scientific literacy for all ["The Lesson Every Child Need Not Learn," July/August], there are two points he fails to address adequately.

First is the notion that a scientifically literate electorate is critical to the health of a modern democracy. Mr. Shamos believes that "no reasonable amount of scientific training could possibly prepare one to form credible judgments on the wide variety of issues the country faces" and that, in any case, even scientific experts disagree on science-policy issues. But when controversial matters involving science arise, what is the scientifically illiterate electorate supposed to do—flip a coin, or side with those who gain the most television time? Even a modest amount of academic exposure to science would enable many people to separate legitimate disagreement from political and *ad hominem* arguments, such as those now infecting the debates over the Strategic Defense Initiative, nuclear winter, genetic engineering, and a plethora of environmental concerns. Carl Sagan the scientist and Carl Sagan the polemicist are not the same person, and it would be helpful if people could distinguish between them.

Second is the need, which Mr. Shamos fails to acknowledge, for certain non-scientists, whose work directly affects science, to appreciate how scientists operate. The actions of politicians and chief executive officers determine which scientific investigations are conducted. Senator Proxmire's Golden Fleece Awards might have served the country better were he not scientifically illiterate.

Scientific literacy for all is unattainable, but improvement in the present, appalling situation is not. Mr. Shamos's position is too pessimistic.

Thomas B. Steel, Jr.
Hofstra University
Hempstead, New York

I believe a scientifically illiterate society will elect government officials who believe in astrology; will so literally interpret religious writings as to permit pseudoscience to be taught as science; will examine environmental issues in simplistic terms; will have no notion of the greatest intellectual accomplishments of mankind. So it is sad to see Morris Shamos give up on making people as scientifically literate as possible.

Stewart Karp
Long Island University
Brookville, New York

Of course it is a waste to force-feed scientific ideas to all children alike. What must be taught instead is the essential skepticism of the scientific method—the nature and significance of scientific evidence and the eternal suspicion of all absolutes. Our failure to do so is evident in the continued acceptance of ancient and medieval absurdities, from pagan magic to fundamentalist theocratic myth.

Maurice O. Burke
Northfield, Illinois

It is unfortunate that grounding in science is no longer considered a requirement for an educated person. Who would dare admit to never having read a play by Shakespeare? But announce that you can't balance your checkbook or understand statistics and you will elicit concurring nods and chuckles.

It is true, as Morris Shamos says, that science has become so specialized, even a good education in basic science does not prepare one to be expert in all science. But the same is true of nonscientific pursuits. That historians, for example, have become experts in particular periods or areas (the history of the military, perhaps, or of science or economics) has not dissuaded us from teaching history.

Bruce J. Sobol, M.D.
Ridgefield, Connecticut

America's system of education suffers from many ills, but the need for understanding science is not, as Morris Shamos says, an empty goal. Science is a way of thinking that incorporates reason and logic. The study of science can teach these thinking skills. Mr. Shamos's comments will be used against many of us who are fighting a difficult battle to enrich our education system. As a scientist, he should be ashamed.

Joyce R. Blueford
Math/Science Nucleus
Fremont, California

Morris Shamos makes the mistake of presuming that literacy is a binary condition—that one is either fully literate or else illiterate. But literacy means only that one has the ability to read and understand; beyond that, there are degrees of literacy. Anyone capable of reading about science with some understanding possesses a degree of scientific literacy.

The key to scientific literacy for the nonscientist is neither memorization of scientific terms nor an intimate understanding of an encyclopedic range of concepts. Rather, all students should be taught the special way in which scientific knowledge is acquired. Any person of average intelligence has the capacity to learn about the methods by which scientists test their theories and to understand that these methods are fundamentally different from those employed in the arts and humanities. The concept of experimental verifiability is central to science, and the understanding of this concept is central to scientific literacy.

Besides, even ordinary citizens can benefit from having some grasp of the fundamental concepts of the physical and biological sciences. The knowledge that it is possible to understand much of the world by applying the laws of science helps free us from superstition and ignorance and gives us some power over our lives.

Scientific literacy for all is by no means an empty goal. The challenge is to train teachers who can make the ideas of science come alive.

Mark H. Shapiro
California State University
Fullerton, California

Should the mayor of Los Angeles know something of plate tectonics? I think so. Should an artist be versed in geometry? Of course. Mr. Shamos's assertion that science courses should not be compulsory raises the same question about other academic disciplines—history, for example. Must we know something about George Washington and Thomas Jefferson to choose the next president? Perhaps not. But we will not drop our high school history requirement. Nor should we drop that of science.

Eugene Krc
El Segundo, California

I would like to pose the following question to Morris Shamos: If requiring science of all students in the hope that one in twenty or thirty will choose it as a career is not an efficient means of directing students into science, what is?

Shane D. Mayor
Forest Hill, Maryland

MORRIS SHAMOS REPLIES TO HIS CRITICS

In challenging the conventional wisdom of science educators, my essay was bound to generate heated debate, but I had hoped that beyond touching some raw nerves, it might evoke *new* insight into an age-old problem. Regrettably, none of the letter writers seems willing to address the essential questions: Why has general education in science failed to impart a basic knowledge of science? Why is science so different from other forms of knowledge as to impose a tougher standard on the notion of literacy? And what incentive does the average person have to expend the effort to become scientifically literate?

Mr. Steel says that appreciation of science is important for *some* nonscientists, and I would hardly disagree; indeed, my position is that *appreciation* of science by *all* is a more realistic goal than scientific literacy for all. Where we disagree is in his view that a "modest amount of academic exposure to what science is" would give many people the knowledge necessary to act as informed and responsible citizens. But this is just what we have now, an electorate with a *little* knowledge of science, which, as we know, can often be more dangerous than no knowledge at all. The answer lies not in exposing everyone to a modest amount of science but in ensuring that we have capable science-policy advisers, individuals truly interested in communicating the effects of science decisions to the public. In medicine, law, economics, government, politics, we do not expect to know the answers to all problems ourselves. Rather, we turn for advice to those we believe to be knowledgeable. Why should science be any different?

Messrs. Burke and Sobol plead for scientific literacy as beneficial to the individual's personal understanding of life. Other scholars and educators have said the same things, some far more poignantly. Who could fail to be moved by the rhetoric of Herbert Spencer, in his famous 1859 essay "What Knowledge Is of Most Worth," or by the reasoned appeals of Thomas Huxley, Jules-Henri Poincaré, J. B. S. Haldane, and John Dewey, to name but a few. Yet, their words fell on deaf ears then, as do the same words today. If anything, it is more difficult now, because of the explosive growth of scientific knowledge, to convince the public of the benefits of being literate in science. Since it is the lack of incentive, rather than a lack of ability among students, that militates against universal scientific literacy, it does not help for Mr. Shapiro to point out the obvious, namely, that any person of average intelligence has the capacity to become literate in science.

By suggesting that literacy means only that one has the ability to read and understand science, Mr. Shapiro falls into a familiar semantic trap that has long plagued the issue of scientific literacy. What shall we mean by "understand"? What depth of understanding makes one literate in science? Substituting one ill-defined term *(understand)* for another *(literacy)* contributes little to clarifying the issue. Mr. Krc makes essentially the same error in suggesting that the mayor of Los Angeles should "know something" of plate tectonics and that an artist should "be versed" in geometry. How much should they know? Somehow, the precision that is said to be characteristic of science is often ignored when scientists speak of education.

I do not, as Mr. Krc suggests, advocate dropping all high school science requirements for nonscience students, though I believe that making science instruction elective for this large group of students would force educators to face up to the challenge of designing more meaningful courses.

Finally, there might be merit to Mr. Mayor's insinuation that we should use a shotgun approach to recruiting students into science careers, if it could be shown that compulsory science education actually achieves this result. But the evidence is that most students who choose careers in science are motivated by factors outside the classroom—mainly by the influence of family, friends, and other role models, or through extracurricular science programs. If, in attracting the one in twenty or thirty students to science through compulsory science education, we also manage to repel a half-dozen or more to the extent that they become antiscience (as seems to occur all too frequently), is science or society really well served?

That there is something about science instruction almost predestined to turn off most students is not a new finding; the education community has been trying for more than a century to instill some degree of scientific literacy in the public, with a notable lack of success. When will we at last admit this failure and turn to other means of getting students at least to appreciate science, to get them to know *what science is about* rather than to know *about science?*

Questions and Suggestions for Writing

1. Of the letters disagreeing with Shamos, which one do you think has the most merit? Why? (If you think two letters are especially meritorious, you need not choose between them; explain the merits of each. If you think none of the letters has merit, take one and point out its weaknesses.)

2. Reread Shamos's reply. If you think his reply to any of the letters is unfair or simplistic, point out the shortcomings.

3. In his reply to Krc, Shamos writes, "I do not, as Mr. Krc suggests, advocate dropping all high school science requirements." Does this remark surprise you? Given Shamos's earlier argument, what case might he make for retaining a high school science requirement?

8

Should the Sale and Use of Drugs Be Legalized?

Gore Vidal

Drugs

It is possible to stop most drug addiction in the United States within a very short time. Simply make all drugs available and sell them at cost. Label each drug with a precise description of what effect—good and bad—the drug will have on the taker. This will require heroic honesty. Don't say that marijuana is addictive or dangerous when it is neither, as millions of people know—unlike "speed," which kills most unpleasantly, or heroin, which is addictive and difficult to kick.

For the record, I have tried—once—almost every drug and liked none, disproving the popular Fu Manchu theory that a single whiff of opium will enslave the mind. Nevertheless many drugs are bad for certain people to take and they should be told why in a sensible way.

Along with exhortation and warning, it might be good for our citizens to recall (or learn for the first time) that the United States was the creation of men who believed that each man has the right to do what he wants with his own life as long as he does not interfere with his neighbor's pursuit of

Gore Vidal (b. 1925), prolific novelist and essayist, is the grandson of Senator T. P. Gore, who for thirty years represented Oklahoma. Vidal himself entered politics in 1960, when he ran (unsuccessfully) as a Democratic-Liberal candidate for Congress. This article first appeared in the New York Times, *1970.*

happiness (that his neighbor's idea of happiness is persecuting others does confuse matters a bit).

This is a startling notion to the current generation of Americans. They reflect a system of public education which has made the Bill of Rights, literally, unacceptable to a majority of high school graduates (see the annual Purdue reports) who now form the "silent majority"—a phrase which that underestimated wit Richard Nixon took from Homer who used it to describe the dead.

Now one can hear the warning rumble begin: If everyone is allowed to take drugs everyone will and the GNP will decrease, the Commies will stop us from making everyone free, and we shall end up a race of zombies, passively murmuring "groovy" to one another. Alarming thought. Yet it seems most unlikely that any reasonably sane person will become a drug addict if he knows in advance what addiction is going to be like.

Is everyone reasonably sane? No. Some people will always become drug addicts just as some people will always become alcoholics, and it is just too bad. Every man, however, has the power (and should have the legal right) to kill himself if he chooses. But since most men don't, they won't be mainliners either. Nevertheless, forbidding people things they like or think they might enjoy only makes them want those things all the more. This psychological insight is, for some mysterious reason, perennially denied our governors.

It is a lucky thing for the American moralist that our country has always existed in a kind of time-vacuum: we have no public memory of anything that happened before last Tuesday. No one in Washington today recalls what happened during the years alcohol was forbidden to the people by a Congress that thought it had a divine mission to stamp out Demon Rum—launching, in the process, the greatest crime wave in the country's history, causing thousands of deaths from bad alcohol, and creating a general (and persisting) contempt among the citizenry for the laws of the United States.

The same thing is happening today. But the government has learned nothing from past attempts at prohibition, not to mention repression.

Last year when the supply of Mexican marijuana was slightly curtailed by the Feds, the pushers got the kids hooked on heroin and deaths increased dramatically, particularly in New York. Whose fault? Evil men like the Mafiosi? Permissive Dr. Spock?[1] Wild-eyed Dr. Leary?[2] No.

The Government of the United States was responsible for those deaths. The bureaucratic machine has a vested interest in playing cops and robbers. Both the Bureau of Narcotics and the Mafia want strong laws

[1]**Dr. Spock** Benjamin Spock, pediatrician and author of books on child rearing that in the 1950s seemed permissive when compared to earlier books. [All notes are the editors'.]

[2]**Dr. Leary** Timothy Leary, a teacher at Harvard who in the 1960s urged students to experiment with drugs and to drop out of middle-class society.

against the sale and use of drugs because if drugs are sold at cost there would be no money in it for anyone.

If there was no money in it for the Mafia, there would be no friendly playground pushers, and addicts would not commit crimes to pay for the next fix. Finally, if there was no money in it, the Bureau of Narcotics would wither away, something they are not about to do without a struggle.

Will anything sensible be done? Of course not. The American people   12 are as devoted to the idea of sin and its punishment as they are to making money—and fighting drugs is nearly as big a business as pushing them. Since the combination of sin and money is irresistible (particularly to the professional politician), the situation will only grow worse.

Questions and Suggestions for Writing ══════════════════

1. On the basis of this essay, characterize Vidal. What *persona* does his tone convey? (On *persona* and tone, see pp. 78–81.)

2. In paragraph 2 is Vidal setting up a *straw man*, (a theory that he attributes to the opposition but a theory in fact so weak that no one holds it)? And, also in this paragraph, is he wrongly suggesting that a sample of one person—Vidal himself—is an adequate sample of the population?

3. In paragraph 3 he says that "each man has the right to do what he wants with his own life as long as he does not interfere with his neighbor's pursuit of happiness." Can one fairly respond that if someone becomes an addict, that person *does* interfere "with his neighbor's pursuit of happiness," perhaps by becoming a menace, or perhaps by eventually becoming a tax burden?

4. Vidal argues (para. 10) that curtailment of illegal shipments of marijuana from Mexico by the federal government made the government "responsible" for the death of young Americans who switched to heroin (para. 9). Present Vidal's reasoning in syllogistic form. Do you agree with his conclusion? Why, or why not?

5. In paragraph 8 Vidal says that "the government has learned nothing from past attempts at prohibition." Does it follow that because the attempt to prohibit alcohol failed, the attempt to prohibit drugs will also fail? Explain.

6. Vidal refers (para. 7) to the Prohibition era (1916–32) as the cause of "the greatest crime wave in history." Consult some resources in your library on the history of Prohibition, and write a 500-word essay evaluating Vidal's claim.

7. If alcohol were illegal, there would of course be some drinkers, but surely everyone would agree that fewer people would abuse alcohol than abuse it now. And surely eveyone would agree that there would (for example) be fewer deaths due to drunk driving. That is, the legalization of alcohol certainly has had some unintended bad effects. Can it be argued that Vidal does not give enough weight to the bad effects that legalization of drugs would produce, and that therefore his argument is of no force?

8. Vidal published this essay in 1970, long before "crack" became the drug of choice. Do you think that what he says may have made sense in 1970 but makes no sense now? Why?

Louis Nizer

How about Low-Cost Drugs for Addicts?

We are losing the war against drug addiction. Our strategy is wrong. I propose a different approach.

The government should create clinics, manned by psychiatrists, that would provide drugs for nominal charges or even free to addicts under controlled regulations. It would cost the government only 20 cents for a heroin shot, for which the addicts must now pay the mob more than $100, and there are similar price discrepancies in cocaine, crack, and other such substances.

Such a service, which would also include the staff support of psychiatrists and doctors, would cost a fraction of what the nation now spends to maintain the land, sea, and air apparatus necessary to interdict illegal imports of drugs. There would also be a savings of hundreds of millions of dollars from the elimination of the prosecutorial procedures that stifle our courts and overcrowd our prisons.

We see in our newspapers the triumphant announcements by government agents that they have intercepted huge caches of cocaine, the street prices of which are in the tens of millions of dollars. Should we be gratified? Will this achievement reduce the number of addicts by one? All it will do is increase the cost to the addict of his illegal supply.

Many addicts who are caught committing a crime admit that they have mugged or stolen as many as six or seven times a day to accumulate the $100 needed for a fix. Since many of them need two or three fixes a day, particularly for crack, one can understand the terror in our streets and homes. It is estimated that there are in New York City alone 200,000 addicts, and this is typical of cities across the nation. Even if we were to assume that only a modest percentage of a city's addicts engage in criminal conduct to obtain the money for the habit, requiring multiple muggings and thefts each day, we could nevertheless account for many of the tens of thousands of crimes each day in New York City alone.

Louis Nizer (b. 1902), the author of nine books about his life as a lawyer, is senior partner in a New York law firm. This article appeared on the Op Ed page in the New York Times, *1986.*

Not long ago, a Justice Department division issued a report stating that more than half the perpetrators of murder and other serious crimes were under the influence of drugs. This symbolizes the new domestic terror in our nation. This is why our citizens are unsafe in broad daylight on the most traveled thoroughfares. This is why typewriters and television sets are stolen from offices and homes and sold for a pittance. This is why parks are closed to the public and why murders are committed. This is why homes need multiple locks, and burglary systems, and why store windows, even in the most fashionable areas, require iron gates.

The benefits of the new strategy to control this terrorism would be immediate and profound.

First, the mob would lose the main source of its income. It could not   8
compete against a free supply for which previously it exacted tribute estimated to be hundreds of millions of dollars, perhaps billions, from hopeless victims.

Second, pushers would be put out of business. There would be no purpose in creating addicts who would be driven by desperate compulsion to steal and kill for the money necessary to maintain their habit. Children would not be enticed. The mob's macabre public relations program is to tempt children with free drugs in order to create customers for the future. The wave of street crimes in broad daylight would diminish to a trickle. Homes and stores would not have to be fortresses. Our recreational areas could again be used. Neighborhoods would not be scandalized by sordid street centers where addicts gather to obtain their supply from slimy merchants.

Third, police and other law enforcement authorities, domestic or foreign, would be freed to deal with traditional nondrug crimes.

There are several objections that might be raised against such a salutary solution.

First, it could be argued that by providing free drugs to the addict we   12
would consign him to permanent addiction. The answer is that medical and psychiatric help at the source would be more effective in controlling the addict's descent than the extremely limited remedies available to the victim today. I am not arguing that the new strategy will cure everything. But I do not see many addicts being freed from their bonds under the present system.

In addition, as between the addict's predicament and the safety of our innocent citizens, which deserves our primary concern? Drug-induced crime has become so common that almost every citizen knows someone in his immediate family or among his friends who has been mugged. It is these citizens who should be our chief concern.

Another possible objection is that addicts will cheat the system by obtaining more than the allowable free shot. Without discounting the resourcefulness of the bedeviled addict, it should be possible to have government cards issued that would be punched so as to limit the free supply in accord with medical authorization.

Yet all objections become trivial when matched against the crisis itself. What we are witnessing is the demoralization of a great society: the ruination of its schoolchildren, athletes, and executives, the corrosion of the workforce in general.

Many thoughtful sociologists consider the rapidly spreading drug use 16 the greatest problem that our nation faces—greater and more real and urgent than nuclear bombs or economic reversal. In China, a similar crisis drove the authorities to apply capital punishment to those who trafficked in opium—an extreme solution that arose from the deepest reaches of frustration.

Free drugs will win the war against the domestic terrorism caused by illicit drugs. As a strategy, it is at once resourceful, sensible, and simple. We are getting nowhere in our efforts to hold back the ocean of supply. The answer is to dry up demand.

Questions and Suggestions for Writing

1. List the arguments Nizer attributes to the opposition. Of these, are there any, in your opinion, with which he does not deal adequately. If so, which ones? And why do his counterarguments strike you as unconvincing?

2. Can you think of any counterarguments to Nizer's thesis that Nizer has omitted? If so, state them.

3. Evaluate Nizer's concluding paragraph. Is it effective? Is it a mere repetition of what he has said, or, on the other hand, does it make a claim that goes far beyond what he has demonstrated (presumably at least to his own satisfaction)?

4. Nizer mentions (para. 16) that China has used the death penalty to curb the illegal use of drugs; but he doesn't pursue the point. Write a 250-word essay either supporting or objecting to the idea of using the death penalty to curb illegal use of drugs in the United States.

5. Nizer opposes current laws that make using addictive drugs a criminal offense, and he favors making such drugs available at "nominal charges or even free" (para. 2). He does not consider a third alternative, parallel to our current policies on tobacco and alcohol, namely, allowing private companies to manufacture, sell, and advertise cocaine, heroin, and other such substances as commercial products. Write a 500-word essay arguing the case for or against such a policy.

Lester C. Thurow

U.S. Drug Policy: Colossal Ignorance

The United States' war on drugs has recently led to the attempted ouster of Panama's military leader, the virtual kidnapping of a Honduran, new efforts to burn crops in Bolivia and a proposed Congressional resolution accusing Mexican officials of accepting bribes. Only a short time ago, similar actions were directed at Pakistan, Colombia, Peru, Turkey, and Thailand.

Before we further damage our foreign relations, we should admit the failure of efforts to interdict drug supplies abroad and focus instead on reducing demand for drugs at home.

The current approach has led us to demand actions of others that we would not for a moment tolerate if asked of us. Consider what we would do if a foreign government kidnapped one of our citizens or if its parliament passed a resolution accusing us of complicity with drug dealers.

Moreover, we reject mobilization of our police and armed forces to   4 interdict drugs at American borders, because it would create too much of a temptation for American officials. Yet opportunities for corruption that are unacceptable here are apparently considered acceptable "over there."

Those running our war on drugs understand neither economics nor history nor foreign cultures. Their economic ignorance is colossal. Drug sellers face what in the jargon of the economics profession is known as an inelastic demand curve. This means that if supplies are cut back by 10 percent, prices rise by more than 10 percent, leaving the seller with higher profits than before the cutback.

If our goal is to deprive criminals of large profits from selling drugs, economic theory and history teach us that legalization is the only answer. When liquor sales were legalized after Prohibition, criminals left the bootleg liquor industry because the huge profits available while the government was attempting to stop liquor sales vanished.

We may not wish to legalize drug use. By making it illegal, we make a statement that society has concluded that drug use is not in the self-interest of the individual and the nation. But if we do not legalize products for which there is a huge demand, profits will remain enormous and suppliers will always come forward. Individual sellers can be arrested, but others will take their place.

Viewed from the perspective of a foreign country such as Pakistan,   8 where I once worked as a development economist, United States antidrug

---

Lester C. Thurow (b. 1938), a professor of economics, is dean of the Sloan School of Management at the Massachusetts Institute of Technology. This article appeared on the Op Ed page in the New York Times, *1988.*

policies are simply arrogant. In many places, local peasant families have grown marijuana, coca, or opium for hundreds of years. Suddenly they are ordered not to grow what they have always grown.

Americans would never accede to such a request. Suppose some foreign government asked us to suppress tobacco farmers (perhaps burn their fields) to improve public health?

Not surprisingly, foreign peasants, knowing nothing of our drug problem, expand their production. Sales of drug crops are the best and perhaps the only way to escape generations of poverty. Drug merchants even become local heroes, as seen in Honduras when Washington obtained the extradition of Juan Ramon Matta, a purported drug trafficker.

Americans cannot persuade fellow citizens to quit using drugs, yet we order foreign governments to stop their peasants from growing them. Not surprisingly, they cannot. Their peasants fight back. Military force must be used. Foreign governments either end up losing control of their own countrysides or must begin shooting at their own citizens.

When foreign governments crack down on drug suppliers at America's 12 request, drug suppliers have to start bribing local officials to get their supplies out of the country. Without the enormous profits that have been generated in the United States, such bribes could not be paid.

Who is to be blamed—the Mexicans who take those bribes or the Americans whose purchases make those bribes possible? What is needed is a demand-side solution in the United States, not a supply-side solution in the rest of the world.

Industries disappear only when the demand for their products disappear. The effort to stop drugs has to focus on the user, not the supplier. It involves education programs to prevent addiction, the arrest and incarceration of all users and changes in the social environment of the poor who buy heroin and the rich who buy cocaine. However difficult, all possible solutions lie on the demand side.

A demand-side solution would be expensive. Jailing buyers, educating addicts, and changing the conditions that lead to pathological behavior—none of these are cheap. But effective interdiction of drugs at our borders would require an enormous army of guards. Foreign interdiction is often advocated as a cheap alternative to expensive, politically divisive policies at home, but that view is a mirage.

The war on drugs is not going to be won on the streets of Karachi; 16 Medellín, Colombia; or Mexico City. It can be won only on the streets of New York and Los Angeles. If we do not want to pay the costs of winning the war on drugs in America, there is no "there" where it can be won.

Questions and Suggestions for Writing

1. Thurow distinguishes (para. 7) between legalizing the *production* of drugs and legalizing their *use*. He evidently favors the former and opposes the latter. Can

this distinction be explained, or is Thurow inconsistent in not favoring or opposing both?

2. Thurow argues (para. 15) that a "demand-side solution" to the drug problem "will be expensive," but that a "supply-side solution" is impossible. Define the terms "demand-side solution" and "supply-side solution."

3. Thurow implies (paras. 8–9) that it is unfair for our government to try to get Pakistani farmers to stop opium production, when our government would resist any foreign government that tried to force our farmers to end tobacco production. Do you agree that it is unfair? Evaluate the analogy on which Thurow relies.

4. What strategies does Thurow employ in an effort to make this argument clear, convincing, and appealing?

Charles B. Rangel

Legalize Drugs? Not on Your Life

The escalating drug crisis is beginning to take its toll on many Americans. And now growing numbers of well-intentioned officials and other opinion leaders are saying that the best way to fight drugs is to legalize them. But what they're really admitting is that they're willing to abandon a war that we have not even begun to fight.

For example, the newly elected and promising Mayor of Baltimore, Kurt Schmoke, at a meeting of the United States Conference of Mayors, called for a full-scale study of the feasibility of legalization. His comments could not have come at a worse time, for we are in the throes of the worst drug epidemic in our history.

Here we are talking about legalization, and we have yet to come up with any formal national strategy or any commitment from the administration on fighting drugs beyond mere words. We have never fought the war on drugs like we have fought other legitimate wars—with all the forces at our command.

Just the thought of legalization brings up more problems and concerns 4 than already exist.

Advocates of legalization should be reminded, for example, that it's not as simple as opening up a chain of friendly neighborhood pharmacies. Press them about some of the issues and questions surrounding this pro-

Charles B. Rangel (b. 1930), a Democratic congressman from New York, is chairman of the House Select Committee on Narcotics Abuse and Control. This article appeared in the New York Times, *1988.*

posed legalization, and they never seem to have any answers. At least not any logical, well thought out ones.

Those who tout legalization remind me of fans sitting in the cheap seats at the ballpark. They may have played the game, and they may think they know all the rules, but from where they're sitting they can't judge the action.

Has anybody ever considered which narcotic and psychotropic drugs would be legalized?

Would we allow all drugs to become legally sold and used, or would   8 we select the most abused few, such as cocaine, heroin, and marijuana?

Who would administer the dosages—the state or the individual?

What quantity of drugs would each individual be allowed to get?

What about addicts: Would we not have to give them more in order to satisfy their craving, or would we give them enough to just whet their appetites?

What do we do about those who are experimenting? Do we sell them   12 the drugs, too, and encourage them to pick up the habit?

Furthermore, will the government establish tax-supported facilities to sell these drugs?

Would we get the supply from the same foreign countries that support our habit now, or would we create our own internal sources and "dope factories," paying people the minimum wage to churn out mounds of cocaine and bales of marijuana?

Would there be an age limit on who can purchase drugs, as exists with alcohol? What would the market price be and who would set it? Would private industry be allowed to have a stake in any of this?

What are we going to do about underage youngsters—the age group   16 hardest hit by the crack crisis? Are we going to give them identification cards? How can we prevent adults from purchasing drugs for them?

How many people are projected to become addicts as a result of the introduction of cheaper, more available drugs sanctioned by government?

Since marijuana remains in a person's system for weeks, what would we do about pilots, railroad engineers, surgeons, police, cross-country truckers, and nuclear plant employees who want to use it during off-duty hours? And what would be the effect on the health insurance industry?

Many of the problems associated with drug abuse will not go away just because of legalization. For too long we have ignored the root cause, failing to see the connection between drugs and hopelessness, helplessness, and despair.

We often hear that legalization would bring an end to the bloodshed   20 and violence that has often been associated with the illegal narcotics trade. The profit will be taken out of it, so to speak, as will be the urge to commit crime to get money to buy drugs. But what gives anybody the impression that legalization would deter many jobless and economically deprived people from resorting to crime to pay for their habits?

Even in a decriminalized atmosphere, money would still be needed to support habits. Because drugs would be cheaper and more available, people would want more and would commit more crime. Does anybody really think the black market would disappear? There would always be opportunities for those who saw profit in peddling larger quantities, or improved versions, of products that are forbidden or restricted.

Legalization would completely undetermine any educational effort we undertake to persuade kids about the harmful effects of drugs. Today's kids have not yet been totally lost to the drug menace, but if we legalize these substances they'll surely get the message that drugs are O.K.

Not only would our young people realize that the threat of jail and punishment no longer exists. They would pick up the far more damaging message that the use of illegal narcotics does not pose a significant enough health threat for the government to ban its use.

If we really want to do something about drug abuse, let's end this 24 nonsensical talk about legalization right now.

Let's put the pressure on our leaders to first make the drug problem a priority issue on the national agenda, then let's see if we can get a coordinated national battle plan that would include the deployment of military personnel and equipment to wipe out this foreign-based national security threat. Votes by the House and more recently the Senate to involve the armed forces in the war on drugs are steps in the right direction.

Finally, let's take this legalization issue and put it where it belongs—amid idle chitchat as cocktail glasses knock together at social events.

Questions and Suggestions for Writing

1. Evaluate Rangel's title and his first paragraph.

2. In paragraphs 7–18 Rangel asks a series of tough questions, with the implication that his opponents cannot answer all of them satisfactorily. Do you think that some or even all of the questions can be answered? Do you find Rangel's strategy here effective? Why, or why not?

3. In paragraph 22 Rangel argues that "legalization would completely undermine any educational effort we undertake to persuade kids about the harmful effects of drugs." Do you agree? Might you reply that alcohol and tobacco are legal, yet we take steps to educate people about their dangers? (Or have efforts at educating people about alcohol and tobacco failed, perhaps for the reason Rangel gives?)

4. In paragraph 25, Rangel supports the idea of mobilizing "the armed forces" in a "national battle plan" in the "war on drugs." What role in this "war" do you think could or should be assigned to the army, the navy, the air force? Defend or criticize Rangel's proposal in an essay of 250–500 words.

5. Which, if any, of Rangel's objections to legalization do you find especially compelling? What makes them compelling? Which (if any) of his arguments against legalization do you find especially weak? What makes them weak?

Tom Morganthau

Should Drugs Be Legal?

Twenty-five years after America's latest fling with psychoactive substances began, there is new talk of legalizing drugs—one symptom of the heated atmosphere that now pervades the debate on national narcotics policy. After spending at least $16 billion in a futile effort to roll back the flood tide of cocaine entering this country, Ronald Reagan called for yet another high-level task force to cope with what he termed the "national emergency" of narcotics abuse. It was a stunning reversal: only last February the president called his administration's war on drugs "an untold American success story."

The new vogue for legalization is a tacit acknowledgment that the war is being lost. Despite the trendy debate, however, no political realist believes that Washington or the nation is ready to consider legalizing drugs as a legitimate policy option. Drugs are now the voting public's No. 1 concern, and politicians everywhere seem hell-bent on demonstrating that they are ready to out-tough the opposition on the drug issue. Congress, for example, now seems likely to raise federal spending on drug enforcement and prevention, and it may even mobilize the U.S. military for emergency antismuggling duty.

Clearly the most radical step would be ending America's seventy-four-year-long prohibition on drugs. The idea has attracted a surprising amount of support in recent weeks—and some of those who have joined the debate, such as editor and columnist William F. Buckley, Jr., and economist Milton Friedman, have impeccably conservative credentials. The Inter-American Dialogue, a blue-chip foreign policy group, recently released a report arguing that it is time to consider the possibility of selective drug legalization. Others who have raised the question of legalization include Mayor Kurt Schmoke of Baltimore, Mayor Marion Barry of Washington and U.S. Representatives Fortney Stark of California and Steny Hoyer of Maryland. Like other critics of current policy, Schmoke says his goal is to insure that every possible solution to the drug crisis gets a hearing. "I know we can't prosecute our way out of this situation," he says.

The argument for legalization comes down to the notion that America's prohibition on drugs imposes too large a cost in terms of tax dollars, draconian law-enforcement tactics and potential infringement of civil liberties. Its proponents are logical, sincere, and well intended—but they are also demonstrably wrong. Legalizing drugs would undoubtedly increase drug abuse and addiction, perhaps to catastrophic levels. And

4

Morganthau (b. 1943), on the staff of Newsweek, *wrote this article in 1988, with the assistance of Peter McKillop, Gregory Cerio, and Richard Sandza.*

though legalization might reduce drug-related crime, the social morality of making drugs freely available is questionable, to say the least.

The new advocates of legalization have nothing in common with Timothy Leary; they do not defend unbridled chemical hedonism, or even using drugs at all. Instead, they are influenced by a style of cost-benefit policy analysis derived from political economics: in the case of drugs, they ask, what are the societal costs of prohibition? The billions spent annually by federal, state, and local law enforcement agencies is only one such cost. Others, less easily quantified, include the enormous rise in violence and mayhem on the streets of major cities, the destruction of neighborhoods, the rise of powerful drug-trafficking organizations and even, some would argue, the strains on U.S. foreign policy now imposed by the goal of preventing drug smuggling from abroad. Many proponents of legalization also are motivated by a strong concern for civil liberties, and some share the libertarian belief that government has no right to prevent individuals from pursuing pleasure—even self-destructive pleasure—so long as no one else is harmed.

The advocates of legalization foresee a much simpler world—a society in which the criminal side effects of America's prohibition on drugs would quickly disappear. No more violence, no more pushers, no more drug gangs—and no more police raids, border searches, official corruption, or overcrowded prisons. Proposals for regulating the sale of legalized drugs vary, and not all would-be legalizers think that every drug should be made licit. But many recognize at least tacitly that there is no logical reason for legalizing one drug without legalizing all drugs—and some, like New York criminologist Georgette Bennett, explicitly support total decriminalization. "There is no question we have a very big drug problem in this country," Bennett says. "The question is, is our current policy the best way to deal with it? My answer is no: by making drugs a criminal matter, we have in fact made the problem worse. If we decriminalize, at least we would only have a massive public health problem on our hands, instead of a massive crime problem, a massive corruption problem and a massive foreign policy problem."

Legalization, in the view of its proponents, would have other benefits as well. Professor Ethan A. Nadelmann of Princeton University's Woodrow Wilson School of Public and International Affairs argues that government could regulate the purity and potency of drugs available on the market, which would reduce the risk of accidental death due to poisoning and overdose. Government could also tax the sale of drugs and use the proceeds to finance both the treatment of drug addicts and alcoholics and a more ambitious program to prevent drug and alcohol abuse. The fact that alcohol and tobacco are legal while drugs are not, Nadelmann says, sends the wrong message to the young, since the total medical costs of alcohol and tobacco use are greater than the medical costs of drug abuse. Citing federal studies, Nadelmann notes that an estimated 18 million Americans are regarded as alcohol abusers and that alcohol and tobacco together are responsible for some 400,000 deaths a year—while the death toll from all illegal drugs combined was only 3,562 in 1985. "I can't guarantee that drug use will not increase [if drugs are legalized], and that's why I prefer not being called an advocate of legalizing drugs," Nadelmann says. "But the argument for legalization depends on the fact that drugs are dangerous and that therefore the vast majority of Americans will not become drug addicts."

But the critical question about legalization is whether that assurance   8 is good enough. How many Americans would use drugs if they were legalized, and how many would then become addicted? Currently, according to federal estimates, there are 5 million to 6 million regular cocaine users, more than half a million heroin users and at least 18 million pot smokers. About 1.5 million to 2 million Americans are addicted to heroin or cocaine. And while Bennett, for one, believes legalization would lead to a decrease in drug abuse, especially if government launched a vigorous drug-education campaign, that prediction may be tragically optimistic.

In truth, the reverse is far more likely: drug use will surely increase, and the only question is, by how much? Legalizing drugs, as U.S. Attorney Rudolph Giuliani of New York argues, is morally equivalent to societal approval for what is now taboo behavior, and combining legalization with anti-drug-abuse education is a flagrant example of sending society a mixed message. Giuliani's conclusion: A great many Americans would ignore the antidrug propaganda, and drug use overall would inevitably increase. Dr. Robert DuPont, the former head of the National Institute on Drug Abuse, argues that the potential market for legal drugs can be compared to the number of Americans who now use alcohol—140 million persons—and that up to 50 million Americans would eventually use cocaine. If DuPont is right, and if the ratio of addicts to nonaddicted users remains the same as it is now—approximately 1 to 5—it is plausible to expect an addicted population of 10 million persons.

Legalization, in short, is at best a high-stakes gamble—"a very dangerous social experiment," as Dr. Edward Senay of the University of Chicago puts it, "that could have a lot of disastrous consequences." Cocaine itself is the biggest gamble of all. Although research into cocaine's effects on the user is still incomplete, Dr. Wayne Wiebel of the University of Illinois School of Public Health says it "is probably the most addictive substance that our society has ever used on a widespread basis." Cocaine is most addictive when it is injected intravenously or smoked in the form of crack. While federal researchers have not yet been able to estimate the prevalence of crack use nationwide, there is no question from police reports that crack is now the drug of choice in inner city neighborhoods.

That is why, to those who see the realities of addiction at close range, the idea of legalizing cocaine or other hard drugs is simply a nightmare. Even assuming that crime and the costs of crime would be reduced, the

open availability of cocaine and other addictive substances can only com-
pound the mammoth social problems of the inner city. While it may be
true, as proponents argue, that most Americans would be able to avoid
addiction, millions of others would not. Legalization, then, is an inequita-
ble trade-off that is based on a failure of empathy for society's victims: all
those who do not use drugs would gain the benefits of reduced crime,
while all those who are addicted (or who will become addicted in the
drug-filled future) would be condemned to a brutal struggle with their
dependency. To psychiatrist Mitchell Rosenthal, president of Phoenix
House Foundation, a New York-based network of drug-treatment centers,
such reasoning is immoral, elitist, and racist—a case of "writing off hundreds and hundreds of thousands of people, their families, and their
children." And to many in the ghetto it is one more example of a social
order that provides abundant opportunities for self-destruction, but very
few for hope.

Questions and Suggestions for Writing

1. Morganthau claims (para. 4) to have pinpointed the three main reasons now
   advocated by those who favor drugs. What are the three reasons he gives? Read
   the essays by Vidal (p. 314) and Thurow (p. 320), and write a 500-word essay
   evaluating Morganthau's claim to have given the opposition's view.

2. Morganthau claims (para. 9) that if drugs were legalized, "drug use will surely
   increase." (See also para. 4.) After reading the essays by Vidal (p. 314), Nizer
   (p. 317), and Thurow (p. 320), write a 500-word essay evaluating their posi-
   tion(s) on this prediction, and explaining whether you agree with them or with
   Morganthau.

3. In paragraph 9, summarizing Rudolph Giuliani's view, Morganthau suggests
   that "combining legalization with anti-drug-abuse education is a flagrant
   example of sending society a mixed message." Might one reply that our society
   treats alcohol and tobacco in precisely this fashion? If you agree with this
   response to Morganthau and Giuliani, would you go on to argue that this
   objection against legalizing drugs is therefore of no weight?

4. In paragraph 10 Morganthau says, "Legalization, in short, is a high-stakes
   gamble." Does his essay persuade you that the risk is too dangerous to take, and
   that drugs should therefore continue to be illegal? If so, exactly what in his
   arguments do you find especially persuasive?

9

Whose Right to Life Is It Anyway?

Ellen Willis

Putting Women Back into the Abortion Debate

Some years ago I attended a New York Institute for the Humanities seminar on the new right. We were a fairly heterogeneous group of liberals and lefties, feminists and gay activists, but on one point nearly all of us agreed: the right-to-life movement was a dangerous antifeminist crusade. At one session I argued that the attack on abortion had significance far beyond itself, that it was the linchpin of the right's social agenda. I got a lot of supporting comments and approving nods. It was too much for Peter Steinfels, a liberal Catholic, author of *The Neoconservatives*, and executive editor of *Commonweal*. Right-to-lifers were not all right-wing fanatics, he protested. "You have to understand," he said plaintively, "that many of us see abortion as a *human life issue*." What I remember best was his air of frustrated isolation. I don't think he came back to the seminar after that.

Things are different now. I often feel isolated when I insist that abortion is, above all, a *feminist issue*. Once people took for granted that

Ellen Willis (b. 1941) was educated at Barnard College and the University of California, Berkeley. She has been a freelance writer since 1966, publishing in such journals as The New Yorker, Rolling Stone, *and* The Village Voice, *where this essay first appeared in 1985.*

abortion was an issue of sexual politics and morality. Now, abortion is most often discussed as a question of "life" in the abstract. Public concern over abortion centers almost exclusively on fetuses; women and their bodies are merely the stage on which the drama of fetal life and death takes place. Debate about abortion—if not its reality—has become sexlessly scholastic. And the people most responsible for this turn of events are, like Peter Steinfels, on the left.

The left wing of the right-to-life movement is a small, seemingly eccentric minority in both "progressive" and antiabortion camps. Yet it has played a critical role in the movement: by arguing that opposition to abortion can be separated from the right's antifeminist program, it has given antiabortion sentiment legitimacy in left-symp and (putatively) profeminist circles. While left antiabortionists are hardly alone in emphasizing fetal life, their innovation has been to claim that a consistent "pro-life" stand involves opposing capital punishment, supporting disarmament, demanding government programs to end poverty, and so on. This is of course a leap the right is neither able nor willing to make. It's been liberals—from Garry Wills to the Catholic bishops—who have supplied the mass media with the idea that prohibiting abortion is part of a "seamless garment" of respect for human life.

Having invented this countercontext for the abortion controversy, left   4 antiabortionists are trying to impose it as the only legitimate context for debate. Those of us who won't accept their terms and persist in seeing opposition to abortion, antifeminism, sexual repression, and religious sectarianism as the real seamless garment have been accused of obscuring the issue with demagoguery. Last year *Commonweal*—perhaps the most important current forum for left antiabortion opinion—ran an editorial demanding that we shape up: "Those who hold that abortion is immoral believe that the biological dividing lines of birth or viability should no more determine whether a developing member of the species is denied or accorded essential rights than should the biological dividing lines of sex or race or disability or old age. This argument is open to challenge. Perhaps the dividing lines are sufficiently different. Pro-choice advocates should state their reasons for believing so. They should meet the argument on its own grounds. . . ."

In other words, the only question we're allowed to debate—or the only one *Commonweal* is willing to entertain—is "Are fetuses the moral equivalent of born human beings?" And I can't meet the argument on its own grounds because I don't agree that this is the key question, whose answer determines whether one supports abortion or opposes it. I don't doubt that fetuses are alive, or that they're biologically human—what else would they be? I do consider the life of a fertilized egg less precious than the well-being of a woman with feelings, self-consciousness, a history, social ties; and I think fetuses get closer to being human in a moral sense as they come closer to birth. But to me these propositions are intuitively self-evident. I wouldn't know how to justify them to a "nonbeliever," nor do I see the point of trying.

I believe the debate has to start in a different place—with the recognition that fertilized eggs develop into infants inside the bodies of women. Pregnancy and birth are active processes in which a woman's body shelters, nourishes, and expels a new life; for nine months she is immersed in the most intimate possible relationship with another being. The growing fetus makes considerable demands on her physical and emotional resources, culminating in the cataclysmic experience of birth. And childbearing has unpredictable consequences; it always entails some risk of injury or death.

For me all this has a new concreteness: I had a baby last year. My much-desired and relatively easy pregnancy was full of what antiabortionists like to call "inconveniences." I was always tired, short of breath; my digestion was never right; for three months I endured a state of hormonal siege; later I had pains in my fingers, swelling feet, numb spots on my legs, the dread hemorrhoids. I had to think about everything I ate. I developed borderline glucose intolerance. I gained fifty pounds and am still overweight; my shape has changed in other ways that may well be permanent. Psychologically, my pregnancy consumed me—though I'd happily bought the seat on the roller coaster, I was still terrified to be so out of control of my normally tractable body. It was all bearable, even interesting—even, at times, transcendent—because I wanted a baby. Birth was painful, exhausting, and wonderful. If I hadn't wanted a baby it would only have been painful and exhausting—or worse. I can hardly imagine what it's like to have your body and mind taken over in this way when you not only don't look forward to the result, but positively dread it. The thought appalls me. So as I see it, the key question is "Can it be moral, under any circumstances, to make a woman bear a child against her will?"

From this vantage point, *Commonweal*'s argument is irrelevant, for in a society that respects the individual, no "member of the species" in *any* stage of development has an "essential right" to make use of someone else's body, let alone in such all-encompassing fashion, without that person's consent. You can't make a case against abortion by applying a general principle about everybody's human rights; you have to show exactly the opposite—that the relationship between fetus and pregnant woman is an exception, one that justifies depriving women of their right to bodily integrity. And in fact all antiabortion ideology rests on the premise—acknowledged or simply assumed—that women's unique capacity to bring life into the world carries with it a unique obligation that women cannot be allowed to "play God" and launch only the lives they welcome.

Yet the alternative to allowing women this power is to make them impotent. Criminalizing abortion doesn't just harm individual women with unwanted pregnancies, it affects all women's sense of themselves. Without control of our fertility we can never envision ourselves as free, for our biology makes us constantly vulnerable. Simply because we are female our physical integrity can be violated, our lives disrupted and transformed, at any time. Our ability to act in the world is hopelessly compromised by our sexual being.

Ah, sex—it does have a way of coming up in these discussions, despite all. When pressed, right-to-lifers of whatever political persuasion invariably point out that pregnancy doesn't happen by itself. The leftists often give patronizing lectures on contraception (though some find only "natural birth control" acceptable), but remain unmoved when reminded that contraceptives fail. Openly or implicitly they argue that people shouldn't have sex unless they're prepared to procreate. (They are quick to profess a single standard—men as well as women should be sexually "responsible." Yes, and the rich as well as the poor should be allowed to sleep under bridges.) Which amounts to saying that if women want to lead heterosexual lives they must give up any claim to self-determination, and that they have no right to sexual pleasure without fear.

Opposing abortion, then, means accepting that women must suffer sexual disempowerment and a radical loss of autonomy relative to men: if fetal life is sacred, the self-denial basic to women's oppression is also basic to the moral order. Opposing abortion means embracing a conservative sexual morality, one that subordinates pleasure to reproduction: if fetal life is sacred, there is no room for the view that sexual passion—or even sexual love—for its own sake is a human need and a human right. Opposing abortion means tolerating the inevitable double standard, by which men may accept or reject sexual restrictions in accordance with their beliefs, while women must bow to them out of fear . . . or defy them at great risk. However much *Commonweal*'s editors and those of like mind want to believe their opposition to abortion is simply about saving lives, the truth is that in the real world they are shoring up a particular sexual culture, whose rules are stacked against women. I have yet to hear any left right-to-lifers take full responsibility for that fact or deal seriously with its political implications.

Unfortunately, their fuzziness has not lessened their appeal—if any- 12 thing it's done the opposite. In increasing numbers liberals and leftists, while opposing antiabortion laws, have come to view abortion as an "agonizing moral issue" with some justice on both sides, rather than an issue—however emotionally complex—of freedom versus repression, or equality versus hierarchy, that affects their political self-definition. This above-the-battle stance is attractive to leftists who want to be feminist good guys but are uneasy or ambivalent about sexual issues, not to mention those who want to ally with "progressive" factions of the Catholic church on Central America, nuclear disarmament, or populist economics without that sticky abortion question getting in the way.

Such neutrality is a way of avoiding the painful conflict over cultural issues that continually smolders on the left. It can also be a way of coping with the contradictions of personal life at a time when liberation is a dream deferred. To me the fight for abortion has always been the cutting edge of feminism, precisely because it denies that anatomy is destiny, that female biology dictates women's subordinate status. Yet recently I've found it hard to focus on the issue, let alone summon up the militance needed to stop the antiabortion tanks. In part that has to do with second-round weariness—do we really have to go through all these things twice?—in part with my life now.

Since my daughter's birth my feelings about abortion—not as a political demand but as a personal choice—have changed. In this society, the difference between the situation of a childless woman and of a mother is immense; the fear that having a child will dislodge one's tenuous hold on a nontraditional life is excruciating. This terror of being forced into the sea-change of motherhood gave a special edge to my convictions about abortion. Since I've made that plunge voluntarily, with consequences still unfolding, the terror is gone; I might not want another child, for all sorts of reasons, but I will never again feel that my identity is at stake. Different battles with the culture absorb my energy now. Besides, since I've experienced the primal, sensual passion of caring for an infant, there will always be part of me that does want another. If I had an abortion today, it would be with conflict and sadness unknown to me when I had an abortion a decade ago. And the antiabortionists' imagery of dead babies hits me with new force. Do many women—left, feminist women—have such feelings? Is this the sort of "ambivalence about abortion" that in the present atmosphere slides so easily into self-flagellating guilt?

Some left antiabortionists, mainly pacifists—Juli Loesch, Mary Meehan, and other "feminists for life"; Jim Wallis and various writers for Wallis's radical evangelical journal *Sojourners*—have tried to square their position with concern for women. They blame the prevalence of abortion on oppressive conditions—economic injustice, lack of child care and other social supports for mothers, the devaluation of childrearing, men's exploitative sexual behavior and refusal to take equal responsibility for children. They disagree on whether to criminalize abortion now (since murder is intolerable no matter what the cause) or to build a long-term moral consensus (since stopping abortion requires a general social transformation), but they all regard abortion as a desperate solution to desperate problems, and the women who resort to it as more sinned against than sinning.

This analysis grasps an essential feminist truth: that in a male- 16 supremacist society no choice a woman makes is genuinely free or entirely in her interest. Certainly many women have had abortions they didn't want or wouldn't have wanted if they had any plausible means of caring for a child; and countless others wouldn't have gotten pregnant in the first place were it not for inadequate contraception, sexual confusion and guilt, male pressure, and other stigmata of female powerlessness. Yet forcing a woman to bear a child she doesn't want can only add injury to insult, while refusing to go through with such a pregnancy can be a woman's first step toward taking hold of her life. And many women who have abortions are "victims" only of ordinary human miscalculation, technological failure, or the vagaries of passion, all bound to exist in any society, however utopian. There will always be women who, at any given moment, want sex but don't want a child; some of these women will get pregnant; some of them will have abortions. Behind the victim theory of abortion is the implicit belief that women are always ready to be mothers, if only conditions are right, and that sex for pleasure rather than procreation is not only "irresponsible" (i.e., bad) but something men impose on women, never something women actively seek. Ironically, left right-to-lifers see abortion as always coerced (it's "exploitation" and "violence against women"), yet regard motherhood—which for most women throughout history has been inescapable, and is still our most socially approved role—as a positive choice. The analogy to the feminist antipornography movement goes beyond borrowed rhetoric: the antiporners, too, see active female lust as surrender to male domination and traditionally feminine sexual attitudes as expressions of women's true nature.

This Orwellian version of feminism, which glorifies "female values" and dismisses women's struggles for freedom—particularly sexual freedom—as a male plot, has become all too familiar in recent years. But its use in the abortion debate has been especially muddleheaded. Somehow we're supposed to leap from an oppressive patriarchal society to the egalitarian one that will supposedly make abortion obsolete without ever allowing women to see themselves as people entitled to control their reproductive function rather than be controlled by it. How women who have no power in this most personal of areas can effectively fight for power in the larger society is left to our imagination. A "New Zealand feminist" quoted by Mary Meehan in a 1980 article in *The Progressive* says, "Accepting short-term solutions like abortion only delays the implementation of real reforms like decent maternity and paternity leaves, job protection, high-quality child care, community responsibility for dependent people of all ages, and recognition of the economic contribution of childminders"— as if these causes were progressing nicely before legal abortion came along. On the contrary, the fight for reproductive freedom is the foundation of all the others, which is why antifeminists resist it so fiercely.

As "pro-life" pacifists have been particularly concerned with refuting charges of misogyny, the liberal Catholics at *Commonweal* are most exercised by the claim that antiabortion laws violate religious freedom. The editorial quoted above hurled another challenge at the proabortion forces:

> It is time, finally, for the pro-choice advocates and editorial writers to abandon, once and for all, the argument that abortion [*sic*] is a religious "doctrine" of a single or several churches being imposed on those of other

persuasions in violation of the First Amendment. . . . Catholics and their bishops are accused of imposing their "doctrine" on abortion, but not their "doctrine" on the needs of the poor, or their "doctrine" on the arms race, or their "doctrine" on human rights in Central America. . . .

The briefest investigation into Catholic teaching would show that the church's case against abortion is utterly unlike, say, its belief in the Real Presence, known with the eyes of faith alone, or its insistence on a Sunday obligation, applicable only to the faithful. The church's moral teaching on abortion. . . . is for the most part like its teaching on racism, warfare, and capital punishment, based on ordinary reasoning common to believers and nonbelievers. . . .

This is one more example of right-to-lifers' tendency to ignore the sexual ideology underlying their stand. Interesting, isn't it, how the editorial neglects to mention that the church's moral teaching on abortion jibes neatly with its teaching on birth control, sex, divorce, and the role of women. The traditional, patriarchal sexual morality common to these teachings is explicitly religious, and its chief defenders in modern times have been the more conservative churches. The Catholic and evangelical Christian churches are the backbone of the organized right-to-life movement and—a few Nathansons and Hentoffs notwithstanding—have provided most of the movement's activists and spokespeople.

Furthermore, the Catholic hierarchy has made opposition to abortion 20 a litmus test of loyalty to the church in a way it has done with no other political issue—witness Archbishop O'Connor's harassment of Geraldine Ferraro during her vice-presidential campaign. It's unthinkable that a Catholic bishop would publicly excoriate a Catholic officeholder or candidate for taking a hawkish position on the arms race or Central America or capital punishment. Nor do I notice anyone trying to read William F. Buckley out of the church for his views on welfare. The fact is there is no accepted Catholic "doctrine" on these matters comparable to the church's absolutist condemnation of abortion. While differing attitudes toward war, racism, and poverty cut across religious and secular lines, the sexual values that mandate opposition to abortion are the bedrock of the traditional religious world view, and the source of the most bitter conflict with secular and religious modernists. When churches devote their considerable political power, organizational resources, and money to translating those values into law, I call that imposing their religious beliefs on me—whether or not they're technically violating the First Amendment.

Statistical studies have repeatedly shown that people's views on abortion are best predicted by their opinions on sex and "family" issues, not on "life" issues like nuclear weapons or the death penalty. That's not because we're inconsistent but because we comprehend what's really at stake in the abortion fight. It's the antiabortion left that refuses to face the contradiction in its own position: you can't be wholeheartedly for "life"—or for such progressive aspirations as freedom, democracy, equality—and condone the subjugation of women. The seamless garment is full of holes.

Questions and Suggestions for Writing

1. What does Ellen Willis mean when she insists, in her second paragraph, that abortion is "a *feminist issue*"? Whether or not you agree, write a paragraph explaining her point. You may want to begin simply by saying, "When Ellen Willis says abortion is 'a *feminist issue*,' she means. . . ."

2. Willis claims that "all antiabortion ideology rests on the premise . . . that woman's unique capacity to bring life into the world carries with it a unique moral obligation. . . ." Do you agree (a) that this belief is crucial to antiabortion ideology, and (b) that it is false? How do you explain the fact that in the antiabortion essay by John Noonan (p. 354), he does not mention this crucial "premise"? How do you think he might try to defend it?

3. After describing the physical and psychological difficulties of pregnancy, Willis says (para. 8):

   > in a society that respects the individual, no "member of the species" in *any* stage of development has an "essential right" to make use of someone else's body, let alone in such all-encompassing fashion, without that person's consent. You can't make a case against abortion by applying a general principle about everybody's human rights; you have to show exactly the opposite—that the relationship between fetus and pregnant woman is an exception, one that justifies depriving women of their right to bodily integrity.

   Do you accept all of Willis's declarations? Any of them? Why, or why not? And (another topic) consider the expression, "without that person's consent." Suppose a woman takes no precautions against becoming pregnant—possibly she even wants to become pregnant—but at a late stage in pregnancy decides she does not wish to bear a child. Can she withdraw her "consent" at any time?

4. In the previous question we asked you to consider Willis's expression, "without that person's consent." Here is a related problem: The relationship between fetus and pregnant woman is different from all other relationships, but is it relevant to point out that women are not alone in having their bodies possessed, so to speak, by others? In time of war, men—but not women—are drafted; the interruption of their normal career causes considerable hardship. At the very least, a draftee is required to give up months or even several years of his life, and to live in circumstances that severely interfere with his privacy and his autonomy. And of course he may in fact be required to yield his life.

5. Do you think (in contrast to Willis) that persons who are opposed to capital punishment and to increased military spending—persons who are, so to speak, "pro-life"—must, if they are to be consistent, also oppose abortion? Why, or why not?

Judith Jarvis Thomson

A Defense of Abortion *

Most opposition to abortion relies on the premise that the fetus is a human being, a person, from the moment of conception. The premise is argued for, but, as I think, not well. Take, for example, the most common argument. We are asked to notice that the development of a human being from conception through birth into childhood is continuous; then it is said that to draw a line, to choose a point in this development and say "before this point the thing is not a person, after this point it is a person" is to make an arbitrary choice, a choice for which in the nature of things no good reason can be given. It is concluded that the fetus is, or anyway that we had better say it is, a person from the moment of conception. But this conclusion does not follow. Similar things might be said about the development of an acorn into an oak tree, and it does not follow that acorns are oak trees, or that we had better say they are. Arguments of this form are sometimes called "slippery slope arguments"—the phrase is perhaps self-explanatory—and it is dismaying that opponents of abortion rely on them so heavily and uncritically.[1]

I am inclined to agree, however, that the prospects for "drawing a line" in the development of the fetus look dim. I am inclined to think also that we shall probably have to agree that the fetus has already become a human person well before birth. Indeed, it comes as a surprise when one first learns how early in its life it begins to acquire human characteristics. By the tenth week, for example, it already has a face, arms and legs,

---

* Judith Jarvis Thomson, "A Defense of Abortion," *Philosophy & Public Affairs* 1, no. 1 (Fall 1971). Copyright © 1971 by Princeton University Press. Reprinted by permission of Princeton University Press.

[1] I am very much indebted to James Thomson for discussion, criticism, and many helpful suggestions.

Judith Thomson (b. 1929), educated at Barnard, Columbia, and Cambridge, has taught philosophy at the Massachusetts Institute of Technology since the 1960s. Her most recent book, Rights, Restitution, and Risk *(1986), is a selection of her much-admired essays on philosophical questions raised by moral, legal, and political issues.*

The publication of Thomson's essay on abortion, reprinted here, antedates by two years the ruling of the Supreme Court, in Roe v. Wade (1973), in which almost all legal restrictions on abortions were lifted. Hitherto, the laws of most states allowed abortion only if the mother's life was endangered by bringing the pregnancy to term, or the neonate would be born deformed, or the pregnancy was owing to rape or incest. The Court reasoned that such restrictions were unconstitutional invasions of the pregnant woman's "privacy." Few Supreme Court decisions in the past generation have proved to be so controversial.

fingers and toes; it has internal organs, and brain activity is detectable.[2] On the other hand, I think that the premise is false, that the fetus is not a person from the moment of conception. A newly fertilized ovum, a newly implanted clump of cells, is no more a person than an acorn is an oak tree. But I shall not discuss any of this. For it seems to me to be of great interest to ask what happens if, for the sake of argument, we allow the premise. How, precisely, are we supposed to get from there to the conclusion that abortion is morally impermissible? Opponents of abortion commonly spend most of their time establishing that the fetus is a person, and hardly any time explaining the step from there to the impermissibility of abortion. Perhaps they think the step too simple and obvious to require much comment. Or perhaps instead they are simply being economical in argument. Many of those who defend abortion rely on the premise that the fetus is not a person, but only a bit of tissue that will become a person at birth; and why pay out more arguments than you have to? Whatever the explanation, I suggest that the step they take is neither easy nor obvious, that it calls for closer examination than it is commonly given, and that when we do give it this closer examination we shall feel inclined to reject it.

I propose, then, that we grant that the fetus is a person from the moment of conception. How does the argument go from here? Something like this, I take it. Every person has a right to life. So the fetus has a right to life. No doubt the mother has a right to decide what shall happen in and to her body; everyone would grant that. But surely a person's right to life is stronger and more stringent than the mother's right to decide what happens in and to her body, and so outweighs it. So the fetus may not be killed; an abortion may not be performed.

It sounds plausible. But now let me ask you to imagine this. You wake 4 up in the morning and find yourself back to back in bed with an unconscious violinist. A famous unconscious violinist. He has been found to have a fatal kidney ailment, and the Society of Music Lovers has canvassed all the available medical records and found that you alone have the right blood type to help. They have therefore kidnapped you, and last night the violinist's circulatory system was plugged into yours, so that your kidneys can be used to extract poisons from his blood as well as your own. The director of the hospital now tells you, "Look, we're sorry the Society of Music Lovers did this to you—we would never have permitted it if we had known. But still, they did it, and the violinist now is plugged into you. To unplug you would be to kill him. But never mind, it's only for nine months. By then he will have recovered from his ailment, and can safely be unplugged from you." Is it morally incumbent on you to accede to this

[2]Daniel Callahan, *Abortion: Law, Choice and Morality* (New York, 1970), p. 373. This book gives a fascinating survey of the available information on abortion. The Jewish tradition is surveyed in David M. Feldman, *Birth Control in Jewish Law* (New York, 1968), Part 5; the Catholic tradition in John T. Noonan, Jr., "An Almost Absolute Value in History," in *The Morality of Abortion*, ed. John T. Noonan, Jr. (Cambridge, Mass., 1970).

situation? No doubt it would be very nice of you if you did, a great kindness. But do you *have* to accede to it? What if it were not nine months, but nine years? Or longer still? What if the director of the hospital says, "Tough luck, I agree, but you've now got to stay in bed, with the violinist plugged into you, for the rest of your life. Because remember this. All persons have a right to life, and violinists are persons. Granted you have a right to decide what happens in and to your body, but a person's right to life outweighs your right to decide what happens in and to your body. So you cannot ever be unplugged from him." I imagine you would regard this as outrageous, which suggests that something really is wrong with the plausible-sounding argument I mentioned a moment ago.

In this case, of course, you were kidnapped; you didn't volunteer for the operation that plugged the violinist into your kidneys. Can those who oppose abortion on the ground I mentioned make an exception for a pregnancy due to rape? Certainly. They can say that persons have a right to life only if they didn't come into existence because of rape; or they can say that all persons have a right to life, but that some have less of a right to life than others, in particular, that those who came into existence because of rape have less. But these statements have a rather unpleasant sound. Surely the question of whether you have a right to life at all, or how much of it you have, shouldn't turn on the question of whether or not you are the product of a rape. And in fact the people who oppose abortion on the ground I mentioned do not make this distinction, and hence do not make an exception in case of rape.

Nor do they make an exception for a case in which the mother has to spend the nine months of her pregnancy in bed. They would agree that would be a great pity, and hard on the mother; but all the same, all persons have a right to life, the fetus is a person, and so on. I suspect, in fact, that they would not make an exception for a case in which, miraculously enough, the pregnancy went on for nine years, or even the rest of the mother's life.

Some won't even make an exception for a case in which continuation of the pregnancy is likely to shorten the mother's life; they regard abortion as impermissible even to save the mother's life. Such cases are nowadays very rare, and many opponents of abortion do not accept this extreme view. All the same, it is a good place to begin; a number of points of interest come out in respect to it.

1. Let us call the view that abortion is impermissible even to save the mother's life "the extreme view." I want to suggest first that it does not issue from the argument I mentioned earlier without the addition of some fairly powerful premises. Suppose a woman has become pregnant, and now learns that she has a cardiac condition such that she will die if she carries the baby to term. What may be done for her? The fetus, being a person, has a right to life, but as the mother is a person too, so has she a

right to life. Presumably they have an equal right to life. How is it supposed to come out that an abortion may not be performed? If mother and child have an equal right to life, shouldn't we perhaps flip a coin? Or should we add to the mother's right to life her right to decide what happens in and to her body, which everybody seems to be ready to grant—the sum of her rights now outweighing the fetus' right to life?

The most familiar argument here is the following. We are told that performing the abortion would be directly killing[3] the child, whereas doing nothing would not be killing the mother, but only letting her die. Moreover, in killing the child, one would be killing an innocent person, for the child has committed no crime, and is not aiming at his mother's death. And then there are a variety of ways in which this might be continued. (1) But as directly killing an innocent person is always and absolutely impermissible, an abortion may not be performed. Or, (2) as directly killing an innocent person is murder, and murder is always and absolutely impermissible, an abortion may not be performed.[4] Or, (3) as one's duty to refrain from directly killing an innocent person is more stringent than one's duty to keep a person from dying, an abortion may not be performed. Or, (4) if one's only options are directly killing an innocent person or letting a person die, one must prefer letting the person die, and thus an abortion may not be performed.[5]

Some people seem to have thought that these are not further premises which must be added if the conclusion is to be reached, but that they follow from the very fact that an innocent person has a right to life.[6] But this seems to me to be a mistake, and perhaps the simplest way to show this

---

[3]The term "direct" in the arguments I refer to is a technical one. Roughly, what is meant by *direct killing* is either killing as an end in itself, or killing as a means to some end; for example, the end of saving someone else's life. See note 6, below, for an example of its use.

[4]Cf. *Encyclical Letter of Pope Pius XI on Christian Marriage*, St. Paul Editions (Boston, n.d.), p. 32: "however much we may pity the mother whose health and even life is gravely imperiled in the performance of the duty allotted to her by nature, nevertheless what could ever be a sufficient reason for excusing in any way the direct murder of the innocent? This is precisely what we are dealing with here." Noonan (*The Morality of Abortion*, p. 43) reads this as follows: "What cause can ever avail to excuse in any way the direct killing of the innocent? For it is a question of that."

[5]The thesis in (4) is in an interesting way weaker than those in (1), (2), and (3): they rule out abortion even in cases in which both mother *and* child will die if the abortion is not performed. By contrast, one who held the view expressed in (4) could consistently say that one needn't prefer letting two persons die to killing one.

[6]Cf. the following passage from Pius XII, *Address to the Italian Catholic Society of Midwives:* "The baby in the maternal breast has the right to life immediately from God— Hence there is no man, no human authority, no science, no medical, eugenic, social, economic or moral 'indication' which can establish or grant a valid juridical ground for a direct deliberate disposition of an innocent human life, that is a disposition which looks to its destruction either as an end or as a means to another end perhaps in itself not illicit.—The baby, still not born, is a man in the same degree and for the same reason as the mother" (quoted in Noonan, *The Morality of Abortion*, p. 45).

is to bring out that while we must certainly grant that innocent persons have a right to life, the theses in (1) through (4) are all false. Take (2), for example. If directly killing an innocent person is murder, and thus is impermissible, then the mother's directly killing the innocent person inside her is murder, and thus is impermissible. But it cannot seriously be thought to be murder if the mother performs an abortion on herself to save her life. It cannot seriously be said that she *must* refrain, that she *must* sit passively by and wait for her death. Let us look again at the case of you and the violinist. There you are, in bed with the violinist, and the director of the hospital says to you, "It's all most distressing, and I deeply sympathize, but you see this is putting an additional strain on your kidneys, and you'll be dead within the month. But you have to stay where you are all the same. Because unplugging you would be directly killing an innocent violinist, and that's murder, and that's impermissible." If anything in the world is true, it is that you do not commit murder, you do not do what is impermissible, if you reach around to your back and unplug yourself from that violinist to save your life.

The main focus of attention in writings on abortion has been on what a third party may or may not do in answer to a request from a woman for an abortion. This is in a way understandable. Things being as they are, there isn't much a woman can safely do to abort herself. So the question asked is what a third party may do, and what the mother may do, if it is mentioned at all, is deduced, almost as an afterthought, from what it is concluded that third parties may do. But it seems to me that to treat the matter in this way is to refuse to grant to the mother that very status of person which is so firmly insisted on for the fetus. For we cannot simply read off what a person may do from what a third party may do. Suppose you find yourself trapped in a tiny house with a growing child. I mean a very tiny house, and a rapidly growing child—you are already up against the wall of the house and in a few minutes you'll be crushed to death. The child on the other hand won't be crushed to death; if nothing is done to stop him from growing he'll be hurt, but in the end he'll simply burst open the house and walk out a free man. Now I could well understand it if a bystander were to say, "There's nothing we can do for you. We cannot choose between your life and his, we cannot be the ones to decide who is to live, we cannot intervene." But it cannot be concluded that you too can do nothing, that you cannot attack it to save your life. However innocent the child may be, you do not have to wait passively while it crushes you to death. Perhaps a pregnant woman is vaguely felt to have the status of house, to which we don't allow the right of self-defense. But if the woman houses the child, it should be remembered that she is a person who houses it.

I should perhaps stop to say explicitly that I am not claiming that 12 people have a right to do anything whatever to save their lives. I think, rather, that there are drastic limits to the right of self-defense. If someone threatens you with death unless you torture someone else to death, I think you have not the right, even to save your life, to do so. But the case under consideration here is very different. In our case there are only two people involved, one whose life is threatened, and one who threatens it. Both are innocent: the one who is threatened is not threatened because of any fault, the one who threatens does not threaten because of any fault. For this reason we may feel that we bystanders cannot intervene. But the person threatened can.

In sum, a woman surely can defend her life against the threat to it posed by the unborn child, even if doing so involves its death. And this shows not merely that the theses in (1) through (4) are false; it shows also that the extreme view of abortion is false, and so we need not canvass any other possible ways of arriving at it from the argument I mentioned at the outset.

2. The extreme view could of course be weakened to say that while abortion is permissible to save the mother's life, it may not be performed by a third party, but only by the mother herself. But this cannot be right, either. For what we have to keep in mind is that the mother and the unborn child are not like two tenants in a small house which has, by an unfortunate mistake, been rented to both: the mother *owns* the house. The fact that she does adds to the offensiveness of deducing that the mother can do nothing from the supposition that third parties can do nothing. But it does more than this: it casts a bright light on the supposition that third parties can do nothing. Certainly it lets us see that a third party who says "I cannot choose between you" is fooling himself if he thinks this is impartiality. If Jones has found and fastened on a certain coat, which he needs to keep him from freezing, but which Smith also needs to keep him from freezing, then it is not impartiality that says "I cannot choose between you" when Smith owns the coat. Women have said again and again "This body is *my* body!" and they have reason to feel angry, reason to feel that it has been like shouting into the wind. Smith, after all, is hardly likely to bless us if we say to him, "Of course it's your coat, anybody would grant that it is. But no one may choose between you and Jones who is to have it."

We should really ask what it is that says "no one may choose" in the face of the fact that the body that houses the child is the mother's body. It may be simply a failure to appreciate this fact. But it may be something more interesting, namely the sense that one has a right to refuse to lay hands on people, even where it would be just and fair to do so, even where justice seems to require that somebody do so. Thus justice might call for somebody to get Smith's coat back from Jones, and yet you have a right to refuse to be the one to lay hands on Jones, a right to refuse to do physical violence to him. This, I think, must be granted. But then what should be said is not "no one may choose," but only "*I* cannot choose," and indeed not even this, but "*I* will not *act*," leaving it open that somebody else can or should, and in particular that anyone in a position of authority, with the job of securing people rights, both can and should. So this is no difficulty. I have not been arguing that any given third party must accede to the mother's request that he perform an abortion to save her life, but only that he may.

I suppose that in some views of human life the mother's body is only 16 on loan to her, the loan not being one which gives her any prior claim to it. One who held this view might well think it impartiality to say "I cannot choose." But I shall simply ignore this possibility. My own view is that if a human being has any just, prior claim to anything at all, he has a just, prior claim to his own body. And perhaps this needn't be argued for here anyway, since, as I mentioned, the arguments against abortion we are looking at do grant that the woman has a right to decide what happens in and to her body.

But although they do grant it, I have tried to show that they do not take seriously what is done in granting it. I suggest the same thing will reappear even more clearly when we turn away from cases in which the mother's life is at stake, and attend, as I propose we now do, to the vastly more common cases in which a woman wants an abortion for some less weighty reason than preserving her own life.

3. Where the mother's life is not at stake, the argument I mentioned at the outset seems to have a much stronger pull. "Everyone has a right to life, so the unborn person has a right to life." And isn't the child's right to life weightier than anything other than the mother's own right to life, which she might put forward as ground for an abortion?

This argument treats the right to life as if it were unproblematic. It is not, and this seems to me to be precisely the source of the mistake.

For we should now, at long last, ask what it comes to, to have a right to 20 life. In some views having a right to life includes having a right to be given at least the bare minimum one needs for continued life. But suppose that what in fact *is* the bare minimum a man needs for continued life is something he has no right at all to be given? If I am sick unto death, and the only thing that will save my life is the touch of Henry Fonda's cool hand on my fevered brow, then all the same, I have no right to be given the touch of Henry Fonda's cool hand on my fevered brow. It would be frightfully nice of him to fly in from the West Coast to provide it. It would be less nice, though no doubt well meant, if my friends flew out to the West Coast and carried Henry Fonda back with them. But I have no right at all against anybody that he should do this for me. Or again, to return to the story I told earlier, the fact that for continued life that violinist needs the continued use of your kidneys does not establish that he has a right to be given the continued use of your kidneys. He certainly has no right against you that *you* should give him continued use of your kidneys. For nobody has any right to use your kidneys unless you give him such a right; and nobody has the right against you that you shall give him this right—if you do allow him to go on using your kidneys, this is a kindness on your part, and not something he can claim from you as his due. Nor has he any right against anybody else that *they* should give him continued use of your kidneys. Certainly he had no right against the Society of Music Lovers that they should plug him into you in the first place. And if you now start to unplug yourself, having learned that you will otherwise have to spend nine years in bed with him, there is nobody in the world who must try to prevent you, in order to see to it that he is given something he has a right to be given.

Some people are rather stricter about the right to life. In their view, it does not include the right to be given anything, but amounts to, and only to, the right not to be killed by anybody. But here a related difficulty arises. If everybody is to refrain from killing that violinist, then everybody must refrain from doing a great many different sorts of things. Everybody must refrain from slitting his throat, everybody must refrain from shooting him—and everybody must refrain from unplugging you from him. But does he have a right against everybody that they shall refrain from unplugging you from him? To refrain from doing this is to allow him to continue to use your kidneys. It could be argued that he has a right against us that *we* should allow him to continue to use your kidneys. That is, while he had no right against us that we should give him the use of your kidneys, it might be argued that he anyway has a right against us that we shall not now intervene and deprive him of the use of your kidneys. I shall come back to third-party interventions later. But certainly the violinist has no right against you that *you* shall allow him to continue to use your kidneys. As I said, if you do allow him to use them, it is a kindness on your part, and not something you owe him.

The difficulty I point to here is not peculiar to the right to life. It reappears in connection with all the other natural rights; and it is something which an adequate account of rights must deal with. For present purposes it is enough just to draw attention to it. But I would stress that I am not arguing that people do not have a right to life—quite to the contrary, it seems to me that the primary control we must place on the acceptability of an account of rights is that it should turn out in that account to be a truth that all persons have a right to life. I am arguing only that having a right to life does not guarantee having either a right to be given the use of or a right to be allowed continued use of another person's body—even if one needs it for life itself. So the right to life will not serve the opponents of abortion in the very simple and clear way in which they seem to have thought it would.

4. There is another way to bring out the difficulty. In the most ordinary sort of case, to deprive someone of what he has a right to is to treat him unjustly. Suppose a boy and his small brother are jointly given a box of chocolates for Christmas. If the older boy takes the box and refuses to give his brother any of the chocolates, he is unjust to him, for the brother has been given a right to half of them. But suppose that, having learned that otherwise it means nine years in bed with that violinist, you unplug yourself from him. You surely are not being unjust to him, for you gave him no right to use your kidneys, and no one else can have given him any such right. But we have to notice that in unplugging yourself, you are killing him; and violinists, like everybody else, have a right to life, and thus in the view we are considering just now, the right not to be killed. So here you do what he supposedly has a right you shall not do, but you do not act unjustly to him in doing it.

The emendation which may be made at this point is this: the right to 24 life consists not in the right not to be killed, but rather in the right not to be killed unjustly. This runs a risk of circularity, but never mind: it would enable us to square the fact that the violinist has a right to life with the fact that you do not act unjustly toward him in unplugging yourself, thereby killing him. For if you do not kill him unjustly, you do not violate his right to life, and so it is no wonder you do him no injustice.

But if this emendation is accepted, the gap in the argument against abortion stares us plainly in the face: it is by no means enough to show that the fetus is a person, and to remind us that all persons have a right to life— we need to be shown also that killing the fetus violates its right to life, i.e., that abortion is unjust killing. And is it?

I suppose we may take it as a datum that in a case of pregnancy due to rape the mother has not given the unborn person a right to the use of her body for food and shelter. Indeed, in what pregnancy could it be supposed that the mother has given the unborn person such a right? It is not as if there were unborn persons drifting about the world, to whom a woman who wants a child says "I invite you in."

But it might be argued that there are other ways one can have acquired a right to the use of another person's body than by having been invited to use it by that person. Suppose a woman voluntarily indulges in intercourse, knowing of the chance it will issue in pregnancy, and then she does become pregnant; is she not in part responsible for the presence, in fact the very existence, of the unborn person inside her? No doubt she did not invite it in. But doesn't her partial responsibility for its being there itself give it a right to the use of her body?[7] If so, then her aborting it would be more like the boy's taking away the chocolates, and less like your un-plugging yourself from the violinist—doing so would be depriving it of what it does have a right to, and thus would be doing it an injustice.

And then, too, it might be asked whether or not she can kill it even to 28 save her own life: If she voluntarily called it into existence, how can she now kill it, even in self-defense?

---

[7]The need for a discussion of this argument was brought home to me by members of the Society for Ethical and Legal Philosophy, to whom this paper was originally presented.

The first thing to be said about this is that it is something new. Opponents of abortion have been so concerned to make out the independence of the fetus, in order to establish that it has a right to life, just as its mother does, that they have tended to overlook the possible support they might gain from making out that the fetus is *dependent* on the mother, in order to establish that she has a special kind of responsibility for it, a responsibility that gives it rights against her which are not possessed by any independent person—such as an ailing violinist who is a stranger to her.

On the other hand, this argument would give the unborn person a right to its mother's body only if her pregnancy resulted from a voluntary act, undertaken in full knowledge of the chance a pregnancy might result from it. It would leave out entirely the unborn person whose existence is due to rape. Pending the availability of some further argument, then, we would be left with the conclusion that unborn persons whose existence is due to rape have no right to the use of their mothers' bodies, and thus that aborting them is not depriving them of anything they have a right to and hence is not unjust killing.

And we should also notice that it is not at all plain that this argument really does go even as far as it purports to. For there are cases and cases, and the details make a difference. If the room is stuffy, and I therefore open a window to air it, and a burglar climbs in, it would be absurd to say, "Ah, now he can stay, she's given him a right to the use of her house—for she is partially responsible for his presence there, having voluntarily done what enabled him to get in, in full knowledge that there are such things as burglars, and that burglars burgle." It would be still more absurd to say this if I had had bars installed outside my windows, precisely to prevent burglars from getting in, and a burglar got in only because of a defect in the bars. It remains equally absurd if we imagine it is not a burglar who climbs in, but an innocent person who blunders or falls in. Again, suppose it were like this: people-seeds drift about in the air like pollen, and if you open your windows, one may drift in and take root in your carpets or upholstery. You don't want children, so you fix up your windows with fine mesh screens, the very best you can buy. As can happen, however, and on very, very rare occasions does happen, one of the screens is defective; and a seed drifts in and takes root. Does the person-plant who now develops have a right to the use of your house? Surely not—despite the fact that you voluntarily opened your windows, you knowingly kept carpets and upholstered furniture, and you knew that screens were sometimes defective. Someone may argue that you are responsible for its rooting, that it does have a right to your house, because after all you *could* have lived out your life with bare floors and furniture, or with sealed windows and doors. But this won't do—for by the same token anyone can avoid a pregnancy due to rape by having a hysterectomy, or anyway by never leaving home without a (reliable!) army.

It seems to me that the argument we are looking at can establish at 32 most that there are *some* cases in which the unborn person has a right to the use of its mother's body, and therefore some cases in which abortion is unjust killing. There is room for much discussion and argument as to precisely which, if any. But I think we should sidestep this issue and leave it open, for at any rate the argument certainly does not establish that all abortion is unjust killing.

5. There is room for yet another argument here, however. We surely must all grant that there may be cases in which it would be morally indecent to detach a person from your body at the cost of his life. Suppose you learn that what the violinist needs is not nine years of your life, but only one hour: all you need do to save his life is to spend one hour in that bed with him. Suppose also that letting him use your kidneys for that one hour would not affect your health in the slightest. Admittedly you were kidnapped. Admittedly you did not give anyone permission to plug him into you. Nevertheless it seems to me plain you *ought* to allow him to use your kidneys for that hour—it would be indecent to refuse.

Again, suppose pregnancy lasted only an hour, and constituted no threat to life or health. And suppose that a woman becomes pregnant as a result of rape. Admittedly she did not voluntarily do anything to bring about the existence of a child. Admittedly she did nothing at all which would give the unborn person a right to the use of her body. All the same it might well be said, as in the newly emended violinist story, that she ought to allow it to remain for that hour—that it would be indecent in her to refuse.

Now some people are inclined to use the term "right" in such a way that it follows from the fact that you ought to allow a person to use your body for the hour he needs, that he has a right to use your body for the hour he needs, even though he has not been given that right by any person or act. They may say that it follows also that if you refuse, you act unjustly toward him. This use of the term is perhaps so common that it cannot be called wrong; nevertheless it seems to me to be an unfortunate loosening of what we would do better to keep a tight rein on. Suppose that box of chocolates I mentioned earlier had not been given to both boys jointly, but was given only to the older boy. There he sits, stolidly eating his way through the box, his small brother watching enviously. Here we are likely to say "You ought not to be so mean. You ought to give your brother some of those chocolates." My own view is that it just does not follow from the truth of this that the brother has any right to any of the chocolates. If the boy refuses to give his brother any, he is greedy, stingy, callous—but not unjust. I suppose that the people I have in mind will say it does follow that the brother has a right to some of the chocolates, and thus that the boy does act unjustly if he refuses to give his brother any. But the effect of saying this is to obscure what we should keep distinct, namely the difference between the boy's refusal in this case and the boy's refusal in the earlier case, in which the box was given to both boys jointly, and in which the small brother thus had what was from any point of view clear title to half.

A further objection to so using the term "right" that from the fact that A ought to do a thing for B, it follows that B has a right against A that A do it for him, is that it is going to make the question of whether or not a man has a right to a thing turn on how easy it is to provide him with it; and this seems not merely unfortunate, but morally unacceptable. Take the case of Henry Fonda again. I said earlier that I had no right to the touch of his cool hand on my fevered brow, even though I needed it to save my life. I said it would be frightfully nice of him to fly in from the West Coast to provide me with it, but that I had no right against him that he should do so. But suppose he isn't on the West Coast. Suppose he has only to walk across the room, place a hand briefly on my brow—and lo, my life is saved. Then surely he ought to do it, it would be indecent to refuse. Is it to be said "Ah, well, it follows that in this case she has a right to the touch of his hand on her brow, and so it would be an injustice in him to refuse?" So that I have a right to it when it is easy for him to provide it, though no right when it's hard? It's rather a shocking idea that anyone's rights should fade away and disappear as it gets harder and harder to accord them to him.

So my own view is that even though you ought to let the violinist use your kidneys for the one hour he needs, we should not conclude that he has a right to do so—we would say that if you refuse, you are, like the boy who owns all the chocolates and will give none away, self-centered and callous, indecent in fact, but not unjust. And similarly, that even supposing a case in which a woman pregnant due to rape ought to allow the unborn person to use her body for the hour he needs, we should not conclude that he has a right to do so; we should conclude that she is self-centered, callous, indecent, but not unjust, if she refuses. The complaints are no less grave; they are just different. However, there is no need to insist on this point. If anyone does wish to deduce "he has a right" from "you ought," then all the same he must surely grant that there are cases in which it is not morally required of you that you allow that violinist to use your kidneys, and in which he does not have a right to use them, and in which you do not do him an injustice if you refuse. And so also for mother and unborn child. Except in such cases as the unborn person has a right to demand it—and we were leaving open the possibility that there may be such cases—nobody is morally *required* to make large sacrifices, of health, of all other interests and concerns, of all other duties and commitments, for nine years, or even for nine months, in order to keep another person alive.

6. We have in fact to distinguish between two kinds of Samaritan: the Good Samaritan and what we might call the Minimally Decent Samaritan. The story of the Good Samaritan, you will remember, goes like this:

> A certain man went down from Jerusalem to Jericho, and fell among thieves, which stripped him of his raiment, and wounded him, and departed, leaving him half dead.
>
> And by chance there came down a certain priest that way; and when he saw him, he passed by on the other side.
>
> And likewise a Levite, when he was at the place, came and looked on him, and passed by on the other side.
>
> But a certain Samaritan, as he journeyed, came where he was; and when he saw him he had compassion on him.
>
> And went to him, and bound up his wounds, pouring in oil and wine, and set him on his own beast, and brought him to an inn, and took care of him.
>
> And on the morrow, when he departed, he took out two pence, and gave them to the host, and said unto him, "Take care of him; and whatsoever thou spendest more, when I come again, I will repay thee."
>
> (Luke 10:30–35)

The Good Samaritan went out of his way, at some cost to himself, to help one in need of it. We are not told what the options were, that is, whether or not the priest and the Levite could have helped by doing less than the Good Samaritan did, but assuming they could have, then the fact they did nothing at all shows they were not even Minimally Decent Samaritans, not because they were not Samaritans, but because they were not even minimally decent.

These things are a matter of degree, of course, but there is a difference, and it comes out perhaps most clearly in the story of Kitty Genovese, who, as you will remember, was murdered while thirty-eight people watched or listened, and did nothing at all to help her. A Good Samaritan would have rushed out to give direct assistance against the murderer. Or perhaps we had better allow that it would have been a Splendid Samaritan who did this, on the ground that it would have involved a risk of death for himself. But the thirty-eight not only did not do this, they did not even trouble to pick up a phone to call the police. Minimally Decent Samaritanism would call for doing at least that, and their not having done it was monstrous.

After telling the story of the Good Samaritan, Jesus said "Go, and do 40 thou likewise." Perhaps he meant that we are morally required to act as the Good Samaritan did. Perhaps he was urging people to do more than is morally required of them. At all events it seems plain that it was not morally required of any of the thirty-eight that he rush out to give direct assistance at the risk of his own life, and that it is not morally required of anyone that he give long stretches of his life—nine years or nine months— to sustaining the life of a person who has no special right (we were leaving open the possibility of this) to demand it.

Indeed, with one rather striking class of exceptions, no one in any country in the world is *legally* required to do anywhere near as much as this for anyone else. The class of exceptions is obvious. My main concern here is not the state of the law in respect to abortion, but it is worth drawing attention to the fact that in no state in this country is any man compelled by law to be even a Minimally Decent Samaritan to any person; there is no law under which charges could be brought against the thirty-eight who stood by while Kitty Genovese died. By contrast, in most states in this country women are compelled by law to be not merely Minimally Decent Samaritans, but Good Samaritans to unborn persons inside them. This doesn't by itself settle anything one way or the other, because it may well be argued that there should be laws in this country—as there are in many European countries—compelling at least Minimally Decent Samaritanism.[8] But it does show that there is a gross injustice in the existing state of the law. And it shows also that the groups currently working against liberalization of abortion laws, in fact working toward having it declared unconstitutional for a state to permit abortion, had better start working for the adoption of Good Samaritan laws generally, or earn the charge that they are acting in bad faith.

I should think, myself, that Minimally Decent Samaritan laws would be one thing, Good Samaritan laws quite another, and in fact highly improper. But we are not here concerned with the law. What we should ask is not whether anybody should be compelled by law to be a Good Samaritan, but whether we must accede to a situation in which somebody is being compelled—by nature, perhaps—to be a Good Samaritan. We have, in other words, to look now at third-party interventions. I have been arguing that no person is morally required to make large sacrifices to sustain the life of another who has no right to demand them, and this even where the sacrifices do not include life itself; we are not morally required to be Good Samaritans or anyway Very Good Samaritans to one another. But what if a man cannot extricate himself from such a situation? What if he appeals to us to extricate him? It seems to me plain that there are cases in which we can, cases in which a Good Samaritan would extricate him. There you are, you were kidnapped, and nine years in bed with that violinist lie ahead of you. You have your own life to lead. You are sorry, but you simply cannot see giving up so much of your life to the sustaining of his. You cannot extricate yourself, and ask us to do so. I should have thought that—in light of his having no right to the use of your body—it was obvious that we do not have to accede to your being forced to give up so much. We can do what you ask. There is no injustice to the violinist in our doing so.

[8]For a discussion of the difficulties involved and a survey of the European experience with such laws, see *The Good Samaritan and the Law,* ed. James M. Ratcliffe (New York, 1966).

7. Following the lead of the opponents of abortion, I have throughout been speaking of the fetus merely as a person, and what I have been asking is whether or not the argument we began with, which proceeds only from the fetus's being a person, really does establish its conclusion. I have argued that it does not.

But of course there are arguments and arguments, and it may be said that I have simply fastened on the wrong one. It may be said that what is important is not merely the fact that the fetus is a person, but that it is a person for whom the woman has a special kind of responsibility issuing from the fact that she is its mother. And it might be argued that all my analogies are therefore irrelevant—for you do not have that special kind of responsibility for that violinist, Henry Fonda does not have that special kind of responsibility for me. And our attention might be drawn to the fact that men and women both *are* compelled by law to provide support for their children. 44

I have in effect dealt (briefly) with this argument in section 4 above; but a (still briefer) recapitulation now may be in order. Surely we do not have any such "special responsibility" for a person unless we have assumed it, explicitly or implicitly. If a set of parents do not try to prevent pregnancy, do not obtain an abortion, and then at the time of birth of the child do not put it out for adoption, but rather take it home with them, then they have assumed responsibility for it, they have given it rights, and they cannot *now* withdraw support from it at the cost of its life because they now find it difficult to go on providing for it. But if they have taken all reasonable precautions against having a child, they do not simply by virtue of their biological relationship to the child who comes into existence have a special responsibility for it. They may wish to assume responsibility for it, or they may not wish to. And I am suggesting that if assuming responsibility for it would require large sacrifices, then they may refuse. A Good Samaritan would not refuse—or anyway, a Splendid Samaritan, if the sacrifices that had to be made were enormous. But then so would a Good Samaritan assume responsibility for that violinist; so would Henry Fonda, if he is a Good Samaritan, fly in from the West Coast and assume responsibility for me.

8. My argument will be found unsatisfactory on two counts by many of those who want to regard abortion as morally permissible. First, while I do argue that abortion is not impermissible, I do not argue that it is always permissible. There may well be cases in which carrying the child to term requires only Minimally Decent Samaritanism of the mother, and this is a standard we must not fall below. I am inclined to think it a merit of my account precisely that it does *not* give a general yes or a general no. It allows for and supports our sense that, for example, a sick and desperately frightened fourteen-year-old schoolgirl, pregnant due to rape, may *of* *course* choose abortion, and that any law which rules this out is an insane law. And it also allows for and supports our sense that in other cases resort to abortion is even positively indecent. It would be indecent in the woman to request an abortion, and indecent in a doctor to perform it, if she is in her seventh month, and wants the abortion just to avoid the nuisance of postponing a trip abroad. The very fact that the arguments I have been drawing attention to treat all cases of abortion, or even all cases of abortion in which the mother's life is not at stake, as morally on a par ought to have made them suspect at the outset.

Secondly, while I am arguing for the permissibility of abortion in some cases, I am not arguing for the right to secure the death of the unborn child. It is easy to confuse these two things in that up to a certain point in the life of the fetus it is not able to survive outside the mother's body; hence removing it from her body guarantees its death. But they are importantly different. I have argued that you are not morally required to spend nine months in bed, sustaining the life of that violinist; but to say this is by no means to say that if, when you unplug yourself, there is a miracle and he survives, you then have a right to turn around and slit his throat. You may detach yourself even if this costs him his life; you have no right to be guaranteed his death, by some other means, if unplugging yourself does not kill him. There are some people who will feel dissatisfied by this feature of my argument. A woman may be utterly devastated by the thought of a child, a bit of herself, put out for adoption and never seen or heard of again. She may therefore want not merely that the child be detached from her, but more, that it die. Some opponents of abortion are inclined to regard this as beneath contempt—thereby showing insensitivity to what is surely a powerful source of despair. All the same, I agree that the desire for the child's death is not one which anybody may gratify, should it turn out to be possible to detach the child alive.

At this place, however, it should be remembered that we have only 48 been pretending throughout that the fetus is a human being from the moment of conception. A very early abortion is surely not the killing of a person, and so is not dealt with by anything I have said here.

Questions and Suggestions for Writing

1. Do you agree with Thomson that it would be permissible for you—that is, you have the right—to pull out the plug on the violinist in her hypothetical example? If you think you do not have this right, how would you argue for your view?

2. Thomson offers an artificial case—a violinist plugged into the reader—as a way of refuting the argument that a fetus's right to life outweighs the mother's right to decide what happens to her body. Why do you, or why do you not, find this example helpful in thinking about abortion? John Noonan (p. 354) dismisses Thomson's artificial case of the violinist as a "caricature" of the relationship of a

pregnant woman to a fetus. Try to plug yourself into Thomson's mind, and write a reply (500 words) defending the analogy. (Notice that Thomson herself early in her essay acknowledges that her analogy has difficulties.)

3. Thomson argues that, just as the plugged-in violinist has no right to the use of your kidneys unless you *give* him that right, so too the fetus has no right to use its mother's body unless she *gives* it the right. Evaluate this argument. Are the two cases really parallel?

4. Why do you, or why do you not, accept Thomson's view (para. 30) that "unborn persons whose existence is due to rape have no right to the use of their mothers' bodies, and thus that aborting them is not depriving them of anything they have a right to and hence is not unjust killing"? Even if you accept this argument, do you accept the argument that she offers in her next paragraph, to the effect that if during sex a woman takes reasonable precautions against pregnancy and nevertheless becomes pregnant, the fetus is an illegitimate intruder with no right to use the mother's body?

5. In paragraph 41 Thomson says, "In no state in this country is any man compelled by law to be even a Minimally Decent Samaritan to any person. . . . By contrast, in most states in this country women are compelled by law to be not merely Minimally Decent Samaritans, but Good Samaritans to unborn persons inside them. . . . [I]t does show that there is a gross injustice in the existing state of the law." But given the facts that women may elect to have abortions, and that fathers as well as mothers may be convicted of child abuse, is Thomson muddying the water by suggesting that women are subjected to exalted standards that men are exempt from?

6. Thomson argues that even if a touch of the late Henry Fonda's hand would have saved her from death, Fonda was under no moral obligation to save her. A little later in the essay she argues not only that the law does not require us to be Good Samaritans, but also that (para. 42) "we are not morally required to be Good Samaritans or anyway Very Good Samaritans to one another." Why do you, or why do you not, agree with her point about the moral requirement?

7. If you have read Noonan's essay, write two paragraphs, one characterizing Noonan as you perceive him through his essay, and the other characterizing Thomson. Among the topics you may want to consider are these: Is the author serious—or stuffy? Does the author seem humane? Does the author seem thoughtful—or merely ingenious? If both of these professors were teaching at your school, would you want to take a course with one, or both? Why? (Holden Caulfield's test for a good author was that you'd want to call him [or her] up on the telephone. Which of these two authors would you rather call? Why?)

8. Thomson argues that a pregnant woman is under no obligation to save the fetus, even if we assume that the fetus is a person, especially because it may mean undergoing nine difficult months. But almost no one would say that a mature son or daughter has the right to kill a totally dependent aged parent— let's say an eighty-year-old with Alzheimer's disease—even though the son or daughter may be put into very difficult circumstances for years. Does Thomson's essay allow us to suggest that she probably would find the killing of the parent morally acceptable?

John Noonan

How to Argue about Abortion

At the heart of the debate about abortion is the relation of person to person in social contexts. Analogies, metaphors, and methods of debate which do not focus on persons and which do not attend to the central contexts are mischievous. Their use arises from a failure to appreciate the distinctive character of moral argument—its requirement that values be organically related and balanced, its dependence on personal vision, and its rootedness in social experience. I propose here to examine various models and methods used in the debate on abortion distinguishing those such as fantasized situations, hard cases, and linear metaphors, all of which do not work, from the balancing, seeing, and appeal to human experience which I believe to be essential. I shall move from models and metaphors which take the rule against abortion as the expression of a single value to the consideration of ways of argument intended to suggest the variety of values which have converged in the formulation of the rule. The values embodied in the rule are various because abortion is an aspect of the relation of person to person, and persons are larger than single values; and abortion is an act in a social context which cannot be reduced to a single value. I write as a critic of abortion, with no doubt a sharper eye for the weaknesses of its friends than of its foes, but my chief aim is to suggest what arguments count.

ARTIFICIAL CASES

One way of reaching the nub of a moral issue is to construct a hypothetical situation endowed with precisely the characteristics you believe are crucial in the real issue you are seeking to resolve. Isolated from the clutter of detail in the real situation, these characteristics point to the proper solution. The risk is that the features you believe crucial you will enlarge to the point of creating a caricature. The pedagogy of your illustration will be blunted by the uneasiness caused by the lack of correspondence between the fantasized situation and the real situation to be judged. Such is the case with two recent efforts by philosophers, Judith Jarvis Thomson and Michael Tooley, to construct arguments justifying abortion.

A member of the Bar of Massachusetts and of the Bar of the Supreme Court, Noonan (b. 1926) has taught law at the University of Notre Dame and the University of California, Berkeley. In 1985 he was appointed to the bench of the U.S. Circuit Court of Appeals.

Suppose, says Thomson, a violinist whose continued existence depends on acquiring new kidneys. Without the violinist's knowledge—he remains innocent—a healthy person is kidnapped and connected to him so that the violinist now shares the use of healthy kidneys. May the victim of the kidnapping break the connection and thereby kill the violinist? Thomson intuits that the normal judgment will be Yes. The healthy person should not be imposed upon by a lifelong physical connection with the violinist. This construct, Thomson contends, bears upon abortion by establishing that being human does not carry with it a right to life which must be respected by another at the cost of serious inconvenience.[1]

This ingenious attempt to make up a parallel to pregnancy imagines a   4 kidnapping; a serious operation performed on the victim of the kidnapping; and a continuing interference with many of the activities of the victim. It supposes that violinist and victim were unrelated. It supposes nothing by which the victim's initial aversion to his yoke-mate might be mitigated or compensated. It supposes no degree of voluntariness. The similitude to pregnancy is grotesque. It is difficult to think of another age or society in which a caricature of this sort could be seriously put forward as a paradigm illustrating the moral choice to be made by a mother.

While Thomson focuses on this fantasy, she ignores a real case from which American tort law has generalized. On a January night in Minnesota, a cattle buyer, Orlando Depue, asked a family of farmers, the Flateaus, with whom he had dined, if he could remain overnight at their house. The Flateaus refused and, although Depue was sick and had fainted, put him out of the house into the cold night. Imposing liability on the Flateaus for Depue's loss of his frostbitten fingers the court said, "In the case at bar defendants were under no contract obligation to minister to plaintiff in his distress; but humanity demanded they do so, if they understood and appreciated his condition. . . . The law as well as humanity required that he not be exposed in his helpless condition to the merciless elements."[2] Depue was a guest for supper although not a guest after supper. The American Law Institute, generalizing, has said that it makes no difference whether the helpless person is a guest or a trespasser. He has the privilege of staying. His host has the duty not to injure him or put him into an environment where he becomes nonviable. The obligation arises when one person "understands and appreciates" the condition of the other.[3] Although the analogy is not exact, the case seems closer to the mother's situation than the case imagined by Thomson; and the emotional response of the Minnesota judges seems to be a truer reflection of what humanity requires.

[1] Judith Thomson, "A Defense of Abortion," *Philosophy & Public Affairs* I (Princeton, N.J.: Princeton University Press, 1972) 48–49, 55–56.
[2] *Depue v. Flateau* 100 Minn. 299, 111 W.W. 1 (1907).
[3] American Law Institute, *Restatement of Torts*, Second (1965) sec. 197.

Michael Tooley's artificial case in defense of abortion is put forward in the course of an even broader defense by him of infanticide, horror of which he likens to other unreasoned cultural taboos. He attacks "the potentiality principle," the principle that the fetus or baby is entitled to respect because the fetus or baby will develop into an adult human being with an admitted right to life. He does so in this way. Suppose, he says, a chemical which could be injected into a kitten which would enable it to develop into a cat possessed of the brain and psychological capabilities of adult human beings. It would not be wrong, he intuits, to refrain from giving a kitten the chemical and to kill the kitten instead. Would it be wrong, he asks, to kill a kitten who had been injected? To do so would be to prevent the development of a rational adult cat. Yet, Tooley intuits, the answer must be that it would not be wrong to kill the injected kitten. Potentiality for rational adulthood, he concludes, does not enhance a kitten's claim to life, or a fetus's.[4]

Leaving the world of humans altogether, Tooley, like Thomson, has fashioned a hypothetical to give light on a very abstract question, "Who has a right to life?" The hypothetical is framed as though the subject of this question were indifferent. To get an answer we are asked to test our reactions to a fantasy. We do not have the experience to tell us what we would decide if we were confronted by his hypothetical cat or hypothetical kitten. Cat lovers would probably respond very differently from dog lovers. We are asked to respond to a construct, and to respond we need to see or feel the flesh and blood of a humanoid.

Cats may be treated on their own merits, apart from chemical injections, as humans. But then the work of personification is consciously done by attention to the human analogues. I may cite here as conclusive authority *Old Possum's Book of Practical Cats*, which also incidentally shows that personification is not dependent on naming.[5]

8

[4]Michael Tooley, "Abortion and Infanticide." *Philosophy & Public Affairs* II (Princeton, N.J.: Princeton University Press, 1973) 60–62.
[5]With Cats, some say, one rule is true:
Don't speak till you are spoken to.
Myself. I do not hold with that—
I say, you should ad-dress a Cat.
But always keep in mind that he
Resents familiarity.
I bow, and taking off my hat,
Ad-dress him in this form: O CAT!
But if he is the Cat next door,
Whom I have often met before
(He comes to see me in my flat)
I greet him with an OOPSA CAT!
I think I've heard them call him James—
But we've not got so far as names.
Before a Cat will condescend *[continued]*

HARD CASES AND EXCEPTIONS

In the presentation of permissive abortion to the American public, major emphasis has been put on situations of great pathos—the child deformed by thalidomide, the child affected by rubella, the child known to suffer from Tay-Sachs disease or Downs syndrome, the raped adolescent, the exhausted mother of small children. These situations are not imagined, and the cases described are not analogies to those where abortion might be sought; they are themselves cases to which abortion is a solution. Who could deny the poignancy of their appeal?

Hard cases make bad law, runs the venerable legal adage, but it seems to be worse law if the distress experienced in situations such as these is not taken into account. If persons are to be given preeminence over abstract principle, should not exceptions for these cases be made in the most rigid rule against abortion? Does not the human experience of such exceptions point to a more sweeping conclusion—the necessity of abandoning any uniform prohibition of abortion, so that all the elements of a particular situation may be weighted by the woman in question and her doctor?

So far, fault can scarcely be found with this method of argumentation, this appeal to common experience. But the cases are oversimplified if focus is directed solely on the parents of a physically defective child or on the mother in the cases of rape or psychic exhaustion. The situations are very hard for the parents or the mother; they are still harder for the fetus who is threatened with death. If the fetus is a person as the opponents of abortion contend, its destruction is not the sparing of suffering by the sacrifice of a principle but by the sacrifice of a life. Emotion is a proper element in moral response, but to the extent that the emotion generated by these cases

To treat you as a trusted friend,
Some little token of esteem
Is needed, like a dish of cream;
And you might now and then supply
Some caviare, or Strassburg Pie,
Some potted grouse, or salmon paste—
He's sure to have his personal taste.
(I know a Cat, who makes a habit
Of eating nothing else but rabbit,
And when he's finished, licks his paws
So's not to waste the onion sauce.)
A Cat's entitled to expect
These evidences of respect.
And so in time you reach your aim,
And finally call him by his NAME.

T.S. Eliot, from "The Ad-dressing of Cats," in *Old Possum's Book of Practical Cats* (New York: Harcourt Brace, 1939) in Eliot, *The Complete Poems and Plays, 1909–1950* (New York: Harcourt Brace, 1952) 170–171. [Copyright 1939 by T.S. Eliot; renewed 1971 by Esme Valerie Eliot. Reprinted by permission of Harcourt Brace Jovanovich, Inc., and Faber and Faber Ltd.]

obscures the claims of the fetus, this kind of argumentation fosters erroneous judgment.

In three of the cases—the child deformed by drugs, disease, or genetic   12
defect—the neglect of the child's point of view seems stained by hypocrisy. Abortion is here justified as putting the child out of the misery of living a less than normal life: The child is not consulted as to the choice. Experience, which teaches that even the most seriously incapacitated prefer living to dying, is ignored. The feelings of the parents are the actual consideration, and these feelings are treated with greater tenderness than the fetal desire to live. The common unwillingness to say frankly that the abortion is sought for the parents' benefit is testimony, unwillingly given, to the intuition that such self-preference by the parents is difficult for society or for the parents themselves to accept.

The other kind of hard case does not mask preference for the parent by a pretense of concern for the fetus. The simplest situation is that of a pregnancy due to rape—in presentations to some legislatures it was usual to add a racist fillip by supposing a white woman and a black rapist—but this gratuitous pandering to bias is not essential. The fetus, unwanted in the most unequivocal way, is analogized to an invader of the mother's body—is it even appropriate to call her a mother when she did nothing to assume the special fiduciary cares of motherhood? If she is prevented from having an abortion, she is being compelled for nine months to be reminded of a traumatic assault. Do not her feelings override the right to life of her unwanted tenant?

Rape arouses fear and a desire for revenge, and reference to rape evokes emotion. The emotion has been enough for the state to take the life of the rapist.[6] Horror of the crime is easily extended to horror of the product, so that the fetal life becomes forfeit too. If horror is overcome, adoption appears to be a more humane solution than abortion. If the rape case is not being used as a stalking horse by proponents of abortion—if there is a desire to deal with it in itself—the solution is to assure the destruction of the sperm in the one to three days elapsing between insemination and impregnation.

Generally, however, the rape case is presented as a way of suggesting a general principle, a principle which could be formulated as follows: Every unintended pregnancy may be interrupted if its continuation will cause emotional distress to the mother. Pregnancies due to bad planning or bad luck are analogized to pregnancies due to rape; they are all involuntary.[7] Indeed many pregnancies can without great difficulty be assimilated to the hard case, for how often do persons undertake an act of sexual intercourse

---

[6]See Note, "Constitutional Law: Capital Punishment for Rape Constitutes Cruel and Unusual Punishment When No Life Is Taken or Endangered," *Minnesota Law Review* 95 (1971) 56.

[7]See Thomson, op. cit.: "A Defense of Abortion," 59.

consciously intending that a child be the fruit of that act? Many pregnancies are unspecified by a particular intent, are unplanned, are in this sense involuntary. Many pregnancies become open to termination if only the baby consciously sought has immunity.

This result is unacceptable to those who believe that the fetus is 16 human. It is acceptable to those who do not believe the fetus is human, but to reach it they do not need the argument based on the hard case. The result would follow immediately from the mother's dominion over a portion of her body. Opponents of abortion who out of consideration for the emotional distress caused by rape will grant the rape exception must see that the exception can be generalized to destroy the rule. If, on other grounds they believe the rule good, they must deny the exception which eats it up.

DIRECT AND INDIRECT

From paradigmatic arguments, I turn to metaphors and especially those which, based on some spatial image, are misleading. I shall begin with "direct" and "indirect" and their cousins, "affirmative" and "negative." In the abortion argument "direct" and "indirect," "affirmative" and "negative" occur more frequently in these kinds of questions: If one denies that a fetus may be killed directly, but admits that indirect abortion is permissible, is he guilty of inconsistency? If one maintains that there is a negative duty not to kill fetuses, does he thereby commit himself to an affirmative obligation of assuring the safe delivery of every fetus? If one agrees that there is no affirmative duty to actualize as many spermatic, ovoid, embryonic, or fetal potentialities as possible, does one thereby concede that it is generally permissible to take steps to destroy fertilized ova? The argumentative implications of these questions can be best unraveled by looking at the force of the metaphors invoked.

"Direct" and "indirect" appeal to our experience of line-drawing and of travel. You reach a place on a piece of paper by drawing a straight or crooked line—the line is direct or indirect. You go to a place without detours or you go in a roundabout fashion—your route is direct or indirect. In each instance, whether your path is direct or indirect your destination is the same. The root experience is that you can reach the same spot in ways distinguished by their immediacy and the amount of ground covered. "Indirectly" says you proceed more circuitously and cover more ground. It does not, however, say anything of the reason why you go circuitously. You may go indirectly because you want to cover more ground or because you want to disguise your destination.

The ambiguity in the reason for indirectness—an ambiguity present in the primary usage of the term—carries over when "indirect" is applied metaphorically to human intentions. There may be a reason for doing something indirectly—you want to achieve another objective besides the indirect action. You may also act indirectly to conceal from another or from yourself what is your true destination. Because of this ambiguity in the reason for indirection, "indirect" is apt to cause confusion when applied in moral analysis.

Defenders of an absolute prohibition of abortion have excepted the 20 removal of a fertilized ovum in an ectopic pregnancy and the removal of a cancerous uterus containing an embryo. They have characterized the abortion involved as "indirect." They have meant that the surgeon's attention is focused on correcting a pathological condition dangerous to the mother and he only performs the operation because there is no alternative way of correcting it.[8] But the physician has to intend to achieve not only the improvement of the mother but the performance of action by which the fertilized ovum becomes nonviable. He necessarily intends to perform an abortion, he necessarily intends to kill. To say that he acts indirectly is to conceal what is being done. It is a confusing and improper use of the metaphor.[9]

A clearer presentation of the cases of the cancerous uterus and the ectopic pregnancy would acknowledge them to be true exceptions to the absolute inviolability of the fetus. Why are they not exceptions which would eat up the rule? It depends on what the rule is considered to be. The principle that can be discerned in them is, whenever the embryo is a danger to the life of the mother, an abortion is permissible. At the level of reason nothing more can be asked of the mother. The exceptions do eat up any rule of preferring the fetus to the mother—any rule of fetus first. They do not destroy the rule that the life of the fetus has precedence over other interests of the mother. The exceptions of the ectopic pregnancy and the cancerous uterus are special cases of the general exception to the rule against killing, which permits one to kill in self-defense. Characterization of this kind of killing as "indirect" does not aid analysis.[10]

It is a basic intuition that one is not responsible for all the consequences of one's acts. By living at all one excludes others from the air one breathes, the food one eats. One cannot foresee all the results which will flow from any given action. It is imperative for moral discourse to be able to distinguish between injury foreseeably inflicted on another, and the harm which one may unknowingly bring about. "Direct" and "indirect"

[8]See my "An Almost Absolute Value in History," Noonan, ed., *The Morality of Abortion* (Cambridge, Mass.: Harvard University Press, 1970) 46–50.

[9]To say that the act is in itself good seems to me to be an impossible supposition—there is no human act "in itself" apart from intent. See, for a contrary analysis, Germain Grisez, *Abortion: The Myths, the Realities, and the Arguments* (Washington: Corpus Books, 1970) 329.

[10]For a comparable analysis of the use of direct and indirect in constitutional law, see D.J. Farage, "That Which 'Directly' Affects Interstate Commerce," *Dickinson Law Review* XLII (Carlisle, Pa.: Dickinson Law School, 1937) 71.

are sometimes used to distinguish the foreseen consequence from the un-considered or unknown consequence. This usage does not justify terming abortion to save a mother's life "indirect." In the case of terminating the ectopic pregnancy, the cancerous uterus, the life-threatening fetus gener-ally, one considers precisely the consequence, the taking of the fetal life.

Just as one intuits that one is not responsible for all the consequences, so one intuits that one is not called to right all wrongs. No one is bound to do the impossible. There is, therefore, an intuitive difference between the duty to refrain from doing harm to anyone and the duty to help everyone in distress. The duty to refrain is possible of fulfillment if it refers only to conscious infliction of harm. The duty to help is impossible if one is going to develop as a human being, getting educated, earning a living, marrying, raising a family, and so forth. The needs of other human beings are subordinated or postponed by everyone to the fulfillment of many of one's own needs, and rightly so. The distinction between affirmative and nega-tive duties, another linear metaphor, rests on this universal experience. The terms do have a basis in moral life. Their usefulness in moral analysis, however, is not great. The crucial distinction is not between negative and affirmative, but between limited and unlimited duty.

It is possible to state the duty not to kill the fetus as the duty to care for the fetus. Opponents of abortion, however, do not commit thereby them-selves to the position that all fertilized ova must be born. A pregnant woman may, for example, take the chance of killing the baby by going for a walk or a drive instead of staying safely in bed. She is not responsible for all the consequences of her acts. She is not called to help the fetus in every possible way. The negative duty or the convertible affirmative duty ex-cludes acts which have a high probability of death for the fetus, but not those with a low probability of death. Similarly, one has a duty not to kill one's older children, and a duty to care for them, but no duty to keep them free from all risk of harm. No inconsistency exists in not equating a limited negative duty with an unlimited affirmative duty; no inconsistency exists in rejecting high risk acts and approving low risk acts.[11]

LINE-DRAWING

The prime linear metaphor is, of course, line-drawing. It is late in the history of moral thought for anyone to suppose that an effective moral retort is, "Yes, but where do you draw the line?" or to make the inference that, because any drawing of a line requires a decision, all line-drawing is arbitrary. One variant or another of these old ploys is, however, frequently used in the present controversy. From living cell to dying corpse a con-

---

[11]For analysis of affirmative and negative duties in tort law, see John G. Fleming, *The Law of Torts* (Sydney: Law Book Co., 2 ed., 1961) 148–151.

tinuum exists. Proponents of abortion are said to be committed to murder, to euthanasia, or, at a minimum, to infanticide. Opponents are alleged to be bound to condemn contraception—after all, spermatozoa are living human cells. Even if contraception is admitted and infanticide rejected, the range of choice is still large enough for the line drawn to be challenged—is it to be at nidation, at formation of the embryo, at quickening, at viability, at birth? Whoever adopts one point is asked why he does not move forward or backward by one stage of development. The difficulty of presenting apodictic[12] reasons for preferring one position is made to serve as proof that the choice may be made as best suits the convenience of an individual or the state.[13]

The metaphor of line-drawing distracts attention from the nature of the moral decision. The metaphor suggests an empty room composed of indistinguishable gray blocks. In whatever way the room is divided, there are gray blocks on either side of the line. Or if the metaphor is taken more mathematically, it suggests a series of points, which, wherever bisected, are fungible with each other. What is obscured in the spatial or mathematical model is the variety of values whose comparison enters into any moral decision. The model appeals chiefly to those novices in moral reasoning who believe that moral judgment is a matter of pursuing a principle to its logical limit. Single-mindedly looking at a single value, they ask, if this is good, why not more of it? In practice, however, no one can be so single-hearted. Insistence on this kind of logical consistency becomes the preserve of fanatics or of controversialists eager to convict their adversaries of inconsistency. If more than one good is sought by a human being, he must bring the goods he seeks into relationship with each other; he must limit one to maintain another; he must mix them.[14]

The process of choosing multiple goods occurs in many particular contexts—in eating, in studying, in painting. No one supposes that those who take the first course must forgo dessert, that the election of English means History shall not be studied, that the use of blue excludes red. Linear models for understanding choice in these matters are readily per-

---

[12]**apodictic** A reason is *apodictic* when it is self-evidently true. [Editors' note]

[13]Even Roger Wertheimer, who has made a good explication of the antiabortion argument from the point of view of one who does not accept it, ends his article by a question-begging device—the burden of proof of fetal humanity, he says, is on the state. Wertheimer, "Understanding the Abortion Argument," *Philosophy & Public Affairs* I (op. cit. 1971) 94–95. From the viewpoint of opponents of abortion, his argument may be reshaped: the state has the burden of proving that its actions are legitimate; laws which permit the killing of the fetus seriously threaten human life; they may be sustained only if the state can show that the fetus is not human; and this cannot be done.

[14]For an example of the controversialist's use of line-drawing, see Glanville Williams, *The Sanctity of Life and the Criminal Law* (New York: Knopf, 1957) 104. For an approach which does not recognize that values must be cut off—that insists we must be "open" to basic values, see Grisez, *Abortion: The Myths, the Realities, and the Arguments* (op. cit.) 310–321. Grisez is followed by John Finnis. "The Rights and Wrongs of Abortion." *Philosophy & Public Affairs* II (op. cit. 1973) 126.

ceived as inappropriate. The commitment to values, the cutting off of values, and the mixing of values accompany each other.

Is, however, the choice of the stage of development which should not 28 be destroyed by abortion a choice requiring the mixing of multiple goods? Is not the linear model appropriate when picking a point on the continuum of life? Are not the moral choices which require commitment and mixing made only after the selection of the stage at which a being becomes a person? To these related questions the answers must all be negative. To recognize a person is a moral decision; it depends on objective data but it also depends on the perceptions and inclinations and ends of the decision makers; it cannot be made without commitment and without consideration of alternative values. Who is a person? This is not a question asked abstractly, in the air, with no purpose in mind. To disguise the personal involvement in the response to personhood is to misconceive the issue of abortion from the start.

Those who identify the rational with the geometrical, the algebraic, the logical may insist that, if the fundamental recognition of personhood depends upon the person who asks, then the arbitrariness of any position on abortion is conceded. If values must be mixed even in identifying the human, who can object to another's mixture? The issue becomes like decisions in eating, studying, and painting, a matter of discretion. A narrow rationalism of this kind uses "taste" as the ultimate epithet for the nonrational. It does not acknowledge that each art has its own rules. It claims for itself alone the honorable term "reason."

As this sort of monopoly has become unacceptable in general philosophy, so it is unnecessary to accept it here. Taste, that is perceptiveness, is basic; and if it cannot be disputed, it can be improved by experience. Enology, painting, or moral reasoning all require basic aptitude, afford wide ranges of options, have limits beyond which a choice can be counterproductive, and are better done by the experienced than by amateurs. Some persons may lack almost any capacity for undertaking one or another of them. Although all men are moral beings, not all are proficient at moral judgment, so that morality is not a democratic business. Selecting multiple goods, those who are capable of the art perceive, test, mix, and judge. The process has little in common with line-drawing. In the case of abortion, it is the contention of its opponents that in such a process the right response to the data is that the fetus is a human being.[15]

BALANCING

The process of decision-making just described is better caught by the term "balancing." In contrast to line-drawing, balancing is a metaphor

[15]E.g., my article. "Deciding Who is Human." *Natural Law Forum* XII (South Bend, Ind: Notre Dame School of Law, 1968) 134–140.

helpful in understanding moral judgment. Biologically understood, balancing is the fundamental metaphor for moral reasoning. A biological system is in balance when its parts are in the equilibrium necessary for it to live. To achieve such equilibrium, some parts—the heart, for example—must be preserved at all costs; others may be sacrificed to maintain the whole. Balance in the biological sense does not demand an egalitarian concern for every part, but an ordering and subordination which permit the whole function. So in moral reasoning the reasoner balances values.

The mistaken common reading of this metaphor is to treat it as equivalent to weighing, so that balancing is understood as an act of quantitative comparison analogous to that performed by an assayer or a butcher. This view tacitly supposes that values are weights which are tangible and commensurate. One puts so many units on one pan of the scales and matches them with so many units on the other to reach a "balanced" judgment. To give a personal example, Daniel Callahan has questioned my position, that the value of innocent life cannot be sacrificed to achieve the other values which abortion might secure. The "force of the rule," he writes, "is absolutist, displaying no 'balance' at all."[16] He takes balancing in the sense of weighing and wonders how one value can be so heavy.

That justice often consists in the fair distribution or exchange of goods as in the familiar Aristotelian examples has no doubt worked to confirm a quantitative approach. Scales as the symbol of justice seem to suggest the antiquity of the quantitative meaning of balance. But the original sense of the scales was otherwise. In Egypt where the symbol was first used, a feather, the Egyptian hieroglyphic for truth, turned the balance. As put by David Daube in his illuminating analysis of the ancient symbolism, "The slightest turning of the scales—'but in the estimation of a hair'—will decide the issue, and the choice is between salvation and annihilation."[17] Not a matching of weights, but a response to reality was what justice was seen to require, and what was at stake was not a slight overweighing in one direction or the other, but salvation. Moral choice, generally, has this character of a hair separating good from evil.

A fortiori then, in moral judgment, where more values are in play than in any system of strict law or commutative justice, balancing is a misleading metaphor if it suggests a matching of weights. It is an indispensable metaphor if it stands for the equilibrium of a living organism making the choices necessary for its preservation. A single value cannot be pursued to the point of excluding all other values. This is the caricature of moral argument I have already touched on in connection with the metaphor of line-drawing. But some values are more vital than others, as the heart is

[16]Daniel Callahan, *Abortion: Law, Choice, and Morality* (New York: Macmillan, 1970) 430–431.
[17]David Daube. "The Scales of Justice," *Juridical Review* LXIII (So. Hackensack, N.J.: Rothman, 1951) 113.

more vital to the body than the hand. A balanced moral judgment requires a sense of the limits, interrelations, and priority of values. It is the position of those generally opposed to abortion that a judgment preferring interests less than human life to human life is unbalanced, that a judgment denying a mother's fiduciary responsibility to her child is unbalanced, that a judgment making killing a principal part of the profession of a physician is unbalanced, that a judgment permitting agencies of the state to procure and pay for the destruction of the offspring of the poor or underprivileged is unbalanced. They contend that such judgments expand the right limits of a mother's responsibility for herself, destroy the fiduciary relation which is a central paradigm for the social bond, fail to relate to the physician's service to life and the state's care for its citizens. At stake in the acceptance of abortion is not a single value, life, against which the suffering of the mother or parents may be balanced. The values to be considered are the child's life, the mother's faithfulness to her dependent, the physician's commitment to preserving life; and in the United States today abortion cannot be discussed without awareness that if law does not prohibit it, the state will fund it, so that the value of the state's abstention from the taking of life is also at issue. The judgment which accepts abortion, it is contended, is unbalanced in subordinating these values to the personal autonomy of the mother and the social interest in population control.

SEEING

The metaphor of balancing points to the process of combining values. But we do not combine values like watercolors. We respond to values situated in subjects. "Balancing" is an inadequate metaphor for moral thinking in leaving out of account the central moral transaction—the response of human beings to other human beings.[18] In making moral judgments we respond to those human beings whom we see.

The metaphor of sight is a way of emphasizing the need for perception, whether by eyes or ears or touch, of those we take as subjects to whom we respond. Seeing in any case is more than the registration of a surface. It is a penetration yielding some sense of the other's structure, so that the experiencing of another is never merely visual or auditory or tactile. We see the features and comprehend the humanity at the same time. Look at the fetus, say the anti-abortionists, and you will see humanity. How long, they ask, can a man turn his head and pretend that he just doesn't see?

An accusation of blindness, however, does not seem to advance moral argument. A claim to see where others do not see is a usual claim of charlatans. "Illumination" or "enlightenment" appear to transcend experi-

[18]See Enda McDonagh. "The Structure and the Basis of the Moral Experience," *Irish Theological Quarterly* XXXVIII, No. 1 (Maynooth, Ireland: St. Patrick's College, 1971) 3–20.

ence and make moral disputation impossible. "Visionary" is often properly a term of disparagement. Is not an appeal to sight the end of rational debate?

In morals, as in epistemology, there is nonetheless no substitute for perception. Are animals within the range of beings with a right to life, and babies not, as Michael Tooley has recently suggested? Should trees be persons, as Christopher Stone has recently maintained?[19] Questions of this kind are fundamentally frivolous for they point to the possibility of moral argument while attempting to deny the foundation of moral argument, our ability to recognize human persons. If a person could in no way perceive another person to be like himself, he would be incapable of moral response. If a person cannot perceive a cat or a tree as different from himself, he cuts off the possibility of argument. Debate should not end with pointing, but it must begin there.

Is there a contradiction in the opponents of abortion appealing to perception when fetuses are normally invisible? Should one not hold that until beings are seen they have not entered the ranks of society? Falling below the threshold of sight, do not fetuses fall below the threshold of humanity? If the central moral transaction is response to the other person, are not fetuses peculiarly weak subjects to elicit our response? These questions pinpoint the principal task of the defenders of the fetus—to make the fetus visible. The task is different only in degree from that assumed by defenders of other persons who have been or are "overlooked." For centuries, color acted as a psychological block to perception, and the blindness induced by color provided a sturdy basis for discrimination. Minorities of various kinds exist today who are "invisible" and therefore unlikely to be "heard" in the democratic process. Persons literally out of sight of society in prisons and mental institutions are often not "recognized" as fellow humans by the world with which they have "lost touch." In each of these instances those who seek to vindicate the rights of the unseen must begin by calling attention to their existence. "Look" is the exhortation they address to the callous and the negligent.[20]

Perception of fetuses is possible with not substantially greater effort 40 than that required to pierce the physical or psychological barriers to recognizing other human beings. The main difficulty is everyone's reluctance to accept the extra burdens of care imposed by an expansion of the numbers in whom humanity is recognized. It is generally more convenient

[19]Michael Tooley, "Abortion and Infanticide." 64–65: Christopher Stone. "Should Trees Have Standing? Toward Legal Rights for Natural Objects." 45 *Southern California Law Review* (Los Angeles: Univ. So. Calif., 1972) 450–501. The same position on trees is taken by Justice William O. Douglas, dissenting, in *Sierra Club v. Morton*, 405 *United States Reports*, (1972) 727.

[20]On our complaisance if we cannot see mutilations or the mutilated. David Daube, *Legal Problems in Medical Advance* (Jerusalem, 1971) 19–22. See also the extensive treatment of the meaning of touch in Ashley Montagu, *Touching* (New York: Columbia, 1972).

to have to consider only one's kin, one's peers, one's country, one's race. Seeing requires personal attention and personal response. The emotion generated by identification with a human form is necessary to overcome the inertia which is protected by a vision restricted to a convenient group. If one is willing to undertake the risk that more will be required in one's action, fetuses may be seen in multiple ways—circumstantially, by the observation of a pregnant woman; photographically, by pictures of life in the womb; scientifically, in accounts written by investigators of prenatal life and child psychologists; visually, by observing a blood transfusion or an abortion while the fetus is alive or by examination of a fetal corpse after death.[21] The proponent of abortion is invited to consider the organism kicking the mother, swimming peacefully in amniotic fluid, responding to the prick of an instrument, being extracted from the womb, sleeping in death. Is the kicker or swimmer similar to him or to her? Is the response to pain like his or hers? Will his or her own face look much different in death?

RESPONSE

Response to the fetus begins with grasp of the data which yield the fetus's structure. That structure is not merely anatomical form; it is dynamic—we apprehend the fetus's origin and end. It is this apprehension which makes response to the nameless fetus different from the conscious analogizing that goes on when we name a cat. Seeing, we are linked to the being in the womb by more than an inventory of shared physical characteristics and by more than a number of made-up psychological characteristics. The weakness of the being as potential recalls our own potential state, the helplessness of the being evokes the human condition of contingency. We meet another human subject.

Seeing is impossible apart from experience, but experience is the most imprecise of terms. What kind of experience counts, and whose? There are experiences which only women and usually only those within ages of 14 to 46 who are fertile can have: conceiving a child, carrying a child, having an abortion, being denied an abortion, giving birth. There are experiences only a fetus can have: being carried, being aborted, being born. There is the experience of obstetricians who regularly deliver children and occasionally abort them; there is the differently textured experience of the professional abortionist. There is the experience of nurses who prepare the mother for abortion, care for her after the abortion, and dispose of the aborted fetus. There is the experience of physicians, social workers, and

---

[21]See, e.g., Beth Day and H. M. I. Liley, *Modern Motherhood: Pregnancy, Childbirth, and the Newborn Baby* (1967 ed.) 23–24, 30–31. In the brief of the state in *Roe v. Wade*, Supreme Court of the United States, October Term, 1970, number 980, possibly the most effective argument was the photograph of an outstretched fetal hand; it was recognizably a human hand.

ministers, who advise a woman to have an abortion or not to have one. There is the experience of those who enforce a law against abortion, and those who stealthily or openly, for profit or for conscience's sake, defy it. There is the experience of those who have sexual intercourse knowing that abortion is or is not a remedy if an accidental pregnancy should result. There is the experience of society at large of a pattern of uncontrolled abortion or of its regulation.

Some arguments are unduly exclusivist in the experience they will admit. Those who suggest that abortion is peculiarly a matter for women disqualify men because the unique experience of pregnancy is beyond their achievement. Yet such champions of abortion do not regularly disqualify sterile women whose experience of pregnancy must be as vicarious as a man's. Tertullian taught that only those who have known motherhood themselves have a right to speak from experience on the choices presented by abortion.[22] Yet even Tertullian did not go so far as to say that only mothers who had both given birth and had had abortions were qualified to speak. Efforts of this sort to restrict those who are competent rest on a confusion between the relevant and the personal. You do not have to be a judge to know that bribery is evil or a slave to know that slavery is wrong. Vicarious experience, in this as in other moral matters, is a proper basis for judgment.

Vicarious experience appears strained to the outer limit when one is asked to consider the experience of the fetus. No one remembers being born, no one knows what it is like to die. Empathy may, however, supply for memory, as it does in other instances when we refer to the experience of infants who cannot speak or to the experience of death by those who cannot speak again. The experience of the fetus is no more beyond our knowledge than the experience of the baby and the experience of the dying.

Participation in an abortion is another sort of experience relevant to moral judgment. Generals are not thought of as the best judges of the morality of war, nor is their experience thought to be unaffected by their profession, but they should be heard, when the permissibility of war is urged. Obstetricians are in an analogous position, their testimony subject to a discount. The testimony of professional abortionists is also relevant, although subject to an even greater discount. Nurses are normally more disinterested witnesses. They speak as ones who have empathized with the female patient, disposed of the fetal remains, and, like the Red Cross in wartime, have known what the action meant by seeing the immediate consequences.

The experience of individuals becomes a datum of argument through autobiography and testimony, inference and empathy. The experience of a society has to be captured by the effort of sociologists and novelists,

[22]Tertullian, *De anima* (ed. J.H. Wasink, 1947) 25.5.

historians and lawyers, psychologists and moralists; and it is strongly affected by the prism of the medium used. Typically the proponents of abortion have put emphasis on quantitative evidence—for example, on the number of abortions performed in the United States or in the world at large. The assumption underlying this appeal to experience is that what is done by a great many persons cannot be bad, is indeed normal. This assumption, often employed when sexual behavior is studied, is rarely favored when racial discrimination or war are considered. It is a species of natural law, identifying the usual with the natural. The experience appealed to counts as argument only for those who accept this identification and consider the usual the good.

Psychological evidence has been called upon by the opponents of abortion. Trauma and guilt have been found associated with the election of abortion. The inference is made that abortion is the cause of this unhappiness. As in many arguments based on social consequences, however, the difficulty is to isolate the cause. Do persons undergoing abortion have character predispositions which would in any event manifest themselves in psychic disturbance? Do they react as they do because of social conditioning which could be changed to encourage a positive attitude to abortion? Is the act of abortion at the root of their problems or the way in which the process is carried out? None of these questions is settled; the evidence is most likely to be convincing to those already inclined to believe that abortion is an evil.[23]

Another kind of experience is that embedded in law. In Roman law where children generally had little status independent of their parents, the fetus was "a portion of the mother or her viscera." This view persisted in nineteenth-century American tort law, Justice Holmes in a leading case describing the fetus as "a part of the body of the mother." In recent years, however, the tort cases have asked, in Justice Bok's phrase, if the fetus is a person; and many courts have replied affirmatively. The change, a striking revolution in torts law, came from the courts incorporating into their thought new biological data on the fetus as a living organism.[24] Evidence on how the fetus is now perceived is also provided by another kind of case where abortion itself is not involved—the interpretation in wills and trusts of gifts to "children" or "issue." In these cases a basic question is, "What is the common understanding of people when they speak of children?" The answer, given repeatedly by American courts, is that "the average testator" speaking of children means to include a being who has been conceived but not born.[25] Free from the distorting pressures of the conflict over abortion,

48

[23]See Callahan, *Abortion: Law, Choice and Morality* (op. cit.) 67–71.

[24]On this development, see Noonan, ed., *The Morality of Abortion* (op. cit.) 6–7, 226–230; William Prosser, *Handbook of the Law of Torts* (St. Paul: West Publ. Co., 3d ed., 1964) sec. 56; Edwin W. Patterson, *Law in a Scientific Age* (New York: Columbia, 1963) 65.

[25]A. James Casner, ed., *American Law of Property* (Boston: Little, Brown, 1952) vol. VII, sec. 22.3; 249; sec. 22, 42, 358.

this evidence of the common understanding suggests that social experience has found the fetus to be within the family of man.

The most powerful expression of common experience is that given by art and literature. Birth has almost everywhere been celebrated in painting. The Nativity has been a symbol of gladness not only because of its sacral significance, but because of its human meaning—"joy that a man is born into the world." Abortion, in contrast, has rarely been the subject of art. Unlike other forms of death, abortion has not been seen by painters as a release, a sacrifice, or a victory. Characteristically it has stood for sterility, futility, and absurdity. Consider, for example, Orozco's mural, "Gods of the Modern World" in the Baker Library at Dartmouth College.[26] Academia is savagely satirized by portraying professors as impotent attendants in an operating room in which truth is stillborn. Bottled fetuses in the foreground attest the professors' habitual failure. The entire force of the criticism of academic achievement comes from the painter's knowledge that everyone will recognize abortion as a grave defeat and the bottling of dead fetuses as a travesty of healthy birth. Whoever sees such a painting sees how mankind has commonly experienced abortion.

In contemporary American literature, John Updike's *Couples* comments directly upon abortion, using it at a crucial turn as both event and symbol. Piet Hanema, married to Angela, has promiscuously pursued other married women, among them Foxy Whitman, who is now pregnant by him. They have this exchange:

> All I know is what *I* honestly want. I want this damn thing to stop growing inside me.
>
> Don't cry.
>
> Nature is *so* stupid. It has all my maternal glands working, do you know what that means, Piet? You know what the great thing about being pregnant I found out was? It's something I just couldn't have imagined. You're never alone. When you have a baby inside you you are not alone. It's a person.[27]

To procure the abortion it becomes necessary for Piet to surrender his own wife Angela to Freddy, who has access to the abortionist. Embarked upon his course Piet does not stop at this act, which destroys his own marriage irretrievably. Foxy's feelings at the time of the abortion are then described through Piet:

> Not until days later, after Foxy had survived the forty-eight hours alone in the house with Toby and the test of Ken's return from Chicago, did Piet learn, not from Freddy but from her as told by Freddy, that at the moment of anesthesia she had panicked; she had tried to strike the

---

[26]Reproduced in *The Orozco Frescoes at Dartmouth* (Dartmouth College, 1934).
[27]*Couples* (New York: Knopf, 1968) 360.

Negress pressing the sweet, sweet mask to her face and through the first waves of ether had continued to cry that she should go home, that she was supposed to have this baby, that the child's father was coming to smash the door down with a hammer and would stop them.[28]

Updike's only comment as an author is given as Piet then goes to Foxy's 52 house: "Death, once invited in, leaves his muddy bootprints everywhere."[29] The elements of the experience of abortion are here: the hatred of the depersonalized burden growing, willy-nilly, in the womb; the sense of a baby, a person, one's own child; the desperate desire to be rid of the burden extinguishing all other considerations; the ineffectual hope of delivery the moment before the child's death. A mask covers the human face of the mother. Symbolically the abortion seals a course of infidelity. Conclusively it becomes death personified.

THE EXPERIENCE OF CHRISTIANS

Ethics generally or Christian ethics specifically do not exist in the fashion of some impersonal science, so that one can say with professorial pomposity, "Ethics teaches." Ethics exists in particular men and women formulating rules and sharing values within particular communities. For the Christian, vicarious experience of special significance is the experience of the religious community of which he or she is a part. Reference to that experience distinguishes the ethics done by Christians from the ethics done by Hindus or humanists. No one makes up an ethical position out of whole cloth. Everyone speaks from inside an environment.[30] The Christian speaks not only from a vantage point in a civil society, but as a member of an ecclesial community which is both contemporary and historical. It is in this sense that there is an experience which Christians share and consequent on it, an ethics done by Christians. The experience of Christians does not cancel other social experience. A Christian forming an ethical position cannot ignore other social experience. He or she incorporates such experience with the experience of Christians in formulating a response.

Since a time contemporaneous with the composition of the Gospels, the teaching of Christians has been that abortion is a denial of human love and the destruction of a being created in the image of God. In nineteen centuries of Christian life, the social discipline enforcing the teaching has varied and the possibility of exceptions to it has been explored. The teaching itself has remained firm. At one level the teaching appears impersonal—the assertion of a rule. But the rule protects values of life,

[28]Ibid., 378–379.

[29]Ibid., 380.

[30]Cf. Josef Fuchs, S.J., "The Absoluteness of Moral Terms," *Gregorianum* LII (Rome: Pontificia Universita Gregoriana, 1971) 453.

responsibility, and love located in persons, and these values are what the Christian community has held dear in responding to human persons in the light of the Christian's imitation of Christ. The rule against abortion is founded on the experience of Christians. It was formed early, maintained for several centuries in a hostile society, then reflected in the law of professedly Christian nations, and accepted in each generation by the community of believers as embodying the requirements of the love of neighbor and of God.[31]

To be uninterested in the history of this Christian conviction is perhaps an unexceptionable stand for a non-Christian; for a Christian it is to disavow the community in time. New moral insights, as experience changes and consciousness develops, are always possible and welcome. But to be genuine development, such insights must take into account the response of the community in the past. To ignore the earlier response is to cut oneself off from the community as it has historically existed. As members of this community, we are called to respond to persons today taking seriously the values of persons in the past.

This response to the community is integrally linked for the Christian 56 to faith. His or her own experience living as a Christian person is to be taken into account. The Christian person responds to the persons, the friends, who are encountered. At the center of the circle of friends, past and present, to whom the Christian responds, is Jesus, so that our response is not to dead history—let the dead bury the dead—but to one who has called us as likenesses and friends.

Questions and Suggestions for Writing

1. In paragraph 6 Noonan summarizes an artificial case set forth by Michael Tooley, about a kitten that, because of an injection, will develop into a "cat possessed of the brain and psychological capabilities of adult human beings." Tooley intuits (Noonan reports) that it would not be wrong to kill the kitten. Does your intuition lead you to the same conclusion? Whether it does or not, on reflection do you think it would be wrong to kill such a kitten? Finally, do you think that this artificial case is helpful in thinking about the morality of abortion? Why, or why not?

2. Why do you think Noonan decided to discuss "artificial cases" at the opening of his essay, rather than later? In fact, why does he include "artificial cases," for he finds them of no use in thinking about issues?

3. Noonan says that opponents of abortion contend that "the fetus is human" and that it is a "person." Could there be humans who are not persons? Persons who are not humans? What aspects of being a human or a person does Noonan

---

[31]On this history, see my "An Almost Absolute Value in History," Noonan, ed. *The Morality of Abortion* (op. cit.) 8–50.

attribute to the fetus? What aspects of being a human or a person does he concede that the fetus lacks? How would he reply to the objection that (a) persons are rational—have the power to think, to reason; and (b) no fetus is rational?

4. In discussing "hard cases," Noonan speaks (para. 12) of "the fetal desire to live." Do you accept this assertion? And do you accept the position, set forth in this paragraph, that in the cases of severely deformed children, "The feelings of the parents are the actual consideration"?

5. In the first sentence of the section called "Direct and Indirect" (para. 17), what does Noonan mean by "paradigmatic arguments"?

6. Noonan favors solving the problem of pregnancy owing to rape either by "adoption" or by "destruction of the sperm in the one to three days elapsed between insemination and impregnation." What reason(s) does he have against destruction of the fertilized ovum two or three days later? A week or a month later?

7. Why does Noonan reject what he calls (para. 21) the "rule of fetus first"?

8. In paragraph 21 Noonan says that abortion is morally acceptable when it is performed in order to save the life of the mother. How well does he support this assertion? Might one argue against his view, on the ground that the mother has lived as an adult, and it is now only fair to let the fetus have a chance at a mature human life?

9. Write a paragraph in which you explain what Noonan means by "line-drawing" and "balancing," and why he thinks "balancing" is a better metaphor than "line-drawing" to describe ethical decision-making. You may quote a few phrases, but the paragraph should consist chiefly of your own words.

10. Why do you think Noonan reserved "The Experience of Christians" for the end of his essay? Would it have made a good beginning? Why, or why not?

10

Should Hiroshima
Have Been Bombed?

Paul Fussell

Hiroshima: A Soldier's View

Many years ago in New York I saw on the side of a bus a whiskey ad which I've remembered all this time, for it's been for me a model of the brief poem. Indeed, I've come upon few short poems subsequently that evinced more genuine poetic talent. The ad consisted of two lines of "free verse," thus:

> In life, experience is the great teacher.
> In Scotch, Teacher's is the great experience.

For present purposes we can jettison the second line (licking our lips ruefully as it disappears), leaving the first to encapsulate a principle whose banality suggests that it enshrines a most useful truth. I bring up the

Paul Fussell, born in 1924 in Pasadena, California, served as a combat officer in Europe during World War II. He has taught at Connecticut College and Rutgers University, and now teaches at the University of Pennsylvania. A specialist in English literature of the eighteenth century, he has also written a book about World War I as well as essays for popular magazines such as Harper's *and* The New Republic *on widely varied subjects, including travel, gun control, and* The Boy Scout Handbook. *The essay reprinted here first appeared in* The New Republic, *a liberal weekly, in 1981.*

matter this August, the thirty-sixth anniversary of the A-bombing of Hiroshima and Nagasaki, to focus on something suggested by the long debate about the ethics, if any, of that affair: namely, the importance of experience, sheer vulgar experience, in influencing, if not determining, one's views about the first use of the bomb. And the experience I'm talking about is that of having come to grips, face to face, with an enemy who designs your death. The experience is common to those in the infantry and the Marines and even the line Navy, to those, in short, who fought the Second World War mindful always that their mission was, as they were repeatedly told, "to close with the enemy and destroy him." I think there's something to be learned about that war, as well as about the tendency of historical memory unwittingly to resolve ambiguity, by considering some of the ways testimonies emanating from experience complicate attitudes about the cruel ending of that cruel war.

"What did you do in the Great War, Daddy?" The recruiting poster deserves ridicule and contempt, of course, but its question is embarrassingly relevant here. The problem is one that touches on the matter of social class in America. Most of those with firsthand experience of the war at its worst were relatively inarticulate and have remained silent. Few of those destined to be destroyed if the main islands had had to be invaded went on to become our most eloquent men of letters or our most impressive ethical theorists or professors of history or international jurists. The testimony of experience has come largely from rough diamonds like James Jones and William Manchester, who experienced the war in the infantry and the Marine Corps. Both would agree with the point, if not perhaps the tone, of a remark about Hiroshima made by a naval officer menaced by the kamikazes off Okinawa: "Those were the best burned women and children I ever saw." Anticipating objection from the inexperienced, Jones, in his book *WWII*, is careful to precede his chapter on Hiroshima with one detailing the plans already in motion for the infantry assaults on the home islands of Kyushu, scheduled for November 1945, and ultimately Honshu. The forthcoming invasion of Kyushu, he notes, "was well into its collecting and stockpiling stages before the war ended." (The island of Saipan was designated a main ammunition and supply base for the invasion, and if you visit it today you can see some of the assembled stuff still sitting there.) "The assault troops were chosen and already in training," Jones reminds us, and he illuminates the situation by the light of experience:

> What it must have been like to some old-timer buck sergeant or staff sergeant who had been through Guadalcanal or Bougainville or the Philippines, to stand on some beach and watch this huge war machine beginning to stir and move all around him and know that he very likely had survived this far only to fall dead on the dirt of Japan's home islands, hardly bears thinking about.

On the other hand, John Kenneth Galbraith is persuaded that the Japanese would have surrendered by November without an invasion. He thinks the atom bombs were not decisive in bringing about the surrender and he implies that their use was unjustified. What did he do in the war? He was in the Office of Price Administration in Washington, and then he was director of the United States Strategic Bombing Survey. He was thirty-seven in 1945, and I don't demand that he experience having his ass shot off. I just note that he didn't. In saying this I'm aware of its offensive implications ad hominem. But here I think that approach justified. What's at stake in an infantry assault is so entirely unthinkable to those without experience of one, even if they possess very wide-ranging imaginations and sympathies, that experience is crucial in this case.

A similar remoteness from experience, as well as a similar rationalistic abstraction, seems to lie behind the reaction of an anonymous reviewer of William Manchester's *Goodbye Darkness: A Memoir of the Pacific War* for the *New York Review of Books*. First of all the reviewer dislikes Manchester's calling the enemy Nips and Japs, but what really shakes him (her?) is this passage:

> After Biak the enemy withdrew to deep caverns. Rooting them out became a bloody business which reached its ultimate horrors in the last months of the war. You think of the lives which would have been lost in an invasion of Japan's home islands—a staggering number of Americans but millions more of Japanese—and you thank God for the atomic bomb.

Thank God for the atomic bomb. From this, "one recoils," says the reviewer. One does, doesn't one?

In an interesting exchange last year in the *New York Review of Books*, ⁴ Joseph Alsop and David Joravsky set forth the by now familiar arguments on both sides of the debate. You'll be able to guess which sides they chose once you know that Alsop experienced capture by the Japanese at Hong Kong in 1942 and that Joravsky made no mortal contact with the Japanese: a young soldier, he was on his way to the Pacific when the war ended. The editors of the *New York Review* have given their debate the tendentious title "Was the Hiroshima Bomb Necessary?"—surely an unanswerable question (unlike "Was It Effective?") and one suggesting the intellectual difficulties involved in imposing ex post facto a rational ethics on this event. Alsop focuses on the power and fanaticism of War Minister Anami, who insisted that Japan fight to the bitter end, defending the main islands with the same means and tenacity with which it had defended Iwo and Okinawa. He concludes: "Japanese surrender could never have been obtained, at any rate without the honor-satisfying bloodbath envisioned by . . . Anami, if the hideous destruction of Hiroshima and Nagasaki had not finally galvanized the peace advocates into tearing up the entire Japanese book of rules." The Japanese planned to deploy the undefeated bulk of their ground forces, over two million men, plus 10,000 kamikaze planes, in a suicidal defense. That fact, says Alsop, makes it absurd to "hold the common view, by now hardly challenged by anyone, that the decision to drop the two bombs on Japan was wicked in itself, and that President Truman and all others who joined in making or who [like Oppenheimer] assented to this decision shared in the wickedness." And in explanation of "the two bombs" Alsop adds: "The true, climactic, and successful effort of the Japanese peace advocates . . . did not begin in deadly earnest until *after* the second bomb had destroyed Nagasaki. The Nagasaki bomb was thus the trigger to all the developments that led to peace."

Joravsky, now a professor of history at Northwestern, argues on the other hand that those who decided to use the bomb on cities betray defects of "reason and self-restraint." It all needn't have happened, he asserts, "if the U.S. government had been willing to take a few more days and to be a bit more thoughtful in opening the age of nuclear warfare." But of course in its view it wasn't doing that: that's a historian's tidy hindsight. The government was ending the war conclusively, as well as irrationally re-membering Pearl Harbor with a vengeance. It didn't know then what everyone knows now about leukemia and carcinoma and birth defects. History, as Eliot's "Gerontion" notes,

> has many cunning passages, contrived corridors
> And issues, deceives with whispering ambitions,
> Guides us by vanities. . . .
> > Think
> Neither fear nor courage saves us. Unnatural vices
> Are fathered by our heroism. Virtues
> Are forced upon us by our impudent crimes.

Understanding the past means feeling its pressure on your pulses and that's harder than Javorsky thinks.

The Alsop–Javorsky debate, which can be seen as reducing finally to a collision between experience and theory, was conducted with a certain civilized respect for evidence. Not so the way the new scurrilous agitprop[1] *New Statesman* conceives those favoring the bomb and those opposing. They are, on the one hand, says Bruce Page, "the imperialist class-forces acting through Harry Truman," and, on the other, those representing "the humane, democratic virtues"—in short, "fascists" opposed to "populists." But ironically the bomb saved the lives not of any imperialists but only of the low and humble, the quintessentially democratic huddled masses—the conscripted enlisted men manning the fated invasion divisions. Bruce Page was nine years old when the war ended. For a man of that experience,

[1]agitprop Propaganda meant to agitate, especially Communist propaganda. [Editors' note]

phrases like "imperialist class-forces" come easily, and the issues look perfectly clear.

He's not the only one to have forgotten, if he ever knew, the savagery of the Pacific war. The dramatic postwar Japanese success at hustling and merchandising and tourism has (happily, in many ways) effaced for most people important elements of the assault context in which Hiroshima should be viewed. It is easy to forget what Japan was like before it was first destroyed and then humiliated, tamed, and constitutionalized by the West. "Implacable, treacherous, barbaric"—those were Admiral Halsey's[2] characterizations of the enemy, and at the time few facing the Japanese would deny that they fit to a T. One remembers the captured American airmen locked for years in packing crates, the prisoners decapitated, the gleeful use of bayonets on civilians. The degree to which Americans register shock and extraordinary shame about the Hiroshima bomb correlates closely with lack of information about the war.

And the savagery was not just on one side. There was much sadism   8 and brutality—undeniably racist—on ours. No Marine was fully persuaded of his manly adequacy who didn't have a well-washed Japanese skull to caress and who didn't have a go at treating surrendering Japs as rifle targets. Herman Wouk remembers it correctly while analyzing Ensign Keith in *The Caine Mutiny:* "Like most of the naval executioners of Kwajalein, he seemed to regard the enemy as a species of animal pest." And the enemy felt the same way about us: "From the grim and desperate taciturnity with which the Japanese died, they seemed on their side to believe they were contending with an invasion of large armed ants." Hiroshima seems to follow in natural sequence: "This obliviousness on both sides to the fact that the opponents were human beings may perhaps be cited as the key to the many massacres of the Pacific war." Since the Japanese resisted so madly, let's pour gasoline into their emplacements and light it and shoot the people afire who try to get out. Why not? Why not blow them all up? Why not, indeed, drop a new kind of big bomb on them? Why allow one more American high school kid to see his intestines blown out of his body and spread before him in the dirt while he screams when we can end the whole thing just like that?

On Okinawa, only weeks before Hiroshima, 123,000 Japanese and Americans *killed* each other. "Just awful" was the comment not of some pacifist but of MacArthur. One million American casualties was his estimate of the cost of the forthcoming invasion. And that invasion was not just a hypothetical threat, as some theorists have argued. It was genuinely in train, as I know because I was to be in it. When the bomb ended the war

---

[2]**Admiral Halsey** William F. ("Bull") Halsey (1882–1959) commanded the U.S. 3rd Fleet during 1944 and 1945 and directed the successful naval operations against Japan in the western Pacific. [Editors' note]

I was in the 45th Infantry Division, which had been through the European war to the degree that it had needed to be reconstituted two or three times. We were in a staging area near Reims, ready to be shipped across the United States for final preparation in the Philippines. My division was to take part in the invasion of Honshu in March 1946. (The earlier invasion of Kyushu was to be carried out by 700,000 infantry already in the Pacific.) I was a twenty-one-year-old second lieutenant leading a rifle platoon. Although still officially in one piece, in the German war I had already been wounded in the leg and back severely enough to be adjudged, after the war, 40 percent disabled. But even if my legs buckled whenever I jumped out of the back of the truck, my condition was held to be satisfactory for whatever lay ahead. When the bombs dropped and news began to circulate that "Operation Olympic" would not, after all, take place, that we would not be obliged to run up the beaches near Tokyo assault-firing while being mortared and shelled, for all the fake manliness of our façades we cried with relief and joy. We were going to live. We were going to grow up to adulthood after all. When the *Enola Gay* dropped its package, "There were cheers," says John Toland, "over the intercom; it meant the end of the war."

Those who cried and cheered are very different from high-minded, guilt-ridden GIs we're told about by the late J. Glenn Gray in *The Warriors* (1959). During the war in Europe Gray was an interrogator in the Counter Intelligence Corps, and in that capacity he underwent the war at division level. After the war he became a professor of philosophy at Colorado College (never, I've thought, the venue of very much reality) and a distinguished editor of Heidegger. There's no doubt that Gray's outlook on everything was noble and elevated. But *The Warriors*, his meditation on modern soldiering, gives every sign of remoteness from experience. Division headquarters is miles behind the places where the soldiers experience terror and madness and relieve these pressures by sadism. "When the news of the atomic bombing of Hiroshima and Nagasaki came," Gray asks us to believe, "many an American soldier felt shocked and ashamed." But why, we ask? Because we'd bombed civilians? We'd been doing that for years and, besides the two bombs, wiped out 10,000 Japanese troops, not now often mentioned, John Hersey's kindly physicians and Jesuit priests being more touching. Were Gray's soldiers shocked and ashamed because we'd obliterated whole towns? We'd done that plenty of times. If at division headquarters some felt shocked and ashamed, down in the rifle companies none did, although Gray says they did:

> The combat soldier knew better than did Americans at home what those bombs meant in suffering and injustice. The man of conscience realized intuitively that the vast majority of Japanese in both cities were no more, if no less, guilty of the war than were his own parents, sisters, or brothers.

I find this canting nonsense: the purpose of dropping the bombs was not to "punish" people but to stop the war. To intensify the shame he insists we feel, Gray seems willing to fiddle the facts. The Hiroshima bomb, he says, was dropped "without any warning." But actually, two days before, 720,000 leaflets were dropped on the city urging everyone to get out and indicating that the place was going to be obliterated. Of course few left.

Experience whispers that the pity is not that we used the bomb to end the Japanese war but that it wasn't ready earlier to end the German one. If only it could have been rushed into production faster and dropped at the right moment on the Reich chancellery or Berchtesgaden or Hitler's military headquarters in East Prussia or—Wagnerian *coup de théâtre*[3]—at Rommel's phony state funeral, most of the Nazi hierarchy could have been pulverized immediately, saving not just the embarrassment of the Nuremburg trials but the lives of about four million Jews, Poles, Slavs, gypsies, and other "sub-humans," not to mention the lives and limbs of millions of Allied and Axis soldiers. If the bomb could have been ready even as late as July 1944, it could have reinforced the Von Stauffenberg plot and ended the war then and there. If the bomb had only been ready in time, the men of my infantry platoon would not have been killed and maimed.

All this is not to deny that like the Russian revolution, the atomic 12 bombing of Japan was a vast historical tragedy, and every passing year magnifies the dilemma into which it has thrown the contemporary world. As with the Russian revolution there are two sides—that's why it's a tragedy rather than a disaster—and unless we are simple-mindedly cruel, like Bruce Page, we need to be painfully aware of both at once. To observe that from the viewpoint of the war's victims-to-be the bomb was precisely the right thing to drop is to purchase no immunity from horror. See, for example, the new book *Unforgettable Fire: Pictures Drawn by Atomic Bomb Survivors*, issued by the Japan Broadcasting Corporation and distributed here by Pantheon Books. It presents a number of amateur colored-pencil, pastel, and water-color depictions of the scene of the Hiroshima bombing made by the middle-aged and elderly survivors for a peace exhibition in 1975. In addition to the heartrending pictures the book offers brief moments of memoir, not for the weak-stomached:

> While taking my severely wounded wife out to the riverbank . . . , I was
> horrified indeed at the sight of a stark naked man standing in the rain
> with his eyeball in his palm. He looked to be in great pain but there was
> nothing I could do for him. I wonder what became of him. Even today, I
> vividly remember the sight. It was simply miserable.

The drawings and paintings, whose often childish style makes them doubly touching, are of skin hanging down, breasts torn off, people bleeding and

---

[3]**Wagnerian coup de théâtre** An unexpected and dramatic event, of the sort found in the operas of Richard Wagner (1813–1883). [Editors' note]

burning, dying mothers nursing dead babies. A bloody woman holds a bloody child in the ruins of a house, and the artist remembers her calling, "Please help this child! Someone, please help this child. Please help! Someone, please." As Samuel Johnson said of the smothering of the innocent Desdemona[4] in another tragedy, "It is not to be endured." Nor, we should notice, is an infantryman's account of having his arm blown off in the Arno Valley in Italy in 1944:

> I wanted to die and die fast. I wanted to forget this miserable world. I cursed the war, I cursed the people who were responsible for it, I cursed God for putting me here . . . to suffer for something I never did or knew anything about. For this was hell, and I never imagined anything or anyone could suffer so bitterly. I screamed and cursed. Why? Why? What had I done to deserve this? But no answer came. I yelled for medics, because subconsciously I wanted to live. I tried to apply my right hand over my bleeding stump, but I didn't have the strength to hold it. I looked to the left of me and saw the bloody mess that was once my left arm; its fingers and palm were turned upward, like a flower looking to the sun for its strength.

The future scholar-critic of rhetoric who writes *The History of Canting in the Twentieth Century* will find much to study in the utterances of those who dilate on the wickedness of the bomb-droppers. He will realize that such utterance can perform for the speaker a valuable double function. First, it can display the fineness of his moral weave. And second, by implication it can also inform the audience that during the war he was not socially so unfortunate as to find himself at the cutting edge of the ground forces, where he might have had to compromise the pure clarity of his moral vision by the experience of weighing his own life against other people's. Down there, which is where the other people were in the war, is the place where coarse self-interest is the rule. When the young soldier with the wild eyes comes at you firing, do you shoot him in the foot, hoping he'll be hurt badly enough to drop or mis-aim the gun with which he is going to kill you, or do you shoot him in the chest and make certain he stops being your mortal enemy? It would be stupid to expect soldiers to be very sensitive humanitarians ("Moderation in war is imbecility"—Admiral of the Fleet Lord Fisher); actually, only the barest decencies can be expected of them. They didn't start the war, except in the terrible sense hinted in Frederic Manning's observation based on his experience in the Great War: "War is waged by men; not by beasts, or by gods. It is a peculiarly human activity. To call it a crime against mankind is to miss at least half its significance; it is also the punishment of a crime." Knowing that fact by experience, soldiers have every motive for wanting a war stopped, by any means.

[4]**Desdemona** Heroine in Shakespeare's *Othello*. [Editors' note]

The predictable stupidity, parochialism, and greed in the postwar international mismanagement of the whole nuclear problem should not tempt us to misimagine the circumstances of the bomb's first "use." Nor should our well-justified fears and suspicions occasioned by the capture of the nuclear business by the mendacious classes (cf. Three Mile Island) tempt us to infer retrospectively extraordinary corruption, cruelty, and swinishness in those who decided to drop the bomb. Times change. Harry Truman was not a fascist, but a democrat. He was as close to a real egalitarian as we've seen in high office for a very long time. He is the only president in my lifetime who ever had the experience of commanding a small unit of ground troops obliged to kill people. He knew better than his subsequent critics what he was doing. The past, which as always did not know the future, acted in ways that ask to be imagined before they are condemned. Or even before they are simplified.

Questions and Suggestions for Writing

1. In his first paragraph, after quoting a whiskey advertisement, Fussell says that the "banality" of the ad "enshrines a most useful truth." Think of another "banal" line that seems to you to "enshrine a most useful truth," and then use it in the opening paragraph of an essay that is on some aspect of atomic warfare. (Write only the first paragraph, not the entire essay.)

2. Disparaging the opinion of John Kenneth Galbraith (para. 2), Fussell writes,

   > What did he do in the war? He was in the Office of Price Administration in Washington, and then he was director of the United States Strategic Bombing Survey. He was thirty-seven in 1945, and I don't demand that he experience having his ass shot off. I just note that he didn't. I'm aware of its offensive implications ad hominem. But here I think that approach justified.

   An ad hominem argument is directed personally at the arguer, rather than at the argument. Do you believe Fussell's comment about Galbraith's activities during the war is appropriate to this argument? Why?

3. In paragraph 4 Fussell characterizes as "unanswerable" the question of whether the Hiroshima bomb was "necessary." Why might someone think this question is unanswerable? Do you, perhaps, believe that either Connor (p. 386) or Alperovitz (p. 389) provides a satisfactory answer?

4. In paragraph 13 Fussell observes that in trenches, "coarse self-interest is the rule." Does he think that this self-interest justifies any methods of warfare or only explains why experienced combat soldiers believe such methods are justified?

5. Fussell's argument is, essentially, this: Those who had firsthand experience of fighting in World War II, and who were about to experience more of it in the Pacific, felt that "the bomb was precisely the right thing to drop." Let's assume that most (perhaps all) of Fussell's fellow soldiers felt (and feel) that way. But was it *right* for the United States to use the atomic bomb against a mostly

civilian population in order to save the lives of American (and indeed of Japanese) soldiers? (In the next essay in this book, Michael Walzer addresses this topic.)

6. Fussell's attack is hard-hitting. Does he hit below the belt? Does he alienate his reader by his methods of argument? Or does he always manage to keep the reader's goodwill? Explain.

7. Fussell says that the critics of the decision to drop the atom bomb on Japan are guilty of "cant"; that is, he accuses them of being hypocrites. Elaborate this charge in explicit detail, perhaps writing two paragraphs, totaling some 250 words. Then in another paragraph or two evaluate it, indicating whether and why you find the charge convincing or not.

Michael Walzer

Hiroshima: An Act of Terrorism

Paul Fussell's defense of the bombing of Hiroshima (*TNR*, August 22 and 29) is written, as he tells us repeatedly, from the standpoint of the ordinary GI. And that standpoint is human, all too human: let anyone die but me! There are no humanitarians in the foxholes. I can almost believe that. But Fussell's recital does remind me a little uneasily of the speech of that Conradian villain Gentleman Brown (in *Lord Jim*): "When it came to saving one's life in the dark, one didn't care who else went—three, thirty, three hundred people. . . ." And Brown went on to boast, very much as Fussell wants to do, that he made Jim wince with this "despairing frankness": "He very soon left off coming the righteous over me. . . ."

But we shouldn't be intimidated, and we shouldn't leave off, but accept the risks of righteousness. After all, Fussell's argument isn't only the argument of ordinary soldiers. It is also and more importantly the argument of ordinary generals—best expressed, I think, by the Prussian general von Moltke in 1880: "The greatest kindness in war is to bring it to a speedy conclusion. It should be allowable, with that end in view, to employ all means save those that are absolutely objectionable." But von Moltke, a stolid professional, probably still believed that the wholesale slaughter of civilians was "absolutely objectionable." With Fussell, it seems, there are no limits at all; anything goes, so long as it helps to bring the boys home.

Since 1980 Walzer (b. 1935) has been a member of the Institute for Advanced Study, at Princeton. His books on political morality include Obligations *(1970),* Just and Unjust Wars *(1977), and* Spheres of Justice *(1983). The essay reprinted here originally appeared in 1981 in* The New Republic, *as a response to the essay by Paul Fussell on page 374. The title of Walzer's essay, taken from the essay itself, is the editors'.*

Nor is this the argument only of GIs and generals. The bombing of Hiroshima was an act of terrorism; its purpose was political, not military. The goal was to kill enough civilians to shake the Japanese government and force it to surrender. And this is the goal of every terrorist campaign. Happily, none of today's terrorist movements have yet been able to kill on the scale of the modern state, and so they have not enjoyed successes as dramatic as the one Fussell describes. But their ordinary members, the terrorists in the foxholes, as it were, must think much as he does: if only we could kill enough people, not a dozen here and there, in a pub, a bus station, or a supermarket, but a whole city full, we could end the struggle once and for all, liberate our land, get the British out of Ireland, force the Israelis to accept a PLO state, and so on. To the boys of the IRA, to young Palestinians in Lebanon, that argument is surely as attractive as it was to the young Paul Fussell on his way to the Pacific in 1945. It is the same argument.

What is wrong with it? If war is indeed a tragedy, if its suffering is   4 inevitable, then nothing is wrong with it. War is war, and what happens, happens. In fact, however, war imposes choices on officers and enlisted men alike. "There wasn't a single soldier," says an Israeli officer who fought in the Six-Day War,[1] "who didn't at some stage have to decide, to choose, to make a moral decision. . . ." Fussell, who has written so beautifully about the literature of war, must know this to be true. And he must also know that there is a moral argument, different from his own argument, that shapes these military choices. Perhaps that argument is most often expounded by those professors far from the battlefield for whom he has such contempt. But it is an argument as old as war itself and one that many soldiers have believed and struggled to live by. It holds, most simply, that combat should be a struggle between combatants, and that noncombatants—civilian men, women, and children—should be protected as far as possible against its cruelties. "The soldier, be he friend or foe," wrote Douglas MacArthur, "is charged with the protection of the weak and the unarmed. It is the very essence and reason of his being . . . a sacred trust." Like policemen, firemen, and sailors at sea, soldiers have a responsibility to accept risks themselves rather than impose risks on ordinary citizens. That is a hard requirement when the soldiers are conscripts. Still, they are trained and armed for war and ordinary citizens are not; and that is a practical difference that makes a moral difference.

Consider how the risks of police work might be reduced, and how many more criminals might be caught, if we permitted the police to ignore the rights of ordinary citizens, to fire indiscriminately into crowds, to

---

[1]**Six-Day War** On June 5, 1967, with Arab troops mobilized on its borders, Israel launched air attacks on Egyptian, Syrian, and Jordanian air bases, and its land forces invaded and occupied the Sinai, Jerusalem's Old City, Jordan's West Bank, the Gaza Strip, and the Golan Heights. The United Nations secured a ceasefire on June 10. [Editors' note.]

punish the innocent relatives of criminals, and so on. But we don't grant such permissions. Nor are soldiers permitted comparable acts, even if they carry with them the promise of success.

There is a code. It is no doubt often broken, particularly in the heat of battle. But honorable men live by it while they can. Hiroshima was a violation of that code. So was the earlier terror bombing of cities— Hamburg, Dresden, Tokyo—but Hiroshima was worse because it was even more terrifying. Its long-term effects were literally unknowable by the men who decided to impose them. And the effects were not imposed, any more than those of the earlier bombing, in the heat of battle, face-to-face with enemy soldiers who aim to kill and have already killed comrades and friends. Though there were soldiers in Hiroshima, they were not the targets of the attack (or else we would have attacked a military base); the city was the target and all its inhabitants.

Fussell writes (again) as a democrat, on behalf of "the low and humble, the quintessentially democratic huddled masses—the conscripted enlisted men manning the fated invasion divisions." Given that standpoint, one might have expected him to question the U.S. demand for unconditional surrender that made the invasion of the Japanese islands seem absolutely necessary. There were people in the U.S. government in 1945 who thought a negotiated settlement possible without an invasion and without the use of the atomic bomb. Surely some attempt should have been made—not only for the sake of our own soldiers, but also for those other "huddled masses," the civilian inhabitants of Hiroshima (and Nagasaki too). Why don't they figure in Fussell's democratic reckoning! If Harry Truman's first responsibility was to American soldiers, he was not without responsibility elsewhere; no man is. And if one is reckoning, what about all the future victims of a politics and warfare from which restraint has been banished? Given the state of our political and moral order, with which Hiroshima probably has something to do, aren't we all more likely to be the victims than the beneficiaries of terrorist attacks?

Questions and Suggestions for Writing

1. In his third paragraph Walzer writes:

> The bombing of Hiroshima was an act of terrorism; its purpose was political, not military. The goal was to kill enough civilians to shake the Japanese government and force it to surrender. And this is the goal of every terrorist campaign.

First, explain in your own words the distinction Walzer makes between a military action and a terrorist action. Second, consider a famous remark of Karl von Clausewitz (1780–1831): "War is not merely a political act, but also a political instrument, a continuation of political relations, a carrying out of the same by other means." When you think about it, do you find this comment more helpful than Walzer's attempt to distinguish between a military action (i.e., war) and a political action? Or do you think that it remains useful to distinguish between war and politics, and military actions and terrorist actions? What would Walzer say about the Japanese attack on Pearl Harbor? Was it, too, "an act of terrorism"? If not, what was it?

2. In his closing paragraph, Walzer draws attention to Fussell's appeal to "democratic reckoning," and cites three considerations that Fussell ignores. What are they? Do they show that by Fussell's own criterion he should have opposed rather than favored the bomb?

3. Walzer insists that the aerial bombing of German and Japanese cities in 1945 violated the "code" of decent warfare. But he never mentions any violations of that "code" by the Germans or Japanese. Is this a flaw in his criticism of Fussell? Explain.

4. In paragraph 5 Walzer argues by analogy against Fussell. Restate Walzer's argument by making the analogy at each step. Do you find it convincing? How might Fussell reply?

5. Walzer calls attention (para. 4) to the traditional distinction between combatants and noncombatants, and to the traditional belief that noncombatants "should be protected, as far as possible, against [war's] cruelties." Can one successfully argue that these principles applied only in the past, when (for the most part) armies fought battles in relatively unpopulated places, and when warfare was mainly a matter of soldier against soldier? Today's most powerful weapons are not wielded by soldiers facing other soldiers. Technology has so changed the nature of warfare that a "combatant," pushing a button, can be far from the battlefield. Moreover, one might say that warfare today is mostly a matter of high-tech weaponry, rather than of soldiers, and thus the persons engaged in making weapons—whether scientists in universities or clerks filing documents in office buildings—are part of the combatant force. Write an essay of 500 to 750 words, evaluating Walzer's contention that noncombatants should be protected, as far as possible, from the cruelties of war. Take account of his comparison with police work.

John Connor

The U.S. Was Right

Forty years ago this week in Hiroshima: the dreadful flash, the wrist watches fused forever at 8:16 A.M. The question still persists: Should we have dropped the atomic bomb?

In August 1985, on the fortieth anniversary of the dropping of atomic bombs on Japan, the New York Times *invited two specialists to comment on the event. Both of their essays are reprinted here. John Connor (b. 1930), professor of anthropology at California State University, Sacramento, was attached to General MacArthur's headquarters in Tokyo in 1949 and 1950.*

History seldom gives decisive answers, but recently declassified documents point to a clear judgment: Yes, it was necessary to drop the bomb. It was needed to end the war. It saved countless American and Japanese lives.

In the early summer of 1945, Japan, under tight control of the militarists, was an implacable, relentless adversary. The Japanese defended territory with a philosophy we had seldom encountered: Soldiers were taught that surrender was worse than death. There was savage resistance to the end in battle after battle.

Of the 5,000-man Japanese force at Tarawa in November 1943, only seventeen remained alive when the island was taken. When Kwajalein was invaded in February 1944, Japanese officers slashed at American tanks with samurai swords; their men held grenades against the sides of tanks in an effort to disable them.

On Saipan, less than 1,000 of the 32,000 defending Japanese troops survived. Casualties among the Japanese-ruled civilians on the island numbered 10,000. Parents bashed their babies' brains out on rocky cliff sides, then leaped to their deaths. Others cut each other's throats; children threw grenades at each other. America suffered 17,000 casualties.

Just 660 miles southeast of Tokyo, Iwo Jima's garrison was told to defend the island as if it were Tokyo itself. They did. In the first day of fighting, there were more American casualties than during D-Day in Normandy. At Okinawa—only 350 miles south of Kyushu—more than 110,000 Japanese soldiers and 100,000 civilians were killed. Kamikaze attacks cost the Navy alone some 10,000 casualties. The Army and Marines lost more than 50,000 men.

In the early summer of 1945, the invasion of Japan was imminent and everyone in the Pacific was apprehensive. The apprehension was justified, because our intelligence was good: With a system code-named "Magic," it had penetrated Japanese codes even before Pearl Harbor. "Magic" would play a crucial role in the closing days of the war.

Many have maintained that the bomb was unnecessary because in the closing days of the war intercepted Japanese diplomatic messages disclosed a passionate desire for peace. While that is true, it is irrelevant. The Japanese government remained in the hands of the militarists: *Their* messages indicated a willingness to fight to the death.

Japanese planes, gasoline, and ammunition had been hoarded for the coming invasion. More than 5,000 aircraft had been hidden everywhere to be used as suicide weapons, with only enough gas in their tanks for a one-way trip to the invasion beaches. More than two million men were moving into positions to defend the home islands.

The object was to inflict such appalling losses that the Americans would agree to a treaty more favorable than unconditional surrender. The Army Chief of Staff, General George C. Marshall, estimated potential American casualties as high as a million.

The willingness of the Japanese to die was more than empty bravado. Several of my colleagues at Kyushu University told me that as boys of fourteen or fifteen, they were being trained to meet the Americans on the beaches with little more than sharpened bamboo spears. They had no illusions about their chances for survival.

The Potsdam declaration calling for unconditional surrender was 12 beamed to Japan on July 27. On July 30, the Americans were informed that Japan would officially ignore the ultimatum. A week later, the bomb was dropped.

Could we not have warned the Japanese in advance, critics asked, and dropped a demonstration bomb? That alternative was vetoed on the grounds the bomb might not work, or that the plane carrying it might be shot down. Moreover, it is questionable how effective a demonstration bomb might have been. The militarists could have imposed a news black-out as complete as the one imposed after the disastrous battle of Midway and continued on their suicidal course. That is exactly what happened at Hiroshima. Within hours, the Japanese government sent in a team of scientists to investigate the damage. Their report was immediately suppressed and was not made public until many years after the war.

After midnight on August 10, a protracted debate took place in an air-raid shelter deep inside the Imperial Palace. The military insisted that Japan should hold out for terms far better than unconditional surrender. The peace faction favored accepting the Potsdam declaration, providing that the emperor would be retained. The two factions remained at an impasse. At 2 A.M., Prime Minister Kantaro Suzuki asked the emperor to decide. In a soft, deliberate voice, the emperor expressed his great longing for peace. The war had ended.

It was impossible, in August 1945, to predict the awesome shadow the bomb would cast on humanity. The decision to drop it seemed both simple and obvious. Without it, the militarists might have prevailed, an invasion ordered. And the loss of both American and Japanese lives would have been awesome.

The atomic bomb accomplished what it had been designed to do. It 16 ended the war.

Questions and Suggestions for Writing

1. What is Connor's thesis? Where do you first find it? Where else does he state it? Are these statements in effective positions? Explain.

2. Jot down the reasons Connor gives to justify dropping the atomic bomb on Hiroshima. In reading and rereading the essay, do you find his evidence persuasive, or do some questions and doubts come to mind? If questions and doubts arise, jot them down.

3. One might say that the essayist argues two points: America needed the bomb to win the war without enormous American casualties, and, second, dropping the bomb was right. Which of these two theses gets more attention? Does Connor

assume that if we needed to win the war without further heavy losses, then using the bomb was morally right?

4. Connor concludes his essay by defending the bombing of Hiroshima in terms of its purpose and its effectiveness in achieving that purpose. Does this reasoning show that he implicitly takes the position that *any* weapon that our side could use to win the war was justifiable? Does his argument require him, in consistency, to condemn the massive aerial bombardment of Tokyo and Dresden earlier in 1945 because those raids did *not* "end the war"?

5. Connor mentions only one alternative to dropping the bomb on Hiroshima— dropping instead "a demonstration bomb." Why does he think this alternative would have failed in its purpose? Were there other alternatives that he ignores? (In this connection, read the next essay, by Alperovitz.)

6. You may have been told to avoid (in general) writing short, choppy sentences and undeveloped paragraphs. Connor's final paragraph consists of only two sentences, one of them very short. Is the paragraph faulty? Explain.

7. Connor never mentions dropping the bomb on Nagasaki three days after the bomb on Hiroshima. Could he defend this act in exactly the same way as he defends the bombing of Hiroshima, or would he need to construct a somewhat different argument? Set forth your answer in one or two paragraphs.

Gar Alperovitz

The U.S. Was Wrong

Though it has not yet received broad public attention, there exists overwhelming historical evidence that President Harry S. Truman knew he could almost certainly end World War II without using the atomic bomb: The United States had cracked the Japanese code, and a stream of documents released over the last forty years show that Mr. Truman had two other options.

The first option was to clarify America's surrender terms to assure the Japanese we would not remove their emperor. The second was simply to await the expected Soviet declaration of war—which, United States intelligence advised, appeared likely to end the conflict on its own.

Gar Alperovitz was born in Racine, Wisconsin, in 1935 and educated at the University of Wisconsin, the University of California (Berkeley), and Cambridge University. He has served as a congressional assistant, a member of the U.S. Senate staff, and a special assistant to the Department of State. He has written several books, including Atomic Diplomacy: Hiroshima and Potsdam *(1965; revised edition, 1985). This article first appeared in the* New York Times, *1985.*

Instead, Hiroshima was bombed August 6, 1945, and Nagasaki on August 9. The planned date for the Soviet Union's entry into the war against Japan was August 8.

The big turning point was the emperor's continuing June-July decision   4 to open surrender negotiations through Moscow. Top American officials—and, most critically, the president—understood the move was extraordinary: Mr. Truman's secret diaries, lost until 1978, call the key intercepted message "the telegram from Jap Emperor asking for peace."

Other documents—among them newly discovered secret memorandums from William J. Donovan, director of the Office of Strategic Services—show that Mr. Truman was personally advised of Japanese peace initiatives through Swiss and Portuguese channels as early as three months before Hiroshima. Moreover, Mr. Truman told several officials he had no objection in principle to Japan's keeping the emperor, which seemed the only sticking point.

American leaders were sure that if he so chose "the Mikado could stop the war with a royal word"—as one top presidential aide put it. Having decided to use the bomb, however, Mr. Truman was urged by Secretary of State James F. Byrnes not to give assurances to the emperor before the weapon had been demonstrated.

Additional official records, including minutes of top-level White House planning meetings, show the president was clearly advised of the importance of a Soviet declaration of war: It would pull the rug out from under Japanese military leaders who were desperately hoping the powerful Red Army would stay neutral.

General George C. Marshall in mid-June told Mr. Truman that "the   8 impact of Russian entry on the already hopeless Japanese may well be the decisive action levering them into capitulation at that time or shortly thereafter if we land."

A month later, the American-British Combined Intelligence Staffs advised their chiefs of the critical importance of a Red Army attack. As the top British general, Sir Hastings Ismay, summarized the conclusions for Prime Minister Winston Churchill: "If and when Russia came into the war against Japan, the Japanese would probably wish to get out on almost any terms short of the dethronement of the Emperor."

Mr. Truman's private diaries also record his understanding of the significance of this option. On July 17, 1945, when Stalin confirmed that the Red Army would march, Mr. Truman privately noted: "Fini Japs when that comes about."

There was plenty of time: The American invasion of Japan was not scheduled until the spring of 1946. Even a preliminary landing on the island of Kyushu was still three months in the future.

General Dwight D. Eisenhower, appalled that the bomb would be   12 used in these circumstances, urged Mr. Truman and Secretary of War Henry L. Stimson not to drop it. In his memoirs, he observed that weeks before Hiroshima, Japan had been seeking a way to surrender. "It wasn't necessary," he said in a later interview, "to hit them with that awful thing."

The man who presided over the Joint Chiefs of Staff, Admiral William D. Leahy, was equally shocked: "The use of this barbarous weapon at Hiroshima and Nagasaki was of no material assistance in our war against Japan. The Japanese were already defeated and ready to surrender."

Why, then, was the bomb used?

American leaders rejected the most obvious option—simply waiting for the Red Army attack—out of political, not military, concerns.

As the diary of one official put it, they wanted to end the war before 16 Moscow got "in so much on the kill." Secretary of the Navy James V. Forrestal's diaries record that Mr. Byrnes "was most anxious to get the Japanese affair over with before the Russians got in."

United States leaders had also begun to think of the atomic bomb as what Secretary Stimson termed the "master card" of diplomacy. President Truman postponed his Potsdam meeting with Stalin until July 17, 1945—one day after the first successful nuclear test—to be sure the atomic bomb would strengthen his hand before confronting the Soviet leader on the shape of a postwar settlement.

To this day, we do not know with absolute certainty Mr. Truman's personal attitudes on several key issues. Yet we do know that his most important adviser, Secretary of State Byrnes, was convinced that dropping the bomb would serve crucial long-range diplomatic purposes.

As one atomic scientist, Leo Szilard, observed: "Mr. Byrnes did not argue that it was necessary to use the bomb against the cities of Japan in order to win the war. Mr. Byrnes' . . . view [was] that our possessing and demonstrating the bomb would make Russia more manageable."

Questions and Suggestions for Writing

1. In a few sentences summarize Alperovitz's essay.

2. If you have read Connor's essay (p. 386), do you find in it convincing (or at least substantial) evidence that Alperovitz ignores or distorts? If so, what is this evidence?

3. Suppose someone argued that although with hindsight we can now see that the bomb was not needed to end the war, President Truman could not have seen this fact in the summer of 1945. Does Alperovitz's evidence refute such an argument? Explain.

4. Alperovitz does not comment explicitly on Truman's character or morality, but, drawing on this essay, what do you think he thinks of Truman as a human being? Support your answer with evidence. Then consider another question: Does Alperovitz in this essay present evidence that supports what you take to be his view of Truman? Explain.

11

Can the Death Penalty Ever Be Justified?

Edward I. Koch

Death and Justice:
How Capital Punishment Affirms Life

Last December a man named Robert Lee Willie, who had been convicted of raping and murdering an eighteen-year-old woman, was executed in the Louisiana state prison. In a statement issued several minutes before his death, Mr. Willie said: "Killing people is wrong. . . . It makes no difference whether it's citizens, countries, or governments. Killing is wrong." Two weeks later in South Carolina, an admitted killer named Joseph Carl Shaw was put to death for murdering two teenagers. In an appeal to the governor for clemency, Mr. Shaw wrote: "Killing is wrong when I did it. Killing is wrong when you do it. I hope you have the courage and moral strength to stop the killing."

It is a curiosity of modern life that we find ourselves being lectured on morality by cold-blooded killers. Mr. Willie previously had been convicted of aggravated rape, aggravated kidnapping, and the murders of a Louisiana deputy and a man from Missouri. Mr. Shaw committed another murder a week before the two for which he was executed, and admitted

---

Edward I. Koch (b. 1924), long active in Democratic politics, was mayor of New York from 1978 to 1989. This essay first appeared in The New Republic, *1985.*

mutilating the body of the fourteen-year-old girl he killed. I can't help wondering what prompted these murderers to speak out against killing as they entered the deathhouse door. Did their newfound reverence for life stem from the realization that they were about to lose their own?

Life is indeed precious, and I believe the death penalty helps to affirm this fact. Had the death penalty been a real possibility in the minds of these murderers, they might well have stayed their hand. They might have shown moral awareness before their victims died, and not after. Consider the tragic death of Rosa Velez, who happened to be home when a man named Luis Vera burglarized her apartment in Brooklyn. "Yeah, I shot her," Vera admitted. "She knew me, and I knew I wouldn't go to the chair."

During my twenty-two years in public service, I have heard the pros   4
and cons of capital punishment expressed with special intensity. As a district leader, councilman, congressman, and mayor, I have represented constituencies generally thought of as liberal. Because I support the death penalty for heinous crimes of murder, I have sometimes been the subject of emotional and outraged attacks by voters who find my position reprehensible or worse. I have listened to their ideas. I have weighed their objections carefully. I still support the death penalty. The reasons I maintain my position can be best understood by examining the arguments most frequently heard in opposition.

1. The death penalty is "barbaric." Sometimes opponents of capital punishment horrify with tales of lingering death on the gallows, of faulty electric chairs, or of agony in the gas chamber. Partly in response to such protests, several states such as North Carolina and Texas switched to execution by lethal injection. The condemned person is put to death painlessly, without ropes, voltage, bullets, or gas. Did this answer the objections of death penalty opponents? Of course not. On June 22, 1984, the *New York Times* published an editorial that sarcastically attacked the new "hygienic" method of death by injection, and stated that "execution can never be made humane through science." So it's not the method that really troubles opponents. It's the death itself they consider barbaric.

Admittedly, capital punishment is not a pleasant topic. However, one does not have to like the death penalty in order to support it any more than one must like radical surgery, radiation, or chemotherapy in order to find necessary these attempts at curing cancer. Ultimately we may learn how to cure cancer with a simple pill. Unfortunately, that day has not yet arrived. Today we are faced with the choice of letting the cancer spread or trying to cure it with the methods available, methods that one day will almost certainly be considered barbaric. But to give up and do nothing would be far more barbaric and would certainly delay the discovery of an eventual cure. The analogy between cancer and murder is imperfect, because murder is not the "disease" we are trying to cure. The disease is injustice.

We may not like the death penalty, but it must be available to punish crimes of cold-blooded murder, cases in which any other form of punishment would be inadequate and, therefore, unjust. If we create a society in which injustice is not tolerated, incidents of murder—the most flagrant form of injustice—will diminish.

2. No other major democracy uses the death penalty. No other major democracy—in fact, few other countries of any description—are plagued by a murder rate such as that in the United States. Fewer and fewer Americans can remember the days when unlocked doors were the norm and murder was a rare and terrible offense. In America the murder rate climbed 122 percent between 1963 and 1980. During that same period, the murder rate in New York City increased by almost 400 percent, and the statistics are even worse in many other cities. A study at M.I.T. showed that based on 1970 homicide rates a person who lived in a large American city ran a greater risk of being murdered than an American soldier in World War II ran of being killed in combat. It is not surprising that the laws of each country differ according to differing conditions and traditions. If other countries had our murder problem, the cry for capital punishment would be just as loud as it is here. And I daresay that any other major democracy where 75 percent of the people supported the death penalty would soon enact it into law.

3. An innocent person might be executed by mistake. Consider the 8 work of Hugo Adam Bedau, one of the most implacable foes of capital punishment in this country. According to Mr. Bedau, it is "false sentimentality to argue that the death penalty should be abolished because of the abstract possibility that an innocent person might be executed." He cites a study of the 7,000 executions in this country from 1893 to 1971, and concludes that the record fails to show that such cases occur. The main point, however, is this. If government functioned only when the possibility of error didn't exist, government wouldn't function at all. Human life deserves special protection, and one of the best ways to guarantee that protection is to assure that convicted murderers do not kill again. Only the death penalty can accomplish this end. In a recent case in New Jersey, a man named Richard Biegenwald was freed from prison after serving eighteen years for murder; since his release he has been convicted of committing four murders. A prisoner named Lemuel Smith, who, while serving four life sentences for murder (plus two life sentences for kidnapping and robbery) in New York's Green Haven Prison, lured a woman corrections officer into the chaplain's office and strangled her. He then mutilated and dismembered her body. An additional life sentence for Smith is meaningless. Because New York has no death penalty statute, Smith has effectively been given a license to kill.

But the problem of multiple murder is not confined to the nation's penitentiaries. In 1981, 91 police officers were killed in the line of duty in this country. Seven percent of those arrested in the cases that have been solved had a previous arrest for murder. In New York City in 1976 and 1977, 85 persons arrested for homicide had a previous arrest for murder. Six of these individuals had two previous arrests for murder, and one had four previous murder arrests. During those two years the New York police were arresting for murder persons with a previous arrest for murder on the average of one every 8.5 days. This is not surprising when we learn that in 1975, for example, the median time served in Massachusetts for homicide was less than two and a half years. In 1976 a study sponsored by the Twentieth Century Fund found that the average time served in the United States for first-degree murder is ten years. The median time served may be considerably lower.

4. Capital punishment cheapens the value of human life. On the contrary, it can be easily demonstrated that the death penalty strengthens the value of human life. If the penalty for rape were lowered, clearly it would signal a lessened regard for the victims' suffering, humiliation, and personal integrity. It would cheapen their horrible experience, and expose them to an increased danger of recurrence. When we lower the penalty for murder, it signals a lessened regard for the value of the victim's life. Some critics of capital punishment, such as columnist Jimmy Breslin, have suggested that a life sentence is actually a harsher penalty for murder than death. This is sophistic nonsense. A few killers may decide not to appeal a death sentence, but the overwhelming majority make every effort to stay alive. It is by exacting the highest penalty for the taking of human life that we affirm the highest value of human life.

5. The death penalty is applied in a discriminatory manner. This factor no longer seems to be the problem it once was. The appeals process for a condemned prisoner is lengthy and painstaking. Every effort is made to see that the verdict and sentence were fairly arrived at. However, assertions of discrimination are not an argument for ending the death penalty but for extending it. It is not justice to exclude everyone from the penalty of the law if a few are found to be so favored. Justice requires that the law be applied equally to all.

6. Thou Shalt Not Kill. The Bible is our greatest source of moral   12
inspiration. Opponents of the death penalty frequently cite the sixth of the Ten Commandments in an attempt to prove that capital punishment is divinely proscribed. In the original Hebrew, however, the Sixth Commandment reads "Thou Shalt Not Commit Murder," and the Torah specifies capital punishment for a variety of offenses. The biblical viewpoint has

been upheld by philosophers throughout history. The greatest thinkers of the nineteenth century—Kant, Locke, Hobbes, Rousseau, Montesquieu, and Mill—agreed that natural law properly authorizes the sovereign to take life in order to vindicate justice. Only Jeremy Bentham was ambivalent. Washington, Jefferson, and Franklin endorsed it. Abraham Lincoln authorized executions for deserters in wartime. Alexis de Tocqueville, who expressed profound respect for American institutions, believed that the death penalty was indispensable to the support of social order. The United States Constitution, widely admired as one of the seminal achievements in the history of humanity, condemns cruel and inhuman punishment, but does not condemn capital punishment.

7. The death penalty is state-sanctioned murder. This is the defense with which Messrs. Willie and Shaw hoped to soften the resolve of those who sentenced them to death. By saying in effect, "You're no better than I am," the murderer seeks to bring his accusers down to his own level. It is also a popular argument among opponents of capital punishment, but a transparently false one. Simply put, the state has rights that the private individual does not. In a democracy, those rights are given to the state by the electorate. The execution of a lawfully condemned killer is no more an act of murder than is legal imprisonment an act of kidnapping. If an individual forces a neighbor to pay him money under threat of punishment, it's called extortion. If the state does it, it's called taxation. Rights and responsibilities surrendered by the individual are what give the state its power to govern. This contract is the foundation of civilization itself.

Everyone wants his or her rights, and will defend them jealously. Not everyone, however, wants responsibilities, especially the painful responsibilities that come with law enforcement. Twenty-one years ago a woman named Kitty Genovese was assaulted and murdered on a street in New York. Dozens of neighbors heard her cries for help but did nothing to assist her. They didn't even call the police. In such a climate the criminal understandably grows bolder. In the presence of moral cowardice, he lectures us on our supposed failings and tries to equate his crimes with our quest for justice.

The death of anyone—even a convicted killer—diminishes us all. But we are diminished even more by a justice system that fails to function. It is an illusion to let ourselves believe that doing away with capital punishment removes the murderer's deed from our conscience. The rights of society are paramount. When we protect guilty lives, we give up innocent lives in exchange. When opponents of capital punishment say to the state, "I will not let you kill in my name," they are also saying to murderers: "You can kill in your *own* name as long as I have an excuse for not getting involved."

It is hard to imagine anything worse than being murdered while 16 neighbors do nothing. But something worse exists. When those same neighbors shrink back from justly punishing the murderer, the victim dies twice.

Questions and Suggestions for Writing

1. In his first argument Koch draws an analogy between cancer and murder, and observes that imperfect as today's cures for cancer are, "to give up and do nothing would be far more barbaric." What is the relevance of this comment in the context of the analogy and the dispute over the death penalty?

2. In his third argument Koch describes a convicted but unexecuted recidivist murderer as someone who "has effectively been given a license to kill." But a license to kill, as in a deer-hunter's license, entitles the holder to engage in lawful killing. (Think of the fictional hero, James Bond—Agent 007—who, we are told, had a real "license to kill.") What is the difference between really having a license and "effectively" having one? How might the opponent of the death penalty reply to Koch's position here?

3. Koch distinguishes between the "median" time served by persons convicted of murder but not sentenced to death, and the "average" time they serve, and he adds that the former "may be considerably longer" than the latter. Explain the difference between a "median" and an "average." Is knowing one of these more important for certain purposes than the other? Why?

4. Koch identifies seven arguments against the death penalty, and he rejects them all. Which of the seven arguments seems to you to be the strongest objection to the death penalty? Which the weakest? Why? Does Koch effectively refute the strongest argument? Can you think of any argument(s) against the death penalty that he neglects?

5. Koch says he supports the death penalty "for heinous crimes of murder." Does he imply that all murders are "heinous crimes," or only some? If the latter, what criteria seem to you to be the appropriate ones to distinguish the "heinous" murders from the rest? Why these criteria?

6. Koch asserts that the death penalty helps to "affirm" the idea that "life is indeed precious." Yet opponents of the death penalty often claim the reverse, arguing that capital punishment undermines the idea that human life is precious. Write an essay of 500 words in which you explain what it means to assert that life is precious, and why one of the two positions—support for or opposition to the death penalty—best supports (or is consistent with) this principle.

David Bruck

The Death Penalty

Mayor Ed Koch contends that the death penalty "affirms life." By failing to execute murderers, he says, we "signal a lessened regard for the value of the victim's life." Koch suggests that people who oppose the death penalty are like Kitty Genovese's neighbors, who heard her cries for help but did nothing while an attacker stabbed her to death.

This is the standard "moral" defense of death as punishment: even if executions don't deter violent crime any more effectively than imprisonment, they are still required as the only means we have of doing justice in response to the worst of crimes.

Until recently, this "moral" argument had to be considered in the abstract, since no one was being executed in the United States. But the death penalty is back now, at least in the southern states, where every one of the more than thirty executions carried out over the last two years has taken place. Those of us who live in those states are getting to see the difference between the death penalty in theory, and what happens when you actually try to use it.

South Carolina resumed executing prisoners in January with the electrocution of Joseph Carl Shaw. Shaw was condemned to death for helping to murder two teenagers while he was serving as a military policeman at Fort Jackson, South Carolina. His crime, propelled by mental illness and PCP, was one of terrible brutality. It is Shaw's last words ("Killing was wrong when I did it. It is wrong when you do it. . . .") that so outraged Mayor Koch: he finds it "a curiosity of modern life that we are being lectured on morality by cold-blooded killers." And so it is. 4

But it was not "modern life" that brought this curiosity into being. It was capital punishment. The electric chair was J. C. Shaw's platform. (The mayor mistakenly writes that Shaw's statement came in the form of a plea to the governor for clemency: Actually Shaw made it only seconds before his death, as he waited, shaved and strapped into the chair, for the switch to be thrown.) It was the chair that provided Shaw with celebrity and an opportunity to lecture us on right and wrong. What made this weird moral reversal even worse is that J. C. Shaw faced his own death with undeniable dignity and courage. And while Shaw died, the TV crews recorded another "curiosity" of the death penalty—the crowd gathered outside the

---

David Bruck (b. 1949) graduated from Harvard College and received his law degree from the University of South Carolina. His practice is devoted almost entirely to the defense of persons under death sentence, through the South Carolina Office of Appellate Defense. The essay reprinted here originally appeared in 1985 in The New Republic *as a response to the essay by Edward I. Koch on p. 392.*

death-house to cheer on the executioner. Whoops of elation greeted the announcement of Shaw's death. Waiting at the penitentiary gates for the appearance of the hearse bearing Shaw's remains, one demonstrator started yelling, "Where's the beef?"

For those who had to see the execution of J. C. Shaw, it wasn't easy to keep in mind that the purpose of the whole spectacle was to affirm life. It will be harder still when Florida executes a cop-killer named Alvin Ford. Ford has lost his mind during his years of death-row confinement, and now spends his days trembling, rocking back and forth, and muttering unintelligible prayers. This has led to litigation over whether Ford meets a centuries-old legal standard for mental competency. Since the Middle Ages, the Anglo-American legal system has generally prohibited the execution of anyone who is too mentally ill to understand what is about to be done to him and why. If Florida wins its case, it will have earned the right to electrocute Ford in his present condition. If it loses, he will not be executed until the state has first nursed him back to some semblance of mental health.[1]

We can at least be thankful that this demoralizing spectacle involves a prisoner who is actually guilty of murder. But this may not always be so. The ordeal of Lenell Jeter—the young black engineer who recently served more than a year of a life sentence for a Texas armed robbery that he didn't commit—should remind us that the system is quite capable of making the very worst sort of mistake. That Jeter was eventually cleared is a fluke. If the robbery had occurred at 7 P.M. rather than 3 P.M., he'd have had no alibi, and would still be in prison today. And if someone had been killed in that robbery, Jeter probably would have been sentenced to death. We'd have seen the usual execution-day interviews with state officials and the victim's relatives, all complaining that Jeter's appeals took too long. And Jeter's last words from the gurney would have taken their place among the growing literature of death-house oration that so irritates the mayor.

Koch quotes Hugo Adam Bedau, a prominent abolitionist, to the 8 effect that the record fails to establish that innocent defendants have been executed in the past. But this doesn't mean, as Koch implies, that it hasn't happened. All Bedau was saying was that doubts concerning executed prisoners' guilt are almost never resolved. Bedau is at work now on an effort to determine how many wrongful death sentences may have been imposed: his list of murder convictions since 1900 in which the state eventually *admitted* error is some four hundred cases long. Of course, very few of these cases involved actual executions: the mistakes that Bedau documents were uncovered precisely because the prisoner was alive and

---

[1]Florida lost its case to execute Ford. On 26 June 1986 the Supreme Court barred execution of convicted murderers who have become so insane that they do not know they are about to be executed nor the reason for it. If Ford regains his sanity, however, he can be executed. [Editors' note]

able to fight for his vindication. The cases where someone is executed are the very cases in which we're least likely to learn that we got the wrong man.

I don't claim that executions of entirely innocent people will occur very often. But they will occur. And other sorts of mistakes already have. Roosevelt Green was executed in Georgia two days before J. C. Shaw. Green and an accomplice kidnapped a young woman. Green swore that his companion shot her to death after Green had left, and that he knew nothing about the murder. Green's claim was supported by a statement that his accomplice made to a witness after the crime. The jury never resolved whether Green was telling the truth, and when he tried to take a polygraph examination a few days before his scheduled execution, the state of Georgia refused to allow the examiner into the prison. As the pressure for symbolic retribution mounts, the courts, like the public, are losing patience with such details. Green was electrocuted on January 9, while members of the Ku Klux Klan rallied outside the prison.

Then there is another sort of arbitrariness that happens all the time. Last October, Louisiana executed a man named Ernest Knighton. Knighton had killed a gas station owner during a robbery. Like any murder, this was a terrible crime. But it was not premeditated, and is the sort of crime that very rarely results in a death sentence. Why was Knighton electrocuted when almost everyone else who committed the same offense was not? Was it because he was black? Was it because his victim and all 12 members of the jury that sentenced him were white? Was it because Knighton's court-appointed lawyer presented no evidence on his behalf at his sentencing hearing? Or maybe there's no reason except bad luck. One thing is clear: Ernest Knighton was picked out to die the way a fisherman takes a cricket out of a bait jar. No one cares which cricket gets impaled on the hook.

Not every prisoner executed recently was chosen that randomly. But many were. And having selected these men so casually, so blindly, the death penalty system asks us to accept that the purpose of killing each of them is to affirm the sanctity of human life.

The death penalty states are also learning that the death penalty is 12 easier to advocate than it is to administer. In Florida, where executions have become almost routine, the governor reports that nearly a third of his time is spent reviewing the clemency requests of condemned prisoners. The Florida Supreme Court is hopelessly backlogged with death cases. Some have taken five years to decide, and the rest of the Court's work waits in line behind the death appeals. Florida's death row currently holds more than 230 prisoners. State officials are reportedly considering building a special "death prison" devoted entirely to the isolation and electrocution of the condemned. The state is also considering the creation of a special public defender unit that will do nothing else but handle death penalty appeals. The death penalty, in short, is spawning death agencies.

And what is Florida getting for all of this? The state went through almost all of 1983 without executing anyone: its rate of intentional homicide declined by 17 percent. Last year Florida executed eight people—the most of any state, and the sixth highest total for any year since Florida started electrocuting people back in 1924. Elsewhere in the U.S. last year, the homicide rate continued to decline. But in Florida, it actually rose by 5.1 percent.

But these are just the tiresome facts. The electric chair has been a centerpiece of each of Koch's recent political campaigns, and he knows better than anyone how little the facts have to do with the public's support for capital punishment. What really fuels the death penalty is the justifiable frustration and rage of people who see that the government is not coping with violent crime. So what if the death penalty doesn't work? At least it gives us the satisfaction of knowing that we got one or two of the sons of bitches.

Perhaps we want retribution on the flesh and bone of a handful of convicted murderers so badly that we're willing to close our eyes to all of the demoralization and danger that come with it. A lot of politicians think so, and they may be right. But if they are, then let's at least look honestly at what we're doing. This lottery of death both comes from and encourages an attitude toward human life that is not reverent, but reckless.

And that is why the mayor is dead wrong when he confuses such fury 16 with justice. He suggests that we trivialize murder unless we kill murderers. By that logic, we also trivialize rape unless we sodomize rapists. The sin of Kitty Genovese's neighbors wasn't that they failed to stab her attacker to death. Justice does demand that murderers be punished. And common sense demands that society be protected from them. But neither justice nor self-preservation demands that we kill men whom we have already imprisoned.

The electric chair in which J. C. Shaw died earlier this year was built in 1912 at the suggestion of South Carolina's governor at the time, Cole Blease. Governor Blease's other criminal justice initiative was an impassioned crusade in favor of lynch law. Any lesser response, the governor insisted, trivialized the loathsome crimes of interracial rape and murder. In 1912 a lot of people agreed with Governor Blease that a proper regard for justice required both lynching and the electric chair. Eventually we are going to learn that justice requires neither.

Questions and Suggestions for Writing

1. After three introductory paragraphs Bruck devotes two paragraphs to Shaw's execution. In a sentence or two, explicitly state the point he is making in his discussion of this execution. Then, in another sentence or two (or three) indicate the degree to which this point refutes Koch's argument.

2. In paragraph 7, Bruck refers to the case of Lenell Jeter, an innocent man who was condemned to a life sentence. Evaluate this point as a piece of evidence used to support an argument against the death penalty.

3. In paragraph 8, Bruck says that "the state eventually *admitted* error" in some four hundred cases. He goes on: "Of course, very few of these cases involved actual executions." How few is "very few"? Why do you suppose Bruck doesn't specify the number? If, say, it is only two, in your opinion does that affect Bruck's point?

4. Discussing the case of Roosevelt Green, Bruck points out that Green offered to take a polygraph test but "the state of Georgia refused to allow the examiner into the prison." In a paragraph evaluate the state's position on this matter.

5. In paragraph 13 Bruck points out that although "last year" (1984) the state executed eight people, the homicide rate in Florida rose 5.1 percent, whereas elsewhere in the United States the homicide rate declined. What do you make of these figures? What do you think Koch would make of them?

6. In his next-to-last paragraph Bruck says that Koch "suggests that we trivialize murder unless we kill murderers. By that logic, we also trivialize rape unless we sodomize rapists." Do you agree that this statement brings out the absurdity of Koch's thinking?

7. Evaluate Bruck's final paragraph (a) as a concluding paragraph, and (b) as a piece of argumentation.

8. Bruck, writing early in 1985, stresses that all the "more than thirty" executions in the nation "in the last two years" have taken place in the South. Why does he think this figure points to a vulnerability in Mayor Koch's argument? Would Bruck's argument here be spoiled if some executions were to occur outside of the South? (By the way, where exactly have most of the recent executions in the nation occurred?)

9. Bruck argues that the present death-penalty system—in practice even if not in theory—utterly fails to "affirm the sanctity of human life." Do you think Bruck would, or should, concede that at least in theory it is possible for a death-penalty system to be no more offensive to the value of human life than, say, a system of imprisonment is offensive to the value of human liberty, or a system of fines is offensive to the value of human property?

10. Can Bruck be criticized for implying that cases like those he cites—Shaw, Ford, Green, and Knightson in particular—are the rule, rather than the exception? Does either Bruck or Koch cite any evidence to help settle this question?

11. Write a paragraph explaining which of these events seems to you to be the more unseemly: a condemned prisoner, on the threshold of execution, lecturing the rest of us on the immorality of killing; or the crowd that bursts into cheers outside a prison when it learns that a scheduled execution has been carried out.

Jacob J. Vellenga

Christianity and the Death Penalty

The Church at large is giving serious thought to capital punishment. Church councils and denominational assemblies are making strong pronouncements against it. We are hearing such arguments as: "Capital punishment brutalizes society by cheapening life." "Capital punishment is morally indefensible." "Capital punishment is no deterrent to murder." "Capital punishment makes it impossible to rehabilitate the criminal."

But many of us are convinced that the Church should not meddle with capital punishment. Church members should be strong in supporting good legislation, militant against wrong laws, opposed to weak and partial law enforcement. But we should be sure that what we endorse or what we oppose is intimately related to the common good, the benefit of society, the establishment of justice, and the upholding of high moral and ethical standards.

There is a good reason for saying that opposition to capital punishment is not for the common good but sides with evil; shows more regard for the criminal than the victim of the crime; weakens justice and encourages murder; is not based on Scripture but on a vague philosophical system that makes a fetish of the idea that the taking of life is wrong, under every circumstance, and fails to distinguish adequately between killing and murder, between punishment and crime.

Capital punishment is a controversial issue upon which good people are divided, both having high motives in their respective convictions. But capital punishment should not be classified with social evils like segregation, racketeering, liquor traffic, and gambling.

These evils are clearly antisocial, while capital punishment is a matter of jurisprudence established for the common good and benefit of society. Those favoring capital punishment are not to be stigmatized as heartless, vengeful, and lacking in mercy, but are to be respected as advocating that which is the best for society as a whole. When we stand for the common good, we must of necessity be strongly opposed to that behavior which is contrary to the common good.

From time immemorial the conviction of good society has been that life is sacred, and he who violates the sacredness of life through murder must pay the supreme penalty. This ancient belief is well expressed in Scripture: "Only you shall not eat flesh with its life, that is, its blood. For

The Reverend Mr. Vellenga (1939–1977) served on the National Board of Administration of the United Presbyterian Church from 1948 to 1954. He also served the United Presbyterian Church in the United States as Associate Executive. The essay reprinted here first appeared in Christianity Today, *1959.*

your lifeblood I will surely require a reckoning; of every beast I will require it and of man; of every man's brother I will require the life of man. Whoever sheds the blood of man, by man shall his blood be shed; for God made man in his own image" (Gen. 9:4–6, RSV). Life is sacred. He who violates the law must pay the supreme penalty, just because life is sacred. Life is sacred since God made man in His image. There is a distinction here between murder and penalty.

Many who oppose capital punishment make a strong argument out of the Sixth Commandment: "Thou shalt not kill" (Exod. 20:13). But they fail to note the commentary on that Commandment which follows: "Whoever strikes a man so that he dies shall be put to death. . . . If a man willfully attacks another to kill him treacherously, you shall take him from my altar that he may die" (Exod. 21:12,14). It is faulty exegesis to take a verse of Scripture out of its context and interpret it without regard to its qualifying words.

The Exodus reference is not the only one referring to capital punishment. In Leviticus 24:17 we read: "He who kills a man shall be put to death." Numbers 35:30–34 goes into more detail on the subject: "If any one kills a person, the murderer shall be put to death on the evidence of witnesses; but no person shall be put to death on the testimony of one witness. Moreover you shall accept no ransom for the life of a murderer who is guilty of death; but he shall be put to death. . . . You shall not thus pollute the land in which you live; for blood pollutes the land, and no expiation can be made for the land, for the blood that is shed in it, except by the blood of him who shed it. You shall not defile the land in which you live, in the midst of which I dwell; for I the Lord dwell in the midst of the people of Israel." (Compare Deut. 17:6–7 and 19:11–13.)

Deuteronomy 19:4–6,10 distinguishes between accidental killing and willful murder: "If any one kills his neighbor unintentionally without having been at enmity with him in time past . . . he may flee to one of these cities [cities of refuge] and save his life; lest the avenger of blood in hot anger pursue the manslayer and overtake him, because the way is long, and wound him mortally, though the man did not deserve to die, since he was not at enmity with his neighbor in time past. . . . lest innocent blood be shed in your land which the Lord your God gives you for an inheritance, and so the guilt of bloodshed be upon you."

The cry of the prophets against social evils was not only directed against discrimination of the poor, and the oppression of widows and orphans, but primarily against laxness in the administration of justice. They were opposed to the laws being flouted and criminals not being punished. A vivid expression of the prophet's attitude is recorded in Isaiah: "Justice is turned back, and righteousness stands afar off; for truth has fallen in the public squares, and uprightness cannot enter. . . . The Lord saw it and it displeased him that there was no justice. He saw that there was no man, and wondered that there was no one to intervene; then his own arm brought him victory, and his righteousness upheld him. He put on righteousness as a breastplate, and a helmet of salvation upon his head; he put on garments of vengeance for clothing and wrapped himself in a fury as a mantle. According to their deeds, so will he repay, wrath to his adversaries, requital to his enemies" (Isa. 59:14–18).

The teachings of the New Testament are in harmony with the Old Testament. Christ came to fulfill the law, not to destroy the basic principles of law and order, righteousness and justice. In Matthew 5:17–20 we read: "Think not that I have come to abolish the law and the prophets; I have come not to abolish them but to fulfill them. For truly, I say to you, till heaven and earth pass away, not an iota, not a dot, will pass from the law until all is accomplished. . . . For I tell you, unless your righteousness exceeds that of the scribes and Pharisees, you will never enter the kingdom of heaven."

Then Christ speaks of hate and murder: "You have heard that it was 12 said to the men of old, 'You shall not kill; and whoever kills shall be liable to judgment [capital punishment].' But I say to you that everyone who is angry with his brother shall be liable to judgment [capital punishment]" (Matt. 5:21–22). It is evident that Jesus was not condemning the established law of capital punishment, but was actually saying that hate deserved capital punishment. Jesus was not advocating doing away with capital punishment but urging his followers to live above the law so that law and punishment could not touch them. To live above the law is not the same as abrogating it.

The Church, the Body of Christ, has enough to do to evangelize and educate society to live above the law and positively to influence society to high and noble living by maintaining a wide margin between right and wrong. The early Christians did not meddle with laws against wrongdoing. Paul expresses this attitude in his letter to the Romans: "Therefore, he who resists the authorities resists what God has appointed, and those who resist will incur judgment. For rulers are not a terror to good conduct, but to bad. . . . for he is God's servant for your good. But if you do wrong, be afraid, for he does not bear the sword in vain; he is the servant of God to execute his wrath on the wrongdoer" (13:2–4).

The early Christians suffered many injustices and were victims of inhuman treatment. Many became martyrs because of their faith. Consequently, they were often tempted to take the law in their own hands. But Paul cautioned them: "Beloved, never avenge yourselves, but leave it to the wrath of God; for it is written, 'Vengeance is mine, I will repay, says the Lord.' No, 'if your enemy is hungry, feed him; if he is thirsty, give him drink; for by so doing you will heap burning coals upon his head'" (Rom. 12: 19–21).

There is not a hint of indication in the New Testament that laws should be changed to make it lenient for the wrongdoer. Rather, the whole trend is that the Church leave matters of justice and law enforcement to the government in power. "Let every person be subject to the governing authorities. For there is no authority except from God, and those that exist have been instituted by God" (Rom. 13:1). Note the juxtaposition of love to enemies with a healthy respect for government. The Christian fellowship is not to take law in its own hands, for God has government in his economy in order to take care of matters of justice.

Jesus's words on loving one's enemies, turning the other cheek, and walking the second mile were not propaganda to change jurisprudence, but they were meant to establish a new society not merely made up of law-abiding citizens but those who lived a life higher than the law, so that stealing, adultery, and murder would become inoperative, but not annulled. The law of love, also called the law of liberty, was not presented to do away with the natural laws of society, but to inaugurate a new concept of law written on the heart where the mainsprings of action are born. The Church is ever to strive for superior law and order, not to advocate a lower order that makes wrongdoing less culpable. 16

Love and mercy have no stability without agreement on basic justice and fair play. Mercy always infers a tacit recognition that justice and rightness are to be expected. Lowering the standards of justice is never to be a substitute for the concept of mercy. The Holy God does not show mercy contrary to his righteousness but in harmony with it. This is why the awful Cross was necessary and a righteous Christ had to hang on it. This is why God's redemption is always conditioned by one's heart attitude. There is no forgiveness for anyone who is unforgiving. "Forgive us our debts, as we forgive our debtors" (Matt. 6:12). There is no mercy for anyone who will not be merciful. "Blessed are the merciful for they shall obtain mercy" (Matt. 5:7). There is striking similarity to these verses in Psalm 18:25–26: "With the loyal thou dost show thyself loyal; with the blameless man thou dost show thyself blameless; with the pure thou dost show thyself pure; and with the crooked thou dost show thyself perverse."

Professor C. S. Lewis in his recent book *Reflections on the Psalms* deals with the difficult subject of the spirit of hatred which is in some of the Psalms. He points out that these hatreds had a good motivation. "Such hatreds are the kind of thing that cruelty and injustice, by a sort of natural law, produce. . . . Not to perceive it at all—not even to be tempted to resentment—to accept it as the most ordinary thing in the world—argues a terrifying insensibility. Thus the absence of anger, especially that sort of anger which we call indignation, can, in my opinion, be a most alarming symptom. . . . If the Jews cursed more bitterly than the Pagans this was, I think, at least in part because they took right and wrong more seriously."

Vindictiveness is a sin, but only because a sense of justice has gotten out of hand. The check on revenge must be in the careful and exact administering of justice by society's government. This is the clear teaching of Scripture in both the Old and New Testaments. The Church and individual Christians should be active in their witness to the Gospel of love and forgiveness and ever lead people to the high law of love of God and our neighbors as ourselves; but meanwhile wherever and whenever God's love and mercy are rejected, as in crime, natural law and order must prevail, not as extraneous to redemption but as part of the whole scope of God's dealings with man.

The argument that capital punishment rules out the possibility of 20 repentance for crime is unrealistic. If a wanton killer does not repent when the sentence of death is upon him, he certainly will not repent if he has twenty to fifty years of life imprisonment ahead of him.

We, who are supposed to be Christian, make too much of physical life. Jesus said, "And do not fear those who kill the body but cannot kill the soul; rather fear him who can destroy both soul and body in hell" (Matt. 10:28). Laxness in law tends to send both soul and body to hell. It is more than a pious remark when a judge says to the condemned criminal: "And may God have mercy on your soul." The sentence of death on a killer is more redemptive than the tendency to excuse his crime as no worse than grand larceny.

It is significant that when Jesus voluntarily went the way of the Cross he chose the capital punishment of his day as his instrument to save the world. And when he gave redemption to the repentant thief he did not save him from capital punishment but gave him Paradise instead which was far better. We see again that mercy and forgiveness are something different than being excused from wrongdoing.

No one can deny that the execution of a murderer is a horrible spectacle. But we must not forget that murder is more horrible. The supreme penalty should be exacted only after the guilt is established beyond the shadow of a doubt and only for wanton, willful, premeditated murder. But the law of capital punishment must stand, no matter how often a jury recommends mercy. The law of capital punishment must stand as a silent but powerful witness to the sacredness of God-given life. Words are not enough to show that life is sacred. Active justice must be administered when the sacredness of life is violated.

It is recognized that this article will only impress those who are 24 convinced that the Scriptures of the Old and New Testament are the supreme authority of faith and practice. If one accepts the authority of Scripture, then the issue of capital punishment must be decided on what Scripture actually teaches and not on the popular, naturalistic ideas of sociology and penology that prevail today. One generation's thinking is not enough to comprehend the implications of the age-old problem of murder. We need the best thinking of the ages on how best to deal with crime and punishment. We need the Word of God to guide us.

Questions and Suggestions for Writing

1. Vellenga claims (para. 4) that the death penalty "should not be classified with social evils like segregation, racketeering, liquor traffic, and gambling." What

is his point in insisting on this contrast? Would it be an effective reply to him to say: "You are right—capital punishment should be classified with social evils like child abuse, the torture of suspects, and punishing juveniles the same as adults." Explain.

2. Vellenga cites biblical passages (paras. 7–9) in support of the death penalty. In consistency, should he also support carrying out executions by stoning, as the Bible does (see Leviticus 24:16), and the death penalty for witchcraft and adultery? (See Exodus 12:18 and Leviticus 20:10.) Explain why or why not, in an essay of 100 words.

3. Vellenga omits discussion of two important New Testament passages concerning the death penalty. In one, Jesus confronts a crowd about to stone a woman taken in adultery, as Jewish law required in that day. Jesus refuses to participate, saying "He that is without sin among you, let him first cast a stone at her" (John 8:1–11). In the other, the apostle Paul observes: "Recompense to no man evil for evil. . . . Avenge not yourselves . . . for it is written, Vengeance is mine; I will repay, saith the Lord" (Romans 12:17–19). How would you square these passages with Vellenga's account (paras. 11–16) of the New Testament's position on crime and punishment?

4. Vellenga contrasts the proper punishment for murder with being "excused" from punishment (paras. 21–22). Does he imply that a life sentence for murder amounts to such an "excuse"? If not, why does he bring in the point at all?

5. Vellenga observes (para. 23) that "the law of capital punishment must stand, no matter how often a jury recommends mercy." Is he implying that the laws requiring juries in capital cases to decide whether to sentence the convicted murderer to death or to prison should be repealed in favor of a mandatory death penalty? Or is he implying that juries should in effect ignore the law, that is, that they should *always* sentence to death? Or do you think he means something else altogether? In any case, do you agree that such laws should be repealed? Or ignored? Does it matter that since 1976, the Supreme Court has ruled that a mandatory death penalty for murder is unconstitutional? (See the case of *Woodson v. North Carolina.*) Explain your position in an essay of 250 words.

6. In paragraph 24 Vellenga says:

> If one accepts the authority of Scripture, then the issue of capital punishment must be decided on what Scripture actually teaches and not on the popular, naturalistic ideas of sociology and penology that prevail today.

By Vellenga's reasoning, must we say that slavery is acceptable even though "popular, naturalistic ideas . . . that prevail today" condemn it? If you think slavery is intolerable, despite the acceptance of it in the Hebrew Bible and in the New Testament, are you committed to thinking (even if you are a devout Jew or Christian) that the Bible does not offer a guide to how to judge capital punishment?

Ernest van den Haag

The Deterrent Effect of the Death Penalty

Crime is going to be with us as long as there is any social order articulated by laws. There is no point making laws that prohibit some action or other (e.g., murder or theft) unless there is some temptation to commit it. And however harsh the threats of the law, they will not restrain some people, whether because they discount the risk of punishment or because they are exposed to extraordinary temptation. They may hope for an immense profit; or be passionately angry or vindictive; or be in such misery that they feel they have nothing to lose. Thus, I repeat, the problem every society must attempt to solve (in part by means of punishment) is not eliminating crime but controlling it.

That threats will not deter everybody all the time must be expected. And it must also be expected that persons committed to criminal activity— career criminals—are not likely to be restrained by threats; nor are persons strongly under the influence of drugs or intoxicated by their own passions. However, if threats are not likely to deter habitual offenders, they are likely to help deter people from *becoming* habitual offenders.

People are not deterred by exactly calculating the size of the threat and the actual risk of suffering punishment against the likely benefit of the crime they consider committing. Few people calculate at all. Rather, the effect of threats is to lead most people to ignore criminal opportunities most of the time. One just does not consider them—any more than the ordinary person sitting down for lunch starts calculating whether he could have Beluga caviar and champagne instead of his usual hamburger and beer. He is not accustomed to caviar, and one reason he is not accustomed to it is that it costs too much. He does not have to calculate every time to know as much. Similarly, he is not accustomed to breaking the law, and one reason is that it costs too much. He does not need to calculate.

It is quite a different matter if one asks, not: "Do threats deter?" but rather: "How much does one threat deter compared to another?" Does the more severe threat deter significantly more? Does the added deterrence warrant the added severity? Thus, no one pondering the death penalty will contend that it does not deter. The question is: Does it deter more than alternative penalties proposed, such as life imprisonment or any lengthy term of imprisonment?

4

Ernest van den Haag (b. 1914) is the author of several books, including Punishing Criminals *(1975), and formerly a professor of jurisprudence at Fordham University Law School in New York. The following is excerpted from* The Death Penalty Pro and Con: A Debate *(1983).*

In the past many attempts were made to determine whether the death penalty deters the crimes for which it was threatened—capital crimes— more than other penalties, usually life imprisonment, mitigated by parole (and amounting therefore to something like ten years in prison in most cases). Most of these attempts led to ambiguous results, often rendered more ambiguous by faulty procedures and research methods. Frequently, contiguous states—one with and the other without the death penalty— were compared. Or states were compared before and after abolition. Usually these comparisons were based on the legal availability or un- availability of the death penalty rather than on the presence or absence of executions and on their frequency. But what matters is whether the death penalty is practiced, not whether theoretically it is available. Finally, nobody would assert that the death penalty—or any crime-control measure—is the only determinant of the frequency of the crime. The number of murders certainly depends as well on the proportion of young males in the population, on income distribution, on education, on the proportion of various races in the population, on local cultural traditions, on the legal definition of murder, and on other such factors.

Comparisons must take all of these matters into account if they are to evaluate the effect threatened penalties may have in deterring crimes. In contiguous states, influential factors other than the death penalty may differ; they may even differ in the same state before and after abolition. Hence, differences (or equalities) in capital crime frequencies cannot simply be ascribed to the presence or absence of the death penalty. More- over, one does not know how soon a change in penalties will make a difference, if it ever does, or whether prospective murderers will know that the death penalty has been abolished in Maine and kept in Vermont. They certainly will know whether or not there is a death penalty in the United States. But in contiguous states? Or within a short time after abolition or reinstatement?

Theoretically, experiments to avoid all these difficulties are possible. But they face formidable obstacles in practice. If, for instance, the death penalty were threatened for murders committed on Monday, Wednesday, and Friday, and life imprisonment for murders committed on Tuesday, Thursday, and Saturday, we would soon see which days murderers prefer, i.e., how much the death penalty deters on Monday, Wednesday, and Friday over and above life imprisonment threatened for murders com- mitted on the other days. If we find no difference, the abolitionist thesis that the death penalty adds no deterrence over and above the threat of life imprisonment would be confirmed.

In the absence of such experiments, none of the available studies seems 8 conclusive. Recently such studies have acquired considerable mathemati- cal sophistication, and some of the more sophisticated studies have con- cluded, contrary to what used to be accepted scholarly opinion, that the death penalty can be shown to deter over and above life imprisonment. Thus, Isaac Ehrlich, in a study published in the *American Economic Review* (June 1975), concluded that, over the period 1933–1969, "an additional execution per year . . . may have resulted on the average in 7 or 8 fewer murders."

Other studies published since Ehrlich's contend that his results are due to the techniques and periods he selected, and that different techniques and periods yield different results. Despite a great deal of research on all sides, one cannot say that the statistical evidence is conclusive. Nobody has claimed to have *disproved* that the death penalty may deter more than life imprisonment. But one cannot claim, either, that it has been proved statistically in a conclusive manner that the death penalty does deter more than alternative penalties. This lack of proof does not amount to disproof. However, abolitionists insist that there ought to be proof positive.

Unfortunately, there is little proof of the sort sought by those who oppose the death penalty, for the deterrent effect of any sort of punishment. Nobody has statistically shown that 4 years in prison deter more than 2, or 20 more than 10. We assume as much. But I know of no statistical proof. One may wonder why such proof is demanded for the death penalty but not for any other. To be sure, death is more serious a punishment than any other. But 10 years in prison are not exactly trivial either. . . .

If it is difficult, perhaps impossible, to prove statistically—and just as hard to disprove—that the death penalty deters more from capital crimes than available alternative punishments do (such as life imprisonment), why do so many people believe so firmly that the death penalty is a more effective deterrent?

Some are persuaded by irrelevant arguments. They insist that the 12 death penalty at least makes sure that the person who suffered it will not commit other crimes. True. Yet this confuses incapacitation with a specific way to bring it about: death. Death is the surest way to bring about the most total incapacitation, and it is irrevocable. But does incapacitation need to be that total? And is irrevocability necessarily an advantage? Obviously it makes correcting mistakes and rehabilitation impossible. What is the advantage of execution, then, over alternative ways of achieving the desired incapacitation?

More important, the argument for incapacitation confuses the elimination of one murderer (or of any number of murderers) with a reduction in the homicide rate. But the elimination of any specific number of actual or even of potential murderers—and there is some doubt that the actual murderers of the past are the most likely future (potential) murderers— will not affect the homicide rate, except through deterrence. There are enough potential murderers around to replace all those incapacitated. Deterrence may prevent the potential from becoming actual murderers.

But incapacitation of some or all actual murderers is not likely to have much effect by itself. Let us then return to the question: Does capital punishment deter more than life imprisonment?

Science, logic, or statistics often have been unable to prove what common sense tells us to be true. Thus, the Greek philosopher Zeno some 2,000 years ago found that he could not show that motion is possible; indeed, his famous paradoxes appear to show that motion is impossible. Though nobody believed them to be true, nobody succeeded in showing the fallacy of these paradoxes until the rise of mathematical logic less than a hundred years ago. But meanwhile, the world did not stand still. Indeed, nobody argued that motion should stop because it had not been shown to be logically possible. There is no more reason to abolish the death penalty than there was to abolish motion simply because the death penalty has not been, and perhaps cannot be, shown statistically to be a deterrent over and above other penalties. Indeed, there are two quite satisfactory, if non-statistical, indications of the marginal deterrent effect of the death penalty.

In the first place, our experience shows that the greater the threatened penalty, the more it deters. Ceteris paribus, the threat of 50 lashes, deters more than the threat of 5; a $1,000 fine deters more than a $10 fine; 10 years in prison deter more than 1 year in prison—just as, conversely, the promise of a $1,000 reward is a greater incentive than the promise of a $10 reward, etc. There may be diminishing returns. Once a reward exceeds, say, $1 million, the additional attraction may diminish. Once a punishment exceeds, say, 10 years in prison (net of parole), there may be little additional deterrence in threatening additional years. We know hardly anything about diminishing returns of penalties. It would still seem likely, however, that the threat of life in prison deters more than any other term of imprisonment.

The threat of death may deter still more. For it is a mistake to regard 16 the death penalty as though it were of the same kind as other penalties. If it is not, then diminishing returns are unlikely to apply. And death differs significantly, in kind, from any other penalty. Life in prison is still life, however unpleasant. In contrast, the death penalty does not just threaten to make life unpleasant—it threatens to take life altogether. This difference is perceived by those affected. We find that when they have the choice between life in prison and execution, 99 percent of all prisoners under sentence of death prefer life in prison. By means of appeals, pleas for commutation, indeed by all means at their disposal, they indicate that they prefer life in prison to execution.

From this unquestioned fact a reasonable conclusion can be drawn in favor of the superior deterrent effect of the death penalty. Those who have the choice in practice, those whose choice has actual and immediate effects on their life and death, fear death more than they fear life in prison or any other available penalty. If they do, it follows that the threat of the death penalty, all other things equal, is likely to deter more than the threat of life in prison. One is most deterred by what one fears most. From which it follows that whatever statistics fail, or do not fail, to show, the death penalty is likely to be more deterrent than any other.

Suppose now one is not fully convinced of the superior deterrent effect of the death penalty. I believe I can show that even if one is genuinely uncertain as to whether the death penalty adds to deterrence, one should still favor it, from a purely deterrent viewpoint. For if we are not sure, we must choose either to (1) trade the certain death, by execution, of a convicted murderer for the probable survival of an indefinite number of murder victims whose future murder is less likely (whose survival is more likely)—if the convicted murderer's execution deters prospective murderers, as it might, or to (2) trade the certain survival of the convicted murderer for the probable loss of the lives of future murder victims more likely to be murdered because the convicted murderer's nonexecution might not deter prospective murderers, who could have been deterred by executing the convicted murderer.

To restate the matter: If we were quite ignorant about the marginal deterrent effects of execution, we would have to choose—like it or not—between the certainty of the convicted murderer's death by execution and the likelihood of the survival of future victims of other murderers on the one hand, and on the other his certain survival and the likelihood of the death of new victims. I'd rather execute a man convicted of having murdered others than to put the lives of innocents at risk. I find it hard to understand the opposite choice.

Questions and Suggestions for Writing

1. Van den Haag mentions (para. 5) several factors relevant to the volume of murder. Easy availability of handguns (not to mention automatic rifles) is not one of them. Read the essays by Desuka (p. 196) and Selib (p. 201) and explain in 100 words whether you think effective gun control would reduce the volume of murder in the United States.

2. Van den Haag proposes (para. 7) an ideal but impractical experiment that he thinks would settle the question whether the death penalty deters. Modifying his example, suppose there was conclusive evidence that the police were ineffective in catching murderers who commit their crimes on Mondays, Wednesdays, and Fridays, but were effective in arresting those who murder on Tuesdays, Thursdays, and Saturdays. If you planned to murder someone, which day(s) of the week would you choose for the crime, and why?

3. Van den Haag distinguishes (para. 13) between the death penalty as a *deterrent* and as *incapacitative*, and argues that in the latter role the death penalty cannot reduce the crime rate. What is his argument, and do you agree?

4. Van den Haag defends the death penalty as a deterrent, not because of strong evidence but by appeal to "common sense" (para. 14). How reliable are appeals to common sense, anyway? Suppose someone defended the proposition that the sun moves around the earth, and not the earth around the sun, because it's obvious, common sense, as anyone can see. Why should we reject this appeal to common sense (if we should) and accept van den Haag's (if we should)?

5. Van den Haag implies (paras. 16–17) that because death row prisoners prefer to have their sentences commuted to life in prison, the threat of death in general may be a better deterrent than the threat of even a long prison sentence. Lay out this argument, step by step, and explain whether you think it is sound. On what assumptions does it rest? Are they vulnerable to criticism?

6. Van den Haag's final argument (para. 18) appears to assume that the convicted murderer whose execution is in question is really guilty. But suppose he's not, or that the evidence against him is not really conclusive. Do you think this affects the force of van den Haag's argument? Why, or why not?

Stephen Nathanson

What If the Death Penalty Did Save Lives?

I would not deny that if the death penalty prevented murders more successfully than other punishments, this would be a powerful argument in its favor. To grant this, however, is not the same as saying that deterrence is the only relevant factor or that it is by itself decisive. The morality of the death penalty, like the morality of many other acts and policies, depends on many diverse factors. For this reason, many different sorts of reasons bear on our assessment of it. We cannot deduce the moral rightness or wrongness of the death penalty from just one general principle, not even from a plausible principle like "protect innocent life whenever possible." Nonetheless, if the death penalty were a superior deterrent, that would introduce a very weighty moral consideration into the balance of reasons, and the greater its deterrent power (the more lives it could be credited with saving), the weightier that reason would be.

In spite of this, it is easy to see that evidence of superior deterrent power would not by itself show that the death penalty was morally legitimate. We can see this by imagining some punishment that it is plausible to believe would be an extremely effective deterrent and yet that we would regard as immoral in spite of the fact that it saved lives.

Stephen Nathanson (b. 1943), a professor of philosophy at Northeastern University, is the author of The Ideal of Rationality *(1985). The following is excerpted from his book,* An Eye for an Eye? The Morality of Punishing by Death *(1987).*

Imagine, for example, that we were to adopt a policy of punishing murderers by administering prolonged and extraordinarily painful forms of torture, to be followed by eventual execution. Instead of aiming for "humane" forms of execution, we would select the most awful forms of execution in the belief that the more awful the process, the more powerful the deterrent. It is certainly plausible to believe that this sort of policy would have greater deterrent power than the death penalty as now administered. (It might also stimulate violence, as the brutalization hypothesis suggests, but we can leave this possibility aside for the sake of our thought experiment.) Even if this form of punishment were remarkably successful as a deterrent, I doubt that we would think that it was morally permissible to impose it. Such a punishment would require extraordinary callousness to administer, and we would surely condemn it as barbaric.

Or, suppose we adopted the following punishment for murder. We 4 would execute not only the person who committed the murder but also the three people in the world who were of greatest personal significance to the murderer. We could imagine a postconviction hearing in which a report was presented, assessing the murderer's relationship to other people and concluding with a judgment about which three people meant the most to the murderer. All of them would then be executed. If we were solely interested in making potential murderers "think twice," this policy would probably work much better than the death penalty as currently practiced. Yet, again, this particular practice would be truly abhorrent, and it would remain abhorrent, even if it saved more lives than other punishments.

What these examples show is that superior deterrent power is not the only issue. A punishment may save more lives and yet involve society in such ghastly practices that we would reject it as immoral.

To establish in principle that a punishment with superior deterrent power may be immoral is a matter of considerable significance. Nonetheless, by itself, it does not show that the death penalty is sufficiently ghastly to merit rejection. The death penalty would qualify as sufficiently bad in itself to be rejected by the absolute pacifist, for whom all killing is immoral, or by the person who finds executions inherently barbaric. These reactions, however, are not widely shared. Most people believe that killing is morally permissible in some circumstances, and most people think that executions can be carried out in a way that is sufficiently humane to bring them within the bounds of civility. I am not sure that the second of these judgments is correct, but I see no effective way to argue against it.[1]

I will not then try to argue that executions are on a par with torture or with the practice of executing those whom murderers care about. Rather, having shown that superior deterrent power by itself would not guarantee

---

[1]For an attempt to show that executions are inhumane in the same way that torture is, see Jeffrey Reiman, "Justice, Civilization, and the Death Penalty," *Philosophy and Public Affairs* 14 (1985): 134–42.

the morality of punishing by death, I want to see whether there are other factors that would call into question the morality of executions, even if executions were the most effective way to save lives.

One of the most powerful objections to the death penalty arises from 8 the possibility of executing innocent people. I take it that we would not *knowingly* execute innocent people even if this had a positive deterrent effect on the homicide rate. If this is true, then we should be deeply disturbed if we could predict that, under a death penalty system, we would unintentionally execute innocent persons. If we could predict that among the effects of instituting the death penalty would be the execution of innocent persons, this would count heavily against the death penalty, even if we could predict that another effect would be a decrease in the homicide rate.

The problem of executing the innocent is, at a certain level, quite simple. Executing innocent people would be a dreadful effect of the death penalty, and it would not be a possible effect of long term imprisonment, a possible alternative to executions. Hence, we could have a severe punishment that did not threaten to result in our killing innocent people. To maintain the death penalty is to be willing to risk innocent lives.

No one could dismiss the relevance or force of this argument, and no one could deny that executing innocent persons is a terrible act. Nonetheless, this argument raises extraordinarily difficult issues of what has sometimes been called "moral arithmetic." There would be no problem, of course, if the number of innocent people executed were larger than the number of innocent lives saved. Nor, I take it, would there be a problem if the numbers were equal. But, the issue becomes much murkier in the situation in which more innocent lives are saved by deterrence than are lost through erroneous executions.

Suppose that there were a net gain in lives saved but that the number of lives saved was extremely small. Then, I think, we would reject the death penalty and forgo the added deterrence it provides. Our decision would be supported by the idea that it is worse for us actually to kill innocent people than it is for us to fail to prevent the deaths of innocent people. The moral significance of the distinction between the harms we cause and those we fail to prevent has been called into question by some recent thinkers.[2] Nonetheless, we generally do distinguish between failing to save a life (say, by not contributing to famine relief) and actually killing someone (by taking away his food, for example). While the failure to protect is morally bad, the active killing seems much worse. So, if innocents are to die, it is better that we not be the agents of their deaths.

If, however, the number of innocents likely to be executed by mistake 12 is very small and the number of potential homicide victims whose lives can

[2]One noteworthy example is Peter Singer, *Practical Ethics* (Cambridge: Cambridge University Press, 1979), Ch. 8.

be saved is very large, then we might well conclude that morality requires us to execute murderers. If this were our judgment, we would then be under a great deal of pressure to try to specify what "very large" and "very small" mean in this context. How many lives must be saved by executions in order for us to be justified in accepting the death penalty, even though we know that some innocent people will be executed?

I fear that I have nothing very helpful to say about how to approach the "moral arithmetic" in this case.

Nonetheless, I think we can reach several conclusions related to the problem of executing innocent people. First, if the death penalty is to be justified, we must have good reason to believe that our system is on the whole quite reliable and that very few innocent people will ever be executed. We must do our utmost to provide stringent safeguards that will make such executions highly unlikely—even if this means bearing extra legal costs, putting up with long delays, and sometimes seeing death sentences overturned for what appear to be merely "legal technicalities." Moreover, we must be confident that these safeguards will work.

Second, we must have reason to believe that the number of lives saved is *substantial*. Superior deterrent power cannot mean simply that a few lives are likely to be saved. If we assume that some innocents will be executed and that it is worse for us actively to kill a person than it is for us to fail in our efforts to prevent someone's death, then executions can be justified only if they lead to substantial savings of lives.

Finally, it must be the case that there are no feasible, morally prefer- 16 able alternatives to the death penalty, no policies that are available to us and that would be equally effective in saving these innocent lives. If there were other morally acceptable policies that did not involve the possibility of executing innocents and yet that were as effective in preventing murders, then we would be morally bound to try these alternatives. If it turned out, for example, that homicide rates could be lowered through greater controls on the availability of guns, or if homicide rates are related to unemployment rates so that lowering unemployment would (along with its other benefits) lower the homicide rate, then it would be our duty to adopt these alternatives to the death penalty. It would be immoral for us to adopt the death penalty if we could predict that some innocent people would be executed and if we knew that alternative policies could save lives equally well.

The problem of executing innocent people is not imaginary or purely hypothetical. The most thorough study available on the execution of innocents has recently been carried out by Hugo Bedau and Michael Radelet.[3] They claim to have found that for the period 1900 to 1980, about 350

---

[3]H. Bedau and M. Radelet, "Miscarriages of Justice in Potentially Capital Cases," *Stanford Law Review* 40 (1987).

people were wrongfully convicted of capital offenses. Of these, 139 were sentenced to death, and 23 were actually executed.

These figures may be reassuring to some. One might react by thinking that the number of errors is small and that most of those wrongfully convicted were not after all executed. Somehow, it might be thought, the system was able to correct these errors in time. A closer look is less reassuring, however, for the evidence that led to a particular person's escaping execution has usually appeared by chance or resulted from the efforts of people outside the legal process. Only in 37 cases, about 10 percent of the cases, were errors discovered by officials. Moreover, as time passes and with the death of those executed, further evidence regarding their cases becomes increasingly difficult to gather. It is plausible to suppose that unknown cases remain and that the number of innocent persons executed is larger than the 23 that Bedau and Radelet have verified. . . .

In a study of the death penalty in Georgia since the *Gregg* decision, Ursula Bentele reports on the case of Jerry Banks, a man who discovered two dead bodies while hunting.[4] Banks went to a road and stopped a car, asking the driver to report the deaths to the police. Banks waited for the police, and when they arrived, he led them to the bodies. One month later, Banks, a black man, was charged with the murder. He was tried, convicted, and sentenced to death, in spite of the fact that a neighbor testified that Banks had been at her home at the time when the shooting occurred. Moreover, the driver whom Banks had signaled and who phoned the police was never called as a witness, and a detective testified that he did not know his identity. In fact, this person, a Mr. Eberhardt, had left his name with the police, had made himself available to the grand jury, had spoken with the judge who conducted the trial, and had made a statement for the sheriff. The Supreme Court of Georgia, in ordering a new trial, specifically noted that the sheriff and other officers knew the identity of this witness but "either intentionally or inadvertently" kept it from Banks and his lawyer.

Banks was tried a second time and again convicted and sentenced to 20 death, apparently because of ineffective work by his lawyer. Only after this second death sentence did two new attorneys discover evidence that the murder weapon could not have been Banks's hunting rifle. They found witnesses who had reported hearing rapid fire shots that could not have come from Banks's shotgun. Others reported that they had seen two white men arguing shortly before the murder took place. Several of the witnesses had actually reported what they had seen to the police, but the reports were ignored and were not introduced at Banks's second trial.

In a second appeal, Banks again won a new trial. This time, after seven years of legal proceedings stretching from 1974 through 1981, all charges against him were dropped.

[4]"The Death Penalty in Georgia: Still Arbitrary," *Washington University Law Quarterly* 62 (1985): 597–600.

While this case may not be typical, the Bedau–Radelet study shows that it is far from unique. The occurrence of such cases is sufficient to call into question our confidence that the awesome responsibility of dealing with crimes that may lead to execution is treated with appropriate care by officials. In the Banks case, physical evidence and witnesses' reports were lost, neglected, or suppressed. If the new attorneys had not intervened on his behalf after the second trial, he would have been executed, and the error might never have come to light.

In considering the problem of executing innocent people, then, we are not dealing with a merely hypothetical problem. With the best will in the world, our system will make mistakes. What Bentele's description of the Banks case and the Bedau–Radelet study clearly indicate is that we cannot count on the best will in the world being exercised by those involved in prosecuting and judging people accused of murder. This is a distressing but important fact about the criminal justice system.

A person can be wrongfully executed even if he or she actually did kill someone. As we have already seen, neither morality nor the law treats all killings as equally bad. In order to determine that a person has committed the type of killing for which the law sanctions execution, the crime must be distinguished from other killings that are not capital offenses. Finally, even after conviction for first degree murder, difficult issues concerning mitigating and aggravating circumstances must be considered. . . .[5]

[W]hen we are toting up the costs of the death penalty, we need to include not only the execution of those who were factually innocent of any crime whatever but also those cases in which the accused were guilty of a killing but nonetheless did not satisfy the legal criteria for execution. We need to recall as well the haziness of these criteria and the resulting fact that many who have been condemned to die would not strike most people as those who were most deserving of death.[6]

That wrongful executions of this sort occur is perhaps best revealed by the history of punishments for rape. While rape is a very serious crime, most people would not think that punishment by death is morally required for it. A similar judgment was reached by the Supreme Court in 1977. It ruled that execution is a disproportionately severe punishment for the crime of rape and thus constitutes a cruel and unusual punishment. Nonetheless, between 1930 and 1964, 455 people—90 percent of whom were black—were executed for rape in the United States.[7]

Even in the case of killings, the facts are complicated, and leniency and severity in sentencing are the products of numerous factors, many of

---

[5]For a powerful and illuminating discussion of these issues, the reader is again referred to Charles Black, *Capital Punishment: The Inevitability of Caprice and Mistake*, 2d ed. (New York: Norton, 1981).

[6]For some comparisons of cases, see U. Bentele, "The Death Penalty in Georgia: Still Arbitrary," *Washington University Law Quarterly* 62 (1985): 585–91.

[7]H. Bedau, *The Death Penalty in America*, 3d ed. (New York: Oxford University Press, 1982), Table 2–3–2.

them irrelevant to the nature of the crime. There is no reason to believe that our system will cease to be arbitrary and discriminatory in these ways. Even a death penalty system that deterred murders and hence saved more lives than one that imposed imprisonment alone would continue to be flawed by uneven justice. As long as racial, class, religious, and economic bias continue to be important determinants of who is executed, the death penalty will both create and perpetuate injustice.

To recall an earlier example, imagine that 100 executions per year save 28 more lives than no executions at all. Imagine further that of all those convicted of murder, the only ones who are executed have red hair. Consider how such people would regard the criminal justice system. Or, to bring home the point, imagine that instead of red heads, those executed are always members of some group (racial, ethnic, religious, or professional) to which *you* belong. Each of us would be deeply disturbed by such a pattern. We would feel strongly that members of our group were being treated unjustly, that our lives were not being treated as significant, that we alone were paying the price for added deterrence. Yet because of our increased exposure to executions, we would be gaining less from the decrease in homicide rates. Whatever the target group might be, this practice would be an expression of the strongest contempt and lack of regard for its members. The injustice would be obvious.

All of the defects of such an arbitrary system remain and continue to constitute a serious objection to the death penalty. Even if it were a more effective deterrent than imprisonment, an arbitrarily administered death penalty would be morally unjust, and it would be cruel and unusual in the sense affirmed by the Supreme Court in *Furman v. Georgia.*

Philosophers are especially fond of "what if?" questions. Such questions allow us to alter factual contingencies and are sometimes helpful in revealing the principles that underlie our judgments. So, let us ask, "What if the deterrent power of the death penalty were so great that it would be extremely difficult to deny its use?"

Suppose, for example, that every execution of a person for murder saved 10,000 lives. If that were the effect of the death penalty, it would be difficult for almost all of us to deny that it was justified, even if it possessed all the defects I have described. What does this show?

One might think that it shows that the death penalty is theoretically 32 justifiable and hence that it offends no deep principles. If the world were a little different and the death penalty were more clearly a superior deterrent, then it would be morally permissible.

I think that this conclusion is mistaken. In this instance, the "what if?" question and the imaginary case of saving thousands by killing one are not helpful. They distort our thinking about the death penalty rather than helping to clarify it. We can see the distorting effects of the example by noting that we could construct a similar argument for the view that there is nothing deeply wrong with executing purely innocent people. Suppose that by executing a person who was totally innocent of any crime, we could get the same life-saving effects. Kill one innocent person—perhaps in a gruesome, torturous manner—and 10,000 others who would have been murder victims will be spared.

Even if we were to decide that executing an innocent person was the morally best thing to do *in this situation*, that would do nothing to show that knowingly executing innocent persons is not fundamentally wrong in our world. It would not show that if only things were a little different, executing innocent persons would be permissible. So, likewise, the fact that we can imagine the death penalty having extreme life-protecting powers does not show that it is not deeply defective in our world. It does not show that the only thing that matters is deterrence.

In this instance, stretching our imaginations may have the effect of breaking down our ability to make a moral assessment. Our moral understanding breaks down here because we have a clash between the prohibition against performing a ghastly act, an act that is a paradigm of immorality, and the injunction that we perform an act that will result in the saving of many, many lives. Where the stakes are so high, the gains on one side so great, it may be that any moral rule or principle can be overwhelmed. Yet, this does nothing to show that in normal circumstances, we ought to treat these principles as if they had no moral importance.

Such examples are in the end totally irrelevant to our reflections about the death penalty.[8] In our world, the system of law and punishment does not operate in this way. No magical and extraordinary effects flow from the punishment of individual criminals. Rather, there are numerous actions that involve many different people, and it is the patterns formed by these actions that have overall social effects like the deterrence of homicide. It is the pattern of treatment of criminals that serves to deter. Likewise, it is the pattern of how we treat even those who violate the laws that reveals the extent to which concerns for justice and human dignity play a part in our lives.

It is highly unlikely that the death penalty will ever operate so effectively as to save many more lives than other, less severe punishments. Yet, given its defects, it would have to save many more lives in order for it to be a genuine candidate for moral legitimacy. If it had this positive effect, we would be faced with an anguished choice, just as we would be faced with an anguished choice if we found that executing innocent people saved many lives. Fortunately, all of this is merely hypothetical. We have no reason to believe that the death penalty does save more lives than other punishments, and so we need not actually confront this choice.

[8]Charles Black argues against the relevance of several imaginary and hypothetical situations in *Capital Punishment: The Inevitability of Caprice and Mistake*, 2d ed. (New York: Norton, 1981), 157–74.

Questions and Suggestions for Writing

1. Nathanson believes (paras. 3–5) that some punishments are too "barbaric" to use even if they proved to be very effective deterrents. Later (para. 25) he cites the ruling of the Supreme Court in *Coker v. Georgia* (1977), holding that the death penalty for rape was a "cruel and unusual punishment" and therefore unconstitutional. Is this what Nathanson meant by a "barbaric" though effective punishment? Or did the Court really mean something else altogether? Go to your library and read the Court's reasoning in the *Coker* case, and write a 250-word essay on the topic.

2. Nathanson rejects "barbaric" punishments (paras. 3–5), but he does not object on this ground to life imprisonment. Yet why is this not barbaric, and no less barbaric than death? Or why is whipping (say, ten lashes) more barbaric, if it is, than a year in prison? If you were convicted of a serious crime, and could choose your sentence, which would you choose, prison or whipping? (or, say, having your hand cut off instead of serving ten years in prison?) Defend your choice in an essay of 250 words.

3. In this century in the United States, executions have been carried out by firing squad, hanging, the electric chair, the gas chamber, and most recently by lethal injection. Which of these methods do you think is most humane, and why? The least humane? Write a 500-word essay explaining your views.

4. Suppose someone objected to Nathanson that he seems to expect the criminal justice system to be virtually infallible before he will allow any executions, whereas we know that no human institution is infallible. Certainly, parole boards are not, for they sometimes release convicted murderers who murder again. Nathanson's demands, therefore, are too strong. How might Nathanson reply?

5. Nathanson reflects on the problem of "moral arithmetic" (paras. 10–13) and concludes that he has "nothing very helpful to say" on it. But, surely, saving more lives rather than fewer is better. Consider the so-called trolley problem: You are at the control of a runaway streetcar, and all you can do is to throw the switch ahead. As you can see, if you go down the left track, you will surely hit and kill twenty innocent people, whereas if you go down the right track, you will hit and kill only one. You know nothing about any of these people, there is no way to warn them, etc. Surely, it is better to throw the switch so that you kill only the one, and not the twenty! Why might Nathanson argue that, true though this moral arithmetic is, it sheds little or no light on the trade-off between the murders prevented only by the death penalty (via deterrence or incapacitation, or both) and innocent persons executed?

Vivian Berger

Rolling the Dice to Decide Who Dies

Since 1984, when the Court of Appeals held unconstitutional the last vestige of the death penalty in New York State, New York has been one of fewer than a third of the states in this country that do not provide for capital punishment. In each of the past few years, however, our Legislature has passed bills reauthorizing death as the sanction for certain types of murder. Governor Cuomo, a committed opponent of capital punishment as was Governor Carey before him, has consistently vetoed these efforts. But sooner or later the governor will relinquish office. Surely, therefore, a time will come when the state acquires as chief executive someone who either supports execution or declines to counter the lawmakers' wishes. Then New Yorkers, acting through their elected officials, will have to regard the death penalty as more than a mere symbolic gesture—a banner to wave in the war against crime.

Because that point may be in the offing, the New York Bar, whose collective opinion should weigh heavily in the final decision whether we remain an abolitionist state, must begin to think seriously about the issues. I, like our governor, fervently oppose capital punishment; and I do so based on considerable experience with how it operates, not just with the rhetoric that surrounds it. I hope to persuade those of you who have no opinion on the subject and perhaps even some who currently favor reviving the death sentence in New York that such a course has nothing to commend it. To the contrary, reinstatement would amount to a giant step backward in this state's historical march toward a decent and efficient system of justice.

To plunge yourself right into the reality of capital punishment, imagine that you are sitting on a jury in Georgia or Florida or some other death-penalty state in the following cases. Your awesome task is to determine whether the defendant should receive life imprisonment or death. Even if you could in fact never sentence a person to die, you must try to envision that possibility—for the prosecution would have struck you for cause unless you had indicated on voir-dire that you would consider the option of death. Here are the five cases in cameo:

#1. A 19-year-old man, John, and his companion stole a young woman's purse on the street, pushed her to the ground, and jumped into their

Vivian Berger (b. 1944), a professor of law at Columbia University in New York, is a founding member of the New York Lawyers against the Death Penalty. She wrote this article for the October 1988 issue of the New York State Bar Journal. *Footnotes, chiefly legal citations, have been omitted.*

nearby car. A taxi driver, observing the theft, sought to block their getaway with his cab. The defendant, John, shot and killed him. It was his first violent offense.

#2. A 19-year-old man, Joe, tried to grab the purse of a 54-year-old woman in a shopping center parking lot. She resisted and began screaming. They struggled for the purse and Joe shot her once in the side, killing her. He had prior misdemeanor convictions for shoplifting and simple battery as well as a felony conviction for theft.

#3. A 21-year-old man, Robert, drove up to an all-night self-service station and filled his tank. He was paying for the gas with a "hot" credit card when the attendant, a college student, became suspicious that the card was stolen. Robert then shot the attendant once, killing him instantly, in order to avoid being arrested for the credit-card theft. Robert had previous convictions for an unarmed juvenile robbery and the burglary of a store.

#4. A 20-year-old man, Nickie, who was under the influence of drugs, broke into a neighbor's apartment and bludgeoned her and her 8-year-old daughter to death with a hammer. He said later that he had done it because he liked to see blood. Nickie had past convictions for robbery and attempted aggravated rape.

#5. A 26-year-old man, Stephen, together with a 17-year-old friend, burglarized the home of an elderly widow for whom the friend had done yard work. They were planning to rob her. The woman ended by being raped, beaten, and strangled as well as robbed. The defendant, Stephen, admitted that the two of them had raped and robbed her. He insisted, however (and no witness supported or contradicted his story) that only the friend had killed the victim and that he, Stephen, had tried in vain to stop the murder. He had previously committed an unarmed "date rape."

Ask yourself which, if any, of these men you would have sentenced to life in prison and which to death. Next, try to guess how the actual jurors decided these cases. In fact, #1, John, the purse-snatcher who shot the cabbie, received life. #2, Joe, the other purse-snatcher who shot the 54-year-old woman, was sentenced to die. #3, Robert, the credit-card thief who shot the attendant at the gas service station, got death as well; he is one of my clients. #4, Nickie, the hammer-bludgeoner who liked to see blood, got life imprisonment. Finally, #5, Stephen, who robbed and raped and may (or may not) have strangled the widow, was sentenced to death; he is also my client.

Whether or not you called any of the cases correctly, you might want to ask yourself: "Did the divergent results make sense?" If there was a pattern, I must say it eludes me. But for the moment, taking some liberties with the facts and treating my examples as hypothetical instead of the true accounts which they are, I want the reader to consider the possibility that jurors in a couple of the cases that ended in death might likelier have opted for life imprisonment if they had received some more information. For example, suppose the sentencing jurors had heard that Joe had been the incredibly abused child of a violent alcoholic father and a battered, helpless, incompetent mother? That the father had made a game of placing Joe and his siblings in a tight circle and throwing heavy objects like glass ashtrays into the air for the pleasure of seeing who would be hit? That Joe had at last run away from home at the age of 12, camped for some months in a Dempsey dumpster, and then been taken in by a man who sheltered him in return for homosexual favors? That during his one, too-brief experience in foster care when he was nine, Joe responded with great affection and excellent behavior to the love and attention of his foster mother? Or, to take another example, suppose the jury had known that Stephen had an IQ in the high 50's or low 60's? That confronted once with a power mower that wasn't running, Stephen put water from a hose inside it because he had seen others fill the machine but never realized that not *any* type of liquid would do?

Of course, no one knows how real jurors would have reacted to the scenarios I described. But experts in capital defense work agree that no matter how appalling the crime, twelve not unduly sentimental jurors may well decide to spare a defendant when shown that he is a human being with some explanation if not excuse for his horrible acts. Yet while the jurors routinely hear the worst things about the defendant, including usually his criminal record, what is shocking is that in so many cases they hear *nothing* else about him that might be deemed relevant to sentence. (Why this occurs, and what it means for the operation of capital punishment, I will explore further shortly.) What they *do* necessarily learn is the race of both defendant and victim. If I had recounted some more examples of the type I asked you to judge as a juror and told you the race of the persons involved, or at least the victim's, you might have begun to detect a pattern that did not emerge from the *pertinent* data. To this topic, too, I will soon return. But what I hope I have done thus far is to give the reader a "slice of death." At the very least, by relating these sadly prosaic stories, I wanted to scotch the notion which so many people have that death is reserved for special cases: the serial killers, the depraved torturers, the Mafia hit men. In New York we deal with the Joes and Stephens each week by the hundreds.

A bit of history sheds some light on how Capital Punishment U.S.A. acquired its present salient features. The watershed came when the United States Supreme Court handed down the landmark *Furman v. Georgia* in 1972. *Furman* invalidated all existing death sentence statutes as violative of the Eighth Amendment's ban on cruel and unusual punishment and thus depopulated state death rows of their 629 occupants. Although there was no majority opinion and only Justices Brennan and Marshall would have held execution to be intrinsically cruel and unusual, Justice Stewart captured the essence of the centrist justices' view—that the death penalty *as actually*   12 *applied* was unconstitutionally arbitrary—in his famous analogy between the imposition of a capital sentence and the freakishness of a strike of lightning. Being "struck" by a capital sentence was cruel and unusual in the same way as being hit by a lightning bolt: the event was utterly capricious and random.

But worse, if possible, than death sentences that are entirely arbitrary in the sense that a strike of lightning is freakish are those imposed on invidious grounds: where the lightning rod is race, religion, gender, or class. As Justice Douglas trenchantly remarked: "The Leopolds and Loebs are given prison terms, not sentenced to death." Blacks, however, were disproportionately sentenced to die, especially for the rape of white females. Indeed, the abolitionist campaign, which culminated in the *Furman* decision, had its genesis in the effort to eliminate capital punishment for rape. So perhaps, historically, the death penalty was really less "unusual" than "cruel": an invisible hand, and clearly a white one, was sorting out whites from blacks and thereby creating a pattern of results that many decent people abhorred.

Probably the justices hoped and believed that after *Furman* the death penalty in the United States would remain dead; if so, they were wrong. Many legislatures simply determined to try until they got it right. And in 1976, in *Gregg v. Georgia* and its four companion cases, a majority of the Court upheld the post-*Furman* capital punishment statutes of Georgia, Florida, and Texas against a challenge to their facial validity, while simultaneously nullifying the revised laws of two other states. Those states had sought to resolve the randomness problem identified in *Furman* by ensuring that lightning would strike *all* persons convicted of murder in the first degree, rather than just a hapless few. In rejecting this tack, the Court noted that mandatory death sentence laws did not really resolve the problem but instead "simply papered [it] over" since juries responded by refusing to convict certain arbitrarily chosen defendants of first-degree murder.

More importantly, though, the justices ratified the so-called guided discretion statutes at issue in three of the five cases. The Court specifically approved some features of the new statutes which it expected would reduce the capriciousness of capital punishment and at the same time further the goal of individualization in sentencing. Thus, to take Georgia's law as a sample, the *Gregg* majority endorsed its provision for separate trials on guilt and penalty and automatic appellate review of sentences of death. The bifurcated trial innovation permitted the admission of evidence relevant only to sentence (for instance, the defendant's prior convictions) in a way that would not prejudice the jury in deciding guilt or innocence. The Court also emphasized that, at the penalty trial, not only did the state have to prove some aggravating circumstances beyond the fact of the murder itself (for example, torture or a previous record of criminal violence) but also defendants had the opportunity to offer evidence in mitigation—brave-conduct medals, or thrown ashtrays and waterlogged mowers.

It is basically under these post-*Gregg* schemes that Capital Punish- 16
ment U.S.A. has been operating for over a decade. Until recently, however, only a handful of executions occurred every year. But in the mid-80s, in the wake of four adverse Supreme Court decisions—after a period in which the Court had overturned the capital sentence in 14 out of 15 cases, the engine of death acquired new steam. In 1984 alone, there were 21 executions (almost twice as many as in all of the years following *Gregg*); 1985 and 1986 saw 18 apiece, and the body count continues to grow. Thus, *Furman II* is hardly on the horizon now. That being so, if our next governor permits the enactment of capital statutes, the Court will surely not "veto" them: members of the Bar should understand that New York will have not dead-letter laws but dying defendants.

Why should New Yorkers oppose this result? Some believe that capital punishment inherently violates human dignity. But because many disagree with that view and my expertise is only lawyering, not moral philosophy, I leave it to others to debate the ultimate ethical issues. I take my stand with an eminent colleague, Professor Charles L. Black, Jr. Like me, refusing to resolve the basic clash of values, he reminds us wisely that there is "no abstract capital punishment." Asked how he would feel about the death penalty if only its administration were perfected, the professor replies: "What would you do if an amoeba were taught to play the piano?" In other words, it's a silly question; capital punishment *is* as it *does*. Therefore, the often high-flown rhetoric bandied about by the pros and antis assumes, in my view, second place to the homely facts that make the American "legal system not good enough to choose people to die." I end with a few of the reasons why, which I hope that those who support or are open to reviving the death sentence in New York take deeply to heart.

Consider, first, the arbitrariness of the death penalty—how, in the real world, capital punishment must be forever married to caprice. From the initial decision to charge through the determination of sentence, the criminal justice system in general is rife with unreviewable discretion. The capital setting provides all of the same opportunities (and several more) for virtually unconstrained choice: the players roll the dice in a game where the stakes consist of life or death. Non-exhaustively, the prosecutor must decide such things as whether to charge capital murder instead of a lesser degree of homicide; whether to plea bargain with the accused or, in a multidefendant case, whether to grant one of the defendants immunity or some other concession in return for cooperating with the state; and whether, if the defendant is convicted of a potentially capital charge, to move the case to the penalty phase and attempt to obtain a verdict of death. Many of those choices and especially the likelihood of plea bargaining will be dramatically affected by factors that have little or nothing to do with the nature of the crime or the strength of the evidence. These factors include geography (district attorneys have different policies on capital punishment, not to speak of varying amounts of dollars to spend on costly capital litigation); political concerns like the proximity of an election; the perceived acumen and aggressiveness of defense counsel; and the desires of the victim's family.

Other players than the prosecutor occupy key roles, too, of course. These include the judge and jury and, depending on local practice, the governor, administrative board, or both, who may be requested to grant clemency. Jurors, it is worth noting, not only possess the completely unreviewable discretion to acquit or compromise on lesser charges; they are also asked, in penalty trials, to determine such intrinsically fuzzy questions as "Will the defendant kill again?" or "Was this murder especially heinous, atrocious, or cruel?" or "Do the aggravating circumstances outweigh the proof in mitigation?" The latter inquiry forces jurors to try to assess how, for instance, the fact that the murder occurred during the course of a robbery and was committed to eliminate a witness should be balanced against the facts that the defendant was high on crack, is a first offender, and has a wife and three children who love him. Could *you* meaningfully weigh such factors?

Consider, second, that these sources of arbitrariness are exacerbated 20 by extreme variations in the performance of defense counsel. Ineffective assistance of counsel completely permeates the penalty phase of capital trials in the post-*Gregg* era. With regard to cases like Stephen's and Joe's and the others with which I began this piece, I pointed out how often the jury hears nothing personal about the defendant even when substantial mitigating proof is readily available, yet I did not explain this phenomenon. The explanation is simply that many defense attorneys do little or nothing by way of investigation geared to sentencing issues and hence do not themselves learn what they should be spreading before the jury. Why do attorneys drop the ball at the penalty phase with such depressing regularity? Some lack the knowledge, experience, or will to assume the role demanded of them in the unique capital setting. Lawyers find it easier to hunt for what one whom I know called "eyeball witnesses" than to construct a psychodrama about a protagonist who is frequently hostile, uncommunicative, beset with mental or emotional problems, or all of the above—especially when to do so involves searching out potential witnesses (family, friends, neighbors, teachers) who, like the client, usually hail from a different racial or socioeconomic milieu from counsel. Others curtail their investigations on account of shockingly low compensation. Still others "throw in the towel" once the verdict of guilt is in. Whatever the causes of these derelictions, most or all can be expected both to cross jurisdictional lines and to continue into the future.

Consider, finally, the last but hardly the least point in my brief against the death penalty—racial discrimination in sentencing. In its modern guise, racial bias focuses primarily on the race of the *victim*, not the defendant. Sophisticated studies by social scientists have demonstrated that murderers of whites are much likelier to be sentenced to death than murderers of blacks. In Georgia, for instance, Professor David Baldus's prizewinning study revealed that, after one accounted for dozens of variables that might legitimately affect punishment, the killer of a white stood a *4.3 times* greater chance of receiving death than did a person who killed a black! The reason for these results is clear and as firmly rooted in our history as prejudice against the black defendant: white society places a premium upon white life. New Yorkers inclined to discount such division on grounds of race as a regional Southern phenomenon need only recall the tensions evoked by the Howard Beach and Goetz trials to see how very wrong they are. In any event, capital punishment only magnifies inequalities of race that persist in the criminal justice system and in American society generally.

Last term, the Supreme Court rejected a challenge, grounded on the damning Baldus statistics, to the death penalty as applied in Georgia. Assuming the validity of the study, the Court nonetheless held 5–4 in *McCleskey v. Kemp* that unless a capital defendant could prove that some specific actor or actors purposely discriminated in his case, thereby causing his sentence of death, neither the Eighth Amendment nor Equal Protection was offended. I hope, however, that New Yorkers will be offended by, and wary of, the prospect of even risking racially tainted sentencing where a person's life is at stake.

There is no good reason to take that risk. The death penalty has not been shown to deter murder. Administering it with even the minimum amount of decency will further increase the logjams in our crowded courts and will likely cost more in the end than the alternative of long-term imprisonment. At worst, some innocent men and women will be executed as time goes by. At best, the guilty we choose to kill will be morally indistinguishable from the rest whose lives we opt to spare. New York cannot—in any sense of the word—afford to resurrect such a bankrupt system. Thoughtful citizens should be proud that our last two governors have resisted the siren call of capital "justice." The Bar, therefore, should strongly support the principled and pragmatic stance of opposition to capital punishment.

Questions and Suggestions for Writing

1. Write a 100-word essay on the question whether a state governor should veto a death penalty law if he or she is personally opposed to capital punishment.

2. During the presidential campaign of 1988, the death penalty was frequently mentioned by then Vice President Bush, who was for it, and by his opponent, Governor Dukakis, who was against it. Do some research on the campaign and

write a 100-word essay on the question whether the pro–capital punishment position of the Republicans was largely what Berger calls "a mere symbolic gesture" (para. 1).

3. Relying only on the information Berger gives in paragraphs 3–8 about those five cases, decide how you would sentence each defendant; then compare your results with those that actually occurred (para. 9). Write a 500-word essay defending your proposed sentences whether or not they agree with those the juries actually handed down.

4. Take into account the additional information Berger supplies in paragraph 10 about the five cases she discusses, and write a 250-word essay explaining why this additional evidence would or would not cause you to change your proposed sentences.

5. Defenders of the death penalty often arouse support for capital punishment by describing murderers as "savage beasts" or as "hopeless recidivists" and the like, whereas Berger (para. 11) arouses opposition to it by telling the reader "sadly prosaic stories" about "the Johns and the Stephens." To what extent do you think such techniques shed light on the morality of the death penalty? On the appropriate legal punishment for the crime of murder?

6. Berger quotes (para. 13) Justice Douglas's reference to Leopold and Loeb. Who were they, and why are their cases relevant to the death penalty controversy? Do some library research to find out, and write a 500-word essay on the lessons of the Leopold and Loeb case. (*Hint:* The case occurred in Chicago in the 1920s, and involved the famous defense attorney, Clarence Darrow.)

7. In response to Berger's point about the "arbitrariness" of the death penalty system (paras. 18–19), a death penalty advocate might reply: Since all murderers really deserve to die anyway, why make so much out of the arbitrary way in which only some are actually sentenced to death and executed? What's so unfair about the good luck of all those who aren't executed even though they deserve it? How might Berger reply?

8. In response to Berger's point about the "racial discrimination" in sentencing (para. 21), a defender of the death penalty might object: The solution to the problem of racial discrimination in death sentencing is not abolishing the death penalty; it is sentencing and executing more whites who kill blacks and more blacks who kill blacks. How might Berger reply?

Part Three

MODELS OF ARGUMENT: ENDURING QUESTIONS

12

Do We Have Inalienable Rights?

Plato

Crito

(Scene: A room in the State prison at Athens in the year 399 B.C. The time is half an hour before dawn, and the room would be almost dark but for the light of a little oil lamp. There is a pallet bed against the back wall. At the head of it a small table supports the lamp; near the foot of it Crito is sitting patiently on a stool. He is an old man, kindly, practical, simple-minded; at present he is suffering from acute emotional strain. On the bed lies Socrates asleep. He stirs, yawns, opens his eyes and sees Crito.)

 Socrates: Here already, Crito? Surely it is still early?

 Crito: Indeed it is.

 Socrates: About what time?

 Crito: Just before dawn.

   4

 Plato (427–347 B.C.), an Athenian aristocrat by birth, was the student of one great philosopher (Socrates) and the teacher of another (Aristotle). His legacy of more than two dozen dialogues—imaginary discussions between Socrates and one or more other speakers, usually young Athenians—has been of such influence that the whole of Western philosophy can be characterized, A. N. Whitehead wrote, as "a series of footnotes to Plato." Plato's interests encompassed the full range of topics in philosophy: ethics, politics, logic, metaphysics, epistemology, aesthetics, psychology, and education.

 The selection reprinted here, Crito, is the third of four dialogues telling the story of the final days of Socrates (469–399 B.C.). The first in the sequence, Euthyphro,

Socrates: I wonder that the warder paid any attention to you.

Crito: He is used to me now, Socrates, because I come here so often; besides, he is under some small obligation to me.

Socrates: Have you only just come, or have you been here for long?

Crito: Fairly long.

Socrates: Then why didn't you wake me at once, instead of sitting by my bed so quietly?

Crito: I wouldn't dream of such a thing, Socrates. I only wish I were not so sleepless and depressed myself. I have been wondering at you, because I saw how comfortably you were sleeping; and I deliberately didn't wake you because I wanted you to go on being as comfortable as you could. I have often felt before in the course of my life how fortunate you are in your disposition, but I feel it more than ever now in your present misfortune when I see how easily and placidly you put up with it.

---

portrays Socrates in his typical role, questioning someone about his beliefs (in this case, the young aristocrat, Euthyphro). The discussion is focused on the nature of piety, but the conversation breaks off before a final answer is reached—perhaps none is possible—because Socrates is on his way to stand trial before the Athenian assembly. He has been charged with "preaching false gods" (heresy) and "corrupting the youth" by causing them to doubt or disregard the wisdom of their elders. (How faithful to any actual event or discussion Euthyphro and Plato's other Socratic dialogues really are, scholars cannot say with assurance.)

In Apology, the second dialogue in the sequence, Plato (who remains entirely in the background, as he does in all the dialogues) recounts Socrates' public reply to the charges against him. During the speech, Socrates explains his life, reminding his fellow citizens that if he is (as the oracle had pronounced) "the wisest of men," then it is only because he knows that he doesn't know what others believe or pretend they do know. The dialogue ends with Socrates being found guilty and duly sentenced to death.

The third in the series is Crito, but we will postpone comment on it for a moment, and glance at the fourth dialogue, Phaedo, in which Plato portrays Socrates' final philosophical discussion. The topic, appropriately, is whether the soul is immortal. It ends with Socrates, in the company of his closest friends, bidding them a last farewell and drinking the fatal cup of hemlock.

Crito, the whole text of which is reprinted here, is the third in this sequence. It is the debate provoked by Crito, an old friend and admirer of Socrates. He visits Socrates in prison and urges him to escape while he still has the chance. After all, Crito argues, the guilty verdict was wrong and unfair, few Athenians really want to have Socrates put to death, his family and friends will be distraught, and so forth. Socrates will not have it. He patiently but firmly examines each of Crito's arguments and explains why it would be wrong to follow his advice.

Plato's Crito thus ranks with Sophocles' tragedy Antigone as one of the first explorations in Western literature of the perennial theme of our responsibility for obeying laws that challenge our conscientious moral convictions. Antigone concludes that she must disobey the law of Creon, tyrant of Thebes; Socrates concludes that he must obey the law of democratic Athens.

In Crito, we have not only a superb illustration of Socratic dialogue and argument, but also a portrait of a virtuous thinker at the end of a long life reflecting on its course and on the moral principles that have guided him. We see Socrates living "an examined life," the only life he thought was worth living.

Socrates: Well, really, Crito, it would be hardly suitable for a man of my age to resent having to die.

Crito: Other people just as old as you are get involved in these misfortunes, Socrates, but their age doesn't keep them from resenting it when they find themselves in your position.

Socrates: Quite true. But tell me, why have you come so early?

Crito: Because I bring bad news, Socrates; not so bad from your point of view, I suppose, but it will be very hard to bear for me and your other friends, and I think that I shall find it hardest of all.

Socrates: Why, what is this news? Has the boat come in from Delos— the boat which ends my reprieve when it arrives?[1]

Crito: It hasn't actually come in yet, but I expect that it will be here today, judging from the report of some people who have just arrived from Sunium and left it there. It's quite clear from their account that it will be here today; and so by tomorrow, Socrates, you will have to—to end your life.

Socrates: Well, Crito, I hope that it may be for the best; if the gods will it so, so be it. All the same, I don't think it will arrive today.

Crito: What makes you think that?

Socrates: I will try to explain. I think I am right in saying that I have to die on the day after the boat arrives?

Crito: That's what the authorities say, at any rate.

Socrates: Then I don't think it will arrive on this day that is just beginning, but on the day after. I am going by a dream that I had in the night, only a little while ago. It looks as though you were right not to wake me up.

Crito: Why, what was the dream about?

Socrates: I thought I saw a gloriously beautiful woman dressed in white robes, who came up to me and addressed me in these words: "Socrates, to the pleasant land of Phthia on the third day thou shalt come."

Crito: Your dream makes no sense, Socrates.

Socrates: To my mind, Crito, it is perfectly clear.

Crito: Too clear, apparently. But look here, Socrates, it is still not too late to take my advice and escape. Your death means a double calamity for me. I shall not only lose a friend whom I can never possibly replace, but besides a great many people who don't know you and me very well will be sure to think that I let you down, because I could have saved you if I had been willing to spend the money; and what could be more contemptible than to get a name for thinking more of money than of your friends? Most

---

[1]**Delos . . . arrives** Ordinarily execution was immediately carried out, but the day before Socrates' trial was the first day of an annual ceremony that involved sending a ship to Delos. When the ship was absent—in this case for about a month—executions could not be performed. As Crito goes on to say, Socrates could easily escape, and indeed he could have left the country before being tried. [All notes are the editors'.]

people will never believe that it was you who refused to leave this place although we tried our hardest to persuade you.

Socrates: But my dear Crito, why should we pay so much attention to what "most people" think? The really reasonable people, who have more claim to be considered, will believe that the facts are exactly as they are.

Crito: You can see for yourself, Socrates, that one has to think of 28 popular opinion as well. Your present position is quite enough to show that the capacity of ordinary people for causing trouble is not confined to petty annoyances, but has hardly any limits if you once get a bad name with them.

Socrates: I only wish that ordinary people *had* an unlimited capacity for doing harm; then they might have an unlimited power for doing good; which would be a splendid thing, if it were so. Actually they have neither. They cannot make a man wise or stupid; they simply act at random.

Crito: Have it that way if you like; but tell me this, Socrates. I hope that you aren't worrying about the possible effects on me and the rest of your friends, and thinking that if you escape we shall have trouble with informers for having helped you to get away, and have to forfeit all our property or pay an enormous fine, or even incur some further punishment? If any idea like that is troubling you, you can dismiss it altogether. We are quite entitled to run that risk in saving you, and even worse, if necessary. Take my advice, and be reasonable.

Socrates: All that you say is very much in my mind, Crito, and a great deal more besides.

Crito: Very well, then, don't let it distress you. I know some people 32 who are willing to rescue you from here and get you out of the country for quite a moderate sum. And then surely you realize how cheap these informers are to buy off; we shan't need much money to settle them; and I think you've got enough of my money for yourself already. And then even supposing that in your anxiety for my safety you feel that you oughtn't to spend my money, there are these foreign gentlemen staying in Athens who are quite willing to spend theirs. One of them, Simmias of Thebes, has actually brought the money with him for this very purpose; and Cebes and a number of others are quite ready to do the same. So as I say, you mustn't let any fears on these grounds make you slacken your efforts to escape; and you mustn't feel any misgivings about what you said at your trial, that you wouldn't know what to do with yourself if you left this country. Wherever you go, there are plenty of places where you will find a welcome; and if you choose to go to Thessaly, I have friends there who will make much of you and give you complete protection, so that no one in Thessaly can interfere with you.

Besides, Socrates, I don't even feel that it is right for you to try to do what you are doing, throwing away your life when you might save it. You are doing your best to treat yourself in exactly the same way as your enemies would, or rather did, when they wanted to ruin you. What is more, it seems to me that you are letting your sons down too. You have it in your power to finish their bringing up and education, and instead of that you are proposing to go off and desert them, and so far as you are concerned they will have to take their chance. And what sort of chance are they likely to get? The sort of thing that usually happens to orphans when they lose their parents. Either one ought not to have children at all, or one ought to see their upbringing and education through to the end. It strikes me that you are taking the line of least resistance, whereas you ought to make the choice of a good man and a brave one, considering that you profess to have made goodness your object all through life. Really, I am ashamed, both on your account and on ours your friends'; it will look as though we had played something like a coward's part all through this affair of yours. First there was the way you came into court when it was quite unnecessary—that was the first act; then there was the conduct of the defense—that was the second; and finally, to complete the farce, we get this situation, which makes it appear that we have let you slip out of our hands through some lack of courage and enterprise on our part, because we didn't save you, and you didn't save yourself, when it would have been quite possible and practicable, if we had been any use at all.

There, Socrates; if you aren't careful, besides the suffering there will be all this disgrace for you and us to bear. Come, make up your mind. Really it's too late for that now; you ought to have it made up already. There is no alternative; the whole thing must be carried through during this coming night. If we lose any more time, it can't be done, it will be too late. I appeal to you, Socrates, on every ground; take my advice and please don't be unreasonable!

Socrates: My dear Crito, I appreciate your warm feelings very much— that is, assuming that they have some justification; if not, the stronger they are, the harder they will be to deal with. Very well, then; we must consider whether we ought to follow your advice or not. You know that this is not a new idea of mine; it has always been my nature never to accept advice from any of my friends unless reflection shows that it is the best course that reason offers. I cannot abandon the principles which I used to hold in the past simply because this accident has happened to me; they seem to me to be much as they were, and I respect and regard the same principles now as before. So unless we can find better principles on this occasion, you can be quite sure that I shall not agree with you; not even if the power of the people conjures up fresh hordes of bogies to terrify our childish minds, by subjecting us to chains and executions and confiscations of our property.

Well, then, how can we consider the question most reasonably? Suppose that we begin by reverting to this view which you hold about people's opinions. Was it always right to argue that some opinions should be taken seriously but not others? Or was it always wrong? Perhaps it was right before the question of my death arose, but now we can see clearly that it was a mistaken persistence in a point of view which was really irresponsible nonsense. I should like very much to inquire into this problem, Crito, with your help, and to see whether the argument will appear in any different light to me now that I am in this position, or whether it will remain the same; and whether we shall dismiss it or accept it.

Serious thinkers, I believe, have always held some such view as the one which I mentioned just now: that some of the opinions which people entertain should be respected, and others should not. Now I ask you, Crito, don't you think that this is a sound principle?—You are safe from the prospect of dying tomorrow, in all human probability; and you are not likely to have your judgment upset by this impending calamity. Consider, then; don't you think that this is a sound enough principle, that one should not regard all the opinions that people hold, but only some and not others? What do you say? Isn't that a fair statement?

Crito: Yes, it is.

Socrates: In other words, one should regard the good ones and not the bad?

Crito: Yes.   40

Socrates: The opinions of the wise being good, and the opinions of the foolish bad?

Crito: Naturally.

Socrates: To pass on, then: what do you think of the sort of illustration that I used to employ? When a man is in training, and taking it seriously, does he pay attention to all praise and criticism and opinion indiscriminately, or only when it comes from the one qualified person, the actual doctor or trainer?

Crito: Only when it comes from the one qualified person.   44

Socrates: Then he should be afraid of the criticism and welcome the praise of the one qualified person, but not those of the general public.

Crito: Obviously.

Socrates: So he ought to regulate his actions and exercises and eating and drinking by the judgment of his instructor, who has expert knowledge, rather than by the opinions of the rest of the public.

Crito: Yes, that is so.   48

Socrates: Very well. Now if he disobeys the one man and disregards his opinion and commendations, and pays attention to the advice of the many who have no expert knowledge, surely he will suffer some bad effect?

Crito: Certainly.

Socrates: And what is this bad effect? Where is it produced?—I mean, in what part of the disobedient person?

Crito: His body, obviously; that is what suffers.   52

Socrates: Very good. Well now, tell me, Crito—we don't want to go through all the examples one by one—does this apply as a general rule, and above all to the sort of actions which we are trying to decide about: just and unjust, honorable and dishonorable, good and bad? Ought we to be guided and intimidated by the opinion of the many or by that of the one— assuming that there is someone with expert knowledge? Is it true that we ought to respect and fear this person more than all the rest put together; and that if we do not follow his guidance we shall spoil and mutilate that part of us which, as we used to say, is improved by right conduct and destroyed by wrong? Or is this all nonsense?

Crito: No, I think it is true, Socrates.

Socrates: Then consider the next step. There is a part of us which is improved by healthy actions and ruined by unhealthy ones. If we spoil it by taking the advice of nonexperts, will life be worth living when this part is once ruined? The part I mean is the body; do you accept this?

Crito: Yes.   56

Socrates: Well, is life worth living with a body which is worn out and ruined in health?

Crito: Certainly not.

Socrates: What about the part of us which is mutilated by wrong actions and benefited by right ones? Is life worth living with this part ruined? Or do we believe that this part of us, whatever it may be, in which right and wrong operate, is of less importance than the body?

Crito: Certainly not.   60

Socrates: It is really more precious?

Crito: Much more.

Socrates: In that case, my dear fellow, what we ought to consider is not so much what people in general will say about us but how we stand with the expert in right and wrong, the one authority, who represents the actual truth. So in the first place your proposition is not correct when you say that we should consider popular opinion in questions of what is right and honorable and good, or the opposite. Of course one might object "All the same, the people have the power to put us to death."

Crito: No doubt about that! Quite true, Socrates; it is a possible   64
objection.

Socrates: But so far as I can see, my dear fellow, the argument which we have just been through is quite unaffected by it. At the same time I should like you to consider whether we are still satisfied on this point: that the really important thing is not to live, but to live well.

Crito: Why, yes.

Socrates: And that to live well means the same thing as to live honorably or rightly?

Crito: Yes.   68

Socrates: Then in the light of this agreement we must consider whether or not it is right for me to try to get away without an official discharge. If it turns out to be right, we must make the attempt; if not, we must let it drop. As for the considerations you raise about expense and reputation and bringing up children, I am afraid, Crito, that they represent the reflections of the ordinary public, who put people to death, and would bring them back to life if they could, with equal indifference to reason. Our real duty, I fancy, since the argument leads that way, is to consider one question only, the one which we raised just now: Shall we be acting rightly in paying money and showing gratitude to these people who are going to rescue me, and in escaping or arranging the escape ourselves, or shall we really be acting wrongly in doing all this? If it becomes clear that such conduct is wrong, I cannot help thinking that the question whether we are sure to die, or to suffer any other ill effect for that matter, if we stand our ground and take no action, ought not to weigh with us at all in comparison with the risk of doing what is wrong.

Crito: I agree with what you say, Socrates; but I wish you would consider what we ought to *do*.

Socrates: Let us look at it together, my dear fellow; and if you can challenge any of my arguments, do so and I will listen to you; but if you can't, be a good fellow and stop telling me over and over again that I ought to leave this place without official permission. I am very anxious to obtain your approval before I adopt the course which I have in mind; I don't want to act against your convictions. Now give your attention to the starting point of this inquiry—I hope that you will be satisfied with my way of stating it—and try to answer my questions to the best of your judgment.

Crito: Well, I will try. 72

Socrates: Do we say that one must never willingly do wrong, or does it depend upon circumstances? Is it true, as we have often agreed before, that there is no sense in which wrongdoing is good or honorable? Or have we jettisoned all our former convictions in these last few days? Can you and I at our age, Crito, have spent all these years in serious discussions without realizing that we were no better than a pair of children? Surely the truth is just what we have always said. Whatever the popular view is, and whether the alternative is pleasanter than the present one or even harder to bear, the fact remains that to do wrong is in every sense bad and dishonorable for the person who does it. Is that our view, or not?

Crito: Yes, it is.

Socrates: Then in no circumstances must one do wrong.

Crito: No. 76

Socrates: In that case one must not even do wrong when one is wronged, which most people regard as the natural course.

Crito: Apparently not.

Socrates: Tell me another thing, Crito: Ought one to do injuries or not?

Crito: Surely not, Socrates. 80

Socrates: And tell me: is it right to do an injury in retaliation, as most people believe, or not?

Crito: No, never.

Socrates: Because, I suppose, there is no difference between injuring people and wronging them.

Crito: Exactly. 84

Socrates: So one ought not to return a wrong or an injury to any person, whatever the provocation is. Now be careful, Crito, that in making these single admissions you do not end by admitting something contrary to your real beliefs. I know that there are and always will be few people who think like this; and consequently between those who do think so and those who do not there can be no agreement on principle; they must always feel contempt when they observe one another's decisions. I want even you to consider very carefully whether you share my views and agree with me, and whether we can proceed with our discussion from the established hypothesis that it is never right to do a wrong or return a wrong or defend one's self against injury by retaliation; or whether you dissociate yourself from any share in this view as a basis for discussion. I have held it for a long time, and still hold it; but if you have formed any other opinion, say so and tell me what it is. If, on the other hand, you stand by what we have said, listen to my next point.

Crito: Yes, I stand by it and agree with you. Go on.

Socrates: Well, here is my next point, or rather question. Ought one to fulfill all one's agreements, provided that they are right, or break them?

Crito: One ought to fulfill them.

88

Socrates: Then consider the logical consequence. If we leave this place without first persuading the State to let us go, are we or are we not doing an injury, and doing it in a quarter where it is least justifiable? Are we or are we not abiding by our just agreements?

Crito: I can't answer your question, Socrates; I am not clear in my mind.

Socrates: Look at it in this way. Suppose that while we were preparing to run away from here (or however one should describe it) the Laws and Constitution of Athens were to come and confront us and ask this question: "Now, Socrates, what are you proposing to do? Can you deny that by this act which you are contemplating you intend, so far as you have the power, to destroy us, the Laws, and the whole State as well? Do you imagine that a city can continue to exist and not be turned upside down, if the legal judgments which are pronounced in it have no force but are nullified and destroyed by private persons?"—how shall we answer this question, Crito, and others of the same kind? There is much that could be said, especially by a professional advocate, to protest against the invalidation of this law which enacts that judgments once pronounced shall be binding. Shall we say "Yes, I do intend to destroy the laws, because the State wronged me by passing a faulty judgment at my trial"? Is this to be our answer, or what?

Crito: What you have just said, by all means, Socrates.

92

Socrates: Then what supposing the Laws say "Was there provision for this in the agreement between you and us, Socrates? Or did you undertake to abide by whatever judgments the State pronounced?" If we expressed surprise at such language, they would probably say: "Never mind our language, Socrates, but answer our questions; after all, you are accustomed to the method of question and answer. Come now, what charge do you bring against us and the State, that you are trying to destroy us? Did we not give you life in the first place? Was it not through us that your father married your mother and begot you? Tell us, have you any complaint against those of us Laws that deal with marriage?" "No, none," I should say. "Well, have you any against the laws which deal with children's upbringing and education, such as you had yourself? Are you not grateful to those of us Laws which were instituted for this end, for requiring your father to give you a cultural and physical education?" "Yes," I should say. "Very good. Then since you have been born and brought up and educated, can you deny, in the first place, that you were our child and servant, both you and your ancestors? And if this is so, do you imagine that what is right for us is equally right for you, and that whatever we try to do to you, you are justified in retaliating? You did not have equality of rights with your father, or your employer (supposing that you had had one), to enable you to retaliate; you were not allowed to answer back when you were scolded or to hit back when you were beaten, or to do a great many other things of the same kind. Do you expect to have such license against your country and its laws that if we try to put you to death in the belief that it is right to do so, you on your part will try your hardest to destroy your country and us its Laws in return? And will you, the true devotee of goodness, claim that you are justified in doing so? Are you so wise as to have forgotten that compared with your mother and father and all the rest of your ancestors your country is something far more precious, more venerable, more sacred, and held in greater honor both among gods and among all reasonable men? Do you not realize that you are even more bound to respect and placate the anger of your country than your father's anger? That if you cannot persuade your country you must do whatever it orders, and patiently submit to any punishment that it imposes, whether it be flogging or imprisonment? And if it leads you out to war, to be wounded or killed, you must comply, and it is right that you should do so; you must not give way or retreat or abandon your position. Both in war and in the law courts and everywhere else you must do whatever your city and your country commands, or else persuade it in accordance with universal justice; but violence is a sin even against your parents, and it is a far greater sin against your country—What shall we say to this, Crito?—that what the Laws say is true, or not?

Crito: Yes, I think so.

Socrates: "Consider, then, Socrates," the Laws would probably continue, "whether it is also true for us to say that what you are now trying to do to us is not right. Although we have brought you into the world and reared you and educated you, and given you and all your fellow citizens a share in all the good things at our disposal, nevertheless by the very fact of granting our permission we openly proclaim this principle: that any Athenian, on attaining to manhood and seeing for himself the political organization of the State and us its Laws, is permitted, if he is not satisfied with us, to take his property and go away wherever he likes. If any of you chooses to go to one of our colonies, supposing that he should not be satisfied with us and the State, or to emigrate to any other country, not one of us Laws hinders or prevents him from going away wherever he likes, without any loss of property. On the other hand, if any one of you stands his ground when he can see how we administer justice and the rest of our public organization, we hold that by so doing he has in fact undertaken to do anything that we tell him; and we maintain that anyone who disobeys is guilty of doing wrong on three separate counts: first because we are his parents, and secondly because we are his guardians; and thirdly because, after promising obedience, he is neither obeying us nor persuading us to change our decision if we are at fault in any way; and although all our orders are in the form of proposals, not of savage commands, and we give him the choice of either persuading us or doing what we say, he is actually doing neither. These are the charges, Socrates, to which we say that you will be liable if you do what you are contemplating; and you will not be the least culpable of your fellow countrymen, but one of the most guilty." If I said "Why do you say that?" they would no doubt pounce upon me with perfect justice and point out that there are very few people in Athens who have entered into this agreement with them as explicitly as I have. They would say "Socrates, we have substantial evidence that you are satisfied with us and with the State. You would not have been so exceptionally reluctant to cross the borders of your country if you had not been exceptionally attached to it. You have never left the city to attend a festival or for any other purpose, except on some military expedition; you have never traveled abroad as other people do, and you have never felt the impulse to acquaint yourself with another country or constitution; you have been content with us and with our city. You have definitely chosen us, and undertaken to observe us in all your activities as a citizen; and as the crowning proof that you are satisfied with our city, you have begotten children in it. Furthermore, even at the time of your trial you could have proposed the penalty of banishment, if you had chosen to do so; that is, you could have done then with the sanction of the State what you are now trying to do without it. But whereas at that time you made a noble show of indifference if you had to die, and in fact preferred death, as you said, to banishment, now you show no respect for your earlier professions, and no regard for us, the Laws, whom you are trying to destroy; you are behaving like the lowest type of menial, trying to run away in spite of the contracts and undertakings by which you agreed to live as a member of our State. Now first answer this question: Are we or are we not speaking the truth when we say that you have undertaken, in deed if not in word, to live your life as a citizen in obedience to us?" What are we to say to that, Crito? Are we not bound to admit it?

Crito: We cannot help it, Socrates.

Socrates: "It is a fact, then," they would say, "that you are breaking covenants and undertakings made with us, although you made them under no compulsion or misunderstanding, and were not compelled to decide in

96

a limited time; you had seventy years in which you could have left the country, if you were not satisfied with us or felt that the agreements were unfair. You did not choose Sparta or Crete—your favorite models of good government—or any other Greek or foreign state; you could not have absented yourself from the city less if you had been lame or blind or decrepit in some other way. It is quite obvious that you stand by yourself above all other Athenians in your affection for this city and for us its Laws;—who would care for a city without laws? And now, after all this, are you not going to stand by your agreement? Yes, you are, Socrates, if you will take our advice; and then you will at least escape being laughed at for leaving the city.

"We invite you to consider what good you will do to yourself or your friends if you commit this breach of faith and stain your conscience. It is fairly obvious that the risk of being banished and either losing their citizenship or having their property confiscated will extend to your friends as well. As for yourself, if you go to one of the neighboring states, such as Thebes or Megara, which are both well governed, you will enter them as an enemy to their constitution[2] and all good patriots will eye you with suspicion as a destroyer of law and order. Incidentally you will confirm the opinion of the jurors who tried you that they gave a correct verdict; a destroyer of laws might very well be supposed to have a destructive influence upon young and foolish human beings. Do you intend, then, to avoid well governed states and the higher forms of human society? And if you do, will life be worth living? Or will you approach these people and have the impudence to converse with them? What arguments will you use, Socrates? The same which you used here, that goodness and integrity, institutions and laws, are the most precious possessions of mankind? Do you not think that Socrates and everything about him will appear in a disreputable light? You certainly ought to think so. But perhaps you will retire from this part of the world and go to Crito's friends in Thessaly? That is the home of indiscipline and laxity, and no doubt they would enjoy hearing the amusing story of how you managed to run away from prison by arraying yourself in some costume or putting on a shepherd's smock or some other conventional runaway's disguise, and altering your personal appearance. And will no one comment on the fact that an old man of your age, probably with only a short time left to live, should dare to cling so greedily to life, at the price of violating the most stringent laws? Perhaps not, if you avoid irritating anyone. Otherwise, Socrates, you will hear a good many humiliating comments. So you will live as the toady and slave of all the populace, literally "roistering in Thessaly," as though you had left this country for Thessaly to attend a banquet there; and where will your discussions about goodness and uprightness be then, we should like to know? But of course you want to live for your children's sake, so that you

[2]**as an enemy to their constitution** As a lawbreaker.

may be able to bring them up and educate them. Indeed! by first taking them off to Thessaly and making foreigners of them, so that they may have that additional enjoyment? Or if that is not your intention, supposing that they are brought up here with you still alive, will they be better cared for and educated without you, because of course your friends will look after them? Will they look after your children if you go away to Thessaly, and not if you go away to the next world? Surely if those who profess to be your friends are worth anything, you must believe that they would care for them.

"No, Socrates; be advised by us your guardians, and do not think more of your children or of your life or of anything else than you think of what is right; so that when you enter the next world you may have all this to plead in your defense before the authorities there. It seems clear that if you do this thing, neither you nor any of your friends will be the better for it or be more upright or have a cleaner conscience here in this world, nor will it be better for you when you reach the next. As it is, you will leave this place, when you do, as the victim of a wrong done not by us, the Laws, but by your fellow men. But if you leave in that dishonorable way, returning wrong for wrong and evil for evil, breaking your agreements and covenants with us, and injuring those whom you least ought to injure—yourself, your friends, your country, and us—then you will have to face our anger in your lifetime, and in that place beyond when the laws of the other world know that you have tried, so far as you could, to destroy even us their brothers, they will not receive you with a kindly welcome. Do not take Crito's advice, but follow ours."

That, my dear friend Crito, I do assure you, is what I seem to hear 100 them saying, just as a mystic seems to hear the strains of music; and the sound of their arguments rings so loudly in my head that I cannot hear the other side. I warn you that, as my opinion stands at present, it will be useless to urge a different view. However, if you think that you will do any good by it, say what you like.

Crito: No, Socrates, I have nothing to say.

Socrates: Then give it up, Crito, and let us follow this course, since God points out the way.

Questions and Suggestions for Writing

1. State as precisely as you can all the arguments Crito uses to try to convince Socrates that he ought to escape. Which of these arguments seems to you to be the best? the worst? Why?

2. Socrates says to Crito, "I cannot abandon the principles which I used to hold in the past simply because this accident [the misfortune of being convicted by the Athenian assembly and then sentenced to death] has happened to me. . . ." Does this remark strike you as self-righteous? stubborn? smug? stupid? Explain.

3. Socrates declares that "serious thinkers" have always held the view that "some of the opinions which people entertain should be respected, and others not." There are two main alternatives to this principle: (a) One should respect *all* the opinions that others hold, and (b) one should respect *none* of the opinions of others. Socrates attacks (a) but he ignores (b). What are his objections to (a)? Do you find them convincing? Can you think of any convincing arguments against (b)?

4. As Socrates shows in his reply to Crito, he seems ready to believe that there are "experts in right and wrong"—that is, persons with expert opinion or even authoritative knowledge on matters of right and wrong conduct—and that their advice should be sought and followed. Do you agree? Consider the thesis that there are no such experts, and write a 500-word essay defending or attacking it.

5. Socrates, as he comments to Crito, believes that "it is never right to do a wrong or to return a wrong or defend oneself against injury by retaliation." He does not offer any argument for this thesis in the dialogue (although he does elsewhere). It was a very strange doctrine in his day, and even now it is not generally accepted. Write a 1,000-word essay defending or attacking this thesis.

6. Socrates seems to argue: Because (a) no one ought to do wrong, and because (b) it would injure the state for someone in Socrates' position to escape, because (c) this act would break a "just agreement" between the citizen and his state, therefore (d) no one in Socrates' position should escape. Do you think this argument is valid? If not, what further assumptions would be needed to make it valid? Do you think the argument is sound (i.e., both valid and true in all its premises)? If not, explain. If you had to attack premise (b) or (c), which do you think is the more vulnerable, and why?

7. In the imaginary speech by the laws of Athens to Socrates, especially in paragraph 93, the Laws convey a picture of the supremacy of the state over the individual—and Socrates seems to assent to this picture. Do you? Why, or why not?

8. The Laws (para. 93) claim that if Socrates were to escape, he would be "guilty of doing wrong on three separate accounts." What are they? Do you agree with all or any? Why, or why not? Read the essay by Martin Luther King, Jr., "Letter from Birmingham Jail," (p. 498) and decide how King would respond to the judgment of the Laws of Athens.

9. At the end of their peroration (para. 99), the Laws of Athens say to Socrates: Take your punishment as prescribed, and at your death "you will leave this place . . . as the victim of a wrong done not by us, the Laws, but by your fellow men." To what wrong do the Laws allude? Do you agree that it is men and not laws who perpetrated this wrong? If you were in Socrates' position, would it matter to you if you were being wronged not by laws but only by men? Explain.

Jean-Jacques Rousseau

From *The Social Contract*

I. THE SUBJECT OF THE FIRST BOOK

Man is born free, and everywhere he is in chains. Many a man believes himself to be the master of others who is, no less than they, a slave. How did this change take place? I do not know. What can make it legitimate? To this question I hope to be able to furnish an answer. . . .

II. OF PRIMITIVE SOCIETIES

The oldest form of society—and the only natural one—is the family. Children remain bound to their father for only just so long as they feel the need of him for their self-preservation. Once that need ceases the natural bond is dissolved. From then on, the children, freed from the obedience which they formerly owed, and the father, cleared of his debt of responsibility to them, return to a condition of equal independence. If the bond remain operative it is no longer something imposed by nature, but has become a matter of deliberate choice. The family is a family still, but by reason of convention only.

This shared liberty is a consequence of man's nature. Its first law is that of self-preservation: its first concern is for what it owes itself. As soon as a man attains the age of reason he becomes his own master, because he alone can judge of what will best assure his continued existence.

Jean-Jacques Rousseau (1712–1778) was born in Geneva of a family of French origin. His mother died in childbirth, and he was raised by a rather neglectful father, from whom he ran away at age sixteen. He led a wandering existence, holding jobs such as music teacher, clerk, and footman. Much of his early life, according to his Confessions, *was spent in vagabondage (possibly, however, Rousseau was boasting of imaginary adventures), but in 1745 he settled in Paris, where he found a woman to support him. She bore him five children, all of whom were placed in orphanages.*

Rousseau wrote about music, politics, education, and himself. The selection reprinted here comes from The Social Contract *(1762), a treatise on the source and nature of government, and especially on its authority over its citizens. Rousseau's views placed him in the so-called contractarian tradition that includes such predecessors as Thomas Hobbes and John Locke, with whom he shared the view that the right of some persons to govern others derives from the consent of the governed. On Rousseau's version of the contract theory, the "natural right" of each person to self-government in a hypothetical "state of nature" must be overcome by transferring ("alienating") the right of government to the whole community. In exchange, the citizen receives such legal rights as the government deems appropriate. The following excerpt focuses on these ideas.*

We may, therefore, if we will, regard the family as the basic model of   4
all political associations. The ruler is the father writ large: the people are,
by analogy, his children, and all, ruler and people alike, alienate their
freedom only so far as it is to their advantage to do so. The only difference
is that, whereas in the family the father's love for his children is sufficient
reward to him for the care he has lavished on them, in the State, the
pleasure of commanding others takes its place, since the ruler is not in a
relation of love to his people.

Grotius[1] denies that political power is ever exercised in the interests of
the governed, and quotes the institution of slavery in support of his contention. His invariable method of arguing is to derive Right from Fact.[2] It
might be possible to adopt a more logical system of reasoning, but none
which would be more favorable to tyrants.

According to Grotius, therefore, it is doubtful whether the term
"human race" belongs to only a few hundred men, or whether those few
hundred men belong to the human race. From the evidence of his book it
seems clear that he holds by the first of these alternatives, and on this point
Hobbes is in agreement with him. If this is so, then humanity is divided
into herds of livestock, each with its "guardian" who watches over his
charges only that he may ultimately devour them.

Just as the shepherd is superior in kind to his sheep, so, too, the
shepherds of men, or, in other words, their rulers, are superior in kind to
their peoples. This, according to Philo, was the argument advanced by
Caligula, the Emperor, who drew from the analogy the perfectly true
conclusion that either Kings are Gods or their subjects brute beasts.

The reasoning of Caligula, of Hobbes, and of Grotius is fundamen-   8
tally the same. Far earlier, Aristotle, too, had maintained that men are not
by nature equal, but that some are born to be slaves, others to be masters.[3]

Aristotle was right: but he mistook the effect for the cause. Nothing is
more certain than that a man born into a condition of slavery is a slave by
nature. A slave in fetters loses everything—even the desire to be freed from
them. He grows to love his slavery, as the companions of Ulysses grew to
love their state of brutish transformation.[4]

If some men are by nature slaves, the reason is that they have been
made slaves *against* nature. Force made the first slaves: cowardice has
perpetuated the species.

[1]**Grotius** Hugo Grotius (1583–1645), a Dutch jurist and humanist, was "the father of
international law" and the author of *De jure belli et pacis* (1625). [Editors' note]

[2]"Learned researches into Public Right are, too often, but the record of ancient abuses, and
it is but a waste of time to pursue such a line of inquiry. . . ." (*Traité des interêts de la France
avec ses voisins*, par M. le Marquis d'Argenson, published by Rey of Amsterdam). This is
precisely the error of which Grotius is guilty.

[3]*Politics*, Book I, Ch. 5.

[4] See the short Treatise by Plutarch, entitled *That Beasts Make Use of Reason.*

I have made no mention of King Adam or of the Emperor Noah, the father of three great Monarchs who divided up the universe between them, as did the children of Saturn, whom some have been tempted to identify with them. I trust that I may be given credit for my moderation, since, being descended in a direct line from one of these Princes, and quite possibly belonging to the elder branch, I may, for all I know, were my claims supported in law, be even now the legitimate Sovereign of the Human Race. However that may be, all will concur in the view that Adam was King of the World, as was Robinson Crusoe of his island, only so long as he was its only inhabitant, and that the great advantage of empire held on such terms was that the Monarch, firmly seated on his throne, had no need to fear rebellions, conspiracy, or war.

III. OF THE RIGHT OF THE STRONGEST

However strong a man, he is never strong enough to remain master always, unless he transform his Might into Right, and Obedience into Duty. Hence we have come to speak of the Right of the Strongest, a right which, seemingly assumed in irony, has, in fact, become established in principle. But the meaning of the phrase has never been adequately explained. Strength is a physical attribute, and I fail to see how any moral sanction can attach to its effects. To yield to the strong is an act of necessity, not of will. At most it is the result of a dictate of prudence. How, then, can it become a duty? 12

Let us assume for a moment that some such Right does really exist. The only deduction from this premise is inexplicable gibberish. For to admit that Might makes Right is to reverse the process of effect and cause. The mighty man who defeats his rival becomes heir to his Right. So soon as we can disobey with impunity, disobedience becomes legitimate. And, since the Mightiest is always right, it merely remains for us to become possessed of Might. But what validity can there be in a Right which ceases to exist when Might changes hands? If a man be constrained by Might to obey, what need has he to obey by Duty? And if he is not constrained to obey, there is no further obligation on him to do so. It follows, therefore, that the word Right adds nothing to the idea of Might. It becomes, in this connection, completely meaningless.

Obey the Powers that be. If that means Yield to Force, the precept is admirable but redundant. My reply to those who advance it is that no case will ever be found of its violation. All power comes from God. Certainly, but so do all ailments. Are we to conclude from such an argument that we are never to call in the doctor? If I am waylaid by a footpad at the corner of a wood, I am constrained by force to give him my purse. But if I can manage to keep it from him, is it my duty to hand it over? His pistol is also a symbol of Power. It must, then, be admitted that Might does not create Right, and that no man is under an obligation to obey any but the legitimate powers of the State. And so I continually come back to the question I first asked.

IV. OF SLAVERY

Since no man has natural authority over his fellows, and since Might can produce no Right, the only foundation left for legitimate authority in human societies is Agreement.

If a private citizen, says Grotius, can alienate his liberty and make 16 himself another man's slave, why should not a whole people do the same, and subject themselves to the will of a King? The argument contains a number of ambiguous words which stand in need of explanation. But let us confine our attention to one only—*alienate*. To alienate means to give or to sell. Now a man who becomes the slave of another does not give himself. He sells himself in return for bare subsistence, if for nothing more. But why should a whole people sell themselves? So far from furnishing subsistence to his subjects, a King draws his own from them, and from them alone. According to Rabelais, it takes a lot to keep a King. Do we, then, maintain that a subject surrenders his person on condition that his property be taken too? It is difficult to see what he will have left.

It will be said that the despot guarantees civil peace to his subjects. So be it. But how are they the gainers if the wars to which his ambition may expose them, his insatiable greed, and the vexatious demands of his Ministers cause them more loss than would any outbreak of internal dissension? How do they benefit if that very condition of civil peace be one of the causes of their wretchedness? One can live peacefully enough in a dungeon, but such peace will hardly, of itself, ensure one's happiness. The Greeks imprisoned in the cave of Cyclops lived peacefully while awaiting their turn to be devoured.

To say that a man gives himself for nothing is to commit oneself to an absurd and inconceivable statement. Such an act of surrender is illegitimate, null, and void by the mere fact that he who makes it is not in his right mind. To say the same thing of a whole People is tantamount to admitting that the People in question are a nation of imbeciles. Imbecility does not produce Right.

Even if a man can alienate himself, he cannot alienate his children. They are born free, their liberty belongs to them, and no one but themselves has a right to dispose of it. Before they have attained the age of reason their father may make, on their behalf, certain rules with a view to ensuring their preservation and well-being. But any such limitation of

their freedom of choice must be regarded as neither irrevocable nor unconditional, for to alienate another's liberty is contrary to the natural order,
and is an abuse of the father's rights. It follows that an arbitrary government can be legitimate only on condition that each successive generation
of subjects is free either to accept or to reject it, and if this is so, then the
government will no longer be arbitrary.

When a man renounces his liberty he renounces his essential man- 20
hood, his rights, and even his duty as a human being. There is no compensation possible for such complete renunciation. It is incompatible with
man's nature, and to deprive him of his free will is to deprive his actions of
all moral sanction. The convention, in short, which sets up on one side an
absolute authority, and on the other an obligation to obey without question, is vain and meaningless. Is it not obvious that where we can demand
everything we owe nothing? Where there is no mutual obligation, no
interchange of duties, it must, surely, be clear that the actions of the
commanded cease to have any moral value? For how can it be maintained
that my slave has any "right" against me when everything that he has is my
property? His right being *my* right, it is absurd to speak of it as ever
operating to my disadvantage.

Grotius, and those who think like him, have found in the fact of war
another justification for the so-called "right" of slavery. They argue that
since the victor has a *right* to kill his defeated enemy, the latter may, if he
so wish, ransom his life at the expense of his liberty, and that this compact
is the more legitimate in that it benefits both parties.

But it is evident that this alleged *right* of a man to kill his enemies
is not in any way a derivative of the state of war, if only because men, in
their primitive condition of independence, are not bound to one another
by any relationship sufficiently stable to produce a state either of war or
of peace. They are not *naturally* enemies. It is the link between *things*
rather than between *men* that constitutes war, and since a state of war
cannot originate in simple personal relations, but only in relations
between things, private hostility between man and man cannot obtain
either in a state of nature where there is no generally accepted system
of private property, or in a state of society where law is the supreme
authority.

Single combats, duels, personal encounters are incidents which do not
constitute a "state" of anything. As to those private wars which were
authorized by the Ordinances of King Louis IX and suspended by the
Peace of God, they were merely an abuse of Feudalism—that most absurd
of all systems of government, so contrary was it to the principles of Natural
Right and of all good polity.

War, therefore, is something that occurs not between man and man, 24
but between States. The individuals who become involved in it are enemies
only by accident. They fight not as men or even as citizens, but as soldiers:

not as members of this or that national group, but as its defenders.[5] A State can have as its enemies only other States, not men at all, seeing that there can be no true relationship between things of a different nature.

This principle is in harmony with that of all periods, and with the constant practice of every civilized society. A declaration of war is a warning, not so much to Governments as to their subjects. The foreigner—whether king, private person, or nation as a whole—who steals, murders, or holds in durance the subjects of another country without first declaring war on that country's Prince, acts not as an enemy but as a brigand. Even when war has been joined, the just Prince, though he may seize all public property in enemy territory, yet respects the property and possessions of individuals, and, in so doing, shows his concern for those rights on which his own laws are based. The object of war being the destruction of the enemy State, a commander has a perfect right to kill its defenders so long as their arms are in their hands: but once they have laid them down and have submitted, they cease to be enemies, or instruments employed by an enemy, and revert to the condition of men, pure and simple, over whose lives no one can any longer exercise a rightful claim. Sometimes it is possible to destroy a State without killing any of its subjects, and nothing in war can be claimed as a right save what may be necessary for the accomplishment of the victor's end. These principles are not those of Grotius, nor are they based on the authority of poets, but derive from the Nature of Things, and are founded upon Reason.

The Right of Conquest finds its sole sanction in the Law of the Strongest. If war does not give to the victor the right to massacre his defeated enemies, he cannot base upon a nonexistent right any claim to the further one of enslaving them. We have the right to kill our enemies only when we cannot enslave them. It follows, therefore, that the right to enslave cannot be deduced from the right to kill, and that we are guilty of enforcing an iniquitous exchange if we make a vanquished foeman purchase with his liberty that life over which we have no right. Is it not obvious that once we begin basing the right of life and death on the

---

[5] The Romans, who, more than any other nation, had a genuine understanding of, and respect for, the legal implications of war, carried their scruples in this matter so far that a citizen was forbidden to volunteer except for a particular campaign and against a specific enemy. When the legion in which Cato the Younger performed his first period of military service under Popilius was reformed, his father wrote to the latter explaining that if he wished to keep the young man under his command he must administer the oath over again, since the first one was now annulled, and consequently Cato could not be called upon to bear arms against the enemy. At the same time he wrote to his son telling him to be sure not to appear on parade until he had renewed his oath. I am aware that such particular instances as the siege of Clusium may be quoted against me, but my reply would be that I am concerned to cite only laws and customs. It was very seldom that the Romans transgressed their laws, and few peoples have had better ones.

right to enslave, and the right to enslave on the right of life and death, we are caught in a vicious circle? Even if we assume the existence of this terrible right to kill all and sundry, I still maintain that a man enslaved, or a People conquered, in war is under no obligation to obey beyond the point at which force ceases to be operative. If the victor spares the life of his defeated opponent in return for an equivalent, he cannot be said to have shown him mercy. In either case he destroys him, but in the latter case he derives value from his act, while in the former he gains nothing. His authority, however, rests on no basis but that of force. There is still a state of war between the two men, and it conditions the whole relationship in which they stand to one another. The enjoyment of the Rights of War presupposes that there has been no treaty of Peace. Conqueror and conquered have, to be sure, entered into a compact, but such a compact, far from liquidating the state of war, assumes its continuance.

Thus, in whatever way we look at the matter, the "Right" to enslave has no existence, not only because it is without legal validity, but because the very term is absurd and meaningless. The words *Slavery* and *Right* are contradictory and mutually exclusive. Whether we be considering the relation of one man to another man, or of an individual to a whole People, it is equally idiotic to say—"You and I have made a compact which represents nothing but loss to you and gain to me. I shall observe it so long as it pleases me to do so—and so shall you, until I cease to find it convenient."

VI. OF THE SOCIAL PACT

I assume, for the sake of argument, that a point was reached in the history of mankind when the obstacles to continuing in a state of nature were stronger than the forces which each individual could employ to the end of continuing in it. The original state of Nature, therefore, could no longer endure, and the human race would have perished had it not changed its manner of existence.

Now, since men can by no means engender new powers, but can only unite and control those of which they are already possessed, there is no way in which they can maintain themselves save by coming together and pooling their strength in a way that will enable them to withstand any resistance exerted upon them from without. They must develop some sort of central direction and learn to act in concert.

Such a concentration of powers can be brought about only as the consequence of an agreement reached between individuals. But the self-preservation of each single man derives primarily from his own strength and from his own freedom. How, then, can he limit these without, at the same time, doing himself an injury and neglecting that care which it is his duty to devote to his own concerns? This difficulty, in so far as it is relevant to my subject, can be expressed as follows:

"Some form of association must be found as a result of which the whole strength of the community will be enlisted for the protection of the person and property of each constituent member, in such a way that each, when united to his fellows, renders obedience to his own will, and remains as free as he was before." That is the basic problem of which the Social Contract provides the solution.

The clauses of this Contract are determined by the Act of Association 32 in such a way that the least modification must render them null and void. Even though they may never have been formally enunciated, they must be everywhere the same, and everywhere tacitly admitted and recognized. So completely must this be the case that, should the social compact be violated, each associated individual would at once resume all the rights which once were his, and regain his natural liberty, by the mere fact of losing the agreed liberty for which he renounced it.

It must be clearly understood that the clauses in question can be reduced, in the last analysis, to one only, to wit, the complete alienation by each associate member to the community of *all his rights*. For, in the first place, since each has made surrender of himself without reservation, the resultant conditions are the same for all: and, because they are the same for all, it is in the interest of none to make them onerous to his fellows.

Furthermore, this alienation having been made unreservedly, the union of individuals is as perfect as it well can be, none of the associated members having any claim against the community. For should there be any rights left to individuals, and no common authority be empowered to pronounce as between them and the public, then each, being in some things his own judge, would soon claim to be so in all. Were that so, a state of Nature would still remain in being, the conditions of association becoming either despotic or ineffective.

In short, whoso gives himself to all gives himself to none. And, since there is no member of the social group over whom we do not acquire precisely the same rights as those over ourselves which we have surrendered to him, it follows that we gain the exact equivalent of what we lose, as well as an added power to conserve what we already have.

If, then, we take from the social pact everything which is not essential 36 to it, we shall find it to be reduced to the following terms: "Each of us contributes to the group his person and the powers which he wields as a person, and we receive into the body politic each individual as forming an indivisible part of the whole."

As soon as the act of association becomes a reality, it substitutes for the person of each of the contracting parties a moral and collective body made up of as many members as the constituting assembly has votes, which body receives from this very act of constitution its unity, its dispersed *self*, and its will. The public person thus formed by the union of individuals was known in the old days as a *City*, but now as the *Republic* or *Body Politic*.[6] This, when it fulfill's a passive role, is known by its members as *The State*, when an active one, as *The Sovereign People*, and, in contrast to other similar bodies, as a *Power*. In respect of the constituent associates, it enjoys the collective name of *The People*, the individuals who compose it being known as *Citizens* in so far as they share in the sovereign authority, as *Subjects* in so far as they owe obedience to the laws of the State. But these different terms frequently overlap, and are used indiscriminately one for the other. It is enough that we should realize the difference between them when they are employed in a precise sense.

VII. OF THE SOVEREIGN

It is clear from the above formula that the act of association implies a mutual undertaking between the body politic and its constituent members. Each individual comprising the former contracts, so to speak, with himself and has a twofold function. As a member of the sovereign people he owes a duty to each of his neighbors, and, as a Citizen, to the sovercign people as a whole. . . .

To the benefits conferred by the status of citizenship might be added that of Moral Freedom, which alone makes a man his own master. For to be subject to appetite is to be a slave, while to obey the laws laid down by society is to be free. But I have already said enough on this point, and am not concerned here with the philosophical meaning of the word *liberty*.

---

[6] The true meaning of the word "City" has been almost entirely lost by the moderns, most of whom think that a Town and a City are identical, and that to be a Burgess is the same thing as to be a Citizen. They do not know that houses may make a town, but that only citizens can make a City. This same error cost the people of Carthage dear in the past. I have never anywhere read that the title *"cives"* could be conferred on the subject of a Prince, not even upon the Macedonians of ancient times, nor upon the English in our own day, though the latter are more nearly in the enjoyment of freedom than any other people. Only the French use *citizens* as a familiar word, the reason for this being that they have no true apprehension of its meaning, as may be seen by anyone who consults a French dictionary. Were it otherwise, they would fall, by adopting it, into the crime of *lèse-majesté*. In their mouths it is held to express not so much legal standing as quality. When Bodin speaks of "our citizens and burgesses," he commits a grave blunder in giving the same meaning to the two words. Not so deceived is M. d'Alembert, who, in his article on Geneva, properly distinguishes between the four Orders (five, if foreigners be counted) which go to make up our city, of which two only constitute the Republic. No French author known to me understands the meaning of the word "Citizen."

IX. OF REAL PROPERTY

Each individual member of the Community gives himself to it at the 40 moment of its formation. What he gives is the whole man as he then is, with all his qualities of strength and power, and everything of which he stands possessed. Not that, as a result of this act of gift, such possessions, by changing hands and becoming the property of the Sovereign, change their nature. Just as the resources of strength upon which the City can draw are incomparably greater than those at the disposition of any single individual, so, too, is public possession when backed by a greater power. It is made more irrevocable, though not, so far, at least, as regards foreigners, more legitimate. For the State, by reason of the Social Contract which, within it, is the basis of all Rights, is the master of all its members' goods, though, in its dealings with other Powers, it is so only by virtue of its rights as first occupier, which come to it from the individuals who make it up.

The Right of "first occupancy," though more real than the "Right of the strongest," becomes a genuine right only after the right of property has been established. All men have a natural right to what is necessary to them. But the positive act which establishes a man's claim to any particular item of property limits him to that and excludes him from all others. His share having been determined, he must confine himself to that, and no longer has any claim on the property of the community. That is why the right of "first occupancy," however weak it be in a state of nature, is guaranteed to every man enjoying the status of citizen. In so far as he benefits from this right, he withholds his claim, not so much from what is another's, as from what is not specifically his.

In order that the right of "first occupancy" may be legalized, the following conditions must be present. (1) There must be no one already living on the land in question. (2) A man must occupy only so much of it as is necessary for his subsistence. (3) He must take possession of it, not by empty ceremony, but by virtue of his intention to work and to cultivate it, for that, in the absence of legal title, alone constitutes a claim which will be respected by others.

In effect, by according the right of "first occupancy" to a man's needs and to his will to work, are we not stretching it as far as it will go? Should not some limits be set to this right? Has a man only to set foot on land belonging to the community to justify his claim to be its master? Just because he is strong enough, at one particular moment, to keep others off, can be demand that they shall never return? How can a man or a People take possession of vast territories, thereby excluding the rest of the world from their enjoyment, save by an act of criminal usurpation, since, as the result of such an act, the rest of humanity is deprived of the amenities of dwelling and subsistence which nature has provided for their common enjoyment? When Nuñez Balboa, landing upon a strip of coast, claimed the Southern Sea and the whole of South America as the property of the crown of Castille, was he thereby justified in dispossessing its former inhabitants, and in excluding from it all the other princes of the earth? Grant that, and there will be no end to such vain ceremonies. It would be open to His Catholic Majesty to claim from his Council Chamber possession of the whole Universe, only excepting those portions of it already in the ownership of other princes.

One can understand how the lands of individuals, separate but con- 44 tiguous, become public territory, and how the right of sovereignty, extending from men to the land they occupy, becomes at once real and personal— a fact which makes their owners more than ever dependent, and turns their very strength into a guarantee of their fidelity. This is an advantage which does not seem to have been considered by the monarchs of the ancient world, who, claiming to be no more than kings of the Persians, the Scythians, the Macedonians, seem to have regarded themselves rather as the rulers of men than as the masters of countries. Those of our day are cleverer, for they style themselves kings of France, of Spain, of England, and so forth. Thus, by controlling the land, they can be very sure of controlling its inhabitants.

The strange thing about this act of alienation is that, far from depriving its members of their property by accepting its surrender, the Community actually establishes their claim to its legitimate ownership, and changes what was formerly mere usurpation into a right, by virtue of which they may enjoy possession. As owners they are Trustees for the Commonwealth. Their rights are respected by their fellow citizens and are maintained by the united strength of the community against any outside attack. From ceding their property to the State—and thus, to themselves— they derive nothing but advantage, since they have, so to speak, acquired all that they have surrendered. This paradox is easily explained once we realize the distinction between the rights exercised by the Sovereign and by the Owner over the same piece of property, as will be seen later.

It may so happen that a number of men begin to group themselves into a community before ever they own property at all, and that only later, when they have got possession of land sufficient to maintain them all, do they either enjoy it in common or parcel it between themselves in equal lots or in accordance with such scale of proportion as may be established by the sovereign. However this acquisition be made, the right exercised by each individual over his own particular share must always be subordinated to the overriding claim of the Community as such. Otherwise there would be no strength in the social bond, nor any real power in the exercise of sovereignty.

I will conclude this chapter, and the present Book, with a remark which should serve as basis for every social system: that, so far from destroying natural equality, the primitive compact substitutes for it a moral and legal equality which compensates for all those physical inequalities from which men suffer. However unequal they may be in bodily strength or in intellectual gifts, they become equal in the eyes of the law, and as a result of the compact into which they have entered.[7] . . .

[FROM THE SECOND BOOK]

V. OF THE RIGHT OF LIFE AND DEATH

It will be asked how the single citizen, having no right over his own life, can transfer that same right to the sovereign. How can he give to another what is not his to give? This problem seems difficult of solution only because it is badly formulated. Every man has the right to risk his life with the object of preserving it. Has it ever been seriously argued that he who throws himself from a window to escape from fire is guilty of suicide? Or has that same crime ever been imputed to the man who perishes at sea in a storm, the danger of which he knew not when he embarked?

The social treaty has, as its aim, the safety of the contracting parties. Who wills the end wills also the means, and the means in this case are inseparable from certain risks, even from certain mortal accidents. He who would preserve his own life at other's cost is under an obligation to give his own for him should the necessity arise. Now, the citizen is no longer judge of the peril to which the law would have him expose his person; and, when the prince says to him, "It is expedient, in the interests of the State, that you should die," die he must, since only on that condition has he lived, till then, in safety. His life is not now, as it once was, merely nature's gift to him. It is something that he holds, on terms, from the State.

The penalty of death inflicted on criminals may be regarded in much the same way. That he may be saved from dying beneath the assassin's knife the citizen must be ready to pay with his life should he himself elect to play the assassin's part. So far from a man disposing of his own life under the terms of the compact, the sole object of that instrument is to preserve it. It is unlikely that any of the contracting parties will scheme to get himself hanged.

Furthermore, the evil-doer who attacks the fabric of social right becomes, by reason of his crime, a rebel and a traitor to his country. By violating its laws he ceases to be a member of it, and may almost be said to have made war upon it. The preservation, therefore, of the State is seen to be incompatible with his own continued existence. One of the two must perish, and, when the guilty man is put to death, it is as an enemy rather than as a citizen. His trial and sentence constitute the proof and declara-

---

[7] Under a bad government such equality is but apparent and illusory. It serves only to keep the poor man confined within the limits of his poverty, and to maintain the rich in their usurpation. In fact, laws are always beneficial to the "haves" and injurious to the "have-nots." Whence it follows that life in a social community can thrive only when all its citizens have something, and none have too much.

tion that he has broken the terms of the social treaty, and that, consequently, he is no longer a member of the State. Now, since he has always admitted that that is what he was, if only tacitly by reason of his residence, he must be separated from the body politic either by exile, as one who has infringed the compact, or by death as a public enemy. For such an enemy is not a moral person, but a man; and, in such a case, the right of war involves the killing of the vanquished.

But, it may be said, the condemnation of a criminal is an ad hoc act. 52 Agreed. I would point out also that it is an act which does not pertain to the sovereign. It is a right which he can confer without exercising it himself. All my ideas are consistent, but I cannot express them all at once.

When punishments are frequent it is always a sign that the government is weak or lazy. There is no man, be he ever so bad, who cannot be made good for something. No man should be put to death, even to serve as an example, unless his continued existence is a source of danger.

As to the right of pardon, of exempting the guilty from the punishment decreed by law and pronounced by the judge, this belongs only to him who is above both law and judge—in other words, to the sovereign. But this right is not clearly defined, and its employment is very rare. In a well-governed State there are few punishments, not because pardons are frequent, but because criminals are few. The great number of crimes which occur when the State is in a condition of decadence confers immunity on the criminals. In the days of the Roman Republic neither the Senate nor the Consuls ever attempted to pardon the guilty. Even the People did not do so, though they sometimes revoked their own judgment. When pardons wax plentiful it is a sure sign that crimes will soon have no need of them, and everyone can see what that means. But I can hear my heart murmuring and checking my pen. Let us leave such questions to the Just Man who has never been at fault: who has never, in his own person, stood in need of pardon.

Questions and Suggestions for Writing

1. Rousseau opens his essay with a paradox: "Man is born free, and everywhere he is in chains." Why is this an effective way to launch into his subject? If Rousseau were alive today, do you think he would still assert this same paradox? Why, or why not? By the time he is finished, has he resolved this paradox? Explain.

2. What does Rousseau think of the idea that "rulers are superior in kind to their peoples" (para. 7)?

3. Consider this argument: The strongest people (however you define strength) are the best people; the right thing to do is whatever the best people advise or demand; therefore strength is what underlies right conduct—in short, Might makes Right. How would Rousseau respond to this argument, in light of paragraphs 12–15?

4. What does it mean to *alienate* one's liberty or property? Do you think (as Hugo Grotius did, see para. 16) that a person can alienate his or her liberty? What does Rousseau think?

5. Rousseau declares that when a person "renounces his liberty he renounces his essential manhood, his rights" (para. 20); yet he also declares (para. 33) that the essence of the social contract is "the complete alienation" by each person of "all his rights." Do these two passages contradict each other? Explain.

6. Rousseau claims that "we have the right to kill our enemies only when we cannot enslave them" (para. 26). Do you think Rousseau should oppose the death penalty for ordinary criminals (not for prisoners of war) in favor of lifelong imprisonment at hard labor, which is roughly equal to enslaving them? Is the remark quoted above consistent with what Rousseau later says (see paras. 48–54) about the death penalty? Explain.

7. Suppose, after reading paragraphs 30 through 40, one were to object that Rousseau's argument really lays the basis for totalitarianism—the complete surrender of each person to society or the state, with no basis in any natural rights to challenge whatever the government chooses to do. How might Rousseau reply?

8. Rousseau concludes (para. 47) that his theory of the social contract provides a basis for "moral and legal equality" of all persons despite their natural inequality. What is his argument for this conclusion? Do you think it is sound? Explain.

9. Rousseau claims that when there is a "great number of crimes" owing to the way society has fallen into "a condition of decadence," this decadence "confers immunity on the criminals" (para. 54). What does he mean by this claim? Would you agree? Why, or why not?

Thomas Jefferson

The Declaration of Independence

When in the course of human events, it becomes necessary for one people to dissolve the political bands which have connected them with another, and to assume among the Powers of the earth, the separate and

---

Thomas Jefferson (1743–1826) was a congressman, the governor of Virginia, the first Secretary of State, and the president of the United States, but he said he wished to be remembered for only three things: drafting the Declaration of Independence, writing the Virginia Statute for Religious Freedom, and founding the University of Virginia. All three were efforts to promote freedom.

Jefferson was born in Virginia, and educated at William and Mary College in Williamsburg, Virginia. After graduating he studied law, was admitted to the bar,

equal station to which the Laws of Nature and of Nature's God entitle them, a decent respect to the opinions of mankind requires that they should declare the causes which impel them to the separation.

We hold these truths to be self-evident, that all men are created equal, that they are endowed by their Creator with certain unalienable Rights, that among these are Life, Liberty and the pursuit of Happiness.

That to secure these rights, Governments are instituted among Men, deriving their just powers from the consent of the governed.

That whenever any Form of Government becomes destructive of these ends, it is the Right of the People to alter or to abolish it, and to institute a new Government, laying its foundation on such principles and organizing its powers in such form, as to them shall seem most likely to effect their Safety and Happiness. Prudence, indeed, will dictate that Governments long established should not be changed for light and transient causes; and accordingly all experience hath shown that mankind are more disposed to suffer, while evils are sufferable, than to right themselves by abolishing the forms to which they are accustomed. But when a long train of abuses and usurpations pursuing invariably the same Object evinces a design to reduce them under absolute Despotism, it is their right, it is their duty, to throw off such government, and to provide new Guards for their future security.

Such has been the patient sufferance of these Colonies; and such is now the necessity which constrains them to alter their former Systems of Government. The history of the present King of Great Britain is a history of repeated injuries and usurpations, all having in direct object the establishment of an absolute Tyranny over these States. To prove this, let Facts be submitted to a candid world.

He has refused his Assent to Laws, the most wholesome and necessary for the public good.

He has forbidden his Governors to pass Laws of immediate and pressing importance, unless suspended in their operation till his Assent should be obtained; and when so suspended, he has utterly neglected to attend to them.

He has refused to pass other Laws for the accommodation of large districts of people, unless those people would relinquish the right of Representation in the Legislature, a right inestimable to them and formidable to tyrants only.

He has called together legislative bodies at places unusual, uncomfort-

---

and in 1769 was elected to the Virginia House of Burgesses, his first political office. In 1776 he went to Philadelphia as a delegate to the second Continental Congress, where he was elected to a committee of five to write the Declaration of Independence. Jefferson drafted the document, which was then subjected to some changes by the other members of the committee and by the Congress. Although he was unhappy with the changes (especially with the deletion of a passage against slavery), his claim to have written the Declaration is just.

able, and distant from the depository of their Public Records, for the sole purpose of fatiguing them into compliance with his measures.

He has dissolved Representative Houses repeatedly, for opposing with manly firmness his invasions on the rights of the people.

He has refused for a long time, after such dissolutions, to cause others to be elected; whereby the Legislative Powers, incapable of Annihilation, have returned to the People at large for their exercise; the State remaining in the mean time exposed to all the dangers of invasion from without, and convulsions within.

He has endeavored to prevent the population of these States, for that   12 purpose obstructing the Laws of Naturalization of Foreigners; refusing to pass others to encourage their migration hither, and raising the conditions of new Appropriations of Lands.

He has obstructed the Administration of Justice, by refusing his Assent to Laws for establishing Judiciary Powers.

He has made Judges dependent on his Will alone, for the tenure of their offices, and the amount and payment of their salaries.

He has erected a multitude of New Offices, and sent hither swarms of Officers to harass our People, and eat out their substance.

He has kept among us, in time of peace, Standing Armies without the   16 consent of our Legislature.

He has affected to render the Military independent of and superior to the Civil Power.

He has combined with others to subject us to jurisdictions foreign to our constitution, and unacknowledged by our laws; giving his Assent to their acts of pretended Legislation:

For quartering large bodies of armed troops among us:

For protecting them, by a mock Trial, from Punishment for any   20 Murders which they should commit on the Inhabitants of these States:

For cutting off our Trade with all parts of the world:

For imposing Taxes on us without our Consent:

For depriving us in many cases, of the benefits of Trial by Jury:

For transporting us beyond Seas to be tried for pretended offenses: 24

For abolishing the free System of English Laws in a Neighbouring Province, establishing therein an Arbitrary government, and enlarging its boundaries so as to render it at once an example and fit instrument for introducing the same absolute rule into these Colonies:

For taking away our Charters, abolishing our most valuable Laws, and altering fundamentally the Forms of our Governments.

For suspending our own Legislatures, and declaring themselves invested with Power to legislate for us in all cases whatsoever.

He has abdicated Government here, by declaring us out of his Protec-   28 tion and waging War against us.

He has plundered our seas, ravaged our Coasts, burnt our towns and destroyed the Lives of our people.

He is at this time transporting large Armies of foreign Mercenaries to compleat the works of death, desolation and tyranny, already begun with circumstances of Cruelty & perfidy scarcely paralleled in the most barbarous ages, and totally unworthy the Head of a civilized nation.

He has constrained our fellow Citizens taken Captive on the high Seas to bear Arms against their Country, to become the executioners of their friends and Brethren, or to fall themselves by their Hands.

He has excited domestic insurrections amongst us, and has endeavored 32 to bring on the inhabitants of our frontiers, the merciless Indian Savages, whose known rule of warfare, is an undistinguished destruction of all ages, sexes and conditions.

In every stage of these Oppressions We Have Petitioned for Redress in the most humble terms: Our repeated petitions have been answered only by repeated injury. A Prince, whose character is thus marked by every act which may define a Tyrant, is unfit to be the ruler of a free People.

Nor have We been wanting in attention to our British brethren. We have warned them from time to time of attempts by their legislature to extend an unwarrantable jurisdiction over us. We have reminded them of the circumstances of our emigration and settlement here. We have appealed to their native justice and magnanimity and we have conjured them by the ties of our common kindred to disavow these usurpations, which would inevitably interrupt our connections and correspondence. They too have been deaf to the voice of justice and of consanguinity. We must, therefore, acquiesce in the necessity, which denounces our Separation, and hold them, as we hold the rest of mankind, Enemies in War, in Peace Friends.

We, therefore, the Representatives of the United States of America, in General Congress, Assembled, appealing to the Supreme Judge of the world for the rectitude of our intentions, do, in the Name, and by Authority of the good People of these Colonies, solemnly publish and declare, That these United Colonies are, and of Right ought to be, Free and Independent States; that they are Absolved from all Allegiance to the British Crown, and that all political connection between them and the State of Great Britain, is and ought to be totally dissolved; and that as Free and Independent States, they have full power to levy War, conclude Peace, contract Alliances, establish Commerce, and to do all other Acts and Things which Independent States may of right do. And for the support of this Declaration, with a firm reliance on the protection of Divine Providence, we mutually pledge to each other our lives, our Fortunes and our sacred Honor.

Questions and Suggestions for Writing

1. According to the first paragraph, for what audience was the Declaration written? What other audiences do you think the document was (in one way or another) addressed to?

2. The Declaration states that it is intended to "prove" that the acts of the government of George III had as their "direct object the establishment of an absolute tyranny" in the American colonies. Write an essay of 500 to 750 words showing whether the evidence offered in the Declaration "proves" this claim to your satisfaction. (You will, of course, want to define "absolute tyranny.") If you think further evidence is needed to "prove" the colonists' point, indicate what this evidence might be.

3. Paying special attention to the paragraphs beginning "That whenever any Form of Government" (para. 4), "In every stage" (para. 33), and "Nor have We been wanting" (para. 34), in a sentence or two set forth the image of themselves that the colonists seek to convey.

4. In the Declaration of Independence it is argued that the colonists are entitled to certain things, and that under certain conditions they may behave in a certain way. Make explicit the syllogism that Jefferson is arguing.

5. What evidence does Jefferson offer to support his major premise? His minor premise?

6. The Declaration cites "certain unalienable rights" and mentions three: "life, liberty and the pursuit of happiness." What is an unalienable right? If someone has an unalienable (or inalienable) right, does that imply that he or she also has certain duties? If so, what are these duties? John Locke, a century earlier (1690), asserted that all men have a natural right to "life, liberty, and property." Do you think that the decision to drop "property" from this list and substitute "pursuit of happiness" made an improvement?

7. The Declaration ends thus: "We mutually pledge to each other our lives, our Fortunes and our sacred Honor." Is it surprising that Honor is put in the final, climactic position? Is this a better ending than "our Fortunes, our sacred Honor, and our lives," or than "our sacred Honor, our lives, and our fortunes?" Why?

8. King George III has asked you to reply, on his behalf, to the colonists, in 500 to 750 words. Write his reply. (*Caution:* A good reply will probably require you to do some reading about the period.)

9. Write a declaration of your own, setting forth in 500 to 750 words why some group is entitled to independence. You may want to argue that adolescents should not be compelled to attend school, or that animals should not be confined in zoos, or that persons who use drugs should be able to buy them legally. Begin with a premise, then set forth facts illustrating the unfairness of the present condition, and conclude by stating what the new condition will mean to society.

The National Assembly of France

Declaration of the Rights of Man and Citizen

The representatives of the French people, organized in National Assembly, considering that ignorance, forgetfulness, or contempt of the rights of man are the sole causes of the public miseries and of the corruption of governments, have resolved to set forth in a solemn declaration the natural, inalienable, and sacred rights of man, in order that this declaration, being ever present to all the members of the social body, may unceasingly remind them of their rights and their duties: in order that the acts of the legislative power and those of the executive power may be each moment compared with the aim of every political institution and thereby may be more respected; and in order that the demands of the citizens, grounded henceforth upon simple and incontestable principles, may always take the direction of maintaining the constitution and the welfare of all.

In consequence, the National Assembly recognizes and declares, in the presence and under the auspices of the Supreme Being, the following rights of man and citizen.

1. Men are born and remain free and equal in rights. Social distinctions can be based only upon public utility.
2. The aim of every political association is the preservation of the natural and imprescriptible rights of man. These rights are liberty, property, security, and resistance to oppression.
3. The source of all sovereignty is essentially in the nation; no body, no individual can exercise authority that does not proceed from it in plain terms.
4. Liberty consists in the power to do anything that does not injure others; accordingly, the exercise of the natural rights of each man has for its only limits those that secure to the other members of society the enjoyment of these same rights. These limits can be determined only by law.
5. The law has the right to forbid only such actions as are injurious to society. Nothing can be forbidden that is not interdicted by the law and no one can be constrained to do that which it does not order.
6. Law is the expression of the general will. All citizens have the right to take part personally or by their representatives in its formation. It must be the same for all, whether it protects or punishes. All citizens being equal

---

Drafted originally by the Constituent Assembly in the summer of 1789, at the onset of the French Revolution, the final version reprinted here became the preamble to the Constitution of France adopted on September 3, 1791.

in its eyes, are equally eligible to all public dignities, places, and employments, according to their capacities, and without other distinction than that of their virtues and their talents.

7. No man can be accused, arrested, or detained except in the cases determined by the law and according to the forms that it has prescribed. Those who procure, expedite, execute, or cause to be executed arbitrary orders ought to be punished: but every citizen summoned or seized in virtue of the law ought to render instant obedience; he makes himself guilty by resistance.

8. The law ought to establish only penalties that are strictly and obviously necessary and no one can be punished except in virtue of a law established and promulgated prior to the offence and legally applied.

9. Every man being presumed innocent until he has been pronounced guilty, if it is thought indispensable to arrest him, all severity that may not be necessary to secure his person ought to be strictly suppressed by law.

10. No one ought to be disturbed on account of his opinions, even religious, provided their manifestation does not derange the public order established by law.

11. The free communication of ideas and opinions is one of the most precious of the rights of man; every citizen then can freely speak, write, and print, subject to responsibility for the abuse of this freedom in the cases determined by law.

12. The guarantee of the rights of man and citizen requires a public force; this force then is instituted for the advantage of all and not for the personal benefit of those to whom it is entrusted.

13. For the maintenance of the public force and for the expenses of administration a general tax is indispensable; it ought to be equally apportioned among all the citizens according to their means.

14. All the citizens have the right to ascertain, by themselves or by their representatives, the necessity of the public tax, to consent to it freely, to follow the employment of it, and to determine the quota, the assessment, the collection, and the duration of it.

15. Society has the right to call for an account from every public agent of its administration.

16. Any society in which the guarantee of the rights is not secured or the separation of powers not determined has no constitution at all.

17. Property being a sacred and inviolable right, no one can be deprived of it unless a legally established public necessity evidently demands it, under the condition of a just and prior indemnity.

Questions and Suggestions for Writing

1. In its preamble, the French Declaration refers to "the rights of man and citizen." Which of the rights listed in the seventeen articles are rights of man,

and which are rights only of citizens? Or is it impossible to divide up the rights in this way? Explain.

2. In the preamble and in article 2, the "rights of man and citizen" are described as "natural," "inalienable," "sacred," and "imprescriptible." What do these adjectives mean?

3. Find a copy of the Bill of Rights, the first ten amendments to the U.S. Constitution, which were also adopted in the year 1791. Compare the two lists of rights. Which are found on both lists? Which are found only in the Bill of Rights? Found only in the French Declaration? Can you suggest any explanation for the discrepancies? For the common elements?

4. Reread the excerpt from Rousseau's *Social Contract* (p. 447). Which, if any, of the rights affirmed in the French Declaration do you think he would have approved of? Which, if any, would he have rejected? Explain.

5. Article 8 mentions some things that the law "ought" to do, and some things that it "can" do. Can you explain these features of the law by reference to any of the rights explicitly mentioned elsewhere in the Declaration? Or must you have recourse to rights unstated, left implicit in the Declaration? Explain.

6. Article 8 lays down the requirement that penalties are to be imposed only to the extent they are "strictly and obviously necessary." Compare this with the eighth amendment in the Bill of Rights, which prohibits "cruel and unusual punishment." Suppose you believe that torture of terrorists is morally wrong; which of these two provisions, the French or the American, would you prefer to rely on to argue that such torture ought to be unconstitutional? Why? Explain.

7. In articles 13 and 14, reference is made to the necessity to tax, and to tax proportionately "according to [the citizens'] means." What right(s), if any, do you think underlie the government's right to tax the citizens? If you can think of no such right(s), then where does the government get the authority to tax?

Jeremy Bentham

From *Anarchical Fallacies*

The revolution, which threw the government into the hands of the penners and adopters of this declaration, having been the effect of insurrection, the grand object evidently is to justify the cause. But by justifying it, they invite it: in justifying past insurrection, they plant and cultivate a propensity to perpetual insurrection in time future; they sow the seeds of

---

Jeremy Bentham (1748–1832) was the leading English utilitarian philosopher and law reformer of the nineteenth century. Favorably disposed toward the American Revolution, he recoiled in horror (as did many of his countrymen) at the violent excesses unleashed by the French Revolution.

anarchy broad-cast: in justifying the demolition of existing authorities, they undermine all future ones, their own consequently in the number. Shallow and reckless vanity!—They imitate in their conduct the author of that fabled law, according to which the assassination of the prince upon the throne gave to the assassin a title to succeed him. *"People, behold your rights! If a single article of them be violated, insurrection is not your right only, but the most sacred of your duties."* Such is the constant language, for such is the professed object of this source and model of all laws—this self-consecrated oracle of all nations.

The more *abstract*—that is, the more *extensive* the proposition is, the more liable is it to involve a fallacy. Of fallacies, one of the most natural modifications is that which is called *begging the question*—the abuse of making the abstract proposition resorted to for proof, a lever for introducing, in the company of *other* propositions that are nothing to the purpose, the very proposition which is admitted to stand in need of proof.

Is the provision in question fit in point of expediency to be passed into a law for the government of the French nation? That, mutatis mutandis, would have been the question put in England: that was the proper question to have been put in relation to each provision it was proposed should enter into the composition of the body of French laws.

Instead of that, as often as the utility of a provision appeared (by reason of the wideness of its extent, for instance) of a doubtful nature, the way taken to clear the doubt was to assert it to be a provision fit to be made law for all men—for all Frenchmen—and for all Englishmen, for example, into the bargain. This medium of proof was the more alluring, inasmuch as to the advantage of removing opposition, was added the pleasure, the sort of titillation so exquisite to the nerve of vanity in a French heart—the satisfaction, to use a homely, but not the less apposite proverb, of teaching grandmothers to suck eggs. Hark! ye citizens of the other side of the water! Can you tell us what rights you have belonging to you? No, that you can't. It's *we* that understand rights: not our own only, but yours into the bargain; while you poor simple souls! know nothing about the matter.

Hasty generalization, the great stumbling-block of intellectual vanity!—hasty generalization, the rock that even genius itself is so apt to split upon!—hasty generalization, the bane of prudence and of science! . . .

The great enemies of public peace are the selfish and dissocial passions:—necessary as they are—the one to the very existence of each individual, the other to his security. On the part of these affections, a deficiency in point of strength is never to be apprehended: all that is to be apprehended in respect of them, is to be apprehended on the side of their excess. Society is held together only by the sacrifices that men can be induced to make of the gratifications they demand: to obtain these sacrifices is the great difficulty, the great task of government. What has been the object, the perpetual and palpable object, of this declaration of pretended rights? To add as much force as possible to these passions, already but too strong,—to burst the cords that hold them in,—to say to the selfish passions, there—everywhere—is your prey!—to the angry passions, there—everywhere—is your enemy.

Such is the morality of this celebrated manifesto, rendered famous by the same qualities that gave celebrity to the incendiary of the Ephesian temple.

The logic of it is of a piece with its morality:—a perpetual vein of 8 nonsense, flowing from a perpetual abuse of words,—words having a variety of meanings, where words with single meanings were equally at hand,—the same words used in a variety of meanings in the same page,— words used in meanings not their own, where proper words were equally at hand,—words and propositions of the most unbounded signification, turned loose without any of those exceptions or modifications which are so necessary on every occasion to reduce their import within the compass, not only of right reason, but even of the design in hand, of whatever nature it may be;—the same inaccuracy, the same inattention in the penning of this cluster of truths on which the fate of nations was to hang, as if it had been an oriental tale, or an allegory for a magazine:—stale epigrams, instead of necessary distinctions,—figurative expressions preferred to simple ones,— sentimental conceit as trite as they are unmeaning, preferred to apt and precise expressions,—frippery ornament preferred to the majestic simplicity of good sound sense,—and the acts of the senate loaded and disfigured by the tinsel of the playhouse.

In a play or a novel, an improper word is but a word: and the impropriety, whether noticed or not, is attended with no consequences. In a body of laws—especially of laws given as constitutional and fundamental ones—an improper word may be a national calamity:—and civil war may be the consequence of it. Out of one foolish word may start a thousand daggers.

Imputations like these may appear general and declamatory—and rightly so, if they stood alone: but they will be justified even to satiety by the details that follow. Scarcely an article, which in rummaging it, will not be found a true Pandora's box.

In running over the several articles, I shall on the occasion of each article point out, in the first place, the errors it contains in theory; and then, in the second place, the mischiefs it is pregnant with in practice.

The criticism is verbal:—true, but what else can it be? Words—words 12 without a meaning, or with a meaning too flatly false to be maintained by anybody, are the stuff it is made of. Look to the letter, you find nonsense— look beyond the letter, you find nothing.

ARTICLE I

Men (all men) are born and remain free, and equal in respect of rights. Social distinctions cannot be founded, but upon common utility. . . .

All men are born free? All men remain free? No, not a single man: not a single man that ever was, or is, or will be. All men, on the contrary, are born in subjection, and the most absolute subjection—the subjection of a helpless child to the parents on whom he depends every moment for his existence. In this subjection every man is born—in this subjection he continues for years—for a great number of years—and the existence of the individual and of the species depends upon his so doing.

What is the state of things to which the supposed existence of these supposed rights is meant to bear reference?—a state of things prior to the existence of government, or a state of things subsequent to the existence of government? If to a state prior to the existence of government, what would the existence of such rights as these be to the purpose, even if it were true, in any country where there is such a thing as government? If to a state of things subsequent to the formation of government—if in a country where there is a government, in what single instance—in the instance of what single government, is it true? Setting aside the case of parent and child, let any man name that single government under which any such equality is recognised.

All men born free? Absurd and miserable nonsense! When the great 16 complaint—a complaint made perhaps by the very same people at the same time, is—that so many men are born slaves. Oh! but when we acknowledge them to be born slaves, we refer to the laws in being; which laws being void, as being contrary to those laws of nature which are the efficient causes of those rights of man that we are declaring, the men in question are free in one sense, though slaves in another;—slaves, and free, at the same time:—free in respect of the laws of nature—slaves in respect of the pretended human laws, which, though called laws, are no laws at all, as being contrary to the laws of nature. For such is the difference—the great and perpetual difference, betwixt the good subject, the rational censor of the laws, and the anarchist—between the moderate man and the man of violence. The rational censor, acknowledging the existence of the law he disapproves, proposes the repeal of it: the anarchist, setting up his will and fancy for a law before which all mankind are called upon to bow down at the first word—the anarchist, trampling on truth and decency, denies the validity of the law in question,—denies the existence of it in the character of a law, and calls upon all mankind to rise up in a mass, and resist the execution of it.

All men are born equal in rights. The rights of the heir of the most indigent family equal to the rights of the heir of the most wealthy? In what case is this true? I say nothing of hereditary *dignities and powers.* Inequalities such as these being proscribed under and by the French government in France, are consequently proscribed by that government under every other government, and consequently have no existence anywhere. For the total subjection of every other government to French government, is a fundamental principle in the law of universal independence—the

French law. Yet neither was this true at the time of issuing this Declaration of Rights, nor was it meant to be so afterwards. The 13th article, which we shall come to in its place, proceeds on the contrary supposition: for, considering its other attributes, inconsistency could not be wanting to the list. It can scarcely be more hostile to all other laws than it is at variance with itself.

All men (i.e., all human creatures of both sexes) *remain equal in rights.* All men, meaning doubtless all human creatures. The apprentice, then, is equal in rights to his master; he has as much liberty with relation to the master, as the master has with relation to him; he has as much right to command and to punish him; he is as much owner and master of the master's house, as the master himself. The case is the same as between ward and guardian. So again as between wife and husband. The madman has as good a right to confine anybody else, as anybody else has to confine him. The idiot has as much right to govern everybody, as anybody can have to govern him. The physician and the nurse, when called in by the next friend of a sick man seized with a delirium, have no more right to prevent his throwing himself out of the window, than he has to throw them out of it. All this is plainly and incontestably included in this article of the Declaration of Rights: in the very words of it, and in the meaning—if it have any meaning. Was this the meaning of the authors of it?—or did they mean to admit this explanation as to some of the instances, and to explain the article away as to the rest? Not being idiots, nor lunatics, nor under a delirium, they would explain it away with regard to the madman, and the man under a delirium. Considering that a child may become an orphan as soon as it has seen the light, and that in that case, if not subject to government, it must perish, they would explain it away, I think, and contradict themselves, in the case of guardian and ward. In the case of master and apprentice, I would not take upon me to decide; it may have been their meaning to proscribe that relation altogether;—at least, this may have been the case, as soon as the repugnancy between that institution and this oracle was pointed out; for the professed object and destination of it is to be the standard of truth and falsehood, of right and wrong, in everything that relates to government. But to this standard, and to this article of it, the subjection of the apprentice to the master is flatly and diametrically repugnant. If it do not proscribe and exclude this inequality, it proscribes none: if it do not do this mischief, it does nothing. . . .

Article II

The end in view of every political association is the preservation of the natural and imprescriptible rights of man. These rights are liberty, property, security, and resistance to oppression.

Sentence 1. The end in view of every political association, is the 20
preservation of the natural and imprescriptible rights of man.

More confusion—more nonsense,—and the nonsense, as usual, dangerous nonsense. The words can scarcely be said to have a meaning: but if they have, or rather if they had a meaning, these would be the propositions either asserted or implied:

1. That there are such things as rights anterior to the establishment of governments: for natural, as applied to rights, if it mean anything, is meant to stand in opposition to *legal*,—to such rights as are acknowledged to owe their existence to government, and are consequently posterior in their date to the establishment of government.

2. That these rights *can not* be abrogated by government: for *can* not is implied in the form of the word imprescriptible, and the sense it wears when so applied, is the cut-throat sense above explained.

3. That the governments that exist derive their origin from formal 24 associations, or what are now called *conventions:* associations entered into by a partnership contract, with all the members for partners,—entered into at a day prefixed, for a predetermined purpose, the formation of a new government where there was none before (for as to formal meetings holden under the controul of an existing government, they are evidently out of question here) in which it seems again to be implied in the way of inference, though a necessary and an unavoidable inference, that all governments (that is, self-called governments, knots of persons exercising the powers of government) that have had any other origin than an association of the above description, are illegal, that is, no governments at all; resistance to them, and subversion of them, lawful and commendable; and so on.

Such are the notions implied in this first part of the article. How stands the truth of things? That there are no such things as natural rights— no such things as rights anterior to the establishment of government—no such things as natural rights opposed to, in contradistinction to, legal: that the expression is merely figurative; that when used in the moment you attempt to give it a literal meaning it leads to error, and to that sort of error that leads to mischief—to the extremity of mischief.

We know what it is for men to live without government—and living without government, to live without rights: we know what it is for men to live without government, for we see instances of such a way of life—we see it in many savage nations, or rather races of mankind; for instance, among the savages of New South Wales, whose way of living is so well known to us: no habit of obedience, and thence no government—no government, and thence no laws—no laws, and thence no such things as rights—no security—no property:—liberty, as against regular controul, the controul of laws and government—perfect; but as against all irregular controul, the mandates of stronger individuals, none. In this state, at a time earlier than the commencement of history—in this same state, judging from analogy, we, the inhabitants of the part of the globe we call Europe, were;—no government, consequently no rights; no rights, consequently no property—no legal security—no legal liberty: security not more than belongs to beasts—forecast and sense of insecurity keener—consequently in point of happiness below the level of the brutal race.

In proportion to the want of happiness resulting from the want of rights, a reason exists for wishing that there were such things as rights. But reasons for wishing there were such things as rights, are not rights;—a reason for wishing that a certain right were established, is not that right— want is not supply—hunger is not bread.

That which has no existence cannot be destroyed—that which cannot 28 be destroyed cannot require anything to preserve it from destruction. *Natural rights* is simple nonsense: natural and imprescriptible rights, rhetorical nonsense,—nonsense upon stilts. But this rhetorical nonsense ends in the old strain of mischievous nonsense: for immediately a list of these pretended natural rights is given, and those are so expressed as to present to view legal rights. And of these rights, whatever they are, there is not, it seems, any one of which any government *can*, upon any occasion whatever, abrogate the smallest particle.

So much for terrorist language. What is the language of reason and plain sense upon this same subject? That in proportion as it is *right* or *proper*, i.e., advantageous to the society in question, that this or that right—a right to this or that effect—should be established and maintained, in that same proportion it is *wrong* that it should be abrogated: but that as there is no *right*, which ought not to be maintained so long as it is upon the whole advantageous to the society that it should be maintained, so there is no right which, when the abolition of it is advantageous to society, should not be abolished. To know whether it would be more for the advantage of society that this or that right should be maintained or abolished, the time at which the question about maintaining or abolishing is proposed, must be given, and the circumstances under which it is proposed to maintain or abolish it; the right itself must be specifically described, not jumbled with an undistinguishable heap of others, under any such vague general terms as property, liberty, and the like.

One thing, in the midst of all this confusion, is but too plain. They know not of what they are talking under the name of natural rights and yet they would have them imprescriptible—proof against all the power of the laws—pregnant with occasions summoning the members of the community to rise up in resistance against the laws. What, then, was their object in declaring the existence of imprescriptible rights, and without specifying a single one by any such mark as it could be known by? This and no other—to excite and keep up a spirit of resistance to all laws—a spirit of insurrection against all governments—against the governments of all other nations instantly—against the government of their own nation—against the government they themselves were pretending to establish—even that, as soon as their own reign should be at an end. In us is the perfection of virtue and wisdom: in all mankind besides, the extremity of wickedness and folly. Our will shall consequently reign without controul, and for ever: reign now we are living—reign after we are dead.

All nations—all future ages—shall be, for they are predestined to be, our slaves.

Future governments will not have honesty enough to be trusted with 32 the determination of what rights shall be maintained, what abrogated— what laws kept in force, what repealed. Future subjects (I should say future citizens, for French government does not admit of subjects) will not have wit enough to be trusted with the choice whether to submit to the determination of the government of their time, or to resist it. Governments, citizens—all to the end of time—all must be kept in chains.

Such are their maxims—such their premises—for it is by such premises only that the doctrine of imprescriptible rights and unrepealable laws can be supported.

What is the real source of these imprescriptible rights—these unrepealable laws? Power turned blind by looking from its own height: self-conceit and tyranny exalted into insanity. No man was to have any other man for a servant, yet all men were forever to be their slaves. Making laws with imposture in their mouths, under pretence of declaring them—giving for laws anything that came uppermost, and these unrepealable ones, on pretence of finding them ready made. Made by what? Not by a God—they allow of none; but by their goddess, Nature.

The origination of governments from a contract is a pure fiction, or in other words, a falsehood. It never has been known to be true in any instance; the allegation of it does mischief, by involving the subject in error and confusion, and is neither necessary nor useful to any good purpose.

All governments that we have any account of have been gradually 36 established by habit, after having been formed by force; unless in the instance of governments formed by individuals who have been emancipated, or have emancipated themselves, from governments already formed, the governments under which they were born—a rare case, and from which nothing follows with regard to the rest. What signifies it how governments are formed? Is it the less proper—the less conducive to the happiness of society—that the happiness of society should be the one object kept in view by the members of the government in all their measures? Is it the less the interest of men to be happy—less to be wished that they may be so—less the moral duty of their governors to make them so, as far as they can, at Mogadore than at Philadelphia?

Whence is it, but from government, that contracts derive their binding force? Contracts came from government, not government from contracts. It is from the habit of enforcing contracts, and seeing them enforced, that governments are chiefly indebted for whatever disposition they have to observe them.

Sentence 2. These rights (these imprescriptible as well as natural rights,) are liberty, property, security, and resistance to oppression.

Observe the extent of these pretended rights, each of them belonging to every man, and all of them without bounds. Unbounded liberty; that is, amongst other things, the liberty of doing or not doing on every occasion whatever each man pleases:—Unbounded property; that is, the right of doing with everything around him (with every *thing* at least, if not with every person,) whatsoever he pleases; communicating that right to anybody, and withholding it from anybody:—Unbounded security; that is, security for such his liberty, for such his property, and for his person, against every defalcation that can be called for on any account in respect of any of them:—Unbounded resistance to oppression; that is, unbounded exercise of the faculty of guarding himself against whatever unpleasant circumstance may present itself to his imagination or his passions under that name. . . .

Unbounded liberty—I must still say unbounded liberty;—for though 40 the next article but one returns to the charge, and gives such a definition of liberty as seems intended to set bounds to it, yet in effect the limitation amounts to nothing; and when, as here, no warning is given of any exception in the texture of the general rule, every exception which turns up is, not a confirmation but a contradiction of the rule: liberty, without any pre-announced or intelligible bounds; and as to the other rights, they remain unbounded to the end: rights of man composed of a system of contradictions and impossibilities.

In vain would it be said, that though no bounds are here assigned to any of these rights, yet it is to be understood as taken for granted, and tacitly admitted and assumed, that they are to have bounds; viz. such bounds as it is understood will be set them by the laws. Vain, I say, would be this apology; for the supposition would be contradictory to the express declaration of the article itself, and would defeat the very object which the whole declaration has in view. It would be self-contradictory, because these rights are, in the same breath in which their existence is declared, declared to be imprescriptible; and imprescriptible, or, as we in England should say, indefeasible, means nothing unless it exclude the interference of the laws.

It would be not only inconsistent with itself, but inconsistent with the declared and sole object of the declaration, if it did not exclude the interference of the laws. It is against the laws themselves, and the laws only, that this declaration is levelled. It is for the hands of the legislator and all legislators, and none but legislators, that the shackles it provides are intended,—it is against the apprehended encroachments of legislators that the rights in question, the liberty and property, and so forth, are intended to be made secure,—it is to such encroachments, and damages, and dangers, that whatever security it professes to give has respect. Precious security for unbounded rights against legislators, if the extent of those rights in every direction were purposely left to depend upon the will and pleasure of those very legislators!

Nonsensical or nugatory, and in both cases, mischievous: such is the alternative.

So much for all these pretended indefeasible rights in the lump: their inconsistency with each other, as well as the inconsistency of them in the character of indefeasible rights with the existence of government and all peaceable society, will appear still more plainly when we examine them one by one.

1. *Liberty*, then, is imprescriptible—incapable of being taken away— out of the power of any government ever to take away: liberty,—that is, every branch of liberty—every individual exercise of liberty; for no line is drawn—no distinction—no exception made. What these instructors as well as governors of mankind appear not to know, is, that all rights are made at the expense of liberty—all laws by which rights are created or confirmed. No right without a correspondent obligation. Liberty, as against the coercion of the law, may, it is true, be given by the simple removal of the obligation by which that coercion was applied—by the simple repeal of the coercing law. But as against the coercion applicable by individual to individual, no liberty can be given to one man but in proportion as it is taken from another. All coercive laws, therefore (that is, all laws but constitutional laws, and laws repealing or modifying coercive laws) and in particular all laws creative of liberty, are, as far as they go, abrogative of liberty. Not here and there a law only—not this or that possible law, but almost all laws, are therefore repugnant to these natural and imprescriptible rights: consequently null and void, calling for resistance and insurrection, and so on, as before.

Laws creative of rights of property are also struck at by the same anathema. How is property given? By restraining liberty; that is, by taking it away so far as is necessary for the purpose. How is your house made yours? By debarring every one else from the liberty of entering it without your leave. But

2. *Property*. Property stands second on the list,—proprietary rights are in the number of the natural and imprescriptible rights of man—of the rights which a man is not indebted for to the laws, and which cannot be taken from him by the laws. Men—that is, every man (for a general expression given without exception is an universal one) has a right to property, to proprietary rights, *a right which* cannot be taken away from him by the laws. To proprietary rights. Good: but in relation to what subject? for as to proprietary rights—without a subject to which they are referable—without a subject in or in relation to which they can be exercised—they will hardly be of much value, they will hardly be worth

taking care of, with so much solemnity. In vain would all the laws in the world have ascertained that I have a right to something. If this be all they have done for me—if there be no specific subject in relation to which my proprietary rights are established, I must either take what I want without right, or starve. As there is no such subject specified with relation to each man, or to any man (indeed how could there be?) the necessary inference (taking the passage literally) is, that every man has all manner of proprietary rights with relation to every subject of property without exception: in a word, that every man has a right to everything. Unfortunately, in most matters of property, what is every man's right is no man's right; so that the effect of this part of the oracle, if observed, would be, not to establish property, but to extinguish it—to render it impossible ever to be revived: and this is one of the rights declared to be imprescriptible.

It will probably be acknowledged, that according to this construction, 48 the clause in question is equally ruinous and absurd:—and hence the inference may be, that this was not the construction—this was not the meaning in view. But by the same rule, every possible construction which the words employed can admit of, might be proved not to have been the meaning in view: nor is this clause a whit more absurd or ruinous than all that goes before it, and a great deal of what comes after it. And, in short, if this be not the meaning of it, what is? Give it a sense—give it any sense whatever,—it is mischievous:—to save it from that imputation, there is but one course to take, which is to acknowledge it to be nonsense.

Thus much would be clear, if anything were clear in it, that according to this clause, whatever proprietary rights, whatever property a man once has, no matter how, being imprescriptible, can never be taken away from him by any law: or of what use or meaning is the clause? So that the moment it is acknowledged in relation to any article, that such article is my property, no matter how or when it became so, that moment it is acknowledged that it can never be taken away from me: therefore, for example, all laws and all judgments, whereby anything is taken away from me without my free consent—all taxes, for example, and all fines—are void, and, as such, call for resistance and insurrection, and so forth, as before.

3. *Security.* Security stands the third on the list of these natural and imprescriptible rights which laws did not give, and which laws are not in any degree to be suffered to take away. . . .

Security for person is the branch that seems here to have been understood:—security for each man's person, as against all those hurtful or disagreeable impressions (exclusive of those which consist in the mere disturbance of the enjoyment of liberty) by which a man is affected in his person; loss of life—loss of limbs—loss of the use of limbs—wounds, bruises, and the like. All laws are null and void, then, which on any account or in any manner seek to expose the person of any man to any risk—which appoint capital or other corporal punishment—which expose a man to personal hazard in the service of the military power against foreign enemies, or in that of the judicial power against delinquents:—all laws which, to preserve the country from pestilence, authorize the immediate execution of a suspected person, in the event of his transgressing certain bounds.

4. *Resistance to oppression.* Fourth and last in the list of natural and imprescriptible rights, resistance to oppression—meaning, I suppose, the right to resist oppression. What is oppression? Power misapplied to the prejudice of some individual. What is it that a man has in view when he speaks of oppression? Some exertion of power which he looks upon as misapplied to the prejudice of some individual—to the producing on the part of such individual some suffering, to which (whether as forbidden by the laws or otherwise) we conceive he ought not to have been subjected. . . . 52

Whenever you are about to be oppressed, you have a right to resist oppression: whenever you conceive yourself to be oppressed, conceive yourself to have a right to make resistance, and act accordingly. In proportion as a law of any kind—any act of power, supreme or subordinate, legislative, administrative, or judicial, is unpleasant to a man, especially if, in consideration of such its unpleasantness, his opinion is, that such act of power ought not to have been exercised, he of course looks upon it as oppression: as often as anything of this sort happens to a man—as often as anything happens to a man to inflame his passions,—this article for fear his passions should not be sufficiently inflamed of themselves, sets itself to work to blow the flame and urges him to resistance. Submit not to any decree or other act of power, of the justice of which you are not yourself perfectly convinced. . . .

Questions and Suggestions for Writing

1. In paragraph 2, Bentham explains the fallacy of "begging the question." Look in the appendix of this book (p. 722) and compare the definition there of this fallacy. Why does Bentham think the French Declaration commits this fallacy? Do you agree?

2. In paragraph 5, Bentham accuses the French authors of the Declaration (p. 465) of committing the fallacy of "hasty generalization." Can you cite any particular passage in the Declaration to which Bentham might point as an example of this fallacy?

3. In paragraph 8, Bentham compares the "logic" of the Declaration with its "morality." What does he mean by these two terms in this context?

4. In paragraphs 14–16, Bentham appears to contradict the claim of the French Declaration (and of Rousseau, too; see p. 447) that "all men [that is, all persons] are born free." What is Bentham's argument against the truth of this proposition? Suppose Rousseau or some other advocate of this proposition wanted to defend it despite Bentham's objections; how might it be defended?

5. In paragraphs 16–18, Bentham attacks the Declaration for its affirmation of the equality of all persons. What is Bentham's criticism? Do you agree or not? Explain.

6. Bentham attacks the doctrine of natural rights with three general criticisms (paras. 22–24) which he amplifies at some length (paras. 25–37). What are they? Can you think of any replies to his criticisms? Write a 500-word essay stating in your own words his critique and presenting your evaluation of it.

7. Calling something with which you disagree "Nonsense" is surely no refutation, it is merely abusive. Is Bentham guilty of this fault when he declares that "natural and imprescriptible rights" is "nonsense on stilts" (para. 28)? Explain. (And, by the way, what do you make of his metaphor, "nonsense on stilts"?)

8. Bentham attacks the Declaration for claiming that all persons have an "unbounded right" to liberty and property (paras. 39–44). Does the Declaration really make such a claim? In any case, what is Bentham's objection to it? Do you agree with him, or not? Explain.

9. In regard to property, Bentham says, "What is every man's right is no man's right" (para. 47). He says this, apparently, because it is paradoxical and by this means he refutes, or at least ridicules, the whole idea. But is he right to do so? Think of a public beach or a public garden: Doesn't everyone have a right to it (that is, to use it) and yet no one has a right to it (that is, no one person owns it)? So where's the paradox after all? How might Bentham reply?

10. Bentham writes as if the alleged "right to resist oppression" was the worst "anarchical fallacy" of them all (see paras. 52–53). Do you agree? Reread the Declaration of Independence (p. 460) for its discussion of the right of resistance to oppressive government, and decide what Bentham would say about Jefferson's argument on this point.

Elizabeth Cady Stanton

Declaration of Sentiments and Resolutions

When, in the course of human events, it becomes necessary for one portion of the family of man to assume among the people of the earth a position different from that which they have hitherto occupied, but one to

---

Elizabeth Cady Stanton (1815–1902), a lawyer's daughter and journalist's wife, proposed in 1848 a convention to address the "social, civil, and religious condition and rights of women." Responding to Stanton's call, women from all over the Northeast convened in the village of Seneca Falls, New York. Her Declaration, adopted by the Seneca Falls Convention—but only after vigorous debate and some amendments by others—became the platform for the women's movement in this country.

which the laws of nature and of nature's God entitle them, a decent respect to the opinions of mankind requires that they should declare the causes that impel them to such a course.

We hold these truths to be self-evident: that all men and women are created equal; that they are endowed by their Creator with certain inalienable rights; that among these are life, liberty, and the pursuit of happiness; that to secure these rights governments are instituted, deriving their just powers from the consent of the governed. Whenever any form of government becomes destructive of these ends, it is the right of those who suffer from it to refuse allegiance to it, and to insist upon the institution of a new government, laying its foundation on such principles, and organizing its powers in such form, as to them shall seem most likely to effect their safety and happiness. Prudence, indeed, will dictate that governments long established should not be changed for light and transient causes; and accordingly all experience hath shown that mankind are more disposed to suffer, while evils are sufferable, than to right themselves by abolishing the forms to which they were accustomed. But when a long train of abuses and usurpations, pursuing invariably the same object, evinces a design to reduce them under absolute despotism, it is their duty to throw off such government, and to provide new guards for their future security. Such has been the patient sufferance of the women under this government, and such is now the necessity which constrains them to demand the equal station to which they are entitled.

The history of mankind is a history of repeated injuries and usurpations on the part of man toward woman, having in direct object the establishment of an absolute tyranny over her. To prove this, let facts be submitted to a candid world.

He has never permitted her to exercise her inalienable right to the 4 elective franchise.

He has compelled her to submit to laws, in the formation of which she had no voice.

He has withheld from her rights which are given to the most ignorant and degraded men—both natives and foreigners.

Having deprived her of this first right of a citizen, the elective franchise, thereby leaving her without representation in the halls of legislation, he has oppressed her on all sides.

He has made her, if married, in the eye of the law, civilly dead. 8

He has taken from her all right in property, even to the wages she earns.

He has made her, morally, an irresponsible being, as she can commit many crimes with impunity, provided they be done in the presence of her husband. In the covenant of marriage, she is compelled to promise obedience to her husband, he becoming to all intents and purposes, her master—the law giving him power to deprive her of her liberty, and to administer chastisement.

He has so framed the laws of divorce, as to what shall be the proper causes, and in case of separation, to whom the guardianship of the children shall be given, as to be wholly regardless of the happiness of women—the law, in all cases, going upon a false supposition of the supremacy of man, and giving all power into his hands.

After depriving her of all rights as a married woman, if single, and the owner of property, he has taxed her to support a government which recognizes her only when her property can be made profitable to it.   12

He has monopolized nearly all the profitable employments, and from those she is permitted to follow, she receives but a scanty remuneration. He closes against her all the avenues to wealth and distinction which he considers most honorable to himself. As a teacher of theology, medicine, or law, she is not known.

He has denied her the facilities for obtaining a thorough education, all colleges being closed against her.

He allows her in Church, as well as State, but a subordinate position, claiming Apostolic authority for her exclusion from the ministry, and, with some exceptions, from any public participation in the affairs of the Church.

He has created a false public sentiment by giving to the world a different code of morals for men and women, by which moral delinquencies which exclude women from society, are not only tolerated, but deemed of little account in man.   16

He has usurped the prerogative of Jehovah himself, claiming it as his right to assign for her a sphere of action, when that belongs to her conscience and to her God.

He has endeavored, in every way that he could, to destroy her confidence in her own powers, to lessen her self-respect, and to make her willing to lead a dependent and abject life.

Now, in view of this entire disfranchisement of one-half the people of this country, their social and religious degradation—in view of the unjust laws above mentioned, and because women do feel themselves aggrieved, oppressed, and fraudulently deprived of their most sacred rights, we insist that they have immediate admission to all the rights and privileges which belong to them as citizens of the United States.

In entering upon the great work before us, we anticipate no small amount of misconception, misrepresentation, and ridicule; but we shall use every instrumentality within our power to effect our object. We shall employ agents, circulate tracts, petition the State and National legislatures, and endeavor to enlist the pulpit and the press in our behalf. We hope this Convention will be followed by a series of Conventions embracing every part of the country.   20

[The following resolutions were discussed by Lucretia Mott, Thomas and Mary Ann McClintock, Amy Post, Catharine A. F. Stebbins, and others, and were adopted:]

Whereas, The great precept of nature is conceded to be, that "man shall pursue his own true and substantial happiness." Blackstone in his Commentaries remarks, that this law of Nature being coeval with mankind, and dictated by God himself, is of course superior in obligation to any other. It is binding over all the globe, in all countries, and at all times; no human laws are of any validity if contrary to this, and such of them as are valid, derive all their force, and all their validity, and all their authority, mediately and immediately, from this original; therefore,

Resolved, That such laws as conflict, in any way, with the true and substantial happiness of woman, are contrary to the great precept of nature and of no validity, for this is "superior in obligation to any other."

Resolved, That all laws which prevent woman from occupying such a station in society as her conscience shall dictate, or which place her in a position inferior to that of man, are contrary to the great precept of nature, and therefore of no force or authority.

Resolved, That woman is man's equal—was intended to be so by the 24 Creator, and the highest good of the race demands that she should be recognized as such.

Resolved, That the women of this country ought to be enlightened in regard to the laws under which they live, that they may no longer publish their degradation by declaring themselves satisfied with their present position, nor their ignorance, by asserting that they have all the rights they want.

Resolved, That inasmuch as man, while claiming for himself intellectual superiority, does accord to woman moral superiority, it is preeminently his duty to encourage her to speak and teach, as she has an opportunity, in all religious assemblies.

Resolved, That the same amount of virtue, delicacy, and refinement of behavior that is required of woman in the social state, should also be required of man, and the same transgressions should be visited with equal severity on both man and woman.

Resolved, That the objection of indelicacy and impropriety, which is 28 so often brought against woman when she addresses a public audience, comes with a very ill-grace from those who encourage, by their attendance, her appearance on the stage, in the concert, or in feats of the circus.

Resolved, That woman has too long rested satisfied in the circumscribed limits which corrupt customs and a perverted application of the Scriptures have marked out for her, and that it is time she should move in the enlarged sphere which her great Creator has assigned her.

Resolved, That it is the duty of the women of this country to secure to themselves their sacred right to the elective franchise.

Resolved, That the equality of human rights results necessarily from the fact of the identity of the race in capabilities and responsibilities.

Resolved, therefore, That, being invested by the Creator with the 32 same capabilities, and the same consciousness of responsibility for their exercise, it is demonstrably the right and duty of woman, equally with man, to promote every righteous cause by every righteous means; and especially in regard to the great subjects of morals and religion, it is self-evidently her right to participate with her brother in teaching them, both in private and in public, by writing and by speaking, by any instrumentalities proper to be used, and in any assemblies proper to be held; and this being a self-evident truth growing out of the divinely implanted principles of human nature, any custom or authority adverse to it, whether modern or wearing the hoary sanction of antiquity, is to be regarded as a self-evident falsehood, and at war with mankind.

[At the last session Lucretia Mott offered and spoke to the following resolution:]

Resolved, That the speedy success of our cause depends upon the zealous and untiring efforts of both men and women, for the overthrow of the monopoly of the pulpit, and for the securing to woman an equal participation with men in the various trades, professions, and commerce.

Questions and Suggestions for Writing

1. Stanton echoes the Declaration of Independence because she wishes to associate her ideas and the movement she supports with a document and a movement that her readers esteem. And of course she must have believed that if readers esteem the Declaration of Independence, they must grant the justice of her goals. Does her strategy work, or does it backfire by making her essay seem strained?

2. When Stanton insists that women have an "inalienable right to the elective franchise" (para. 3), what does she mean by inalienable? By elective franchise? If you have read Bentham's criticism of natural rights (p. 467), decide whether he would agree with Stanton that women have such a right. Do you think he would agree that women should have this right equally with men under law? Why, or why not?

3. Stanton complains that men have made women, "in the eyes of the law, civilly dead" (para. 8). What does she mean by civilly dead? How is it possible for a person to be biologically alive yet civilly dead?

4. Stanton objects that women are "not known" as teachers of "theology, medicine, or law" (para. 13). Is this still true today? Do some research in your library, and then write three 100-word biographical sketches, one each on a well-known woman professor of theology, of medicine, and of law.

5. How might you go about proving (rather than merely asserting) that, as paragraph 24 says, "woman is man's equal—was intended so by the Creator"?

6. The Declaration claims that women have "the same capabilities" as men (para. 32). Yet in 1848 Stanton and the others at Seneca Falls knew, or should have

known, that history recorded no example of an outstanding woman philosopher to compare with Plato or Kant, a great composer to compare with Beethoven or Chopin, a scientist to compare with Galileo or Newton, or a creative mathematician to compare with Euclid or Descartes. Do these facts contradict the Declaration's claim? If not, why not? How else but by different intellectual capabilities do you think such facts are to be explained?

7. Stanton's Declaration is almost 150 years old. Have all of the issues she raised been satisfactorily resolved? If not, which ones remain?

8. In our society, children have very few rights. For instance, a child cannot decide to drop out of elementary school or high school, and a child cannot decide to leave his or her parents in order to reside with some other family that he or she finds more compatible. Whatever your view of children's rights, compose the best Declaration of the Rights of Children that you can compose.

The General Assembly of the United Nations

Universal Declaration of Human Rights

PREAMBLE

Whereas recognition of the inherent dignity and of the equal and inalienable rights of all members of the human family is the foundation of freedom, justice, and peace in the world,

Whereas disregard and contempt for human rights have resulted in barbarous acts which have outraged the conscience of mankind, and the advent of a world in which human beings shall enjoy freedom of speech and belief and freedom from fear and want has been proclaimed as the highest aspiration of the common people,

Whereas it is essential, if man is not to be compelled to have recourse, as a last resort, to rebellion against tyranny and oppression, that human rights should be protected by the rule of law,

Whereas it is essential to promote the development of friendly relations between nations,

Whereas the peoples of the United Nations have in the Charter reaffirmed their faith in fundamental human rights, in the dignity and

---

Adopted in 1948 in the General Assembly by a vote of 48 to 0 (with South Africa, Soviet Union, and Saudi Arabia among the abstainers), this Declaration is now the most influential international manifesto of human rights. It arose from the human rights provisions in the Charter of the United Nations, adopted in 1945, and the several Conventions and Covenants it has inspired have treaty status in international law. These include the Convention on Genocide (1948) and the International Covenant on Economic, Social, and Cultural Rights (1966) and on Civil and Political Rights (1966).

worth of the human person and in the equal rights of men and women and have determined to promote social progress and better standards of life in larger freedom,

Whereas Member States have pledged themselves to achieve, in cooperation with the United Nations, the promotion of universal respect for and observance of human rights and fundamental freedoms,

Whereas a common understanding of these rights and freedoms is of the greatest importance for the full realization of this pledge.

Now, therefore, the General Assembly *proclaims*

This universal declaration of human rights as a common standard of achievement for all peoples and all nations, to the end that every individual and every organ of society, keeping this Declaration constantly in mind, shall strive by teaching and education to promote respect for these rights and freedoms and by progressive measures, national and international, to secure their universal and effective recognition and observance, both among the peoples of Member States themselves and among the peoples of territories under their jurisdiction.

ARTICLE 1

All human beings are born free and equal in dignity and rights. They are endowed with reason and conscience and should act toward one another in a spirit of brotherhood.

ARTICLE 2

Everyone is entitled to all the rights and freedoms set forth in this Declaration, without distinction of any kind, such as race, color, sex, language, religion, political or other opinion, national or social origin, property, birth, or other status.

Furthermore, no distinction shall be made on the basis of the political, jurisdictional, or international status of the country or territory to which a person belongs, whether it be independent, trust, non-self-governing or under any other limitation of sovereignty.

ARTICLE 3

Everyone has the right to life, liberty, and security of person.

ARTICLE 4

No one shall be held in slavery or servitude; slavery and the slave trade shall be prohibited in all their forms.

ARTICLE 5

No one shall be subjected to torture or to cruel, inhuman, or degrading treatment or punishment.

ARTICLE 6

Everyone has the right to recognition everywhere as a person before the law.

ARTICLE 7

All are equal before the law and are entitled without any discrimination to equal protection of the law. All are entitled to equal protection against any discrimination in violation of this Declaration and against any incitement to such discrimination.

ARTICLE 8

Everyone has the right to an effective remedy by the competent national tribunals for acts violating the fundamental rights granted him by the constitution or by law.

ARTICLE 9

No one shall be subjected to arbitrary arrest, detention, or exile.

ARTICLE 10

Everyone is entitled in full equality to a fair and public hearing by an independent and impartial tribunal, in the determination of his rights and obligations and of any criminal charge against him.

ARTICLE 11

1. Everyone charged with a penal offense has the right to be presumed innocent until proved guilty according to law in a public trial at which he has had all the guarantees necessary for his defense.

2. No one shall be held guilty of any penal offense on account of any act or omission which did not constitute a penal offense, under national or international law, at the time when it was committed. Nor shall a heavier penalty be imposed than the one that was applicable at the time the penal offense was committed.

ARTICLE 12

No one shall be subjected to arbitrary interference with his privacy, family, home, or correspondence, nor to attacks upon his honor and reputation. Everyone has the right to the protection of the law against such interference or attacks.

ARTICLE 13

1. Everyone has the right to freedom of movement and residence within the borders of each State.

2. Everyone has the right to leave any country, including his own, and to return to his country.

ARTICLE 14

1. Everyone has the right to seek and to enjoy in other countries asylum from persecution.
2. This right may not be invoked in the case of prosecutions genuinely arising from nonpolitical crimes or from acts contrary to the purposes and principles of the United Nations.

ARTICLE 15

1. Everyone has the right to a nationality.
2. No one shall be arbitrarily deprived of his nationality nor denied the right to change his nationality.

ARTICLE 16

1. Men and women of full age, without any limitation due to race, nationality, or religion, have the right to marry and to found a family. They are entitled to equal rights as to marriage, during marriage and at its dissolution.
2. Marriage shall be entered into only with the free and full consent of the intending spouses.
3. The family is the natural and fundamental group unit of society and is entitled to protection by society and the State.

ARTICLE 17

1. Everyone has the right to own property alone as well as in association with others.
2. No one shall be arbitrarily deprived of his property.

ARTICLE 18

Everyone has the right to freedom of thought, conscience, and religion; this right includes freedom to change his religion or belief, and freedom, either alone or in community with others and in public or private, to manifest his religion or belief in teaching, practice, worship, and observance.

ARTICLE 19

Everyone has the right to freedom of opinion and expression; this right includes freedom to hold opinions without interference and to seek, receive, and impart information and ideas through any media and regardless of frontiers.

ARTICLE 20

1. Everyone has the right to freedom of peaceful assembly and association.

2. No one may be compelled to belong to an association.

ARTICLE 21

1. Everyone has the right to take part in the government of his country, directly or through freely chosen representatives.

2. Everyone has the right of equal access to public service in his country.

3. The will of the people shall be the basis of the authority of government; this will shall be expressed in periodic and genuine elections which shall be by universal and equal suffrage and shall be held by secret vote or by equivalent free voting procedures.

ARTICLE 22

Everyone, as a member of society, has the right to social security and is entitled to realization, through national effort and international cooperation and in accordance with the organization and resources of each State, of the economic, social, and cultural rights indispensable for his dignity and the free development of his personality.

ARTICLE 23

1. Everyone has the right to work, to free choice of employment, to just and favorable conditions of work and to protection against unemployment.

2. Everyone, without any discrimination, has the right to equal pay for equal work.

3. Everyone who works has the right to just and favorable remuneration ensuring for himself and his family an existence worthy of human dignity, and supplemented, if necessary, by other means of social protection.

4. Everyone has the right to form and to join trade unions for the protection of his interests.

ARTICLE 24

Everyone has the right to rest and leisure, including reasonable limitation of working hours and periodic holidays with pay.

ARTICLE 25

1. Everyone has the right to a standard of living adequate for the health and well-being of himself and of his family, including food,

clothing, housing, and medical care and necessary social services, and the right to security in the event of unemployment, sickness, disability, widowhood, old age, or other lack of livelihood in circumstances beyond his control.

2. Motherhood and childhood are entitled to special care and assistance. All children, whether born in or out of wedlock, shall enjoy the same social protection.

ARTICLE 26

1. Everyone has the right to education. Education shall be free, at least in the elementary and fundamental stages. Elementary education shall be compulsory. Technical and professional education shall be made generally available and higher education shall be equally accessible to all on the basis of merit.

2. Education shall be directed to the full development of the human personality and to the strengthening of respect for human rights and fundamental freedoms. It shall promote understanding, tolerance, and friendship among all nations, racial or religious groups, and shall further the activities of the United Nations for the maintenance of peace.

3. Parents have a prior right to choose the kind of education that shall be given to their children.

ARTICLE 27

1. Everyone has the right freely to participate in the cultural life of the community, to enjoy the arts, and to share in scientific advancement and its benefits.

2. Everyone has the right to the protection of the moral and material interests resulting from any scientific, literary, or artistic production of which he is the author.

ARTICLE 28

Everyone is entitled to a social and international order in which the rights and freedoms set forth in this Declaration can be fully realized.

ARTICLE 29

1. Everyone has duties to the community in which alone the free and full development of his personality is possible.

2. In the exercise of his rights and freedoms, everyone shall be subject only to such limitations as are determined by law solely for the purpose of securing due recognition and respect for the rights and freedoms of others and of meeting the just requirements of morality, public order, and the general welfare in a democratic society.

3. These rights and freedoms may in no case be exercised contrary to the purposes and principles of the United Nations.

ARTICLE 30

Nothing in this Declaration may be interpreted as implying for any State, group, or person any right to engage in any activity or to perform any act aimed at the destruction of any of the rights and freedoms set forth herein.

Questions and Suggestions for Writing

1. Obtain a copy of the Bill of Rights (1791), the first ten amendments to the United States Constitution. Which items listed there are also included in the U.N. Declaration? Are any listed in the former but omitted from the latter? Can you explain the agreements and discrepancies between these two sets of rights?

2. Compare the provisions of the U.N. Declaration with the French Declaration (p. 465). Which items appear in both documents? Which appear only in the U.N. Declaration? Can you explain the agreements and disagreements between these two documents?

3. Article 2 prohibits discrimination on several grounds, but age is not one of them. Do you think that our rights—or at least some of them—should depend on how old (or young) we are? Or is ageism an objectionable prejudice, like racism or sexism? Explain.

4. Do you think Article 5 implicitly prohibits the death penalty? Why, or why not?

5. If a government requires a passport and a visa before it allows a person to enter or leave the country, does this constitute a violation of Article 13 section 2? Why, or why not?

6. Article 26 section 1 declares that elementary education is "compulsory." Does this mean that everyone has a *right* to attend elementary school, or a *duty* to do so? Or does it mean something else? Explain.

7. Suppose a government passed a law prohibiting a woman from giving birth to more than two children during her lifetime. Would such a legal prohibition violate any of the human rights listed in this Declaration? Why, or why not?

Maurice Cranston

Economic and Social Rights

. . . Some politicians, indeed, have a vested interest in keeping talk about human rights as meaningless as possible. For there are those who do not want to see human rights become positive rights by genuine enactments; hence the more nebulous, unrealistic, or absurd the concept of human rights is made out to be, the better such men are pleased.

I believe that a philosophically respectable concept of human rights has been muddled, obscured, and debilitated in recent years by an attempt to incorporate into it specific rights of a different logical category. The traditional human rights are political and civil rights such as the right to life, liberty, and a fair trial. What are now being put forward as universal human rights are economic and social rights, such as the right to unemployment insurance, old-age pensions, medical services, and holidays with pay. There is both a philosophical and a political objection to this. The philosophical objection is that the new theory of human rights does not make sense. The political objection is that the circulation of a confused notion of human rights hinders the effective protection of what are correctly seen as human rights.

At the United Nations interest in political and civil rights has tended over the years to give way to consideration of economic and social rights. . . . In 1966, the two sets of rights were accorded more or less equal status in the simultaneous reception by the General Assembly of the two Covenants, the one on political and civil, the other on economic and social rights. And while the great majority of governments has procrastinated in the matter of ratifying either Covenant, the Covenant on economic and social rights has proved the more popular. There is one good reason for this easy popularity of the second covenant: and that is that the rights it names are not universal human rights at all.

There is nothing essentially difficult about transforming political and   4
civil rights into positive rights. All that is needed is an international court with real powers of enforcement. But the so-called economic and social rights cannot be transformed into positive rights by analogous innovations. A right is like a duty in that it must pass the test of practicability. It is not my duty to do what it is physically impossible for me to do. You cannot reasonably say that it was my duty to have jumped into the River Thames at Richmond to rescue a drowning child if I was nowhere near Richmond at the time the child was drowning. What is true of duties is equally true of

Maurice Cranston (b. 1920) is the author of several books, including a biography of John Locke, and is a professor of political science at the University of London. This excerpt is from his book What Are Human Rights? *(1973).*

rights. If it is impossible for a thing to be done, it is absurd to claim it as a right. At present it is utterly impossible, and will be for a long time yet, to provide "holidays with pay"[1] for everybody in the world. For millions of people who live in those parts of Asia, Africa, and South America where industrialisation has hardly begun, such claims are vain and idle.

The traditional "political and civil rights" can (as I have said) be readily secured by legislation; and generally they can be secured by fairly simple legislation. Since those rights are for the most part rights against government interference with a man's activities, a large part of the legislation needed has to do no more than restrain the government's own executive arm. This is no longer the case when we turn to "the right to work," "the right to social security," and so forth. For a government to provide social security it needs to do more than make laws; it has to have access to great capital wealth, and many governments in the world today are still poor. The government of India, for example, simply cannot command the resources that would guarantee each one of over 500 million inhabitants of India "a standard of living adequate for the health and well-being of himself and his family," let alone "holidays with pay."

Another test of a human right is that it shall be a genuinely universal moral right. This the so-called human right to holidays with pay plainly cannot pass. For it is a right that is necessarily limited to those persons who are *paid* in any case, that is to say, to the *employé* class. Since not everyone belongs to this class, the right cannot be a universal right, a right which, in the terminology of the Universal Declaration, "everyone" has. That the right to a holiday with pay is for many people a real moral right, I would not for one moment deny. But it is a right . . . which can be claimed by members of a specific class of persons *because* they are members of that class.

A further test of a human right, or universal moral right, is the test of *paramount importance*. Here the distinction is less definite, but no less crucial. And here again there is a parallel between rights and duties. It is a paramount duty to relieve great distress, as it is not a paramount duty to give pleasure. It would have been my duty to rescue the drowning child at Richmond if I had been there at the time; but it is not, in the same sense, my duty to give Christmas presents to the children of my neighbours. This difference is obscured in the cruder type of utilitarian philosophy which analyses moral goodness in terms of the greatest happiness of the greatest number: but common sense does not ignore it. Common sense knows that fire engines and ambulances are essential services, whereas fun fairs and holiday camps are not. Liberality and kindness are reckoned moral virtues; but they are not moral duties in the sense that the obligation to rescue a drowning child is a moral duty.

---

[1] **holidays** British English for vacation. [Editors' note]

It is worth considering the circumstances in which ordinary people   8
find themselves invoking the language of human rights. I suggest they are
situations like these:

A black student in South Africa is awarded a scholarship to Oxford,
and then refused a passport by the South African government simply
because he is black. We feel this is clear invasion of the human right to
freedom of movement. Jews are annihilated by the Nazi government,
simply because they are Jews. We feel this is a manifest abuse (an atrocious
abuse) of the human right to life. In several countries men are held in
prison indefinitely without trial. We feel this is a gross invasion of the
human right to liberty and to a fair trial on any criminal charge.

In considering cases of this kind, we are confronted by matters which
belong to a totally different moral dimension from questions of social
security and holidays with pay. A human right is something of which no
one may be deprived without a grave affront to justice. There are certain
deeds which should never be done, certain freedoms which should never be
invaded, some things which are supremely sacred. If a Declaration of
Human Rights is what it purports to be, a declaration of universal moral
rights, it should be confined to this sphere of discourse. If rights of another
class are introduced, the effect may even be to bring the whole concept of
human rights into disrepute. "It would be a splendid thing," people might
say, "for everyone to have holidays with pay, a splendid thing for everyone
to have social security, a splendid thing to have equality before the law, and
freedom of speech, and the right to life. One day perhaps, this beautiful
ideal may be realised. . . ."

Thus the effect of a Universal Declaration which is overloaded with
affirmations of so-called human rights which are not human rights at all is
to push *all* talk of human rights out of the clear realm of the morally
compelling into the twilight world of utopian aspiration. In the Universal
Declaration of 1948 there indeed occurs the phrase "a common standard of
achievement" which brands that Declaration as an attempt to translate
rights into ideals. And however else one might choose to define moral
rights, they are plainly *not* ideals or aspirations.

Much has been made of the difference between a right and a duty, and   12
the distinction is of course important. But Tom Paine was surely correct
when he pointed out that there could be no rights without duties. To speak
of a universal right is to speak of a universal duty; to say that all men have
a right to life is to impose on all men the duty of respecting human life, to
put all men under the same prohibition against attacking, injuring, or
endangering the life of any other human being. Indeed, if this universal
duty were not imposed, what sense could be made of the concept of a
universal human right?

The so-called economic and social rights, insofar as they are intelligible at all, impose no such universal duty. They are rights to be given things,

things such as a decent income, schools, and social services. But who is called upon to do the giving? Whose duty is it? When the authors of the United Nations Covenant on Economic and Social Rights assert that "everyone has the right to social security," are they saying that everyone ought to subscribe to some form of worldwide social security system from which each in turn may benefit in case of need? If something of this kind is meant, why do the United Nations Covenants make no provision for instituting such a system? And if no such system exists, where is the obligation, and where the right? To impose on men a "duty" which they cannot possibly perform is as absurd in its way, though perhaps not as cruel, as bestowing on them a "right" which they cannot possibly enjoy.

To deny that the "economic and social rights" are the universal moral rights of all men is not to deny that they may be the moral rights of some men. In the moral criticism of legal rights, it is certainly arguable that the privileges of some members of a certain community ought to be extended to other members (and perhaps all members) of that community. But this matter is correctly seen as a problem of *socialisation* or *democratisation*— that is, the extension of privileges and immunities—rather than as a problem about the universal rights of all men: and the case for any such specific claims to an extension of legal rights must be argued on other grounds.

When at the time of the French Revolution Babeuf[2] claimed the right of the people to education, he was speaking about the rights of Frenchmen, and not of man. To claim economic and social rights for the members of a given community is a reasonable exercise. And, moreover, in the case of Babeuf, his claim for a popular right to education was fortified by some relevant arguments: he said, rightly or wrongly, that the wealth of France was produced by the working classes of France, and that those people had therefore earned the right to education. To assert a right which is thus local (i.e., a right of Frenchmen) and earned, is to assert a right which belongs to a different logical category from rights which are universal and not necessarily earned.

It has often been said that a particular man's duties derive from his 16 station: and in a similar way, a particular man's situation in the world will govern the system of rights which he can claim. A miner in Pittsburgh will be able to justify the claim to a great many rights which include some economic and social rights; a miner in Durham will be able to sustain a fairly similar range of rights, but by no means an identical one. A beggar in Calcutta will not be able to produce anything like the same number of just entitlements in the sphere of economic and social benefits; but he has exactly the same rights as the two other men to political and civil rights.

---

[2] **Babeuf** Jacques (Graechus) Babeuf (1760–97) led a radical egalitarian faction during the French Revolution; later generations often regarded him as a forerunner of Marxist Communism. [Editors' note]

Human rights, indeed, are possessed by the basest criminal. The *New York Times* published not long ago a photograph of the president of the Central African Republic, Monsieur Jean-Bédel Bokassa, in the courtyard of the prison at Bangui. The president was wearing his full regalia, with decorations and medals, and he was personally commanding his soldiers to beat with clubs prisoners who had been convicted of theft. "Thieves must all die," he announced. "There will be no more theft in the Central African Republic." According to the *New York Times*, "Of the 46 men beaten, at least three died. Their corpses were put on public display the next day with the battered survivors, many of whom appeared near death."

This case is peculiarly odious for several reasons. Had the convicts been publicly shot, as were thieves in Nigeria in that same year, the régime could well be accused of employing the kind of cruel and inhuman punishment which is proscribed by Article 5 of the Universal Declaration, but at least the Nigerian régime could quote the practice of eighteenth-century Europe as a precedent for the use of capital punishment for theft. But the president of the Central African Republic could hardly claim to be using punishment at all: the penalty was not one imposed by a court of justice (for the court had already imposed the lawful penalty, imprisonment). What President Bokassa was doing was adding to that penalty a further additional suffering, prescribed by his arbitrary will—the beating to death, or near, of certain convicts—as a means of promoting public order through terror. The smile of the president in the press photographs of the occasion adds one ghoulish refinement to the scene.

Even if such methods *did* protect public order—and the experience of the public shootings of thieves in Nigeria suggests that they do not—the use of torture at the pleasure of a despot is precisely the kind of thing which declarations of the Rights of Man are meant to outlaw, and which the United Nations at its inception was expected to banish from the earth. This is a matter of moral urgency which is far removed from questions of holidays with pay.

Questions and Suggestions for Writing

1. Cranston distinguishes between "traditional human rights" and "economic and social rights" (para. 2), and he gives a few examples of each. Examine both the French Declaration (p. 465) and the U.N. Declaration (p. 484) and decide regarding each of the rights in these documents which are traditional and which are socioeconomic. Are there any that seem to you to be both? Neither? Explain.

2. What does Cranston mean (para. 4) by "transforming" a human right into a "positive" right? Why does he argue that this cannot be done with socioeconomic rights? Do you agree or not? Explain.

3. Cranston mentions several tests of genuine human rights. Draw up a list of his tests, and decide whether any of the following pass them all: the right to life, the right to vote, the right to emigrate.

4. Cranston describes a human right as "something of which no one may be deprived without a grave affront to justice" (para. 10). He also says that "a universal right is a universal duty" (para. 12). Is either of these statements intended to serve as a definition of a human right? Why, or why not? In any case, can you think of a better definition?

5. Cranston denies that human rights are "ideals or aspirations" (para. 11). What argument, if any, does he offer for this view? Do you agree? Explain.

6. Cranston regards the need for greater provision of economic and social benefits as "a problem of *socialisation* or *democratisation*," but not as "a problem about the universal rights of all men" (para. 14). Consider a country in which the government refuses to allow elections and due process of law in criminal trials. Which way would Cranston describe these problems, and why? Would you agree?

7. Why does Cranston argue (para. 16) that a Pittsburgh miner and a Calcutta beggar have the same rights but not the same "entitlements in the sphere of economic and social benefits"? Do you agree?

8. Cranston claims that declarations of rights have always been intended to "outlaw . . . the use of torture at the pleasure of a despot" (para. 19). Would he allow that rights have any role in objecting to the behavior of a government that refuses to allocate resources for health care for the needy but readily grants generous tax advantages for the wealthy and budgets considerable funds for police to put down hunger riots? Why, or why not?

Martin Luther King, Jr.

Letter from Birmingham Jail

A CALL FOR UNITY*

April 12, 1963

We the undersigned clergymen are among those who, in January, issued "An Appeal for Law and Order and Common Sense," in dealing with racial problems in Alabama. We expressed understanding that honest

*In 1963 King was arrested in Birmingham, Alabama, for participating in a march for which no parade permit had been issued by the city officials. In jail he wrote a response to a letter he had received from eight local clergymen. Their letter titled "A Call for Unity" is printed here, followed by King's response.

Martin Luther King, Jr. (1929–1968) was born in Atlanta and educated at Morehouse College, Crozer Theological Seminary, and Boston University. In 1954

convictions in racial matters could properly be pursued in the courts, but urged that decisions of those courts should in the meantime be peacefully obeyed.

Since that time there had been some evidence of increased forebearance and a willingness to face facts. Responsible citizens have undertaken to work on various problems which cause racial friction and unrest. In Birmingham, recent public events have given indication that we all have opportunity for a new constructive and realistic approach to racial problems.

However, we are now confronted by a series of demonstrations by some of our Negro citizens, directed and led in part by outsiders. We recognize the natural impatience of people who feel that their hopes are slow in being realized. But we are convinced that these demonstrations are unwise and untimely.

We agree rather with certain local Negro leadership which has called 4 for honest and open negotiation of racial issues in our area. And we believe this kind of facing of issues can best be accomplished by citizens of our own metropolitan area, white and Negro, meeting with their knowledge and experience of the local situation. All of us need to face that responsibility and find proper channels for its accomplishment.

Just as we formerly pointed out that "hatred and violence have no sanction in our religious and political traditions," we also point out that such actions as incite to hatred and violence, however technically peaceful those actions may be, have not contributed to the resolution of our local problems. We do not believe that these days of new hope are days when extreme measures are justified in Birmingham.

We commend the community as a whole, and the local news media and law enforcement officials in particular, on the calm manner in which these demonstrations have been handled. We urge the public to continue to show restraint should the demonstrations continue, and the law enforcement officials to remain calm and continue to protect our city from violence.

We further strongly urge our own Negro community to withdraw support from these demonstrations, and to unite locally in working peacefully for a better Birmingham. When rights are consistently denied, a cause should be pressed in the courts and in negotiations among local leaders, and not in the streets. We appeal to both our white and Negro citizenry to observe the principles of law and order and common sense.

---

he was called to serve as a Baptist minister in Montgomery, Alabama. During the next two years he achieved national fame when, using a policy of nonviolent resistance, he successfully led the boycott against segregated bus lines in Montgomery. He then organized the Southern Christian Leadership Conference, which furthered civil rights, first in the South and then nationwide. In 1964 he was awarded the Nobel Peace Prize. Four years later he was assassinated in Memphis, Tennessee, while supporting striking garbage workers.

C.C.J. Carpenter, D.D., L.L.D., Bishop of Alabama; Joseph A. Durick, D.D., Auxiliary Bishop, Diocese of Mobile-Birmingham; Rabbi Milton L. Grafman, Temple Emanu-El, Birmingham, Alabama; Bishop Paul Hardin, Bishop of the Alabama–West Florida Conference of the Methodist Church; Bishop Nolan B. Harmon, Bishop of the North Alabama Conference of the Methodist Church; George M. Murray, D.D., L.L.D., Bishop Coadjutor, Episcopal Diocese of Alabama; Edward V. Ramage, Moderator, Synod of the Alabama Presbyterian Church in the United States; Earl Stallings, Pastor, First Baptist Church, Birmingham, Alabama.

LETTER FROM BIRMINGHAM JAIL

April 16, 1963

My Dear Fellow Clergymen:

While confined here in the Birmingham city jail, I came across your recent statement calling my present activities "unwise and untimely."[1] Seldom do I pause to answer criticism of my work and ideas. If I sought to answer all the criticisms that cross my desk, my secretaries would have little time for anything other than such correspondence in the course of the day, and I would have no time for constructive work. But since I feel that you are men of genuine good will and that your criticisms are sincerely set forth, I want to try to answer your statement in what I hope will be patient and reasonable terms.

I think I should indicate why I am here in Birmingham, since you have been influenced by the view which argues against "outsiders coming in." I have the honor of serving as president of the Southern Christian Leadership Conference, an organization operating in every southern state, with headquarters in Atlanta, Georgia. We have some eighty-five affiliated organizations across the South, and one of them is the Alabama Christian Movement for Human Rights. Frequently we share staff, educational and financial resources with our affiliates. Several months ago the affiliate here in Birmingham asked us to be on call to engage in a non-violent direct-action program if such were deemed necessary. We readily consented, and when the hour came we lived up to our promise. So I, along with several members of my staff, am here because I was invited here. I am here because I have organizational ties here.

[1] Author's note: This response to a published statement by eight fellow clergymen from Alabama (Bishop C.C.J. Carpenter, Bishop Joseph A. Durick, Rabbi Milton L. Grafman, Bishop Paul Hardin, Bishop Nolan B. Harmon, the Reverend George M. Murray, the Reverend Edward V. Ramage, and the Reverend Earl Stallings) was composed under somewhat constricting circumstances. Begun on the margins of the newspaper in which the statement appeared while I was in jail, the letter was continued on scraps of writing paper supplied by a friendly Negro trusty, and concluded on a pad my attorneys were eventually permitted to leave me. Although the text remains in substance unaltered, I have indulged in the author's prerogative of polishing it for publication.

But more basically, I am in Birmingham because injustice is here. Just as the prophets of the eighth century B.C. left their villages and carried their "thus saith the Lord" far beyond the boundaries of their home towns, and just as the Apostle Paul left his village of Tarsus and carried the gospel of Jesus Christ to the far corners of the Greco-Roman world, so am I compelled to carry the gospel of freedom beyond by own home town. Like Paul, I must constantly respond to the Macedonian call for aid.

Moreover, I am cognizant of the interrelatedness of all communities 4 and states. I cannot sit idly by in Atlanta and not be concerned about what happens in Birmingham. Injustice anywhere is a threat to justice everywhere. We are caught in an inescapable network of mutuality, tied in a single garment of destiny. Whatever affects one directly, affects all indirectly. Never again can we afford to live with the narrow, provincial "outside agitator" idea. Anyone who lives inside the United States can never be considered an outsider anywhere within its bounds.

You deplore the demonstrations taking place in Birmingham. But your statement, I am sorry to say, fails to express a similar concern for the conditions that brought about the demonstrations. I am sure that none of you would want to rest content with the superficial kind of social analysis that deals merely with effects and does not grapple with underlying causes. It is unfortunate that demonstrations are taking place in Birmingham, but it is even more unfortunate that the city's white power structure left the Negro community with no alternative.

In any nonviolent campaign there are four basic steps: collection of the facts to determine whether injustices exist; negotiation; self-purification; and direct action. We have gone through all these steps in Birmingham. There can be no gainsaying the fact that racial injustice engulfs this community. Birmingham is probably the most thoroughly segregated city in the United States. Its ugly record of brutality is widely known. Negroes have experienced grossly unjust treatment in the courts. There have been more unsolved bombings of Negro homes and churches in Birmingham than in any other city in the nation. These are the hard, brutal facts of the case. On the basis of these conditions, Negro leaders sought to negotiate with the city fathers. But the latter consistently refused to engage in good-faith negotiation.

Then, last September, came the opportunity to talk with leaders of Birmingham's economic community. In the course of the negotiations, certain promises were made by the merchants—for example, to remove the stores' humiliating racial signs. On the basis of these promises, the Reverend Fred Shuttlesworth and the leaders of the Alabama Christian Movement for Human Rights agreed to a moratorium on all demonstrations. As the weeks and months went by, we realized that we were the victims of a broken promise. A few signs, briefly removed, returned; the others remained.

As in so many past experiences, our hopes had been blasted, and the 8 shadow of deep disappointment settled upon us. We had no alternative except to prepare for direct action, whereby we would present our very bodies as a means of laying our case before the conscience of the local and the national community. Mindful of the difficulties involved, we decided to undertake a process of self-purification. We began a series of workshops on nonviolence, and we repeatedly asked ourselves: "Are you able to accept blows without retaliating?" "Are you able to endure the ordeal of jail?" We decided to schedule our direct-action program for the Easter season, realizing that except for Christmas, this is the main shopping period of the year. Knowing that a strong economic-withdrawal program would be the by-product of direct action, we felt that this would be the best time to bring pressure to bear on the merchants for the needed change.

Then it occurred to us that Birmingham's mayoralty election was coming up in March, and we speedily decided to postpone action until after election day. When we discovered that the Commissioner of Public Safety, Eugene "Bull" Connor, had piled up enough votes to be in the run-off, we decided again to postpone action until the day after the run-off so that the demonstrations could not be used to cloud the issues. Like many others, we waited to see Mr. Connor defeated, and to this end we endured postponement after postponement. Having aided in this community need, we felt that our direct-action program could be delayed no longer.

You may well ask: "Why direct action? Why sit-ins, marches, and so forth? Isn't negotiation a better path?" You are quite right in calling for negotiation. Indeed, this is the very purpose of direct action. Nonviolent direct action seeks to create such a crisis and foster such a tension that a community which has constantly refused to negotiate is forced to confront the issue. It seeks so to dramatize the issue that it can no longer be ignored. My citing the creation of tension as part of the work of the nonviolent-resister may sound rather shocking. But I must confess that I am not afraid of the word "tension." I have earnestly opposed violent tension, but there is a type of constructive, nonviolent tension which is necessary for growth. Just as Socrates felt that it was necessary to create a tension in the mind so that individuals could rise from the bondage of myths and half-truths to the unfettered realm of creative analysis and objective appraisal, so must we see the need for nonviolent gadflies to create the kind of tension in society that will help men rise from the dark depths of prejudice and racism to the majestic heights of understanding and brotherhood.

The purpose of our direct-action program is to create a situation so crisis-packed that it will inevitably open the door to negotiation. I therefore concur with you in your call for negotiation. Too long has our beloved Southland been bogged down in a tragic effort to live in monologue rather than dialogue.

One of the basic points in your statement is that the action that I and 12 my associates have taken in Birmingham is untimely. Some have asked: "Why didn't you give the new city administration time to act?" The only answer that I can give to this query is that the new Birmingham administration must be prodded about as much as the outgoing one, before it will act. We are sadly mistaken if we feel that the election of Albert Boutwell as mayor will bring the millennium to Birmingham. While Mr. Boutwell is a much more gentle person than Mr. Connor, they are both segregationists, dedicated to maintenance of the status quo. I have hope that Mr. Boutwell will be reasonable enough to see the futility of massive resistance to desegregation. But he will not see this without pressure from devotees of civil rights. My friends, I must say to you that we have not made a single gain in civil rights without determined legal and nonviolent pressure. Lamentably, it is an historical fact that privileged groups seldom give up their privileges voluntarily. Individuals may see the moral light and voluntarily give up their unjust posture; but, as Reinhold Niebuhr has reminded us, groups tend to be more immoral than individuals.

We know through painful experience that freedom is never voluntarily given by the oppressor; it must be demanded by the oppressed. Frankly, I have yet to engage in a direct-action campaign that was "well timed" in the view of those who have not suffered unduly from the disease of segregation. For years now I have heard the word "Wait!" It rings in the ear of every Negro with piercing familiarity. This "Wait" has almost always meant "Never." We must come to see, with one of our distinguished jurists, that "justice too long delayed is justice denied."

We have waited for more than 340 years for our constitutional and God-given rights. The nations of Asia and Africa are moving with jetlike speed toward gaining political independence, but we still creep at horse-and-buggy pace toward gaining a cup of coffee at a lunch counter. Perhaps it is easy for those who have never felt the stinging darts of segregation to say, "Wait." But when you have seen vicious mobs lynch your mothers and fathers at will and drown your sisters and brothers at whim; when you have seen hate-filled policemen curse, kick, and even kill your black brothers and sisters; when you see the vast majority of your twenty million Negro brothers smothering in an airtight cage of poverty in the midst of an affluent society; when you suddenly find your tongue twisted and your speech stammering as you seek to explain to your six-year-old daughter why she can't go to the public amusement park that has just been advertised on television, and see tears welling up in her eyes when she is told that Funtown is closed to colored children, and see ominous clouds of inferiority beginning to form in her little mental sky, and see her beginning to distort her personality by developing an unconscious bitterness toward white people; when you have to concoct an answer for a five-year-old son who is asking: "Daddy, why do white people treat colored people so mean?"; when you take a cross-country drive and find it necessary to sleep night after night in the uncomfortable corners of your automobile because no motel will accept you; when you are humiliated day in and day out by nagging signs reading "white" and "colored"; when your first name becomes "nigger," your middle name becomes "boy" (however old you are) and your last name becomes "John," and your wife and mother are never given the respected title "Mrs."; when you are harried by day and haunted by night by the fact that you are a Negro, living constantly at tiptoe stance, never quite knowing what to expect next, and are plagued with inner fears and outer resentments; when you are forever fighting a degenerating sense of "nobodiness"—then you will understand why we find it difficult to wait. There comes a time when the cup of endurance runs over, and men are no longer willing to be plunged into the abyss of despair. I hope, sirs, you can understand our legitimate and unavoidable impatience.

You express a great deal of anxiety over our willingness to break laws. This is certainly a legitimate concern. Since we so diligently urge people to obey the Supreme Court's decision of 1954 outlawing segregation in the public schools, at first glance it may seem rather paradoxical for us consciously to break laws. One may well ask: "How can you advocate breaking some laws and obeying others?" The answer lies in the fact that there are two types of laws: just and unjust. I would be the first to advocate obeying just laws. One has not only a legal but a moral responsibility to obey just laws. Conversely, one has a moral responsibility to disobey unjust laws. I would agree with St. Augustine that "an unjust law is no law at all."

Now, what is the difference between the two? How does one deter- 16 mine whether a law is just or unjust? A just law is a man-made code that squares with the moral law or the law of God. An unjust law is a code that is out of harmony with the moral law. To put it in the terms of St. Thomas Aquinas: An unjust law is a human law that is not rooted in eternal law and natural law. Any law that uplifts human personality is just. Any law that degrades human personality is unjust. All segregation statutes are unjust because segregation distorts the soul and damages the personality. It gives the segregator a false sense of superiority and the segregated a false sense of inferiority. Segregation, to use the terminology of the Jewish philosopher Martin Buber, substitutes an "I–it" relationship for an "I–thou" relationship and ends up relegating persons to the status of things. Hence segregation is not only politically, economically, and sociologically unsound, it is morally wrong and sinful. Paul Tillich has said that sin is separation. Is not segregation an existential expression of man's tragic separation, his awful estrangement, his terrible sinfulness? Thus it is that I can urge men to obey the 1954 decision of the Supreme Court, for it is morally right; and I can urge them to disobey segregation ordinances, for they are morally wrong.

Let us consider a more concrete example of just and unjust laws. An unjust law is a code that a numerical or power majority group compels a minority group to obey but does not make binding on itself. This is *difference* made legal. By the same token, a just law is a code that a majority compels a minority to follow and that it is willing to follow itself. This is *sameness* made legal.

Let me give another explanation. A law is unjust if it is inflicted on a minority that, as a result of being denied the right to vote, had no part in enacting or devising the law. Who can say that the legislature of Alabama which set up that state's segregation laws was democratically elected? Throughout Alabama all sorts of devious methods are used to prevent Negroes from becoming registered voters, and there are some counties in which, even though Negroes constitute a majority of the population, not a single Negro is registered. Can any law enacted under such circumstances be considered democratically structured?

Sometimes a law is just on its face and unjust in its application. For instance, I have been arrested on a charge of parading without a permit. Now, there is nothing wrong in having an ordinance which requires a permit for a parade. But such an ordinance becomes unjust when it is used to maintain segregation and to deny citizens the First Amendment privilege of peaceful assembly and protest.

I hope you are able to see the distinction I am trying to point out. In 20 no sense do I advocate evading or defying the law, as would the rabid segregationist. That would lead to anarchy. One who breaks an unjust law must do so openly, lovingly, and with a willingness to accept the penalty. I submit that an individual who breaks a law that conscience tells him is unjust, and who willingly accepts the penalty of imprisonment in order to arouse the conscience of the community over its injustice, is in reality expressing the highest respect for law.

Of course, there is nothing new about this kind of civil disobedience. It was evidenced sublimely in the refusal of Shadrach, Meshach, and Abednego to obey the laws of Nebuchadnezzar, on the ground that a higher moral law was at stake. It was practiced superbly by the early Christians, who were willing to face hungry lions and the excruciating pain of chopping blocks rather than submit to certain unjust laws of the Roman Empire. To a degree, academic freedom is a reality today because Socrates practiced civil disobedience. In our own nation, the Boston Tea Party represented a massive act of civil disobedience.

We should never forget that everything Adolf Hitler did in Germany was "legal" and everything the Hungarian freedom fighters did in Hungary was "illegal." It was "illegal" to aid and comfort a Jew in Hitler's Germany. Even so, I am sure that, had I lived in Germany at the time, I would have aided and comforted my Jewish brothers. If today I lived in a Communist country where certain principles dear to the Christian faith are suppressed, I would openly advocate disobeying that country's anti-religious laws.

I must make two honest confessions to you, my Christian and Jewish brothers. First, I must confess that over the past few years I have been gravely disappointed with the white moderate. I have almost reached the regrettable conclusion that the Negro's great stumbling block in his stride toward freedom is not the White Citizen's Counciler or the Ku Klux

Klanner, but the white moderate, who is more devoted to "order" than to justice; who prefers a negative peace which is the absence of tension to a positive peace which is the presence of justice; who constantly says: "I agree with you in the goal you seek, but I cannot agree with your methods of direct action"; who paternalistically believes he can set the timetable for another man's freedom; who lives by a mythical concept of time and who constantly advises the Negro to wait for a "more convenient season." Shallow understanding from people of good will is more frustrating than absolute misunderstanding from people of ill will. Lukewarm acceptance is much more bewildering than outright rejection.

I had hoped that the white moderate would understand that law and order exist for the purpose of establishing justice and that when they fail in this purpose they become the dangerously structured dams that block the flow of social progress. I had hoped that the white moderate would understand that the present tension in the South is a necessary phase of the transition from an obnoxious negative peace, in which the Negro passively accepted his unjust plight, to a substantive and positive peace, in which all men will respect the dignity and worth of human personality. Actually, we who engage in nonviolent direct action are not the creators of tension. We merely bring to the surface the hidden tension that is already alive. We bring it out in the open, where it can be seen and dealt with. Like a boil that can never be cured so long as it is covered up but must be opened with all its ugliness to the natural medicines of air and light, injustice must be exposed, with all the tension its exposure creates, to the light of human conscience and the air of national opinion before it can be cured.

In your statement you assert that our actions, even though peaceful, must be condemned because they precipitate violence. But is this a logical assertion? Isn't this like condemning a robbed man because his possession of money precipitated the evil act of robbery? Isn't this like condemning Socrates because his unswerving commitment to truth and his philosophical inquiries precipitated the act by the misguided populace in which they made him drink hemlock? Isn't this like condemning Jesus because his unique God-consciousness and never-ceasing devotion to God's will precipitated the evil act of crucifixion? We must come to see that, as the federal courts have consistently affirmed, it is wrong to urge an individual to cease his efforts to gain his basic constitutional rights because the quest may precipitate violence. Society must protect the robbed and punish the robber.

I had also hoped that the white moderate would reject the myth concerning time in relation to the struggle for freedom. I have just received a letter from a white brother in Texas. He writes: "All Christians know that the colored people will receive equal rights eventually, but it is possible that you are in too great a religious hurry. It has taken Christianity almost two thousand years to accomplish what it has. The teachings of

Christ take time to come to earth." Such an attitude stems from a tragic misconception of time, from the strangely irrational notion that there is something in the very flow of time that will inevitably cure all ills. Actually, time itself is neutral; it can be used either destructively or constructively. More and more I feel that the people of ill will have used time much more effectively than have the people of good will. We will have to repent in this generation not merely for the hateful words and actions of the bad people but for the appalling silence of the good people. Human progress never rolls in on wheels of inevitability; it comes through the tireless efforts of men willing to be co-workers with God, and without this hard work, time itself becomes an ally of the forces of social stagnation. We must use time creatively, in the knowledge that the time is always ripe to do right. Now is the time to make real the promise of democracy and transform our pending national elegy into a creative psalm of brotherhood. Now is the time to lift our national policy from the quicksand of racial injustice to the solid rock of human dignity.

You speak of our activity in Birmingham as extreme. At first I was rather disappointed that fellow clergymen would see my nonviolent efforts as those of an extremist. I began thinking about the fact that I stand in the middle of two opposing forces in the Negro community. One is a force of complacency, made up in part of Negroes who, as a result of long years of oppression, are so drained of self-respect and a sense of "somebodiness" that they have adjusted to segregation; and in part of a few middle-class Negroes who, because of a degree of academic and economic security and because in some ways they profit by segregation, have become insensitive to the problems of the masses. The other force is one of bitterness and hatred, and it comes perilously close to advocating violence. It is expressed in the various black nationalist groups that are springing up across the nation, the largest and best-known being Elijah Muhammad's Muslim movement. Nourished by the Negro's frustration over the continued existence of racial discrimination, this movement is made up of people who have lost faith in America, who have absolutely repudiated Christianity, and who have concluded that the white man is an incorrigible "devil."

I have tried to stand between these two forces, saying that we need 28 emulate neither the "do-nothingism" of the complacent nor the hatred and despair of the black nationalist. For there is the more excellent way of love and nonviolent protest. I am grateful to God that, through the influence of the Negro church, the way of nonviolence became an integral part of our struggle.

If this philosophy had not emerged, by now many streets of the South would, I am convinced, be flowing with blood. And I am further convinced that if our white brothers dismiss as "rabble-rousers" and "outside agitators" those of us who employ nonviolent direct action, and if they refuse to support our nonviolent efforts, millions of Negroes will, out of frustration and despair, seek solace and security in black-nationalist ideologies—a development that would inevitably lead to a frightening racial nightmare.

Oppressed people cannot remain oppressed forever. The yearning for freedom eventually manifests itself, and that is what has happened to the American Negro. Something within has reminded him of his birthright of freedom, and something without has reminded him that it can be gained. Consciously or unconsciously, he has been caught up by the *Zeitgeist*, and with his black brothers of Africa and his brown and yellow brothers of Asia, South America, and the Caribbean, the United States Negro is moving with a sense of great urgency toward the promised land of racial justice. If one recognizes this vital urge that has engulfed the Negro community, one should readily understand why public demonstrations are taking place. The Negro has many pent-up resentments and latent frustrations, and he must release them. So let him march; let him make prayer pilgrimages to the city hall; let him go on freedom rides—and try to understand why he must do so. If his repressed emotions are not released in nonviolent ways, they will seek expression through violence; this is not a threat but a fact of history. So I have not said to my people: "Get rid of your discontent." Rather, I have tried to say that this normal and healthy discontent can be channeled into the creative outlet of nonviolent direct action. And now this approach is being termed extremist.

But though I was initially disappointed at being categorized as an extremist, as I continued to think about the matter I gradually gained a measure of satisfaction from the label. Was not Jesus an extremist for love: "Love your enemies, bless them that curse you, do good to them that hate you, and pray for them which despitefully use you, and persecute you." Was not Amos an extremist for justice: "Let justice roll down like waters and righteousness like an ever-flowing stream." Was not Paul an extremist for the Christian gospel: "I bear in my body the marks of the Lord Jesus." Was not Martin Luther an extremist: "Here I stand; I cannot do otherwise, so help me God." And John Bunyan: "I will stay in jail to the end of my days before I make a butchery of my conscience." And Abraham Lincoln: "This nation cannot survive half slave and half free." And Thomas Jefferson: "We hold these truths to be self-evident, that all men are created equal. . . ." So the question is not whether we will be extremists, but what kind of extremists we will be. Will we be extremists for hate or for love? Will we be extremists for the preservation of injustice or for the extension of justice? In that dramatic scene on Calvary's hill three men were crucified. We must never forget that all three were crucified for the same crime—the crime of extremism. Two were extremists for immorality, and thus fell below their environment. The other, Jesus Christ, was an extremist for love, truth, and goodness, and thereby rose above his environment. Perhaps the South, the nation, and the world are in dire need of creative extremists.

I had hoped that the white moderate would see this need. Perhaps I 32 was too optimistic; perhaps I expected too much. I suppose I should have realized that few members of the oppressor race can understand the deep groans and passionate yearnings of the oppressed race, and still fewer have the vision to see that injustice must be rooted out by strong, persistent, and determined action. I am thankful, however, that some of our white brothers in the South have grasped the meaning of this social revolution and committed themselves to it. They are still all too few in quantity, but they are big in quality. Some—such as Ralph McGill, Lillian Smith, Harry Golden, James McBride Dabbs, Ann Braden, and Sarah Patton Boyle— have written about our struggle in eloquent and prophetic terms. Others have marched with us down nameless streets of the South. They have languished in filthy, roach-infested jails, suffering the abuse and brutality of policemen who view them as "dirty nigger-lovers." Unlike so many of their moderate brothers and sisters, they have recognized the urgency of the moment and sensed the need for powerful "action" antidotes to combat the disease of segregation.

Let me take note of my other major disappointment. I have been so greatly disappointed with the white church and its leadership. Of course, there are some notable exceptions. I am not unmindful of the fact that each of you has taken some significant stands on this issue. I commend you, Reverend Stallings, for your Christian stand on this past Sunday, in welcoming Negroes to your worship service on a nonsegregated basis. I commond the Catholic leaders of this state for integrating Spring Hill College several years ago.

But despite these notable exceptions, I must honestly reiterate that I have been disappointed with the church. I do not say this as one of those negative critics who can always find something wrong with the church. I say this as a minister of the gospel, who loves the church; who was nurtured in its bosom; who has been sustained by its spiritual blessings and who will remain true to it as long as the cord of life shall lengthen.

When I was suddenly catapulted into the leadership of the bus protest in Montgomery, Alabama, a few years ago, I felt we would be supported by the white church. I felt that the white ministers, priests, and rabbis of the South would be among our strongest allies. Instead, some have been outright opponents, refusing to understand the freedom movement and misrepresenting its leaders; all too many others have been more cautious than courageous and have remained silent behind the anesthetizing security of stained-glass windows.

In spite of my shattered dreams, I came to Birmingham with the hope 36 that the white religious leadership of this community would see the justice of our cause and, with deep moral concern, would serve as the channel through which our just grievances could reach the power structure. I had hoped that each of you would understand. But again I have been disappointed.

I have heard numerous southern religious leaders admonish their worshipers to comply with a desegregation decision because it is the law, but I have longed to hear white ministers declare: "Follow this decree because integration is morally right and because the Negro is your brother." In the midst of blatant injustices inflicted upon the Negro, I have watched white churchmen stand on the sideline and mouth pious irrelevancies and sanctimonious trivialities. In the midst of a mighty struggle to rid our nation of racial and economic injustice, I have heard many ministers say: "Those are social issues, with which the gospel has no real concern." And I have watched many churches commit themselves to a completely otherworldly religion which makes a strange, unbiblical distinction between body and soul, between the sacred and the secular.

I have traveled the length and breadth of Alabama, Mississippi, and all the other southern states. On sweltering summer days and crisp autumn mornings I have looked at the South's beautiful churches with their lofty spires pointing heavenward. I have beheld the impressive outlines of her massive religious-education buildings. Over and over I have found myself saying: "What kind of people worship here? Who is their God? Where were their voices when the lips of Governor Barnett dripped with words of interposition and nullification? Where were they when Governor Wallace gave a clarion call for defiance and hatred? Where were their voices of support when bruised and weary Negro men and women decided to rise from the dark dungeons of complacency to the bright hills of creative protest?"

Yes, these questions are still in my mind. In deep disappointment I have wept over the laxity of the church. But be assured that my tears have been tears of love. There can be no deep disappointment where there is not deep love. Yes, I love the church. How could I do otherwise? I am in the rather unique position of being the son, the grandson, and the great-grandson of preachers. Yes, I see the church as the body of Christ. But, oh! How we have blemished and scarred that body through social neglect and through fear of being nonconformists.

There was a time when the church was very powerful—in the time 40 when the early Christians rejoiced at being deemed worthy to suffer for what they believed. In those days the church was not merely a thermometer that recorded the ideas and principles of popular opinion; it was a thermostat that transformed the mores of society. Whenever the early Christians entered a town, the people in power became disturbed and immediately sought to convict the Christians for being "disturbers of the peace" and "outside agitators." But the Christians pressed on, in the conviction that they were "a colony of heaven," called to obey God rather than man. Small in number, they were big in commitment. They were too God-intoxicated to be "astronomically intimidated." By their effort and example they brought an end to such ancient evils as infanticide and gladiatorial contests.

Things are different now. So often the contemporary church is a weak, ineffectual voice with an uncertain sound. So often it is an archdefender of the status quo. Far from being disturbed by the presence of the church, the power structure of the average community is consoled by the church's silent—and often even vocal—sanction of things as they are.

But the judgment of God is upon the church as never before. If today's church does not recapture the sacrificial spirit of the early church, it will lose its authenticity, forfeit the loyalty of millions, and be dismissed as an irrelevant social club with no meaning for the twentieth century. Every day I meet young people whose disappointment with the church has turned into outright disgust.

Perhaps I have once again been too optimistic. Is organized religion too inextricably bound to the status quo to save our nation and the world? Perhaps I must turn my faith to the inner spiritual church, the church within the church, as the true *ekklesia* and the hope of the world. But again I am thankful to God that some noble souls from the ranks of organized religion have broken loose from the paralyzing chains of conformity and joined us as active partners in the struggle for freedom. They have left their secure congregations and walked the streets of Albany, Georgia, with us. They have gone down the highways of the South on tortuous rides for freedom. Yes, they have gone to jail with us. Some have been dismissed from their churches, have lost the support of their bishops and fellow ministers. But they have acted in the faith that right defeated is stronger than evil triumphant. Their witness has been the spiritual salt that has preserved the true meaning of the gospel in these troubled times. They have carved a tunnel of hope through the dark mountain of disappointment.

I hope the church as a whole will meet the challenge of this decisive 44 hour. But even if the church does not come to the aid of justice, I have no despair about the future. I have no fear about the outcome of our struggle in Birmingham, even if our motives are at present misunderstood. We will reach the goal of freedom in Birmingham and all over the nation, because the goal of America is freedom. Abused and scorned though we may be, our destiny is tied up with America's destiny. Before the pilgrims landed at Plymouth, we were here. Before the pen of Jefferson etched the majestic words of the Declaration of Independence across the pages of history, we were here. For more than two centuries our forebears labored in this country without wages; they made cotton king; they built the homes of their masters while suffering gross injustice and shameful humiliation— and yet out of a bottomless vitality they continued to thrive and develop. If the inexpressible cruelties of slavery could not stop us, the opposition we now face will surely fail. We will win our freedom because the sacred heritage of our nation and the eternal will of God are embodied in our echoing demands.

Before closing I feel impelled to mention one other point in your statement that has troubled me profoundly. You warmly commended the

Birmingham police force for keeping "order" and "preventing violence." I doubt that you would have so warmly commended the police force if you had seen its dogs sinking their teeth into unarmed, nonviolent Negroes. I doubt that you would so quickly commend the policemen if you were to observe their ugly and inhumane treatment of Negroes here in the city jail; if you were to watch them push and curse old Negro women and young Negro girls; if you were to see them slap and kick old Negro men and young boys; if you were to observe them, as they did on two occasions, refuse to give us food because we wanted to sing our grace together. I cannot join you in your praise of the Birmingham police department.

It is true that the police have exercised a degree of discipline in handling the demonstrators. In this sense they have conducted themselves rather "nonviolently" in public. But for what purpose? To preserve the evil system of segregation. Over the past few years I have consistently preached that nonviolence demands that the means we use must be as pure as the ends we seek. I have tried to make clear that it is wrong to use immoral means to attain moral ends. But now I must affirm that it is just as wrong, or perhaps even more so, to use moral means to preserve immoral ends. Perhaps Mr. Connor and his policemen have been rather nonviolent in public, as was Chief Pritchett in Albany, Georgia, but they have used the moral means of nonviolence to maintain the immoral end of racial injustice. As T. S. Eliot has said: "The last temptation is the greatest treason: To do the right deed for the wrong reason."

I wish you had commended the Negro sit-inners and demonstrators of Birmingham for their sublime courage, their willingness to suffer, and their amazing discipline in the midst of great provocation. One day the South will recognize its real heroes. They will be the James Merediths, with the noble sense of purpose that enables them to face jeering and hostile mobs, and with the agonizing loneliness that characterizes the life of the pioneer. They will be old, oppressed, battered Negro women, symbolized in a seventy-two-year-old woman in Montgomery, Alabama, who rose up with a sense of dignity and with her people decided not to ride segregated buses, and who responded with ungrammatical profundity to one who inquired about her weariness: "My feets is tired, but my soul is at rest." They will be the young high school and college students, the young ministers of the gospel and a host of their elders, courageously and non-violently sitting in at lunch counters and willingly going to jail for conscience' sake. One day the South will know that when these disinherited children of God sat down at lunch counters, they were in reality standing up for what is best in the American dream and for the most sacred values in our Judaeo-Christian heritage, thereby bringing our nation back to those great wells of democracy which were dug deep by the founding fathers in their formulation of the Constitution and the Declaration of Independence.

Never before have I written so long a letter. I'm afraid it is much too 48 long to take your precious time. I can assure you that it would have been much shorter if I had been writing from a comfortable desk, but what else can one do when he is alone in a narrow jail cell, other than write long letters, think long thoughts, and pray long prayers?

If I have said anything in this letter that overstates the truth and indicates an unreasonable impatience, I beg you to forgive me. If I have said anything that understates the truth and indicates my having a patience that allows me to settle for anything less than brotherhood, I beg God to forgive me.

I hope this letter finds you strong in the faith. I also hope that circumstances will soon make it possible for me to meet each of you, not as an integrationist or a civil-rights leader but as a fellow clergyman and a Christian brother. Let us all hope that the dark clouds of racial prejudice will soon pass away and the deep fog of misunderstanding will be lifted from our fear-drenched communities, and in some not too distant tomorrow the radiant stars of love and brotherhood will shine over our great nation with all their scintillating beauty.

Yours for the cause of Peace and Brotherhood,
Martin Luther King, Jr.

Questions and Suggestions for Writing

1. In his first five paragraphs, how does King assure his audience that he is not a meddlesome intruder but a man of good will?

2. In paragraph 3 King refers to Hebrew prophets and to the Apostle Paul, and later (para. 10) to Socrates. What is the point of these references?

3. In paragraph 11 what does King mean when he says that "our beloved Southland" has long tried to "live in monologue rather than dialogue"?

4. King begins paragraph 23 with "I must make two honest confessions to you, my Christian and Jewish brothers." What would have been gained or lost if he had used this paragraph as his opening?

5. King's last three paragraphs do not advance his argument. What do they do?

6. Why does King advocate breaking unjust laws "openly, lovingly" (para. 20)? What does he mean by these words? What other motives or attitudes do these words rule out?

7. Construct two definitions of "civil disobedience," and explain whether and to what extent it is easier (or harder) to justify civil disobedience, depending on how you have defined the expression.

8. If you feel that you wish to respond to King's letter on some point, write a letter nominally addressed to King. You may, if you wish, adopt the persona of one of the eight clergymen whom King initially addressed.

9. King writes (para. 46) that "nonviolence demands that the means we use must be as pure as the ends we seek." How do you think King would evaluate the following acts of civil disobedience: (a) occupying a college administration building in order to press a demand for divestment in South Africa; (b) sailing on a collision course with a whaling ship to protest against whaling; (c) trespassing on a nuclear site to protest against the arms race? Set down your answer in an essay of 500 words.

13

What Are the Bounds of Free Speech?

Plato

"The Greater Part of the Stories Current Today We Shall Have to Reject"

"What kind of education shall we give them then? We shall find it difficult to improve on the time-honored distinction between the physical training we give to the body and the education we give to the mind and character."

For a biographical note about Plato (427–347 B.C.), see page 433. This selection from Plato's Republic, *one of his best known and longest dialogues, is about the education suitable for the rulers of an ideal society.*

Republic *begins, typically, with an investigation into the nature of justice. Socrates (who speaks for Plato) convincingly explains to Glaucon that we cannot reasonably expect to achieve a just society unless we devote careful attention to the moral education of the young men who are scheduled in later life to become the rulers. (Here as elsewhere, Plato's elitism and aristocratic bias shows itself; as readers of* Republic *soon learn, Plato is no admirer of democracy or of a classless society.) Plato cares as much about what the educational curriculum should exclude as what it should include. His special target was the common practice in his day of using for pedagogy the Homeric tales and other stories about the gods. He readily embraces the principle of censorship, as the excerpt explains, because he thinks it is a necessary means to achieve the ideal society.*

"True."

"And we shall begin by educating mind and character, shall we not?"

"Of course."

"In this education you would include stories, would you not?"

"Yes."

"These are of two kinds, true stories and fiction.[1] Our education must use both, and start with fiction."

"I don't know what you mean."

"But you know that we begin by telling children stories. These are, in general, fiction, though they contain some truth. And we tell children stories before we start them on physical training."

"That is so."

"That is what I meant by saying that we must start to educate the mind before training the body."

"You are right," he said.

"And the first step, as you know, is always what matters most, particularly when we are dealing with those who are young and tender. That is the time when they are easily molded and when any impression we choose to make leaves a permanent mark."

"That is certainly true."

"Shall we therefore readily allow our children to listen to any stories made up by anyone, and to form opinions that are for the most part the opposite of those we think they should have when they grow up?"

"We certainly shall not."

"Then it seems that our first business is to supervise the production of stories, and choose only those we think suitable, and reject the rest. We shall persuade mothers and nurses to tell our chosen stories to their children, and by means of them to mold their minds and characters which are more important than their bodies. The greater part of the stories current today we shall have to reject."

"Which are you thinking of?"

"We can take some of the major legends as typical. For all, whether major or minor, should be cast in the same mold and have the same effect. Do you agree?"

"Yes: but I'm not sure which you refer to as major."

"The stories in Homer and Hesiod and the poets. For it is the poets who have always made up fictions and stories to tell to men."

"What sort of stories do you mean and what fault do you find in them?"

"The worst fault possible," I replied, "especially if the fiction is an ugly one."

[1]The Greek word *pseudos* and its corresponding verb meant not only "fiction"—stories, tales—but also "what is not true" and so, in suitable contexts, "lies": and this ambiguity should be borne in mind. [Editors' note: All the footnotes are by the translator, but some notes have been omitted.]

"And what is that?"

"Misrepresenting the nature of gods and heroes, like a portrait painter whose portraits bear no resemblance to their originals."

"That is a fault which certainly deserves censure. But give me more details."

"Well, on the most important of subjects, there is first and foremost the foul story about Ouranos[2] and the things Hesiod says he did, and the revenge Cronos took on him. While the story of what Cronos did, and what he suffered at the hands of his son, is not fit as it is to be lightly repeated to the young and foolish, even if it were true; it would be best to say nothing about it, or if it must be told, tell it to a select few under oath of secrecy, at a rite which required, to restrict it still further, the sacrifice not of a mere pig but of something large and difficult to get."

"These certainly are awkward stories."

"And they shall not be repeated in our state, Adeimantus," I said. "Nor shall any young audience be told that anyone who commits horrible crimes, or punishes his father unmercifully, is doing nothing out of the ordinary but merely what the first and greatest of the gods have done before."

"I entirely agree," said Adeimantus, "that these stories are unsuitable."

"Nor can we permit stories of wars and plots and battles among the gods; they are quite untrue, and if we want our prospective guardians to believe that quarrelsomeness is one of the worst of evils, we must certainly not let them be told the story of the Battle of the Giants or embroider it on robes, or tell them other tales about many and various quarrels between gods and heroes and their friends and relations. On the contrary, if we are to persuade them that no citizen has ever quarrelled with any other, because it is sinful, our old men and women must tell children stories with this end in view from the first, and we must compel our poets to tell them similar stories when they grow up. But we can admit to our state no stories about Hera being tied up by her son, or Hephaestus being flung out of Heaven by his father for trying to help his mother when she was getting a beating, nor any of Homer's Battles of the Gods, whether their intention is allegorical or not. Children cannot distinguish between what is allegory and what isn't, and opinions formed at that age are usually difficult to eradicate or change; we should therefore surely regard it as of the utmost importance that the first stories they hear shall aim at encouraging the highest excellence of character."

"Your case is a good one," he agreed, "but if someone wanted details, and asked what stories we were thinking of, what should we say?"

---

[2]**Ouranos** (the sky), the original supreme god, was castrated by his son Cronos to separate him from Gaia (mother earth). Cronos was in turn deposed by Zeus in a struggle in which Zeus was helped by the Titans.

To which I replied, "My dear Adeimantus, you and I are not engaged on writing stories but on founding a state. And the founders of a state, though they must know the type of story the poet must produce, and reject any that do not conform to that type, need not write them themselves."

"True: but what are the lines on which our poets must work when they deal with the gods?"

"Roughly as follows," I said. "God must surely always be represented as he really is, whether the poet is writing epic, lyric, or tragedy."

"He must."

"And in reality of course god is good, and he must be so described."

"Certainly."

"But nothing good is harmful, is it?"[3]

"I think not."

"Then can anything that is not harmful do harm?"

"No."

"And can what does no harm do evil?"

"No again."

"And can what does no evil be the cause of any evil?"

"How could it?"

"Well then; is the good beneficial?"

"Yes."

"So it must be the cause of well-being."

"Yes."

"So the good is not the cause of everything, but only of states of well-being and not of evil."

"Most certainly," he agreed.

"Then god, being good, cannot be responsible for everything, as is commonly said, but only for a small part of human life, for the greater part of which he has no responsibility. For we have a far smaller share of good than of evil, and while god must be held to be sole cause of good, we must look for some factors other than god as cause of the evil."

"I think that's very true," he said.

"So we cannot allow Homer or any other poet to make such a stupid mistake about the gods, as when he says that

> Zeus has two jars standing on the floor of his palace, full of fates, good in
> one and evil in the other

and that the man to whom Zeus allots a mixture of both has 'varying fortunes sometimes good and sometimes bad,' while the man to whom he

---

[3]The reader of the following passage should bear the following ambiguities in mind: (1) the Greek word for good (*agathos*) can mean (a) morally good, (b) beneficial or advantageous; (2) the Greek word for evil (*kakos*) can also mean harm or injury; (3) the adverb of *agathos* (*eu*-well) can imply either morally right or prosperous. The word translated "cause of" could equally well be rendered "responsible for."

allots unmixed evil is 'chased by ravening despair over the face of the earth.'[4] Nor can we allow references to Zeus as 'dispenser of good and evil.' And we cannot approve if it is said that Athene and Zeus prompted the breach of solemn treaty and oath by Pandarus, or that the strife and contentions of the gods were due to Themis and Zeus. Nor again can we let our children hear from Aeschylus that

> God implants a fault in man, when he wishes to destroy a house utterly.

No: We must forbid anyone who writes a play about the sufferings of Niobe (the subject of the play from which these last lines are quoted), or the house of Pelops, or the Trojan war, or any similar topic, to say they are acts of god; or if he does he must produce the sort of interpretation we are now demanding, and say that god's acts were good and just, and that the sufferers were benefited by being punished. What the poet must not be allowed to say is that those who were punished were made wretched through god's action. He may refer to the wicked as wretched because they needed punishment, provided he makes it clear that in punishing them god did them good. But if a state is to be run on the right lines, every possible step must be taken to prevent anyone, young or old, either saying or being told, whether in poetry or prose, that god, being good, can cause harm or evil to any man. To say so would be sinful, inexpedient, and inconsistent."

"I should approve of a law for this purpose and you have my vote for it," he said.

"Then of our laws laying down the principles which those who write or speak about the gods must follow, one would be this: *God is the cause, not of all things, but only of good.*"

"I am quite content with that," he said.

Questions and Suggestions for Writing

1. In the beginning of the dialogue Plato says that adults recite fictions to very young children, and that these fictions help to mold character. Think of some stories that you heard or read when young, such as "Snow White and the Seven Dwarfs" or "Ali Baba and the Forty Thieves." Try to think of a story that, in the final analysis, is not in accord with what you consider to be proper morality, such as a story in which a person triumphs through trickery, or a story in which evil actions—perhaps murders—are set forth without unfavorable comment. (Was it naughty of Jack to kill the giant?) Upon reflection, do you think children should not be told such stories? Why, or why not? Or think of the early film westerns, in which, on the whole, the Indians (except for an occasional Uncle Tonto) are depicted as bad guys and the whites (except for an occasional

---

[4]Quotations from Homer are generally taken from the translations by Dr. Rieu in the *Penguin* series. At times (as here) the version quoted by Plato differs slightly from the accepted text.

coward or rustler) are depicted as good guys. Many people who now have gray hair enjoyed such films in their childhood. Are you prepared to say that such films are not damaging? Or, on the other hand, are you prepared to say they are damaging and should be prohibited?

2. It is often objected that censorship of reading matter and of television programs available to children underrates their ability to think for themselves and to discount the dangerous, obscene, and tawdry. Do you agree with this objection? Does Plato?

3. Plato says that allowing poets to say what they please about the gods in his ideal state would be "inconsistent." Explain what he means by this criticism, and then explain why you agree or disagree with it.

4. Do you believe that parents should censor the "fiction" their children encounter (literature, films, pictures, rock lyrics), but that the community should not censor the "fiction" of adults? Write an essay of 500 words on one of these topics: "Censorship and Rock Lyrics"; "X-rated Films"; "Ethnic Jokes." (These topics are broadly worded; you can narrow one, and offer whatever thesis you wish.)

5. Were you taught that any of the founding fathers ever acted disreputably, or that any American hero had any serious moral flaw? Or that America ever acted immorally in its dealings with other nations? Do you think it appropriate for children to hear such things?

John Stuart Mill

From *On Liberty*

INTRODUCTORY

The object of this essay is to assert one very simple principle, as entitled to govern absolutely the dealings of society with the individual in the way of compulsion and control, whether the means used be physical

---

John Stuart Mill (1806–1873), one of England's most influential philosophers and essayists in the nineteenth century, was blessed with a precocious genius that enabled him to master foreign languages, mathematics, and other studies with equal ease. From his infancy he was raised by his formidable father, James Mill, for an arduous and ambitious career as a teacher, writer, editor, conversationalist, and public servant. (His Autobiography *[1873] tells the story of his youth with vivid detail.) For half a century he was active in the literary, cultural, and political life of London, but today even his major books—notably,* System of Logic *(1843) and* Principles of Political Economy *(1848)—are studied only by specialists. Several of his shorter pieces, however, continue to be widely read, including* Utilitarianism *(1863),* Subjection of Women *(1869), and the most influential of them all,* On Liberty *(1859), from which we reprint a substantial excerpt.*

force in the form of legal penalties or the moral coercion of public opinion. That principle is that the sole end for which mankind are warranted, individually or collectively, in interfering with the liberty of action of any of their number is self-protection. That the only purpose for which power can be rightfully exercised over any member of a civilized community, against his will, is to prevent harm to others. His own good, either physical or moral, is not a sufficient warrant. He cannot rightfully be compelled to do or forbear because it will be better for him to do so, because it will make him happier, because, in the opinions of others, to do so would be wise or even right. These are good reasons for remonstrating with him, or reasoning with him, or persuading him, or entreating him, but not for compelling him or visiting him with any evil in case he do otherwise. To justify that, the conduct from which it is desired to deter him must be calculated to produce evil to someone else. The only part of the conduct of anyone for which he is amenable to society is that which concerns others. In the part which merely concerns himself, his independence is, of right, absolute. Over himself, over his own body and mind, the individual is sovereign.

It is, perhaps, hardly necessary to say that this doctrine is meant to apply only to human beings in the maturity of their faculties. We are not speaking of children or of young persons below the age which the law may fix as that of manhood or womanhood. Those who are still in a state to require being taken care of by others must be protected against their own actions as well as against external injury. For the same reason we may leave out of consideration those backward states of society in which the race itself may be considered as in its nonage. The early difficulties in the way of spontaneous progress are so great that there is seldom any choice of means for overcoming them; and a ruler full of the spirit of improvement is warranted in the use of any expedients that will attain an end perhaps

---

In this essay, Mill sets himself the task of stating a general principle that would appeal to his readers and serve to distinguish between the area of an individual's conduct that ought to be completely free from supervision and the area of conduct that is properly supervised, regulated, and even punished by government. Mill does not write for those with fascist or totalitarian sympathies, or for readers still in thrall to traditional (tribal, sectarian) ways of life. Such outlooks would grant to government an all-encompassing authority that Mill utterly rejects. He takes for granted an audience of sympathetic liberals, who prize freedom and individualism and yet recognize that these values are not absolutes without limit.

Mill is also a utilitarian; that is, he believes individual conduct or government policy is justified or condemned depending on whether (in Jeremy Bentham's famous phrase) it conduces to "the greatest good of the greatest number." Where a person's conduct has virtually no effect for good or ill on the interests of others, then the utilitarian criterion is equivalent to the ideal of enlightened self-interest. But because most of what we say and do does affect others, predicting and evaluating that influence can become crucial, as it is for Mill, in deciding whether speech or action ought to be tolerated rather than restricted.

otherwise unattainable. Despotism is a legitimate mode of government in dealing with barbarians, provided the end be their improvement and the means justified by actually effecting that end. Liberty, as a principle, has no application to any state of things anterior to the time when mankind have become capable of being improved by free and equal discussion. Until then, there is nothing for them but implicit obedience to an Akbar or a Charlemagne,[1] if they are so fortunate as to find one. But as soon as mankind have attained the capacity of being guided to their own improvement by conviction or persuasion (a period long since reached in all nations with whom we need here concern ourselves), compulsion, either in the direct form or in that of pains and penalties for noncompliance, is no longer admissible as a means to their own good, and justifiable only for the security of others. . . .

There is a sphere of action in which society, as distinguished from the individual, has, if any, only an indirect interest: comprehending all that portion of a person's life and conduct which affects only himself or, if it also affects others, only with their free, voluntary, and undeceived consent and participation. When I say only himself, I mean directly and in the first instance; for whatever affects himself may affect others through himself; and the objection which may be grounded on this contingency will receive consideration in the sequel. This, then, is the appropriate region of human liberty. It comprises, first, the inward domain of consciousness, demanding liberty of conscience in the most comprehensive sense, liberty of thought and feeling, absolute freedom of opinion and sentiment on all subjects, practical or speculative, scientific, moral, or theological. The liberty of expressing and publishing opinions may seem to fall under a different principle, since it belongs to that part of the conduct of an individual which concerns other people, but, being almost of as much importance as the liberty of thought itself and resting in great part on the same reasons, is practically inseparable from it. Secondly, the principle requires liberty of tastes and pursuits, of framing the plan of our life to suit our own character, of doing as we like, subject to such consequences as may follow, without impediment from our fellow creatures, so long as what we do does not harm them, even though they should think our conduct foolish, perverse, or wrong. Thirdly, from this liberty of each individual follows the liberty, within the same limits, of combination among individuals; freedom to unite for any purpose not involving harm to others: the persons combining being supposed to be of full age and not forced or deceived.

No society in which these liberties are not, on the whole, respected is 4 free, whatever may be its form of government; and none is completely free in which they do not exist absolute and unqualified. The only freedom

---

[1]**Akbar . . . Charlemagne** Akbar (1542–1605), Mogul Emperor of India; Charlemagne (742–815), King of the Franks, and later Emperor of the West. [All notes are the editors'.]

which deserves the name is that of pursuing our own good in our own way, so long as we do not attempt to deprive others of theirs or impede their efforts to obtain it. Each is the proper guardian of his own health, whether bodily or mental and spiritual. Mankind are greater gainers by suffering each other to live as seems good to themselves than by compelling each to live as seems good to the rest. . . .

OF THE LIBERTY OF THOUGHT AND DISCUSSION

The time, it is to be hoped, is gone by when any defense would be necessary of the "liberty of the press" as one of the securities against corrupt or tyrannical government. No argument, we may suppose, can now be needed against permitting a legislature or an executive, not identified in interest with the people, to prescribe opinions to them and determine what doctrines or what arguments they shall be allowed to hear. This aspect of the question, besides, has been so often and so triumphantly enforced by preceding writers that it need not be specially insisted on in this place. Though the law of England, on the subject of the press, is as servile to this day as it was in the time of the Tudors,[2] there is little danger of its being actually put in force against political discussion except during some temporary panic when fear of insurrection drives ministers and judges from their propriety; and, speaking generally, it is not, in constitutional countries, to be apprehended that the government, whether completely responsible to the people or not, will often attempt to control the expression of opinion, except when in doing so it makes itself the organ of the general intolerance of the public. Let us suppose, therefore, that the government is entirely at one with the people, and never thinks of exerting any power of coercion unless in agreement with what it conceives to be their voice. But I deny the right of the people to exercise such coercion, either by themselves or by their government. The power itself is illegitimate. The best government has no more title to it than the worst. It is as noxious, or more noxious, when exerted in accordance with public opinion than when in opposition to it. If all mankind minus one were of one opinion, mankind would be no more justified in silencing that one person than he, if he had the power, would be justified in silencing mankind. Were an opinion a personal possession of no value except to the owner, if to be obstructed in the enjoyment of it were simply a private injury, it would make some difference whether the injury was inflicted only on a few persons or on many. But the peculiar evil of silencing the expression of an opinion is that it is robbing the human race, posterity as well as the existing generation—those who dissent from the opinion, still more than those who

[2]**the time of the Tudors** The period in England from the reign of Henry VII through the reign of Queen Elizabeth I; i.e., 1485–1603.

hold it. If the opinion is right, they are deprived of the opportunity of exchanging error for truth; if wrong, they lose, what is almost as great a benefit, the clearer perception and livelier impression of truth produced by its collision with error. . . .

We have now recognized the necessity to the mental well-being of mankind (on which all their other well-being depends) of freedom of opinion, and freedom of the expression of opinion, on four distinct grounds, which we will now briefly recapitulate:

First, if any opinion is compelled to silence, that opinion may, for aught we can certainly know, be true. To deny this is to assume our own infallibility.

Secondly, though the silenced opinion be an error, it may, and very commonly does, contain a portion of truth; and since the general or prevailing opinion on any subject is rarely or never the whole truth, it is only by the collision of adverse opinions that the remainder of the truth has any chance of being supplied. 8

Thirdly, even if the received opinion be not only true, but the whole truth; unless it is suffered to be, and actually is, vigorously and earnestly contested, it will, by most of those who receive it, be held in the manner of a prejudice, with little comprehension or feeling of its rational grounds. And not only this, but, fourthly, the meaning of the doctrine itself will be in danger of being lost or enfeebled, and deprived of its vital effect on the character and conduct: the dogma becoming a mere formal profession, inefficacious for good, but cumbering the ground and preventing the growth of any real and heartfelt conviction from reason or personal experience.

Before quitting the subject of freedom of opinion, it is fit to take some notice of those who say that the free expression of all opinions should be permitted on condition that the manner be temperate, and do not pass the bounds of fair discussion. Much might be said on the impossibility of fixing where these supposed bounds are to be placed; for if the test be offense to those whose opinions are attacked, I think experience testifies that this offense is given whenever the attack is telling and powerful, and that every opponent who pushes them hard, and whom they find it difficult to answer, appears to them, if he shows any strong feeling on the subject, an intemperate opponent. But this, though an important consideration in a practical point of view, merges in a more fundamental objection. Undoubtedly, the manner of asserting an opinion, even though it be a true one, may be very objectionable and may justly incur severe censure. But the principal offenses of the kind are such as it is mostly impossible, unless by accidental self-betrayal, to bring home to conviction. The gravest of them is, to argue sophistically, to suppress facts or arguments, to misstate the elements of the case, or misrepresent the opposite opinion. But all this, even to the most aggravated degree, is so continually done in perfect good faith by persons who are not considered, and in many other respects may not deserve to be considered, ignorant or incompetent, that it is rarely possible, on adequate grounds, conscientiously to stamp the misrepresentation as morally culpable, and still less could law presume to interfere with this kind of controversial misconduct. With regard to what is commonly meant by intemperate discussion, namely invective, sarcasm, personality, and the like, the denunciation of these weapons would deserve more sympathy if it were ever proposed to interdict them equally to both sides; but it is only desired to restrain the employment of them against the prevailing opinion; against the unprevailing they may not only be used without general disapproval, but will be likely to obtain for him who uses them the praise of honest zeal and righteous indignation. Yet whatever mischief arises from their use is greatest when they are employed against the comparatively defenseless; and whatever unfair advantage can be derived by any opinion from this mode of asserting it accrues almost exclusively to received opinions. The worst offense of this kind which can be committed by a polemic is to stigmatize those who hold the contrary opinion as bad and immoral men. To calumny of this sort, those who hold any unpopular opinion are peculiarly exposed, because they are in general few and uninfluential, and nobody but themselves feels much interested in seeing justice done them; but this weapon is, from the nature of the case, denied to those who attack a prevailing opinion: they can neither use it with safety to themselves, nor, if they could, would it do anything but recoil on their own cause. In general, opinions contrary to those commonly received can only obtain a hearing by studied moderation of language and the most cautious avoidance of unnecessary offense, from which they hardly ever deviate even in a slight degree without losing ground, while unmeasured vituperation employed on the side of the prevailing opinion really does deter people from professing contrary opinions and from listening to those who profess them. For the interest, therefore, of truth and justice it is far more important to restrain this employment of vituperative language than the other; and, for example, if it were necessary to choose, there would be much more need to discourage offensive attacks on infidelity than on religion. It is, however, obvious that law and authority have no business with restraining either, while opinion ought, in every instance, to determine its verdict by the circumstances of the individual case—condemning everyone, on whichever side of the argument he places himself, in whose mode of advocacy either want of candor, or malignity, bigotry, or intolerance of feeling manifest themselves; but not inferring these vices from the side which a person takes, though it be the contrary side of the question to our own; and giving merited honor to everyone, whatever opinion he may hold, who has calmness to see and honesty to state what his opponents and their opinions really are, exaggerating nothing to their discredit, keeping nothing back which tells, or can be supposed to tell, in their favor. This is the real morality of public discussion; and if often violated, I am happy to think that there are many controversialists who to a great extent observe it, and a still greater number who conscientiously strive toward it.

OF THE LIMITS TO THE AUTHORITY OF SOCIETY OVER THE INDIVIDUAL

What, then, is the rightful limit to the sovereignty of the individual over himself? Where does the authority of society begin? How much of human life should be assigned to individuality, and how much to society?

Each will receive its proper share if each has that which more par-   12 ticularly concerns it. To individuality should belong the part of life in which it is chiefly the individual that is interested; to society, the part which chiefly interests society.

Though society is not founded on a contract, and though no good purpose is answered by inventing a contract in order to deduce social obligations from it, everyone who receives the protection of society owes a return for the benefit, and the fact of living in society renders it indispensable that each should be bound to observe a certain line of conduct toward the rest. This conduct consists, first, in not injuring the interests of one another, or rather certain interests which, either by express legal provision or by tacit understanding, ought to be considered as rights; and secondly, in each person's bearing his share (to be fixed on some equitable principle) of the labors and sacrifices incurred for defending the society or its members from injury and molestation. These conditions society is justified in enforcing at all costs to those who endeavor to withhold fulfillment. Nor is this all that society may do. The acts of an individual may be hurtful to others or wanting in due consideration for their welfare, without going to the length of violating any of their constituted rights. The offender may then be justly punished by opinion, though not by law. As soon as any part of a person's conduct affects prejudicially the interests of others, society has jurisdiction over it, and the question whether the general welfare will or will not be promoted by interfering with it becomes open to discussion. But there is no room for entertaining any such question when a person's conduct affects the interests of no persons besides himself, or needs not affect them unless they like (all the persons concerned being of full age and the ordinary amount of understanding). In all such cases, there should be perfect freedom, legal and social, to do the action and stand the consequences. . . .

The distinction here pointed out between the part of a person's life which concerns only himself and that which concerns others, many persons will refuse to admit. How (it may be asked) can any part of the conduct of a member of society be a matter of indifference to the other members? No person is an entirely isolated being; it is impossible for a person to do anything seriously or permanently hurtful to himself without mischief reaching at least to his near connections, and often far beyond them. If he injures his property, he does harm to those who directly or indirectly derived support from it, and usually diminishes, by a greater or less amount, the general resources of the community. If he deteriorates his bodily or mental faculties, he not only brings evil upon all who depended on him for any portion of their happiness, but disqualifies himself for rendering the services which he owes to his fellow creatures generally, perhaps becomes a burden on their affection or benevolence; and if such conduct were very frequent hardly any offense that is committed would detract more from the general sum of good. Finally, if by his vices or follies a person does no direct harm to others, he is nevertheless (it may be said) injurious by his example, and ought to be compelled to control himself for the sake of those whom the sight or knowledge of his conduct might corrupt or mislead.

And even (it will be added) if the consequences of misconduct could be confined to the vicious or thoughtless individual, ought society to abandon to their own guidance those who are manifestly unfit for it? If protection against themselves is confessedly due to children and persons under age, is not society equally bound to afford it to persons of mature years who are equally incapable of self-government? If gambling, or drunkenness, or incontinence, or idleness, or uncleanliness are as injurious to happiness, and as great a hindrance to improvement, as many or most of the acts prohibited by law, why (it may be asked) should not law, so far as is consistent with practicability and social convenience, endeavor to repress these also? And as a supplement to the unavoidable imperfections of law, ought not opinion at least to organize a powerful police against these vices and visit rigidly with social penalties those who are known to practice them? There is no question here (it may be said) about restricting individuality, or impeding the trial of new and original experiments in living. The only things it is sought to prevent are things which have been tried and condemned from the beginning of the world until now—things which experience has shown not to be useful or suitable to any person's individuality. There must be some length of time and amount of experience after which a moral or prudential truth may be regarded as established; and it is merely desired to prevent generation after generation from falling over the same precipice which has been fatal to their predecessors.

I fully admit that the mischief which a person does to himself may 16 seriously affect, both through their sympathies and their interests, those nearly connected with him and, in a minor degree, society at large. When, by conduct of this sort, a person is led to violate a distinct and assignable obligation to any other person or persons, the case is taken out of the self-regarding class and becomes amenable to moral disapprobation in the proper sense of the term. If, for example, a man, through intemperance or extravagance, becomes unable to pay his debts, or, having undertaken the moral responsibility of a family, becomes from the same cause incapable of supporting or educating them, he is deservedly reprobated and might be justly punished; but it is for the breach of duty to his family or creditors, not for the extravagance. If the resources which ought to have been devoted to them had been diverted from them for the most prudent investment, the moral culpability would have been the same. George Barnwell[3] murdered his uncle to get money for his mistress, but if he had done it to set himself up in business, he would equally have been hanged. Again, in the frequent case of a man who causes grief to his family by addiction to bad habits, he deserves reproach for his unkindness or ingratitude; but so he may for cultivating habits not in themselves vicious, if they are painful to those with whom he passes his life, or who from personal ties are dependent on him for their comfort. Whoever fails in the consideration generally due to the interests and feelings of others, not being compelled by some more imperative duty, or justified by allowable self-preference, is a subject of moral disapprobation for that failure, but not for the cause of it, nor for the errors, merely personal to himself, which may have remotely led to it. In like manner, when a person disables himself, by conduct purely self-regarding, from the performance of some definite duty incumbent on him to the public, he is guilty of a social offense. No person ought to be punished simply for being drunk; but a soldier or a policeman should be punished for being drunk on duty. Whenever, in short, there is a definite damage, or a definite risk of damage, either to an individual or to the public, the case is taken out of the province of liberty and placed in that of morality or law. . . .

But the strongest of all the arguments against the interference of the public with purely personal conduct is that, when it does interfere, the odds are that it interferes wrongly and in the wrong place. On questions of social morality, of duty to others, the opinion of the public, that is, of an overruling majority, though often wrong, is likely to be still oftener right, because on such questions they are only required to judge of their own interests, of the manner in which some mode of conduct, if allowed to be practiced, would affect themselves. But the opinion of a similar majority, imposed as a law on the minority, on questions of self-regarding conduct is quite as likely to be wrong as right, for in these cases public opinion means, at the best, some people's opinion of what is good or bad for other people, while very often it does not even mean that—the public, with the most perfect indifference, passing over the pleasure or convenience of those whose conduct they censure and considering only their own preference. There are many who consider as an injury to themselves any conduct which they have a distaste for, and resent it as an outrage to their feelings; as a religious bigot, when charged with disregarding the religious feelings of others, has been known to retort that they disregard his feelings by

---

[3]**George Barnwell** An apprentice in a popular ballad and in George Lillo's play, *The London Merchant* (1731).

persisting in their abominable worship or creed. But there is no parity between the feeling of a person for his own opinion and the feeling of another who is offended at his holding it, no more than between the desire of a thief to take a purse and the desire of the right owner to keep it. And a person's taste is as much his own peculiar concern as his opinion or his purse. It is easy for anyone to imagine an ideal public which leaves the freedom and choice of individuals in all uncertain matters undisturbed and only requires them to abstain from modes of conduct which universal experience has condemned. But where has there been seen a public which set any such limit to its censorship? Or when does the public trouble itself about universal experience? In its interferences with personal conduct it is seldom thinking of anything but the enormity of acting or feeling differently from itself; and this standard of judgment, thinly disguised, is held up to mankind as the dictate of religion and philosophy by nine-tenths of all moralists and speculative writers. These teach that things are right because they are right; because we feel them to be so. They tell us to search in our own minds and hearts for laws of conduct binding on ourselves and on all others. What can the poor public do but apply these instructions and make their own personal feelings of good and evil, if they are tolerably unanimous in them, obligatory on all the world?

The evil here pointed out is not one which exists only in theory; and it may perhaps be expected that I should specify the instances in which the public of this age and country improperly invests its own preferences with the character of moral laws. I am not writing an essay on the aberrations of existing moral feeling. That is too weighty a subject to be discussed parenthetically, and by way of illustration. Yet examples are necessary to show that the principle I maintain is of serious and practical moment, and that I am not endeavoring to erect a barrier against imaginary evils. And it is not difficult to show, by abundant instances, that to extend the bounds of what may be called moral police until it encroaches on the most unquestionably legitimate liberty of the individual is one of the most universal of all human propensities. . . .

Without dwelling upon supposititious cases[4] there are, in our own day, gross usurpations upon the liberty of private life actually practiced, and still greater ones threatened with some expectation of success, and opinions propounded which assert an unlimited right in the public not only to prohibit by law everything which it thinks wrong, but, in order to get at what it thinks wrong, to prohibit a number of things which it admits to be innocent.

Under the name of preventing intemperance, the people of one English colony, and of nearly half the United States, have been interdicted by law[5] from making any use whatever of fermented drinks, except for medi- [20]

[4]**supposititious cases** Cases depending on a supposition; hypothetical cases.
[5]**law** The Maine Liquor Law (1851) prohibited the manufacture, sale, and use of intoxicating drinks, with some exceptions.

cal purposes, for prohibition of their sale is in fact, as it is intended to be, prohibition of their use. And though the impracticability of executing the law has caused its repeal in several of the States which had adopted it, including the one from which it derives its name, an attempt has notwithstanding been commenced, and is prosecuted with considerable zeal by many of the professed philanthropists, to agitate for a similar law in this country. The association, or "Alliance," as it terms itself, which has been formed for this purpose, has acquired some notoriety through the publicity given to a correspondence between its secretary and one of the very few English public men who hold that a politician's opinions ought to be founded on principles. Lord Stanley's share in this correspondence is calculated to strengthen the hopes already built on him, by those who know how rare such qualities as are manifested in some of his public appearances unhappily are among those who figure in political life. The organ of the Alliance, who would "deeply deplore the recognition of any principle which could be wrested to justify bigotry and persecution," undertakes to point out the "broad and impassable barrier" which divides such principles from those of the association. "All matters relating to thought, opinion, conscience, appear to me," he says, "to be without the sphere of legislation; all pertaining to social act, habit, relation, subject only to a discretionary power vested in the State itself, and not in the individual, to be within it." No mention is made of a third class, different from either of these, viz., acts and habits which are not social, but individual; although it is to this class, surely, that the act of drinking fermented liquors belongs. Selling fermented liquors, however, is trading, and trading is a social act. But the infringement complained of is not on the liberty of the seller, but on that of the buyer and consumer; since the State might just as well forbid him to drink wine as purposely make it impossible for him to obtain it. The secretary, however, says, "I claim, as a citizen, a right to legislate whenever my social rights are invaded by the social act of another." And now for the definition of these "social rights": "If anything invades my social rights, certainly the traffic in strong drink does. It destroys my primary right of security by constantly creating and stimulating social disorder. It invades my right of equality by deriving a profit from the creation of a misery I am taxed to support. It impedes my right to free moral and intellectual development by surrounding my path with dangers and by weakening and demoralizing society, from which I have a right to claim mutual aid and intercourse." A theory of "social rights" the like of which probably never before found its way into distinct language: being nothing short of this— that it is the absolute social right of every individual that every other individual shall act in every respect exactly as he ought; that whosoever fails thereof in the smallest particular violates my social right and entitles me to demand from the legislature the removal of the grievance. So monstrous a principle is far more dangerous than any single interference with liberty; there is no violation of liberty which it would not justify; it acknowledges no right to any freedom whatever, except perhaps to that of holding opinions in secret, without ever disclosing them; for the moment an opinion which I consider noxious passes anyone's lips, it invades all the "social rights" attributed to me by the Alliance. The doctrine ascribes to all mankind a vested interest in each other's moral, intellectual, and even physical perfection, to be defined by each claimant according to his own standard. . . .

Questions and Suggestions for Writing

1. Mill claims (para. 1) that the purpose of his essay is "to assert one very simple principle." Some critics have maintained that he asserts *two* principles. Who is right, Mill or these critics?

2. In his second paragraph, Mill grants two major exceptions to his principle barring state interference with personal conduct. What are these exceptions? Are you willing to agree with him? Explain why, preferably in two paragraphs.

3. In several places in his essay Mill describes what freedom (liberty) is, but he never quite comes out and explicitly defines it. Try to help him out with an explicit definition of your own that faithfully expresses Mill's ideas.

4. Mill gives three main reasons against censorship of the press. One of them (as he later expresses it in para. 7) is that "All silencing of discussion is an assumption of infallibility." Do you agree?

5. Would Mill agree that "Sticks and stones can break my bones, but words can never hurt me"? Do you agree?

6. How adequate is Mill's distinction (para. 12) between a person's conduct that affects the interests of others, and conduct that affects no one else? What objections to it does Mill himself anticipate? Can you think of troubling borderline cases that put the distinction in doubt?

7. Mill allows (para. 16) that a person who injures a pedestrian while driving "under the influence" (as we euphemistically say) may be punished—but so long as his drunkenness injures no one, or no one but himself, he may not be punished. Write an essay of 500 to 750 words either attacking or defending Mill's position. (By the way, do the laws on this matter currently in force in your state coincide with Mill's position, or not?)

8. Would Mill agree with Susan Brownmiller (p. 548) in defending legal regulation of obscene and pornographic materials, or would he agree with Susan Jacoby (p. 8) in leaving such publications unregulated? Explain.

9. Suppose you believed that cigarette manufacture, distribution, sale, use, and advertising should be made illegal, or that these should at least be severely regulated. Would you find an ally or a hostile critic in Mill? Explain.

John Marshall Harlan and Harry A. Blackmun

Paul Robert Cohen, Appellant, v. State of California

Justice Harlan delivered the opinion of the Court.

This case may seem at first blush too inconsequential to find its way into our books, but the issue it presents is of no small constitutional significance.

Appellant Paul Robert Cohen was convicted in the Los Angeles Municipal Court of violating that part of California Penal Code § 415 which prohibits "maliciously and willfully disturb[ing] the peace or quiet of any neighborhood or person, . . . by . . . offensive conduct. . . ." He was given 30 days' imprisonment. The facts upon which his conviction rests are detailed in the opinion of the Court of Appeal of California, Second Appellate District, as follows:

> On April 26, 1968 the defendant was observed in the Los Angeles County Courthouse in the corridor outside of Division 20 of the Municipal Court wearing a jacket bearing the words "Fuck the Draft" which were plainly visible. There were women and children present in the corridor. The defendant was arrested. The defendant testified that he wore the jacket as a means of informing the public of the depth of his feelings against the Vietnam War and the draft.
>
> The defendant did not engage in, nor threaten to engage in, nor did anyone as the result of his conduct in fact commit or threaten to commit any act of violence. The defendant did not make any loud or unusual noise, nor was there any evidence that he uttered any sound prior to his arrest.

In affirming the conviction the Court of Appeal held that "offensive conduct" means "behavior which has a tendency to provoke *others* to acts of violence or to in turn disturb the peace," and that the State had proved this element because, on the facts of this case, "[i]t was certainly reasonably foreseeable that such conduct might cause others to rise up to commit a violent act against the person of the defendant or attempt to forceably

4

During the 1960s, draft-age men often protested against the Selective Service System on grounds that it was administered unfairly and that it was being used to provide troops to fight an unjust war in Vietnam. Protest took varied forms, including civil disobedience and violent resistance. Peaceful objections were far more frequent, but in some cases it was hard to tell whether the protest was lawful or not. The conduct of Paul Robert Cohen is one of these borderline cases. Cohen was convicted in 1968 in Los Angeles of a misdemeanor for behaving in a manner that violated a California statute forbidding "tumultuous or offensive conduct." Cohen argued that his conduct was protected by the United States Constitution as

remove his jacket." The California Supreme Court declined review by a divided vote. We brought the case here, postponing the consideration of the question of our jurisdiction over this appeal to a hearing of the case on the merits. We now reverse.

The question of our jurisdiction need not detain us long. Throughout the proceedings below, Cohen consistently claimed that, as construed to apply to the facts of this case, the statute infringed his rights to freedom of expression guaranteed by the First and Fourteenth Amendments of the Federal Constitution. That contention has been rejected by the highest California state court in which review could be had. Accordingly, we are fully satisfied that Cohen has properly invoked our jurisdiction by this appeal.

I

In order to lay hands on the precise issue which this case involves, it is useful first to canvass various matters which this record does *not* present.

The conviction quite clearly rests upon the asserted offensiveness of the *words* Cohen used to convey his message to the public. The only "conduct" which the State sought to punish is the fact of communication. Thus, we deal here with a conviction resting solely upon "speech," not upon any separately identifiable conduct which allegedly was intended by Cohen to be perceived by others as expressive of particular views but which, on its face, does not necessarily convey any message and hence arguably could be regulated without effectively repressing Cohen's ability to express himself. Further, the State certainly lacks power to punish Cohen for the underlying content of the message the inscription conveyed. At least so long as there is no showing of an intent to incite disobedience to or disruption of the draft. Cohen could not, consistently with the First and Fourteenth Amendments, be punished for asserting the evident position on the inutility or immorality of the draft his jacket reflected.

Appellant's conviction, then, rests squarely upon his exercise of the "freedom of speech" protected from arbitrary governmental interference by the Constitution and can be justified, if at all, only as a valid regulation of the manner in which he exercised that freedom, not as a permissible prohibition on the substantive message it conveys. This does not end the

8

an act of "free speech," but the California Court of Appeals disagreed and upheld his conviction. He appealed to the United States Supreme Court, and won by a vote of six to three. Excerpted here is the majority opinion, written by Associate Justice John Marshall Harlan (1899–1971), one of the most respected jurists to sit on the Court during the past generation. The facts of the case are briefly set out by Harlan in his opening paragraphs. We also reprint the main argument of the brief dissenting opinion, written by Associate Justice Harry A. Blackmun (b. 1908). Legal citations have been omitted.

inquiry, of course, for the First and Fourteenth Amendments have never been thought to give absolute protection to every individual to speak whenever or wherever he pleases, or to use any form of address in any circumstances that he chooses. In this vein, too, however, we think it important to note that several issues typically associated with such problems are not presented here.

In the first place, Cohen was tried under a statute applicable throughout the entire State. Any attempt to support this conviction on the ground that the statute seeks to preserve an appropriately decorous atmosphere in the courthouse where Cohen was arrested must fail in the absence of any language in the statute that would have put appellant on notice that certain kinds of otherwise permissible speech or conduct would nevertheless, under California law, not be tolerated in certain places. No fair reading of the phrase "offensive conduct" can be said sufficiently to inform the ordinary person that distinctions between certain locations are thereby created.[1]

In the second place, as it comes to us, this case cannot be said to fall within those relatively few categories of instances where prior decisions have established the power of government to deal more comprehensively with certain forms of individual expression simply upon a showing that such a form was employed. This is not, for example, an obscenity case. Whatever else may be necessary to give rise to the States' broader power to prohibit obscene expression, such expression must be, in some significant way, erotic. It cannot plausibly be maintained that this vulgar allusion to the Selective Service System would conjure up such psychic stimulation in anyone likely to be confronted with Cohen's crudely defaced jacket.

This Court has also held that the States are free to ban the simple use, without a demonstration of additional justifying circumstances, of so-called "fighting words," those personally abusive epithets which, when addressed to the ordinary citizen, are, as a matter of common knowledge, inherently likely to provoke violent reaction. While the four-letter word displayed by Cohen in relation to the draft is not uncommonly employed in a personally provocative fashion, in this instance it was clearly not "directed to the person of the hearer." No individual actually or likely to be present could reasonably have regarded the words on appellant's jacket as a direct personal insult. Nor do we have here an instance of the exercise of the State's police power to prevent a speaker from intentionally provoking a given group to hostile reaction. There is, as noted above, no showing that anyone who saw Cohen was in fact violently aroused or that appellant intended such a result.

---

[1]It is illuminating to note what transpired when Cohen entered a courtroom in the building. He removed his jacket and stood with it folded over his arm. Meanwhile, a policeman sent the presiding judge a note suggesting that Cohen be held in contempt of court. The judge declined to do so and Cohen was arrested by the officer only after he emerged from the courtroom.

Finally, in arguments before this Court much has been made of the 12
claim that Cohen's distasteful mode of expression was thrust upon unwilling or unsuspecting viewers, and that the State might therefore legitimately act as it did in order to protect the sensitive from otherwise
unavoidable exposure to appellant's crude form of protest. Of course, the
mere presumed presence of unwitting listeners or viewers does not serve
automatically to justify curtailing all speech capable of giving offense.
While this Court has recognized that government may properly act in
many situations to prohibit intrusion into the privacy of the home of
unwelcome views and ideas which cannot be totally banned from the
public dialogue, we have at the same time consistently stressed that "we
are often 'captives' outside the sanctuary of the home and subject to
objectionable speech." The ability of government, consonant with the
Constitution, to shut off discourse solely to protect others from hearing it
is, in other words, dependent upon a showing that substantial privacy
interests are being invaded in an essentially intolerable manner. Any
broader view of this authority would effectively empower a majority to
silence dissidents simply as a matter of personal predilections.

In this regard, persons confronted with Cohen's jacket were in a quite
different posture than, say, those subjected to the raucous emissions of
sound trucks blaring outside their residences. Those in the Los Angeles
courthouse could effectively avoid further bombardment of their sensibilities simply by averting their eyes. And, while it may be that one has a
more substantial claim to a recognizable privacy interest when walking
through a courthouse corridor than, for example, strolling through Central
Park, surely it is nothing like the interest in being free from unwanted
expression in the confines of one's own home. Given the subtlety and
complexity of the factors involved, if Cohen's "speech" was otherwise
entitled to constitutional protection, we do not think the fact that some
unwilling "listeners" in a public building may have been briefly exposed to
it can serve to justify this breach of the peace conviction where, as here,
there was no evidence that persons powerless to avoid appellant's conduct
did in fact object to it, and where that portion of the statute upon which
Cohen's conviction rests evinces no concern, either on its face or as construed by the California courts, with the special plight of the captive
auditor, but, instead, indiscriminately sweeps within its prohibitions all
"offensive conduct" that disturbs "any neighborhood or person."[2]

---

[2]In fact, other portions of the same statute do make some such distinctions. For example,
the statute also prohibits disturbing "the peace or quiet . . . by loud or unusual noise" and
using "vulgar, profane or indecent language within the presence or hearing of women or
children, in a loud or boisterous manner." . . . This second quoted provision in particular
serves to put the actor on much fairer notice as to what is prohibited. It also buttresses our
view that the "offensive conduct" portion, as construed and applied in this case, cannot
legitimately be justified in this Court as designed or intended to make fine distinctions
between differently situated recipients.

II

Against this background, the issue flushed by this case stands out in bold relief. It is whether California can excise, as "offensive conduct," one particular scurrilous epithet from the public discourse, either upon the theory of the court below that its use is inherently likely to cause violent reaction or upon a more general assertion that the States, acting as guardians of public morality, may properly remove this offensive word from the public vocabulary.

The rationale of the California court is plainly untenable. At most it reflects an "undifferentiated fear or apprehension of disturbance [which] is not enough to overcome the right to freedom of expression." We have been shown no evidence that substantial numbers of citizens are standing ready to strike out physically at whoever may assault their sensibilities with execrations like that uttered by Cohen. There may be some persons about with such lawless and violent proclivities, but that is an insufficient base upon which to erect, consistently with constitutional values, a governmental power to force persons who wish to ventilate their dissident views into avoiding particular forms of expression. The argument amounts to little more than the self-defeating proposition that to avoid physical censorship of one who has not sought to provoke such a response by a hypothetical coterie of the violent and lawless, the States may more appropriately effectuate that censorship themselves.

Admittedly, it is not so obvious that the First and Fourteenth Amendments must be taken to disable the States from punishing public utterance of this unseemly expletive in order to maintain what they regard as a suitable level of discourse within the body politic. We think, however, that examination and reflection will reveal the shortcoming of a contrary viewpoint. 16

At the outset, we cannot overemphasize that, in our judgment, most situations where the State has a justifiable interest in regulating speech will fall within one or more of the various established exceptions, discussed above but not applicable here, to the usual rule that governmental bodies may not prescribe the form or content of individual expression. Equally important to our conclusion is the constitutional backdrop against which our decision must be made. The constitutional right of free expression is powerful medicine in a society as diverse and populous as ours. It is designed and intended to remove governmental restraints from the arena of public discussion, putting the decision as to what views shall be voiced largely into the hands of each of us, in the hope that use of such freedom will ultimately produce a more capable citizenry and more perfect polity and in the belief that no other approach would comport with the premise of individual dignity and choice upon which our political system rests.

To many, the immediate consequence of this freedom may often appear to be only verbal tumult, discord, and even offensive utterance.

These are, however, within established limits, in truth necessary side effects of the broader enduring values which the process of open debate permits us to achieve. That the air may at times seem filled with verbal cacophony is, in this sense, not a sign of weakness but of strength. We cannot lose sight of the fact that, in what otherwise might seem a trifling and annoying instance of individual distasteful abuse of a privilege, these fundamental societal values are truly implicated. That is why "[w]holly neutral futilities . . . come under the protection of free speech as fully as do Keats' poems or Donne's sermons," and why "so long as the means are peaceful, the communication need not meet standards of acceptability."

Against this perception of the constitutional policies involved, we discern certain more particularized considerations that peculiarly call for reversal of this conviction. First, the principle contended for by the State seems inherently boundless. How is one to distinguish this from any other offensive word? Surely the State has no right to cleanse public debate to the point where it is grammatically palatable to the most squeamish among us. Yet no readily ascertainable general principle exists for stopping short of that result were we to affirm the judgment below. For, while the particular four-letter word being litigated here is perhaps more distasteful than most others of its genre, it is nevertheless often true that one man's vulgarity is another's lyric. Indeed, we think it is largely because governmental officials cannot make principled distinctions in this area that the Constitution leaves matters of taste and style so largely to the individual.

Additionally, we cannot overlook the fact, because it is well illustrated 20 by the episode involved here, that much linguistic expression serves a dual communicative function: it conveys not only ideas capable of relatively precise, detached explication, but otherwise inexpressible emotions as well. In fact, words are often chosen as much for their emotive as their cognitive force. We cannot sanction the view that the Constitution, while solicitous of the cognitive content of individual speech, has little or no regard for that emotive function which, practically speaking, may often be the more important element of the overall message sought to be communicated. Indeed, as Mr. Justice Frankfurter has said, "[o]ne of the prerogatives of American citizenship is the right to criticize public men and measures—and that means not only informed and responsible criticism but the freedom to speak foolishly and without moderation."

Finally, and in the same vein, we cannot indulge the facile assumption that one can forbid particular words without also running a substantial risk of suppressing ideas in the process. Indeed, governments might soon seize upon the censorship of particular words as a convenient guise for banning the expression of unpopular views. We have been able, as noted above, to discern little social benefit that might result from running the risk of opening the door to such grave results.

It is, in sum, our judgment that, absent a more particularized and compelling reason for its actions, the State may not, consistently with the

First and Fourteenth Amendments, make the simple public display here involved of this single four-letter expletive a criminal offense. Because that is the only arguably sustainable rationale for the conviction here at issue, the judgment below must be

Reversed

    Justice Blackmun, with whom The Chief Justice and Justice Black join.

    I dissent:

    Cohen's absurd and immature antic, in my view, was mainly conduct and little speech. The California Court of Appeal appears so to have described it, and I cannot characterize it otherwise. . . .

Questions and Suggestions for Writing

1. After reading the facts of the case, do you agree with the dissenting opinion that what Cohen did was "mainly conduct and little speech"? Does it matter if this evaluation is correct?

2. State briefly and in your own words the several kinds of issues that, in the majority's opinion, the Cohen case does *not* involve. If the case doesn't involve them, why does the majority discuss them?

3. In Part II of the majority opinion, the Court gives its reasons for reversing Cohen's conviction. State those reasons in your own words, perhaps in three or four sentences.

4. Suppose Cohen's behavior and arrest had occurred in a neighborhood office of the Selective Service System (a local draft board), rather than in the county court house. Do you think this circumstance might have affected the Court's judgment? Explain, in an essay of 250 words.

5. Suppose, contrary to fact, there had been evidence that Cohen's conduct actually had "provoked others to acts of violence or to disturb the peace." In an essay of 250 to 500 words indicate whether you think this evidence should have led the majority to uphold his conviction, and why.

Irving Kristol

Pornography, Obscenity, and the Case for Censorship

I

Being frustrated is disagreeable, but the real disasters in life begin when you get what you want. For almost a century now, a great many intelligent, well-meaning and articulate people—of a kind generally called liberal or intellectual, or both—have argued eloquently against any kind of censorship of art and/or entertainment. And within the past ten years, the courts and the legislatures of most Western nations have found these arguments persuasive—so persuasive that hardly a man is now alive who clearly remembers what the answers to these arguments were. Today, in the United States and other democracies, censorship has to all intents and purposes ceased to exist.

Is there a sense of triumphant exhilaration in the land? Hardly. There is, on the contrary, a rapidly growing unease and disquiet. Somehow, things have not worked out as they were supposed to, and many notable civil libertarians have gone on record as saying this was not what they meant at all. They wanted a world in which *Desire under the Elms* could be produced, or *Ulysses*[1] published, without interference by philistine busybodies holding public office. They have got that, of course; but they have also got a world in which homosexual rape takes place on the stage, in which the public flocks during lunch hours to witness varieties of professional fornication, in which Times Square has become little more than a hideous market for the sale and distribution of printed filth that panders to all known (and some fanciful) sexual perversions.

But disagreeable as this may be, does it really matter? Might not our unease and disquiet be merely a cultural hangover—a "hangup," as they say? What reason is there to think that anyone was ever corrupted by a book?

---

[1]*Desire under the Elms* . . . *Ulysses* Respectively, a play by Eugene O'Neill (1888–1953) and a novel by James Joyce (1882–1941). [Editors' note]

Kristol (b. 1920), a professor at New York University and coeditor of the journal The Public Interest, *describes himself as a "neoconservative." According to Kristol, in* Reflections of a Neoconservative *(1984), neoconservativism is "a current of thought emerging out of the academic-intellectual world and provoked by disillusionment with contemporary liberalism." In a sense, Kristol might call himself a neoliberal, for he says, in his collection of essays, that he wants "a return to the original sources of liberal vision and liberal energy so as to correct the warped version of liberalism that is today's orthodoxy." The following is excerpted from* On the Democratic Idea in America *(1972).*

This last question, oddly enough, is asked by the very same people 4 who seem convinced that advertisements in magazines or displays of violence on television do indeed have the power to corrupt. It is also asked, incredibly enough and in all sincerity, by people—e.g., university professors and schoolteachers—whose very lives provide all the answers one could want. After all, if you believe that no one was ever corrupted by a book, you have also to believe that no one was ever improved by a book (or a play or a movie). You have to believe, in other words, that all art is morally trivial and that, consequently, all education is morally irrelevant. No one, not even a university professor, really believes that.

To be sure, it is extremely difficult, as social scientists tell us, to trace the effects of any single book (or play or movie) on an individual reader or any class of readers. But we all know, and social scientists know it too, that the ways in which we use our minds and imaginations do shape our characters and help define us as persons. That those who certainly know this are nevertheless moved to deny it merely indicates how a dogmatic resistance to the idea of censorship can—like most dogmatism—result in a mindless insistence on the absurd.

I have used these harsh terms—"dogmatism" and "mindless"— advisedly. I might also have added "hypocritical." For the plain fact is that none of us is a complete civil libertarian. We all believe that there is some point at which the public authorities ought to step in to limit the "self expression" of an individual or a group, even where this might be seriously intended as a form of artistic expression, and even where the artistic transaction is between consenting adults. A playwright or theatrical director might, in this crazy world of ours, find someone willing to commit suicide on the stage, as called for by the script. We would not allow that— any more than we would permit scenes of real physical torture on the stage, even if the victim were a willing masochist. And I know of no one, no matter how free in spirit, who argues that we ought to permit gladiatorial contests in Yankee Stadium, similar to those once performed in the Colosseum at Rome—even if only consenting adults were involved.

The basic point that emerges is one that Professor Walter Berns has powerfully argued: no society can be utterly indifferent to the ways its citizens publicly entertain themselves.[2] Bearbaiting and cockfighting are prohibited only in part out of compassion for the suffering animals; the main reason they were abolished was because it was felt that they debased and brutalized the citizenry who flocked to witness such spectacles. And the question we face with regard to pornography and obscenity is whether, now that they have such strong legal protection from the Supreme Court, they can or will brutalize and debase our citizenry. We are, after all, not

[2]This is as good a place as any to express my profound indebtedness to Walter Berns's superb essay, "Pornography vs. Democracy," in the winter 1971 issue of *The Public Interest*.

dealing with one passing incident—one book, or one play, or one movie. We are dealing with a general tendency that is suffusing our entire culture.

I say pornography *and* obscenity because, though they have different dictionary definitions and are frequently distinguishable as "artistic" genres, they are nevertheless in the end identical in effect. Pornography is not objectionable simply because it arouses sexual desire or lust or prurience in the mind of the reader or spectator; this is a silly Victorian notion. A great many nonpornographic works—including some parts of the Bible—excite sexual desire very successfully. What is distinctive about pornography is that, in the words of D. H. Lawrence, it attempts "to do dirt on [sex] . . . [It is an] insult to a vital human relationship."

In other words, pornography differs from erotic art in that its whole purpose is to treat human beings obscenely, to deprive human beings of their specifically human dimension. That is what obscenity is all about. It is light years removed from any kind of carefree sensuality—there is no continuum between Fielding's *Tom Jones* and the Marquis de Sade's *Justine*. These works have quite opposite intentions. To quote Susan Sontag: "What pornographic literature does is precisely to drive a wedge between one's existence as a full human being and one's existence as a sexual being—while in ordinary life a healthy person is one who prevents such a gap from opening up." This definition occurs in an essay *defending* pornography—Miss Sontag is a candid as well as gifted critic—so the definition, which I accept, is neither tendentious nor censorious.

Along these same lines, one can point out—as C. S. Lewis pointed out some years back—that it is no accident that in the history of all literatures obscene words, the so-called "four-letter words," have always been the vocabulary of farce or vituperation. The reason is clear; they reduce men and women to some of their mere bodily functions—they reduce man to his animal component, and such a reduction is an essential purpose of farce or vituperation.

Similarly, Lewis also suggested that it is not an accident that we have no offhand, colloquial, neutral terms—not in any Western European language at any rate—for our most private parts. The words we do use are either (a) nursery terms, (b) archaisms, (c) scientific terms, or (d) a term from the gutter (i.e., a demeaning term). Here I think the genius of language is telling us something important about man. It is telling us that man is an animal with a difference: he has a unique sense of privacy, and a unique capacity for shame when this privacy is violated. Our "private parts" are indeed private, and not merely because convention prescribes it. This particular convention is indigenous to the human race. In practically all primitive tribes, men and women cover their private parts; and in practically all primitive tribes, men and women do not copulate in public.

It may well be that Western society, in the latter half of the twentieth century, is experiencing a drastic change in sexual mores and sexual relationships. We have had many such "sexual revolutions" in the past—the bourgeois family and bourgeois ideas of sexual propriety were themselves established in the course of a revolution against eighteenth-century "licentiousness"—and we shall doubtless have others in the future. It is, however, highly improbable (to put it mildly) that what we are witnessing is the Final Revolution which will make sexual relations utterly un-problematic, permit us to dispense with any kind of ordered relationships between the sexes, and allow us freely to redefine the human condition. And so long as humanity has not reached that utopia, obscenity will remain a problem.

II

One of the reasons it will remain a problem is that obscenity is not merely about sex, any more than science fiction is about science. Science fiction, as every student of the genre knows, is a peculiar vision of power: what it is really about is politics. And obscenity is a peculiar vision of humanity: what it is really about is ethics and metaphysics.

Imagine a man—a well-known man, much in the public eye—in a hospital ward, dying an agonizing death. He is not in control of his bodily functions, so that his bladder and his bowels empty themselves of their own accord. His consciousness is overwhelmed and extinguished by pain, so that he cannot communicate with us, nor we with him. Now, it would be, technically, the easiest thing in the world to put a television camera in his hospital room and let the whole world witness this spectacle. We don't do it—at least we don't do it as yet—because we regard this as an *obscene* invasion of privacy. And what would make the spectacle obscene is that we would be witnessing the extinguishing of humanity in a human animal.

Incidentally, in the past our humanitarian crusaders against capital punishment understood this point very well. The abolitionist literature goes into great physical detail about what happens to a man when he is hanged or electrocuted or gassed. And their argument was—and is—that what happens is shockingly obscene, and that no civilized society should be responsible for perpetrating such obscenities, particularly since in the nature of the case there must be spectators to ascertain that this horror was indeed being perpetrated in fulfillment of the law.

Sex—like death—is an activity that is both animal and human. There are human sentiments and human ideals involved in this animal activity. But when sex is public, the viewer does not see—cannot see—the senti-ments and the ideals. He can only see the animal coupling. And that is why, when men and women make love, as we say, they prefer to be alone—because it is only when you are alone that you can make love, as distinct from merely copulating in an animal and casual way. And that, too, is why those who are voyeurs, if they are not irredeemably sick, also 16 feel ashamed at what they are witnessing. When sex is a public spectacle, a human relationship has been debased into a mere animal connection.

It is also worth noting that this making of sex into an obscenity is not a mutual and equal transaction but rather an act of exploitation by one of the partners—the male partner. I do not wish to get into the complicated question as to what, if any, are the essential differences—as distinct from conventional and cultural differences—between male and female. I do not claim to know the answer to that. But I do know—and I take it as a sign that has meaning—that pornography is, and always has been, a man's work; that women rarely write pornography; and that women tend to be indifferent consumers of pornography.[3] My own guess, by way of explanation, is that a woman's sexual experience is ordinarily more suffused with human emotion than is man's, that men are more easily satisfied with autoerotic activities, and that men can therefore more easily take a more "technocratic" view of sex and its pleasures. Perhaps this is not correct. But whatever the explanation, there can be no question that pornography is a form of "sexism," as the women's liberation movement calls it, and that the instinct of women's liberation has been unerring in perceiving that when pornography is perpetrated, it is perpetrated against them, as part of a conspiracy to deprive them of their full humanity.

But even if all this is granted, it might be said—and doubtless will be said—that I really ought not to be unduly concerned. Free competition in the cultural marketplace—it is argued by people who have never otherwise had a kind word to say for laissez-faire—will automatically dispose of the problem. The present fad for pornography and obscenity, it will be asserted, is just that, a fad. It will spend itself in the course of time; people will get bored with it, will be able to take it or leave it alone in a casual way, in a "mature way," and, in sum, I am being unnecessarily distressed about the whole business. The *New York Times*, in an editorial, concludes hopefully in this vein.

> In the end . . . the insensate pursuit of the urge to shock, carried from one excess to a more abysmal one, is bound to achieve its own antidote in total boredom. When there is no lower depth to descend to, ennui will erase the problem.

I would like to be able to go along with this line of reasoning, but I cannot. I think it is false, and for two reasons, the first psychological, the second political.

The basic psychological fact about pornography and obscenity is that 20 it appeals to and provokes a kind of sexual regression. The sexual pleasure one gets from pornography and obscenity is autoerotic and infantile; put

[3]There are, of course, a few exceptions. *L'Histoire d'O*, for instance, was written by a woman. It is unquestionably the most *melancholy* work of pornography ever written. And its theme is precisely the dehumanization accomplished by obscenity.

bluntly, it is a masturbatory exercise of the imagination, when it is not masturbation pure and simple. Now, people who masturbate do not get bored with masturbation, just as sadists don't get bored with sadism, and voyeurs don't get bored with voyeurism.

In other words, infantile sexuality is not only a permanent temptation for the adolescent or even the adult—it can quite easily become a permanent, self-reinforcing neurosis. It is because of an awareness of this possibility of regression toward the infantile condition, a regression which is always open to us, that all the codes of sexual conduct ever devised by the human race take such a dim view of autoerotic activities and try to discourage autoerotic fantasies. Masturbation is indeed a perfectly natural autoerotic activity, as so many sexologists blandly assure us today. And it is precisely because it is so perfectly natural that it can be so dangerous to the mature or maturing person, if it is not controlled or sublimated in some way. That is the true meaning of Portnoy's complaint.[4] Portnoy, you will recall, grows up to be a man who is incapable of having an adult sexual relationship with a woman; his sexuality remains fixed in an infantile mode, the prisoner of his autoerotic fantasies. Inevitably, Portnoy comes to think, in a perfectly *infantile* way, that it was all his mother's fault.

It is true that, in our time, some quite brilliant minds have come to the conclusion that a reversion to infantile sexuality is the ultimate mission and secret destiny of the human race. I am thinking in particular of Norman O. Brown, for whose writings I have the deepest respect. One of the reasons I respect them so deeply is that Mr. Brown is a serious thinker who is unafraid to face up to the radical consequences of his radical theories. Thus, Mr. Brown knows and says that for his kind of salvation to be achieved, humanity must annul the civilization it has created—not merely the civilization we have today, but all civilization—so as to be able to make the long descent backward into animal innocence.

And that is the point. What is at stake is civilization and humanity, nothing less. The idea that "everything is permitted," as Nietzsche put it, rests on the premise of nihilism and has nihilistic implications. I will not pretend that the case against nihilism and for civilization is an easy one to make. We are here confronting the most fundamental of philosophical questions, on the deepest levels. In short, the matter of pornography and obscenity is not a trivial one, and only superficial minds can take a bland and untroubled view of it.

In this connection, I must also point out those who are primarily 24 against censorship on liberal grounds tell us not to take pornography or obscenity seriously, while those who are for pornography and obscenity on radical grounds take it very seriously indeed. I believe the radicals— writers like Susan Sontag, Herbert Marcuse, Norman O. Brown, and even Jerry Rubin—are right, and the liberals are wrong. I also believe that those

---

[4]**Portnoy's complaint** Title of a novel (1969) by Philip Roth. [Editors' note]

young radicals at Berkeley, some seven years ago, who provoked a major confrontation over the public use of obscene words, showed a brilliant political instinct. And once Mark Rudd could publicly ascribe to the president of Columbia a notoriously obscene relationship to his mother, without provoking any kind of reaction, the S.D.S.[5] had already won the day. The occupation of Columbia's buildings merely ratified their victory. Men who show themselves unwilling to defend civilization against nihilism are not going to be either resolute or effective in defending the university against anything.

III

I am already touching upon a political aspect of pornography when I suggest that it is inherently and purposefully subversive of civilization and its institutions. But there is another and more specifically political aspect, which has to do with the relationship of pornography and/or obscenity to democracy, and especially to the quality of public life on which democratic government ultimately rests.

Though the phrase "the quality of life" trips easily from so many lips these days, it tends to be one of those clichés with many trivial meanings and no large, serious one. Sometimes it merely refers to such externals as the enjoyment of cleaner air, cleaner water, cleaner streets. At other times it refers to the merely private enjoyment of music, painting, or literature. Rarely does it have anything to do with the way the citizen in a democracy views himself—his obligations, his intentions, his ultimate self-definition.

Instead, what I would call the "managerial" conception of democracy is the predominant opinion among political scientists, sociologists, and economists, and has, through the untiring efforts of these scholars, become the conventional journalistic opinion as well. The root idea behind this "managerial" conception is that democracy is a "political system" (as they say) which can be adequately defined in terms of—can be fully reduced to—its mechanical arrangements. Democracy is then seen as a set of rules and procedures, and *nothing but* a set of rules and procedures, whereby majority rule and minority rights are reconciled into a state of equilibrium. If everyone follows these rules and procedures, then a democracy is in working order. I think this is a fair description of the democratic idea that currently prevails in academia. One can also fairly say that it is now the liberal idea of democracy par excellence.

I cannot help but feel that there is something ridiculous about being 28 this kind of democrat, and I must further confess to having a sneaking sympathy for those of our young radicals who also find it ridiculous. The

[5]S.D.S. Students for a Democratic Society, a radical group active in the 1960s. [Editors' note]

absurdity is the absurdity of idolatry, of taking the symbolic for the real, the means for the end. The purpose of democracy cannot possibly be the endless functioning of its own political machinery. The purpose of any political regime is to achieve some version of the good life and the good society. It is not at all difficult to imagine a perfectly functioning democracy which answers all questions except one—namely, why should anyone of intelligence and spirit care a fig for it?

There is, however, an older idea of democracy—one which was fairly common until about the beginning of this century—for which the conception of the quality of public life is absolutely crucial. This idea starts from the proposition that democracy is a form of self-government, and that if you want it to be a meritorious polity, you have to care about what kind of people govern it. Indeed, it puts the matter more strongly and declares that if you want self-government, you are only entitled to it if that "self" is worthy of governing. There is no inherent right to self-government if it means that such government is vicious, mean, squalid, and debased. Only a dogmatist and a fanatic, an idolater of democratic machinery, could approve of self-government under such conditions.

And because the desirability of self-government depends on the character of the people who govern, the older idea of democracy was very solicitous of the condition of this character. It was solicitous of the individual self, and felt an obligation to educate it into what used to be called "republican virtue." And it was solicitous of that collective self which we call public opinion and which, in a democracy, governs us collectively. Perhaps in some respects it was nervously oversolicitous—that would not be surprising. But the main thing is that it cared, cared not merely about the machinery of democracy but about the quality of life that this machinery might generate.

And because it cared, this older idea of democracy had no problem in principle with pornography and/or obscenity. It censored them—and it did so with a perfect clarity of mind and a perfectly clear conscience. It was not about to permit people capriciously to corrupt themselves. Or, to put it more precisely: In this version of democracy, the people took some care not to let themselves be governed by the more infantile and irrational parts of themselves.

I have, it may be noticed, uttered that dreadful word *censorship*. And 32 I am not about to back away from it. If you think pornography and/or obscenity is a serious problem, you have to be for censorship. I will go even further and say that if you want to prevent pornography and/or obscenity from becoming a problem, you have to be for censorship. And lest there be any misunderstanding as to what I am saying, I will put it as bluntly as possible: If you care for the quality of life in our American democracy, then you have to be for censorship.

But can a liberal be for censorship? Unless one assumes that being a liberal *must* mean being indifferent to the quality of American life, then the answer has to be yes, a liberal can be for censorship—but he ought to favor a liberal form of censorship.

Is that a contradiction in terms? I do not think so. We have no problem in contrasting *repressive* laws governing alcohol and drugs and tobacco with laws *regulating* (i.e., discouraging the sale of) alcohol and drugs and tobacco. Laws encouraging temperance are not the same thing as laws that have as their goal prohibition or abolition. We have not made the smoking of cigarettes a criminal offense. We have, however, and with good liberal conscience, prohibited cigarette advertising on television, and may yet, again with good liberal conscience, prohibit it in newspapers and magazines. The idea of restricting individual freedom, in a liberal way, is not at all unfamiliar to us.

I therefore see no reason why we should not be able to distinguish repressive censorship from liberal censorship of the written and spoken word. In Britain, until a few years ago, you could perform almost any play you wished, but certain plays, judged to be obscene, had to be performed in private theatrical clubs, which were deemed to have a "serious" interest in theater. In the United States, all of us who grew up using public libraries are familiar with the circumstances under which certain books could be circulated only to adults, while still other books had to be read in the library reading room, under the librarian's skeptical eye. In both cases, a small minority that was willing to make a serious effort to see an obscene play or read an obscene book could do so. But the impact of obscenity was circumscribed and the quality of public life was only marginally affected.[6]

I am not saying it is easy in practice to sustain a distinction between liberal and repressive censorship, especially in the public realm of a democracy, where popular opinion is so vulnerable to demagoguery. Moreover, an acceptable system of liberal censorship is likely to be exceedingly difficult to devise in the United States today, because our educated classes, upon whose judgment a liberal censorship must rest, are so convinced that there is no such thing as a problem of obscenity, or even that there is no such thing as obscenity at all. But, to counterbalance this, there is the further, fortunate truth that the tolerable margin for error is quite large, and single mistakes or single injustices are not all that important.

This possibility of error, of course, occasions much distress among artists and academics. It is a fact, one that cannot and should not be denied, that any system of censorship is bound, upon occasion, to treat unjustly a particular work of art—to find pornography where there is only gentle eroticism, to find obscenity where none really exists, or to find both where its existence ought to be tolerated because it serves a larger moral

[6]It is fairly predictable that someone is going to object that this point of view is "elitist"— that, under a system of liberal censorship, the rich will have privileged access to pornography and obscenity. Yes, of course, they will—just as, at present, the rich have privileged access to heroin if they want it. But one would have to be an egalitarian maniac to object to this state of affairs on the grounds of equality.

purpose. Though most works of art are not obscene, and though most obscenity has nothing to do with art, there are some few works of art that are, at least in part, pornographic and/or obscene. There are also some few works of art that are in the special category of the comic-ironic "bawdy" (Boccaccio, Rabelais). It is such works of art that are likely to suffer at the hands of the censor. That is the price one has to be prepared to pay for censorship—even liberal censorship.

But just how high is this price? If you believe, as so many artists seem to believe today, that art is the only sacrosanct activity in our profane and vulgar world—that any man who designates himself an artist thereby acquires a sacred office—then obviously censorship is an intolerable form of sacrilege. But for those of us who do not subscribe to this religion of art, the costs of censorship do not seem so high at all.

If you look at the history of American or English literature, there is precious little damage you can point to as a consequence of the censorship that prevailed throughout most of that history. Very few works of literature—of real literary merit, I mean—ever were suppressed; and those that were, were not suppressed for long. Nor have I noticed, now that censorship of the written word has to all intents and purposes ceased in this country, that hitherto suppressed or repressed masterpieces are flooding the market. Yes, we can now read *Fanny Hill* and the Marquis de Sade. Or, to be more exact, we can now openly purchase them, since many people were able to read them even though they were publicly banned, which is as it should be under a liberal censorship. So how much have literature and the arts gained from the fact that we can all now buy them over the counter, that, indeed, we are all now encouraged to buy them over the counter? They have not gained much that I can see.

And one might also ask a question that is almost never raised: how 40 much has literature lost from the fact that everything is now permitted? It has lost quite a bit, I should say. In a free market, Gresham's law can work for books or theater as efficiently as it does for coinage—driving out the good, establishing the debased. The cultural market in the United States today is being preempted by dirty books, dirty movies, dirty theater. A pornographic novel has a far better chance of being published today than a nonpornographic one, and quite a few pretty good novels are not being published at all simply because they are not pornographic, and are therefore less likely to sell. Our cultural condition has not improved as a result of the new freedom. American cultural life wasn't much to brag about twenty years ago; today one feels ashamed for it.

Just one last point which I dare not leave untouched. If we start censoring pornography or obscenity, shall we not inevitably end up censoring political opinion? A lot of people seem to think this would be the case—which only shows the power of doctrinaire thinking over reality. We had censorship of pornography and obscenity for 150 years, until almost yesterday, and I am not aware that freedom of opinion in this country was in any way diminished as a consequence of this fact. Fortunately for those of us who are liberal, freedom is not indivisible. If it were, the case for liberalism would be indistinguishable from the case for anarchy; and they are two very different things.

But I must repeat and emphasize: what kind of laws we pass governing pornography and obscenity, what kind of censorship—or, since we are still a federal nation, what kinds of censorship—we institute in our various localities may indeed be difficult matters to cope with; nevertheless the real issue is one of principle. I myself subscribe to a liberal view of the enforcement problem: I think that pornography should be illegal *and* available to anyone who wants it so badly as to make a pretty strenuous effort to get it. We have lived with under-the-counter pornography for centuries now, in a fairly comfortable way. But the issue of principle, of whether it should be over or under the counter, has to be settled before we can reflect on the advantages and disadvantages of alternative modes of censorship. I think the settlement we are living under now, in which obscenity and democracy are regarded as equals, is wrong; I believe it is inherently unstable; I think it will, in the long run, be incompatible with any authentic concern for the quality of life in our democracy.

Questions and Suggestions for Writing

1. If you find some of Kristol's sentences particularly effective as examples of persuasive writing, copy out two or three and then explain *why* they are effective.

2. In his second paragraph Kristol refers to Eugene O'Neill's *Desire under the Elms* (1924) and James Joyce's *Ulysses* (1922). If you have read either of these works, write a paragraph in which you explain why some members of an earlier generation might have wanted to censor them.

3. In his second paragraph Kristol implies that a play ought not to show such an act as a homosexual rape. Is it relevant to inquire about the context of the scene? That is, is it relevant to ask whether the rape is presented as acceptable, or is presented as abominable? Or is the presentation of homosexual rape inherently unacceptable?

4. In paragraph 4 Kristol says, "If you believe that no one was ever corrupted by a book, you have also to believe that no one was ever improved by a book (or a play or a movie). You have to believe, in other words, that all art is morally trivial and that, consequently, all education is morally irrelevant." If you think a reply can be made, make it, perhaps in an essay of 500 words.

5. In paragraph 6 Kristol says that as civil libertarians we are all hypocrites, and he cites our presumed intolerance of an exhibition in which someone would really commit suicide. Jot down the chief arguments you would use in arguing for or against allowing such an exhibition.

6. Is Kristol's distinction between pornography and erotic art clear to you? If so, rephrase it in your own words. If not, what makes it obscure, and how could it be made clearer?

7. In paragraphs 33 and 34, arguing for "a liberal form of censorship," Kristol makes a distinction between "*repressive* laws" and "laws *regulating* (i.e., discouraging the sale of) alcohol and drugs and tobacco." He points out that regulatory laws prohibit cigarette advertisements on television. What forms might laws "regulating" but not "repressing" pornography take? Would you favor such laws? Why? Write an essay of 500 to 750 words explaining how "liberal censorship" might work, and on what moral principles it is supposedly based.

8. Kristol admits (para. 37) that "any system of censorship is bound, upon occasion, to treat unjustly a particular work of art." But this, he says, "is the price one has to be prepared to pay." Are you prepared to pay it? Why?

9. In the eighteenth century the German writer and critic Gotthold Ephraim Lessing wrote: "The object of art is pleasure, and pleasure is not indispensable. What kind and what degree of pleasure shall be permitted may justly depend on the lawgiver." Taking this as your text, but drawing also on Kristol's essay, write an essay of 500 words, supporting or rebutting Lessing.

10. Look again at paragraph 38, and analyze Kristol's persuasive methods. How does his choice of words help to support his point?

Susan Brownmiller

Let's Put Pornography Back in the Closet

Free speech is one of the great foundations on which our democracy rests. I am old enough to remember the Hollywood Ten, the screenwriters who went to jail in the late 1940s because they refused to testify before a congressional committee about their political affiliations. They tried to use the First Amendment as a defense, but they went to jail because in those days there were few civil liberties lawyers around who cared to champion the First Amendment right to free speech, when the speech concerned the Communist party.

The Hollywood Ten were correct in claiming the First Amendment. Its high purpose is the protection of unpopular ideas and political dissent.

Susan Brownmiller (b. 1935), a graduate of Cornell University, is the founder of Women against Pornography, and the author of several books, including Against Our Will: Men, Women, and Rape *(1975). The essay reprinted here is from* Take Back the Night *(1980), a collection of essays edited by Laura Lederer. The book has been called "the manifesto of antipornography feminism."*

In the dark, cold days of the 1950s, few civil libertarians were willing to declare themselves First Amendment absolutists. But in the brighter, though frantic, days of the 1960s, the principle of protecting unpopular political speech was gradually strengthened.

It is fair to say now that the battle has largely been won. Even the American Nazi party has found itself the beneficiary of the dedicated, tireless work of the American Civil Liberties Union. But—and please notice the quotation marks coming up—"To equate the free and robust exchange of ideas and political debate with commercial exploitation of obscene material demeans the grand conception of the First Amendment and its high purposes in the historic struggle for freedom. It is a misuse of the great guarantees of free speech and free press."

I didn't say that, although I wish I had, for I think the words are   4 thrilling. Chief Justice Warren Burger said it in 1973, in the United States Supreme Court's majority opinion in *Miller v. California*. During the same decades that the right to political free speech was being strengthened in the courts, the nation's obscenity laws also were undergoing extensive revision.

It's amazing to recall that in 1934 the question of whether James Joyce's *Ulysses* should be banned as pornographic actually went before the Court. The battle to protect *Ulysses* as a work of literature with redeeming social value was won. In later decades, Henry Miller's *Tropic* books, *Lady Chatterley's Lover* and the *Memoirs of Fanny Hill* also were adjudged not obscene. These decisions have been important to me. As the author of *Against Our Will*, a study of the history of rape that does contain explicit sexual material, I shudder to think how my book would have fared if James Joyce, D. H. Lawrence, and Henry Miller hadn't gone before me.

I am not a fan of *Chatterley* or the *Tropic* books, I should quickly mention. They are not to my literary taste, nor do I think they represent female sexuality with any degree of accuracy. But I would hardly suggest that we ban them. Such a suggestion wouldn't get very far anyway. The battle to protect these books is ancient history. Time does march on, quite methodically. What, then, is unlawfully obscene, and what does the First Amendment have to do with it?

In the Miller case of 1973 (not Henry Miller, by the way, but a porn distributor who sent unsolicited stuff through the mails), the Court came up with new guidelines that it hoped would strengthen obscenity laws by giving more power to the states. What it did in actuality was throw everything into confusion. It set up a three-part test by which materials can be adjudged obscene. The materials are obscene if they depict patently offensive, hard-core sexual conduct; lack serious scientific, literary, artistic, or political value; and appeal to the prurient interest of an average person—as measured by contemporary community standards.

"Patently offensive," "prurient interest," and "hard-core" are indeed   8 words to conjure with. "Contemporary community standards" are what we're trying to redefine. The feminist objection to pornography is not based on prurience, which the dictionary defines as lustful, itching desire. We are not opposed to sex and desire, with or without the itch, and we certainly believe that explicit sexual material has its place in literature, art, science, and education. Here we part company rather swiftly with old-line conservatives who don't want sex education in the high schools, for example.

No, the feminist objection to pornography is based on our belief that pornography represents hatred of women, that pornography's intent is to humiliate, degrade, and dehumanize the female body for the purpose of erotic stimulation and pleasure. We are unalterably opposed to the presentation of the female body being stripped, bound, raped, tortured, mutilated, and murdered in the name of commercial entertainment and free speech.

These images, which are standard pornographic fare, have nothing to do with the hallowed right of political dissent. They have everything to do with the creation of a cultural climate in which a rapist feels he is merely giving in to a normal urge and a woman is encouraged to believe that sexual masochism is healthy, liberated fun. Justice Potter Stewart once said about hard-core pornography, "You know it when you see it," and that certainly used to be true. In the good old days, pornography looked awful. It was cheap and sleazy, and there was no mistaking it for art.

Nowadays, since the porn industry has become a multimillion dollar business, visual technology has been employed in its service. Pornographic movies are skillfully filmed and edited, pornographic still shots using the newest tenets of good design artfully grace the covers of *Hustler*, *Penthouse*, and *Playboy*, and the public—and the courts—are sadly confused.

The Supreme Court neglected to define "hard-core" in the Miller   12 decision. This was a mistake. If "hard-core" refers only to explicit sexual intercourse, then that isn't good enough. When women or children or men—no matter how artfully—are shown tortured or terrorized in the service of sex, that's obscene. And "patently offensive," I would hope, to our "contemporary community standards."

Justice William O. Douglas wrote in his dissent to the Miller case that no one is "compelled to look." This is hardly true. To buy a paper at the corner newsstand is to subject oneself to a forcible immersion in pornography, to be demeaned by an array of dehumanized, chopped-up parts of the female anatomy, packaged like cuts of meat at the supermarket. I happen to like my body and I work hard at the gym to keep it in good shape, but I am embarrassed for my body and for the bodies of all women when I see the fragmented parts of us so frivolously, and so flagrantly, displayed.

Some constitutional theorists (Justice Douglas was one) have maintained that any obscenity law is a serious abridgement of free speech. Others (and Justice Earl Warren was one) have maintained that the First Amendment was never intended to protect obscenity. We live quite compatibly with a host of free-speech abridgements. There are restraints against false and misleading advertising or statements—shouting "fire" without cause in a crowded movie theater, etc.—that do not threaten, but strengthen, our societal values. Restrictions on the public display of pornography belong in this category.

The distinction between permission to publish and permission to display publicly is an essential one and one which I think consonant with First Amendment principles. Justice Burger's words which I quoted above support this without question. We are not saying "Smash the presses" or "Ban the bad ones," but simply "Get the stuff out of our sight." Let the legislatures decide—using realistic and humane contemporary community standards—what can be displayed and what cannot. The courts, after all, will be the final arbiters.

Questions and Suggestions for Writing

1. Objecting to Justice Douglas's remark that no one is "'compelled to look'" (para. 13), Brownmiller says, "This is hardly true. To buy a paper at the corner newsstand is to subject oneself to forcible immersion in pornography, to be demeaned by an array of dehumanized, chopped-up parts of the female anatomy, packaged like cuts of meat at the supermarket." Is this true at your local newsstand, or are the sex magazines kept in one place, relatively remote from the newspapers?

2. When Brownmiller attempts to restate the "three-part test" for obscenity established by the Supreme Court in *Miller v. California*, she writes (para. 7): "The materials are obscene if they depart . . ." and so on. She should have written: "The materials are obscene if and only if they depart . . ." and so on. Explain what is wrong here with her "if," and why "if and only if" is needed.

3. In her next-to-last paragraph, Brownmiller reminds us that we already live quite comfortably with some "free-speech abridgements." The examples she gives are that we may not falsely shout "Fire" in a crowded theater, and we may not issue misleading advertisements. Do you think that these widely accepted restrictions are valid evidence in arguing in behalf of limiting the display of what Brownmiller considers pornography? Why?

4. Brownmiller insists that defenders of the First Amendment, who will surely oppose laws that interfere with the freedom to publish, need not go on to condemn laws that regulate the freedom to "display publicly" pornographic publications. Do you agree? Suppose a publisher insists he cannot sell his product at a profit unless he is permitted to display it to advantage, and so restriction on the latter amounts to interference with his freedom to publish. How might Brownmiller reply?

5. In her last paragraph Brownmiller says that "contemporary community standards" should be decisive. Can it be argued that, because standards vary from one community to another, and from time to time even in the same place, her recommendation subjects the rights of a minority to the whims of a majority?

The Bill of Rights, after all, was supposed to safeguard constitutional rights from the possible tyranny of the majority.

6. How does Brownmiller's objection to pornography agree and disagree with the position taken by Irving Kristol in the preceding selection?

7. When Brownmiller accuses "the public and the courts" of being "sadly confused," what does she think they are "confused" about? The definition of "pornography" or "obscenity"? The effects of such literature on men and women? Or is it something else?

14

What Is the Ideal Society?

Thomas More

From *Utopia*

[A DAY IN UTOPIA]

And now for their working conditions. Well, there's one job they all
do, irrespective of sex, and that's farming. It's part of every child's education. They learn the principles of agriculture at school, and they're taken

---

*The son of a prominent London lawyer, More (1478–1535) served as a page in
the household of the Archbishop of Canterbury, went to Oxford, and then studied
law in London. More's charm, brilliance, and gentle manner caused Erasmus, the
great Dutch humanist who became his friend during a visit to London, to write to
a friend: "Did nature ever create anything kinder, sweeter, or more harmonious
than the character of Thomas More?"*

*More served in Parliament, became a diplomat, and after holding several impor-
tant positions in the government of Henry VIII rose to become Lord Chancellor.
But when Henry married Anne Boleyn, broke from the Church of Rome, and
established himself as head of the Church of England, More refused to subscribe to
the Act of Succession and Supremacy. Condemned to death as a traitor, he still
refused to accept Henry as head of the church, and so was executed in 1535,
nominally for treason but really because he would not recognize the king rather
than the pope as the head of his church. A moment before the ax fell, More
displayed a bit of the whimsy for which he was known: When he put his head on
the block, he brushed his beard aside, commenting that his beard had done no
offense to the king. In 1886 the Roman Catholic Church beatified More, and in*

for regular outings into the fields near the town, where they not only watch farm work being done, but also do some themselves, as a form of exercise.

Besides farming which, as I say, is everybody's job, each person is taught a special trade of his own. He may be trained to process wool or flax, or he may become a stonemason, a blacksmith, or a carpenter. Those are the only trades that employ any considerable quantity of labor. They have no tailors or dressmakers, since everyone on the island wears the same sort of clothes—except that they vary slightly according to sex and marital status—and the fashion never changes. These clothes are quite pleasant to look at, they allow free movement of the limbs, they're equally suitable for hot and cold weather—and the great thing is, they're all home-made. So everybody learns one of the other trades I mentioned, and by everybody I mean the women as well as the men—though the weaker sex are given the lighter jobs, like spinning and weaving, while the men do the heavier ones.

Most children are brought up to do the same work as their parents, since they tend to have a natural feeling for it. But if a child fancies some other trade, he's adopted into a family that practices it. Of course, great care is taken, not only by the father, but also by the local authorities, to see that the foster father is a decent, respectable type. When you've learned one trade properly, you can, if you like, get permission to learn another— and when you're an expert in both, you can practice whichever you prefer, unless the other one is more essential to the public.

The chief business of the Stywards[1]—in fact, practically their only   4
business—is to see that nobody sits around doing nothing, but that everyone gets on with his job. They don't wear people out, though, by keeping them hard at work from early morning till late at night, like cart horses.

---

[1]**Stywards** In Utopia, each group of thirty households elects a styward; each town has two hundred stywards, who elect the mayor. [All notes are by the editors.]

1935, the four-hundredth anniversary of his death, it canonized him as St. Thomas More.

More wrote Utopia *(1514–1515) in Latin, the international language of the day. The book's name, however, is Greek for "no place" (ou topos), with a pun on "good place" (eu topos).* Utopia *owes something to Plato's* Republic, *and something to then-popular accounts of voyagers such as Amerigo Vespucci.* Utopia *purports to record an account given by a traveler named Hytholodaeus (Greek for "learned in nonsense"), who allegedly visited Utopia. The work is playful, but it is also serious. In truth, it is hard to know exactly where it is serious, and how serious it is. One inevitably wonders, for example, if More the devoted Roman Catholic could really have advocated euthanasia. And could More the persecutor of heretics really have approved of the religious tolerance practiced in Utopia? Is he perhaps in effect saying, "Let's see what reason, unaided by Christian revelation, can tell us about an ideal society"? But if so is he nevertheless also saying, very strongly, that Christian countries, though blessed with the revelation of Christ's teachings, are far behind these unenlightened pagans?* Utopia *has been widely praised by all sorts of readers—from Roman Catholics to communists—but for all sorts of reasons.*

The selection here is about one twelfth of the book.

That's just slavery—and yet that's what life is like for the working classes nearly everywhere else in the world. In Utopia they have a six-hour working day—three hours in the morning, then lunch—then a two-hour break—then three more hours in the afternoon, followed by supper. They go to bed at 8 P.M., and sleep for eight hours. All the rest of the twenty-four they're free to do what they like—not to waste their time in idleness or self-indulgence, but to make good use of it in some congenial activity. Most people spend these free periods on further education, for there are public lectures first thing every morning. Attendance is quite voluntary, except for those picked out for academic training, but men and women of all classes go crowding in to hear them—I mean, different people go to different lectures, just as the spirit moves them. However, there's nothing to stop you from spending this extra time on your trade, if you want to. Lots of people do, if they haven't the capacity for intellectual work, and are much admired for such public-spirited behavior.

After supper they have an hour's recreation, either in the gardens or in the communal dining-halls, according to the time of year. Some people practice music, others just talk. They've never heard of anything so silly and demoralizing as dice, but they have two games rather like chess. The first is a sort of arithmetical contest, in which certain numbers "take" others. The second is a pitched battle between virtues and vices, which illustrates most ingeniously how vices tend to conflict with one another, but to combine against virtues. It also shows which vices are opposed to which virtues, how much strength vices can muster for a direct assault, what indirect tactics they employ, what help virtues need to overcome vices, what are the best methods of evading their attacks, and what ultimately determines the victory of one side or the other.

But here's a point that requires special attention, or you're liable to get the wrong idea. Since they only work a six-hour day, you may think there must be a shortage of essential goods. On the contrary, those six hours are enough, and more than enough to produce plenty of everything that's needed for a comfortable life. And you'll understand why it is, if you reckon up how large a proportion of the population in other countries is totally unemployed. First you have practically all the women—that gives you nearly 50 percent for a start. And in countries where the women *do* work, the men tend to lounge about instead. Then there are all the priests, and members of so-called religious orders—how much work do they do? Add all the rich, especially the landowners, popularly known as nobles and gentlemen. Include their domestic staffs—I mean those gangs of armed ruffians that I mentioned before. Finally, throw in all the beggars who are perfectly hale and hearty, but pretend to be ill as an excuse for being lazy. When you've counted them up, you'll be surprised to find how few people actually produce what the human race consumes.

And now just think how few of these few people are doing essential work—for where money is the only standard of value, there are bound to be dozens of unnecessary trades carried on, which merely supply luxury goods or entertainment. Why, even if the existing labor force were distributed among the few trades really needed to make life reasonably comfortable, there'd be so much overproduction that prices would fall too low for the workers to earn a living. Whereas, if you took all those engaged in nonessential trades, and all who are too lazy to work—each of whom consumes twice as much of the products of other people's labor as any of the producers themselves—if you put the whole lot of them on to something useful, you'd soon see how few hours' work a day would be amply sufficient to supply all the necessities and comforts of life—to which you might add all real and natural forms of pleasure.

[THE HOUSEHOLD]

But let's get back to their social organization. Each household, as I said, comes under the authority of the oldest male. Wives are subordinate to their husbands, children to their parents, and younger people generally to their elders. Every town is divided into four districts of equal size, each with its own shopping center in the middle of it. There the products of every household are collected in warehouses, and then distributed according to type among various shops. When the head of a household needs anything for himself or his family, he just goes to one of these shops and asks for it. And whatever he asks for, he's allowed to take away without any sort of payment, either in money or in kind. After all, why shouldn't he? There's more than enough of everything to go round, so there's no risk of his asking for more than he needs—for why should anyone want to start hoarding, when he knows he'll never have to go short of anything? No living creature is naturally greedy, except from fear of want—or in the case of human beings, from vanity, the notion that you're better than people if you can display more superfluous property than they can. But there's no scope for that sort of thing in Utopia.

[UTOPIAN BELIEFS]

The Utopians fail to understand why anyone should be so fascinated by the dull gleam of a tiny bit of stone, when he has all the stars in the sky to look at—or how anyone can be silly enough to think himself better than other people, because his clothes are made of finer woollen thread than theirs. After all, those fine clothes were once worn by a sheep, and they never turned it into anything better than a sheep.

Nor can they understand why a totally useless substance like gold should now, all over the world, be considered far more important than human beings, who gave it such value as it has, purely for their own convenience. The result is that a man with about as much mental agility as a lump of lead or a block of wood, a man whose utter stupidity is paralleled only by his immorality, can have lots of good, intelligent people at his beck and call, just because he happens to possess a large pile of gold coins. And if by some freak of fortune or trick of the law—two equally effective methods of turning things upside down—the said coins were suddenly transferred to the most worthless member of his domestic staff, you'd soon see the present owner trotting after his money, like an extra piece of currency, and becoming his own servant's servant. But what puzzles and disgusts the Utopians even more is the idiotic way some people have of practically worshipping a rich man, not because they owe him money or are otherwise in his power, but simply because he's rich—although they know perfectly well that he's far too mean to let a single penny come their way, so long as he's alive to stop it.

They get these ideas partly from being brought up under a social system which is directly opposed to that type of nonsense, and partly from their reading and education. Admittedly, no one's allowed to become a full-time student, except for the very few in each town who appear as children to possess unusual gifts, outstanding intelligence, and a special aptitude for academic research. But every child receives a primary education, and most men and women go on educating themselves all their lives during those free periods that I told you about. . . .

In ethics they discuss the same problems as we do. Having dis- 12 tinguished between three types of "good," psychological, physiological, and environmental, they proceed to ask whether the term is strictly applicable to all of them, or only to the first. They also argue about such things as virtue and pleasure. But their chief subject of dispute is the nature of human happiness—on what factor or factors does it depend? Here they seem rather too much inclined to take a hedonistic view, for according to them human happiness consists largely or wholly in pleasure. Surprisingly enough, they defend this self-indulgent doctrine by arguments drawn from religion—a thing normally associated with a more serious view of life, if not with gloomy asceticism. You see, in all their discussions of happiness they invoke certain religious principles to supplement the operations of reason, which they think otherwise ill-equipped to identify true happiness.

The first principle is that every soul is immortal, and was created by a kind God, Who meant it to be happy. The second is that we shall be rewarded or punished in the next world for our good or bad behavior in this one. Although these are religious principles, the Utopians find rational grounds for accepting them. For suppose you didn't accept them? In that case, they say, any fool could tell you what you ought to do. You should go all out for your own pleasure, irrespective of right and wrong. You'd merely have to make sure that minor pleasures didn't interfere with major ones, and avoid the type of pleasure that has painful aftereffects. For what's the sense of struggling to be virtuous, denying yourself the pleasant things of life, and deliberately making yourself uncomfortable, if there's nothing you hope to gain by it? And what *can* you hope to gain by it, if you receive no compensation after death for a thoroughly unpleasant, that is, a thoroughly miserable life?

Not that they identify happiness with every type of pleasure—only with the higher ones. Nor do they identify it with virtue—unless they belong to a quite different school of thought. According to the normal view, happiness is the *summum bonum*[2] toward which we're naturally impelled by virtue—which in their definition means following one's natural impulses, as God meant us to do. But this includes obeying the instinct to be reasonable in our likes and dislikes. And reason also teaches us, first to love and reverence Almighty God, to Whom we owe our existence and our potentiality for happiness, and secondly to get through life as comfortably and cheerfully as we can, and help all other members of our species to do so too.

The fact is, even the sternest ascetic tends to be slightly inconsistent in his condemnation of pleasure. He may sentence *you* to a life of hard labor, inadequate sleep, and general discomfort, but he'll also tell you to do your best to ease the pains and privations of others. He'll regard all such attempts to improve the human situation as laudable acts of humanity— for obviously nothing could be more humane, or more natural for a human being, than to relieve other people's sufferings, put an end to their miseries, and restore their *joie de vivre*, that is, their capacity for pleasure. So why shouldn't it be equally natural to do the same thing for oneself?

Either it's a bad thing to enjoy life, in other words, to experience 16 pleasure—in which case you shouldn't help anyone to do it, but should try to save the whole human race from such a frightful fate—or else, if it's good for other people, and you're not only allowed, but positively obliged to make it possible for them, why shouldn't charity begin at home? After all, you've a duty to yourself as well as to your neighbor, and, if Nature says you must be kind to others, she can't turn round the next moment and say you must be cruel to yourself. The Utopians therefore regard the enjoyment of life—that is, pleasure—as the natural object of all human efforts, and natural, as they define it, is synonymous with virtuous. However, Nature also wants us to help one another to enjoy life, for the very good reason that no human being has a monopoly of her affections. She's equally anxious for the welfare of every member of the species. So of course she tells us to make quite sure that we don't pursue our own interests at the expense of other people's.

On this principle they think it right to keep one's promises in private life, and also to obey public laws for regulating the distribution of "goods"—by which I mean the raw materials of pleasure—provided such

---

[2]**summum bonum** Latin for "the highest good."

laws have been properly made by a wise ruler, or passed by common consent of a whole population, which has not been subjected to any form of violence or deception. Within these limits they say it's sensible to consult one's own interests, and a moral duty to consult those of the community as well. It's wrong to deprive someone else of a pleasure so that you can enjoy one yourself, but to deprive yourself of a pleasure so that you can add to someone else's enjoyment is an act of humanity by which you always gain more than you lose. For one thing, such benefits are usually repaid in kind. For another, the mere sense of having done somebody a kindness, and so earned his affection and goodwill, produces a spiritual satisfaction which far outweighs the loss of a physical one. And lastly—a belief that comes easily to a religious mind—God will reward us for such small sacrifices of momentary pleasure, by giving us an eternity of perfect joy. Thus they argue that, in the final analysis, pleasure is the ultimate happiness which all human beings have in view, even when they're acting most virtuously.

Pleasure they define as any state or activity, physical or mental, which is naturally enjoyable. The operative word is *naturally*. According to them, we're impelled by reason as well as an instinct to enjoy ourselves in any natural way which doesn't hurt other people, interfere with greater pleasures, or cause unpleasant aftereffects. But human beings have entered into an idiotic conspiracy to call some things enjoyable which are naturally nothing of the kind—as though facts were as easily changed as definitions. Now the Utopians believe that, so far from contributing to happiness, this type of thing makes happiness impossible—because, once you get used to it, you lose all capacity for real pleasure, and are merely obsessed by illusory forms of it. Very often these have nothing pleasant about them at all—in fact, most of them are thoroughly disagreeable. But they appeal so strongly to perverted tastes that they come to be reckoned not only among the major pleasures of life, but even among the chief reasons for living.

In the category of illusory pleasure addicts they include the kind of person I mentioned before, who thinks himself better than other people because he's better dressed than they are. Actually he's just as wrong about his clothes as he is about himself. From a practical point of view, why is it better to be dressed in fine woollen thread than in coarse? But he's got it into his head that fine thread is naturally superior, and that wearing it somehow increases his own value. So he feels entitled to far more respect than he'd ever dare to hope for, if he were less expensively dressed, and is most indignant if he fails to get it.

Talking of respect, isn't it equally idiotic to attach such importance to 20 a lot of empty gestures which do nobody any good? For what real pleasure can you get out of the sight of a bared head or a bent knee? Will it cure the rheumatism in your own knee, or make you any less weak in the head? Of course, the great believers in this type of artificial pleasure are those who pride themselves on their "nobility." Nowadays that merely means that they happen to belong to a family which has been rich for several generations, preferably in landed property. And yet they feel every bit as "noble" even if they've failed to inherit any of the said property, or if they have inherited it and then frittered it all away.

Then there's another type of person I mentioned before, who has a passion for jewels, and feels practically superhuman if he manages to get hold of a rare one, especially if it's a kind that's considered particularly precious in his country and period—for the value of such things varies according to where and when you live. But he's so terrified of being taken in by appearances that he refuses to buy any jewel until he's stripped off all the gold and inspected it in the nude. And even then he won't buy it without a solemn assurance and a written guarantee from the jeweler that the stone is genuine. But my dear sir, why shouldn't a fake give you just as much pleasure, if you can't, with your own eyes, distinguish it from a real one? It makes no difference to you whether it's genuine or not—any more than it would to a blind man!

And now, what about those people who accumulate superfluous wealth, for no better purpose than to enjoy looking at it? Is their pleasure a real one, or merely a form of delusion? The opposite type of psychopath buries his gold, so that he'll never be able to use it, and may never even see it again. In fact, he deliberately loses it in his anxiety not to lose it—for what can you call it but lost, when it's put back into the earth, where it's no good to him, or probably to anyone else? And yet he's tremendously happy when he's got it stowed away. Now, apparently, he can stop worrying. But suppose the money is stolen, and ten years later he dies without ever knowing it has gone. Then for a whole ten years he has managed to survive his loss, and during that period what difference has it made to him whether the money was there or not? It was just as little use to him either way.

Among stupid pleasures they include not only gambling—a form of idiocy that they've heard about but never practiced—but also hunting and hawking. What on earth is the fun, they ask, of throwing dice onto a table? Besides, you've done it so often that, even if there was some fun in it at first, you must surely be sick of it by now. How can you possibly enjoy listening to anything so disagreeable as the barking and howling of dogs? And why is it more amusing to watch a dog chasing a hare than to watch one dog chasing another? In each case the essential activity is running—if running is what amuses you. But if it's really the thought of being in at the death, and seeing an animal torn to pieces before your eyes, wouldn't pity be a more appropriate reaction to the sight of a weak, timid, harmless little creature like a hare being devoured by something so much stronger and fiercer?

So the Utopians consider hunting below the dignity of free men, and 24 leave it entirely to butchers, who are, as I told you, slaves. In their view hunting is the vilest department of butchery, compared with which all the others are relatively useful and honorable. An ordinary butcher slaughters livestock far more sparingly, and only because he has to, whereas a hunter kills and mutilates poor little creatures purely for his own amusement. They say you won't find that type of blood lust even among animals, unless they're particularly savage by nature, or have become so by constantly being used for this cruel sport.

There are hundreds of things like that, which are generally regarded as pleasures, but everyone in Utopia is quite convinced that they've got nothing to do with real pleasure, because there's nothing naturally enjoyable about them. Nor is this conviction at all shaken by the argument that most people do actually enjoy them, which would seem to indicate an appreciable pleasure content. They say this is a purely subjective reaction caused by bad habits, which can make a person prefer unpleasant things to pleasant ones, just as pregnant women sometimes lose their sense of taste, and find suet or turpentine more delicious than honey. But however much one's judgment may be impaired by habit or ill health, the nature of pleasure, as of everything else, remains unchanged.

Real pleasures they divide into two categories, mental and physical. Mental pleasures include the satisfaction that one gets from understanding something, or from contemplating truth. They also include the memory of a well-spent life, and the confident expectation of good things to come. Physical pleasures are subdivided into two types. First there are those which fill the whole organism with a conscious sense of enjoyment. This may be the result of replacing physical substances which have been burnt up by the natural heat of the body, as when we eat or drink. Or else it may be caused by the discharge of some excess, as in excretion, sexual intercourse, or any relief of irritation by rubbing or scratching. However, there are also pleasures which satisfy no organic need, and relieve no previous discomfort. They merely act, in a mysterious but quite unmistakable way, directly on our senses, and monopolize their reactions. Such is the pleasure of music.

Their second type of physical pleasure arises from the calm and regular functioning of the body—that is, from a state of health undisturbed by any minor ailments. In the absence of mental discomfort, this gives one a good feeling, even without the help of external pleasures. Of course, it's less ostentatious, and forces itself less violently on one's attention than the cruder delights of eating and drinking, but even so it's often considered the greatest pleasure in life. Practically everyone in Utopia would agree that it's a very important one, because it's the basis of all the others. It's enough by itself to make you enjoy life, and unless you have it, no other pleasure is possible. However, mere freedom from pain, without positive health, they would call not pleasure but anaesthesia.

Some thinkers used to maintain that a uniformly tranquil state of health couldn't properly be termed a pleasure since its presence could only be detected by contrast with its opposite—oh yes, they went very thoroughly into the whole question. But that theory was exploded long ago, 28 and nowadays nearly everybody subscribes to the view that health is most definitely a pleasure. The argument goes like this—illness involves pain, which is the direct opposite of pleasure, and illness is the direct opposite of health, therefore health involves pleasure. They don't think it matters whether you say that illness *is* or merely *involves* pain. Either way it comes to the same thing. Similarly, whether health *is* a pleasure, or merely *produces* pleasure as inevitably as fire produces heat, it's equally logical to assume that where you have an uninterrupted state of health you cannot fail to have pleasure.

Besides, they say, when we eat something, what really happens is this. Our failing health starts fighting off the attacks of hunger, using the food as an ally. Gradually it begins to prevail, and, in this very process of winning back its normal strength, experiences the sense of enjoyment which we find so refreshing. Now, if health enjoys the actual battle, why shouldn't it also enjoy the victory? Or are we to suppose that when it has finally managed to regain its former vigor—the one thing that it has been fighting for all this time—it promptly falls into a coma, and fails to notice or take advantage of its success? As for the idea that one isn't conscious of health except through its opposite, they say that's quite untrue. Everyone's perfectly aware of feeling well, unless he's asleep or actually feeling ill. Even the most insensitive and apathetic sort of person will admit that it's delightful to be healthy—and what is delight, but a synonym for pleasure?

They're particularly fond of mental pleasures, which they consider of primary importance, and attribute mostly to good behavior and a clear conscience. Their favorite physical pleasure is health. Of course, they believe in enjoying food, drink, and so forth, but purely in the interests of health, for they don't regard such things as very pleasant in themselves—only as methods of resisting the stealthy onset of disease. A sensible person, they say, prefers keeping well to taking medicine, and would rather feel cheerful than have people trying to comfort him. On the same principle it's better not to need this type of pleasure than to become addicted to it. For, if you think that sort of thing will make you happy, you'll have to admit that your idea of perfect felicity would be a life consisting entirely of hunger, thirst, itching, eating, drinking, rubbing, and scratching—which would obviously be most unpleasant as well as quite disgusting. Undoubtedly these pleasures should come right at the bottom of the list, because they're so impure. For instance, the pleasure of eating is invariably diluted with the pain of hunger, and not in equal proportions either—for the pain is both more intense and more prolonged. It starts before the pleasure, and doesn't stop until the pleasure has stopped too.

So they don't think much of pleasures like that, except insofar as they're necessary. But they enjoy them all the same, and feel most grateful to Mother Nature for encouraging her children to do things that have to be done so often, by making them so attractive. For just think how dreary life would be, if those chronic ailments, hunger and thirst, could only be cured by foul-tasting medicines, like the rarer types of disease!

They attach great value to special natural gifts such as beauty, 32 strength, and agility. They're also keen on the pleasures of sight, hearing, and smell, which are peculiar to human beings—for no other species admires the beauty of the world, enjoys any sort of scent, except as a method of locating food, or can tell the difference between a harmony and a discord. They say these things give a sort of relish to life.

However, in all such matters they observe the rule that minor pleasures mustn't interfere with major ones, and that pleasure mustn't cause pain—which they think is bound to happen, if the pleasure is immoral. But they'd never dream of despising their own beauty, overtaxing their strength, converting their agility into inertia, ruining their physique by going without food, damaging their health, or spurning any other of Nature's gifts, unless they were doing it for the benefit of other people or of society, in the hope of receiving some greater pleasure from God in return. For they think it's quite absurd to torment oneself in the name of an unreal virtue, which does nobody any good, or in order to steel oneself against disasters which may never occur. They say such behavior is merely self-destructive, and shows a most ungrateful attitude toward Nature—as if one refused all her favors, because one couldn't bear the thought of being indebted to her for anything.

Well, that's their ethical theory, and short of some divine revelation, they doubt if the human mind is capable of devising a better one. We've no time to discuss whether it's right or wrong—nor is it really necessary, for all I undertook was to describe their way of life, not to defend it.

[TREATMENT OF THE DYING]

As I told you, when people are ill, they're looked after most sympathetically, and given everything in the way of medicine or special food that could possibly assist their recovery. In the case of permanent invalids, the nurses try to make them feel better by sitting and talking to them, and do all they can to relieve their symptoms. But if, besides being incurable, the disease also causes constant excruciating pain, some priests and government officials visit the person concerned, and say something like this:

"Let's face it, you'll never be able to live a normal life. You're just a 36 nuisance to other people and a burden to yourself—in fact you're really leading a sort of posthumous existence. So why go on feeding germs? Since your life's a misery to you, why hesitate to die? You're imprisoned in a torture chamber—why don't you break out and escape to a better world? Or say the word, and we'll arrange for your release. It's only common sense to cut your losses. It's also an act of piety to take the advice of a priest, because he speaks for God."

If the patient finds these arguments convincing, he either starves himself to death, or is given a soporific and put painlessly out of his misery. But this is strictly voluntary, and, if he prefers to stay alive, everyone will go on treating him as kindly as ever.

[THE SUMMING UP]

Well, that's the most accurate account I can give you of the Utopian Republic. To my mind, it's not only the best country in the world, but the only one that has any right to call itself a republic. Elsewhere, people are always talking about the public interest, but all they really care about is private property. In Utopia, where there's no private property, people take their duty to the public seriously. And both attitudes are perfectly reasonable. In other "republics" practically everyone knows that, if he doesn't look out for himself, he'll starve to death, however prosperous his country may be. He's therefore compelled to give his own interests priority over those of the public; that is, of other people. But in Utopia, where everything's under public ownership, no one has any fear of going short, as long as the public storehouses are full. Everyone gets a fair share, so there are never any poor men or beggars. Nobody owns anything, but everyone is rich—for what greater wealth can there be than cheerfulness, peace of mind, and freedom from anxiety? Instead of being worried about his food supply, upset by the plaintive demands of his wife, afraid of poverty for his son, and baffled by the problem of finding a dowry for his daughter, the Utopian can feel absolutely sure that he, his wife, his children, his grandchildren, his great-grandchildren, his great-great-grandchildren, and as long a line of descendants as the proudest peer could wish to look forward to, will always have enough to eat and enough to make them happy. There's also the further point that those who are too old to work are just as well provided for as those who are still working.

Now, will anyone venture to compare these fair arrangements in Utopia with the so-called justice of other countries?—in which I'm damned if I can see the slightest trace of justice or fairness. For what sort of justice do you call this? People like aristocrats, goldsmiths, or moneylenders, who either do no work at all, or do work that's really not essential, are rewarded for their laziness or their unnecessary activities by a splendid life of luxury. But laborers, coachmen, carpenters, and farm-hands, who never stop working like cart horses, at jobs so essential that, if they *did* stop working, they'd bring any country to a standstill within twelve months—what happens to them? They get so little to eat, and have such a wretched time, that they'd be almost better off if they *were* cart horses. Then at least, they wouldn't work quite such long hours, their food wouldn't be very much worse, they'd enjoy it more, and they'd have no fears for the future. As it is, they're not only ground down by unrewarding toil in the present, but also worried to death by the prospect of a poverty-stricken old age—since their daily wages aren't enough to support them for one day, let alone leave anything over to be saved up when they're old.

Can you see any fairness or gratitude in a social system which lavishes 40 such great rewards on so-called noblemen, goldsmiths, and people like that, who are either totally unproductive or merely employed in producing luxury goods or entertainment, but makes no such kind provision for farmhands, coal heavers, laborers, carters, or carpenters, without whom society couldn't exist at all? And the climax of ingratitude comes when they're old and ill and completely destitute. Having taken advantage of them throughout the best years of their lives, society now forgets all the sleepless hours they've spent in its service, and repays them for all the vital work they've done, by letting them die in misery. What's more, the wretched earnings of the poor are daily whittled away by the rich, not only through private dishonesty, but through public legislation. As if it weren't unjust enough already that the man who contributes most to society should get the least in return, they make it even worse, and then arrange for injustice to be legally described as justice.

In fact, when I consider any social system that prevails in the modern world, I can't, so help me God, see it as anything but a conspiracy of the rich to advance their own interests under the pretext of organizing society. They think up all sorts of tricks and dodges, first for keeping safe their ill-gotten gains, and then for exploiting the poor by buying their labor as cheaply as possible. Once the rich have decided that these tricks and dodges shall be officially recognized by society—which includes the poor as well as the rich—they acquire the force of law. Thus an unscrupulous minority is led by its insatiable greed to monopolize what would have been enough to supply the needs of the whole population. And yet how much happier even these people would be in Utopia! There, with the simultaneous abolition of money and the passion for money, how many other social problems have been solved, how many crimes eradicated! For obviously the end of money means the end of all those types of criminal behavior which daily punishments are powerless to check: fraud, theft, burglary, brawls, riots, disputes, rebellion, murder, treason, and black magic. And the moment money goes, you can also say goodbye to fear, tension, anxiety, overwork, and sleepless nights. Why, even poverty itself, the one problem that has always seemed to need money for its solution, would promptly disappear if money ceased to exist.

Let me try to make this point clearer. Just think back to one of the years when the harvest was bad, and thousands of people died of starvation. Well, I bet if you'd inspected every rich man's barn at the end of that lean period you'd have found enough corn to have saved all the lives that were lost through malnutrition and disease, and prevented anyone from suffering any ill effects whatever from the meanness of the weather and the soil. Everyone could so easily get enough to eat, if it weren't for that blessed nuisance, money. There you have a brilliant invention which was designed to make food more readily available. Actually it's the only thing that makes it unobtainable.

I'm sure that even the rich are well aware of all this, and realize how much better it would be to have everything one needed, than lots of things one didn't need—to be evacuated altogether from the danger area, than to dig oneself in behind a barricade of enormous wealth. And I've no doubt that either self-interest, or the authority of our Savior Christ—Who was far too wise not to know what was best for us, and far too kind to recommend anything else—would have led the whole world to adopt the Utopian system long ago, if it weren't for that beastly root of all evils, pride. For pride's criterion of prosperity is not what you've got yourself, but what other people haven't got. Pride would refuse to set foot in paradise, if she thought there'd be no underprivileged classes there to gloat over and order about—nobody whose misery could serve as a foil to her own happiness, or whose poverty she could make harder to bear, by flaunting her own riches. Pride, like a hellish serpent gliding through human hearts—or shall we say, like a sucking-fish that clings to the ship of state?—is always dragging us back, and obstructing our progress toward a better way of life.

But as this fault is too deeply ingrained in human nature to be easily   44 eradicated, I'm glad that at least one country has managed to develop a system which I'd like to see universally adopted. The Utopian way of life provides not only the happiest basis for a civilized community, but also one which, in all human probability, will last forever. They've eliminated the root causes of ambition, political conflict, and everything like that. There's therefore no danger of internal dissension, the one thing that has destroyed so many impregnable towns. And as long as there's unity and sound administration at home, no matter how envious neighboring kings may feel, they'll never be able to shake, let alone to shatter, the power of Utopia. They've tried to do so often enough in the past, but have always been beaten back.

Questions and Suggestions for Writing ══════════════

1. More, writing early in the sixteenth century, of course was living in a primarily agricultural society. Laborers were needed on farms; but might More have had any other reason for insisting that all people should do some farming, and that farming should be part of "every child's education"? Do you think everyone should put in some time as a farmer? Why, or why not?

2. More indicates that in the England of his day many people loafed or engaged in unnecessary work (producing luxury goods, for one thing), putting an enormous burden on those who engaged in useful work. Is this condition, or any part of it, true of our society? Explain.

3. The Utopians cannot understand why the people of other nations value gems, gold, and fine clothes. If you value any of these, can you offer an explanation?

4. What arguments can you offer against the Utopians' treatment of persons who are incurably ill and in pain?

5. Summarize More's report of the Utopians' idea of pleasure. (This summary will probably take three or four paragraphs.)

6. More's Utopians cannot understand why anyone takes pleasure in gambling or in hunting. If either activity gives you pleasure, in an essay of 500 words explain why, and offer an argument on behalf of your view.

7. As More makes clear in the part we entitle "The Summing Up," in Utopia there is no private property. In a sentence or two summarize the reasons he gives for this principle, and then in a paragraph evaluate them.

Niccolò Machiavelli

From *The Prince*

ON THOSE THINGS FOR WHICH MEN, AND PARTICULARLY PRINCES, ARE PRAISED OR BLAMED

Now there remains to be examined what should be the methods and procedures of a prince in dealing with his subjects and friends. And because I know that many have written about this, I am afraid that by writing about it again I shall be thought of as presumptuous, since in discussing this material I depart radically from the procedures of others. But since my intention is to write something useful for anyone who understands it, it seemed more suitable to me to search after the effectual truth of the matter rather than its imagined one. And many writers have imagined for themselves republics and principalities that have never been

---

Niccolò Machiavelli (1469–1527) was born in Florence at a time when Italy was divided into five major states: Venice, Milan, Florence, the Papal States, and Naples. Although these states often had belligerent relations with one another as well as with lesser Italian states, under the Medici family in Florence they achieved a precarious balance of power. In 1494, however, Lorenzo de' Medici, who had ruled from 1469 to 1492, died, and two years later Lorenzo's successor was exiled when the French army arrived in Florence. Italy became a field where Spain, France, and Germany competed for power. From 1498 to 1512 Machiavelli held a high post in the diplomatic service of the Florentine Republic, but when the French army reappeared and the Florentines in desperation recalled the Medici, Machiavelli lost his post, was imprisoned, tortured, and then exiled. Banished from Florence, he nevertheless lived in fair comfort on a small estate nearby, writing his

seen nor known to exist in reality; for there is such a gap between how one lives and how one ought to live that anyone who abandons what is done for what ought to be done learns his ruin rather than his preservation: for a man who wishes to make a vocation of being good at all times will come to ruin among so many who are not good. Hence it is necessary for a prince who wishes to maintain his position to learn how not to be good, and to use this knowledge or not to use it according to necessity.

Leaving aside, therefore, the imagined things concerning a prince, and taking into account those that are true, I say that all men, when they are spoken of, and particularly princes, since they are placed on a higher level, are judged by some of these qualities which bring them either blame or praise. And this is why one is considered generous, another miserly (to use a Tuscan word, since "avaricious" in our language is still used to mean one who wishes to acquire by means of theft; we call "miserly" one who excessively avoids using what he has); one is considered a giver, the other rapacious; one cruel, another merciful; one treacherous, another faithful; one effeminate and cowardly, another bold and courageous; one humane, another haughty; one lascivious, another chaste; one trustworthy, another cunning; one harsh, another lenient; one serious, another frivolous; one religious, another unbelieving; and the like. And I know that everyone will admit that it would be a very praiseworthy thing to find in a prince, of the qualities mentioned above, those that are held to be good; but since it is neither possible to have them nor to observe them all completely, because human nature does not permit it, a prince must be prudent enough to know how to escape the bad reputation of those vices that would lose the state for him, and must protect himself from those that will not lose it for him, if this is possible; but if he cannot, he need not concern himself unduly if he ignores these less serious vices. And, moreover, he need not worry about incurring the bad reputation of those vices without which it would be difficult to hold his state; since, carefully taking everything into account, one will discover that something which appears to be a virtue, if pursued, will end in his destruction; while some other thing which seems to be a vice, if pursued, will result in his safety and his well-being.

---

major works and hoping to obtain an office from the Medici. In later years he was employed in a few minor diplomatic missions, but even after the collapse and expulsion of the Medici in 1527, and the restoration of the republic, he did not regain his old position of importance. He died shortly after the restoration.

Our selection comes from The Prince, *which Machiavelli wrote in 1513 during his banishment hoping that it would interest the Medici and thus restore him to favor; but the book was not published until 1532, five years after his death. In this book of twenty-six short chapters, Machiavelli begins by examining different kinds of states, but the work's enduring power resides in the discussions (in chapters 15–18, reprinted here) of qualities necessary to a prince, that is, a head of state. Any such examination obviously is based in part on assumptions about the nature of the citizens of the realm.*

On Generosity and Miserliness

Beginning, therefore, with the first of the above-mentioned qualities, I say that it would be good to be considered generous; nevertheless, generosity used in such a manner as to give you a reputation for it will harm you; because if it is employed virtuously and as one should employ it, it will not be recognized and you will not avoid the reproach of its opposite. And so, if a prince wants to maintain his reputation for generosity among men, it is necessary for him not to neglect any possible means of lavish display; in so doing such a prince will always use up all his resources and he will be obliged, eventually, if he wishes to maintain his reputation for generosity, to burden the people with excessive taxes and to do everything possible to raise funds. This will begin to make him hateful to his subjects, and, becoming impoverished, he will not be much esteemed by anyone; so that, as a consequence of his generosity, having offended many and rewarded few, he will feel the effects of any slight unrest and will be ruined at the first sign of danger; recognizing this and wishing to alter his policies, he immediately runs the risk of being reproached as a miser.

A prince, therefore, unable to use this virtue of generosity in a manner which will not harm himself if he is known for it, should, if he is wise, not worry about being called a miser; for with time he will come to be considered more generous once it is evident that, as a result of his parsimony, his income is sufficient, he can defend himself from anyone who makes war against him, and he can undertake enterprises without overburdening his people, so that he comes to be generous with all those from whom he takes nothing, who are countless, and miserly with all those to whom he gives nothing, who are few. In our times we have not seen great deeds accomplished except by those who were considered miserly; all others were done away with. Pope Julius II, although he made use of his reputation for generosity in order to gain the papacy, then decided not to maintain it in order to be able to wage war; the present King of France has waged many wars without imposing extra taxes on his subjects, only because his habitual parsimony has provided for the additional expenditures; the present King of Spain, if he had been considered generous, would not have engaged in nor won so many campaigns.

Therefore, in order not to have to rob his subjects, to be able to defend himself, not to become poor and contemptible, and not to be forced to become rapacious, a prince must consider it of little importance if he incurs the name of miser, for this is one of those vices that permits him to rule. And if someone were to say: Caesar with his generosity came to rule the empire, and many others, because they were generous and known to be so, achieved very high positions; I reply: you are either already a prince or you are on the way to becoming one; in the first instance such generosity is damaging; in the second it is very necessary to be thought generous. And Caesar was one of those who wanted to gain the principality of Rome; but if, after obtaining this, he had lived and had not moderated his expenditures, he would have destroyed that empire. And if someone were to reply: there have existed many princes who have accomplished great deeds with their armies who have been reputed to be generous; I answer you: a prince either spends his own money and that of his subjects or that of others; in the first case he must be economical; in the second he must not restrain any part of his generosity. And for that prince who goes out with his soldiers and lives by looting, sacking, and ransoms, who controls the property of others, such generosity is necessary; otherwise he would not be followed by his troops. And with what does not belong to you or to your subjects you can be a more liberal giver, as were Cyrus, Caesar, and Alexander; for spending the wealth of others does not lessen your reputation but adds to it; only the spending of your own is what harms you. And there is nothing that uses itself up faster than generosity, for as you employ it you lose the means of employing it, and you become either poor or despised or, in order to escape poverty, rapacious and hated. And above all other things a prince must guard himself against being despised and hated; and generosity leads you to both one and the other. So it is wiser to live with the reputation of a miser, which produces reproach without hatred, than to be forced to incur the reputation of rapacity, which produces reproach along with hatred, because you want to be considered as generous.

ON CRUELTY AND MERCY AND WHETHER IT IS BETTER TO BE LOVED THAN TO BE FEARED OR THE CONTRARY

Proceeding to the other qualities mentioned above, I say that every prince must desire to be considered merciful and not cruel; nevertheless, he must take care not to misuse this mercy. Cesare Borgia[1] was considered cruel; nonetheless, his cruelty had brought order to Romagna, united it, restored it to peace and obedience. If we examine this carefully, we shall see that he was more merciful than the Florentine people, who, in order to avoid being considered cruel, allowed the destruction of Pistoia.[2] Therefore, a prince must not worry about the reproach of cruelty when it is a matter of keeping his subjects united and loyal; for with a very few examples of cruelty he will be more compassionate than those who, out of excessive mercy, permit disorders to continue, from which arise murders

[1]**Cesare Borgia**   The son of Pope Alexander VI, Cesare Borgia (1476–1507) was ruthlessly opportunistic. Encouraged by his father, in 1499 and 1500 he subdued the cities of **Romagna**, the region including Ferrara and Ravenna. [Notes are by the editors unless otherwise specified.]

[2]**Pistoia**   A town near Florence; Machiavelli suggests that the Florentines failed to treat dissenting leaders with sufficient severity.

and plundering; for these usually harm the community at large, while the executions that come from the prince harm one individual in particular. And the new prince, above all other princes, cannot escape the reputation of being called cruel, since new states are full of dangers. And Virgil, through Dido, states: "My difficult condition and the newness of my rule make me act in such a manner, and to set guards over my land on all sides."[3]

Nevertheless, a prince must be cautious in believing and in acting, nor should he be afraid of his own shadow; and he should proceed in such a manner, tempered by prudence and humanity, so that too much trust may not render him imprudent nor too much distrust render him intolerable.

From this arises an argument: whether it is better to be loved than to be feared, or the contrary. I reply that one should like to be both one and the other; but since it is difficult to join them together, it is much safer to be feared than to be loved when one of the two must be lacking. For one can generally say this about men: that they are ungrateful, fickle, simulators and deceivers, avoiders of danger, greedy for gain; and while you work for their good they are completely yours, offering you their blood, their property, their lives, and their sons, as I said earlier, when danger is far away; but when it comes nearer to you they turn away. And that prince who bases his power entirely on their words, finding himself stripped of other preparations, comes to ruin; for friendships that are acquired by a price and not by greatness and nobility of character are purchased but are not owned, and at the proper moment they cannot be spent. And men are less hesitant about harming someone who makes himself loved than one who makes himself feared because love is held together by a chain of obligation which, since men are a sorry lot, is broken on every occasion in which their own self-interest is concerned; but fear is held together by a dread of punishment which will never abandon you.

A prince must nevertheless make himself feared in such a manner that he will avoid hatred, even if he does not acquire love; since to be feared and not to be hated can very well be combined; and this will always be so when he keeps his hands off the property and the women of his citizens and his subjects. And if he must take someone's life, he should do so when there is proper justification and manifest cause; but, above all, he should avoid the property of others; for men forget more quickly the death of their father than the loss of their patrimony. Moreover, the reasons for seizing their property are never lacking; and he who begins to live by stealing always finds a reason for taking what belongs to others; on the contrary, reasons for taking a life are rarer and disappear sooner.

But when the prince is with his armies and has under his command a multitude of troops, then it is absolutely necessary that he not worry about

[3]In *Aeneid* I, 563–564, **Virgil** (70–19 B.C.) puts this line into the mouth of **Dido**, the woman ruler of Carthage.

being considered cruel; for without that reputation he will never keep an army united or prepared for any combat. Among the praiseworthy deeds of Hannibal[4] is counted this: that, having a very large army, made up of all kinds of men, which he commanded in foreign lands, there never arose the slightest dissension, neither among themselves nor against their prince, both during his good and his bad fortune. This could not have arisen from anything other than his inhuman cruelty, which, along with his many other abilities, made him always respected and terrifying in the eyes of his soldiers; and without that, to attain the same effect, his other abilities would not have sufficed. And the writers of history, having considered this matter very little, on the one hand admire these deeds of his and on the other condemn the main cause of them.

And that it be true that his other abilities would not have been sufficient can be seen from the example of Scipio,[5] a most extraordinary man not only in his time but in all recorded history, whose armies in Spain rebelled against him; this came about from nothing other than his excessive compassion, which gave to his soldiers more liberty than military discipline allowed. For this he was censured in the senate by Fabius Maximus, who called him the corruptor of the Roman militia. The Locrians, having been ruined by one of Scipio's officers, were not avenged by him, nor was the arrogance of that officer corrected, all because of his tolerant nature; so that someone in the senate who tried to apologize for him said that there were many men who knew how not to err better than they knew how to correct errors. Such a nature would have, in time, damaged Scipio's fame and glory if he had maintained it during the empire; but, living under the control of the senate, this harmful characteristic of his not only concealed itself but brought him fame.

I conclude, therefore, returning to the problem of being feared and loved, that since men love at their own pleasure and fear at the pleasure of the prince, a wise prince should build his foundation upon that which belongs to him, not upon that which belongs to others: he must strive only to avoid hatred, as has been said.

How a Prince Should Keep His Word

How praiseworthy it is for a prince to keep his word and to live by integrity and not by deceit everyone knows; nevertheless, one sees from the experience of our times that the princes who have accomplished great deeds are those who have cared little for keeping their promises and who

---

[4]**Hannibal** The Carthaginian general (247–183 B.C.) whose crossing of the Alps with elephants and full baggage train is one of the great feats of military history.

[5]**Scipio** Publius Cornelius Scipio Africanus the Elder (235–183 B.C.), the conqueror of Hannibal in the Punic Wars. The munity of which Machiavelli speaks took place in 206 B.C.

have known how to manipulate the minds of men by shrewdness; and in the end they have surpassed those who laid their foundations upon honesty.

You must, therefore, know that there are two means of fighting: one according to the laws, the other with force; the first way is proper to man, the second to beasts; but because the first, in many cases, is not sufficient, it becomes necessary to have recourse to the second. Therefore, a prince must know how to use wisely the natures of the beast and the man. This policy was taught to princes allegorically by the ancient writers, who described how Achilles and many other ancient princes were given to Chiron[6] the Centaur to be raised and taught under his discipline. This can only mean that, having a half-beast and half-man as a teacher, a prince must know how to employ the nature of the one and the other; and the one without the other cannot endure.

Since, then, a prince must know how to make good use of the nature of the beast, he should choose from among the beasts the fox and the lion; for the lion cannot defend itself from traps and the fox cannot protect itself from wolves. It is therefore necessary to be a fox in order to recognize the traps and a lion in order to frighten the wolves. Those who play only the part of the lion do not understand matters. A wise ruler, therefore, cannot and should not keep his word when such an observance of faith would be to his disadvantage and when the reasons which made him promise are removed. And if men were all good, this rule would not be good; but since men are a sorry lot and will not keep their promises to you, you likewise need not keep yours to them. A prince never lacks legitimate reasons to break his promises. Of this one could cite an endless number of modern examples to show how many pacts, how many promises have been made null and void because of the infidelity of princes; and he who has known best how to use the fox has come to a better end. But it is necessary to know how to disguise this nature well and to be a great hypocrite and a liar: and men are so simpleminded and so controlled by their present necessities that one who deceives will always find another who will allow himself to be deceived.

I do not wish to remain silent about one of these recent instances. Alexander VI[7] did nothing else, he thought about nothing else, except to deceive men, and he always found the occasion to do this. And there never was a man who had more forcefulness in his oaths, who affirmed a thing with more promises, and who honored his word less; nevertheless, his tricks always succeeded perfectly since he was well acquainted with this aspect of the world.

16

---

[6]**Chiron** (Kī´ron) A centaur (half man, half horse), who was said in classical mythology to have been the teacher not only of Achilles but also of Theseus, Jason, Hercules, and other heroes.

[7]**Alexander VI** Pope from 1492 to 1503; father of Cesare Borgia.

Therefore, it is not necessary for a prince to have all of the above-mentioned qualities, but it is very necessary for him to appear to have them. Furthermore, I shall be so bold as to assert this; that having them and practicing them at all times is harmful; and appearing to have them useful; for instance, to seem merciful, faithful, humane, forthright, religious, and to be so; but his mind should be disposed in such a way that should it become necessary not to be so, he will be able and know how to change to the contrary. And it is essential to understand this: that a prince, and especially a new prince, cannot observe all those things by which men are considered good, for in order to maintain the state he is often obliged to act against his promise, against charity, against humanity, and against religion. And therefore, it is necessary that he have a mind ready to turn itself according to the way the winds of Fortune and the changeability of affairs require him; and, as I said above, as long as it is possible, he should not stray from the good, but he should know how to enter into evil when necessity commands.

A prince, therefore, must be very careful never to let anything slip from his lips which is not full of the five qualities mentioned above: he should appear, upon seeing and hearing him, to be all mercy, all faithfulness, all integrity, all kindness, all religion. And there is nothing more necessary than to seem to possess this last quality. And men in general judge more by their eyes than their hands; for everyone can see but few can feel. Everyone sees what you seem to be, few perceive what you are, and those few do not dare to contradict the opinion of the many who have the majesty of the state to defend them; and in the actions of all men, and especially of princes, where there is no impartial arbiter, one must consider the final result.[8] Let a prince therefore act to seize and to maintain the state; his methods will always be judged honorable and will be praised by all; for ordinary people are always deceived by appearances and by the outcome of a thing; and in the world there is nothing but ordinary people; and there is no room for the few, while the many have a place to lean on. A certain prince of the present day, whom I shall refrain from naming, preaches nothing but peace and faith, and to both one and the other he is entirely opposed; and both, if he had put them into practice, would have cost him many times over either his reputation or his state.

Questions and Suggestions for Writing

1. In the opening paragraph, Machiavelli claims that a ruler who wishes to keep in power must "learn how not to be good"—that is, must know where and when to ignore the demands of conventional morality. In the rest of the excerpt, does he give any convincing evidence to support this claim? Can you

[8]The Italian original, *si guarda al fine*, has often been mistranslated as "the ends justify the means," something Machiavelli never wrote.[Translators' note]

think of any recent political event in which a political leader violated the requirements of morality, as Machiavelli advises?

2. Machiavelli says in paragraph 1 that "a man who wishes to make a vocation of being good at all times will come to ruin among so many who are not good." (By the way, the passage is ambiguous. "At all times" is, in the original, a squinting modifier. It may look backward, to "being good," or forward, to "will come to ruin," but probably Machiavelli means, "A man who at all times wishes to make a vocation of being good will come to ruin among so many who are not good.") Is this view realistic or cynical? (What is the difference between these two?) Assume for the moment that the view is realistic. Does it follow that society requires a ruler who must act according to the principles Machiavelli sets forth?

3. In his second paragraph Machiavelli claims that it is impossible for a ruler to exhibit *all* the conventional virtues (trustworthiness, liberality, and so on). Why does he make this claim? Do you agree with it?

4. In paragraph 4 Machiavelli cites as examples Pope Julius II, the King of France, the King of Spain, and other rulers. Is he using these examples to illustrate his generalizations, or to provide evidence for them? If you think he is using them to provide evidence, how convincing do you find the evidence? (*Consider:* Could Machiavelli be arguing from a biased sample?)

5. In paragraphs 6–10 Machiavelli argues that it is sometimes necessary for a ruler to be cruel, and so he praises Cesare Borgia and Hannibal. What is it about human nature, according to Machiavelli, that explains this need to have recourse to cruelty? (By the way, how do you think "cruelty" should be defined here?)

6. Machiavelli says that Cesare Borgia's cruelty brought peace to Romagna, and that, on the other hand, the Florentines who sought to avoid being cruel in fact brought pain to Pistoia. Can you think of recent episodes supporting the view that cruelty can be beneficial to society? If so, restate Machiavelli's position, using these examples from recent history. Then go on to write two paragraphs, arguing on behalf of your two examples. Or, if you believe that Machiavelli's point here is fundamentally wrong, explain why, again using current examples.

7. In *The Prince*, Machiavelli is writing about how to be a successful ruler. He explicitly says he is dealing with things as they are, not things as they should be. Do you think that in fact one can write usefully about statecraft without considering ethics? Explain. Or you may want to think about it in this way: The study of politics is often called "political science." Machiavelli can be seen as a sort of scientist, objectively analyzing the nature of governing—without offering any moral judgments. In an essay of 500 words argue for or against the view that the study of politics is rightly called "political science."

8. In paragraph 18 Machiavelli declares that "one must consider the final result." Taking account of the context, do you think the meaning is that (a) any end, goal, or purpose of anyone justifies using any means to reach it, or (b) the end of governing the state, nation, or country justifies using any means to achieve it? Or do you think Machiavelli means both, or something else entirely?

9. Take some important contemporary political figure and in 500 words argue that he or she does or does not act according to Machiavelli's principles.

10. If you have read the selection from More's *Utopia* (p. 553), write an essay of 500 words on one of these two topics: (1) Why More's book is or is not wiser than Machiavelli's, or (2) why one of the books is more interesting than the other.

11. More and Machiavelli wrote their books at almost exactly the same time. Write a dialogue of two or three double-spaced typed pages, in which the two men argue about the nature of the state. (During the argument, they will have to reveal their assumptions about the nature of human beings, and the role of government.)

Karl Marx

From *The Communist Manifesto*

A specter is haunting Europe—the specter of Communism. All the Powers of old Europe have entered into a holy alliance to exorcise this specter; Pope and Czar, Metternich and Guizot, French Radicals[1] and German police spies.

[1]**Metternich and Guizot, French Radicals** Metternich (1773–1859) was the Chancellor of the Austrian empire; Guizot (1787–1874) was a conservative French statesman and historian; the French Radicals were middle-class liberals who during the reign of Louis Philippe (1773–1850) sought a return to a republic. [Notes are by the editors unless otherwise specified.]

Karl Marx (1818–1883) was born in Germany, of a middle-class Jewish family that, to escape the consequences of anti-Jewish laws, had converted to Christianity shortly before Marx was born. Marx himself, however, was an atheist, and, as we will see in a moment, believed in a sort of historical determinism. After studying law, history, and philosophy, he earned a doctorate in philosophy in 1841. In 1843 he married, and for a few months served as an editor for a socialist journal, but when the Prussian authorities suppressed the journal Marx and his wife went to Paris, where in studying socialism he met Friedrich Engels (1820–1895), the son of a rich manufacturer of textiles. Commissioned in 1847 to write a platform for the Communist League—a group consisting originally of German exiles in London but by this time international—Marx and Engels produced The Communist Manifesto, *setting forth the theory and the program of a revolutionary movement. Engels was not especially creative, but he wrote easily (Marx did not) and his facility and his devotion to Marx's ideas made him an ideal collaborator. Engels wrote the first draft, which Marx then completely rewrote. Engels later attributed the work to Marx, though perhaps his modesty and his loyalty caused him to play down his own role. The* Manifesto, *first published in German in 1848, was promptly translated into French, Danish, and Polish, and in 1850 into English.*

Exiled from several European capitals, from 1849 Marx and his wife and children lived a life of poverty in London. He devoted himself chiefly to research,

Where is the party in opposition that has not been decried as communistic by its opponents in power? Where the Opposition that has not hurled back the branding reproach of Communism against the more advanced opposition parties, as well as against its reactionary adversaries?

Two things result from this fact.

1. Communism is already acknowledged by all European Powers to be itself a Power. 4

2. It is high time that Communists should openly, in the face of the whole world, publish their views, their aims, their tendencies, and meet this nursery tale of the specter of Communism with a Manifesto of the party itself.

---

barely supporting his family by occasional journalism and, when extremely hard pressed, by accepting gifts from Engels. In addition to seeking to stimulate awareness in the working class by his writings, Marx helped to found, in 1864, the International Workingmen's Association, a Communist organization. In 1867 he published the first volume of Capital, *the income from which, Marx said, did not cover the cost of the cigars he smoked while writing it. The second and third volumes of* Capital *(1885, 1894) were completed by Engels.*

Of The Communist Manifesto *Engels said: "The fundamental proposition which forms its nucleus belongs to Marx." This proposition, later known as "the materialist conception of history," or "historical materialism," holds that history is essentially the story of changes caused by economic practices: the means of production (for instance land and tools) and exchange engender the ideology (such as the laws, religion, and ethics) of an age. Consequently, each stage of economic development produces unique political and cultural forms, which the class in power falsely claims are eternal principles. Thus, true history records not the exploits of heroes but the struggles between economic classes. As Marx saw it, the bourgeoisie (owners of the means of production) had fulfilled a revolutionary role by overthrowing the feudal society, but now, in the nineteenth century, the bourgeoisie was engaged in an oppressive struggle with a new class of revolutionaries, the proletariat (workers, persons who had nothing to sell but their labor). The proletariat, for reasons specified in the* Manifesto, *would be victorious, and the final stage of evolution would produce a classless society; when the workers own the means of production, no one will be enslaved to another, and no one will be enslaved to further historical (economic) developments.*

Writing in 1888, Engels said that Marx's understanding of economics "is destined to do for history what Darwin's theory has done for biology." The Communist Manifesto is a passionate, fiery work, but as Engels's comparison with Darwin suggests, Marx clearly thought of his theory as scientific and empirical, and thought that the class struggle would result in the survival of the fittest: liberation of the proletariat. By predicting, from an interpretation of the past, the inevitable disappearance of capitalism, this deterministic view set communism apart from the socialism of the day. "Socialism" in the nineteenth century referred chiefly to efforts to alleviate the class struggle and to improve the lot of the worker by tinkering with capitalism; it did not envision (as Marx and Engels did) that a revolution was necessary and inevitable, that capitalism would disappear in its struggle with the proletariat, and that a classless society would be engendered. In this text of The Communist Manifesto *we omit a section, "Socialist and Communist Literature," in which Marx examines what he takes to be the Utopian (i.e., naively unrealistic) errors of socialist movements.*

78 WHAT IS THE IDEAL SOCIETY?

To this end, Communists of various nationalities have assembled in London and sketched the following Manifesto, to be published in the English, French, German, Italian, Flemish, and Danish languages.

Bourgeois and Proletarians[2]

The history of all hitherto existing society[3] is the history of class struggles.

Freeman and slave, patrician and plebeian, lord and serf, guild master and journeyman, in a word, oppressor and oppressed, stood in constant opposition to one another, carried on uninterrupted, now hidden, now open fight, a fight that each time ended, either in a revolutionary reconstitution of society at large, or in the common ruin of the contending classes.

In the earlier epochs of history we find almost everywhere a complicated arrangement of society into various orders, a manifold gradation of social rank. In ancient Rome we have patricians, knights, plebeians, slaves; in the Middle Ages, feudal lords, vassals, guild masters, journeymen, apprentices, serfs; in almost all of these classes, again, subordinate gradations.

The modern bourgeois society that has sprouted from the ruins of feudal society has not done away with class antagonisms. It has but established new classes, new conditions of oppression, new forms of struggle in place of the old ones.

Our epoch, the epoch of the bourgeoisie, possesses, however, this distinctive feature; it has simplified the class antagonisms. Society as a whole is more and more splitting up into two great hostile camps, into two great classes directly facing each other: Bourgeoisie and Proletariat.

From the serfs of the Middle Ages sprang the chartered burghers of the earliest towns. From these burgesses the first elements of the bourgeoisie were developed.

[2][Engels's note] By bourgeoisie is meant the class of modern Capitalists, owners of the means of social production and employers of wage labor. By proletariat, the class of modern wage-laborers who, having no means of production of their own are reduced to selling their labor power in order to live.

[3][Engels's note] That is, all written history. In 1847, the prehistory of society, the social organization existing previous to recorded history, was all but unknown. Since then, Haxthausen discovered common ownership of land in Russia. Maurer proved it to be the social foundation from which all Teutonic races started in history, and by and by village communities were found to be, or to have been, the primitive form of society everywhere from India to Ireland. The inner organization of this primitive communistic society was laid bare, in its typical form, by Morgan's crowning discovery of the true nature of the gens and its relation to the tribe. With the dissolution of these primeval communities society begins to be differentiated into separate and finally antagonistic classes. I have attempted to retrace this process of dissolution in *The Origin of the Family, Private Property, and the State* (Chicago; Charles H. Kerr).

The discovery of America, the rounding of the Cape, opened up fresh ground for the rising bourgeoisie. The East Indian and Chinese markets, the colonization of America, trade with the colonies, the increase in the means of exchange and in commodities generally, gave to commerce, to navigation, to industry, an impulse never before known, and thereby, to the revolutionary element in the tottering feudal society, a rapid development.

The feudal system of industry, under which industrial production was monopolized by closed guilds, now no longer sufficed for the growing wants of the new market. The manufacturing system took its place. The guild masters were pushed on one side by the manufacturing middle class: division of labor between the different corporate guilds vanished in the face of division of labor in each single workshop.

Meantime the markets kept ever growing, the demand ever rising. Even manufacture[4] no longer sufficed. Thereupon, steam and machinery revolutionized industrial production. The place of manufacture was taken by the giant, Modern Industry, the place of the industrial middle class, by industrial millionaires, the leaders of whole industrial armies, the modern bourgeois.

Modern industry has established the world market, for which the 16
discovery of America paved the way. This market has given an immense development to commerce, to navigation, to communication by land. This development has, in its turn, reacted on the extension of industry; and in proportion as industry, commerce, navigation, railways extended, in the same proportion the bourgeoisie developed, increased its capital, and pushed into the background every class handed down from the Middle Ages.

We see, therefore, how the modern bourgeoisie is itself the product of a long course of development, of a series of revolutions in the modes of production and of exchange.

Each step in the development of the bourgeoisie was accompanied by a corresponding political advance of that class. An oppressed class under the sway of the feudal nobility, an armed and self-governing association in the medieval commune, here independent urban republic (as in Italy and Germany), there taxable "third estate"[5] of the monarchy (as in France), afterward, in the period of manufacture proper, serving either the semi-feudal or the absolute monarchy as a counterpoise against nobility, and, in fact, cornerstone of the great monarchies in general, the bourgeoisie has at

---

[4]**manufacture** System of production relying mainly on human power, as opposed to the later industrial system relying on machinery driven by water and steam.

[5][Engels's note] "Commune" was the name taken, in France, by the nascent towns even before they had conquered from their feudal lords and masters, local self-government and political rights as "the Third Estate." Generally speaking, for the economical development of the bourgeoisie, England is here taken as the typical country, for its political development, France.

last, since the establishment of Modern Industry and of the world market, conquered for itself, in the modern representative State, exclusive political sway. The executive of the modern State is but a committee for managing the common affairs of the whole bourgeoisie.

The bourgeoisie, historically, has played a most revolutionary part.

The bourgeoisie, wherever it has got the upper hand, has put an end   20
to all feudal, patriarchal, idyllic relations. It has pitilessly torn asunder the motley feudal ties that bound man to his "natural superiors," and has left no other nexus between man and man than naked self-interest, than callous "cash payment." It has drowned the most heavenly ecstasies of religious fervor, of chivalrous enthusiasm, of Philistine sentimentalism, in the icy water of egotistical calculation. It has resolved personal worth into exchange value, and in place of the numberless indefeasible chartered freedoms, has set up that single, unconscionable freedom—Free Trade. In one word, for exploitation veiled by religious and political illusions, it has substituted naked, shameless, direct, brutal exploitation.

The bourgeoisie has stripped of its halo every occupation hitherto honored and looked up to with reverent awe. It has converted the physician, the lawyer, the priest, the poet, the man of science, into its paid wage laborers.

The bourgeoisie has torn away from the family its sentimental veil, and has reduced the family relation to a mere money relation.

The bourgeoisie has disclosed how it came to pass that the brutal display of vigor in the Middle Ages, which reactionists so much admire, found its fitting complement in the most slothful indolence. It has been the first to show what man's activity can bring about. It has accomplished wonders far surpassing Egyptian pyramids, Roman aqueducts, and Gothic cathedrals; it has conducted expeditions that put in the shade all former Exoduses of nations and crusades.

The bourgeoisie cannot exist without constantly revolutionizing the   24
instruments of production, and thereby the relations of production, and with them the whole relations of society. Conservation of the old modes of production in unaltered form was, on the contrary, the first condition of existence for all earlier industrial classes. Constant revolutionizing of production, uninterrupted disturbance of all social conditions, everlasting uncertainty and agitation distinguish the bourgeois epoch from all earlier ones. All fixed, fast frozen relations, with their train of ancient and venerable prejudices and opinions, are swept away, all new formed ones become antiquated before they can ossify. All that is solid melts into the air, all that is holy is profaned, and man is at last compelled to face with sober senses, his real conditions of life, and his relations with his kind.

The need of a constantly expanding market for its products chases the bourgeoisie over the whole surface of the globe. It must nestle everywhere, settle everywhere, establish connections everywhere.

The bourgeoisie has through its exploitation of the world market given a cosmopolitan character to production and consumption in every country. To the great chagrin of reactionists, it has drawn from under the feet of industry the national ground on which it stood. All old-established national industries have been destroyed or are daily being destroyed. They are dislodged by new industries, whose introduction becomes a life and death question for all civilized nations, by industries that no longer work up indigenous raw material, but raw material drawn from the remotest zones; industries whose products are consumed, not only at home, but in every quarter of the globe. In place of the old wants, satisfied by the productions of the country, we find new wants, requiring for their satisfaction the products of distant lands and climes. In place of the old local and national seclusion and self-sufficiency, we have intercourse in every direction, universal interdependence of nations. And as in material, so also in intellectual production. The intellectual creations of individual nations become common property. National onesidedness and narrowmindedness become more and more impossible, and from the numerous national and local literatures there arises a world literature.

The bourgeoisie, by the rapid improvement of all instruments of production, by the immensely facilitated means of communication, draws all, even the most barbarian nations into civilization. The cheap prices of its commodities are the heavy artillery with which it batters down all Chinese walls, with which it forces the barbarians' intensely obstinate hatred of foreigners to capitulate. It compels all nations, on pain of extinction, to adopt the bourgeois mode of production; it compels them to introduce what it calls civilization into their midst, i.e., to become bourgeois themselves. In a word, it creates a world after its own image.

The bourgeoisie has subjected the country to the rule of the towns. It has created enormous cities, has greatly increased the urban population as compared with the rural and has thus rescued a considerable part of the population from the idiocy of rural life. Just as it has made the country dependent on the towns, so it has made barbarian and semi-barbarian countries dependent on civilized ones, nations of peasants on nations of bourgeois, the East on the West.

The bourgeoisie keeps more and more doing away with the scattered state of the population, of the means of production, and of property. It has agglomerated population, centralized means of production, and has concentrated property in a few hands. The necessary consequence of this was political centralization. Independent, or but loosely connected provinces, with separate interests, laws, governments, and systems of taxation, became lumped together in one nation, with one government, one code of laws, one national class interest, one frontier, and one customs tariff.

The bourgeoisie, during its rule of scarce one hundred years, has created more massive and more colossal productive forces than have all preceding generations together. Subjection of Nature's forces to man, machinery, application of chemistry to industry and agriculture, steam navigation, railways, electric telegraphs, clearing of whole continents for cultivation, canalization of rivers, whole populations conjured out of the ground—what earlier century had even a presentiment that such productive forces slumbered in the lap of social labor?

We see then: The means of production and of exchange on whose foundation the bourgeoisie built itself up, were generated in feudal society. At a certain stage in the development of these means of production and of exchange, the conditions under which feudal society produced and exchanged, the feudal organization of agriculture and manufacturing industry, in one word, the feudal relations of property became no longer compatible with the already developed productive forces; they became so many fetters. They had to burst asunder; they were burst asunder.

Into their places stepped free competition, accompanied by social and political constitution adapted to it, and by economical and political sway of the bourgeois class. 32

A similar movement is going on before our own eyes. Modern bourgeois society with its relations of production, of exchange and of property, a society that has conjured up such gigantic means of production and of exchange, is like the sorcerer who is no longer able to control the powers of the nether world whom he has called up by his spells. For many a decade past, the history of industry and commerce is but the history of the revolt of modern productive forces against modern conditions of production, against the property relations that are the conditions for the existence of the bourgeoisie and of its rule. It is enough to mention the commercial crises that by their periodical return put on its trial, each time more threateningly, the existence of the entire bourgeois society. In these crises a great part not only of the existing products, but also of the previously created productive forces, are periodically destroyed. In these crises there breaks out an epidemic that in all earlier epochs, would have seemed an absurdity—the epidemic of overproduction. Society suddenly finds itself put back into a state of momentary barbarism; it appears as if a famine, a universal war of devastation, had cut off the supply of every means of subsistence; industry and commerce seem to be destroyed; and why? Because there is too much civilization, too much means of subsistence, too much industry, too much commerce. The productive forces at the disposal of society no longer tend to further the development of the conditions of the bourgeois property; on the contrary, they have become too powerful for these conditions by which they are fettered, and as soon as they overcome these fetters they bring disorder into the whole of bourgeois society, endanger the existence of bourgeois property. The conditions of bourgeois society are too narrow to comprise the wealth created by them. And how does the bourgeosie get over these crises? On the one hand by enforced destruction of a mass of productive forces; on the other, by the conquest of new markets, and by the more thorough exploitation of the old ones. That is to say, by paving the way for more extensive and more destructive crises, and by diminishing the means whereby crises are prevented.

The weapons with which the bourgeoisie felled feudalism to the ground are now turned against the bourgeoisie itself.

But not only has the bourgeoisie forged the weapons that bring death to itself; it has also called into existence the men who are to wield those weapons—the modern working class—the proletarians.

In proportion as the bourgeoisie, i.e., capital, is developed, in the same proportion is the proletariat, the modern working class, developed, a class of laborers who live only so long as they find work, and who find work only so long as their labor increases capital. These laborers, who must sell themselves piecemeal, are a commodity, like every other article of commerce, and are consequently exposed to all the vicissitudes of competition, to all the fluctuations of the market.

Owing to the extensive use of machinery and to division of labor, the work of the proletarians has lost all individual character, and, consequently, all charm for the workman. He becomes an appendage of the machine, and it is only the most simple, most monotonous and most easily acquired knack that is required of him. Hence, the cost of production of a workman is restricted almost entirely to the means of subsistence that he requires for his maintenance, and for the propagation of his race. But the price of a commodity, and also of labor, is equal to its cost of production. In proportion, therefore, as the repulsiveness of the work increases the wage decreases. Nay more, in proportion as the use of machinery and division of labor increases, in the same proportion the burden of toil increases, whether by prolongation of the working hours, by increase of the work enacted in a given time, or by increased speed of the machinery, etc.

Modern industry has converted the little workshop of the patriarchal master into the great factory of the industrial capitalist. Masses of laborers, crowded into factories, are organized like soldiers. As privates of the industrial army they are placed under the command of a perfect hierarchy of officers and sergeants. Not only are they the slaves of the bourgeois class and of the bourgeois state, they are daily and hourly enslaved by the machine, by the overlooker, and, above all, by the individual bourgeois manufacturer himself. The more openly this despotism proclaims gain to be its end and aim, the more petty, the more hateful, and the more embittering it is.

The less the skill and exertion or strength implied in manual labor, in other words, the more modern industry becomes developed, the more is the labor of men superseded by that of women. Differences of age and sex have no longer any distinctive social validity for the working class. All are instruments of labor, more or less expensive to use, according to their age and sex.

No sooner is the exploitation of the laborer by the manufacturer, so far at an end, that he receives his wages in cash, than he is set upon by the other portions of the bourgeoisie, the landlord, the shopkeeper, the pawnbroker, etc.

The lower strata of the middle class—the small tradespeople, shopkeepers, and retired tradesmen generally, the handicraftsmen and peasants—all these sink gradually into the proletariat, partly because their diminutive capital does not suffice for the scale on which Modern Industry is carried on, and is swamped in the competition with the large capitalists, partly because their specialized skill is rendered worthless by new methods of production. Thus the proletariat is recruited from all classes of the population.

The proletariat goes through various stages of development. With its birth begins its struggle with the bourgeoisie. At first the contest is carried on by individual laborers, then by the workpeople of a factory, then by the operatives of one trade, in one locality, against the individual bourgeois who directly exploits them. They direct their attacks not against the bourgeois conditions of production, but against the instruments of production themselves; they destroy imported wares that compete with their labor, they smash to pieces machinery, they set factories ablaze, they seek to restore by force the vanished status of the workman of the Middle Ages.

At this stage the laborers still form an incoherent mass scattered over the whole country, and broken up by their mutual competition. If anywhere they unite to form more compact bodies, this is not yet the consequence of their own active union, but of the union of the bourgeoisie, which class, in order to attain its own political ends, is compelled to set the whole proletariat in motion, and is moreover yet, for a time, able to do so. At this stage, therefore, the proletarians do not fight their enemies, but the enemies of their enemies, the remnants of absolute monarchy, the landowners, the nonindustrial bourgeois, the petty bourgeoisie. Thus the whole historical movement is concentrated in the hands of the bourgeoisie, every victory so obtained is a victory for the bourgeoisie.

But with the development of industry the proletariat not only increases in number; it becomes concentrated in greater masses, its strength grows, and it feels that strength more. The various interests and conditions of life within the ranks of the proletariat are more and more equalized, in proportion as machinery obliterates all distinctions of labor, and nearly everywhere reduces wages to the same low level. The growing competition among the bourgeois, and the resulting commercial crisis, make the wages of the workers even more fluctuating. The unceasing improvement of machinery, ever more rapidly developing, makes their livelihood more and more precarious; the collisions between individual workmen and individual bourgeois take more and more the character of collisions between two classes. Thereupon the workers begin to form combinations (Trades' Unions) against the bourgeois; they club together in order to keep up the rate of wages; they found permanent associations in order to make provision beforehand for these occasional revolts. Here and there the contest breaks out into riots.

Now and then the workers are victorious, but only for a time. The real fruit of their battle lies not in the immediate result but in the ever-expanding union of workers. This union is helped on by the improved means of communication that are created by modern industry, and that places the workers of different localities in contact with one another. It was just this contact that was needed to centralize the numerous local struggles, all of the same character, into one national struggle between classes. But every class struggle is a political struggle. And that union, to attain which the burghers of the Middle Ages with their miserable highways, required centuries, the modern proletarians, thanks to railways, achieve in a few years.

This organization of the proletarians into a class, and consequently into a political party, is continually being upset again by the competition between the workers themselves. But it ever rises up again, stronger, firmer, mightier. It compels legislative recognition of particular interests of the workers by taking advantage of the divisions among the bourgeoisie itself. Thus the ten hours' bill in England[6] was carried.

Altogether collisions between the classes of the old society further, in many ways, the course of development of the proletariat. The bourgeoisie finds itself involved in a constant battle. At first with the aristocracy; later on, with those portions of the bourgeoisie itself whose interests have become antagonistic to the progress of industry; at all times, with the bourgeoisie of foreign countries. In all these battles it sees itself compelled to appeal to the proletariat, to ask for its help, and thus, to drag it into the political arena. The bourgeoisie itself, therefore, supplies the proletariat with its own elements of political and general education; in other words, it furnishes the proletariat with weapons for fighting the bourgeoisie.

Further, as we have already seen, entire sections of the ruling classes are, by the advance of industry, precipitated into the proletariat, or are at least threatened in their conditions of existence. These also supply the proletariat with fresh elements of enlightenment and progress.

Finally, in times when the class struggle nears the decisive hour, the process of dissolution going on within the ruling class—in fact, within the whole range of an old society—assumes such a violent, glaring character that a small section of the ruling class cuts itself adrift and joins the revolutionary class, the class that holds the future in its hands. Just as, therefore, at an earlier period, a section of the nobility went over to the bourgeoisie, so now a portion of the bourgeoisie goes over to the proletariat, and in particular, a portion of the bourgeois ideologists, who have

48

----

[6] **the ten hours' bill** Legislation enacted by Parliament in 1847, limiting the working day of factory workers to ten hours.

raised themselves to the level of comprehending theoretically the historical movements as a whole.

Of all the classes that stand face to face with the bourgeoisie today the proletariat alone is a really revolutionary class. The other classes decay and finally disappear in the face of modern industry; the proletariat is its special and essential product.

The lower middle class, the small manufacturer, the shopkeeper, the artisan, the peasant, all these fight against the bourgeoisie, to save from extinction their existence as fractions of the middle class. They are therefore not revolutionary, but conservative. Nay, more; they are reactionary, for they try to roll back the wheel of history. If by chance they are revolutionary, they are so only in view of their impending transfer into the proletariat; they thus defend not their present, but their future interests; they desert their own standpoint to place themselves at that of the proletariat.

The "dangerous class," the social scum, that passively rotting mass   52
thrown off by the lowest layers of old society, may, here and there, be swept into the movement by a proletarian revolution; its conditions of life, however, prepare it far more for the part of a bribed tool of reactionary intrigue.

In the conditions of the proletariat, those of the old society at large are already virtually swamped. The proletarian is without property; his relation to his wife and children has no longer anything in common with the bourgeois family relations; modern industrial labor, modern subjection to capital, the same in England as in France, in America as in Germany, has stripped him of every trace of national character. Law, morality, religion, are to him so many bourgeois prejudices, behind which lurk in ambush just as many bourgeois interests.

All the preceding classes that got the upper hand sought to fortify their already acquired status by subjecting society at large to their conditions of appropriation. The proletarians cannot become masters of the productive forces of society, except by abolishing their own previous mode of appropriation, and thereby also every other previous mode of appropriation. They have nothing of their own to secure and to fortify; their mission is to destroy all previous securities for and insurances of individual property.

All previous historical movements were movements of minorities, or in the interest of minorities. The proletarian movement is the self-conscious, independent movement of the immense majority. The proletariat, the lowest stratum of our present society, cannot stir, cannot raise itself up without the whole superincumbent strata of official society being sprung into the air.

Though not in substance, yet in form, the struggle of the proletariat   56
with the bourgeoisie is at first a national struggle. The proletariat of each country must, of course, first of all settle matters with its own bourgeoisie.

In depicting the most general phases of the development of the proletariat, we traced the more or less veiled civil war, raging within existing society, up to the point where that war breaks out into open revolution, and where the violent overthrow of the bourgeoisie lays the foundations for the sway of the proletariat.

Hitherto every form of society has been based, as we have already seen, on the antagonism of oppressing and oppressed classes. But in order to oppress a class, certain conditions must be assured to it under which it can, at least, continue its slavish existence. The serf, in the period of serfdom, raised himself to membership in the commune, just as the petty bourgeois, under the yoke of feudal absolutism, managed to develop into a bourgeois. The modern laborer, on the contrary, instead of rising with the progress of industry, sinks deeper and deeper below the conditions of existence of his own class. He becomes a pauper, and pauperism develops more rapidly than population and wealth. And here it becomes evident that the bourgeoisie is unfit any longer to be the ruling class in society, and to impose its conditions of existence upon society as an overriding law. It is unfit to rule, because it is incompetent to assure an existence to its slave within his slavery, because it cannot help letting him sink into such a state that it has to feed him, instead of being fed by him. Society can no longer live under this bourgeoisie; in other words, its existence is no longer compatible with society.

The essential condition for the existence, and for the sway of the bourgeois class, is the formation and augmentation of capital; the condition for capital is wage labor. Wage labor rests exclusively on competition between the laborers. The advance of industry, whose involuntary promoter is the bourgeoisie, replaces the isolation of the laborers, due to competition, by their involuntary combination, due to association. The development of Modern Industry, therefore, cuts from under its feet the very foundation on which the bourgeoisie produces and appropriates products. What the bourgeoisie therefore produces, above all, are its own gravediggers. Its fall and the victory of the proletariat are equally inevitable.

Proletarians and Communists

In what relation do the Communists stand to the proletarians as a whole? 60

The Communists do not form a separate party opposed to other working class parties.

They have no interests separate and apart from those of the proletariat as a whole.

They do not set up any sectarian principles of their own, by which to shape and mold the proletarian movement.

The Communists are distinguished from the other working class parties by this only: (1) In the national struggles of the proletarians of the different countries, they point out and bring to the front the common 64 interests of the entire proletariat, independently of all nationality. (2) In the various stages of development which the struggle of the working class against the bourgeoisie has to pass through, they always and everywhere represent the interests of the movement as a whole.

The Communists, therefore, are on the one hand practically the most advanced and resolute section of the working class parties of every country, that section which pushes forward all others; on the other hand, theoretically, they have over the great mass of the proletariat the advantage of clearly understanding the line of march, the conditions, and the ultimate general results of the proletarian movement.

The immediate aim of the Communists is the same as that of all the other proletarian parties: formation of the proletariat into a class, overthrow of the bourgeois supremacy, conquest of political power by the proletariat.

The theoretical conclusions of the Communists are in no way based on ideas or principles that have been invented or discovered by this or that would-be universal reformer.

They merely express, in general terms, actual relations springing from   68
an existing class struggle, from a historical movement going on under our very eyes. The abolition of existing property relations is not at all a distinctive feature of Communism.

All property relations in the past have continually been subject to historical change consequent upon the change in historical conditions.

The French Revolution, for example, abolished feudal property in favor of bourgeois property.

The distinguishing feature of Communism is not the abolition of property generally, but the abolition of bourgeois property. But modern bourgeois private property is the final and most complete expression of the system of producing and appropriating products, that is based on class antagonism, on the exploitation of the many by the few.

In this sense, the theory of the Communists may be summed up in the   72
single sentence: Abolition of private property.

We Communists have been reproached with the desire of abolishing the right of personally acquiring property as the fruit of a man's own labor, which property is alleged to be the groundwork of all personal freedom, activity, and independence.

Hard won, self-acquired, self-earned property! Do you mean the property of the petty artisan and of the small peasant, a form of property that preceded the bourgeois form? There is no need to abolish that; the development of industry has to a great extent already destroyed it, and is still destroying it daily.

Or do you mean modern bourgeois private property?

But does wage labor create any property for the laborer? Not a bit. It   76
creates capital, i.e., that kind of property which exploits wage labor, and which cannot increase except upon condition of getting a new supply of

wage labor for fresh exploitation. Property, in its present form, is based on the antagonism of capital and wage labor. Let us examine both sides of this antagonism.

To be a capitalist is to have not only a purely personal, but a social status in production. Capital is a collective product, and only by the united action of many members, nay, in the last resort, only by the united action of all members of society, can it be set in motion.

Capital is therefore not a personal, it is a social power.

When, therefore, capital is converted into common property, into the property of all members of society, personal property is not thereby transformed into social property. It is only the social character of the property that is changed. It loses its class character.

Let us now take wage labor.   80

The average price of wage labor is the minimum wage, i.e., that quantum of the means of subsistence which is absolutely requisite to keep the laborer in bare existence as a laborer. What, therefore, the wage laborer appropriates by means of his labor, merely suffices to prolong and reproduce a bare existence. We by no means intend to abolish this personal appropriation of the products of labor, an appropriation that is made for the maintenance and reproduction of human life, and that leaves no surplus wherewith to command the labor of others. All that we want to do away with is the miserable character of this appropriation, under which the laborer lives merely to increase capital and is allowed to live only insofar as the interests of the ruling class require it.

In bourgeois society, living labor is but a means to increase accumulated labor. In Communist society accumulated labor is but a means to widen, to enrich, to promote the existence of the laborer.

In bourgeois society, therefore, the past dominates the present; in Communist society the present dominates the past. In bourgeois society, capital is independent and has individuality, while the living person is dependent and has no individuality.

And the abolition of this state of things is called by the bourgeois   84
abolition of individuality and freedom! And rightly so. The abolition of bourgeois individuality, bourgeois independence and bourgeois freedom is undoubtedly aimed at.

By freedom is meant, under the present bourgeois conditions of production, free trade, free selling and buying.

But if selling and buying disappears, free selling and buying disappears also. This talk about free selling and buying, and all the other "brave words" of our bourgeoisie about freedom in general have a meaning, if any, only in contrast with restricted selling and buying, with the fettered traders of the Middle Ages, but have no meaning when opposed to the Communistic abolition of buying and selling, of the bourgeois conditions of production, and of the bourgeoisie itself.

You are horrified at our intending to do away with private property.

But in your existing society private property is already done away with for nine-tenths of the population; its existence for the few is solely due to its non-existence in the hands of those nine-tenths. You reproach us, therefore, with intending to do away with a form of property, the necessary condition for whose existence is the nonexistence of any property for the immense majority of society.

In one word, you reproach us with intending to do away with your property. Precisely so: that is just what we intend.

From the moment when labor can no longer be converted into capital, money, or rent, into a social power capable of being monopolized; i.e., from the moment when individual property can no longer be transformed into bourgeois property, into capital, from the moment, you say, individuality vanishes.

You must, therefore, confess that by "individual" you mean no other person than the bourgeois, than the middle-class owner of property. This person must, indeed, be swept out of the way and made impossible.

Communism deprives no man of the power to appropriate the products of society: all that it does is to deprive him of the power to subjugate the labor of others by means of such appropriation.

It has been objected that upon the abolition of private property all work will cease and universal laziness will overtake us.

According to this, bourgeois society ought long ago to have gone to the dogs through sheer idleness; for those of its members who work acquire nothing, and those who acquire anything do not work. The whole of this objection is but another expression of the tautology: that there can no longer be any wage labor when there is no longer any capital.

All objections urged against the Communistic mode of producing and appropriating material products have, in the same way, been urged against the Communistic modes of producing and appropriating intellectual products. Just as, to the bourgeois, the disappearance of class property is the disappearance of production itself, so the disappearance of class culture is to him identical with the disappearance of all culture.

That culture, the loss of which he laments, is, for the enormous majority, a mere training to act as a machine.

But don't wrangle with us so long as you apply, to our intended abolition of bourgeois property, the standard of your bourgeois notions of freedom, culture, law, etc. Your very ideas are but the outgrowth of the conditions of your bourgeois production and bourgeois property, just as your jurisprudence is but the will of your class made into a law for all, a will whose essential character and direction are determined by the economical conditions of existence of your class.

The selfish misconception that induces you to transform into eternal laws of nature and of reason the social forms springing from your present mode of production and form of property—historical relations that rise and disappear in the progress of production—this misconception you share with every ruling class that has preceded you. What you see clearly in the case of ancient property, what you admit in the case of feudal property, you are of course forbidden to admit in the case of your own bourgeois form of property.

Abolition of the family! Even the most radical flare up at this infamous proposal of the Communists.

On what foundation is the present family, the bourgeois family, based? On capital, on private gain. In its completely developed form this family exists only among the bourgeoisie. But this state of things finds its complement in the practical absence of the family among the proletarians, and in public prostitution.

The bourgeois family will vanish as a matter of course when its complement vanishes, and both will vanish with the vanishing of capital. 100

Do you charge us with wanting to stop the exploitation of children by their parents? To this crime we plead guilty.

But, you will say, we destroy the most hallowed of relations when we replace home education by social.

And your education! Is not that also social, and determined by the social conditions under which you educate; by the intervention, direct or indirect, of society by means of schools, etc.? The Communists have not invented the intervention of society in education; they do but seek to alter the character of that intervention, and to rescue education from the influence of the ruling class.

The bourgeois claptrap about the family and education, about the hallowed correlation of parent and child, become all the more disgusting, the more, by the action of Modern Industry, all family ties among the proletarians are torn asunder and their children transformed into simple articles of commerce and instruments of labor. 104

But you Communists would introduce community of women, screams the whole bourgeoisie chorus.

The bourgeois sees in his wife a mere instrument of production. He hears that the instruments of production are to be exploited in common, and, naturally, can come to no other conclusion, than that the lot of being common to all will likewise fall to the women.

He has not even a suspicion that the real point aimed at is to do away with the status of women as mere instruments of production.

For the rest, nothing is more ridiculous than the virtuous indignation of our bourgeois at the community of women which, they pretend, is to be openly and officially established by the Communists. The Communists have no need to introduce community of women; it has existed almost from time immemorial. 108

Our bourgeois, not content with having the wives and daughters of their proletarians at their disposal, not to speak of common prostitutes, take the greatest pleasure in seducing each other's wives.

Bourgeois marriage is in reality a system of wives in common, and thus, at the most, what the Communists might possibly be reproached with, is that they desire to introduce, in substitution for a hypocritically concealed, an openly legalized community of women. For the rest, it is self-evident that the abolition of the present system of production must bring with it the abolition of the community of women springing from that system, i.e., of prostitution both public and private.

The Communists are further reproached with desiring to abolish countries and nationalities.

The working men have no country. We cannot take from them what 112 they don't possess. Since the proletariat must first of all acquire political supremacy, must rise to be the leading class of the nation, must constitute itself the nation, it is, so far, itself national, though not in the bourgeois sense of the word.

National differences and antagonisms between peoples are daily more and more vanishing, owing to the development of the bourgeoisie, to freedom of commerce, to the world market, to uniformity in the mode of production and in the conditions of life corresponding thereto.

The supremacy of the proletariat will cause them to vanish still faster. United action, of the leading civilized countries at least, is one of the first conditions for the emancipation of the proletariat.

In proportion as the exploitation of one individual by another is put an end to, the exploitation of one nation by another will also be put an end to. In proportion as the antagonism between classes within the nation vanishes, the hostility of one nation to another will come to an end.

The charges against Communism made from a religious, a philosophi- 116 cal, and generally, from an ideological standpoint, are not deserving of serious examination.

Does it require deep intuition to comprehend that man's ideas, views, and conceptions, in one word, man's consciousness, changes with every change in the conditions of his material existence, in his social relations and in his social life?

What else does the history of ideas prove than that intellectual production changes in character in proportion as material production is changed? The ruling ideas of each age have ever been the ideas of its ruling class.

When people speak of ideas that revolutionize society they do but express the fact that within the old society the elements of a new one have been created, and that the dissolution of the old ideas keeps even pace with the dissolution of the old conditions of existence.

When the ancient world was in its last throes the ancient religions 120 were overcome by Christianity. When Christian ideas succumbed in the eighteenth century to rationalist ideas, feudal society fought its death battle with the then revolutionary bourgeoisie. The ideas of religious liberty and freedom of conscience merely gave expression to the sway of free competition within the domain of knowledge.

"Undoubtedly," it will be said, "religious, moral, philosophical, and judicial ideas have been modified in the course of historical development. But religion, morality, philosophy, political science, and law, constantly survived this change.

"There are, besides, eternal truths, such as Freedom, Justice, etc., that are common to all states of society. But Communism abolishes eternal truths, it abolishes all religion and all morality, instead of constituting them on a new basis; it therefore acts in contradiction to all past historical experience."

What does this accusation reduce itself to? The history of all past society has consisted in the development of class antagonisms, antagonisms that assumed different forms at different epochs.

But whatever form they may have taken, one fact is common to all 124 past ages, viz., the exploitation of one part of society by the other. No wonder, then, that the social consciousness of past ages, despite all the multiplicity and variety it displays, moves within certain common forms, or general ideas, which cannot completely vanish except with the total disappearance of class antagonisms.

The Communist revolution is the most radical rupture with traditional property relations; no wonder that its development involves the most radical rupture with traditional ideas.

But let us have done with the bourgeois objections to Communism.

We have seen above that the first step in the revolution by the working class is to raise the proletariat to the position of ruling class, to win the battle of democracy.

The proletariat will use its political supremacy to wrest, by degrees, 128 all capital from the bourgeoisie, to centralize all instruments of production in the hands of the State, i.e., of the proletariat organized as a ruling class; and to increase the total productive forces as rapidly as possible.

Of course, in the beginning, this cannot be effected except by means of despotic inroads on the rights of property, and on the conditions of bourgeois production; by means of measures, therefore, which appear economically insufficient and untenable, but which in the course of the movement outstrip themselves, necessitate further inroads upon the old social order, and are unavoidable as a means of entirely revolutionizing the mode of production.

These measures will of course be different in different countries.

Nevertheless in the most advanced countries the following will be pretty generally applicable:

1. Abolition of property in land and application of all rents of land to public purposes.
2. A heavy progressive or graduated income tax.
3. Abolition of all right of inheritance.
4. Confiscation of the property of all emigrants and rebels.

5. Centralization of credit in the hands of the State, by means of a national bank with State capital and an exclusive monopoly.
6. Centralization of the means of communication and transport in the hands of the State.
7. Extension of factories and instruments of production owned by the State; the bringing into cultivation of waste lands, and the improvement of the soil generally in accordance with a common plan.
8. Equal liability of all to labor. Establishment of industrial armies, especially for agriculture.
9. Combination of agriculture with manufacturing industries; gradual abolition of the distinction between town and country by a more equable distribution of the population over the country.
10. Free education for all children in public schools. Abolition of children's factory labor in its present form. Combination of education with industrial production, etc., etc.

When, in the course of development, class distinctions have disap- 132 peared, and all production has been concentrated in the hands of a vast association of the whole nation, the public power will lose its political character. Political power, properly so called, is merely the organized power of one class for oppressing another. If the proletariat during its contest with the bourgeoisie is compelled, by the force of circumstances, to organize itself as a class, if, by means of a revolution, it makes itself the ruling class, and, as such, sweeps away by force the old conditions of production, then it will, along with these conditions, have swept away the conditions for the existence of class antagonism, and of classes generally, and will thereby have abolished its own supremacy as a class.

In place of the old bourgeois society, with its classes and class antagonisms, we shall have an association in which the free development of each is the condition for the free development of all. . . .

POSITION OF THE COMMUNISTS IN RELATION TO THE VARIOUS EXISTING OPPOSITION PARTIES

[The preceding section] has made clear the relations of the Communists to the existing working class parties, such as the Chartists in England and the Agrarian Reforms[7] in America.

The Communists fight for the attainment of the immediate aims, for the enforcement of the momentary interests of the working class; but in the

[7]**Chartists . . . Agrarian Reforms** The Chartists were a radical English group, seeking reforms in land and labor; "Agrarian Reforms" refers to the National Reform Association, formed in New York in 1845, which demanded nationalization of the land.

movement of the present they also represent and take care of the future of that movement. In France the Communists ally themselves with the Social Democrats[8] against the conservative and radical bourgeoisie, reserving, however, the right to take up a critical position in regard to phrases and illusions traditionally handed down from the great Revolution.

In Switzerland they support the Radicals,[9] without losing sight of the fact that this party consists of antagonistic elements, partly of Democratic Socialists, in the French sense, partly of radical bourgeois.

In Poland they support the party that insists on an agrarian revolution, as the prime condition for national emancipation, that party which fomented the insurrection of Cracow in 1846.

In Germany they fight with the bourgeoisie whenever it acts in a revolutionary way, against the absolute monarchy, the feudal squirearchy, and the petty bourgeoisie.

But they never cease for a single instant to instill into the working class the clearest possible recognition of the hostile antagonism between bourgeoisie and proletariat, in order that the German workers may straightway use, as so many weapons against the bourgeoisie, the social and political conditions that the bourgeoisie must necessarily introduce along with its supremacy, and in order that, after the fall of the reactionary classes in Germany, the fight against the bourgeoisie itself may immediately begin.

The Communists turn their attention chiefly to Germany, because that country is on the eve of a bourgeois revolution, that is bound to be carried out under more advanced conditions of European civilization, and with a more developed proletariat, than that of England was in the seventeenth and of France in the eighteenth century, and because the bourgeois revolution in Germany will be but the prelude to an immediately following proletarian revolution.

In short, the Communists everywhere support every revolutionary movement against the existing social and political order of things.

In all these movements they bring to the front, as the leading question in each, the property question, no matter what its degree of development at the time.

Finally, they labor everywhere for the union and agreement of the democratic parties of all countries.

The Communists disdain to conceal their views and aims. They openly declare that their ends can be attained only by the forcible overthrow of all existing social conditions. Let the ruling classes tremble at a Communistic revolution. The proletarians have nothing to lose but their chains. They have a world to win.

Working men of all countries, unite!

---

[8]**Social Democrats** A French group who proposed labor reforms.
[9]**Radicals** Reformers who advocated nonviolent change.

Questions and Suggestions for Writing ==========

1. Briefly state the thesis of paragraphs 7–59 of *The Communist Manifesto*.

2. Marx, writing in 1848, seems to think that the proletariat consists only of factory workers. If *we* say that the proletariat is sometimes called "the lower class," is it true that today's proletariat consists chiefly of factory workers? Or is "the lower class" highly diverse? How, in fact, would you define "the lower class"? Is it somewhat clearly distinct from "the middle class"? Is the concept of class relevant to our society? Why?

3. Some factory workers—such as workers in the automobile industry—make salaries that many people regard as very good. They also have attractive retirement plans and medical coverage. Can it therefore be argued that Marx was utterly mistaken in his prophecies about the future of the worker, especially in his vision of "two great hostile camps . . . bourgeoisie and proletariat"? If so, is his analysis of the workings of history of no value?

4. Putting aside the question of the development of the worker, if you are aware of any errors in Marx's historical analysis, write an essay of 500 words pointing out that he misinterpreted some part of history.

5. In paragraph 20 Marx says: "The bourgeoisie, wherever it has got the upper hand, has put an end to all feudal, patriarchal, idyllic relations." First, exactly what do the words *feudal, patriarchal*, and *idyllic* mean? Second, considering this combination of words, is Marx here (and later in the paragraph) implying the existence of a prebourgeois world that contradicts his idea of continuing class struggle?

6. In paragraph 23 Marx says that the bourgeoisie "has accomplished wonders far surpassing Egyptian pyramids, Roman aqueducts, and Gothic cathedrals; it has conducted expeditions that put in the shade all former Exoduses of nations and crusades." Here, and elsewhere in *The Communist Manifesto*, do you find a view that seems inconsistent with other passages about the bourgeoisie? If so, write a paragraph pointing out the inconsistencies; if not, write a paragraph reconciling the apparent inconsistencies.

7. Marx occasionally uses metaphors—figures of speech—in his writing, such as "A specter is haunting Europe" (the opening line), and "The cheap prices of its commodities are the heavy artillery with which it batters down all Chinese walls" (para. 27), and "What the bourgeoisie therefore produces, above all, are its own gravediggers" (para. 59). Take any one of his metaphors and paraphrase it, translating it (so to speak) into nonfigurative language. Then, in a sentence or two or three explain which version you think is better, and why.

8. In paragraph 102 Marx writes: "But, you will say, we destroy the most hallowed of relations when we replace home education by social." Can it be argued that our system of public education is communistic? And can it be argued that indeed "home education" is preferable to public education?

9. Marx claims that the triumph of the proletariat is "inevitable." He does not mean, however, that workers need make no effort to prevail over their class enemies, for their triumph is fated to take place whether they make any efforts or not. What does he mean? Do you think he is right?

10. On pages 593–594 Marx lists ten "measures" that are necessary, in his judgment, to transform a capitalist society into a communist society. Write an essay of 750 to 1000 words in which you evaluate the extent to which each of these measures has already come into practice in the United States. Which, if any, of these ten do you favor? Explain why.

11. Marx considers several popular objections to communism (abolition of private property, universal laziness, and so on). Write an essay of 500 to 750 words in which you argue for or against *one* of these objections. Base your argument, where possible, on what you know about some actual communist society, such as Soviet Russia, the People's Republic of China, or Castro's Cuba.

12. Let's assume that we are living in 1848, when *The Communist Manifesto* was published. It is unquestionably a time when most people are desperately poor and (if they are not unemployed and starving) are working long hours. In England, for instance, a bill was introduced in 1833 to limit the working hours of children under thirteen to nine hours a day, six days a week, and to limit the hours of persons between ages thirteen and eighteen to twelve hours a day. Not until 1847, with the Ten Hours' Act (referred to by Marx), was the working day in England limited to ten hours. Because we are living in 1848 we don't know what the late twentieth century will be like. Write an essay of 500 to 750 words explaining why you, a hard-pressed worker who has somehow found time to read *The Communist Manifesto*, have decided to become—or not to become—a Communist.

Virginia Woolf

Professions for Women

When your secretary invited me to come here, she told me that your Society is concerned with the employment of women and she suggested that I might tell you something about my own professional experiences. It is true I am a woman; it is true I am employed, but what professional

---

Virginia Woolf (1882–1942) was born in London, daughter of Leslie Stephen, a distinguished Victorian scholar. She grew up in an atmosphere of learning, and after her father's death she continued to move in a world of intellectuals and writers (the Bloomsbury Group) that included economist John Maynard Keynes and novelist E. M. Forster. In 1912 she married Leonard Woolf, a writer with a special interest in politics. Together they founded the Hogarth Press, which published much important material, including Virginia's own novels and the first English translations of Sigmund Freud. In addition to writing such major novels as Mrs. Dalloway *(1925),* To the Lighthouse *(1927), and* The Waves *(1931), she wrote many essays, chiefly on literature and on feminist causes.*

The essay reprinted here was originally a talk delivered in 1931 to the Women's Service League.

experiences have I had? It is difficult to say. My profession is literature; and in that profession there are fewer experiences for women than in any other, with the exception of the stage—fewer, I mean, that are peculiar to women. For the road was cut many years ago—by Fanny Burney, by Aphra Behn, by Harriet Martineau, by Jane Austen, by George Eliot— many famous women, and many more unknown and forgotten, have been before me, making the path smooth, and regulating my steps. Thus, when I came to write, there were very few material obstacles in my way. Writing was a reputable and harmless occupation. The family peace was not broken by the scratching of a pen. No demand was made upon the family purse. For ten and sixpence one can buy paper enough to write all the plays of Shakespeare—if one has a mind that way. Pianos and models, Paris, Vienna, and Berlin, masters and mistresses, are not needed by a writer. The cheapness of writing paper is, of course, the reason why women have succeeded as writers before they have succeeded in the other professions.

But to tell you my story—it is a simple one. You have only got to figure to yourselves a girl in a bedroom with a pen in her hand. She had only to move that pen from left to right—from ten o'clock to one. Then it occurred to her to do what is simple and cheap enough after all—to slip a few of those pages into an envelope, fix a penny stamp in the corner, and drop the envelope into the red box at the corner. It was thus that I became a journalist; and my effort was rewarded on the first day of the following month—a very glorious day it was for me—by a letter from an editor containing a check for one pound ten shillings and sixpence.[1] But to show you how little I deserve to be called a professional woman, how little I know of the struggles and difficulties of such lives, I have to admit that instead of spending that sum upon bread and butter, rent, shoes and stockings, or butcher's bills, I went out and bought a cat—a beautiful cat, a Persian cat, which very soon involved me in bitter disputes with my neighbors.

What could be easier than to write articles and to buy Persian cats with the profits? But wait a moment. Articles have to be about something. Mine, I seem to remember, was about a novel by a famous man. And while I was writing this review, I discovered that if I were going to review books I should need to do battle with a certain phantom. And the phantom was a woman, and when I came to know her better I called her after the heroine of a famous poem, The Angel in the House. It was she who used to come between me and my paper when I was writing reviews. It was she who bothered me and wasted my time and so tormented me that at last I killed her. You who come of a younger and happier generation may not have heard of her—you may not know what I mean by the Angel in the House. I will describe her as shortly as I can. She was intensely sympathetic. She

---

[1] **one pound ten shillings and sixpence** In 1930, this sum was equivalent to about $7.40. [Editors' note]

was immensely charming. She was utterly unselfish. She excelled in the difficult arts of family life. She sacrificed herself daily. If there was chicken, she took the leg; if there was a draught she sat in it—in short she was so constituted that she never had a mind or a wish of her own, but preferred to sympathize always with the minds and wishes of others. Above all—I need not say it—she was pure. Her purity was supposed to be her chief beauty—her blushes, her great grace. In those days—the last of Queen Victoria—every house had its Angel. And when I came to write I encountered her with the very first words. The shadow of her wings fell on my page; I heard the rustling of her skirts in the room. Directly, that is to say, I took my pen in hand to review that novel by a famous man, she slipped behind me and whispered: "My dear, you are a young woman. You are writing about a book that has been written by a man. Be sympathetic; be tender; flatter; deceive; use all the arts and wiles of our sex. Never let anybody guess that you have a mind of your own. Above all, be pure." And she made as if to guide my pen. I now record the one act for which I take some credit to myself, though the credit rightly belongs to some excellent ancestors of mine who left me a certain sum of money—shall we say five hundred pounds a year?—so that it was not necessary for me to depend solely on charm for my living. I turned upon her and caught her by the throat. I did my best to kill her. My excuse, if I were to be had up in a court of law, would be that I acted in self-defense. Had I not killed her she would have killed me. She would have plucked the heart out of my writing. For, as I found, directly I put pen to paper, you cannot review even a novel without having a mind of your own, without expressing what you think to be the truth about human relations, morality, sex. And all these questions, according to the Angel in the House, cannot be dealt with freely and openly by women; they must charm, they must conciliate, they must—to put it bluntly—tell lies if they are to succeed. Thus, whenever I felt the shadow of her wing or the radiance of her halo upon my page, I took up the inkpot and flung it at her. She died hard. Her fictitious nature was of great assistance to her. It is far harder to kill a phantom than a reality. She was always creeping back when I thought I had despatched her. Though I flatter myself that I killed her in the end, the struggle was severe; it took much time that had better have been spent upon learning Greek grammar; or in roaming the world in search of adventures. But it was a real experience; it was an experience that was bound to befall all women writers at that time. Killing the Angel in the House was part of the occupation of a woman writer.

But to continue my story. The Angel was dead; what then remained? 4 You may say that what remained was a simple and common object—a young woman in a bedroom with an inkpot. In other words, now that she had rid herself of falsehood, that young woman had only to be herself. Ah, but what is "herself"? I mean, what is a woman? I assure you, I do not know. I do not believe that you know. I do not believe that anybody can know until she has expressed herself in all the arts and professions open to human skill. That indeed is one of the reasons why I have come here—out of respect for you, who are in process of showing us by your experiments what a woman is, who are in process of providing us, by your failures and successes, with that extremely important piece of information.

But to continue the story of my professional experiences. I made one pound ten and six by my first review; and I bought a Persian cat with the proceeds. Then I grew ambitious. A Persian cat is all very well, I said; but a Persian cat is not enough. I must have a motor car. And it was thus that I became a novelist—for it is a very strange thing that people will give you a motor car if you will tell them a story. It is a still stranger thing that there is nothing so delightful in the world as telling stories. It is far pleasanter than writing reviews of famous novels. And yet, if I am to obey your secretary and tell you my professional experiences as a novelist, I must tell you about a very strange experience that befell me as a novelist. And to understand it you must try first to imagine a novelist's state of mind. I hope I am not giving away professional secrets if I say that a novelist's chief desire is to be as unconscious as possible. He has to induce in himself a state of perpetual lethargy. He wants life to proceed with the utmost quiet and regularity. He wants to see the same faces, to read the same books, to do the same things day after day, month after month, while he is writing, so that nothing may break the illusion in which he is living—so that nothing may disturb or disquiet the mysterious nosings about, feelings round, darts, dashes, and sudden discoveries of that very shy and illusive spirit, the imagination. I suspect that this state is the same both for men and women. Be that as it may, I want you to imagine me writing a novel in a state of trance. I want you to figure to yourselves a girl sitting with a pen in her hand, which for minutes, and indeed for hours, she never dips into the inkpot. The image that comes to my mind when I think of this girl is the image of a fisherman lying sunk in dreams on the verge of a deep lake with a rod held out over the water. She was letting her imagination sweep unchecked round every rock and cranny of the world that lies submerged in the depths of our unconscious being. Now came the experience, the experience that I believe to be far commoner with women writers than with men. The line raced through the girl's fingers. Her imagination had rushed away. It had sought the pools, the depths, the dark places where the largest fish slumber. And then there was a smash. There was an explosion. There was foam and confusion. The imagination had dashed itself against something hard. The girl was roused from her dream. She was indeed in a state of the most acute and difficult distress. To speak without figure she had thought of something, something about the body, about the passions which it was unfitting for her as a woman to say. Men, her reason told her, would be shocked. The consciousness of what men will say of a woman who speaks the truth about her passions had roused her from her artist's state of unconsciousness. She could write no more. The trance was over. Her imagination could work no longer. This I believe to be a very common experience with women writers—they are impeded by the extreme conventionality of the other sex. For though men sensibly allow themselves great freedom in these respects, I doubt that they realize or can control the extreme severity with which they condemn such freedom in women.

These then were two very genuine experiences of my own. These were two of the adventures of my professional life. The first—killing the Angel in the House—I think I solved. She died. But the second, telling the truth about my own experiences as a body, I do not think I solved. I doubt that any woman has solved it yet. The obstacles against her are still immensely powerful—and yet they are very difficult to define. Outwardly, what is simpler than to write books? Outwardly, what obstacles are there for a woman rather than for a man? Inwardly, I think, the case is very different; she has still many ghosts to fight, many prejudices to overcome. Indeed it will be a long time still, I think, before a woman can sit down to write a book without finding a phantom to be slain, a rock to be dashed against. And if this is so in literature, the freest of all professions for women, how is it in the new professions which you are now for the first time entering?

Those are the questions that I should like, had I time, to ask you. And indeed, if I have laid stress upon these professional experiences of mine, it is because I believe that they are, though in different forms, yours also. Even when the path is nominally open—when there is nothing to prevent a woman from being a doctor, a lawyer, a civil servant—there are many phantoms and obstacles, as I believe, looming in her way. To discuss and define them is I think of great value and importance; for thus only can the labor be shared, the difficulties be solved. But besides this, it is necessary also to discuss the ends and the aims for which we are fighting, for which we are doing battle with these formidable obstacles. Those aims cannot be taken for granted; they must be perpetually questioned and examined. The whole position, as I see it—here in this hall surrounded by women practicing for the first time in history I know not how many different professions—is one of extraordinary interest and importance. You have won rooms of your own in the house hitherto exclusively owned by men. You are able, though not without great labor and effort, to pay the rent. You are earning your five hundred pounds a year. But this freedom is only a beginning; the room is your own, but it is still bare. It has to be furnished; it has to be decorated; it has to be shared. How are you going to furnish it, how are you going to decorate it? With whom are you going to share it, and upon what terms? These, I think, are questions of the utmost importance and interest. For the first time in history you are able to ask them; for the first time you are able to decide for yourselves what the answers should be. Willingly would I stay and discuss those questions and answers—but not tonight. My time is up; and I must cease.

Questions and Suggestions for Writing

1. At the end of the first paragraph, Woolf purports to explain why "women have succeeded as writers before they have succeeded in the other professions." Do you think her explanation is serious? Correct? Write a 250 word essay in which you defend or attack her explanation.

2. Woolf declares herself (paras. 5 and 6) to have been unable to write comfortably about her "passions" and her "own experiences as a body." She also thinks that men have it easier in this respect. Can you think of reasons why this difference should be true, or appear to be true, earlier in this century? Do you think it is true today? Why, or why not?

3. In her final paragraph Woolf says that "even when the path is nominally open" for a woman to become a doctor, lawyer, or civil servant, "there are many phantoms and obstacles . . . looming in her way." In a paragraph explain what she means, and in a second paragraph indicate whether you think her point is valid today.

4. In your library find a copy of John Stuart Mill's *Subjection of Women* (written about seventy-five years before Woolf's essay), read it, and write a 500-word essay focused on one of these questions: (a) Would Mill have approved of Woolf's murdering the Angel in the House? (b) How would Mill explain Woolf's inability to answer the question, "What is a woman?"

5. In the reference section in your library find out what you can about each of the five women Woolf mentions in her first paragraph. Then look up something about the life of Virginia Woolf herself, and write a 500-word essay in which you compare her life and career to the life and career of the one woman among these five most like her.

B. F. Skinner

Education in Walden Two

The quarters for children from one to three consisted of several small playrooms with Lilliputian[1] furniture, a child's lavatory, and a dressing and locker room. Several small sleeping rooms were operated on the same

[1] In Jonathan Swift's *Gulliver's Travels*, Gulliver visits Lilliput, a country whose inhabitants are only six inches tall. [Editors' note]

Until his recent retirement, B[urrhus] F[rederic] Skinner (b. 1904) taught experimental psychology at Harvard University. He is best known for his contributions to behavioral psychology, studying the observable responses of creatures to external physical stimuli. Briefly, for Skinner, behavior is created by reinforcement, which may be influenced by reward or punishment. Skinner's critics charge that he seeks to rob human beings of autonomy, but he replies that our apparent autonomy

principle as the baby-cubicles. The temperature and the humidity were controlled so that clothes or bedclothing were not needed. The cots were double-decker arrangements of the plastic mattresses we had seen in the cubicles. The children slept unclothed, except for diapers. There were more beds than necessary, so that the children could be grouped according to developmental age or exposure to contagious diseases or need for supervision, or for educational purposes.

We followed Mrs. Nash to a large screened porch on the south side of the building, where several children were playing in sandboxes and on swings and climbing apparatuses. A few wore "training pants"; the rest were naked. Beyond the porch was a grassy play yard enclosed by closely trimmed hedges, where other children, similarly undressed, were at play. Some kind of marching game was in progress.

As we returned, we met two women carrying food hampers. They spoke to Mrs. Nash and followed her to the porch. In a moment five or six children came running into the playrooms and were soon using the lavatory and dressing themselves. Mrs. Nash explained that they were being taken on a picnic.

"What about the children who don't go?" said Castle. "What do you   4
do about the green-eyed monster?"

Mrs. Nash was puzzled.

"Jealousy. Envy," Castle elaborated. "Don't the children who stay home ever feel unhappy about it?"

"I don't understand," said Mrs. Nash.

"And I hope you won't try," said Frazier, with a smile. "I'm afraid we   8
must be moving along."

We said good-bye, and I made an effort to thank Mrs. Nash, but she seemed to be puzzled by that too, and Frazier frowned as if I had committed some breach of good taste.

"I think Mrs. Nash's puzzlement," said Frazier, as we left the building, "is proof enough that our children are seldom envious or jealous. Mrs. Nash was twelve years old when Walden Two was founded. It was a little late to undo her early training, but I think we were successful. She's a good

---

is chiefly an illusion: We merely think we act freely, when in fact we are respond-ing to our family, peer group, culture, unconscious prejudices, and other stimuli. Skinner holds that he is helping us to see what really conditions our responses. He has set forth his ideas in several books, notably in Walden Two *(1948),* Science and Human Behavior *(1953),* Beyond Freedom and Dignity *(1971), and* About Be-haviorism *(1974). Our selection comes from* Walden Two, *a book cast in a fictional mode. The title of course alludes ironically to Thoreau's* Walden, *a book celebrat-ing independence.*

In the book, Walden Two *Community was founded by Frazier, formerly a professor of psychology. In the selection that follows, two other professors, Burris (the narrator) and Castle, are visiting the community, along with some younger people, including Barbara and her boyfriend Rodge.*

example of the Walden Two product. She could probably recall the experience of jealousy, but it's not part of her present life."

"Surely that's going too far!" said Castle. "You can't be so godlike as all that! You must be assailed by emotions just as much as the rest of us!"

"We can discuss the question of godlikeness later, if you wish," replied 12 Frazier. "As to emotions—we aren't free of them all, nor should we like to be. But the meaner and more annoying—the emotions which breed unhappiness—are almost unknown here, like unhappiness itself. We don't need them any longer in our struggle for existence, and it's easier on our circulatory system, and certainly pleasanter, to dispense with them."

"If you've discovered how to do that, you are indeed a genius," said Castle. He seemed almost stunned as Frazier nodded assent. "We all know that emotions are useless and bad for our peace of mind and our blood pressure," he went on. "But how arrange things otherwise?"

"We arrange them otherwise here," said Frazier. He was showing a mildness of manner which I was coming to recognize as a sign of confidence.

"But emotions are—fun!" said Barbara. "Life wouldn't be worth living without them."

"Some of them, yes," said Frazier. "The productive and strengthening 16 emotions—joy and love. But sorrow and hate—and the high-voltage excitements of anger, fear, and rage—are out of proportion with the needs of modern life, and they're wasteful and dangerous. Mr. Castle has mentioned jealousy—a minor form of anger, I think we may call it. Naturally we avoid it. It has served its purpose in the evolution of man; we've no further use for it. If we allowed it to persist, it would only sap the life out of us. In a cooperative society there's no jealousy because there's no need for jealousy."

"That implies that you all get everything you want," said Castle. "But what about social possessions? Last night you mentioned the young man who chose a particular girl or profession. There's still a chance for jealousy there, isn't there?"

"It doesn't imply that we get everything we want," said Frazier. "Of course we don't. But jealousy wouldn't help. In a competitive world there's some point to it. It energizes one to attack a frustrating condition. The impulse and the added energy are an advantage. Indeed, in a competitive world emotions work all too well. Look at the singular lack of success of the complacent man. He enjoys a more serene life, but it's less likely to be a fruitful one. The world isn't ready for simple pacifism or Christian humility, to cite two cases in point. Before you can safely train out the destructive and wasteful emotions, you must make sure they're no longer needed."

"How do you make sure that jealousy isn't needed in Walden Two?" I said.

"In Walden Two problems can't be solved by attacking others," said 20 Frazier with marked finality.

"That's not the same as eliminating jealousy, though," I said.

"Of course it's not. But when a particular emotion is no longer a useful part of a behavioral repertoire, we proceed to eliminate it."

"Yes, but how?"

"It's simply a matter of behavioral engineering," said Frazier.   24

"Behavioral engineering?"

"You're baiting me, Burris. You know perfectly well what I mean. The techniques have been available for centuries. We use them in education and in the psychological management of the community. But you're forcing my hand," he added. "I was saving that for this evening. But let's strike while the iron is hot."

We had stopped at the door of the large children's building. Frazier shrugged his shoulders, walked to the shade of a large tree, and threw himself on the ground. We arranged ourselves about him and waited.

"Each of us," Frazier began, "is engaged in a pitched battle with the   28 rest of mankind."

"A curious premise for a Utopia," said Castle. "Even a pessimist like myself takes a more hopeful view than that."

"You do, you do," said Frazier. "But let's be realistic. Each of us has interests which conflict with the interests of everybody else. That's our original sin, and it can't be helped. Now, 'everybody else' we call 'society.' It's a powerful opponent, and it always wins. Oh, here and there an individual prevails for a while and gets what he wants. Sometimes he storms the culture of a society and changes it slightly to his own advantage. But society wins in the long run, for it has the advantage of numbers and of age. Many prevail against one, and men against a baby. Society attacks early, when the individual is helpless. It enslaves him almost before he has tasted freedom. The 'ologies' will tell you how it's done. Theology calls it building a conscience or developing a spirit of selflessness. Psychology calls it the growth of the super-ego.

"Considering how long society has been at it, you'd expect a better job. But the campaigns have been badly planned and the victory has never been secure. The behavior of the individual has been shaped according to revelations of 'good conduct,' never as the result of experimental study. But why not experiment? The questions are simple enough. What's the best behavior for the individual so far as the group is concerned? And how can the individual be induced to behave in that way? Why not explore these questions in a scientific spirit?

"We could do just that in Walden Two. We had already worked out a   32 code of conduct—subject, of course, to experimental modification. The code would keep things running smoothly if everybody lived up to it. Our job was to see that everybody did. Now, you can't get people to follow a useful code by making them into so many jacks-in-the-box. You can't foresee all future circumstances, and you can't specify adequate future conduct. You don't know what will be required. Instead you have to set up certain behavioral processes which will lead the individual to design his own 'good' conduct when the time comes. We call that sort of thing 'self-control.' But don't be misled, the control always rests in the last analysis in the hands of society.

"One of our Planners, a young man named Simmons, worked with me. It was the first time in history that the matter was approached in an experimental way. Do you question that statement, Mr. Castle?"

"I'm not sure I know what you are talking about," said Castle.

"Then let me go on. Simmons and I began by studying the great works on morals and ethics—Plato, Aristotle, Confucius, the New Testament, the Puritan divines, Machiavelli, Chesterfield, Freud—there were scores of them. We were looking for any and every method of shaping human behavior by imparting techniques of self-control. Some techniques were obvious enough, for they had marked turning points in human history. 'Love your enemies' is an example—a psychological invention for easing the lot of an oppressed people. The severest trial of oppression is the constant rage which one suffers at the thought of the oppressor. What Jesus discovered was how to avoid these inner devastations. His technique was to *practice the opposite emotion.* If a man can succeed in 'loving his enemies' and 'taking no thought for the morrow,' he will no longer be assailed by hatred of the oppressor or rage at the loss of his freedom or possessions. He may not get his freedom or possessions back, but he's less miserable. It's a difficult lesson. It comes late in our program."

"I thought you were opposed to modifying emotions and instincts 36 until the world was ready for it," said Castle. "According to you, the principle of 'love your enemies' should have been suicidal."

"It would have been suicidal, except for an entirely unforeseen consequence. Jesus must have been quite astonished at the effect of his discovery. We are only just beginning to understand the power of love because we are just beginning to understand the weakness of force and aggression. But the science of behavior is clear about all that now. Recent discoveries in the analysis of punishment—but I am falling into one digression after another. Let me save my explanation of why the Christian virtues—and I mean merely the Christian techniques of self-control—have not disappeared from the face of the earth, with due recognition of the fact that they suffered a narrow squeak within recent memory.

"When Simmons and I had collected our techniques of control, we had to discover how to teach them. That was more difficult. Current educational practices were of little value, and religious practices scarcely any better. Promising paradise or threatening hell-fire is, we assumed, generally admitted to be unproductive. It is based upon a fundamental fraud which, when discovered, turns the individual against society and nourishes the very thing it tries to stamp out. What Jesus offered in return for loving one's enemies was heaven *on earth*, better known as peace of mind.

"We found a few suggestions worth following in the practices of the clinical psychologist. We undertook to build a tolerance for annoying experiences. The sunshine of midday is extremely painful if you come from a dark room, but take it in easy stages and you can avoid pain altogether. The analogy can be misleading, but in much the same way it's possible to build a tolerance to painful or distasteful stimuli, or to frustration, or to situations which arouse fear, anger, or rage. Society and nature throw these annoyances at the individual with no regard for the development of tolerances. Some achieve tolerances, most fail. Where would the science of immunization be if it followed a schedule of accidental dosages?

"Take the principle of 'Get thee behind me, Satan,' for example," 40 Frazier continued. "It's a special case of self-control by altering the environment. Subclass A 3, I believe. We give each child a lollipop which has been dipped in powdered sugar so that a single touch of the tongue can be detected. We tell him he may eat the lollipop later in the day, provided it hasn't already been licked. Since the child is only three or four, it is a fairly diff——"

"Three or four!" Castle exclaimed.

"All our ethical training is completed by the age of six," said Frazier quietly. "A simple principle like putting temptation out of sight would be acquired before four. But at such an early age the problem of not licking the lollipop isn't easy. Now, what would you do, Mr. Castle, in a similar situation?"

"Put the lollipop out of sight as quickly as possible."

"Exactly. I can see you've been well trained. Or perhaps you dis- 44 covered the principle for yourself. We're in favor of original inquiry wherever possible, but in this case we have a more important goal and we don't hesitate to give verbal help. First of all, the children are urged to examine their own behavior while looking at the lollipops. This helps them to recognize the need for self-control. Then the lollipops are concealed, and the children are asked to notice any gain in happiness or any reduction in tension. Then a strong distraction is arranged—say; an interesting game. Later the children are reminded of the candy and encouraged to examine their reaction. The value of the distraction is generally obvious. Well, need I go on? When the experiment is repeated a day or so later, the children all run with the lollipops to their lockers and do exactly what Mr. Castle would do—a sufficient indication of the success of our training."

"I wish to report an objective observation of my reaction to your story," said Castle, controlling his voice with great precision. "I find myself revolted by this display of sadistic tyranny."

"I don't wish to deny you the exercise of an emotion which you seem to find enjoyable," said Frazier. "So let me go on. Concealing a tempting but forbidden object is a crude solution. For one thing, it's not always feasible. We want a sort of psychological concealment—covering up the candy by paying no attention. In a later experiment the children wear their lollipops like crucifixes for a few hours."

> "'Instead of the cross, the lollipop,
> About my neck was hung,' "[2]

said Castle.

"I wish somebody had taught me that, though," said Rodge, with a glance at Barbara.

"Don't we all?" said Frazier. "Some of us learn control, more or less by 48 accident. The rest of us go all our lives not even understanding how it is possible, and blaming our failure on being born the wrong way."

"How do you build up a tolerance to an annoying situation?" I said.

"Oh, for example, by having the children 'take' a more and more painful shock, or drink cocoa with less and less sugar in it until a bitter concoction can be savored without a bitter face."

"But jealousy or envy—you can't administer them in graded doses," I said.

"And why not? Remember, we control the social environment, too, at 52 this age. That's why we get our ethical training in early. Take this case. A group of children arrive home after a long walk tired and hungry. They're expecting supper; they find, instead, that it's time for a lesson in self-control: they must stand for five minutes in front of steaming bowls of soup.

"The assignment is accepted like a problem in arithmetic. Any groaning or complaining is a wrong answer. Instead, the children begin at once to work upon themselves to avoid any unhappiness during the delay. One of them may make a joke of it. We encourage a sense of humor as a good way of not taking an annoyance seriously. The joke won't be much, according to adult standards—perhaps the child will simply pretend to empty the bowl of soup into his upturned mouth. Another may start a song with many verses. The rest join in at once, for they've learned that it's a good way to make time pass."

Frazier glanced uneasily at Castle, who was not to be appeased.

"That also strikes you as a form of torture, Mr. Castle?" he asked.

"I'd rather be put on the rack," said Castle.   56

"Then you have by no means had the thorough training I supposed. You can't imagine how lightly the children take such an experience. It's a rather severe biological frustration, for the children are tired and hungry

---

[2]An adaptation of a line from S. T. Coleridge's poem, "The Rime of the Ancient Mariner," with "lollipop" substituted for "Albatross." The mariner had wantonly killed an albatross, and the dead bird was placed about his neck as a sign of his sin. [Editors' note]

and they must stand and look at food; but it's passed off as lightly as a five-minute delay at curtain time. We regard it as a fairly elementary test. Much more difficult problems follow."

"I suspected as much," muttered Castle.

"In a later stage we forbid all social devices. No songs, no jokes—merely silence. Each child is forced back upon his own resources—a very important step."

"I should think so," I said. "And how do you know it's successful? You might produce a lot of silently resentful children. It's certainly a dangerous stage." 60

"It is, and we follow each child carefully. If he hasn't picked up the necessary techniques, we start back a little. A still more advanced stage"—Frazier glanced again at Castle, who stirred uneasily—"brings me to my point. When it's time to sit down to the soup, the children count off—heads and tails. Then a coin is tossed and if it comes up heads, the 'heads' sit down and eat. The 'tails' remain standing for another five minutes."

Castle groaned.

"And you call that envy?" I asked.

"Perhaps not exactly," said Frazier. "At least there's seldom any ag- 64 gression against the lucky ones. The emotion, if any, is directed against Lady Luck herself, against the toss of the coin. That, in itself, is a lesson worth learning, for it's the only direction in which emotion has a surviving chance to be useful. And resentment toward things in general, while perhaps just as silly as personal aggression, is more easily controlled. Its expression is not socially objectionable."

Frazier looked nervously from one of us to the other. He seemed to be trying to discover whether we shared Castle's prejudice. I began to realize, also, that he had not really wanted to tell this story. He was vulnerable. He was treading on sanctified ground, and I was pretty sure he had not established the value of most of these practices in an experimental fashion. He could scarcely have done so in the short space of ten years. He was working on faith, and it bothered him.

I tried to bolster his confidence by reminding him that he had a professional colleague among his listeners. "May you not inadvertently teach your children some of the very emotions you're trying to eliminate?" I said. "What's the effect, for example, of finding the anticipation of a warm supper suddenly thwarted? Doesn't that eventually lead to feelings of uncertainty, or even anxiety?"

"It might. We had to discover how often our lessons could be safely administered. But all our schedules are worked out experimentally. We watch for undesired consequences just as any scientist watches for disrupting factors in his experiments.

"After all, it's a simple and sensible program," he went on in a tone of 68 appeasement. "We set up a system of gradually increasing annoyances and frustrations against a background of complete serenity. An easy environment is made more and more difficult as the children acquire the capacity to adjust."

"But *why?*" said Castle. "Why these deliberate unpleasantnesses—to put it mildly? I must say I think you and your friend Simmons are really very subtle sadists."

"You've reversed your position, Mr. Castle," said Frazier in a sudden flash of anger with which I rather sympathized. Castle was calling names, and he was also being unaccountably and perhaps intentionally obtuse. "A while ago you accused me of breeding a race of softies," Frazier continued. "Now you object to toughening them up. But what you don't understand is that these potentially unhappy situations are never very annoying. Our schedules make sure of that. You wouldn't understand, however, because you're not so far advanced as our children."

Castle grew black.

"But what do your children get out of it?" he insisted, apparently 72 trying to press some vague advantage in Frazier's anger.

"What do they get out of it!" exclaimed Frazier, his eyes flashing with a sort of helpless contempt. His lips curled and he dropped his head to look at his fingers, which were crushing a few blades of grass.

"They must get happiness and freedom and strength," I said, putting myself in a ridiculous position in attempting to make peace.

"They don't sound happy or free to me, standing in front of bowls of Forbidden Soup," said Castle, answering me parenthetically while continuing to stare at Frazier.

"If I must spell it out," Frazier began with a deep sigh, "what they get 76 is escape from the petty emotions which eat the heart out of the unprepared. They get the satisfaction of pleasant and profitable social relations on a scale almost undreamed of in the world at large. They get immeasurably increased efficiency, because they can stick to a job without suffering the aches and pains which soon beset most of us. They get new horizons, for they are spared the emotions characteristic of frustration and failure. They get—" His eyes searched the branches of the trees. "Is that enough?" he said at last.

"And the community must gain their loyalty," I said, "when they discover the fears and jealousies and diffidences in the world at large."

"I'm glad you put it that way," said Frazier. "You might have said that they must feel superior to the miserable products of our public schools. But we're at pains to keep any feeling of superiority or contempt under control, too. Having suffered most acutely from it myself, I put the subject first on our agenda. We carefully avoid any joy in a personal triumph which means the personal failure of somebody else. We take no pleasure in the sophistical, the disputative, the dialectical." He threw a vicious glance at Castle. "We don't use the motive of domination, because we are always thinking of the whole group. We could motivate a few geniuses that way—it was certainly my own motivation—but we'd sacrifice some of the happiness of everyone else. Triumph over nature and over oneself, yes. But over others, never."

"You've taken the mainspring out of the watch," said Castle flatly.

"That's an experimental question, Mr. Castle, and you have the wrong 80 answer."

Frazier was making no effort to conceal his feeling. If he had been riding Castle, he was now using his spurs. Perhaps he sensed that the rest of us had come round and that he could change his tactics with a single holdout. But it was more than strategy, it was genuine feeling. Castle's undeviating skepticism was a growing frustration.

"Are your techniques really so very new?" I said hurriedly. "What about the primitive practice of submitting a boy to various tortures before granting him a place among adults? What about the disciplinary techniques of Puritanism? Or of the modern school, for that matter?"

"In one sense you're right," said Frazier. "And I think you've nicely answered Mr. Castle's tender concern for our little ones. The unhappinesses we deliberately impose are far milder than the normal unhappinesses from which we offer protection. Even at the height of our ethical training, the unhappiness is ridiculously trivial—to the well-trained child.

"But there's a world of difference in the way we use these an- 84 noyances," he continued. "For one thing, we don't punish. We never administer an unpleasantness in the hope of repressing or eliminating undesirable behavior. But there's another difference. In most cultures the child meets up with annoyances and reverses of uncontrolled magnitude. Some are imposed in the name of discipline by persons in authority. Some, like hazings, are condoned though not authorized. Others are merely accidental. No one cares to, or is able to, prevent them.

"We all know what happens. A few hardy children emerge, particularly those who have got their unhappiness in doses that could be swallowed. They become brave men. Others become sadists or masochists of varying degrees of pathology. Not having conquered a painful environment, they become preoccupied with pain and make a devious art of it. Others submit—and hope to inherit the earth. The rest—the cravens, the cowards—live in fear for the rest of their lives. And that's only a single field—the reaction to pain. I could cite a dozen parallel cases. The optimist and the pessimist, the contented and the disgruntled, the loved and the unloved, the ambitious and the discouraged—these are only the extreme products of a miserable system.

"Traditional practices are admittedly better than nothing," Frazier went on. "Spartan or Puritan—no one can question the occasional happy result. But the whole system rests upon the wasteful principle of selection. The English public school[3] of the nineteenth century produced brave

[3]**English public schools,** such as Eton and Harrow, are comparable to American private preparatory schools, such as Groton and Exeter, and not at all like American public high schools. [Editors' note]

men—by setting up almost insurmountable barriers and making the most of the few who came over. But selection isn't education. Its crops of brave men will always be small, and the waste enormous. Like all primitive principles, selection serves in place of education only through a profligate use of material. Multiply extravagantly and select with rigor. It's the philosophy of the 'big litter' as an alternative to good child hygiene.

"In Walden Two we have a different objective. We make every man a brave man. They all come over the barriers. Some require more preparation than others, but they all come over. The traditional use of adversity is to select the strong. We control adversity to build strength. And we do it deliberately, no matter how sadistic Mr. Castle may think us, in order to prepare for adversities which are beyond control. Our children eventually experience the 'heartache and the thousand natural shocks that flesh is heir to.' It would be the cruelest possible practice to protect them as long as possible, especially when we *could* protect them so well."

Frazier held out his hands in an exaggerated gesture of appeal.   88

"What alternative *had* we?" he said, as if he were in pain. "What else could we do? For four or five years we could provide a life in which no important need would go unsatisfied, a life practically free of anxiety or frustration or annoyance. What would *you* do? Would you let the child enjoy this paradise with no thought for the future—like an idolatrous and pampering mother? Or would you relax control of the environment and let the child meet accidental frustrations? *But what is the virtue of accident?* No, there was only one course open to us. We had to *design* a series of adversities, so that the child would develop the greatest possible self-control. Call it deliberate, if you like, and accuse us of sadism; there was no other course." Frazier turned to Castle, but he was scarcely challenging him. He seemed to be waiting, anxiously, for his capitulation. But Castle merely shifted his ground.

"I find it difficult to classify these practices," he said. Frazier emitted a disgruntled "Ha!" and sat back. "Your system seems to have usurped the place as well as the techniques of religion."

"Of religion and family culture," said Frazier wearily. "But I don't call it usurpation. Ethical training belongs to the community. As for techniques, we took every suggestion we could find without prejudice as to the source. But not on faith. We disregarded all claims of revealed truth and put every principle to an experimental test. And by the way, I've very much misrepresented the whole system if you suppose that any of the practices I've described are fixed. We try out many different techniques. Gradually we work toward the best possible set. And we don't pay much attention to the apparent success of a principle in the course of history. History is honored in Walden Two only as entertainment. It isn't taken seriously as food for thought. Which reminds me, very rudely, of our original plan for the morning. Have you had enough of emotion? Shall we turn to intellect?"

Frazier addressed these questions to Castle in a very friendly way and   92
I was glad to see that Castle responded in kind. It was perfectly clear,
however, that neither of them had ever worn a lollipop about the neck or
faced a bowl of Forbidden Soup.

Questions and Suggestions for Writing

1. In his preface to *Walden Two* Skinner says the book is "an account of how I
   thought a group of, say, a thousand people might have solved the problems of
   their daily lives with the help of behavioral engineering." And in our selection
   from the book he again uses the expression "behavioral engineering" in paragraph 24. What does this expression mean to you? If you have read the
   selection from More's *Utopia* (p. 553), explain whether or not More seems to be
   advocating behavioral engineering.

2. In the preface to *Walden Two* Skinner says:

   > In spite of our lip service to freedom, we do very little to further the development
   > of the individual. How many Americans can say that they are doing the kinds of
   > things they are best qualified to do and most enjoy doing?

   Think of your closest relatives—let's say your parents, grandparents, siblings,
   uncles, aunts, and cousins—and try to form an impression of how many of
   them "are doing the kinds of things they are best qualified to do and most
   enjoy doing." Then try to imagine whether the number would be larger if they
   had lived in Skinner's Walden Two. Why would the number be larger? Why not?

3. Skinner claims that "jealousy and envy" are missing from the experience of the
   inhabitants of Walden Two. In one paragraph explain the difference between
   these two emotions.

4. In paragraph 12 Frazier says that emotions that breed unhappiness are no
   longer needed "in our struggle for existence," and a few paragraphs later he
   goes on to say that jealousy "has served its purpose in the evolution of man."
   What does he mean? Why might such emotions once have been needed, and
   why, according to Skinner, are they not needed in Walden Two? Frazier claims
   that jealousy, envy, and anger are "useless and bad from our point of view," as
   well as "dangerous." Do you think, for example, that the emotion of resentment when confronted with unpunished wrongdoing can be defended? Explain.

5. In paragraph 35 Frazier characterizes Jesus' 'Love your enemies' as "a psychological invention for easing the lot of an oppressed people." Read the entire
   paragraph, and the next three paragraphs, and then evaluate Frazier's interpretation of Jesus' words.

6. Castle characterizes the lollipop exercise as "sadistic tyranny." In the following
   paragraphs Frazier seeks to justify this and other exercises. Do you find his
   arguments convincing? Why?

7. In Walden Two, "ethical training" seems to consist mainly of acquiring the
   disposition to obey certain rules. Do you think this is an adequate conception
   of "ethical training"?

8. The methods of "ethical training" used in Walden Two were developed, we are told, "experimentally," that is, by trial and error, as Frazier explains. Do you see anything objectionable in such experiments on children? Can you think of any alternatives?

9. Why do you or why do you not plan to use the lollipop and soup exercises on any children you have or may have?

10. In an essay of 500 words explain why you wish you had been brought up in Walden Two, or why you are glad that you weren't.

Martin Luther King, Jr.

I Have a Dream

I am happy to join with you today in what will go down in history as the greatest demonstration for freedom in the history of our nation.

Five score years ago, a great American, in whose symbolic shadow we stand today, signed the Emancipation Proclamation. This momentous decree came as a great beacon light of hope to millions of Negro slaves who had been seared in the flames of withering injustice. It came as a joyous daybreak to end the long night of their captivity. But one hundred years later, the Negro still is not free. One hundred years later, the life of the Negro is still sadly crippled by the manacles of segregation and the chains of discrimination. One hundred years later, the Negro lives on a lonely island of poverty in the midst of a vast ocean of material prosperity. One hundred years later, the Negro is still anguished in the corners of American society and finds himself in exile in his own land. And so we have come here today to dramatize a shameful condition.

In a sense we have come to our nation's capital to cash a check. When the architects of our republic wrote the magnificent words of the Constitution and the Declaration of Independence, they were signing a promissory note to which every American was to fall heir. This note was the promise that all men—yes, Black men as well as white men—would be guaranteed the inalienable rights of life, liberty, and the pursuit of happiness.

It is obvious today that America has defaulted on this promissory note   4 insofar as her citizens of color are concerned. Instead of honoring this sacred obligation, America has given the Negro people a bad check, a

---

For a biographical note about Dr. King (1929–1968), see page 496. "I Have a Dream" was delivered from the steps of the Lincoln Memorial, in Washington, D.C., in 1963, the hundredth anniversary of the Emancipation Proclamation. King's immediate audience consisted of more than 200,000 people who had come to demonstrate for civil rights.

check which has come back marked "insufficient funds." But we refuse to believe that the bank of justice is bankrupt. We refuse to believe that there are insufficient funds in the great vaults of opportunity of this nation; and so we have come to cash this check, a check that will give us upon demand the riches of freedom and the security of justice.

We have also come to this hallowed spot to remind America of the fierce urgency of *now*. This is no time to engage in the luxury of cooling off or to take the tranquilizing drug of gradualism. *Now* is the time to make real the promises of democracy. *Now* is the time to rise from the dark and desolate valley of segregation to the sunlit path of racial justice. *Now* is the time to lift our nation from the quicksands of racial injustice to the solid rock of brotherhood. *Now* is the time to make justice a reality for all of God's children.

It would be fatal for the nation to overlook the urgency of the moment. This sweltering summer of the Negro's legitimate discontent will not pass until there is an invigorating autumn of freedom and equality. Nineteen sixty-three is not an end, but a beginning. And those who hope that the Negro needed to blow off steam and will now be content will have a rude awakening if the nation returns to business as usual. There will be neither rest nor tranquility in America until the Negro is granted his citizenship rights. The whirlwinds of revolt will continue to shake the foundations of our nation until the bright day of justice emerges.

But there is something that I must say to my people who stand on the warm threshold which leads into the palace of justice. In the process of gaining our rightful place, we must not be guilty of wrongful deeds. Let us not seek to satisfy our thirst for freedom by drinking from the cup of bitterness and hatred. We must forever conduct our struggle on the high plane of dignity and discipline. We must not allow our creative protest to degenerate into physical violence. Again and again we must rise to the majestic heights of meeting physical force with soul force. And the marvelous new militancy which has engulfed the Negro community must not lead us to a distrust of all white people; for many of our white brothers, as evidenced by their presence here today, have come to realize that their destiny is tied up with our destiny, and they have come to realize that their freedom is inextricably bound to our freedom.

We cannot walk alone. And as we walk we must make the pledge that 8 we shall always march ahead. We cannot turn back. There are those who are asking the devotees of civil rights, "When will you be satisfied?" We can never be satisfied as long as the Negro is the victim of the unspeakable horrors of police brutality. We can never be satisfied as long as our bodies, heavy with the fatigue of travel, cannot gain lodging in the motels of the highways and the hotels of the cities. We cannot be satisfied as long as the Negro's basic mobility is from a smaller ghetto to a larger one. We can never be satisfied as long as our children are stripped of their selfhood and robbed of their dignity by signs stating "For Whites Only." We cannot be satisfied as long as the Negro in Mississippi cannot vote and a Negro in New York believes he has nothing for which to vote. No, no, we are not satisfied, and we will not be satisfied until justice rolls down like waters and righteousness like a mighty stream.

I am not unmindful that some of you have come here out of great trials and tribulations. Some of you have come fresh from narrow jail cells. Some of you have come from areas where your quest for freedom left you battered by the storms of persecution and staggered by the winds of police brutality. You have been the veterans of creative suffering. Continue to work with the faith that unearned suffering is redemptive.

Go back to Mississippi, and go back to Alabama. Go back to South Carolina. Go back to Georgia. Go back to Louisiana. Go back to the slums and ghettos of our Northern cities, knowing that somehow this situation can and will be changed. Let us not wallow in the valley of despair.

I say to you today, my friends, even though we face the difficulties of today and tomorrow, I still have a dream. It is a dream deeply rooted in the American dream. I have a dream that one day this nation will rise up and live out the true meaning of its creed: "We hold these truths to be self-evident, that all men are created equal." I have a dream that one day, on the red hills of Georgia, sons of former slaves and the sons of former slave owners will be able to sit down together at the table of brotherhood. I have a dream that one day even the state of Mississippi, a state sweltering with the heat of injustice, sweltering with the heat of oppression, will be transformed into an oasis of freedom and justice. I have a dream that my four little children will one day live in a nation where they will not be judged by the color of their skin, but by the content of their character.

I have a dream today. I have a dream that one day down in 12 Alabama—with its vicious racists, with its governor's lips dripping with the words of interposition and nullification—one day right there in Alabama, little Black boys and Black girls will be able to join hands with little white boys and white girls as sisters and brothers.

I have a dream today. I have a dream that one day every valley shall be exalted and every hill and mountain shall be made low, the rough places will be made plain and the crooked places will be made straight, and the glory of the Lord shall be revealed, and all flesh shall see it together.[1]

This is our hope. This is the faith that I go back to the South with. And with this faith we will be able to hew out of the mountain of despair a stone of hope. With this faith we will be able to transform the jangling discords of our nation into a beautiful symphony of brotherhood. With this faith we will be able to work together, to play together, to struggle together, to go to jail together, to stand up for freedom together, knowing that we will be free one day.

---

[1] A quotation from the Bible: Isaiah 40:4–5. [Editors' note]

And this will be the day—this will be the day when all of God's children will be able to sing with new meaning:

> My country,'tis of thee,
> Sweet land of liberty,
>   Of thee I sing;
> Land where my fathers died,
> Land of the Pilgrims' pride,
> From every mountainside
>   Let freedom ring.

And if America is to be a great nation, this must become true.

And so let freedom ring from the prodigious hilltops of New 16 Hampshire. Let freedom ring from the mighty mountains of New York. Let freedom ring from the heightening Alleghenies of Pennsylvania. Let freedom ring from the snow-capped Rockies of Colorado. Let freedom ring from the curvaceous slopes of California.

But not only that. Let freedom ring from Stone Mountain of Georgia. Let freedom ring from Lookout Mountain of Tennessee. Let freedom ring from every hill and molehill of Mississippi. "From every mountainside let freedom ring."

And when this happens—when we allow freedom to ring, when we let it ring from every village and every hamlet, from every state and every city—we will be able to speed up that day when all of God's children, Black men and white men, Jews and Gentiles, Protestants and Catholics, will be able to join hands and sing in the words of the old Negro spiritual: "Free at last! Free at last! Thank God Almighty. We are free at last!"

Questions and Suggestions for Writing

1. Analyze the rhetoric—the oratorical art—of the first paragraph. What, for instance, is gained by saying "Five score years ago" instead of "a hundred years ago"? By metaphorically calling the Emancipation Proclamation "a great beacon light"? By saying that "Negro slaves . . . had been seared in the flames of withering injustice"? And what of the metaphors "daybreak" and "the long night of captivity"?

2. Do the first two paragraphs make an effective opening? Why?

3. In the third and fourth paragraphs King uses the metaphor of a bad check. Rewrite the third paragraph *without* using any of King's metaphors, and then in a paragraph evaluate the difference between King's version and yours.

4. King's highly metaphoric speech of course appeals to emotions. But it also offers *reasons*. What reason(s), for instance, does King give to support his belief that blacks should not resort to physical violence?

5. When King delivered the speech, his audience at the Lincoln Memorial was primarily black. Do you think that the speech is also addressed to whites? Explain.

6. The speech can be divided into three parts: paragraphs 1 through 6; paragraphs 7 ("But there is") through 10; and paragraph 11 ("I say to you today, my friends") to the end. Summarize each of these three parts in a sentence or two, so that the basic organization is evident.

7. King says (para. 11) that his dream is "deeply rooted in the American dream." First, what is the American dream, as King seems to understand it? Second, how does King establish his point—that is, what evidence does he use to convince us—that his dream is the American dream? (On this second issue, for a start one might point out that in the opening paragraph King refers to the Emancipation Proclamation. What other relevant documents does he refer to?)

8. King delivered his speech in 1963, more than twenty years ago. In an essay of 500 words argue that the speech still is—or is not—relevant. Or write an essay of 500 words in which you state what you take to be the "American dream," and argue that it now is or is not readily available to blacks.

Gloria Steinem

Sisterhood

A very, very long time ago (about three or four years), I took a certain secure and righteous pleasure in saying the things that women are supposed to say. I remember with pain—

"My work won't interfere with marriage. After all, I can always keep my typewriter at home." Or:

"I don't want to write about women's stuff. I want to write about foreign policy." Or:

"Black families were forced into matriarchy, so I see why black women have to step back and let their men get ahead." Or:

"I know we're helping Chicano groups that are tough on women, but *that's their culture.*" Or:

Gloria Steinem, born in Toledo, Ohio in 1934, helped to found New York *magazine in 1968, and was a founding editor of* Ms. *in 1971. (The essay reprinted here originally appeared in* Ms. *in 1972.) In 1972* McCall's *magazine named her* Woman of the Year. *Outrageous Acts and Everyday Rebellions (1983) is a collection of some of her essays; her most recent book,* Marilyn *(1986), analyzes the life of Marilyn Monroe.*

"Who would want to join a women's group? I've never been a joiner, have you?" Or (when bragging):

"He says I write like a man."

I suppose it's obvious from the kinds of statements I chose that I was secretly nonconforming. I wasn't married. I was earning a living at a profession I cared about. I had basically—if quietly—opted out of the "feminine" role. But that made it all the more necessary to repeat the conventional wisdom, even to look as conventional as I could manage, if I was to avoid some of the punishments reserved by society for women who don't do as society says. I therefore learned to Uncle Tom with subtlety, logic, and humor. Sometimes, I even believed it myself.

If it weren't for the women's movement, I might still be dissembling away. But the ideas of this great sea-change in women's view of ourselves are contagious and irresistible. They hit women like a revelation, as if we had left a dark room and walked into the sun.

At first my discoveries seemed personal. In fact, they were the same ones so many millions of women have made and are continuing to make. Greatly simplified, they go like this: Women are human beings first, with minor differences from men that apply largely to the single act of reproduction. We share the dreams, capabilities, and weaknesses of all human beings, but our occasional pregnancies and other visible differences have been used—even more pervasively, if less brutally, than racial differences have been used—to create an "inferior" group and an elaborate division of labor. The division is continued for a clear if often unconscious reason: the economic and social profit of males as a group. 4

Once this feminist realization dawned, I reacted in what turned out to be predictable ways. First, I was amazed at the simplicity and obviousness of a realization that made sense, at last, of my life experience. I couldn't figure out why I hadn't seen it before. Second, I realized how far that new vision of life was from the system around us, and how tough it would be to explain this feminist realization at all, much less to get people (especially, though not only, men) to accept so drastic a change.

But I tried to explain. God knows (*she* knows) that women try. We make analogies with other groups that have been marked for subservient roles in order to assist blocked imaginations. We supply endless facts and statistics of injustice, reeling them off until we feel like human information-retrieval machines. We lean heavily on the device of reversal. (If there is a male reader to whom all my *pre*realization statements seem perfectly logical, for instance, let him read each sentence with "men" substituted for "women"—or himself for me—and see how he feels: "My work won't interfere with marriage. . . ."; ". . . Chicano groups that are tough on men. . . ." You get the idea.)

We even use logic. If a woman spends a year bearing and nursing a child, for instance, she is supposed to have the primary responsibility for raising that child to adulthood. That's logic by the male definition, but it often makes women feel children are their only function, keeps them from doing any other kind of work, or discourages them from being mothers at all. Wouldn't it be just as logical to say that the child has two parents, therefore both are equally responsible for child rearing, and the father should compensate for that extra year by spending *more* than half the time caring for the child? Logic is in the eye of the logician.

Occasionally, these efforts at explaining actually succeed. More often, 8 I get the feeling that most women are speaking Urdu and most men are speaking Pali.[1]

Whether joyful or painful, both kinds of reaction to our discovery have a great reward. They give birth to sisterhood.

First, we share the exhilaration of growth and self-discovery, the sensation of having the scales fall from our eyes. Whether we are giving other women this new knowledge or receiving it from them, the pleasure for all concerned is enormous. And very moving.

In the second stage, when we're exhausted from dredging up facts and arguments for the men whom we had previously thought advanced and intelligent, we make another simple discovery: women understand. We may share experiences, make jokes, paint pictures, and describe humiliations that mean little to men, but *women understand.*

The odd thing about these deep and personal connections among 12 women is that they often leap barriers of age, economics, worldly experience, race, culture—all the barriers that, in male or mixed society, seem so impossible to cross.

I remember meeting with a group of women in Missouri who, because they had come in equal numbers from the small town and from its nearby campus, seemed to be split between wives with white gloves welded to their wrists and students with boots who used words like "imperialism" and "oppression." Planning for a child-care center had brought them together, but the meeting seemed hopeless until three of the booted young women began to argue among themselves about a young male professor. The leader of the radicals on campus, he accused all women unwilling to run Mimeograph machines of not being sufficiently devoted to the cause. As for child-care centers, he felt their effect of allowing women to compete with men for jobs was part of a dreaded "feminization" of the American male and American culture.

"He sounds just like my husband," said one of the white-gloved women. "He wants me to have bake sales and collect door-to-door for his Republican party."

The young women had sense enough to take it from there. What difference did boots or white gloves make if they were all getting treated

---

[1]**Urdu . . . Pali** Urdu is the chief language of West Pakistan; Pali is an ancient language of India. [Editors' note]

like servants and children? Before they broke up, they were discussing some subjects that affected them all (like the myth of the vaginal orgasm) and planning to meet every week. "Men think we're whatever it is we do for men," explained one of the housewives. "It's only by getting together with other women that we'll ever find out who we are."

Even racial barriers become a little less formidable once we discover 16 this mutuality of our life experiences as women. At a meeting run by black women domestics who had formed a job cooperative in Alabama, a white housewife asked me about the consciousness-raising sessions or "rap groups" that are often an organic path to feminism. I explained that while men, even minority men, usually had someplace—a neighborhood, a bar, a street corner, something—where they could get together and be themselves, women were isolated in their houses and families; isolated from other females. We had no street corners, no bars, no offices, no territory that was recognized as ours. Rap groups were an effort to create something of our own, a free place—an occasional chance for total honesty and support from our sisters.

As I talked about isolation, about the feeling that there must be something wrong with us if we aren't content to be housekeepers and mothers, tears began to stream down the cheeks of this dignified woman— clearly as much of a surprise to her as to us. For the black women, some distance was bridged by seeing this white woman cry.

"He does it to us both, honey," said the black woman next to her, putting an arm around her shoulders. "If it's your own kitchen or some- body else's, you still don't get treated like people. Women's work just doesn't count."

The meeting ended with the housewife organizing a support group of white women who would extract from their husbands a living wage for domestic workers and help them fight the local authorities who opposed any pay raises; a support group without which the domestic workers felt their small and brave cooperative could not survive.

As for the "matriarchal" argument that I swallowed in prefeminist 20 days, I now understand why many black women resent it and feel that it's the white sociologists' way of encouraging the black community to imitate a white suburban life-style. "If I end up cooking grits for revolutionaries," explained a black woman poet from Chicago, "it isn't my revolution. Black men and women need to work together: you can't have liberation for half a race." In fact, some black women wonder if criticism of the strength they were forced to develop isn't a way to keep half the black community working at lowered capacity and lowered pay, as well as to attribute some of black men's sufferings to black women, instead of to their real source— white racism. I wonder with them.

Looking back at all those male-approved things I used to say, the basic hang-up seems clear—a lack of esteem for women, whatever our race, and for myself.

This is the most tragic punishment that society inflicts on any second-class group. Ultimately the brainwashing works, and we ourselves come to believe our group is inferior. Even if we achieve a little success in the world and think of ourselves as "different," we don't want to associate with our group. We want to identify up, not down (clearly my problem in not wanting to join women's groups). We want to be the only woman in the office, or the only black family on the block, or the only Jew in the club.

The pain of looking back at wasted, imitative years is enormous. Trying to write like men. Valuing myself and other women according to the degree of our acceptance by men—socially, in politics, and in our professions. It's as painful as it is now to hear two grown-up female human beings competing with each other on the basis of their husband's status, like servants whose identity rests on the wealth or accomplishments of their employers.

And this lack of esteem that makes us put each other down is still the 24 major enemy of sisterhood. Women who are conforming to society's expectations view the nonconformists with justifiable alarm. *Those noisy, unfeminine women,* they say to themselves. *They will only make trouble for us all.* Women who are quietly nonconforming, hoping nobody will notice, are even more alarmed because they have more to lose. And that makes sense, too.

The status quo protects itself by punishing all challengers, especially women whose rebellion strikes at the most fundamental social organization: the sex roles that convince half the population that its identity depends on being first in work or in war, and the other half that it must serve as docile, unpaid, or underpaid labor.

In fact, there seems to be no punishment inside the white male club that quite equals the ridicule and personal viciousness reserved for women who rebel. Attractive or young women who act forcefully are assumed to be either unnatural or male-controlled. If they succeed, it could only have been sexually, through men. Old women or women considered unattractive by male standards are accused of acting out of bitterness, because they could not get a man. Any woman who chooses to behave like a full human being should be warned that the armies of the status quo will treat her as something of a dirty joke. That's their natural and first weapon. She will *need* sisterhood.

All of that is meant to be a warning but not a discouragement. There are more rewards than punishments.

For myself, I can now admit anger and use it constructively, where 28 once I would have submerged it and let it fester into guilt or collect for some destructive explosion.

I have met brave women who are exploring the outer edge of human possibility, with no history to guide them, and with a courage to make themselves vulnerable that I find moving beyond the words to express it.

I no longer think that I do not exist, which was my version of that lack of self-esteem afflicting many women. (If male standards weren't natural to me, and they were the only standards, how could I exist?) This means that I am less likely to need male values and approval and am less vulnerable to classic arguments. ("If you don't like me, you're not a real woman"—said by a man who is coming on. "If you don't like me, you can't relate to other people, you're not a real person"—said by anyone who understands blackmail as an art.)

I can sometimes deal with men as equals and therefore can afford to like them for the first time.

I have discovered politics that are not intellectual or superimposed. 32 They are organic. I finally understand why for years I inexplicably identified with "out" groups: I belong to one, too. And I know it will take a coalition of such groups to achieve a society in which, at a minimum, no one is born into a second-class role because of visible difference, because of race or of sex.

I no longer feel strange by myself or with a group of women in public. I feel just fine.

I am continually moved to discover I have sisters.

I am beginning, just beginning, to find out who I am.

Questions and Suggestions for Writing

1. Analyze and evaluate Steinem's opening paragraph.

2. In paragraph 2 what does Steinem mean when she says she "learned to Uncle Tom"?

3. What is Steinem's thesis? How does she support it? Is the support adequate?

4. In paragraph 6 Steinem suggests that if a male reader substitutes "men" for "women" in the sentences in her first paragraph, he will see how absurd her earlier positions were. If you are a male, read the sentences, with the suggested substitution, and then analyze your responses. Do all the sentences now seem offensive? Equally so? If you are a female, do the original sentences strike you as reasonable, or as offensive? Do the revised sentences (with "men" instead of "women") seem reasonable or offensive?

5. In paragraph 7 Steinem appeals to "logic." Is the suggestion she offers in the paragraph logical? Would "fair" be a more appropriate word here than "logical"? Why, or why not? (And what, by the way, does she mean by her final sentence in this paragraph?)

6. This essay originally appeared in *Ms.*, a magazine read chiefly by women. Do you think that the essay is more likely to interest women than men? If you were the editor of a male-oriented magazine such as *Esquire* or *Playboy*, would you publish this essay? Why, or why not? (In your response, make sure that you

give evidence of your familiarity with the contents of the magazine in question.)

7. In paragraph 22 Steinem says that brainwashing works, and if we are members of an oppressed group we "come to believe our group is inferior. Even if we achieve a little success in the world and think of ourselves as 'different,' we don't want to associate with our group." If you know of someone (possibly yourself) who exemplifies Steinem's point, write a sketch of 250 words, letting the reader get a good look at this concrete example. (Do not, however, use anyone's real name, unless you choose to write about a public figure.)

8. In paragraph 30 Steinem speaks of "male standards" and "male values." In a paragraph set forth what you take to be her understanding of these standards and values. Is a "male" standard of value one that men but not women invented? Or one that benefits men (but not women)? Both? Neither?

9. Evaluate Steinem's final paragraph as a conclusion. (Suppose it had been combined with the two preceding paragraphs. Would the effect be different?)

10. Betty Friedan, a leader in the women's movement, writes in *The Second Stage* (1981) that the first stage of the movement was to seek "full participation" in business and politics, but in doing so, many feminists "cast man as enemy and seemed to repudiate the traditional values of the family. In reaction against the feminine mystique, which defined women solely in reference to their relation to men as wives, mothers, and homemakers, we insidiously fell into a feminist mystique, which denied that core of women's personhood that is fulfilled through love, nurture, home." (Notice, by the way, the distinction between "feminine" and "feminist.") Friedan goes on to argue that women must now "move into the second stage—no longer against, but with men." In the second stage, Friedan says, "Women have to say 'No' to standards of success set in terms of men who had wives to take care of all the details of life. . . . In the second stage, the woman will find and use her own strength and style at work, instead of trying so hard to do it man's way." In the second stage, she assumes, unions and companies will provide flexible work plans, "not just to help women but because men will be demanding them." Does Steinem's essay illustrate "first-stage" thinking, marked by a "feminist mystique"? Do you imagine that Steinem might now agree with Friedan? And do you imagine that Friedan's forecast is likely to prove true? Express your responses in an essay of 500 words.

15

What Are the Grounds of Religious Faith?

Paul

1 Corinthians 15

Moreover, brethren, I declare unto you the gospel which I preached unto you, which also ye have received, and wherein ye stand;

By which also ye are saved, if ye keep in memory what I preached unto you, unless ye have believed in vain.

Paul (A.D. 5?–67?), known as Saul before his conversion from Judaism to Christianity, was a native of Tarsus, a commercial town in the land that is now Turkey. Tarsus was part of the Roman Empire, and Saul, though a Jew, was a Roman citizen. After attending a rabbinical school in Jerusalem, Saul set out for Damascus in A.D. 33 or 34 to suppress Christianity there, but on the way he saw a blinding light, heard the voice of Jesus, and experienced a conversion, described in Acts of the Apostles 9:1–22. In later years he traveled widely, preaching Christianity to Jews and gentiles. In 59–61 he was imprisoned in Rome, and he may have been convicted and executed, but nothing certain is known about his death.

Paul seems to have been the first Christian missionary to Corinth, a Roman colony a little to the west of Athens. After his initial visit, probably from 50 to 52, he is reported to have gone to Judea, Syria, Ephesus, and elsewhere. While at Ephesus, however, he heard reports of disorders in Corinth. His letter of response, probably written in about 54, was incorporated into the New Testament as 1 Corinthians, one of his two extant epistles addressed to the Christian community at Corinth. From this letter we reprint Chapter 15.

It is not entirely clear what doctrine(s) of resurrection Paul is opposing in this passage. Perhaps some members of the church did not believe in any form of life

For I delivered unto you first of all that which I also received, how that Christ died for our sins according to the scriptures;

And that he was buried, and that he rose again the third day according to the scriptures: 4

And that he was seen of Cephas, then of the twelve:

After that, he was seen of above five hundred brethren at once; of whom the greater part remain unto this present, but some are fallen asleep.

After that, he was seen of James; then of all the apostles.

And last of all he was seen of me also, as of one born out of due time.   8

For I am the least of the apostles, that am not meet to be called an apostle, because I persecuted the church of God.

But by the grace of God I am what I am: and his grace which was bestowed upon me was not in vain; but I laboured more abundantly than they all: yet not I, but the grace of God which was with me.

Therefore whether it were I or they, so we preach, and so ye believed.

Now if Christ be preached that he rose from the dead, how say some   12 among you that there is no resurrection of the dead?

But if there be no resurrection of the dead, then is Christ not risen:

And if Christ be not risen, then is our preaching vain, and your faith is also vain.

Yea, and we are found false witnesses of God; because we have testified of God that he raised up Christ: whom he raised not up, if so be that the dead rise not.

For if the dead rise not, then is not Christ raised: 16

And if Christ be not raised, your faith is vain; ye are yet in your sins.

Then they also which are fallen asleep in Christ are perished.

If in this life only we have hope in Christ, we are of all men most miserable.

---

after death; perhaps others believed that the resurrection took place at baptism; and perhaps others debated the nature of the resurrection body.

The Interpreter's Bible, *10:12, outlines the fifty-eight verses of Chapter 15 thus:*

A. *The resurrection of Jesus (1–19)*
  1. *The tradition concerning the fact (1–11)*
  2. *The significance of the resurrection (12–19)*
B. *The eschatological drama [i.e., concern with ultimate things, such as death and heaven] (20–34)*
  1. *The order of events (20–28)*
  2. *Ad hominem rebuttal (29–34)*
C. *The resurrection body (35–50)*
  1. *Various types of body (35–41)*
  2. *A spiritual body (42–50)*
D. *The Christian confidence (51–58)*

The translation used here is the Authorized Version (1611), also known as the King James Version.

But now is Christ risen from the dead, and become the firstfruits of 20
them that slept.

For since by man came death, by man came also the resurrection of
the dead.

For as in Adam all die, even so in Christ shall all be made alive.

But every man in his own order: Christ the firstfruits; afterward they
that are Christ's at his coming.

Then cometh the end, when he shall have delivered up the kingdom to 24
God, even the Father; when he shall have put down all rule and all
authority and power.

For he must reign, till he hath put all enemies under his feet.

The last enemy that shall be destroyed is death.

For he hath put all things under his feet. But when he saith all things
are put under him, it is manifest that he is excepted, which did put all
things under him.

And when all things shall be subdued unto him, then shall the Son also 28
himself be subject unto him that put all things under him, that God may
be all in all.

Else what shall they do which are baptized for the dead, if the dead
rise not at all? why are they then baptized for the dead?

And why stand we in jeopardy every hour?

I protest by your rejoicing which I have in Christ Jesus our Lord, I die
daily.

If after the manner of men I have fought with beasts at Ephesus, what 32
advantageth it me, if the dead rise not? let us eat and drink; for to morrow
we die.

Be not deceived: evil communications corrupt good manners.

Awake to righteousness, and sin not; for some have not the knowledge
of God: I speak this to your shame.

But some man will say, How are the dead raised up? and with what
body do they come?

Thou fool, that which thou sowest is not quickened, except it die: 36

And that which thou sowest, thou sowest not that body that shall be,
but bare grain, it may chance of wheat, or of some other grain:

But God giveth it a body as it hath pleased him, and to every seed his
own body.

All flesh is not the same flesh: but there is one kind of flesh of men,
another flesh of beasts, another of fishes, and another of birds.

There are also celestial bodies, and bodies terrestrial: but the glory of 40
the celestial is one, and the glory of the terrestrial is another.

There is one glory of the sun, and another glory of the moon, and
another glory of the stars: for one star differeth from another star in glory.

So also is the resurrection of the dead. It is sown in corruption; it is
raised in incorruption:

It is sown in dishonour; it is raised in glory: it is sown in weakness; it is raised in power:

It is sown a natural body; it is raised a spiritual body. There is a 44 natural body, and there is a spiritual body.

And so it is written, The first man Adam was made a living soul; the last Adam was made a quickening spirit.

Howbeit that was not first which is spiritual, but that which is natural; and afterward that which is spiritual.

The first man is of the earth, earthy: the second man is the Lord from heaven.

As is the earthy, such are they also that are earthy: and as is the 48 heavenly, such are they also that are heavenly.

And as we have borne the image of the earthy, we shall also bear the image of the heavenly.

Now this I say, brethren, that flesh and blood cannot inherit the kingdom of God; neither doth corruption inherit incorruption.

Behold, I shew you a mystery; We shall not all sleep, but we shall all be changed,

In a moment, in the twinkling of an eye, at the last trump: for the 52 trumpet shall sound, and the dead shall be raised incorruptible, and we shall be changed.

For this corruptible must put on incorruption, and this mortal must put on immortality.

So when this corruptible shall have put on incorruption, and this mortal shall have put on immortality, then shall be brought to pass the saying that is written, Death is swallowed up in victory.

O death, where is thy sting? O grave, where is thy victory?

The sting of death is sin; and the strength of sin is the law.   56

But thanks be to God, which giveth us the victory through our Lord Jesus Christ.

Therefore, my beloved brethren, be ye stedfast, unmoveable, always abounding in the work of the Lord, forasmuch as ye know that your labour is not in vain in the Lord.

Questions and Suggestions for Writing

1. Why is belief in the Resurrection of Christ important to Paul? What evidence does he offer to support his belief in it?

2. What leads Paul to the conclusion that the dead are resurrected? What evidence does he offer to support this belief? What conclusion, according to Paul, follows if the dead are not resurrected?

3. In verse 22 Paul speaks of people who are "in Adam," and of others who are "in Christ." Explain the distinction to someone who finds it puzzling. (If you find it

puzzling, check a guide to the Bible, such as *The Interpreter's Bible*, or *A New Catholic Commentary on Holy Scripture*, ed. Reginald C. Fuller et al.)

4. What mistaken belief, according to Paul, leads people to conclude that we should (as he says in verse 32) "eat and drink; for to morrow we die"?

5. In verses 35–50 Paul insists again on bodily resurrection of human beings. In 35–44 he uses an analogy to explain that the body that dies and the body that is resurrected are continuous and yet also are different. Put his analogy into your own words. Do you think analogy is an effective way of making this point? Why? In verse 45 Paul uses a different argument, contrasting Adam ("the first man Adam") with Christ ("the last Adam"). Why do you think he drops the analogy and now offers this evidence? How in verses 46–47 does Paul bring the two points together?

6. In verse 55 Paul says, "O death, where is thy sting? O grave, where is thy victory?" In a paragraph summarize the beliefs (expressed in this selection) that lead Paul to the conclusion that death and the grave are conquered.

Thomas Henry Huxley

From *Agnosticism and Christianity*

Nemo ergo ex me scire quaerat, quod me nescire scio,
nisi forte ut nescire discat.
—AUGUSTINUS, DE CIV. DEI, XII.7.[1]

The present discussion has arisen out of the use, which has become general in the last few years, of the terms "Agnostic" and "Agnosticism."

The people who call themselves "Agnostics" have been charged with

---

[1] "No one, therefore, should seek to learn knowledge from me, for I know that I do not know—unless indeed he wishes to learn that he does not know." St. Augustine, *City of God* XII.7.

Thomas Henry Huxley (1825–1897), born in a London suburb, took a degree in medicine, then studied geology, physiology, and tropical marine life. He published numerous research papers, but he is chiefly known as a popularizer of science, an advocate of scientific education, and a man who sought to apply scientific methods to all fields of knowledge. His two goals, he said, were "To promote the increase of natural knowledge and to forward the application of scientific methods to all the problems of life." Dubbed "Darwin's bulldog," he vigorously advocated the theory of evolution, winning many adherents for Darwinism, partly because of his firm grasp of the subject and partly because of his skill as a writer and speaker. In the famous debate (1860) with Bishop Wilberforce on Darwin's On the Origin of Species by Means of Natural Selection, *when Wilberforce mockingly asked Huxley whether he was descended from an ape on his grandmother's or his grandfather's side, Huxley's telling riposte was that he would not be ashamed to have an ape for*

doing so because they have not the courage to declare themselves "Infidels." It has been insinuated that they have adopted a new name in order to escape the unpleasantness which attaches to their proper denomination. To this wholly erroneous imputation I have replied by showing that the term "Agnostic" did, as a matter of fact, arise in a manner which negatives it; and my statement has not been, and cannot be, refuted. Moreover, speaking for myself, and without impugning the right of any other person to use the term in another sense, I further say that Agnosticism is not properly described as a "negative" creed, nor indeed as a creed of any kind, except insofar as it expresses absolute faith in the validity of a principle, which is as much ethical as intellectual. This principle may be stated in various ways, but they all amount to this: that it is wrong for a man to say that he is certain of the objective truth of any proposition unless he can produce evidence which logically justifies that certainty. This is what Agnosticism asserts; and, in my opinion, it is all that is essential to Agnosticism. That which Agnostics deny and repudiate, as immoral, is the contrary doctrine, that there are propositions which men ought to believe, without logically satisfactory evidence; and that reprobation ought to attach to the profession of disbelief in such inadequately supported propositions. the justification of the Agnostic principle lies in the success which follows upon its application, whether in the field of natural, or in that of civil, history; and in the fact that, so far as these topics are concerned, no sane man thinks of denying its validity.

Still speaking for myself, I add that though Agnosticism is not, and cannot be, a creed, except insofar as its general principle is concerned; yet that the application of that principle results in the denial of, or the suspension of judgment concerning, a number of propositions respecting which our contemporary ecclesiastical "gnostics" profess entire certainty. And, insofar as these ecclesiastical persons can be justified in their old-established custom (which many nowadays think more honored in the breach than the observance) of using opprobrious names to those who differ from them, I fully admit their right to call me and those who think

---

an ancestor, but he would be ashamed to be connected with a man who used his great gifts to obscure the truth.

Huxley's advocacy of Darwinism inevitably drew him to write and to talk about the relation of science to religion. He coined the word agnostic (Greek for "without knowledge") to describe his own position about the existence of God, but he did not see himself as a foe of religion, only as a foe of conventional theology. "A deep sense of religion," he wrote, is "compatible with the absence of theology." Something of this feeling is evident in the words that he asked to have engraved on his tombstone:

Be not afraid, ye waiting hearts that weep
For still He giveth His beloved sleep,
And if an endless sleep He will, so be it.

The selection reprinted here is part of an essay first published in 1892.

with me "Infidels"; all I have ventured to urge is that they must not expect us to speak of ourselves by that title.

The extent of the region of the uncertain, the number of the problems 4 the investigation of which ends in a verdict of not proven, will vary according to the knowledge and the intellectual habits of the individual Agnostic. I do not very much care to speak of anything as "unknowable." What I am sure about is that there are many topics about which I know nothing; and which, so far as I can see, are out of reach of my faculties. But whether these things are knowable by anyone else is exactly one of those matters which is beyond my knowledge, though I may have a tolerably strong opinion as to the probabilities of the case. Relatively to myself, I am quite sure that the region of uncertainty—the nebulous country in which words play the part of realities—is far more extensive than I could wish. Materialism and Idealism; Theism and Atheism; the doctrine of the soul and its mortality or immortality—appear in the history of philosophy like the shades of Scandinavian heroes, eternally slaying one another and eternally coming to life again in a metaphysical "Nifelheim."[2] It is getting on for twenty-five centuries, at least, since mankind began seriously to give their minds to these topics. Generation after generation, philosophy has been doomed to roll the stone uphill; and, just as all the world swore it was at the top, down it has rolled to the bottom again. All this is written in innumerable books; and he who will toil through them will discover that the stone is just where it was when the work began. Hume saw this; Kant saw it; since their time, more and more eyes have been cleansed of the films which prevented them from seeing it; until now the weight and number of those who refuse to be the prey of verbal mystifications has begun to tell in practical life.

It was inevitable that a conflict should arise between Agnosticism and Theology; or rather, I ought to say, between Agnosticism and Ecclesiasticism. For Theology, the science, is one thing; and Ecclesiasticism, the championship of a foregone conclusion[3] as to the truth of a particular form of Theology, is another. With scientific Theology, Agnosticism has no quarrel. On the contrary, the Agnostic, knowing too well the influence of prejudice and idiosyncrasy, even on those who desire most earnestly to be impartial, can wish for nothing more urgently than that the scientific theologian should not only be at perfect liberty to thresh out the matter in his own fashion; but that he should, if he can, find flaws in the Agnostic position; and, even if demonstration is not to be had, that he should put, in their full force, the grounds of the conclusions he thinks probable. The scientific theologian admits the Agnostic principle, however widely his results may differ from those reached by the majority of Agnostics.

[2]In Norse mythology, region of cold and darkness, or the realm of the dead. [Editors' note]
[3]"Let us maintain, before we have proved. This seeming paradox is the secret of happiness." (Dr. Newman, *Tract 85*).

But, as between Agnosticism and Ecclesiasticism, or, as our neighbors across the Channel call it, Clericalism, there can be neither peace nor truce. The Cleric asserts that it is morally wrong not to believe certain propositions, whatever the results of a strict scientific investigation of the evidence of these propositions. He tells us "that religious error is, in itself, of an immoral nature."[4] He declares that he has prejudged certain conclusions, and looks upon those who show cause for arrest of judgment as emissaries of Satan. It necessarily follows that, for him, the attainment of faith, not the ascertainment of truth, is the highest aim of mental life. And, on careful analysis of the nature of this faith, it will too often be found to be, not the mystic process of unity with the Divine, understood by the religious enthusiast; but that which the candid simplicity of a Sunday scholar once defined it to be. "Faith," said this unconscious plagiarist of Tertullian,[5] "is the power of saying you believe things which are incredible."

Now I, and many other Agnostics, believe that faith, in this sense, is an abomination; and though we do not indulge in the luxury of self-righteousness so far as to call those who are not of our way of thinking hard names, we do feel that the disagreement between ourselves and those who hold this doctrine is even more moral than intellectual. It is desirable there should be an end of any mistakes on this topic. If our clerical opponents were clearly aware of the real state of the case, there would be an end of the curious delusion, which often appears between the lines of their writings, that those whom they are so fond of calling "Infidels" are people who not only ought to be, but in their hearts are, ashamed of themselves. It would be discourteous to do more than hint the antipodal opposition of this pleasant dream of theirs to facts.

The clerics and their lay allies commonly tell us that if we refuse to admit that there is good ground for expressing definite convictions about certain topics, the bonds of human society will dissolve and mankind lapse into savagery. There are several answers to this assertion. One is that the bonds of human society were formed without the aid of their theology; and, in the opinion of not a few competent judges, have been weakened rather than strengthened by a good deal of it. Greek science, Greek art, the ethics of old Israel, the social organization of old Rome, contrived to come into being, without the help of anyone who believed in a single distinctive article of the simplest of the Christian creeds. The science, the art, the jurisprudence, the chief political and social theories, of the modern world have grown out of those of Greece and Rome—not by favor of, but in the teeth of, the fundamental teachings of early Christianity, to which science, art, and any serious occupation with the things of this world, were alike despicable.

[4]Dr. Newman, *Essay on Development.*
[5]Roman author and Church Father (ca. 155–ca. 222).

Again, all that is best in the ethics of the modern world, insofar as it has not grown out of Greek thought, or Barbarian manhood, is the direct development of the ethics of old Israel. There is no code of legislation, ancient or modern, at once so just and so merciful, so tender to the weak and poor, as the Jewish law; and, if the Gospels are to be trusted, Jesus of Nazareth himself declared that he taught nothing but that which lay implicitly, or explicitly, in the religious and ethical system of his people.

> "And the scribe said unto him, Of a truth, Teacher, thou hast well said that he is one; and there is none other but he and to love him with all the heart, and with all the understanding, and with all the strength, and to love his neighbor as himself, is much more than all whole burnt offerings and sacrifices." (Mark xii. 32–33)

Here is the briefest of summaries of the teaching of the prophets of Israel of the eighth century; does the Teacher, whose doctrine is thus set forth in his presence, repudiate the exposition? Nay; we are told, on the contrary, that Jesus saw that he "answered discreetly," and replied, "Thou art not far from the kingdom of God."

So that I think that even if the creeds, from the so-called "Apostles" to the so-called "Athanasian," were swept into oblivion; and even if the human race should arrive at the conclusion that, whether a bishop washes a cup or leaves it unwashed, is not a matter of the least consequence, it will get on very well. The causes which have led to the development of morality in mankind, which have guided or impelled us all the way from the savage to the civilized state, will not cease to operate because a number of ecclesiastical hypotheses turn out to be baseless. And, even if the absurd notion that morality is more the child of speculation than of practical necessity and inherited instinct, had any foundation; if all the world is going to thieve, murder, and otherwise misconduct itself as soon as it discovers that certain portions of ancient history are mythical; what is the relevance of such arguments to any one who holds by the Agnostic principle?

Surely, the attempt to cast out Beelzebub by the aid of Beelzebub is a 12 hopeful procedure as compared to that of preserving morality by the aid of immorality. For I suppose it is admitted that an Agnostic may be perfectly sincere, may be competent, and may have studied the question at issue with as much care as his clerical opponents. But, if the Agnostic really believes what he says, the "dreadful consequence" argufier (consistently, I admit, with his own principles) virtually asks him to abstain from telling the truth, or to say what he believes to be untrue, because of the supposed injurious consequences to morality. "Beloved brethren, that we may be spotlessly moral, before all things let us lie," is the sum total of many an exhortation addressed to the "Infidel." Now, as I have already pointed out, we cannot oblige our exhorters. We leave the practical application of the convenient doctrines of "Reserve" and "Nonnatural interpretation" to those who invented them.

I trust that I have now made amends for any ambiguity, or want of fullness, in my previous exposition of that which I hold to be the essence of the Agnostic doctrine. Henceforward, I might hope to hear no more of the assertion that we are necessarily Materialists, Idealists, Atheists, Theists, or any other ists, if experience had led me to think that the proved falsity of a statement was any guarantee against its repetition. And those who appreciate the nature of our position will see, at once, that when Ecclesiasticism declares that we ought to believe this, that, and the other, and are very wicked if we don't, it is impossible for us to give any answer but this: We have not the slightest objection to believe anything you like, if you will give us good grounds for belief, but, if you cannot, we must respectfully refuse, even if that refusal should wreck morality and insure our own damnation several times over. We are quite content to leave that to the decision of the future. The course of the past has impressed us with the firm conviction that no good ever comes of falsehood, and we feel warranted in refusing even to experiment in that direction. . . .

Questions and Suggestions for Writing

1. Review what Huxley calls "the Agnostic principle," and ask yourself: What kind of evidence do I have that logically justifies my certainty that (a) sometimes physical objects are shaped differently from the way they look; (b) a wristwatch can be more or less accurate; and (c) I am not now asleep and dreaming that I am reading this page?

2. When Huxley says (para. 3) that "Agnosticism is not, and cannot be, a creed," what does he mean? Why does he exempt the Agnostic principle from this pronouncement? What is a "creed," anyway? (Look up, as a famous example, the Apostles' Creed.) Do all Jews, or all Christians, have a common creed?

3. Why is Huxley unwilling to call himself an "Infidel" but ready to accept the label "Agnostic"? Does he establish a reasonable distinction between "Infidels" and "Agnostics"? Look up the meaning and etymology of both in a good unabridged dictionary. Do you think that Huxley is an "Infidel," whether or not he likes that designation himself?

4. Write a paragraph explaining, in your own words, what Huxley means by "Ecclesiasticism."

5. Huxley says (para. 5) he has no quarrel with "scientific Theology." What do you think "scientific Theology" is? What would a "scientific theologian" do? What do you think believers such as C. S. Lewis (p. 640) and Arthur A. Cohen (p. 670) would say about "scientific Theology"?

6. Huxley says, in paragraph 9, that "all that is best in the ethics of the modern world . . . is the direct development of the ethics of old Israel." He seems to be very certain about this point. Earlier he says that "it is wrong for a man to say

that he is certain of the objective proof of any proposition unless he can produce evidence which logically justifies that certainty." How might Huxley have gone about trying to offer evidence that would logically justify his assertion about Hebrew ethics?

7. Huxley quotes (para. 9) a passage from the Gospel of St. Mark, in which a questioner commends Jesus for saying that one's chief duty is to love God with all one's heart, and to love one's neighbor as oneself. Huxley's point is that Jesus was teaching the noble Hebraic code of ethics. But suppose that one were to say to the agnostic Huxley that Jesus' ethical teaching (love of neighbor) depends on His belief in God: One loves one's neighbor *because* God has told us to do so, and has given us the idea of love by lovingly creating us. What might Huxley reply?

8. Drawing a sharp contrast between "the attainment of faith" and "the ascertainment of truth," Huxley indicates his preference for the latter. After reading the essays of Lewis and Cohen, write a 500-word essay in which you weigh the pros and cons of Huxley's distinction, his preference for the one rather than the other, and the relevance of both to the religious beliefs of Jews and Christians.

William James

From *The Will to Believe*

What then do we now mean by the religious hypothesis? Science says things are; morality says some things are better than other things; and religion says essentially two things.

William James (1842–1910), brother of Alice James and of the novelist Henry James, was born into a wealthy family in New York City. He at first studied to be a painter, then turned to chemistry and biology, and took a degree in medicine. Though given to depression and hallucinations, it seems that he saved himself by an act of will or of faith: "My first act of free will," he said, "shall be to believe in free will." James accepted a position as instructor in physiology at Harvard, but, considering his uncertain health, he decided that he did not have the strength to do laboratory work, and he turned to philosophy and psychology. "I never had any philosophic instruction, the first lecture on psychology I ever heard being the first I ever gave." He published his first book, Principles of Psychology (1890), when he was forty-eight.

James developed his ideas partly under the influence of Darwin's writing, but he gave Darwinism a decidedly special twist. Impressed by Darwin's findings that "variations" assisted some creatures to survive in a changing environment, James saw the human mind as a potent force, not as a consciousness that merely receives external impressions. "Mental interests, hypotheses, postulates, so far as they are the basis for human action—action which to a great extent transforms the world— help to make the truth which they declare."

In 1897 James published a book of essays titled The Will to Believe. Part of one essay is reprinted here.

First, she says that the best things are the more eternal things, the overlapping things, the things in the universe that throw the last stone, so to speak, and say the final word. "Perfection is eternal"—this phrase of Charles Secrétan—seems a good way of putting this first affirmation of religion, an affirmation which obviously cannot yet be verified scientifically at all.

The second affirmation of religion is that we are better off even now if we believe her first affirmation to be true.

Now, let us consider what the logical elements of this situation are *in case the religious hypothesis in both its branches be really true.* (Of course, we must admit that possibility at the outset. If we are to discuss the question at all, it must involve a living option. If for any of you religion be a hypothesis that cannot, by any living possibility, be true, then you need go no farther. I speak to the "saving remnant" alone.) So proceeding, we see, first, that religion offers itself as a *momentous* option. We are supposed to gain, even now, by our belief, and to lose by our nonbelief, a certain vital good. Secondly, religion is a *forced* option, so far as that good goes. We cannot escape the issue by remaining skeptical and waiting for more light, because, although we do avoid error in that way *if religion be untrue,* we lose the good, *if it be true,* just as certainly as if we positively chose to disbelieve. It is as if a man should hesitate indefinitely to ask a certain woman to marry him because he was not perfectly sure that she would prove an angel after he brought her home. Would he not cut himself off from that particular angel-possibility as decisively as if he went and married someone else? Skepticism, then, is not avoidance of option; it is option of a certain particular kind of risk. *Better risk loss of truth than chance of error*—that is your faith-vetoer's exact position. He is actively playing his stake as much as the believer is; he is backing the field against the religious hypothesis, just as the believer is backing the religious hypothesis against the field. To preach skepticism to us as a duty until "sufficient evidence" for religion be found, is tantamount therefore to telling us, when in presence of religious hypothesis, that to yield to our fear of its being error is wiser and better than to yield to our hope that it may be true. It is not intellect against all passions, then; it is only intellect with one passion laying down its law. And by what, forsooth, is the supreme wisdom of this passion warranted? Dupery for dupery, what proof is there that dupery through hope is so much worse than dupery through fear? I, for one, can see no proof; and I simply refuse obedience to the scientist's command to imitate his kind of option, in a case where my own stake is important enough to give me the right to choose my own form of risk. If religion be true and the evidence for it be still insufficient, I do not wish, by putting your extinguisher upon my nature (which feels to me as if it had after all some business in this matter), to forfeit my sole chance in life of getting upon the winning side—that chance depending, of course, on my willingness to run the risk of acting as if my passional need of taking the world religiously might be prophetic and right.

All this is on the supposition that it really may be prophetic and right, and that, even to us who are discussing the matter, religion is a live hypothesis which may be true. Now, to most of us religion comes in a still further way that makes a veto on our active faith even more illogical. The more perfect and more eternal aspect of the universe is represented in our religions as having personal form. The universe is no longer a mere *It* to us, but a *Thou*, if we are religious; and any relation that may be possible from person to person might be possible here. For instance, although in one sense we are passive portions of the universe, in another we show a curious autonomy, as if we were small active centers on our own account. We feel, too, as if the appeal of religion to us were made to our own active goodwill, as if evidence might be forever withheld from us unless we met the hypothesis halfway. To take a trivial illustration: Just as a man who in a company of gentlemen made no advances, asked a warrant for every concession, and believed no one's word without proof, would cut himself off by such churlishness from all the social rewards that a more trusting spirit would earn—so here, one who should shut himself up in snarling logicality and try to make the gods extort his recognition willy-nilly, or not get it at all, might cut himself off forever from his only opportunity of making the gods' acquaintance. This feeling, forced on us we know not whence, that by obstinately believing that there are gods (although not to do so would be so easy both for our logic and our life) we are doing the universe the deepest service we can, seems part of the living essence of the religious hypothesis. If the hypothesis *were* true in all its parts, including this one, then pure intellectualism, with its veto on our making willing advances, would be an absurdity; and some participation of our sympathetic nature would be logically required. I, therefore, for one, cannot see my way to accepting the agnostic rules for truth-seeking, or willfully agree to keep my willing nature out of the game. I cannot do so for this plain reason, that *a rule of thinking which would absolutely prevent me from acknowledging certain kinds of truth if those kinds of truth were really there, would be an irrational rule.* That for me is the long and short of the formal logic of the situation, no matter what the kinds of truth might materially be.

I confess I do not see how this logic can be escaped. But sad experience makes me fear that some of you may still shrink from radically saying with me, *in abstracto*, that we have the right to believe at our own risk any hypothesis that is live enough to tempt our will. I suspect, however, that if this is so, it is because you have got away from the abstract logical point of view altogether, and are thinking (perhaps without realizing it) of some particular religious hypothesis which for you is dead. The freedom to "believe what we will" you apply to the case of some patent superstition;

and the faith you think of is the faith defined by the schoolboy when he said, "Faith is when you believe something that you know ain't true." I can only repeat that this is misapprehension. *In concreto*, the freedom to believe can only cover living options which the intellect of the individual cannot by itself resolve; and living options never seem absurdities to him who has them to consider. When I look at the religious question as it really puts itself to concrete men, and when I think of all the possibilities which both practically and theoretically it involves, then this command that we shall put a stopper on our heart, instincts, and courage, and *wait*—acting of course meanwhile more or less as if religion were *not* true[1]—till doomsday, or till such time as our intellect and senses working together may have raked in evidence enough—this command, I say, seems to me the queerest idol ever manufactured in the philosophic cave.[2] Were we scholastic absolutists, there might be more excuse. If we had an infallible intellect with its objective certitudes, we might feel ourselves disloyal to such a perfect organ of knowledge in not trusting to it exclusively, in not waiting for its releasing word. But if we are empiricists, if we believe that no bell in us tolls to let us know for certain when truth is in our grasp, then it seems a piece of idle fantasticality to preach so solemnly our duty of waiting for the bell. Indeed we *may* wait if we will—I hope you do not think that I am denying that—but if we do so, we do so at our peril as much as if we believed. In either case we *act*, taking our life in our hands. No one of us ought to issue vetoes to the other, nor should we bandy words of abuse. We ought, on the contrary, delicately and profoundly to respect one another's mental freedom: then only shall we bring about the intellectual republic; then only shall we have that spirit of inner tolerance without which all our outer tolerance is soulless, and which is empiricism's glory; then only shall we live and let live, in speculative as well as in practical things. . . .

Questions and Suggestions for Writing

1. In paragraph 4 James says that for the person who believes that "the religious hypothesis" may indeed be true, religion is a "*forced* option." He goes on to

---

[1]Since belief is measured by action, he who forbids us to believe religion to be true, necessarily also forbids us to act as we should if we did believe it to be true. The whole defense of religious faith hinges upon action. If the action required or inspired by the religious hypothesis is in no way different from that dictated by the naturalistic hypothesis, then religious faith is a pure superfluity, better pruned away, and controversy about its legitimacy is a piece of idle trifling, unworthy of serious minds. I myself believe, of course, that the religious hypothesis gives to the world an expression which specifically determines our reactions, and makes them in a large part unlike what they might be on a purely naturalistic scheme of belief. [James's note]

[2]According to Francis Bacon (1561–1626), in *The Novum Organum*, "The Idols of the Cave are the idols of the individual man," whose judgment may go astray because of heredity, environment, or education. [Editors' note]

clarify his point with the example of a man thinking about getting married. In your own words, and with an example of your own invention, in one or two paragraphs explain James's point to a reader who has not grasped it.

2. Normally a hypothesis is a proposition which (unlike $2 + 2 = 4$) is not necessarily true but which can be tested—and either confirmed or disconfirmed. Moreover, a hypothesis should not be embraced in the absence of adequate evidence or in the face of strong counterevidence, and the truth of a hypothesis should in no way depend on the proposer's belief (or disbelief) in it. Is James's "religious hypothesis" a hypothesis in this sense? Does it have or lack other features crucial to its status as a hypothesis?

3. In paragraph 5 James says that "the universe is no longer a mere *It* to us but a *Thou*, if we are religious." Explain his point in your own words.

4. Reduce the main argument in James's essay to a syllogism. Formulate his major premise, his minor premise, and his conclusion.

5. James is eager to defend "the religious hypothesis" as a "live option" against skeptical criticism. But what, exactly, is the *content* or *meaning* of this hypothesis for James? Is it, for example, such as to make someone who believes it a Christian? Why, or why not? (It may be useful to read the next essay, by C. S. Lewis, before answering this question.)

6. In an essay of 500 words explain whether, for you, Buddhism, Islam, Judaism, or Christianity—or none of them—is a "living option," as James uses that term (para. 4). Devote part of your essay to explaining what conditions enter into something's being a live option.

7. In "Agnosticism and Christianity," the essay preceding James's, Thomas Huxley says (para. 2) that "it is wrong for a man to say that he is certain of the objective proof of any proposition unless he can produce evidence which logically justifies that certainty." Would James agree or disagree, in whole or in part? Explain, in an essay of 500 words—but first read, or reread, Huxley's entire paragraph. Or, in an essay of 500 words, state what you think would be Huxley's reply to James's essay.

8. If you are unconvinced by James's argument, write a 500-word response. If you are convinced by his argument, write a 500-word analysis of his methods of arguing.

C. S. Lewis

What Christians Believe

1. THE RIVAL CONCEPTIONS OF GOD

I have been asked to tell you what Christians believe, and I am going to begin by telling you one thing that Christians do not need to believe. If you are a Christian you do not have to believe that all the other religions are simply wrong all through. If you are an atheist you do have to believe that the main point in all the religions of the whole world is simply one huge mistake. If you are a Christian, you are free to think that all these religions, even the queerest ones, contain at least some hint of the truth. When I was an atheist I had to try to persuade myself that most of the human race have always been wrong about the question that mattered to them most: when I became a Christian I was able to take a more liberal view. But, of course, being a Christian does mean thinking that where Christianity differs from other religions, Christianity is right and they are wrong. As in arithmetic—there is only one right answer to a sum, and all other answers are wrong: but some of the wrong answers are much nearer being right than others.

The first big division of humanity is into the majority, who believe in some kind of God or gods, and the minority who do not. On this point, Christianity lines up with the majority—lines up with ancient Greeks and Romans, modern savages, Stoics, Platonists, Hindus, Mohammedans, etc., against the modern Western European materialist.

Now I go on to the next big division. People who all believe in God can be divided according to the sort of God they believe in. There are two very different ideas on this subject. One of them is the idea that He is beyond good and evil. We humans call one thing good and another thing bad. But according to some people that is merely our human point of view. These people would say that the wiser you become the less you would want to call anything good or bad, and the more clearly you would see that everything is good in one way and bad in another, and that nothing could have been different. Consequently, these people think that long before you got anywhere near the divine point of view the distinction would have disappeared altogether. We call a cancer bad, they would say, because it kills a man; but you might just as well call a successful surgeon bad because he kills a cancer. It all depends on the point of view. The other and opposite idea is that God is quite definitely "good" or "righteous," a God who takes

---

For a biographical note about C. S. Lewis (1898–1963), see page 13. The material reprinted here was originally delivered to the British public, in the early 1940s, in a series of radio addresses.

sides, who loves love and hates hatred, who wants us to behave in one way and not in another. The first of these views—the one that thinks God beyond good and evil—is called Pantheism. It was held by the great Prussian philosopher Hegel and, as far as I can understand them, by the Hindus. The other view is held by Jews, Mohammedans, and Christians.

And with this big difference between Pantheism and the Christian 4 idea of God, there usually goes another. Pantheists usually believe that God, so to speak, animates the universe as you animate your body: that the universe almost *is* God, so that if it did not exist He would not exist either, and anything you find in the universe is a part of God. The Christian idea is quite different. They think God invented and made the universe—like a man making a picture or composing a tune. A painter is not a picture, and he docs not die if his picture is destroyed. You may say, "He's put a lot of himself into it," but you only mean that all its beauty and interest has come out of his head. His skill is not in the picture in the same way that it is in his head, or even in his hands. I expect you see how this difference between Pantheists and Christians hangs together with the other one. If you do not take the distinction between good and bad very seriously, then it is easy to say that anything you find in this world is a part of God. But, of course, if you think some things really bad, and God really good, then you cannot talk like that. You must believe that God is separate from the world and that some of the things we see in it are contrary to His will. Confronted with a cancer or a slum the Pantheist can say, "If you could only see it from the divine point of view, you would realize that this also is God." The Christian replies, "Don't talk damned nonsense."[1] For Christianity is a fighting religion. It thinks God made the world—that space and time, heat and cold, and all the colors and tastes, and all the animals and vegetables, are things that God "made up out of His head" as a man makes up a story. But it also thinks that a great many things have gone wrong with the world that God made and that God insists, and insists very loudly, on our putting them right again.

And, of course, that raises a very big question. If a good God made the world why has it gone wrong? And for many years I simply refused to listen to the Christian answers to this question, because I kept on feeling "whatever you say, and however clever your arguments are, isn't it much simpler and easier to say that the world was not made by any intelligent power? Aren't all your arguments simply a complicated attempt to avoid the obvious?" But then that threw me back into another difficulty.

My argument against God was that the universe seemed so cruel and unjust. But how had I got this idea of *just* and *unjust?* A man does not call a line crooked unless he has some idea of a straight line. What was I comparing this universe with when I called it unjust? If the whole show

[1]One listener complained of the word *damned* as frivolous swearing. But I mean exactly what I say—nonsense that is *damned* is under God's curse, and will (apart from God's grace) lead those who believe it to eternal death.

was bad and senseless from A to Z, so to speak, why did I, who was supposed to be part of the show, find myself in such violent reaction against it? A man feels wet when he falls into water, because man is not a water animal: a fish would not feel wet. Of course I could have given up my idea of justice by saying it was nothing but a private idea of my own. But if I did that, then my argument against God collapsed too—for the argument depended on saying that the world was really unjust, not simply that it did not happen to please my private fancies. Thus in the very act of trying to prove that God did not exist—in other words, that the whole of reality was senseless—I found I was forced to assume that one part of reality—namely my idea of justice—was full of sense. Consequently atheism turns out to be too simple. If the whole universe has no meaning, we should never have found out that it has no meaning: just as, if there were no light in the universe and therefore no creatures with eyes, we should never know it was dark. *Dark* would be without meaning.

2. The Invasion

Very well then, atheism is too simple. And I will tell you another view that is also too simple. It is the view I call Christianity-and-water, the view which simply says there is a good God in Heaven and everything is all right—leaving out all the difficult and terrible doctrines about sin and hell and the devil, and the redemption. Both these are boys' philosophies.

It is no good asking for a simple religion. After all, real things are not simple. They look simple, but they are not. The table I am sitting at looks simple: but ask a scientist to tell you what it is really made of—all about the atoms and how the light waves rebound from them and hit my eye and what they do to the optic nerve and what it does to my brain—and, of course, you find that what we call "seeing a table" lands you in mysteries and complications which you can hardly get to the end of. A child saying a child's prayer looks simple. And if you are content to stop there, well and good. But if you are not—and the modern world usually is not—if you want to go on and ask what is really happening—then you must be prepared for something difficult. If we ask for something more than simplicity, it is silly then to complain that the something more is not simple.

Very often, however, this silly procedure is adopted by people who are not silly, but who, consciously or unconsciously, want to destroy Christianity. Such people put up a version of Christianity suitable for a child of six and make that the object of their attack. When you try to explain the Christian doctrine as it is really held by an instructed adult, they then complain that you are making their heads turn round and that it is all too complicated and that if there really were a God they are sure He would have made "religion" simple, because simplicity is so beautiful, etc. You must be on your guard against these people for they will change their ground every minute and only waste your time. Notice, too, their idea of God "making religion simple": as if "religion" were something God invented, and not His statement to us of certain quite unalterable facts about His own nature.

Besides being complicated, reality, in my experience, is usually odd. It is not neat, not obvious, not what you expect. For instance, when you have grasped that the earth and the other planets all go round the sun, you would naturally expect that all the planets were made to match—all at equal distances from each other, say, or distances that regularly increased, or all the same size, or else getting bigger or smaller as you go farther from the sun. In fact, you find no rhyme or reason (that we can see) about either the sizes or the distances; and some of them have one moon, one has four, one has two, some have none, and one has a ring.

Reality, in fact, is usually something you could not have guessed. That is one of the reasons I believe Christianity. It is a religion you could not have guessed. If it offered us just the kind of universe we had always expected, I should feel we were making it up. But, in fact, it is not the sort of thing anyone would have made up. It has just that queer twist about it that real things have. So let us leave behind all these boys' philosophies— these oversimple answers. The problem is not simple and the answer is not going to be simple either.

What is the problem? A universe that contains much that is obviously 12 bad and apparently meaningless, but containing creatures like ourselves who know that it is bad and meaningless. There are only two views that face all the facts. One is the Christian view that this is a good world that has gone wrong, but still retains the memory of what it ought to have been. The other is the view called Dualism. Dualism means the belief that there are two equal and independent powers at the back of everything, one of them good and the other bad, and that this universe is the battlefield in which they fight out an endless war. I personally think that next to Christianity Dualism is the manliest and most sensible creed on the market. But it has a catch in it.

The two powers, or spirits, or gods—the good one and the bad one— are supposed to be quite independent. They both existed from all eternity. Neither of them made the other, neither of them has any more right than the other to call itself God. Each presumably thinks it is good and thinks the other bad. One of them likes hatred and cruelty, the other likes love and mercy, and each backs its own view. Now what do we mean when we call one of them the Good Power and the other the Bad Power? Either we are merely saying that we happen to prefer the one to the other—like preferring beer to cider—or else we are saying that, whatever the two powers think about it, and whichever we humans, at the moment, happen to like, one of them is actually wrong, actually mistaken, in regarding itself as good. Now if we mean merely that we happen to prefer the first, then we must give up talking about good and evil at all. For good means what you ought to prefer quite regardless of what you happen to like at any given moment. If "being good" meant simply joining the side you happened to fancy, for no real reason, then good would not deserve to be called good. So we must mean that one of the two powers is actually wrong and the other actually right.

But the moment you say that, you are putting into the universe a third thing in addition to the two Powers: some law or standard or rule of good which one of the powers conforms to and the other fails to conform to. But since the two powers are judged by this standard, then this standard, or the Being who made this standard, is farther back and higher up than either of them, and He will be the real God. In fact, what we meant by calling them good and bad turns out to be that one of them is in a right relation to the real ultimate God and the other in a wrong relation to Him.

The same point can be made in a different way. If Dualism is true, then the bad Power must be a being who likes badness for its own sake. But in reality we have no experience of anyone liking badness just because it is bad. The nearest we can get to it is in cruelty. But in real life people are cruel for one of two reasons—either because they are sadists, that is, because they have a sexual perversion which makes cruelty a cause of sensual pleasure to them, or else for the sake of something they are going to get out of it—money, or power, or safety. But pleasure, money, power, and safety are all, as far as they go, good things. The badness consists in pursuing them by the wrong method, or in the wrong way, or too much. I do not mean, of course, that the people who do this are not desperately wicked. I do mean that wickedness, when you examine it, turns out to be the pursuit of some good in the wrong way. You can be good for the mere sake of goodness: you cannot be bad for the mere sake of badness. You can do a kind action when you are not feeling kind and when it gives you no pleasure, simply because kindness is right; but no one ever did a cruel action simply because cruelty is wrong—only because cruelty was pleasant or useful to him. In other words badness cannot succeed even in being bad in the same way in which goodness is good. Goodness is, so to speak, itself: badness is only spoiled goodness. And there must be something good first before it can be spoiled. We called sadism a sexual perversion; but you must first have the idea of a normal sexuality before you can talk of its being perverted: and you can see which is the perversion, because you can explain the perverted from the normal, and cannot explain the normal from the perverted. It follows that this Bad Power, who is supposed to be on an equal footing with the Good Power, and to love badness in the same way as the Good Power loves goodness, is a mere bogy. In order to be bad he must have good things to want and then to pursue in the wrong way: he must have impulses which were originally good in order to be able to pervert them. But if he is bad he cannot supply himself either with good things to desire or with good impulses to pervert. He must be getting both from the Good Power. And if so, then he is not independent. He is part of the Good Power's world: he was made either by the Good Power or by some power above them both.

Put it more simply still. To be bad, he must exist and have intelligence 16 and will. But existence, intelligence, and will are in themselves good. Therefore he must be getting them from the Good Power: even to be bad he must borrow or steal from his opponent. And do you now begin to see why Christianity has always said that the devil is a fallen angel? That is not a mere story for the children. It is a real recognition of the fact that evil is a parasite, not an original thing. The powers which enable evil to carry on are powers given it by goodness. All the things which enable a bad man to be effectively bad are in themselves good things—resolution, cleverness, good looks, existence itself. That is why Dualism, in a strict sense, will not work.

But I freely admit that real Christianity (as distinct from Christianity-and-water) goes much nearer to Dualism than people think. One of the things that surprised me when I first read the New Testament seriously was that it talked so much about a Dark Power in the universe—a mighty evil spirit who was held to be the Power behind death and disease, and sin. The difference is that Christianity thinks this Dark Power was created by God, and was good when he was created, and went wrong. Christianity agrees with Dualism that this universe is at war. But it does not think this is a war between independent powers. It thinks it is a civil war, a rebellion, and that we are living in a part of the universe occupied by the rebel.

Enemy-occupied territory—that is what this world is. Christianity is the story of how the rightful king has landed, you might say landed in disguise, and is calling us all to take part in a great campaign of sabotage. When you go to church you are really listening in to the secret wireless from our friends: that is why the enemy is so anxious to prevent us from going. He does it by playing on our conceit and laziness and intellectual snobbery. I know someone will ask me, "Do you really mean, at this time of day, to reintroduce our old friend the devil—hoofs and horns and all?" Well, what the time of day has to do with it I do not know. And I am not particular about the hoofs and horns. But in other respects my answer is "Yes, I do." I do not claim to know anything about his personal appearance. If anybody really wants to know him better I would say to that person, "Don't worry. If you really want to, you will. Whether you'll like it when you do is another question."

3. THE SHOCKING ALTERNATIVE

Christians, then, believe that an evil power has made himself for the present the Prince of this World. And, of course, that raises problems. Is this state of affairs in accordance with God's will or not? If it is, He is a strange God, you will say: and if it is not, how can anything happen contrary to the will of a being with absolute power?

But anyone who has been in authority knows how a thing can be in 20 accordance with your will in one way and not in another. It may be quite sensible for a mother to say to the children, "I'm not going to go and make you tidy the schoolroom every night. You've got to learn to keep it tidy on your own." Then she goes up one night and finds the Teddy bear and the ink and the French Grammar all lying in the grate. That is against her will. She would prefer the children to be tidy. But on the other hand, it is her will which has left the children free to be untidy. The same thing arises in any regiment, or trade union, or school. You make a thing voluntary and then half the people do not do it. That is not what you willed, but your will has made it possible.

It is probably the same in the universe. God created things which had free will. That means creatures which can go either wrong or right. Some people think they can imagine a creature which was free but had no possibility of going wrong; I cannot. If a thing is free to be good it is also free to be bad. And free will is what has made evil possible. Why, then, did God give them free will? Because free will, though it makes evil possible, is also the only thing that makes possible any love or goodness or joy worth having. A world of automata—of creatures that worked like machines—would hardly be worth creating. The happiness which God designs for His higher creatures is the happiness of being freely, voluntarily united to Him and to each other in an ecstasy of love and delight compared with which the most rapturous love between a man and a woman on this earth is mere milk and water. And for that they must be free.

Of course God knew what would happen if they used their freedom the wrong way: apparently He thought it worth the risk. Perhaps we feel inclined to disagree with Him. But there is a difficulty about disagreeing with God. He is the source from which all your reasoning power comes: you could not be right and He wrong any more than a stream can rise higher than its own source. When you are arguing against Him you are arguing against the very power that makes you able to argue at all: it is like cutting off the branch you are sitting on. If God thinks this state of war in the universe a price worth paying for free will—that is, for making a live world in which creatures can do real good or harm and something of real importance can happen, instead of a toy world which only moves when He pulls the strings—then we may take it it is worth paying.

When we have understood about free will, we shall see how silly it is to ask, as somebody once asked me: "Why did God make a creature of such rotten stuff that it went wrong?" The better stuff a creature is made of— the cleverer and stronger and freer it is—then the better it will be if it goes right, but also the worse it will be if it goes wrong. A cow cannot be very good or very bad; a dog can be both better and worse; a child better and worse still; an ordinary man, still more so; a man of genius, still more so; a superhuman spirit best—or worst—of all.

How did the Dark Power go wrong? Here, no doubt, we ask a question to which human beings cannot give an answer with any certainty. A reasonable (and traditional) guess, based on our own experiences of going wrong, can, however, be offered. The moment you have a self at all, there is a possibility of putting yourself first—wanting to be the center—wanting to be God, in fact. That was the sin of Satan: and that was the sin he taught the human race. Some people think the fall of man had something to do with sex, but that is a mistake. (The story in the Book of Genesis rather suggests that some corruption in our sexual nature followed the fall and was its result, not its cause.) What Satan put into the heads of our remote ancestors was the idea that they could "be like gods"—could set up on their own as if they had created themselves—be their own masters—invent some sort of happiness for themselves outside God, apart from God. And out of that hopeless attempt has come nearly all that we call human history—money, poverty, ambition, war, prostitution, classes, empires, slavery—the long terrible story of man trying to find something other than God which will make him happy.

The reason why it can never succeed is this. God made us: invented us as a man invents an engine. A car is made to run on gasoline, and it would not run properly on anything else. Now God designed the human machine to run on Himself. He Himself is the fuel our spirits were designed to burn, or the food our spirits were designed to feed on. There is no other. That is why it is just no good asking God to make us happy in our own way without bothering about religion. God cannot give us a happiness and peace apart from Himself, because it is not there. There is no such thing.

That is the key to history. Terrific energy is expended—civilizations are built up—excellent institutions devised; but each time something goes wrong. Some fatal flaw always brings the selfish and cruel people to the top and it all slides back into misery and ruin. In fact, the machine conks. It seems to start up all right and runs a few yards, and then it breaks down. They are trying to run it on the wrong juice. That is what Satan has done to us humans.

And what did God do? First of all He left us conscience, the sense of right and wrong: and all through history there have been people trying (some of them very hard) to obey it. None of them ever quite succeeded. Secondly, he sent the human race what I call good dreams: I mean those queer stories scattered all through the heathen religions about a god who dies and comes to life again and, by his death, has somehow given new life to men. Thirdly, He selected one particular people and spent several centuries hammering into their heads the sort of God He was—that there was only one of Him and that He cared about right conduct. Those people were the Jews, and the Old Testament gives an account of the hammering process.

Then comes the real shock. Among these Jews there suddenly turns up 28 a man who goes about talking as if He was God. He claims to forgive sins. He says He has always existed. He says He is coming to judge the world at the end of time. Now let us get this clear. Among Pantheists, like the Indians, anyone might say that he was a part of God, or one with God: there would be nothing very odd about it. But this man, since He was a Jew, could not mean that kind of God. God, in their language, meant the Being outside the world Who had made it and was infinitely different from anything else. And when you have grasped that, you will see that what this man said was, quite simply, the most shocking thing that has ever been uttered by human lips.

One part of the claim tends to slip past us unnoticed because we have heard it so often that we no longer see what it amounts to. I mean the claim to forgive sins: any sins. Now unless the speaker is God, this is really so preposterous as to be comic. We can all understand how a man forgives offenses against himself. You tread on my toe and I forgive you, you steal my money and I forgive you. But what should we make of a man, himself unrobbed and untrodden on, who announced that he forgave you for treading on other men's toes and stealing other men's money? Asinine fatuity is the kindest description we should give of his conduct. Yet this is what Jesus did. He told people that their sins were forgiven, and never waited to consult all the other people whom their sins had undoubtedly injured. He unhesitatingly behaved as if He was the party chiefly concerned, the person chiefly offended in all offenses. This makes sense only if He really was the God whose laws are broken and whose love is wounded in every sin. In the mouth of any speaker who is not God, these words would imply what I can only regard as a silliness and conceit unrivaled by any other character in history.

Yet (and this is the strange, significant thing) even His enemies, when they read the Gospels, do not usually get the impression of silliness and conceit. Still less do unprejudiced readers. Christ says that He is "humble and meek" and we believe Him; not noticing that, if He were merely a man, humility and meekness are the very last characteristics we could attribute to some of His sayings.

I am trying here to prevent anyone saying the really foolish thing that people often say about Him: "I'm ready to accept Jesus as a great moral teacher, but I don't accept His claim to be God." That is the one thing we must not say. A man who was merely a man and said the sort of things Jesus said would not be a great moral teacher. He would either be a lunatic—on a level with the man who says he is a poached egg—or else he would be the Devil of Hell. You must make your choice. Either this man was, and is, the Son of God: or else a madman or something worse. You can shut Him up for a fool, you can spit at Him and kill Him as a demon;

or you can fall at His feet and call Him Lord and God. But let us not come with any patronizing nonsense about His being a great human teacher. He has not left that open to us. He did not intend to.

4. THE PERFECT PENITENT

We are faced, then, with a frightening alternative. This man we are 32 talking about either was (and is) just what He said or else a lunatic, or something worse. Now it seems to me obvious that He was neither a lunatic nor a fiend: and consequently, however strange or terrifying or unlikely it may seem, I have to accept the view that He was and is God. God has landed on this enemy-occupied world in human form.

And now, what was the purpose of it all? What did He come to do? Well, to teach, of course; but as soon as you look into the New Testament or any other Christian writing you will find they are constantly talking about something different—about His death and His coming to life again. It is obvious that Christians think the chief point of the story lies here. They think the main thing He came to earth to do was to suffer and be killed.

Now before I became a Christian I was under the impression that the first thing Christians had to believe was one particular theory as to what the point of this dying was. According to that theory God wanted to punish men for having deserted and joined the Great Rebel, but Christ volunteered to be punished instead, and so God let us off. Now I admit that even this theory does not seem to me quite so immoral and so silly as it used to; but that is not the point I want to make. What I came to see later on was that neither this theory nor any other is Christianity. The central Christian belief is that Christ's death has somehow put us right with God and given us a fresh start. Theories as to how it did this are another matter. A good many different theories have been held as to how it works: what all Christians are agreed on is that it does work. I will tell you what I think it is like. All sensible people know that if you are tired and hungry a meal will do you good. But the modern theory of nourishment—all about the vitamins and proteins—is a different thing. People ate their dinners and felt better long before the theory of vitamins was ever heard of: and if the theory of vitamins is some day abandoned they will go on eating their dinners just the same. Theories about Christ's death are not Christianity: they are explanations about how it works. Christians would not all agree as to how important these theories are. My own church—the Church of England—does not lay down any one of them as the right one. The Church of Rome goes a bit further. But I think they will all agree that the thing itself is infinitely more important than any explanations that theologians have produced. I think they would probably admit that no explanation will ever be quite adequate to the reality. But as I said in the preface to this book, I am only a layman, and at this point we are getting into deep water.

I can only tell you, for what it is worth, how I, personally, look at the matter.

On my view the theories are not themselves the thing you are asked to accept. Many of you no doubt have read Jeans or Eddington. What they do when they want to explain the atom, or something of that sort, is to give you a description out of which you can make a mental picture. But then they warn you that this picture is not what the scientists actually believe. What the scientists believe is a mathematical formula. The pictures are there only to help you to understand the formula. They are not really true in the way the formula is; they do not give you the real thing but only something more or less like it. They are only meant to help, and if they do not help you can drop them. The thing itself cannot be pictured, it can only be expressed mathematically. We are in the same boat here. We believe that the death of Christ is just that point in history at which something absolutely unimaginable from outside shows through into our own world. And if we cannot picture even the atoms of which our own world is built, of course we are not going to be able to picture this. Indeed, if we found that we could fully understand it, that very fact would show it was not what it professes to be—the inconceivable, the uncreated, the thing from beyond nature, striking down into nature like lightning. You may ask what good will it be to us if we do not understand it. But that is easily answered. A man can eat his dinner without understanding exactly how food nourishes him. A man can accept what Christ has done without knowing how it works; indeed, he certainly would not know how it works until he has accepted it.

We are told that Christ was killed for us, that His death has washed out our sins, and that by dying He disabled death itself. That is the formula. That is Christianity. That is what has to be believed. Any theories we build up as to how Christ's death did all this are, in my view, quite secondary: mere plans or diagrams to be left alone if they do not help us, and, even if they do help us, not to be confused with the thing itself. All the same, some of these theories are worth looking at.

The one most people have heard is the one I mentioned before—the one about our being let off because Christ had volunteered to bear a punishment instead of us. Now on the face of it that is a very silly theory. If God was prepared to let us off, why on earth did He not do so? And what possible point could there be in punishing an innocent person instead? None at all that I can see, if you are thinking of punishment in the police-court sense. On the other hand, if you think of a debt, there is plenty of point in a person who has some assets paying it on behalf of someone who has not. Or if you take "paying the penalty," not in the sense of being punished, but in the more general sense of "standing the racket" or "footing the bill," then, of course, it is a matter of common experience that, when one person has got himself into a hole, the trouble of getting him out usually falls on a kind friend.

Now what was the sort of "hole" man had got himself into? He had tried to set up on his own, to behave as if he belonged to himself. In other words, fallen man is not simply an imperfect creature who needs improvement: he is a rebel who must lay down his arms. Laying down your arms, surrendering, saying you are sorry, realizing that you have been on the wrong track and getting ready to start life over again from the ground floor—that is the only way out of a "hole." This process of surrender—this movement full speed astern—is what Christians call repentance. Now repentance is no fun at all. It is something much harder than merely eating humble pie. It means unlearning all the self-conceit and self-will that we have been training ourselves into for thousands of years. It means killing part of yourself, undergoing a kind of death. In fact, it needs a good man to repent. And here comes the catch. Only a bad person needs to repent: only a good person can repent perfectly. The worse you are the more you need it and the less you can do it. The only person who could do it perfectly would be a perfect person—and he would not need it.

Remember, this repentance, this willing submission to humiliation and a kind of death, is not something God demands of you before He will take you back and which He could let you off if He chose: it is simply a description of what going back to Him is like. If you ask God to take you back without it, you are really asking Him to let you go back without going back. It cannot happen. Very well, then, we must go through with it. But the same badness which makes us need it, makes us unable to do it. Can we do it if God helps us? Yes, but what do we mean when we talk of God helping us? We mean God putting into us a bit of Himself, so to speak. He lends us a little of His reasoning powers and that is how we think: He puts a little of His love into us and that is how we love one another. When you teach a child writing, you hold its hand while it forms the letters: that is, it forms the letters because you are forming them. We love and reason because God loves and reasons and holds our hand while we do it. Now if we had not fallen, that would be all plain sailing. But unfortunately we now need God's help in order to do something which God, in His own nature, never does at all—to surrender, to suffer, to submit, to die. Nothing in God's nature corresponds to this process at all. So that the one road for which we now need God's leadership most of all is a road God, in His own nature, has never walked. God can share only what He has: this thing, in His own nature, He has not.

But supposing God became a man—suppose our human nature which 40 can suffer and die was amalgamated with God's nature in one person— then that person could help us. He could surrender His will, and suffer and die, because He was man; and He could do it perfectly because He was God. You and I can go through this process only if God does it in us; but God can do it only if He becomes man. Our attempts at this dying will succeed only if we men share in God's dying, just as our thinking can succeed only because it is a drop out of the ocean of His intelligence: but we cannot share God's dying unless God dies; and He cannot die except by being a man. That is the sense in which He pays our debt, and suffers for us what He Himself need not suffer at all.

I have heard some people complain that if Jesus was God as well as man, then His sufferings and death lose all value in their eyes, "because it must have been so easy for him." Others may (very rightly) rebuke the ingratitude and ungraciousness of this objection; what staggers me is the misunderstanding it betrays. In one sense, of course, those who make it are right. They have even understated their own case. The perfect submission, the perfect suffering, the perfect death were not only easier to Jesus because He was God, but were possible only because He was God. But surely that is a very odd reason for not accepting them? The teacher is able to form the letters for the child because the teacher is grown-up and knows how to write. That, of course, makes it easier for the teacher; and only because it is easier for him can he help the child. If it rejected him because "it's easy for grown-ups" and waited to learn writing from another child who could not write itself (and so had no "unfair" advantage), it would not get on very quickly. If I am drowning in a rapid river, a man who still has one foot on the bank may give me a hand which saves my life. Ought I to shout back (between my gasps) "No, it's not fair! You have an advantage! You're keeping one foot on the bank"? That advantage—call it "unfair" if you like—is the only reason why he can be of any use to me. To what will you look for help if you will not look to that which is stronger than yourself?

Such is my own way of looking at what Christians call the Atonement. But remember this is only one more picture. Do not mistake it for the thing itself: and if it does not help you, drop it.

5. THE PRACTICAL CONCLUSION

The perfect surrender and humiliation were undergone by Christ: perfect because He was God, surrender and humiliation because He was man. Now the Christian belief is that if we somehow share the humility and suffering of Christ we shall also share in His conquest of death and find a new life after we have died and in it become perfect, and perfectly happy, creatures. This means something much more than our trying to follow His teaching. People often ask when the next step in evolution—the step to something beyond man—will happen. But on the Christian view, it has happened already. In Christ a new kind of man appeared: and the new kind of life which began in Him is to be put into us.

How is this to be done? Now, please remember how we acquired the old, ordinary kind of life. We derived it from others, from our father and mother and all our ancestors, without our consent—and by a very curious process, involving pleasure, pain, and danger. A process you would never have guessed. Most of us spend a good many years in childhood trying to guess it: and some children, when they are first told, do not believe it—and I am not sure that I blame them, for it is very odd. Now the God who arranged that process is the same God who arranges how the new kind of life—the Christ life—is to be spread. We must be prepared for it being odd too. He did not consult us when He invented sex: He has not consulted us either when He invented this.

There are three things that spread the Christ life to us: baptism, belief, and that mysterious action which different Christians call by different names—Holy Communion, the Mass, the Lord's Supper. At least, those are the three ordinary methods. I am not saying there may not be special cases where it is spread without one or more of these. I have not time to go into special cases, and I do not know enough. If you are trying in a few minutes to tell a man how to get to Edinburgh you will tell him the trains: he can, it is true, get there by boat or by a plane, but you will hardly bring that in. And I am not saying anything about which of these three things is the most essential. My Methodist friend would like me to say more about belief and less (in proportion) about the other two. But I am not going into that. Anyone who professes to teach you Christian doctrine will, in fact, tell you to use all three, and that is enough for our present purpose.

I cannot myself see why these things should be the conductors of the new kind of life. But then, if one did not happen to know, I should never have seen any connection between a particular physical pleasure and the appearance of a new human being in the world. We have to take reality as it comes to us: there is no good jabbering about what it ought to be like or what we should have expected it to be like. But though I cannot see why it should be so, I can tell you why I believe it is so. I have explained why I have to believe that Jesus was (and is) God. And it seems plain as a matter of history that He taught His followers that the new life was communicated in this way. In other words, I believe it on His authority. Do not be scared by the word *authority*. Believing things on authority only means believing them because you have been told them by someone you think trustworthy. Ninety-nine percent of the things you believe are believed on authority. I believe there is such a place as New York. I have not seen it myself. I could not prove by abstract reasoning that there must be such a place. I believe it because reliable people have told me so. The ordinary man believes in the Solar System, atoms, evolution, and the circulation of the blood on authority—because the scientists say so. Every historical statement in the world is believed on authority. None of us has seen the Norman Conquest or the defeat of the Armada. None of us could prove them by pure logic as you prove a thing in mathematics. We believe them simply because people who did see them have left writings that tell us about them: in fact, on authority. A man who jibbed at authority in other things as some people do in religion would have to be content to know nothing all his life.

Do not think I am setting up baptism and belief and the Holy Communion as things that will do instead of your own attempts to copy Christ. Your natural life is derived from your parents; that does not mean it will stay there if you do nothing about it. You can lose it by neglect, or you can drive it away by committing suicide. You have to feed it and look after it: but always remember you are not making it, you are only keeping up a life you got from someone else. In the same way a Christian can lose the Christ-life which has been put into him, and he has to make efforts to keep it. But even the best Christian that ever lived is not acting on his own steam—he is only nourishing or protecting a life he could never have acquired by his own efforts. And that has practical consequences. As long as the natural life is in your body, it will do a lot toward repairing that body. Cut it, and up to a point it will heal, as a dead body would not. A live body is not one that never gets hurt, but one that can to some extent repair itself. In the same way a Christian is not a man who never goes wrong, but a man who is enabled to repent and pick himself up and begin over again after each stumble—because the Christ-life is inside him, repairing him all the time, enabling him to repeat (in some degree) the kind of voluntary death which Christ Himself carried out.

That is why the Christian is in a different position from other people who are trying to be good. They hope, by being good, to please God if there is one; or—if they think there is not—at least they hope to deserve approval from good men. But the Christian thinks any good he does comes from the Christ-life inside him. He does not think God will love us because we are good, but that God will make us good because He loves us; just as the roof of a greenhouse does not attract the sun because it is bright, but becomes bright because the sun shines on it. 48

And let me make it quite clear that when Christians say the Christ-life is in them, they do not mean simply something mental or moral. When they speak of being "in Christ" or of Christ being "in them," this is not simply a way of saying that they are thinking about Christ or copying Him. They mean that Christ is actually operating through them; that the whole mass of Christians are the physical organism through which Christ acts—that we are His fingers and muscles, the cells of His body. And perhaps that explains one or two things. It explains why this new life is spread not only by purely mental acts like belief, but by bodily acts like baptism and Holy Communion. It is not merely the spreading of an idea; it is more like evolution—a biological or superbiological fact. There is no good trying to be more spiritual than God. God never meant man to be a purely spiritual creature. That is why He uses material things like bread and wine to put the new life into us. We may think this rather crude and unspiritual. God does not: He invented eating. He likes matter. He invented it.

Here is another thing that used to puzzle me. Is it not frightfully unfair that this new life should be confined to people who have heard of Christ and been able to believe in Him? But the truth is God has not told us what His arrangements about the other people are. We do know that no man can be saved except through Christ; we do not know that only those who know Him can be saved through Him. But in the meantime, if you are worried about the people outside, the most unreasonable thing you can do is to remain outside yourself. Christians are Christ's body, the organism through which He works. Every addition to that body enables Him to do more. If you want to help those outside you must add your own little cell to the body of Christ who alone can help them. Cutting off a man's fingers would be an odd way of getting him to do more work.

Another possible objection is this. Why is God landing in this enemy-occupied world in disguise and starting a sort of secret society to undermine the devil? Why is He not landing in force, invading it? Is it that He is not strong enough? Well, Christians think He is going to land in force; we do not know when. But we can guess why He is delaying. He wants to give us the chance of joining His side freely. I do not suppose you and I would have thought much of a Frenchman who waited till the Allies were marching into Germany and then announced he was on our side. God will invade. But I wonder whether people who ask God to interfere openly and directly in our world quite realize what it will be like when He does. When that happens, it is the end of the world. When the author walks on to the stage the play is over. God is going to invade, all right: but what is the good of saying you are on His side then, when you see the whole natural universe melting away like a dream and something else—something it never entered your head to conceive—comes crashing in; something so beautiful to some of us and so terrible to others that none of us will have any choice left? For this time it will be God without disguise; something so overwhelming that it will strike either irresistible love or irresistible horror into every creature. It will be too late then to choose your side. There is no use saying you choose to lie down when it has become impossible to stand up. That will not be the time for choosing: it will be the time when we discover which side we really have chosen, whether we realized it before or not. Now, today, this moment, is our chance to choose the right side. God is holding back to give us that chance. It will not last forever. We must take it or leave it.

Questions and Suggestions for Writing

1. What is Lewis's argumentative strategy in his opening paragraph? Why does he bother to tell us about his atheistic days?

2. Lewis often seeks to clarify his points by giving rather simple examples—of a painter (para. 4), of straight and crooked lines (para. 6), of a fish (para. 6), and

of a car (para. 25). Reread the paragraphs in which these examples are given, and see if you find the examples helpful—or do you find them too simple?

3. In paragraph 44 Lewis talks about sex. Exactly why does he introduce this point?

4. In part 3 of his essay, Lewis refers to "the Dark Power." Reflect on this metaphor: Why "dark"? Why "power"? How much power does Lewis allow that the Dark Power has over us?

5. Lewis accepts Jesus as God because he finds only three alternatives, and rejects all of them. What are these alternatives, and what is Lewis's argument for rejecting each? Do you find this a convincing argument—identifying four possible positions, rejecting three, and concluding that the remaining one must be true?

6. Put yourself in the shoes of Lewis's original audience—persons listening to a radio in the 1940s. Let's assume you were not a believer at the start, and you remained a nonbeliever at the finish. Do you think that you have learned anything—other than, of course, what Lewis believed? And, second, do you think, as a nonbeliever, that you have been addressed courteously and fairly?

7. Lewis says (para. 11) one of his reasons for believing Christianity is that "it is a religion you could not have guessed." In an essay of 500 words explain what he means by this comment, and discuss whether, in general, inability to guess something is a good reason for believing in it.

Bertrand Russell

Why I Am Not a Christian

As your Chairman has told you, the subject about which I am going to speak to you tonight is "Why I Am Not a Christian." Perhaps it would be as well, first of all, to try to make out what one means by the word *Christian*. It is used these days in a very loose sense by a great many people. Some people mean no more by it than a person who attempts to live a good life. In that sense I suppose there would be Christians in all sects and creeds; but I do not think that that is the proper sense of the word, if only because it would imply that all the people who are not Christians—all the Bud-

Bertrand Russell (1872–1970), born in England, made his academic reputation as a mathematician and logician, but he won a popular reputation as a philosopher and social critic. Among his highly readable books are History of Western Philosophy *(1945) and* Why I Am Not a Christian *(1957).*

A pacifist during World War I, Russell was imprisoned in 1916 and deprived of his teaching position at Cambridge University. His unorthodox opinions continued to cause him personal difficulties. In 1938 he was offered a post at the City College of New York, but a judge refused to grant him a visa because of Russell's allegedly

dhists, Confucians, Mohammedans, and so on—are not trying to live a good life. I do not mean by a Christian any person who tries to live decently according to his lights. I think that you must have a certain amount of definite belief before you have a right to call yourself a Christian. The word does not have quite such a full-blooded meaning now as it had in the times of St. Augustine and St. Thomas Aquinas. In those days, if a man said that he was a Christian it was known what he meant. You accepted a whole collection of creeds which were set out with great precision, and every single syllable of those creeds you believed with the whole strength of your convictions.

WHAT IS A CHRISTIAN?

Nowadays it is not quite that. We have to be a little more vague in our meaning of Christianity. I think, however, that there are two different items which are quite essential to anybody calling himself a Christian. The first is one of a dogmatic nature—namely, that you must believe in God and immortality. If you do not believe in those two things, I do not think that you can properly call yourself a Christian. Then, further than that, as the name implies, you must have some kind of belief about Christ. The Mohammedans, for instance, also believe in God and in immortality, and yet they would not call themselves Christians. I think you must have at the very lowest the belief that Christ was, if not divine, at least the best and wisest of men. If you are not going to believe that much about Christ, I do not think you have any right to call yourself a Christian. Of course, there is another sense, which you find in *Whitaker's Almanack* and in geography books, where the population of the world is said to be divided into Christians, Mohammedans, Buddhists, fetish worshipers, and so on; and in that sense we are all Christians. The geography books count us all in, but that is a purely geographical sense, which I suppose we can ignore. Therefore I take it that when I tell you why I am not a Christian I have to tell you two different things: first, why I do not believe in God and in immortality; and, secondly, why I do not think that Christ was the best and wisest of men, although I grant him a very high degree of moral goodness.

But for the successful efforts of unbelievers in the past, I could not take so elastic a definition of Christianity as that. As I said before, in olden days

dangerous views on sex. During the last two decades of his life, Russell's criticism of American foreign policy made him an especially provocative figure in this country.

Reprinted here is one of his most famous essays on religion. An amusing note: On one occasion when he was imprisoned, the jailer asked him his religion. Russell replied that he was an atheist, a remark that puzzled the jailer, but the man, wishing to be friendly, replied, "Ah well, we all believe in the same God, don't we?"

it had a much more full-blooded sense. For instance, it included the belief in hell. Belief in eternal hell-fire was an essential item of Christian belief until pretty recent times. In this country, as you know, it ceased to be an essential item because of a decision of the Privy Council, and from that decision the Archbishop of Canterbury and the Archbishop of York dissented; but in this country our religion is settled by Act of Parliament, and therefore the Privy Council was able to override their Graces and hell was no longer necessary to a Christian. Consequently I shall not insist that a Christian must believe in hell.

THE EXISTENCE OF GOD

To come to this question of the existence of God: it is a large and 4 serious question, and if I were to attempt to deal with it in any adequate manner I should have to keep you here until Kingdom Come, so that you will have to excuse me if I deal with it in a somewhat summary fashion. You know, of course, that the Catholic Church has laid it down as a dogma that the existence of God can be proved by the unaided reason. That is a somewhat curious dogma, but it is one of their dogmas. They had to introduce it because at one time the freethinkers adopted the habit of saying that there were such and such arguments which mere reason might urge against the existence of God, but of course they knew as a matter of faith that God did exist. The arguments and the reasons were set out at great length, and the Catholic Church felt that they must stop it. Therefore they laid it down that the existence of God can be proved by the unaided reason and they had to set up what they considered were arguments to prove it. There are, of course, a number of them, but I shall take only a few.

THE FIRST CAUSE ARGUMENT

Perhaps the simplest and easiest to understand is the argument of the First Cause. (It is maintained that everything we see in this world has a cause, and as you go back in the chain of causes further and further you must come to a First Cause, and to that First Cause you give the name of God.) That argument, I suppose, does not carry very much weight nowadays, because, in the first place, cause is not quite what it used to be. The philosophers and the men of science have got going on cause, and it has not anything like the vitality it used to have; but, apart from that, you can see that the argument that there must be a First Cause is one that cannot have any validity. I may say that when I was a young man and was debating these questions very seriously in my mind, I for a long time accepted the argument of the First Cause, until one day, at the age of eighteen, I read

John Stuart Mill's *Autobiography,* and I there found this sentence: "My father taught me that the question 'Who made me?' cannot be answered, since it immediately suggests the further question 'Who made God?'" That very simple sentence showed me, as I still think, the fallacy in the argument of the First Cause. If everything must have a cause, then God must have a cause. If there can be anything without a cause, it may just as well be the world as God, so that there cannot be any validity in that argument. It is exactly of the same nature as the Hindu's view that the world rested upon an elephant and the elephant rested upon a tortoise; and when they said, "How about the tortoise?" the Indian said, "Suppose we change the subject." The argument is really no better than that. There is no reason why the world could not have come into being without a cause; nor, on the other hand, is there any reason why it should not have always existed. There is no reason to suppose that the world had a beginning at all. The idea that things must have a beginning is really due to the poverty of our imagination. Therefore, perhaps, I need not waste any more time upon the argument about the First Cause.

THE NATURAL LAW ARGUMENT

Then there is a very common argument from natural law. That was a favorite argument all through the eighteenth century, especially under the influence of Sir Isaac Newton and his cosmogony. People observed the planets going around the sun according to the law of gravitation, and they thought that God had given a behest to these planets to move in that particular fashion, and that was why they did so. That was, of course, a convenient and simple explanation that saved them the trouble of looking any further for explanations of the law of gravitation. Nowadays we explain the law of gravitation in a somewhat complicated fashion that Einstein has introduced. I do not propose to give you a lecture on the law of gravitation, as interpreted by Einstein, because that again would take some time; at any rate, you no longer have the sort of natural law that you had in the Newtonian system, where, for some reason that nobody could understand, nature behaved in a uniform fashion. We now find that a great many things we thought were natural laws are really human conventions. You know that even in the remotest depths of stellar space there are still three feet to a yard. That is, no doubt, a very remarkable fact, but you would hardly call it a law of nature. And a great many things that have been regarded as laws of nature are of that kind. On the other hand, where you can get down to any knowledge of what atoms actually do, you will find they are much less subject to law than people thought, and that the laws at which you arrive are statistical averages of just the sort that would emerge from chance. There is, as we all know, a law that if you throw dice you will get double sixes only about once in thirty-six times, and we do not regard that as evidence that the fall of the dice is regulated by design; on the contrary, if the double sixes came every time we should think that there was design. The laws of nature are of that sort as regards a great many of them. They are statistical averages such as would emerge from the laws of chance; and that makes this whole business of natural law much less impressive than it formerly was. Quite apart from that, which represents the momentary state of science that may change tomorrow, the whole idea that natural laws imply a lawgiver is due to a confusion between natural and human laws. Human laws are behests commanding you to behave a certain way, in which way you may choose to behave, or you may choose not to behave; but natural laws are a description of how things do in fact behave, and being a mere description of what they in fact do, you cannot argue that there must be somebody who told them to do that, because even supposing that there were, you are then faced with the question "Why did God issue just those natural laws and no others?" If you say that he did it simply from his own good pleasure, and without any reason, you then find that there is something which is not subject to law, and so your train of natural law is interrupted. If you say, as more orthodox theologians do, that in all the laws which God issues he had a reason for giving those laws rather than others—the reason, of course, being to create the best universe, although you would never think it to look at it—if there were a reason for the laws which God gave, then God himself was subject to law, and therefore you do not get any advantage by introducing God as an intermediary. You have really a law outside and anterior to the divine edicts, and God does not serve your purpose, because he is not the ultimate lawgiver. In short, this whole argument about natural law no longer has anything like the strength that it used to have. I am traveling on in time in my review of the arguments. The arguments that are used for the existence of God change their character as time goes on. They were at first hard intellectual arguments embodying certain quite definite fallacies. As we come to modern times they become less respectable intellectually and more and more affected by a kind of moralizing vagueness.

THE ARGUMENT FROM DESIGN

The next step in this process brings us to the argument from design. You all know the argument from design: Everything in the world is made just so that we can manage to live in the world, and if the world was ever so little different, we could not manage to live in it. That is the argument from design. It sometimes takes a rather curious form; for instance, it is argued that rabbits have white tails in order to be easy to shoot. I do not know how rabbits would view that application. It is an easy argument to parody. You all know Voltaire's remark, that obviously the nose was designed to be such as to fit spectacles. That sort of parody has turned out to be not nearly so wide of the mark as it might have seemed in the eighteenth century, because since the time of Darwin we understand much better why living creatures are adapted to their environment. It is not that their environment was made to be suitable to them but that they grew to be suitable to it, and that is the basis of adaptation. There is no evidence of design about it.

When you come to look into this argument from design, it is a most astonishing thing that people can believe that this world, with all the things that are in it, with all its defects, should be the best that omnipotence and omniscience have been able to produce in millions of years. I really cannot believe it. Do you think that, if you were granted omnipotence and omniscience and millions of years in which to perfect your world, you could produce nothing better than the Ku Klux Klan or the Fascists? Moreover, if you accept the ordinary laws of science, you have to suppose that human life and life in general on this planet will die out in due course: it is a stage in the decay of the solar system; at a certain stage of decay you get the sort of conditions of temperature and so forth which are suitable to protoplasm, and there is life for a short time in the life of the whole solar system. You see in the moon the sort of thing to which the earth is tending—something dead, cold, and lifeless.

I am told that that sort of view is depressing, and people will sometimes tell you that if they believed that, they would not be able to go on living. Do not believe it; it is all nonsense. Nobody really worries much about what is going to happen millions of years hence. Even if they think they are worrying much about that, they are really deceiving themselves. They are worried about something much more mundane, or it may merely be a bad digestion; but nobody is really seriously rendered unhappy by the thought of something that is going to happen to this world millions and millions of years hence. Therefore, although it is of course a gloomy view to suppose that life will die out—at least I suppose we may say so, although sometimes when I contemplate the things that people do with their lives I think it is almost a consolation—it is not such as to render life miserable. It merely makes you turn your attention to other things.

THE MORAL ARGUMENTS FOR DEITY

Now we reach one stage further in what I shall call the intellectual descent that the Theists have made in their argumentations, and we come to what are called the moral arguments for the existence of God. You all know, of course, that there used to be in the old days three intellectual arguments for the existence of God, all of which were disposed of by Immanuel Kant in the *Critique of Pure Reason*; but no sooner had he disposed of those arguments than he invented a new one, a moral argument, and that quite convinced him. He was like many people: in intellectual matters he was skeptical, but in moral matters he believed implicitly in the maxims that he had imbibed at his mother's knee. That illustrates what the psychoanalysts so much emphasize—the immensely stronger hold upon us that our very early associations have than those of later times.

Kant, as I say, invented a new moral argument for the existence of God, and that in varying forms was extremely popular during the nineteenth century. It has all sorts of forms. One form is to say that there would be no right or wrong unless God existed. I am not for the moment concerned with whether there is a difference between right and wrong, or whether there is not: that is another question. The point I am concerned with is that, if you are quite sure there is a difference between right and wrong, you are then in this situation: Is that difference due to God's fiat or is it not? If it is due to God's fiat, then for God himself there is no difference between right and wrong, and it is no longer a significant statement to say that God is good. If you are going to say, as theologians do, that God is good, you must then say that right and wrong have some meaning which is independent of God's fiat, because God's fiats are good and not bad independently of the mere fact that he made them. If you are going to say that, you will then have to say that it is not only through God that right and wrong came into being, but that they are in their essence logically anterior to God. You could, of course, if you liked, say that there was a superior deity who gave orders to the God who made this world, or could take up the line that some of the gnostics took up—a line which I often thought was a very plausible one—that as a matter of fact this world that we know was made by the devil at a moment when God was not looking. There is a good deal to be said for that, and I am not concerned to refute it.

THE ARGUMENT FOR THE REMEDYING OF INJUSTICE

Then there is another very curious form of moral argument, which is this: they say that the existence of God is required in order to bring justice into the world. In the part of this universe that we know there is great injustice, and often the good suffer, and often the wicked prosper, and one hardly knows which of those is the more annoying; but if you are going to have justice in the universe as a whole you have to suppose a future life to redress the balance of life here on earth. So they say that there must be a God, and there must be heaven and hell in order that in the long run there may be justice. That is a very curious argument. If you looked at the matter from a scientific point of view, you would say, "After all, I know only this world. I do not know about the rest of the universe, but so far as one can argue at all on probabilities one would say that probably this world is a fair sample, and if there is injustice here the odds are that there is injustice elsewhere also." Supposing you got a crate of oranges that you opened, and you found all the top layer of oranges bad, you would not argue, "The underneath ones must be good, so as to redress the balance." You would say, "Probably the whole lot is a bad consignment"; and that is really what a scientific person would argue about the universe. He would say, "Here we find in this world a great deal of injustice, and so far as that goes that is a reason for supposing that justice does not rule in the world; and therefore so far as it goes it affords a moral argument against deity and not in favor of one." Of course I know that the sort of intellectual arguments that I have been talking to you about are not what really moves people. What really moves people to believe in God is not any intellectual argument at all. Most people believe in God because they have been taught from early infancy to do it, and that is the main reason.

Then I think that the next most powerful reason is the wish for safety, a sort of feeling that there is a big brother who will look after you. That plays a very profound part in influencing people's desire for a belief in God.

THE CHARACTER OF CHRIST

I now want to say a few words upon a topic which I often think is not quite sufficiently dealt with by Rationalists, and that is the question whether Christ was the best and the wisest of men. It is generally taken for granted that we should all agree that that was so. I do not myself. I think that there are a good many points upon which I agree with Christ a great deal more than the professing Christians do. I do not know that I could go with Him all the way, but I could go with Him much further than most professing Christians can. You will remember that He said, "Resist not evil: but whosoever shall smite thee on thy right cheek, turn to him the other also." That is not a new precept or a new principle. It was used by Lao-tse and Buddha some 500 or 600 years before Christ, but it is not a principle which as a matter of fact Christians accept. I have no doubt that the present Prime Minister,[1] for instance, is a most sincere Christian, but I should not advise any of you to go and smite him on one cheek. I think you might find that he thought this text was intended in a figurative sense.

Then there is another point which I consider excellent. You will remember that Christ said, "Judge not lest ye be judged." That principle I do not think you would find was popular in the law courts of Christian countries. I have known in my time quite a number of judges who were very earnest Christians, and none of them felt that they were acting contrary to Christian principles in what they did. Then Christ says, "Give to him that asketh of thee, and from him that would borrow of thee turn not thou away." That is a very good principle. Your Chairman has re-

[1]Stanley Baldwin.

minded you that we are not here to talk politics, but I cannot help observing that the last general election was fought on the question of how desirable it was to turn away from him that would borrow of thee, so that one must assume that the Liberals and Conservatives of this country are composed of people who do not agree with the teaching of Christ, because they certainly did very emphatically turn away on that occasion.

Then there is one other maxim of Christ which I think has a great deal 16 in it, but I do not find that it is very popular among some of our Christian friends. He says, "If thou wilt be perfect, go and sell that which thou hast, and give to the poor." That is a very excellent maxim, but, as I say, it is not much practiced. All these, I think, are good maxims, although they are a little difficult to live up to. I do not profess to live up to them myself; but then, after all, it is not quite the same thing as for a Christian.

DEFECTS IN CHRIST'S TEACHING

Having granted the excellence of these maxims, I come to certain points in which I do not believe that one can grant either the superlative wisdom or the superlative goodness of Christ as depicted in the Gospels; and here I may say that one is not concerned with the historical question. Historically it is quite doubtful whether Christ ever existed at all, and if He did we do not know anything about Him, so that I am not concerned with the historical question, which is a very difficult one. I am concerned with Christ as He appears in the Gospels, taking the Gospel narrative as it stands, and there one does find some things that do not seem to be very wise. For one thing, He certainly thought that His second coming would occur in clouds of glory before the death of all the people who were living at that time. There are a great many texts that prove that. He says, for instance, "Ye shall not have gone over the cities of Israel till the Son of Man be come." Then He says, "There are some standing here which shall not taste death till the Son of Man comes into His kingdom"; and there are a lot of places where it is quite clear that He believed that His second coming would happen during the lifetime of many then living. That was the belief of His earlier followers, and it was the basis of a good deal of His moral teaching. When He said, "Take no thought for the morrow," and things of that sort, it was very largely because He thought that the second coming was going to be very soon, and that all ordinary mundane affairs did not count. I have, as a matter of fact, known some Christians who did believe that the second coming was imminent. I knew a parson who frightened his congregation terribly by telling them that the second coming was very imminent indeed, but they were much consoled when they found that he was planting trees in his garden. The early Christians did really believe it, and they did abstain from such things as planting trees in their gardens, because they did accept from Christ the belief that the second coming was imminent. In that respect, clearly He was not so wise as some other people have been, and He was certainly not superlatively wise.

THE MORAL PROBLEM

Then you come to moral questions. There is one very serious defect to my mind in Christ's moral character, and that is that He believed in hell. I do not myself feel that any person who is really profoundly humane can believe in everlasting punishment. Christ certainly as depicted in the Gospels did believe in everlasting punishment, and one does find repeatedly a vindictive fury against those people who would not listen to His preaching—an attitude which is not uncommon with preachers, but which does somewhat detract from superlative excellence. You do not, for instance find that attitude in Socrates. You find him quite bland and urbane toward the people who would not listen to him; and it is, to my mind, far more worthy of a sage to take that line than to take the line of indignation. You probably all remember the sort of things that Socrates was saying when he was dying, and the sort of things that he generally did say to people who did not agree with him.

You will find that in the Gospels Christ said, "Ye serpents, ye generation of vipers, how can ye escape the damnation of hell." That was said to people who did not like His preaching. It is not really to my mind quite the best tone, and there are a great many of these things about hell. There is, of course, the familiar text about the sin against the Holy Ghost: "Whosoever speaketh against the Holy Ghost it shall not be forgiven him neither in this World nor in the world to come." That text has caused an unspeakable amount of misery in the world, for all sorts of people have imagined that they have committed the sin against the Holy Ghost, and thought that it would not be forgiven them either in this world or in the world to come. I really do not think that a person with a proper degree of kindliness in his nature would have put fears and terrors of that sort into the world.

Then Christ says, "The Son of Man shall send forth His angels, and 20 they shall gather out of His kingdom all things that offend, and them which do iniquity, and shall cast them into a furnace of fire; there shall be wailing and gnashing of teeth"; and He goes on about the wailing and gnashing of teeth. It comes in one verse after another, and it is quite manifest to the reader that there is a certain pleasure in contemplating wailing and gnashing of teeth, or else it would not occur so often. Then you all, of course, remember about the sheep and the goats; how at the second coming He is going to divide the sheep from the goats, and He is going to say to the goats, "Depart from me, ye cursed, into everlasting fire." He continues, "And these shall go away into everlasting fire." Then He says again, "If thy hand offend thee, cut it off; it is better for thee to enter into life maimed, than having two hands to go into hell, into the fire that never shall be quenched; where the worm dieth not and the fire is not quenched." He repeats that again and again also. I must say that I think all this doctrine, that hell-fire is a punishment for sin, is a doctrine of cruelty. It is a doctrine that put cruelty into the world and gave the world generations of cruel torture; and the Christ of the Gospels, if you could take Him as His chroniclers represent Him, would certainly have to be considered partly responsible for that.

There are other things of less importance. There is the instance of the Gadarene swine, where it certainly was not very kind to the pigs to put the devils into them and make them rush down the hill to the sea. You must remember that He was omnipotent, and He could have made the devils simply go away; but He chose to send them into the pigs. Then there is the curious story of the fig tree, which always rather puzzled me. You remember what happened about the fig tree. "He was hungry; and seeing a fig tree afar off having leaves, He came if haply He might find anything thereon; and when He came to it He found nothing but leaves, for the time of figs was not yet. And Jesus answered and said unto it: "No man eat fruit of thee hereafter for ever' . . . and Peter . . . saith unto Him: 'Master, behold the fig tree which thou cursedst is withered away.'" This is a very curious story, because it was not the right time of year for figs, and you really could not blame the tree. I cannot myself feel that either in the matter of wisdom or in the matter of virtue Christ stands quite as high as some other people known to history. I think I should put Buddha and Socrates above Him in those respects.

THE EMOTIONAL FACTOR

As I said before, I do not think that the real reason why people accept religion has anything to do with argumentation. They accept religion on emotional grounds. One is often told that it is a very wrong thing to attack religion, because religion makes men virtuous. So I am told; I have not noticed it. You know, of course, the parody of that argument in Samuel Butler's book, *Erewhon Revisited*. You will remember that in *Erewhon* there is a certain Higgs who arrives in a remote country, and after spending some time there he escapes from that country in a balloon. Twenty years later he comes back to that country and finds a new religion in which he is worshiped under the name of the "Sun Child," and it is said that he ascended into heaven. He finds that the Feast of the Ascension is about to be celebrated, and he hears Professors Hanky and Panky say to each other that they never set eyes on the man Higgs, and they hope they never will; but they are the high priests of the religion of the Sun Child. He is very indignant, and he comes up to them, and he says, "I am going to expose all this humbug and tell the people of Erewhon that it was only I, the man Higgs, and I went up in a balloon." He was told, "You must not do that, because all the morals of this country are bound round this myth, and if they once know that you did not ascend into heaven they will all become wicked"; and so he is persuaded of that and he goes quietly away.

That is the idea—that we should all be wicked if we did not hold to the Christian religion. It seems to me that the people who have held to it have been for the most part extremely wicked. You find this curious fact, that the more intense has been the religion of any period and the more profound has been the dogmatic belief, the greater has been the cruelty and the worse has been the state of affairs. In the so-called ages of faith, when men really did believe the Christian religion in all its completeness, there was the Inquisition, with its tortures; there were millions of unfortunate women burned as witches; and there was every kind of cruelty practiced upon all sorts of people in the name of religion.

You find as you look around the world that every single bit of progress 24 in humane feeling, every improvement in the criminal law, every step toward the diminution of war, every step toward better treatment of the colored races, or every mitigation of slavery, every moral progress that there has been in the world, has been consistently opposed by the organized churches of the world. I say quite deliberately that the Christian religion, as organized in its churches, has been and still is the principal enemy of moral progress in the world.

How the Churches Have Retarded Progress

You may think that I am going too far when I say that that is still so. I do not think that I am. Take one fact. You will bear with me if I mention it. It is not a pleasant fact, but the churches compel one to mention facts that are not pleasant. Supposing that in this world that we live in today an inexperienced girl is married to a syphilitic man; in that case the Catholic Church says, "This is an indissoluble sacrament. You must endure celibacy or stay together. And if you stay together, you must not use birth control to prevent the birth of syphilitic children." Nobody whose natural sympathies have not been warped by dogma, or whose moral nature was not absolutely dead to all sense of suffering, could maintain that it is right and proper that that state of things should continue.

That is only an example. There are a great many ways in which, at the present moment, the church, by its insistence upon what it chooses to call morality, inflicts upon all sorts of people undeserved and unnecessary suffering. And of course, as we know, it is in its major part an opponent still of progress and of improvement in all the ways that diminish suffering in the world, because it has chosen to label as morality a certain narrow set of rules of conduct which have nothing to do with human happiness; and when you say that this or that ought to be done because it would make for human happiness, they think that has nothing to do with the matter at all.

"What has human happiness to do with morals? The object of morals is not to make people happy."

FEAR, THE FOUNDATION OF RELIGION

Religion is based, I think, primarily and mainly upon fear. It is partly the terror of the unknown and partly, as I have said, the wish to feel that you have a kind of elder brother who will stand by you in all your troubles and disputes. Fear is the basis of the whole thing—fear of the mysterious, fear of defeat, fear of death. Fear is the parent of cruelty, and therefore it is no wonder if cruelty and religion have gone hand in hand. It is because fear is at the basis of those two things. In this world we can now begin a little to understand things, and a little to master them by help of science, which has forced its way step by step against the Christian religion, against the churches, and against the opposition of all the old precepts. Science can help us to get over this craven fear in which mankind has lived for so many generations. Science can teach us, and I think our own hearts can teach us, no longer to look around for imaginary supports, no longer to invent allies in the sky, but rather to look to our own efforts here below to make this world a fit place to live in, instead of the sort of place that the churches in all these centuries have made it.

WHAT WE MUST DO

We want to stand upon our own feet and look fair and square at the world—its good facts, its bad facts, its beauties, and its ugliness; see the world as it is and be not afraid of it. Conquer the world by intelligence and not merely by being slavishly subdued by the terror that comes from it. The whole conception of God is a conception derived from the ancient Oriental despotisms. It is a conception quite unworthy of free men. When you hear people in church debasing themselves and saying that they are miserable sinners, and all the rest of it, it seems contemptible and not worthy of self-respecting human beings. We ought to stand up and look the world frankly in the face. We ought to make the best we can of the world, and if it is not so good as we wish, after all it will still be better than what these others have made of it in all these ages. A good world needs knowledge, kindliness, and courage; it does not need a regretful hankering after the past or a fettering of the free intelligence by the words uttered long ago by ignorant men. It needs a fearless outlook and a free intelligence. It needs hope for the future, not looking back all the time toward a past that is dead, which we trust will be far surpassed by the future that our intelligence can create.

Questions and Suggestions for Writing

1. Russell's talk was originally delivered to the National Secular Society. What sort of a group do you think this Society was? Do you imagine that the audience approved or disapproved of the talk? Do you think that to some extent the talk was geared to the taste of this audience? What evidence can you offer for your view?

2. In a sentence summarize Russell's first paragraph, and in another sentence summarize his second paragraph. Finally, write a third sentence, this one describing and evaluating Russell's strategy in beginning his essay with these two paragraphs.

3. Read and reread Russell's third paragraph, about hell. In the last line of this paragraph, he says, "Consequently I shall not insist that a Christian must believe in hell." "Consequently," of course, suggests that what follows is logically derived from what precedes. State in your own words the reason that Russell offers for the conclusion here. What do you think Russell thought of that reason?

4. In paragraph 8 Russell wonders why an omnipotent and omniscient creator would "produce nothing better than the Ku Klux Klan or the Fascists." Even if you do not believe in an omnipotent and omniscient creator, try to write a one-paragraph response to this point.

5. Many Christians would say that they believe in God because Jesus believed in God. (This point is made by C. S. Lewis, in the preceding essay.) They would add that because historical evidence supports their belief that Jesus did indeed live and die and was resurrected, there can be no reason to doubt Jesus's teachings. Why, in your opinion, does Russell not comment on this argument?

6. Russell discusses the meaning of the term *Christian*, and offers his own definition. Look up in two unabridged dictionaries the definitions of this term, and explain whether Russell's definition agrees with all or any of those in the dictionaries. (By the way, do the dictionaries fully agree with each other?)

7. In paragraph 15 Russell says that many Christians do not practice certain teachings of Jesus. Suppose he is right; does this failing show that Jesus's teachings are wrong? Or that it is unreasonable to believe in Jesus? What, exactly, does Russell's argument prove?

8. In paragraph 21, setting forth what he takes to be some of Jesus's unpleasant teachings and doings, Russell refers to one episode in which exorcised devils entered into swine (Matthew 8:28–34; Mark 5:1–20) and another in which Jesus cursed a fig tree (Matthew 21:19; Mark 11:13–14). In the library examine several Christian commentaries on the Bible (for instance, D. E. Nineham's *The Gospel of St. Mark*, or even *The Interpreter's One-Volume Commentary on the Bible*) to see what explanations believers have offered. Do you find any of these explanations adequate? Why?

9. In paragraph 24 Russell asserts that "every single bit of progress in humane feeling . . . has been consistently opposed by the organized churches of the

world." What evidence does he offer? What evidence can you offer to support or to refute this view?

10. Russell states and criticizes five arguments for God's existence. Whether or not you find any of these arguments wholly convincing, which of them seems to you to be the strongest or the most likely to be sound, and which the weakest? In an essay of 500 words explain your evaluation. Optional: If you believe in God's existence, does it matter to you whether any of these arguments survived Russell's criticisms? Explain.

11. In his next-to-last paragraph Russell says that "fear" is the basis of religion. Many Christians would disagree, and would insist that love is the basis of Christianity. On this issue, where do you stand? Why?

12. In his final paragraph Russell says that people who debase themselves and call themselves "miserable sinners" in fact are "contemptible." If you have done things of which you have been deeply ashamed, do you think your confession (even if only to yourself) is "contemptible"?

13. Putting aside your own views of Christianity, in an essay of 500 to 750 words assess the strengths and the weaknesses of Russell's essay as an argument.

Arthur A. Cohen

Why I Choose to Be a Jew

Until the present day, the Jew could not *choose* to be a Jew—history forced him to accept what his birth had already defined.

During the Middle Ages he was expected to live as a Jew. He could escape by surrendering to Islam or Christianity, but he could *not* choose to remain anonymous. In the nineteenth century, with the growth of nationalism, Christianity became the ally of patriotism. The Jews of Europe were compelled to prove that their religion did not compromise their loyalty to King, Emperor, Kaiser, or Tsar. But no matter how desperately they tried to allay suspicion by assimilation or conversion, the fact of their birth returned to plague them. Finally, in the Europe of Nazism and Communism, the Jew could not choose—on any terms—to exist at all.

In the United States today, it is at last possible to choose *not* to remain a Jew. The mass migrations of Jews from Europe have ended and the immigrant generation which was tied to the European pattern of poverty and voluntary segregation is dying off. Their children, the second generation, were as suspicious of the gentile American society in which they grew

Arthur A. Cohen (1928–1986) was a publisher, novelist, and scholar. This essay, originally published in Harper's, *was one of a series of essays on modern religious beliefs.*

up as they were condescending toward the ghetto world of their parents. The second generation, however, made the Jewish community economically secure and fought anti-Semitism so effectively that, though still present, it is no longer severe. *Their* children—the third generation of Jews now in its twenties and thirties—are able to choose.

For this generation the old arguments no longer hold. It was once   4 possible to appeal to history to prove that Jewish birth was inescapable, but history is no proof to those who are—as many Jews are—indifferent to its evidence. Loyalty to the Jewish people and pride in the State of Israel are no longer enough to justify the choice to be a Jew. The postwar American Jew no longer needs the securities which European Jewry found in Jewish Socialism, Jewish Nationalism, the revival of Hebrew, and the Zionist Movement. *Fear*—the fear of anti-Semitism and *hope*—the hope for the restoration of Israel—are no longer effective reasons for holding on to Jewish identity. The fear has waned and the hope has been fulfilled.

The irresistible forces of history no longer *compel* the Jew to choose Judaism. In many cases, moreover, he is choosing to repudiate Judaism or to embrace Christianity. I do not say the numbers are alarming. That they exist at all is, however, symptomatic. It is only the exceptional—those who are searching deeply or are moved profoundly, who ever reject or embrace. The majority tend more often to undramatic indifference—to slide into the routine of maturity without asking questions for which no meaningful answers have been offered.

Given the freedom to choose I have decided to embrace Judaism. I have not done so out of loyalty to the Jewish people or the Jewish state. My choice was religious. I chose to believe in the God of Abraham, Isaac, and Jacob; to acknowledge the law of Moses as the Word of God; to accept the people of Israel as the holy instrument of divine fulfillment; to await the coming of the Messiah and the redemption of history.

SCAFFOLD OF UNREASON

Many Jews will find my beliefs unfamiliar or unacceptable—perhaps outrageous. The manner in which I arrived at them is not very interesting in itself, but I think two aspects of my experience are worth noting because they are fairly common: I come from a fundamentally unobservant Jewish home and my first religious inclination was to become a Christian.

My parents are both second-generation American Jews whose own   8 parents were moderately religious, but, newly come to America, lacked either the education or the opportunity, patience, and time to transmit to their children their own understanding of Judaism. My parents went to synagogue to observe the great Jewish holidays—Passover, the New Year, and the Day of Atonement—but worship at home, knowledge of the liturgy, familiarity with Hebrew, concern with religious thought and problems, did not occupy them. Their real concern—and they were not unique—was adjusting to American life, achieving security, and passing to their children and those less fortunate the rewards of their struggle.

It would be ungrateful to deny the accomplishments of my parents' generation. They managed to provide their children with secular education and security. But although the flesh was nourished, the spirit was left unattended. When I had finished high school and was ready to leave for college I took with me little sense of what my religion, or any religion, involved. I knew only that in these matters I would have to fend for myself.

When an American Jew studies at an American university it is difficult for him not to be overwhelmed—as I was at the University of Chicago—by the recognition that Western culture is a Christian culture, that Western values are rooted in the Greek and Christian tradition. He may hear such phrases as "Judaeo-Christian tradition" or "the Hebraic element in Western culture," but he cannot be deluded into thinking that this is more than a casual compliment. The University of Chicago, moreover, insisted that its students study seriously the philosophic sources of Western culture, which, if not outspokenly Christian, were surely non-Jewish. I soon found myself reading the classics of Christian theology and devotion—from St. Augustine and St. Anselm through the sermons of Meister Eckhart.

It was not long before my unreligious background, a growing and intense concern with religious problems, and the ready access to compelling Christian literature all combined to produce a crisis—or at least my parents and I flattered ourselves that this normal intellectual experience was a religious crisis. The possibility of being a Christian was, however, altogether real. I was rushed, not to a psychoanalyst, but to a Rabbi—the late Milton Steinberg, one of the most gifted and profound Jewish thinkers of recent years. Leading me gently, he retraced the path backward through Christianity to Judaism, revealing the groundwork of Jewish thought and experience which supported what I have come to regard as the scaffolding of Christian "unreason."

It was extremely important to me to return to Judaism through the medium of Christianity—to choose after having first received the impress of Western education and Christian thought. Since it would have been possible to become a Christian—to accept Christian history as my history, to accept the Christian version of Judaism as the grounds of my own repudiation of Judaism, to believe that a Messiah had redeemed *me*—I could only conclude that Judaism was not an unavoidable fate, but a destiny to be chosen freely.

ACT VERSUS THOUGHT

My own conversion and, I suspect, the conversion of many other Jews to Judaism, was affected, therefore, through study, reflection, and thought. What first seized my attention was not the day-to-day religious life of the Jewish community around me, but rather principles, concepts, and values. I had first to examine the pressing theological claims of a seemingly triumphant Christianity, before I could accept the ancient claims of a dispersed, tormented, and suffering Jewry.

This may sound reasonable enough to a gentile, but I must point out that it is an extremely unconventional attitude for a Jew. Historically, Judaism has often looked with disfavor upon theology. And today, despite the fact that traditional emotional ties can no longer be relied upon to bind the third generation of Jewish life, American Jewish leadership has not seen fit to encourage the examination of the theological bases of Jewish faith. In fact, the leading rabbinical seminaries teach little Jewish theology as such, give scant attention to Jewish philosophic literature, and have allowed the apologetic comparison of religious beliefs to become a moribund discipline. Even practical problems involving some theological insight—the nature of marriage, the Jewish attitude toward converts, the life of prayer—are dispatched with stratospheric platitudes, or not discussed at all.

Why this distrust of theology? I suspect that some Jewish leaders fear—perhaps not unjustifiably—that theological scrutiny of what they mean by God, Israel, and Law might reveal that they have no theology at all. Others no doubt fear—again not unjustifiably—that their unbending interpretations of Jewish Law and life might have to be revised and rethought. Theology often produces a recognition of insufficiency, an awareness that valid doctrine is being held for the wrong reasons and that erroneous doctrine is being used to rationalize right action. But the major Jewish argument against Jewish theology is that it is a Christian pastime— that it may, by insinuation and subtle influence, Christianize Judaism. In this view, Christianity is a religion of faith, dogma, and theology and Judaism is a religion which emphasizes *observance* of God's Law, not speculation about it.

For me this argument is a vast oversimplification. Christianity is not 16 without its own structure of discipline, requirements, and laws—the Roman sacraments and the Lutheran and Anglican liturgy, for example—and this structure does not move with the Holy Spirit as easily as St. Paul might have wished. Judaism, on the other hand, is not tied to the pure act. It has matured through the centuries a massive speculative and mystic tradition which attempts to explain the principles upon which right action are founded. Judaism need not, therefore, regret the renewal of theology. It already has one. It is merely a question of making what is now a minor chord in Jewish tradition sound a more commanding note.

THE SMOKING MOUNTAIN

As a "convert" who thinks that theology must come first, what do I believe?

The convert, I must point out, is unavoidably both a thinker and a believer—he thinks patiently and believes suddenly. Yet belief, by itself, cannot evict the demons of doubt and despair. As a believer I can communicate my beliefs, but as a thinker I cannot guarantee that they are certain or will never change. As all things that record the encounter of God and man, beliefs are subject to the conditions of time and history, and the pitiable limitation of our capacity to understand such enormous mysteries. As I shall try to show, however, the four beliefs which I have already set down lie at the center of my faith as a Jew. They depend upon one another; they form a whole; they differ profoundly from the substance of Christian belief.

First, I chose to believe in the God of Abraham, Isaac, and Jacob. This is to affirm the reality of a God who acts in history and addresses man. Although this God may well be the same as the abstract gods formulated by philosophers, he is still more than these—he is the God who commanded Abraham to quit the land of the Chaldeans and who wrestled with Jacob throughout the night.

The philosopher and the believer must differ in their method. The philosopher begins by examining that portion of reality to which reason allows him access; the believer, however, must at some point move beyond the limits which reason has defined. He may rightly contend that reason points beyond itself, that the rational is real, but that much in human life—evil, suffering, guilt, and love—is terrifyingly real without ever being rationally comprehensible.

Reason may thus push a man to belief, and it is inaccurate to speak of the believer as though he had deserted or betrayed reason. Informed belief demands philosophic criticism and refinement. The believer is bound to uphold his faith in things he cannot see or verify; but he is foolish if he does not try to define what that belief is and clarify the unique ways in which it makes reality meaningful for him.

For me then to believe in the Biblical God, the God of the Patriarchs, the smoking mountain, the burning bush, was not to surrender reason, but to go beyond it. More than accepting the literal words of the Bible, it meant believing in the Lord of History—the God who creates and unfolds history, and observes its tragic rifts and displacements—from the Tower of Babel to the Cold War; who, in his disgust, once destroyed the world with flood and later repented his anger; who, forgoing anger, gave to the world counsels of revelation, commencing with the gift of Torah to Moses and continuing through the inspired writings of the ancient rabbis; and who finally—through his involvement with the work of creation—prepares it for redemption.

It may seem difficult—indeed for many years it was—to consider the Bible, which is the source of this belief, as more than the unreliable account of an obscure Semitic tribe. But gradually I came to discover in it an authentic statement of the grandeur and misery of man's daily existence—a statement which I could accept only if I believed in a God who could be addressed as "Lord, Lord."

THE EXALTED AND THE PICAYUNE

My second belief is an acknowledgment that *the Law of Moses is the*   24 *Word of God*. The Bible tells us that the Word of God broke out over the six hundred thousand Hebrews who assembled at the foot of Sinai. That Word was heard by Moses—he who had been appointed to approach and receive. The Word became human—in its humanity, it undoubtedly suffers from the limitation of our understanding—but it lost none of its divinity.

The Law is always a paradox: it is both the free Word of God and the frozen formality of human laws. But the Law of Moses was vastly different from what we usually understand law to be. It is true that in the days before the Temple was destroyed by Titus in 70 A.D. divine law was the enforceable law of the judge and the court; but later the great rabbis who interpreted it conceived of the revelation of God to Israel, not as law in its common usage, but as *Torah*— teaching.

Torah is a fundamental concept for the Jew. Narrowly conceived, it refers to the Pentateuch—the first five books of the Bible which are the pristine source of all Jewish tradition. In them are the laws of the Sabbath and the festivals; the foundations of family and communal morality; and the essentials of Jewish faith—the unity of God, the election of Israel, and the definition of its special mission. But, broadly conceived, Torah refers to *any* teaching which brings man closer to the true God, who is the God of Israel and the Lord of History.

Torah has two aspects—the actual way of law and observance (the *halachah* as it is called in Hebrew) and the theology of the rabbis which interprets that way (called the *aggadah*). By means of both, according to Jewish tradition, God proposes to lead *all* of his creation to fulfillment, to perfect its imperfections, to mend the brokenness of his creatures. The Jewish people—the guardian of the *halachah* and the *aggadah*— has been elected to be pedagogue to all the nations of the world, to become on its behalf "a kingdom of priests and a holy people."

Jews can achieve holiness—the primary objective, I believe, of their   28 religion—neither by prayer nor meditation alone. Judaism values prayer only in conjunction with the act; it praises study only in relation to life.

God does not propose or suggest ways to achieve holiness; he commands them. According to Torah, he lays upon each Jew "the yoke of the commandments." To observe the Sabbath is as much a commandment as is the obligation to daily prayer; the grace which accompanies eating as essential as the study of sacred literature. Although tradition distinguishes between practical and intellectual commandments, it considers both to be equally the expressed will of God. The arbitrary and the reasonable—the dietary laws and the prohibition of homosexuality for example—both proceed from God.

Judaism begins with an explicit fact: the revelation of Torah. Many of its commandments may seem trivial. But it should not be expected that God will leave the trivial to man and concern himself only with the broad, general, and universal. The corruption of man takes place not only in the province of principle, but in the small and petty routine of life. The Torah is therefore exalted and picayune, universal and particular, occupied equally with principle and the details of practice. It tolerates no separation between the holy and the profane—all that is secular must become sacred, all that is profane must be kept open to the transforming power of God.

The exact degree to which Jews should fulfill all the commandments of the Law is one of the most difficult and perplexing dilemmas for modern Jews. Orthodox Jews are in principle obligated to observe all of Jewish Law, Reform Jews have cut observance to a minimum (though there is a movement to increase it). Conservative Jews stand somewhere in between. I will not attempt it in this space, but I believe it is possible to show that the fundamental question is not whether the Jew performs the required acts of observance, but whether he is truly aware of the sacred intention of these acts. One can, for example, recite the blessings over the food one eats and feel nothing of the sanctity of food; on the other hand one can silently acknowledge the holiness of eating, and fulfill the command of God. Both are needed—the blessing and the inner acknowledgment, but the former is surely incomplete without the latter.

ODD OF GOD

The third of my beliefs is, as I have indicated, simply an element of God's revelation in Torah—that *the Jewish people has been chosen as a special instrument of God.*

The Jews did not request the attentions of God. There is significant truth—truth moreover which the rabbis of the Talmud endorse—in the popular couplet: "How odd of God, to choose the Jews." Odd, and unsolicited. The ancient rabbis disclaim particular merit. If anyone possessed merit, they repeat, it was not the generation that fled Egypt and braved the wilderness for forty years, but the generations of the Biblical patriarchs—Abraham, Isaac, and Jacob. They had no organizer such as Moses, nor strength of numbers, nor the miracles of the well, manna, and quail. They made a covenant with God on sheer trust. The generation of Sinai was *compelled* to become the people of God or perish. A God of History grows impatient with delay. The God of Israel was profoundly impatient on Sinai.

This tradition of election should not be confused with racial pride or an attitude of arrogant exclusion toward others. The Jew believes neither

COHEN • WHY I CHOOSE TO BE A JEW   **677**

that the truth flows in his blood nor that the gentile cannot come to possess it. Judaism is exclusive only in the sense that we affirm we possess important truth which is available to all—everyone can join but only on our terms.

The election of Israel is not a conclusion drawn from history—the survival and endurance of the Jews through twenty centuries of destructive persecution could be no more than blind accident. At best it could be construed as a compliment to the resiliency and stubbornness of the Jewish people. Judaism has insisted however—not as a declaration after the fact, but as a principle of its very existence—that it is both a holy nation chosen by God to be his own and a suffering nation destined to endure martyrdom for his sake. God announces not only that "Ye shall be holy unto me; for I the Lord am Holy, and have separated you from the peoples, that ye should be mine" (Leviticus 20:26) but that "You only have I known of all the families of the earth: therefore I will visit upon you all your iniquities" (Amos 3:2).

Israel is thus called not only to be the example to the nations, but, being the example, is tried all the more sorely for its transgressions. To be sure, this is not a doctrine for the uncourageous. No one even slightly familiar with the agonies of Jewish history could claim that the election of Israel has brought with it particular reward and security. It is however precisely the fact of Jewish suffering which makes its election and mission all the more pertinent to the modern world. To have believed and survived in spite of history is perhaps the only evidence which Judaism can offer to the accuracy of its conviction that it is called to be a holy community.

WOLF AND LAMB

In the face of Christendom and the obvious success which its claims have enjoyed, it may seem foolish or presumptuous for Judaism—a small and insignificant community of believers—to assert my fourth belief: that *Jesus is not the Messiah of which the Bible speaks*, that Christianity has conceived but one more imperfect image of the end, and that *a Messiah is yet to come who will redeem history.*

But there are enduring reasons why Jews cannot accept Jesus as the Messiah. Both Christian and Jew begin with the conviction of the imperfection of man. The Christian argues, however, that creation has been so corrupted by man as to be saved only through the mediation of Jesus. The Jew considers creation imperfect but, rather than corrupt, he finds it rich with unfulfilled possibility. The role of man is to bring creation to that point at which the Messiah can come to glorify man by bringing him the praise of God—not to save him from self-destruction, as Christianity would have it. According to Jewish tradition, Moses died from the kiss of

God. It would be fitting to conceive the advent of the Messiah and the Kingdom of God as the bestowal of a kiss.

This does not mean that God congratulates man for his good works but rather that he shares both in the agony of history and in its sanctification. Judaism does not imagine that every day we are getting better and better, and that finally we will reach a point where the Messiah will come. As likely as not, it seems to me, history is coming closer each day to suicide. The mission of Judaism is not to stave off disaster but to enlarge man's awareness of the Divine Presence.

Jews believe, if they are to remain Jews, that the Messiah has not 40 come. They can accept Jesus of Nazareth as little more than a courageous witness to truths to which his own contemporaries in Pharisaic Judaism by and large subscribed. Jesus was, as Martin Buber has suggested, one in the line of "suffering servants" whom God sends forth to instruct the nations. It is to the dogmatizing work of St. Paul that one must ascribe the transformation of "prophet" into "Christ"—and it is therefore St. Paul who severs Jesus from the life of Israel. The rejection of Jesus must now stand to the end of time.

The role of Israel and Judaism, until the advent of the true Messiah, is to outlast the world and its solutions—to examine its complacencies, to deflate its securities, to put its principles to the test of prophetic judgment. This is an aristocratic and painful mission, for though Judaism may address the world and lay claim to it, it does not seek to convert it.

Judaism does not say "The world is not changed—therefore we do not believe in the Messiah." This is only partially true, for the coming of the Messiah will mean more than a reformed world in which the wolf and lamb shall share bread together and war shall cease. This social image of salvation is true as far as it goes, but it does not go far enough. The Messiah is not a handyman or a plumber—his task does not consist in "mending" a world that is temporarily faulty but is essentially perfect. The world is to be transformed—not reformed—by the Messiah.

This transformation will come to pass, Judaism believes, only when the world wishes it so deeply that it cannot abide itself more a single moment. At that moment the Messiah may come. This moment of expectancy has not yet arrived. The rabbis have taught us that I, and all of the House of Israel, prevent him from coming. Of this there is no question, but we cannot avoid concluding that he has not come.

For the Jew who comfortably repeats the rituals of his religion without 44 confronting the principles of faith which they express, and for the Jew who was not aware that Judaism had any principles of faith at all, this personal statement may seem shocking. But I do not think my position or my background are by any means unique. If, as I have argued, the present generation of American Jews is indeed the first generation of Jews in centuries who are free to choose to believe as Jews, then, in my terms at least, my argument is important. Now as never before it will be possible for the Jewish people and the State of Israel to survive, but for Jewish *religion* to perish. For me, and for other believing Jews, it is crucial for mankind that Judaism survive. The mission of Judaism is not completed nor the task of the Jewish people fulfilled. If the Jewish people is an instrument sharpened by God for his own purposes, it must go on serving that purpose, sustaining its burden, and keeping that trust which alone can bring all men to redemption.

Questions and Suggestions for Writing

1. Much of the essay is about theology. Exactly what is "theology"?

2. In explaining that his choice to be a Jew was a "religious" one, Cohen mentions four things that, as a religious Jew, he now believes. Which if any of these could a Christian believe? (You may want to consult the essay by C. S. Lewis on p. 640.) Which, if any, must a Christian reject?

3. Cohen opens his essay by declaring that for the first time in history a Jew can "choose to be a Jew." Why does he think this opportunity is important? Is his point peculiar to Jews in our time, or could an American Catholic or an American Protestant say the same thing?

4. Cohen expresses a fundamentally respectful attitude toward Christianity. Explain in your own words his reasons. If like Cohen you are not a Christian, are you prepared to adopt the same attitude for the same reasons? Why, or why not?

5. During his discussion, Cohen mentions such biblical miracles (although he doesn't call them that) as "the smoking mountain" and "the burning bush." Go to the library, find a Bible concordance, and locate the passages in the Bible to which he refers. Do you think that a Jew, or a Christian, must believe in these (or other) miracles?

6. Cohen in paragraph 40 refers to Jesus of Nazareth as "little more than a courageous witness to truths" shared with his Jewish countrymen. C. S. Lewis, however, as befits a professing Christian, offers a very different account. Suppose you had to decide which of these interpretations is the sounder. In an essay of 500 words indicate what evidence, were it available, would convince you one way rather than the other?

Carol P. Christ

Why Women Need the Goddess

At the close of Ntozake Shange's stupendously successful Broadway play "For Colored Girls Who Have Considered Suicide When the Rainbow Is Enuf," a tall beautiful black woman rises from despair to cry out, "I found God in myself and I loved her fiercely."[1] Her discovery is echoed by women around the country who meet spontaneously in small groups on full moons, solstices, and equinoxes to celebrate the Goddess as symbol of life and death powers and waxing and waning energies in the universe and in themselves.[2]

> It is the night of the full moon. Nine women stand in a circle, on a rocky hill above the city. The western sky is rosy with the setting sun; in the east the moon's face begins to peer above the horizon. . . . The woman pours out a cup of wine onto the earth, refills it and raises it high. "Hail, Tana, Mother of mothers!" she cries. "Awaken from your long sleep, and return to your children again!"[3]

What are the political and psychological effects of this fierce new love of the divine in themselves for women whose spiritual experience has been focused by the male God of Judaism and Christianity? Is the spiritual dimension of feminism a passing diversion, an escape from difficult but necessary political work? Or does the emergence of the symbol of Goddess among women have significant political and psychological ramifications for the feminist movement?

To answer this question, we must first understand the importance of religious symbols and rituals in human life and consider the effect of male symbolism of God on women. According to anthropologist Clifford Geertz, religious symbols shape a cultural ethos, defining the deepest values of a society and the persons in it. "Religion," Geertz writes "is a system of symbols which act to produce powerful, pervasive, and long-

[1]From the original cast album, Buddah Records, 1976.

[2]See Susan Rennie and Kristen Grimstad, "Spiritual Explorations Cross-Country," *Quest*, 1975, *I* (4), 1975, 49–51; and *WomanSpirit* magazine.

[3]See Starhawk, "Witchcraft and Women's Culture," in [Carol P. Christ and Judith Plaskow, eds., *WomanSpirit Rising* (San Francisco: Harper & Row, 1979)].

Carol P. Christ earned a Ph.D. at Yale University. She has been active in the women's movement since the late 1960s and now teaches in the Department of Women's Studies at San Jose State University.
This essay was originally an address delivered in 1978 at the University of California Santa Cruz Extension conference, "The Great Goddess Re-Emerging." It is reprinted, along with other essays by Christ, in Laughter of Aphrodite: Reflections on a Journey to the Goddess *(1987).*

lasting moods and motivations"[4] in the people of a given culture. A "mood" for Geertz is a psychological attitude such as awe, trust, and respect, while a "motivation" is the *social* and *political* trajectory created by a mood that transforms mythos into ethos, symbol system into social and political reality. Symbols have both psychological and political effects, because they create the inner conditions (deep-seated attitudes and feelings) that lead people to feel comfortable with or to accept social and political arrangements that correspond to the symbol system.

Because religion has such a compelling hold on the deep psyches of so many people, feminists cannot afford to leave it in the hands of the fathers. Even people who no longer "believe in God" or participate in the institutional structure of patriarchal religion still may not be free of the power of the symbolism of God the Father. A symbol's effect does not depend on rational assent, for a symbol also functions on levels of the psyche other than the rational. Religion fulfills deep psychic needs by providing symbols and rituals that enable people to cope with limit situations[5] in human life (death, evil, suffering) and to pass through life's important transitions (birth, sexuality, death). Even people who consider themselves completely secularized will often find themselves sitting in a church or synagogue when a friend or relative gets married, or when a parent or friend has died. The symbols associated with these important rituals cannot fail to affect the deep or unconscious structures of the mind of even a person who has rejected these symbolisms on a conscious level—especially if the person is under stress. The reason for the continuing effect of religious symbols is that the mind abhors a vacuum. Symbol systems cannot simply be rejected, they must be replaced. Where there is not any replacement, the mind will revert to familiar structures at times of crisis, bafflement, or defeat.

Religions centered on the worship of a male God create "moods" and "motivations" that keep women in a state of psychological dependence on men and male authority, while at the same [time] legitimating the *political* and *social* authority of fathers and sons in the institutions of society.

Religious symbol systems focused around exclusively male images of divinity create the impression that female power can never be fully legitimate or wholly beneficent. This message need never be explicitly stated (as, for example, it is in the story of Eve) for its effect to be felt. A woman completely ignorant of the myths of female evil in biblical religion nonetheless acknowledges the anomaly of female power when she prays exclusively to a male God. She may see herself as like God (created in the image of God) only by denying her own sexual identity and affirming God's transcendence of sexual identity. But she can never have the experience that is freely available to every man and boy in her culture, of having

---

[4]"Religion as a Cultural System," in William L. Lessa and Evon V. Vogt, eds., *Reader in Comparative Religion*, 2nd ed. (New York: Harper & Row, 1972), p. 206.
[5]Geertz, p. 210.

her full sexual identity affirmed as being in the image and likeness of God. In Geertz's terms, her "mood" is one of trust in male power as salvific and distrust of female power in herself and other women as inferior or dangerous. Such a powerful, pervasive, and longlasting "mood" cannot fail to become a "motivation" that translates into social and political reality.

In *Beyond God the Father,* feminist theologian Mary Daly detailed the psychological and political ramifications of father religion for women. "If God in 'his' heaven is a father ruling his people," she wrote, "then it is the 'nature' of things and according to divine plan and the order of the universe that society be male dominated. Within this context, a *mystification of roles* takes place: The husband dominating his wife represents God 'himself.' The images and values of a given society have been projected into the realm of dogmas and 'Articles of Faith,' and these in turn justify the social structures which have given rise to them and which sustain their plausibility."[6]

Philosopher Simone de Beauvoir was well aware of the function of patriarchal religion as legitimater of male power. As she wrote, "Man enjoys the great advantage of having a god endorse the code he writes; and since man exercises a sovereign authority over women it is especially fortunate that this authority has been vested in him by the Supreme Being. For the Jews, Mohammedans, and Christians, among others, man is Master by divine right; the fear of God will therefore repress any impulse to revolt in the downtrodden female."[7]

This brief discussion of the psychological and political effects of God religion puts us in an excellent position to begin to understand the significance of the symbol of Goddess for women. In discussing the meaning of the Goddess, my method will first be phenomenological. I will isolate a meaning of the symbol of the Goddess as it has emerged in the lives of contemporary women. I will then discuss its psychological and political significance by contrasting the "moods" and "motivations" engendered by Goddess symbols with those engendered by Christian symbolism. I will also correlate Goddess symbolism with themes that have emerged in the women's movement, in order to show how Goddess symbolism undergirds and legitimates the concerns of the women's movement, much as God symbolism in Christianity undergirded the interests of men in patriarchy. I will discuss four aspects of Goddess symbolism here: the Goddess as affirmation of female power, the female body, the female will, and women's bonds and heritage. There are, of course, many other meanings of the Goddess that I will not discuss here.

The sources for the symbol of the Goddess in contemporary spirituality are traditions of Goddess worship and modern women's experience. The ancient Mediterranean, pre-Christian European, native Ameri-

---

[6]Boston: Beacon Press, 1974, p. 13, italics added.
[7]*The Second Sex*, trans. H. M. Parshley (New York: Alfred A. Knopf, 1953).

can, Mesoamerican, Hindu, African, and other traditions are rich sources for Goddess symbolism. But these traditions are filtered through modern women's experiences. Traditions of Goddesses' subordination to Gods, for example, are ignored. Ancient traditions are tapped selectively and eclecticly, but they are not considered authoritative for modern consciousness. The Goddess symbol has emerged spontaneously in the dreams, fantasies, and thoughts of many women around the country in the past several years. Kirsten Grimstad and Susan Rennie reported that they were surprised to discover widespread interest in spirituality, including the Goddess, among feminists around the country in the summer of 1974.[8] *WomanSpirit* magazine, which published its first issue in 1974 and has contributors from across the United States, has expressed the grass roots nature of the women's spirituality movement. In 1976, a journal, *Lady Unique*, devoted to the Goddess emerged. In 1975, the first women's spirituality conference was held in Boston and attended by 1,800 women. In 1978, a University of Santa Cruz course on the Goddess drew over 500 people. Sources for this essay are these manifestations of the Goddess in modern women's experiences as reported in *WomanSpirit*, *Lady Unique*, and elsewhere, and as expressed in conversations I have had with women who have been thinking about the Goddess and women's spirituality.

The simplest and most basic meaning of the symbol of Goddess is the acknowledgment of the legitimacy of female power as a beneficent and independent power. A woman who echoes Ntozake Shange's dramatic statement, "I found God in myself and I loved her fiercely," is saying "Female power is strong and creative." She is saying that the divine principle, the saving and sustaining power, is in herself, that she will no longer look to men or male figures as saviors. The strength and independence of female power can be intuited by contemplating ancient and modern images of the Goddess. This meaning of the symbol of Goddess is simple and obvious, and yet it is difficult for many to comprehend. It stands in sharp contrast to the paradigms of female dependence on males that have been predominant in Western religion and culture. The internationally acclaimed novelist Monique Wittig captured the novelty and flavor of the affirmation of female power when she wrote, in her mythic work *Les Guerilleres*,

> There was a time when you were not a slave, remember that. You walked alone, full of laughter, you bathed bare-bellied. You say you have lost all recollection of it, remember . . . you say there are no words to describe it, you say it does not exist. But remember. Make an effort to remember. Or, failing that, invent.[9]

[8]See Rennie and Grimstad.

[9]*Les Guerilleres*, trans. David LeVay (New York: Avon Books, 1971), p. 89. Also quoted in Morgan MacFarland, "Witchcraft: The Art of Remembering," *Quest*, 1975, *I* (4), 41.

While Wittig does not speak directly of the Goddess here, she captures the "mood" of joyous celebration of female freedom and independence that is created in women who define their identities through the symbol of Goddess. Artist Mary Beth Edelson expressed the political "motivations" inspired by the Goddess when she wrote,

> The ascending archetypal symbols of the feminine unfold today in the psyche of modern Every woman. They encompass the multiple forms of the Great Goddess. Reaching across the centuries we take the hands of our Ancient Sisters. The Great Goddess alive and well is rising to announce to the patriarchs that their 5,000 years are up—Hallelujah! Here we come.[10]

The affirmation of female power contained in the Goddess symbol has both psychological and political consequences. Psychologically, it means the defeat of the view engendered by patriarchy that women's power is inferior and dangerous. This new "mood" of affirmation of female power also leads to new "motivations"; it supports and undergirds women's trust in their own power and the power of other women in family and society.

If the simplest meaning of the Goddess symbol is an affirmation of the legitimacy and beneficence of female power, then a question immediately arises, "Is the Goddess simply female power writ large, and if so, why bother with the symbol of Goddess at all? Or does the symbol refer to a Goddess 'out there' who is not reducible to a human potential?" The many women who have rediscovered the power of Goddess would give three answers to this question: (1) The Goddess is divine female, a personification who can be invoked in prayer and ritual; (2) the Goddess is symbol of the life, death, and rebirth energy in nature and culture, in personal and communal life and (3) the Goddess is symbol of the affirmation of the legitimacy and beauty of female power (made possible by the new becoming of women in the women's liberation movement). If one were to ask these women which answer is the "correct" one, different responses would be given. Some would assert that the Goddess definitely is *not* "out there," that the symbol of a divinity "out there" is part of the legacy of patriarchal oppression, which brings with it the authoritarianism, hierarchicalism, and dogmatic rigidity associated with biblical monotheistic religions. They might assert that the Goddess symbol reflects the sacred power within women and nature, suggesting the connectedness between women's cycles of menstruation, birth, and menopause, and the life and death cycles of the universe. Others seem quite comfortable with the notion of Goddess as a divine female protector and creator and would find their experience of Goddess limited by the assertion that she is not *also* out there as well as within themselves and in all natural processes. When asked what the symbol of Goddess means, feminist priestess Starhawk replied, "It all

---

[10]"Speaking for Myself," *Lady Unique*, 1976, *I*, 56.

depends on how I feel. When I feel weak, she is someone who can help and protect me. When I feel strong, she is the symbol of my own power. At other times I feel her as the natural energy in my body and the world."[11] How are we to evaluate such a statement? Theologians might call these the words of a sloppy thinker. But my deepest intuition tells me they contain a wisdom that Western theological thought has lost.

To theologians, these differing views of the "meaning" of the symbol [12] of Goddess might seem to threaten a replay of the trinitarian controversies. Is there, perhaps, a way of doing theology, which would not lead immediately into dogmatic controversy, which would not require theologians to say definitively that one understanding is true and the others are false? Could people's relation to a common symbol be made primary and varying interpretations be acknowledged? The diversity of explications of the meaning of the Goddess symbol suggests that symbols have a richer significance than any explications of their meaning can express, a point literary critics have long insisted on. This phenomenological fact suggests that theologians may need to give more than lip service to a theory of symbol in which the symbol is viewed as the primary fact and the meanings are viewed as secondary. It also suggests that a *thea*logy[12] of the Goddess would be very different from the *theo*logy we have known in the West. But to spell out this notion of the primacy of *symbol* in thealogy in contrast to the primacy of the *explanation* in theology would be the topic of another paper. Let me simply state that women, who have been deprived of a female religious symbol system for centuries, are therefore in an excellent position to recognize the power and primacy of symbols. I believe women must develop a theory of symbol and thealogy congruent with their experience at the same time as they "remember and invent" new symbol systems.

A second important implication of the Goddess symbol for women is the affirmation of the female body and the life cycle expressed in it. Because of women's unique position as menstruants, birthgivers, and those who have traditionally cared for the young and the dying, women's connection to the body, nature, and this world has been obvious. Women were denigrated because they seemed more carnal, fleshy, and earthy than the culture-creating males.[13] The misogynist anti*body* tradition in Western thought is symbolized in the myth of Eve who is traditionally viewed as a sexual temptress, the epitome of women's carnal nature. This tradition reaches its nadir in the *Malleus Maleficarum (The Hammer of Evil-Doing Women)*, which states, "All witchcraft stems from carnal lust, which in women is insatiable."[14] The Virgin Mary, the positive female image in

[11]Personal communication.

[12]A term coined by Naomi Goldenberg to refer to reflection on the meaning of the symbol of Goddess.

[13]This theory of the origins of the Western dualism is stated by Rosemary Ruether in *New Woman: New Earth* (New York: Seabury Press, 1975), and elsewhere.

[14]Heinrich Kramer and Jacob Sprenger (New York: Dover, 1971), p. 47.

Christianity does not contradict Christian denigration of the female body and its powers. The Virgin Mary is revered because she, in her perpetual virginity, transcends the carnal sexuality attributed to most women.

The denigration of the female body is expressed in cultural and religious taboos surrounding menstruation, childbirth, and menopause in women. While menstruation taboos may have originated in a perception of the awesome powers of the female body,[15] they degenerated into a simple perception that there is something "wrong" with female bodily functions. Menstruating women were forbidden to enter the sanctuary in ancient Hebrew and premodern Christian communities. Although only Orthodox Jews still enforce religious taboos against menstruant women, few women in our culture grow up affirming their menstruation as a connection to sacred power. Most women learn that menstruation is a curse and grow up believing that the bloody facts of menstruation are best hidden away. Feminists challenge this attitude to the female body. Judy Chicago's art piece "Menstruation Bathroom" broke these menstrual taboos. In a sterile white bathroom, she exhibited boxes of Tampax and Kotex on an open shelf, and the wastepaper basket was overflowing with bloody tampons and sanitary napkins.[16] Many women who viewed the piece felt relieved to have their "dirty secret" out in the open.

The denigration of the female body and its powers is further expressed in Western culture's attitudes toward childbirth.[17] Religious iconography does not celebrate the birthgiver, and there is no theology or ritual that enables a woman to celebrate the process of birth as a spiritual experience. Indeed, Jewish and Christian traditions also had blood taboos concerning the woman who had recently given birth. While these religious taboos are rarely enforced today (again, only by Orthodox Jews), they have secular equivalents. Giving birth is treated as a disease requiring hospitalization, and the woman is viewed as a passive object, anesthetized to ensure her acquiescence to the will of the doctor. The women's liberation movement has challenged these cultural attitudes, and many feminists have joined with advocates of natural childbirth and home birth in emphasizing the need for women to control and take pride in their bodies, including the birth process.

Western culture also gives little dignity to the postmenopausal or aging woman. It is no secret that our culture is based on a denial of aging and death, and that women suffer more severely from this denial than men. Women are placed on a pedestal and considered powerful when they are young and beautiful, but they are said to lose this power as they age. As feminists have pointed out, the "power" of the young woman is illusory,

[15]See Rita M. Gross, "Menstruation and Childbirth as Ritual and Religious Experience in the Religion of the Australian Aborigines," in *The Journal of the American Academy of Religion*, 1977, 45 (4), Supplement 1147–1181.

[16]*Through the Flower* (New York: Doubleday & Company, 1975), plate 4, pp. 106–107.

[17]See Adrienne Rich, *Of Woman Born* (New York: Bantam Books, 1977), Chaps. 6 and 7.

since beauty standards are defined by men, and since few women are considered (or consider themselves) beautiful for more than a few years of their lives. Some men are viewed as wise and authoritative in age, but old women are pitied and shunned. Religious iconography supports this cultural attitude toward aging women. The purity and virginity of Mary and the female saints is often expressed in the iconographic convention of perpetual youth. Moreover, religious mythology associates aging women with evil in the symbol of the wicked old witch. Feminists have challenged cultural myths of aging women and have urged women to reject patriarchal beauty standards and to celebrate the distinctive beauty of women of all ages.

The symbol of Goddess aids the process of naming and reclaiming the female body and its cycles and processes. In the ancient world and among modern women, the Goddess symbol represents the birth, death, and rebirth processes of the natural and human worlds. The female body is viewed as the direct incarnation of waxing and waning, life and death, cycles in the universe. This is sometimes expressed through the symbolic connection between the twenty-eight-day cycles of menstruation and the twenty-eight-day cycles of the moon. Moreover, the Goddess is celebrated in the triple aspect of youth, maturity, and age, or maiden, mother, and crone. The potentiality of the young girl is celebrated in the nymph or maiden aspect of the Goddess. The Goddess as mother is sometimes depicted giving birth, and giving birth is viewed as a symbol for all the creative, life-giving powers of the universe.[18] The life-giving powers of the Goddess in her creative aspect are not limited to physical birth, for the Goddess is also seen as the creator of all the arts of civilization, including healing, writing, and the giving of just law. Women in the middle of life who are not physical mothers may give birth to poems, songs, and books, or nurture other women, men, and children. They too are incarnations of the Goddess in her creative, life-giving aspect. At the end of life, women incarnate the crone aspect of the Goddess. The wise old woman, the woman who knows from experience what life is about, the woman whose closeness to her own death gives her a distance and perspective on the problems of life, is celebrated as the third aspect of the Goddess. Thus, women learn to value youth, creativity, and wisdom in themselves and other women.

The possibilities of reclaiming the female body and its cycles have been expressed in a number of Goddess-centered rituals. Hallie Mountainwing and Barby My Own created a summer solstice ritual to celebrate menstruation and birth. The women simulated a birth canal and birthed each other into their circle. They raised power by placing their hands on each other's bellies and chanting together. Finally they marked each

---

[18]See James Mellaart, *Earliest Civilizations of the Near East* (New York: McGraw-Hill, 1965), p. 92.

other's faces with rich, dark menstrual blood saying, "This is the blood that promises renewal. This is the blood that promises sustenance. This is the blood that promises life."[19] From hidden dirty secret to symbol of the life power of the Goddess, women's blood has come full circle. Other women have created rituals that celebrate the crone aspect of the Goddess. Z. Budapest believes that the crone aspect of the Goddess is predominant in the fall, especially at Halloween, an ancient holiday. On this day, the wisdom of the old woman is celebrated, and it is also recognized that the old must die so that the new can be born.

The "mood" created by the symbol of the Goddess in triple aspect is one of positive, joyful affirmation of the female body and its cycles and acceptance of aging and death as well as life. The "motivations" are to overcome menstrual taboos, to return the birth process to the hands of women, and to change cultural attitudes about age and death. Changing cultural attitudes toward the female body could go a long way toward overcoming the spirit-flesh, mind-body dualisms of Western culture, since, as Ruether has pointed out, the denigration of the female body is at the heart of these dualisms. The Goddess as symbol of the revaluation of the body and nature thus also undergirds the human potential and ecology movements. The "mood" is one of affirmation, awe, and respect for the body and nature, and the "motivation" is to respect the teachings of the body and the rights of all living beings.

A third important implication of the Goddess symbol for women is the positive valuation of will in a Goddess-centered ritual, especially in Goddess-centered ritual magic and spellcasting in womanspirit and feminist witchcraft circles. The basic notion behind ritual magic and spellcasting is energy as power. Here the Goddess is a center or focus of power and energy; she is the personification of the energy that flows between beings in the natural and human worlds. In Goddess circles, energy is raised by chanting or dancing. According to Starhawk, "Witches conceive of psychic energy as having form and substance that can be perceived and directed by those with a trained awareness. The power generated within the circle is built into a cone form, and at its peak is released—to the Goddess, to reenergize the members of the coven, or to do a specific work such as healing."[20] In ritual magic, the energy raised is directed by willpower. Women who celebrate in Goddess circles believe they can achieve their wills in the world.

The emphasis on the will is important for women, because women traditionally have been taught to devalue their wills, to believe that they cannot achieve their will through their own power, and even to suspect that the assertion of will is evil. Faith Wildung's poem "Waiting," from

---

[19]Barby My Own, "Ursa Maior: Menstrual Moon Celebration," in Anne Kent Rush, ed., *Moon, Moon* (Berkeley, Calif., and New York: Moon Books and Random House, 1976), pp. 374–387.

[20]Starhawk, in ["Witchcraft and Women's Culture"].

which I will quote only a short segment, sums up women's sense that their lives are defined not by their own will, but by waiting for others to take the initiative.

> Waiting for my breasts to develop
> Waiting to wear a bra
> Waiting to menstruate
>
> . . .
>
> Waiting for life to begin, Waiting—
> Waiting to be somebody
>
> . . .
>
> Waiting to get married
> Waiting for my wedding day
> Waiting for my wedding night
>
> . . .
>
> Waiting for the end of the day
> Waiting for sleep. Waiting . . .[21]

Patriarchal religion has enforced the view that female initiative and will are evil through the juxtaposition of Eve and Mary. Eve caused the fall by asserting her will against the command of God, while Mary began the new age with her response to God's initiative, "Let it be done to me according to thy word" (Luke 1:38). Even for men, patriarchal religion values the passive will subordinate to divine initiative. The classical doctrines of sin and grace view sin as the prideful assertion of will and grace as the obedient subordination of the human will to the divine initiative or order. While this view of will might be questioned from a human perspective, Valerie Saiving has argued that it has particularly deleterious consequences for women in Western culture. According to Saiving, Western culture encourages males in the assertion of will, and thus it may make some sense to view the male form of sin as an excess of will. But since culture discourages females in the assertion of will, the traditional doctrines of sin and grace encourage women to remain in their form of sin, which is self-negation or insufficient assertion of will.[22] One possible reason the will is denigrated in a patriarchal religious framework is that both human and divine will are often pictured as arbitrary, self-initiated, and exercised without regard for other wills.

In a Goddess-centered context, in contrast, the will is valued. *A woman is encouraged to know her will, to believe that her will is valid, and to believe that her will can be achieved in the world*, three powers traditionally denied to her in patriarchy. In a Goddess-centered framework, a woman's will is not subordinated to the Lord God as king and

---

[21]In Judy Chicago, pp. 213–217.

[22]"The Human Situation: A Feminine View," in *Journal of Religion*, 1960, *40*, 100–112, and reprinted in [*WomanSpirit Rising*].

ruler, nor to men as his representatives. Thus a woman is not reduced to waiting and acquiescing in the wills of others as she is in patriarchy. But neither does she adopt the egocentric form of will that pursues self-interest without regard for the interests of others.

The Goddess-centered context provides a different understanding of the will than that available in the traditional patriarchal religious framework. In the Goddess framework, will can be achieved only when it is exercised in harmony with the energies and wills of other beings. Wise women, for example, raise a cone of healing energy at the full moon or solstice when the lunar or solar energies are at their high points with respect to the earth. This discipline encourages them to recognize that not all times are propitious for the achieving of every will. Similarly, they know that spring is a time for new beginnings in work and love, summer a time for producing external manifestations of inner potentialities, and fall or winter times for stripping down to the inner core and extending roots. Such awareness of waxing and waning processes in the universe discourages arbitrary ego-centered assertion of will, while at the same time encouraging the assertion of individual will in cooperation with natural energies and the energies created by the wills of others. Wise women also have a tradition that whatever is sent out will be returned and this reminds them to assert their wills in cooperative and healing rather than egocentric and destructive ways. This view of will allows women to begin to recognize, claim, and assert their wills without adopting the worst characteristics of the patriarchal understanding and use of will. In the Goddess-centered framework, the "mood" is one of positive affirmation of personal will in the context of the energies of other wills or beings. The "motivation" is for women to know and assert their wills in cooperation with other wills and energies. This of course does not mean that women always assert their wills in positive and life-affirming ways. Women's capacity for evil is, of course, as great as men's. My purpose is simply to contrast the differing attitudes toward the exercise of will per se, and the female will in particular, in Goddess-centered religion and in the Christian God-centered religion.

The fourth and final aspect of Goddess symbolism that I will discuss here is the significance of the Goddess for a revaluation of woman's bonds and heritage. As Virginia Woolf has said, "Chloe liked Olivia," a statement about a woman's relation to another woman, is a sentence that rarely occurs in fiction. Men have written the stories, and they have written about women almost exclusively in their relations to men.[23] The celebrations of women's bonds to each other, as mothers and daughters, as colleagues and coworkers, as sisters, friends, and lovers, is beginning to occur in the new literature and culture created by women in the women's movement. While I believe that the revaluing of each of these bonds is

[23]*A Room of One's Own* (New York: Harcourt Brace Jovanovich, 1928), p. 86.

important, I will focus on the mother-daughter bond, in part because I believe it may be the key to the others.

Adrienne Rich has pointed out that the mother-daughter bond, perhaps the most important of woman's bonds, "resonant with charges . . . the flow of energy between two biologically alike bodies, one of which has lain in amniotic bliss inside the other, one of which has labored to give birth to the other,"[24] is rarely celebrated in patriarchal religion and culture. Christianity celebrates the father's relation to the son and the mother's relation to the son, but the story of mother and daughter is missing. So, too, in patriarchal literature and psychology the mothers and the daughters rarely exist. Volumes have been written about the oedipal complex, but little has been written about the girl's relation to her mother. Moreover, as de Beauvoir has noted, the mother-daughter relation is distorted in patriarchy because the mother must give her daughter over to men in a male-defined culture in which women are viewed as inferior. The mother must socialize her daughter to become subordinate to men, and if her daughter challenges patriarchal norms, the mother is likely to defend the patriarchal structures against her own daughter.[25]

These patterns are changing in the new culture created by women in which the bonds of women to women are beginning to be celebrated. Holly Near has written several songs that celebrate women's bonds and women's heritage. In one of her finest songs she writes of an "old-time woman" who is "waiting to die." A young woman feels for the life that has passed the old woman by and begins to cry, but the old woman looks her in the eye and says, "If I had not suffered, you wouldn't be wearing those jeans/Being an old-time woman ain't as bad as it seems."[26] This song, which Near has said was inspired by her grandmother, expresses and celebrates a bond and a heritage passed down from one woman to another. In another of Near's songs, she sings of "a hiking-boot mother who's seeing the world/For the first time with her own little girl." In this song, the mother tells the drifter who has been traveling with her to pack up and travel alone if he thinks "traveling three is a drag" because "I've got a little one who loves me as much as you need me/And darling, that's loving enough."[27] This song is significant because the mother places her relationship to her daughter above her relationship to a man, something women rarely do in patriarchy.[28]

Almost the only story of mothers and daughters that has been transmitted in Western culture is the myth of Demeter and Persephone that was

[24]Rich, p. 226.

[25]De Beauvoir, pp. 448–449.

[26]"Old Time Woman," lyrics by Jeffrey Langley and Holly Near, from *Holly Near: A Live Album*, Redwood Records, 1974.

[27]"Started Out Fine," by Holly Near from *Holly Near: A Live Album*.

[28]Rich, p. 223.

the basis of religious rites celebrated by women only, the Thesmophoria, and later formed the basis of the Eleusian mysteries, which were open to all who spoke Greek. In this story, the daughter, Persephone, is raped away from her mother, Demeter, by the God of the underworld. Unwilling to accept this state of affairs, Demeter rages and withholds fertility from the earth until her daughter is returned to her. What is important for women in this story is that a mother fights for her daughter and for her relation to her daughter. This is completely different from the mother's relation to her daughter in patriarchy. The "mood" created by the story of Demeter and Persephone is one of celebration of the mother-daughter bond, and the "motivation" is for mothers and daughters to affirm the heritage passed on from mother to daughter and to reject the patriarchal pattern where the primary loyalties of mother and daughter must be to men.

The symbol of Goddess has much to offer women who are struggling 28 to be rid of the "powerful, pervasive, and long-lasting moods and motivations" of devaluation of female power, denigration of the female body, distrust of female will, and denial of the women's bonds and heritage that have been engendered by patriarchal religion. As women struggle to create a new culture in which women's power, bodies, will, and bonds are celebrated, it seems natural that the Goddess would reemerge as symbol of the newfound beauty, strength, and power of women.

Questions and Suggestions for Writing

1. In paragraph 3, Carol P. Christ says that "The symbols associated with . . . important rituals cannot fail to affect the deep or unconscious structures of the mind of even a person who has rejected these symbolisms on a conscious level. . . ." Do you think (perhaps drawing on your own experience) that this statement is true? If so, how might you support your opinion? Before answering the question, reread the entire paragraph. By the way, if you believe that the statement cannot be proved (or disproved), do you think it is irresponsible of Christ to have made such a statement?

2. Reread paragraph 5, in which the writer briefly discusses the story of Eve (Genesis 1:26–3:24). Do you agree with Christ's interpretation of the story? If not, why not? And do you agree with her assertion (also in para. 5) that male readers of the Bible, unlike female readers, have their "full sexual identity affirmed as being in the image and likeness of God"? If not, why not?

3. Christ describes her "method" as "phenomenological" (para. 8). What does she do with this method? Why does she call it "phenomenological"?

4. Paragraph 10 speaks of "the paradigms of female dependence on males that have been predominant in Western religion and culture." Suppose someone told you that he or she didn't quite understand what was meant here. What examples might you offer, in an attempt to clarify the point?

5. In paragraph 12, Christ says that women "have been deprived of a female religious symbol system for centuries." Suppose someone replied that this is not true, at least for Christian women, who have the Virgin Mary. What do you think Carol Christ's reply might be? (Consider also paras. 13 and 16, in which she briefly discusses Mary.)

6. Suppose someone were to criticize Christ's essay as follows: Christ has not made it clear whether she proposes to supplement or to supplant traditional Judeo-Christian male-centered religious belief and practices with female-centered belief and practices. In addition, she has not made it clear whether she expects both men and women to embrace a Goddess religion or whether her emphasis on the Goddess is for women only, and it is impossible to evaluate her ideas unless one is quite clear on these two matters.

     Write a 500-word essay either rejecting or justifying this criticism.

7. A reader of Christ's essay might find it difficult to understand any connection between her views about the "need for the Goddess" and the beliefs and practices of conventional Judaism and Christianity. Rather, Christ's outlook might seem to many to be semipagan and anti-Christian (or perhaps post-Christian). Write a 500-word essay in which you justify or reject such an interpretation.

Appendix: Further Perspectives

A PHILOSOPHER'S VIEW

Stephen Toulmin's Method for Analyzing Arguments

In Chapter 2, we explained the contrast between *deductive* and *inductive* arguments in order to focus on two ways in which we reason: either

> making explicit something hidden in what we already accept (**deduction**)

or

> going beyond what we know to something new (**induction**).

Yet both types of reasoning share some structural features, as we also noticed. Thus, all reasoning is aimed at establishing some **thesis** (or conclusion) and does so by means of some **assumptions** (or premises). These are two basic characteristics that any argument contains.

After a little scrutiny we can in fact point to six (rather than only two) shared by all arguments, deductive and inductive, good and bad alike. Using the vocabulary popularized by Stephen Toulmin in *An Introduction to Reasoning* (1979; second edition 1984), they are as follows:

694

1. THE CLAIM

Every argument has a purpose, goal, or aim, namely, to establish some conclusion (claim or thesis). The point of an argument in favor of equal rights for women might be to defend the following thesis or claim:

Men and women should have equal legal rights.

A more precise formulation of the claim might be

Equal legal rights should become part of the Constitution.

A still more precise formulation might be

Equal legal rights should become constitutional law by amendment.

This is what the controversy over the Equal Rights Amendment was all about.

Consequently, in reading or analyzing someone else's argument, your first question should naturally be: What is the argument intended to prove or establish? What **claim** is it making? Has this claim been precisely formulated, so that it unambiguously asserts what its advocate means?

2. THE GROUNDS

Once we have the argument's purpose or point clearly in mind and thus know what the arguer is claiming to establish, then we can ask for the evidence, reasons, support, in short, for the **grounds** on which the claim is based. These grounds will be the premises from which the claim is derived (in a deductive argument) or which make the claim plausible or probable (in an inductive argument).

Obviously, not every kind of claim can be supported by every kind of ground, and conversely, not every kind of ground gives support for every kind of claim. Thus, if I claim that half the students in the room are women, I can ground my claim in either of two ways. I can count all the women and all the men (suppose the total equals fifty) and thus be in a position to say that the number of women equals fifty divided by two. In this manner I deduce my claim from my premise. Or I can count a sample of, say, ten students, and find that in the sample, five of the students are women, and thus have inductive—plausible but not conclusive—grounds for my claim.

So far, we have merely restated points about premises and conclusions covered in Chapter 2. But now we want to notice four additional features of all kinds of arguments, features we did not consider earlier.

3. WARRANTS

Once we have a grip on the point of an argument, and the evidence or reasons offered in its support, the next question to ask is why these reasons support this conclusion. What is the **warrant,** or guarantee, that the reasons proffered do support the claim or lead to the conclusion? In simple deductive arguments, the warrant takes different forms, as we shall see. In the simplest cases, we can point to the way in which the meanings of the key terms are really equivalent. Thus, if John is taller than Bill, then Bill must be shorter than John because of the meaning in English of "is shorter than" and "is taller than." In this case, the warrant is something we can state quite literally and explicitly.

In other cases, we may need to be more resourceful. A reliable tactic is to think up a simple argument exactly parallel in form and structure to the argument we are trying to defend, and then point out the parallel, correctly mentioning that if one is ready to accept the simpler argument then in consistency one must accept the more controversial argument, because both arguments have exactly the same structure. For example, in her essay on the abortion controversy (see p. 337), Judith Thomson argues that a pregnant woman has the right to an abortion to save her life, even if it involves the death of her unborn child. She anticipates that some readers may balk at her reasoning, and so she offers this parallel argument: Suppose you were locked in a tiny house with another human being, which through no fault of its own is growing uncontrollably, with the result that it is slowly crushing you to death. Of course it would be morally permissible to kill the other person to save your own life. With the reader's presumed agreement on that argument, the parallel to the abortion situation—so Thomson hopes—is obvious.

In simple inductive arguments, we are likely to point to the way in which an observation or set of data constitutes a representative sample of a whole (unexamined) population. Here, the warrant is the representativeness of the sample. Or in plotting a line on a graph through a set of points, we defend one line over alternatives on the ground that it makes the smoothest fit through most of the points. In this case, the warrant is simplicity. Or in defending one hypothesis against competing explanations of a phenomenon, we appeal to the way in which the preferred explanation can be seen as a special case of generally accepted physical laws. Examples of such warrants for inductive reasoning will be offered below (see "A Logician's View," p. 699).

Establishing the warrants for our reasoning—that is, explaining why our grounds really support our claims—can quickly become a highly technical and exacting procedure that goes far beyond our purpose in this book. To do justice to the state of current knowledge about these warrants one would need to take a solid course or two in formal deductive logic and statistical methods. Developing a "feel" for why reasons or grounds are, and in some cases are not, relevant to what they are alleged to support is the most we can hope to do here without recourse to more rigorous techniques.

Even without formal training, however, one can sense that something is wrong with many bad arguments. Here is an example. British professor C. E. M. Joad found himself standing on a station platform, annoyed because he had just missed his train, when another, making an unscheduled stop, pulled up to the platform in front of him. He decided to jump aboard, only to hear the porter say "I'm afraid you'll have to get off, sir. This train doesn't stop here." "In that case," replied Joad, "don't worry. I'm not on it."

4. BACKING

The support or **backing** appropriate for one kind of argument might be quite inappropriate for another kind of argument. Thus, the reasons appropriate to support an amendment to the Constitution are completely different from those appropriate to settle the question of what caused the defeat of Napoleon's invasion of Russia. Arguments for the amendment might be rooted in fairness or perhaps in efficiency, whereas arguments about the military defeat might be rooted in newly discovered historical data. The canons of good argument derive in these two cases from appropriate ways in which the scholarly communities in law and history, respectively, have developed over the years to support, defend, challenge, and undermine a given kind of argument.

Another way of stating this point is to recognize that once one has given reasons for a claim, one is then likely to be challenged to explain why these reasons are good reasons—why, that is, one should believe these reasons rather than regard them skeptically. Why (a simple example) should we accept the testimony of Dr. X when Dr. Y, equally renowned, supports the opposite side? Or: Why is it safe to rest a prediction on a small though admittedly carefully selected sample? Or: Why is it legitimate to argue that (a) if I dream I am the King of France then I must exist, whereas it is illegitimate to argue that (b) if I dream I am the King of France then the King of France must exist? To answer these kinds of challenges is to *back up* one's reasoning, and no argument is any better than its backing.

5. MODAL QUALIFIERS

If we think of the elements of an argument as a set of assertions or propositions, namely

the claim (conclusion, thesis to be established),

the grounds (explicit reasons advanced), and

the backing (implicit assumptions),

then we can focus on a common feature of these elements. Each when formulated will have, explicitly or tacitly, some quantifying or qualifying terms that indicate the scope or degree of the assertion, the extent to which it is alleged to hold or apply.

Thus, *most* but not all heavy smokers cut short their life span by some years because of their use of tobacco; *some* but not all diseases are communicable; *other things being equal*, it is better to score higher than lower on examinations, *usually* though not always the fastest sprinters make the best 800-meter relay team; and so on. A claim that *all* As are Bs cannot be convincing if it rests on no better evidence than that *most* of the As *so far observed* are Bs. The exact scope and strength of our assertions, whether reasons or conclusion, is unclear until we have precisely fixed on these **qualifiers.**

6. POSSIBLE REBUTTALS

Very few arguments of any interest are beyond dispute, conclusively knockdown affairs, in which the claim of the argument is so rigidly tied to its grounds, warrants, and backing, and its qualifiers so precisely orchestrated that it really proves its conclusion beyond any possibility of doubt. On the contrary, most arguments have many counterarguments, and sometimes it is the counterargument that is the more convincing.

Suppose one has taken a sample that appears to be random—an interviewer on your campus accosts the first ten students who pass by her, and seven of them happen to be fraternity or sorority members. She is now ready to argue that seven-tenths of the student body belong to Greek organizations. You believe, however, that such students are in the minority and point out that she happens to have conducted her interview around the corner from the Panhellenic Society's office just off Sorority Row. Her random sample is anything but. The ball is now back in her court as you await her response to your rebuttal.

As this example illustrates, it is safe to say that we do not understand our own arguments very well until we have tried to get a grip on the places in which they are vulnerable to criticism, counterattack, or refutation. Edmund Burke (quoted in Chapter 2 but worth repeating) said, "He that wrestles with us strengthens our nerves, and sharpens our skill. Our antagonist is our helper." Therefore, cultivating alertness to such weak spots, girding one's loins to defend at these places, always helps strengthen one's position.

A LOGICIAN'S VIEW

Deduction, Induction, Fallacies

In Chapter 2 we introduced these terms. Now we will discuss them in greater detail.

DEDUCTION

The basic aim of deductive reasoning is to start with some assumption or premise, and extract from it consequences that are concealed but implicit in it. Thus, taking the simplest case, if I assert

1. The cat is on the mat,

it is a matter of simple deduction to infer that

2. The mat is under the cat.

Everyone would grant that (2) follows from (1)—or, that (2) can be validly deduced from (1)—because of the meaning of the key connective concepts in each proposition. Anyone who understands English knows that, whatever A and B are, if A is *on* B, then B must be *under* A. Thus, in this and all other cases of valid deductive reasoning, we can say not only that we are entitled to *infer* the conclusion from the premise—in this case, infer (2) from (1)—but that the premise *implies* the conclusion. Remember, too, the inference of (2) from (1) does not depend on the truth of (1). (2) follows from (1) whether or not (1) is true; consequently, if (1) is true then so is (2); but if (1) is false then (2) is false, also.

Let's take another example—more interesting, but comparably simple:

3. President Truman was underrated by his critics.

Given (3), a claim amply verified by events of the 1950s, one is entitled to infer

4. The critics underrated President Truman.

On what basis can we argue that (3) implies (4)? The two propositions are equivalent because a rule of English grammar assures us that we can convert the position of subject and predicate phrases in a sentence if we shift from the passive to the active voice (or vice versa).

Both pairs of examples illustrate that in deductive reasoning, our aim is to transform, reformulate, or restate in our conclusion some (or, as in the examples so far, all) of the information in our premises.

Remember, even though a proposition or statement follows from a previous proposition or statement, the statements need not be true. We can see why if we consider another example. Suppose someone asserts or claims that

5. The Hudson River is longer than the Mississippi.

As every student of American geography knows, (5) is false. But, false or not, we can validly deduce from it:

6. The Mississippi is shorter than the Hudson.

This inference is valid (even though the conclusion is untrue) because the conclusion follows logically (more precisely, deductively) from (5): In English, as we know, the meaning of "A is shorter than B," which appears in (6), is simply the converse of "B is longer than A," which appears in (5).

The deductive relation between (5) and (6) reminds us again that the idea of validity, which is so crucial to deduction, is not the same as the idea of truth. False propositions have implications—logical consequences—too, every bit as precisely as do true propositions.

In the three pairs of examples so far, what can we point to as the *warrant* for our claims? We have anticipated that question; the answer in each case is a rule of ordinary English. In the first and third pairs of examples, it is a rule of English semantics; in the second pair it is a rule of English syntax. Change those rules and the inferences will no longer be valid; fail to learn those rules and one will not trust the inferences.

In many cases, of course, the deductive inference or pattern of reasoning is much more complex than that which we have seen in the examples so far. When we introduced the idea of deduction in Chapter 2, we gave as our primary example the syllogism. Here is another example:

7. Texas is larger than California; California is larger than Arizona; therefore, Texas is larger than Arizona.

The conclusion in this syllogism is derivable from the two premises; that is, anyone who asserts the two premises is committed to accepting the conclusion as well, whether or not one thinks of it.

Notice again that the *truth* of the conclusion is not established merely by validity of the inference. The conclusion in this syllogism happens to be true. And the premises of this syllogism imply the conclusion. But the argument also proves the conclusion because both of the premises on which the conclusion depends are true. Even a Californian admits that Texas is larger than California, which in turn is larger than Arizona. In other words, argument (7) is a *sound* argument, because (as we explained in Chapter 2) it is valid and because all its premises are true.

How might we present the warrant for the argument in (7)? Short of a crash course in formal logic, either of two strategies might suffice. One is to argue from the fact that the validity of the inference depends on the meaning of a key concept, *being larger than*, which has the property of *transitivity*, a property that many concepts share (for example, *is equal to*, *is to the right of*, *is smarter than*—all are transitive concepts). Consequently, whatever A, B, and C are, if A is larger than B, and B larger than C, then A will be larger than C. The final step is to substitute Texas, California, and Arizona for A, B, and C, respectively.

A second strategy is to think of representing Texas, California, and Arizona by concentric circles, with the largest for Texas, a smaller circle inside it for California, and a smaller one inside California for Arizona. (This is an adaptation of the technique used in elementary formal logic known as Venn diagrams.) In this manner one can give graphic display to the important fact that the conclusion follows from the premises, because one can literally *see* the conclusion represented by nothing more than a representation of the premises.

Both of these strategies bring out the fact that validity of deductive inference is a purely *formal* property of argument. Each strategy abstracts the form from the content of the propositions involved to show how the concepts in the premises are related to the concepts in the conclusion.

Not all deductive reasoning occurs in syllogisms, however, or at least not in syllogisms like the one in (7). (The term *syllogism* is sometimes used to refer to any deductive argument of whatever form, provided only that it has two premises.) In fact, syllogisms such as (7) are not the commonest form of our deductive reasoning at all. Nor are they the simplest (and of course not the most complex). For something even simpler, but quite familiar, consider this argument:

8. If the horses are loose, then the barn door was left unlocked. The horses are loose. Therefore, the barn door was left unlocked.

Here the pattern of reasoning is called **modus ponens**, which means positing or laying down the minor premise ("the horses are loose"). It is also called **hypothetical syllogism**, because its major premise ("if the horses are loose then the barn door was left unlocked") is a hypothetical or conditional proposition. It has the form: If A then B; A; therefore B. Notice that the content of the assertions represented by A and B do not matter; any set of expressions having the same form or structure will do equally well, including assertions built out of meaningless terms, as in this example:

9. If the slithy toves, then the gyres gimble. The slithy toves. Therefore the gyres gimble.

Argument (9) has exactly the same form as argument (8), and as a piece of deductive inference it is every bit as good. Unlike (8), however, (9) is of no interest to us because none of its assertions make any sense (unless you are a reader of Lewis Carroll's "Jabberwocky," and even then the sense of (9) is doubtful). You cannot, in short, use a valid deductive argument to prove anything unless the premises and the conclusion are *true*, but they can't be true unless they *mean* something in the first place.

This parallel between arguments (8) and (9) shows that deductive validity in an argument rests on the form or structure of the argument, and not on its content or meaning. Consequently, the validity of an argument, by itself, is not a strong recommendation for the argument. It has been said that the Devil can quote Scripture; similarly, an argument can be deductively valid and of no further interest or value whatever, because valid (but false) conclusions can be drawn from false or even meaningless assumptions. Nevertheless, although validity by itself is not enough, it is a necessary condition of any deductive argument that purports to *prove* its conclusion.

Now let us consider another argument with the same form as (8) and (9), only more interesting.

> 10. If President Truman knew the Japanese were about to surrender, then it was immoral of him to order that the atom bombs be dropped. Truman knew the Japanese were about to surrender. Therefore it was immoral of him to order that the atom bombs be dropped.

As in the two previous examples, anyone who assents to the premises must assent to the conclusion, because the form of the three arguments is identical. But do the premises of argument (10) *prove* the conclusion? That depends on whether both premises are true. Well, are they? This turns on a number of considerations, and it is worthwhile pausing to examine this argument closely to illustrate the kinds of things that are involved in answering this question.

Let us begin by examining the second (minor) premise. As some of the readings reprinted in Chapter 10 indicate, the answer is controversial even to this day. History, autobiography, letters, other documentary evidence—all are needed to assemble the evidence to back up the grounds for the thesis or claim made in the conclusion of this valid argument. Evaluating this material effectively will probably involve not only further deductions, but inductive reasoning as well.

Now consider the first (major) premise. Its truth doesn't depend on what history shows, but on what moral principles one accepts. The major premise has the form of a hypothetical proposition ("if . . . then . . ."), and asserts a connection between two very different kinds of things. The antecedent of the hypothetical (the part preceded by "if") mentions facts about Truman's *knowledge*, and the consequent of the hypothetical (the part following "then") mentions facts about the *morality* of his conduct in light of such knowledge. The major premise as a whole can thus be seen as expressing a principle of *moral responsibility*.

Such principles can, of course, be controversial. In this case, for instance, is the principle peculiarly relevant to the knowledge and conduct of a president of the United States? Probably not; it is far more likely that this principle is merely a special case of a more general proposition about anyone's moral responsibility. (After all, we know a great deal more about the conditions of our own moral responsibility than we do about those of high government officials.) We might express this more general principle in this way: If we have knowledge that makes our violent conduct unnecessary, then we are immoral if we act violently anyway. Thus, accepting this general principle can serve as a basis for defending the major premise of argument (10).

We have examined this argument in some detail because it illustrates the kinds of considerations needed to test whether a given argument is not only valid but whether its premises are true—that is, whether its premises really prove the conclusion.

The great value of the form of argument known as hypothetical syllogism, exemplified by arguments (8), (9), and (10), is that the structure of the argument is so simple and so universally applicable in reasoning that it is often both easy and worthwhile to formulate one's claims so that they can be grounded by an argument of this sort.

Before leaving the subject of deductive inference, consider three other forms of argument, each of which can be found in actual use elsewhere in the readings in this volume. The simplest of these is **disjunctive syllogism,** so called because, again, it has two premises, and its major premise is a **disjunction** (that is, a complex assertion built from two or more alternatives joined by the conjunction "or"). For example,

11. Either censorship of television shows is overdue, or our society is indifferent to the education of its youth. Our society is not indifferent to the education of its youth. Therefore, censorship of television is overdue.

Notice, by the way, that the validity of an argument, as in this case, does not turn on pedantic repetition of every word or phrase as the argument moves along; nonessential elements can be dropped, or equivalent expressions substituted for variety, without adverse effect on the reasoning. Thus, in conversation, or in writing, the argument in (11) might actually look like this:

12. Either censorship of television shows is overdue, or our society is indifferent to the education of its youth. But, of course, we aren't indifferent; it's censorship that's overdue.

The key feature of disjunctive syllogism, as the example suggests, is that the conclusion is whichever of the disjuncts (that is, one of the independent clauses in the major premise, such as "society is indifferent to the education of its youth") is left over after the others have been negated in the minor premise. Thus, we could easily have a very complex disjunctive syllogism, with a dozen disjuncts in the major premise, and seven of them denied in the minor premise, leaving a conclusion of the remaining five. Usually, however, the form of the argument is this: Assert a disjunction with two or more disjuncts in the major premise; then deny all but one in the minor premise; and infer validly the remaining disjunct as the conclusion. That was the form of argument (12).

Another type of argument, especially favored by orators and rhetoricians of the past, is the **dilemma**. Ordinarily, we often use the term *dilemma* in the sense of an awkward predicament, as when we say, "His dilemma was that he didn't have enough money to pay the waiter." But when logicians refer to a dilemma, they mean a forced choice between two or more equally unattractive alternatives. For example, the predicament of the United States government during the mid-1980s as it faced the crisis brought on by terrorist attacks on American civilian targets, which were believed, during that time, to be inspired and supported by the Libyan government, can be formulated in a dilemma:

13. If the United States bombs targets in Libya, innocent people will be killed and the Arab world will be angered. If the United States doesn't bomb Libyan targets, then terrorists will go unpunished and the United States will lose respect among other governments. Either the United States bombs Libyan targets or it doesn't. Therefore, in either case unattractive consequences will follow: The innocent will be killed or terrorists will go unpunished.

Notice first the structure of the argument: two conditional propositions asserted as premises, followed by another premise that states a **necessary truth** (the premise, "Either we bomb the Libyans or we don't," is a disjunction of two exhaustive alternatives, and so one of the two alternatives must be true). No doubt the conclusion of this dilemma follows from its premises.

But does the argument prove, as it purports to do, that whatever the United States government does, it will suffer undesirable consequences? If the two conditional premises failed to exhaust the possibilities, then one can escape from the dilemma by going "between the horns"; that is, by finding a third alternative. If (as in this case) that is not possible, one can still ask whether both of the main premises are true. (In this argument, it should be clear that neither of these main premises spells out all or even most of the consequences that could be foreseen.) Even so, in cases where both these conditional premises are true, it may be that the consequences of one alternative are nowhere nearly so bad as those of the other. If that is true, but our reasoning stops before evaluating that fact, we may be guilty of failing to distinguish between the greater and the lesser of two admitted evils. The logic of the dilemma itself cannot decide on this choice for us. Instead, we must bring to bear empirical inquiry and imagination to the evaluation of the grounds of the dilemma itself.

Finally, one of the most powerful and dramatic forms of argument is **reductio ad absurdum** (from the Latin, meaning "reduction to absurdity"). The idea of a reductio argument is to establish a conclusion by refuting its opposite, and it is an especially attractive tactic when what you are refuting is your opponent's position in order to prove your own. For example, in Plato's *Republic*, Socrates asks an old gentleman, Cephalus, to state what right conduct is. Cephalus says that it is paying your debts and keeping your word. Socrates rejects this answer by showing that it leads to a contradiction. He argues that this cannot be the right answer because if we assume that it is, we will be quickly led into contradiction, for in some cases when you keep your word you will nonetheless be doing the wrong thing. For suppose, says Socrates, that you borrowed a weapon from a man, promising to return it when he asks for it, and one day he comes to your door, demanding his weapon and swearing angrily that he intends to murder a neighbor. Keeping your word under those circumstances is absurd, Socrates implies; and the reader of the dialogue is left to infer that Cephalus' definition, which led to this result, is refuted.

Let's take a closer look at a second example. Suppose you are opposed to any form of gun control, whereas I am in favor of gun control. I might try to refute your position by attacking it with a reductio argument. To do that, I start out by assuming the very opposite of what I believe or favor, and try to establish a contradiction that results from following out the consequences of this initial assumption. My argument might look like this:

14. Let's assume your position, namely, that there are no legal restrictions whatever on the sale and ownership of guns. That means that you favor having every neighborhood hardware store selling pistols and rifles to whoever walks in the door. But that's not all. You apparently also favor selling machine guns to children, anti-tank weapons to lunatics, small bore cannons to the near-sighted, as well as guns, and the ammunition to go with them, to anyone with a criminal record. But this is utterly preposterous. No one could favor such a dangerous policy. So the only question worth debating is what *kind* of gun control is necessary.

Now in this example, my reductio of your position on gun control is not based on claiming to show that you have strictly contradicted yourself, for there is no purely logical contradiction in opposing all forms of gun control. Instead, what I have tried to do (just as Socrates did) is to show that there is a contradiction between what you profess—no gun controls whatever—and what you probably really believe, if only you will stop to think about it—no lunatic should be allowed to buy a loaded machine gun. So my refutation of your position rests on whether I succeed in establishing an inconsistency among your own beliefs. If you really believe that lunatics should be free to purchase guns and ammunition then my refutation fails.

In explaining reductio ad absurdum, we have had to rely on another idea fundamental to logic, that of **contradiction**, or inconsistency. (We used this idea, remember, to define validity in Chapter 2.) A deductive argument is valid if and only if affirming the premises and denying the conclusion results in a contradiction.) The opposite of contradiction is **consistency**, a notion of hardly less importance to good reasoning than validity. These concepts deserve a few words of further explanation and illustration. Consider this pair of assertions:

15. Abortion is homicide.
16. Racism is unfair.

No one would plausibly claim that we can infer or deduce (16) from (15), or, for that matter, (15) from (16). This almost goes without saying, because there is no evident connection between (15) and (16). They are unrelated assertions; logically speaking, they are *independent* of each other. In such cases the two assertions are mutually consistent; that is, both could be true. But now consider another proposition:

17. Euthanasia is not murder.

Could a person assert (15) *abortion is homicide* and (17) and be consistent? This question is equivalent to asking whether one could assert the **conjunction** simultaneously, which is what we have here:

18. Abortion is homicide and euthanasia is not murder.

It is not so easy to say whether (18) is consistent or inconsistent. The kinds of moral scruples that might lead one to assert either of its conjuncts (that is, the two independent propositions, *Abortion is homicide* and *Euthanasia is not murder*) might lead to the belief that the other one must be false, and thus to the conclusion that (18) is inconsistent. (Notice that if [15] were the assertion that *Abortion is murder*, instead of *Abortion is homicide*, the problem of asserting consistently both [15] and [17] would be more acute.) Yet, if we think again, we might imagine someone being convinced that there is no inconsistency in asserting that *Abortion is homicide*, say, and that *Euthanasia is not murder*, or even the reverse. (For instance, suppose you believed that the unborn deserve a chance to live, and that putting elderly persons to death in a painless manner and with their consent confers a benefit on them.)

Let us generalize: We can say of any set of propositions that they are *consistent* if and only if all *could be true together*. (Notice that it follows from this definition that propositions that mutually imply each other, as do *The cat is on the mat* and *The mat is under the cat*, are consistent.) Remember that, once again, the truth of the assertions in question does not matter. Propositions can be consistent or not, quite apart from whether they are true. Not so their falsehood: It follows from our definition of consistency that an *inconsistent* proposition must be *false.* (We have relied on this idea in explaining how a reductio ad absurdum works.)

Assertions or claims that are not consistent can take either of two forms. Suppose you assert proposition (15), that abortion is homicide, early in an essay you are writing, but later you say

19. Abortion is harmless.

You have now asserted a position on abortion that is strictly **contrary** to the one with which you began; contrary in the sense that both assertions (15) and (19) cannot be true. It is simply not true that if an abortion involves killing a human being (which is what *homicide* strictly means) then it causes no one any harm (killing a person always causes harm—even if it is excusable, or justifiable, or not wrong, or the best thing to do in the circumstances, and so on). Notice that although (15) and (19) cannot both be true, they can both be false. In fact, many people who are perplexed about the morality of abortion believe precisely this. They concede that abortion does harm the fetus, so (19) must be false; but they also believe that abortion doesn't kill anyone, so (15) must also be false.

Or consider another, simpler case. If you describe the glass as half empty and I describe it as half full, both of us can be right; the two assertions are consistent, even though they sound vaguely incompatible. (This is the reason that disputing over whether the glass is half full or half empty has become the popular paradigm of a futile, purely verbal disagreement.) But if I describe the glass as half empty whereas you insist that it is two-thirds empty, then we have a real disagreement, because the two descriptions are strictly contrary, in that both cannot be true—although both can be false.

This, by the way, enables us to define the difference between a pair of contradictory propositions and a pair of contrary propositions. Two propositions are **contrary** if and only if both cannot be true (although both can be false); two propositions are **contradictory** if and only if one is true and the other is false.

Genuine contradiction, and not merely contrary assertion, is the situation we should expect to find in some disputes. Someone advances a thesis—such as the assertion in (15)—and someone else flatly contradicts it by the simple expedient of negating it, thus:

20. Abortion is not homicide.

If we can trust public opinion polls, many of us are not sure whether to agree with (15) or with (20). But we should agree that whichever is true, *both* cannot be true, and *both* cannot be false. The two assertions, between them, exclude all other possibilities; they pose a forced choice for our belief. (Again, we have met this idea, too, in the reductio ad absurdum.)

Now it is one thing for Jack and Jill in a dispute or argument to contradict each other. It is quite another matter for Jack to contradict himself. One wants (or should want) to avoid self-contradiction because of the embarrassing position in which one then finds oneself. Once I have contradicted myself, what are others to believe I really believe? What, indeed, *do* I believe, for that matter? It may be all right for a poet to glory in self-contradiction on occasion (Walt Whitman wrote, "I contradict myself? Very well, I contradict myself—I contain multitudes"), but the ordinary reasoner is well advised to avoid self-contradiction, whenever possible, except when one has genuinely changed one's mind and is ready to give up the earlier position (assertion) in favor of its opposite, which is what one now believes. But this case, of course, is now no longer one of asserting or claiming both parts of the contradictory pair.

It may be, as Emerson observed, that a "foolish consistency is the hobgoblin of little minds"—that is, it may be shortsighted to purchase a consistency in one's beliefs at the expense of flying in the face of common sense. But making an effort to avoid a foolish inconsistency is the hallmark of serious thinking.

INDUCTION

Unlike deduction, which involves logical thinking we can carry out with regard to any assertion or claim whatever—because every possible statement, true or false, has its logical consequences—induction is relevant to one kind of assertion only; namely, to **empirical** or *factual* claims. Other kinds of assertions (such as definitions, mathematical equations, and moral or legal standards) simply are not the product of inductive reasoning and cannot serve as a basis for further inductive thinking.

And so, in studying the methods of induction, we are exploring tactics and strategies useful in gathering evidence—empirical, observational, experimental—on behalf of a claim or a ground for a claim. Modern science is the product of these methods, though the methods differ somewhat from one science to another because they depend on the theories and technology appropriate to each of the sciences. Here, all we can do is discuss generally the more abstract features of inductive inquiry. For fuller details, you must eventually consult your local physicist, chemist, geologist, or their colleagues and counterparts in other scientific fields.

Observation and Inference

Let us begin with a simple example. Suppose we have evidence (actually, we don't, but that will not matter for our purposes) to the effect that

1. Two hundred thirty persons observed in a sample of 500 smokers have cardiovascular disease.

The basis for asserting (1)—the evidence or ground—would be, presumably, straightforward physical examination of the persons in the sample, one by one, carefully counted.

With this claim in hand, we can think of the purpose and methods of induction as being pointed in both of two opposite directions: toward establishing the basis or ground of the very empirical proposition with which we start, in this example the observation stated in (1); or toward understanding what that observation indicates or suggests as a more general, inclusive, or fundamental fact of nature.

In each case, we start from something we *do* know (or take for granted and treat as a sound starting point)—some fact of nature, perhaps a striking or commonplace event that we have observed and recorded—and then go on to something we do *not* fully know and perhaps cannot directly observe. In the example at hand, only the second of these two orientations is of any interest, and so let us concentrate exclusively on it. (Let us also generously treat as a *method* of induction any regular pattern or style of nondeductive reasoning that we can use on a claim such as that in [1].)

Anyone truly interested in the observed fact that *230 of 500 smokers have cardiovascular disease* is likely to start speculating about, and thus be interested in finding out, whether any or all of several other propositions are also true. For example, one might wonder whether

2. *All* smokers have cardiovascular disease or will develop it during their lifetimes.

This claim is a straightforward generalization of the original observation as reported in claim (1). When we think inductively about the linkage between (1) and (2), we are reasoning from an observed sample (some smokers, that is, 230 of the 500 *observed*) to the entire membership of a more inclusive class (*all* smokers, whether observed or not). The fundamental question raised by reasoning from the narrower claim (1) to the broader claim (2) is whether we have any ground for believing that what is true of *some* members of a class is true of them *all*. So the difference between (1) and (2) is that of *quantity* or scope; and the truth of (2) based on (1) depends on how representative the sample in (1) is.

We can also think inductively about the *relation* between the factors mentioned in (1). Having observed data as reported in (1), we may be tempted to assert a different and profounder kind of claim:

3. Smoking *causes* cardiovascular disease.

Here our interest is not merely in generalizing from a sample to a whole class; it is the far more important one of *explaining* the observation with which we began in claim (1). Certainly the preferred, even if not the only, mode of explanation for a natural phenomenon is a *causal* explanation. In proposition (3), we propose to explain the presence of one phenomenon (cardiovascular disease) by the prior occurrence of another phenomenon (smoking). The observation reported in (1) is now being used as evidence or support for this new conjecture.

Our original claim in (1) asserted no causal relation between anything and anything else; whatever the cause of cardiovascular disease may be, that cause is not observed or mentioned in assertion (1). Similarly, the observation asserted in claim (1) is consistent with many explanations. For example, the explanation of (1) might not be (3), but some other, un-detected, carcinogenic factor unrelated to smoking, for instance, exposure to high levels of radon. And so it is clear that anyone who asserts (3) goes well beyond (1) in the manner characteristic of inductive reasoning. The question one now faces is what can be added to (1), or teased out of it, in order to produce an adequate ground for claiming (3). (We shall return to this example for closer scrutiny.)

But there is a third way to go beyond (1). Instead of a straightforward generalization, as we had in (2), or a pronouncement on the cause of a phenomenon, as in (3), we might have a somewhat more complex and cautious further claim in mind, such as this:

4. Smoking is a factor in the causation of cardiovascular disease in some persons.

This proposition is like (3) in that it advances a claim about causation, and so if (3) is true it constitutes a partial or plausible explanation for (1). But (4) is a weaker claim than (3). That is, other observations, theories, or evidence that would require us to regard (3) as false might not falsify (4); evidence that would support (4) could easily fail to be enough to support (3). Consequently, it is even possible that (4) is true although (3) is false, because (4) allows for other (unmentioned) factors in the causation of cardiovascular disease (genetic or dietary factors, for example) which may not be found in all smokers.

Propositions (2), (3), and (4) differ from proposition (1) in an impor-tant respect. We began by assuming that (1) states an empirical fact, whereas these others do not. Instead, they state *hypotheses* or conjectures, each of which goes beyond the observed facts asserted in (1). Each of (2), (3), and (4) is thus an *inductive inference* from (1). In yet another form, we can say that (2), (3), and (4) are hypotheses relative to (1), even if relative to some other starting point (such as all the information that scientists today really have about smoking and cardiovascular disease) they are not.

Probability

Another way of formulating the last point is to say that whereas proposition (1), a statement of observed fact, has a **probability** of 1.0—that is, it is absolutely certain—the probability of each of the hypotheses stated in (2), (3), and (4) *relative* to (1) is smaller than 1.0. (We need not worry about how much smaller than 1.0 the probabilities are, nor about which of these hypotheses is the most and which the least probable given the evidence in [1].) Relative to some starting point other than (1), however, the probability of these same three hypotheses might be quite different. Of course, it still would not be 1.0, absolute certainty. But it takes only a moment's reflection to realize that, whatever may be the probability of (2) or (3) or (4) relative to (1), those probabilities in each case will be quite different relative to

5. Ten persons observed in a sample of 500 smokers have cardiovascular disease.

The idea that a proposition can have a different probability relative to different bases is fundamental to all inductive reasoning. It can be convincingly illustrated by the following example. Suppose we want to consider the probability of this proposition being true:

6. Susanne Smith will live to be eighty.

Taken as an abstract question of fact, we cannot even guess what the probability is with any assurance. But we can do better than guess; we can in fact even calculate the answer, if we are given some further information. Thus, suppose we are told that

7. Susanne Smith is seventy-nine.

Our original question then becomes one of determining the probability that (6) is true given (7); that is, relative to the evidence contained in proposition (7). No doubt, if Susanne Smith really is seventy-nine, then the probability that she will live to be eighty is greater than if we know only that

8. Susanne Smith is more than nine years old.

Obviously, a lot can happen to Susanne in the seventy years between nine and seventy-nine that is not very likely to happen to her in the one year between seventy-nine and eighty. And so, proposition (6) is more probable relative to proposition (7) than it is relative to proposition (8).

Let us disregard (7) and instead further suppose for the sake of the argument that the following is true:

9. Ninety percent of the women alive at seventy-nine live to be eighty.

Given this additional information, we now have a basis for answering our original question about proposition (6) with some precision. But suppose, in addition to (8), we are also told that

10. Susanne Smith is suffering from inoperable cancer.

and also that

> 11. The survival rate for women suffering from inoperable cancer is 0.6 years (that is, the average life span for women after a diagnosis of inoperable cancer is about seven months).

With this new information, the probability that (6) will be true has changed drastically, all because we can now calculate it in relation to a new body of evidence.

The probability of an event, thus, is not an abstract and fixed number, but a variable number, always relative to some evidence—and given different evidence, one and the same thing can have different probabilities. In other words, the probability of anything is always relative to how much is known (assumed, believed), and because different persons may know different things about a given event, or the same person may know different things at different times, one and the same event can have two or more probabilities. This expression is not a paradox but a logical consequence of the concept of what it is for an event to have (that is, to be assigned) a probability.

If we shift to the *calculation* of probabilities, we find that generally we have two ways in which to do so. One way to proceed is by the method of **a priori** or **equal probabilities**, that is, by reference to the relevant possibilities taken abstractly and apart from any other information. Thus, in an election contest with only two candidates, A and B, each of the candidates has a fifty-fifty chance of winning (whereas in a three-candidate race, each candidate would have one chance in three of winning). Therefore the probability that candidate A will win is 0.5, and the probability that candidate B will win is also 0.5. (The sum of the probabilities of all possible independent outcomes must always equal 1.0, which is obvious enough if you think about it.)

But in politics the probabilities are not reasonably calculated so abstractly. We know that many empirical factors enter into these events, and that a calculation of probabilities in ignorance of those factors is likely to be drastically misleading. In our example of the two-candidate election, suppose candidate A has strong party support and is the incumbent, whereas candidate B represents a party long out of power and is further handicapped by being relatively unknown. No one who knows anything about electoral politics would give B the same chance of winning as A. The two events are not equiprobable in relation to all the information available.

Similarly, suppose hundreds of throws with a given pair of dice reveal that a pair of ones comes up not 1 time in 12, as would be expected if all possible combinations were equally possible, but only 1 time in 100. This information would immediately suggest that either the throws were rigged or the dice are loaded, and in any case that the probability of a pair of ones for these dice is not 0.08 but much less, perhaps 0.01 (that is, 1 in 100).

Probabilities calculated in this way are **relative frequencies;** that is, they are calculated in terms of the observed frequency with which a specified event actually occurs.

Both methods of calculating probabilities are legitimate; in each case the calculation is relative to observed circumstances. But, as the examples show, it is most reasonable to have recourse to the method of equi-probabilities only when few or no other factors affecting possible outcomes are known.

Mill's Methods

Let us return to our earlier example about smoking and cardiovascular disease, and consider in greater detail the question of a causal connection between the two. We began with what we treated as an observed fact (in truth, of course, it is mere supposition) that

1. 230 of an observed sample of 500 smokers had cardiovascular disease.

Our question now is, how might we augment this information so as to strengthen our confidence that

3. Smoking causes cardiovascular disease.

Suppose further examination showed that

12. In the sample of 230 smokers with cardiovascular disease, no other suspected factor (such as genetic predisposition, lack of physical exercise, age over fifty) was also observed.

Such an observation would encourage us to believe that (4), *Smoking is a factor in the causation of cardiovascular disease in some persons,* is true. Why? We are encouraged to believe it because we are inclined to believe also that whatever the cause of a phenomenon is, it must *always* be present when its effect is present. Thus, the inference from (1) to (4) is supported by (12), using **Mill's Method of Agreement,** named after the British philosopher, John Stuart Mill (1806–1873), who first formulated it. It is called a method of agreement because of the way in which it relies on *agreement* among the observed phenomena where a presumed cause is thought to be *present.*

Let us suppose further that in our search for evidence to support (4) we conduct additional research, and discover:

13. In a sample of 500 nonsmokers, selected to be representative of both sexes, different ages, dietary habits, exercise patterns, and so on, none is observed to have cardiovascular disease.

This observation would further encourage us to believe that we had obtained significant additional confirmation of (4), on the ground that factors present (such as male sex, lack of exercise, family history of cardiovascular disease) in cases where the effect is absent (no cardiovascular disease observed) cannot be causal factors. This is an example of **Mill's Method of Difference**, so called because the cause or causal factor of an effect must be *different* from whatever the factors are that are present when the effect is *absent*.

Suppose now that, increasingly confident that we have found the cause of cardiovascular disease, we study our first sample of 230 smokers ill with cardiovascular disease, and discover this:

14. Those who smoke two or more packs of cigarettes daily for ten or more years have cardiovascular disease either much younger or much more severely than those who smoke less.

This is an application of **Mill's Method of Concomitant Variation**, perhaps the most convincing of the three methods. Here we deal not merely with the presence of the conjectured cause (smoking) or the absence of the effect we are studying (cardiovascular disease), as we were previously, but with the more interesting and subtler matter of the *degree and regularity of the correlation* of the supposed cause and effect. According to the observations reported in (14), it strongly appears that the more we have of the "cause" (smoking) the sooner or the more intense the onset of the "effect."

Notice, however, what happens to our confirmation of (4) if instead of the observation reported in (14) we had observed instead:

15. In a representative sample of 500 nonsmokers, cardiovascular disease was observed in 34 cases.

(Let us not pause here to explain what makes a sample more or less representative of a population, although this fact is vital to all statistical reasoning.) Such an observation would lead us almost immediately to suspect some other or additional causal factor: Smoking might indeed be a factor in causing cardiovascular disease, but it can hardly be *the* cause, because (using Mill's Method of Difference) we cannot have the effect, as we do in the observed sample reported in (15), unless we also have the cause.

An observation such as the one in (15), however, is likely to lead us to regard as disconfirmed our hypothesis that smoking causes cardiovascular disease. But we have a fall-back position ready; it is that other causal hypothesis mentioned earlier, namely (4), *Smoking is a factor in the causation of cardiovascular disease in some persons.* Even if (3) stumbles over the evidence in (15), (4) need not. It is still quite possible that smoking is *a* factor in causing this disease, even if it is not the *only* factor.

Confirmation, Mechanism, and Theory

Notice that in the discussion so far, we have spoken of the *confirmation* of a hypothesis, such as our causal claim in (4), but not of its *verification*. (Similarly, we have imagined very different evidence, such as that stated in [15], leading us to speak of the *dis*confirmation of [4], though not of its *falsi*fication.) Confirmation (getting some evidence for) is weaker than verification (getting sufficient evidence to regard as true); and our (imaginary) evidence so far in favor of (4) falls well short of conclusive support. Further research—the study of more representative or much larger samples, for example—might yield very different observations. It might lead us to conclude that although initial research had confirmed our hypothesis about smoking as the cause of cardiovascular disease, the additional information obtained subsequently disconfirmed the hypothesis. Most interesting hypotheses, both in detective stories and in modern science, have confirming and disconfirming evidence simultaneously. The challenge is to evaluate the hypothesis by considering such conflicting evidence.

As long as we confine our observations to *correlations* of the sort reported in our several (imaginary) observations, such as proposition (1), that 230 smokers in a group of 500 have cardiovascular disease, or (12), that 230 smokers with the disease share no other suspected factors, such as lack of exercise, any defense of a *causal* hypothesis such as claim (3), *Smoking causes cardiovascular disease*, or claim (4), *Smoking is a factor in causing the disease*, is not likely to convince the skeptic or lead those with beliefs alternative to (3) and (4) to abandon them and agree with us. Why is that? It is because a causal hypothesis without any account of the *underlying mechanism* by means of which the (alleged) cause produces the effect will seem superficial. Only when we can specify in detail *how* the (alleged) cause produces the effect will the causal hypothesis be convincing.

In other cases, in which no mechanism can be found, we seek instead to embed the causal hypothesis in a larger *theory*, one that rules out as incompatible any causal hypothesis except the favored one. (That is, we appeal to the test of consistency and thereby bring deductive reasoning to bear on our problem.) Thus, perhaps we cannot specify any mechanism— any underlying structure that generates a regular sequence of events, one of which is the effect we are studying—to explain why, for example, the gravitational mass of a body causes it to attract other bodies. But we can embed this claim in a larger body of physical theory that rules out as inconsistent any alternative causal explanations. To do that convincingly in regard to any given causal hypothesis, as this example suggests, requires detailed knowledge of the current state of the relevant body of scientific theory, something far beyond our aim or need to consider in further detail here.

FALLACIES

The straight road on which sound reasoning proceeds gives little latitude for cruising about. Irrationality, carelessness, passionate attachment to one's unexamined beliefs, and the sheer complexity of some issues, not to mention Original Sin, occasionally spoil the reasoning of even the best of us. Although in this book we reprint many varied voices and arguments, we hope we have reprinted no readings that exhibit the most flagrant errors or commit the graver abuses against the canons of good reasoning. Nevertheless, an inventory of those abuses and their close examination can be an instructive (as well as an amusing) exercise. Instructive, because the diagnosis and repair of error helps to fix more clearly the principles of sound reasoning on which such remedial labors depend. Amusing, because we are so constituted that our perception of the non-sense of others can stimulate our mind, warm our heart, and give us comforting feelings of superiority.

The discussion that follows, then, is a quick tour through the twisting lanes, mudflats, forests, and quicksands of the faults that one sometimes encounters in reading arguments that stray from the highway of clear thinking.

We can and do apply the name *fallacy* to many types of errors, mistakes, and confusions in oral and written discourse, in which our reasoning has gone awry. For convenience, we can group the fallacies by referring to the six aspects of reasoning identified in the Toulmin Method, described earlier (p. 694). Let us take up first those fallacies which spoil our *claims* or our *grounds*. These are errors in the meaning, clarity, or sense of a sentence, or of some word or phrase in a sentence, being used in the role of a claim or ground. They are thus not so much errors of *reasoning* as they are errors in *reasons* or in the *claims* that our reasons are intended to support or criticize.

Many Questions

The old saw, "Have you stopped beating your wife?" illustrates the **fallacy of many questions.** This question, as we can readily see, is un-answerable unless both of its implicit presuppositions are true. The questioner presupposes that (a) the addressee has or had a wife, and that (b) he used to beat her. If either of these presuppositions is false, then the question is pointless; it cannot be answered strictly and simply either with a yes or a no.

Amphiboly

Near the center of the town of Concord, Massachusetts, is an empty field with a sign reading "Old Cow Pasture." Hmm. A pasture in former times used by cows? A pasture now in use for old cows? An erstwhile pasture for old cows? The error here is *amphiboly;* the brevity of the sign has produced a group of words that give rise to meanings other than the one the author intended.

Consider a more complex example. Suppose someone asserts *All rights are equal* and also *Everyone has a right to property.* Many people believe both these claims, but their combination involves an amphiboly. On one interpretation, the two claims entail that everyone has an *equal right* to property. (That is, you and I each have an equal right to whatever property we have.) But the two claims can also be interpreted to mean that everyone has a *right to equal* property. (That is, whatever property you have a right to, I have a right to the same, or at least equivalent, property.) The latter interpretation is radically revolutionary, whereas the former is not. Arguments over equal rights often involve this amphiboly.

Death by a Thousand Qualifications

In a letter of recommendation, sent in support of an applicant for a job on your newspaper, you find this sentence: "Young Smith was the best student I've ever taught in an English course." Pretty strong endorsement, you think, except that the letter writer is a very junior faculty member, has been teaching for only two years, is an instructor in the history department, and taught a section of freshman English as a courtesy for a sick colleague, and only eight students were enrolled in the course. Thanks to these implicit qualifications, the letter writer did not lie or exaggerate in his praise; but the effect of his sentence on you, the unwitting reader, is quite misleading. The explicit claim in the letter, and its impact on you, is quite different from the tacitly qualified claim in the mind of the writer.

The **fallacy of death by a thousand qualifications** gets its name from the way a bold assertion can be virtually killed, its true content reduced to nothing, once all the appropriate or necessary qualifications are added to it. To see this effect even more clearly, suppose you come on a remark from a politician describing another country (let's call it Ruritania so as not to offend anyone) as a "democracy"—except that it doesn't have regular elections, lacks a written constitution, has no independent judiciary, prohibits religious worship except of the state-designated deity, and so forth. Some democracy! The unstated qualifications have taken all the content out of the original description.

Equivocation

In a delightful passage in *Alice in Wonderland,* the king asks his messenger, "Who did you pass on the road?" and the messenger replies, "Nobody." This prompts the king to observe, "Of course, nobody walks slower than you," provoking the messenger's sullen response: "I do my best. I'm sure nobody walks much faster than I do." At this the king remarks with surprise, "He can't do that or else he'd have been here first!" (This, by the way, is the classic predecessor of the famous comic dialogue, "Who's on First?" between Abbott and Costello.) The king and the messenger are equivocating on the term *nobody.* The messenger uses it in the normal way as an indefinite pronoun equivalent to "not anyone." But the king uses the word as though it were a proper noun, *Nobody,* the rather odd name of some person. No wonder the king and the messenger talk right past each other.

Equivocation (from the Latin for "equal voice," that is, giving utterance to two meanings at the same time in one word or phrase) can ruin otherwise good reasoning, as in this example: *Euthanasia is a good death; one dies a good death when one dies peacefully in old age; therefore euthanasia is dying peacefully in old age.* The etymology of *euthanasia* is literally "a good death," and so the first premise is true. And the second premise is certainly plausible. But the conclusion of this syllogism is false. Euthanasia cannot be defined as a peaceful death in one's old age, for two reasons. First, euthanasia requires the intervention of another person who kills someone (or lets him die); second, even a very young person can be given euthanasia. The problem arises because "a good death" is used in the second premise in a manner that does not apply to euthanasia. Both meanings of "a good death" are legitimate, but here together they constitute an equivocation that spoils an otherwise valid argument.

The fallacy of equivocation takes us from the discussion of confusions in individual claims or ground to the more troublesome fallacies that infect the linkages between the claims we make and the grounds (or reasons) for them. These are the fallacies that occur in statements that, following the vocabulary of the Toulmin Method, are called the *warrant* of reasoning. Each fallacy is an example of reasoning that involves a **non sequitur;** that is, reasoning in which the *claim* (conclusion) "doesn't follow" from the *grounds* (premises).

Composition

Could an all-star team of professional basketball players beat the Boston Celtics in their heyday, say the team of 1985–1986? Perhaps in one game or two, but probably not in seven of a dozen games in a row. As students of the game know, teamwork is an indispensable part of outstanding performance, and the Celtics are famous for their self-sacrificing style of play.

The **fallacy of composition** can be convincingly illustrated, therefore, in this argument: *A team of five NBA all-stars is the best team in basketball because each of the five players is the best at his position.* The fallacy is called composition because the reasoning commits the error of arguing from the true premise that each member of a group has a certain property to the false conclusion that the group (the composition) itself has the property. (That is, because A is the best player at forward, B is the best center, and so on, therefore the team of A, B . . . is the best team.)

Division

In the Bible, we are told that Jesus had twelve apostles and that Matthew was an apostle. Does it follow that Matthew was twelve? No. To argue in this way from a property of a group to a property of a member of that group is to commit the **fallacy of division.** The example of the Apostles may not be a very tempting instance of this error; here is a classic version that is a bit more interesting. If it is true that the average American family has 1.8 children, does it follow that your brother and sister-in-law are likely to have 1.8 children? If you think it does, you have committed the fallacy of division.

Poisoning the Well

During the 1970s some critics of the Equal Rights Amendment (ERA) argued against it by pointing out that Marx and Engels, as their *Communist Manifesto* proves, favored equality of women and men—and therefore ERA is immoral, or undesirable, and perhaps even a communist plot. This kind of reasoning is an attempt to **poison the well;** that is, an attempt to shift attention from the merits of the argument—the validity of the reasoning, the truth of the claims—to the source or origin of the argument. Such criticism nicely deflects attention from the real issue; namely, whether the view in question is true and what the quality of evidence is in its support. The mere fact that Marx (or Hitler, for that matter) believed something does not show that the belief is false or immoral; just because some scoundrel believes the world is round, that is no reason for you to believe it is flat.

Ad Hominem

Closely allied to poisoning the well is another fallacy, **ad hominem** argument (from the Latin for "against the person"). Since arguments and theories are not natural occurrences but are the creative products of particular persons, a critic can easily yield to the temptation to attack an argument or theory by trying to impeach or undercut the credentials of its author.

The Genetic Fallacy

Another member of the family of related fallacies that includes poisoning the well and ad hominem is the **genetic fallacy.** Here the error takes the form of arguing against some claim by pointing out that its origin (genesis) is tainted or it was invented by someone deserving our contempt. Thus, one might attack the ideas of the Declaration of Independence by pointing out that its principal author, Thomas Jefferson, was a slaveholder. Assuming that it is not anachronistic and inappropriate to criticize a public figure of two centuries ago for practicing slavery, and conceding that slavery is morally outrageous, it is nonetheless fallacious to attack the ideas or even the sincerity of the Declaration by attempting to impeach the credentials of its author. Jefferson's moral faults do not by themselves falsify, make improbable, or constitute counterevidence to the truth or other merits of the claims made in his writings. At most, one's faults cast doubt on one's integrity or sincerity if one makes claims at odds with one's practice.

The genetic fallacy can take other forms less closely allied to ad hominem argument. For example, an opponent of the death penalty might argue:

> Capital punishment arose in barbarous times; but we claim to be civilized; therefore we should discard this relic of the past.

Such reasoning shouldn't be persuasive, because the question of the death penalty for our society must be decided by the degree to which it serves our purposes—justice and defense against crime, presumably—to which its historic origins are irrelevant. The practices of beer- and wine-making are as old as human civilization, but their origin in antiquity is no reason to outlaw them in our time. The curious circumstances in which something originates usually play no role whatever in its validity. Anyone who would argue that nothing good could possibly come from molds and fungi is refuted by Sir Arthur Fleming's discovery of penicillin in the 1940s.

Appeal to Authority

The example of Jefferson can be turned around to illustrate another fallacy. One might easily imagine someone from the South in 1860 defending the slavocracy of that day by appealing to the fact that no less a person than Jefferson—a brilliant public figure, thinker, and leader by any measure—owned slaves. Or, today, one might defend capital punishment on the ground that Abraham Lincoln, surely one of the nation's greatest presidents, signed many death warrants during the Civil War, thereby authorizing the execution of Union soldiers. No doubt the standing and esteem in which such figures as Jefferson and Lincoln are deservedly held amounts to impressive endorsement for whatever acts and practices, policies and institutions, they supported. But the **authority** of these figures in itself is not *evidence* for the truth of their views, and so their authority cannot be a reason for anyone to agree with them. Obviously, Jefferson and Lincoln themselves could not support their beliefs by pointing to the fact that they held them. Because their own authority is no reason for them to believe what they believe, it is no reason for anyone else, either.

Sometimes the appeal to authority is fallacious because the authoritative person is not an expert on the issue in dispute. The fact that a high-energy physicist has won the Nobel Prize is no reason for attaching any special weight to her views on the causes of cancer, the reduction of traffic accidents, or the legalization of marijuana. On the other hand, one would be well advised to attend to her views on the advisability of "Star Wars" (SDI) research, for there may be a connection between the kind of research for which she received the Prize and the research projects in "Star Wars."

All of us depend heavily on the knowledge of various experts and authorities, and so it ill-behooves us to ignore or disregard their views. Conversely, we should resist the temptation to accord their views on diverse subjects the same respect that we grant them in the area of their expertise.

The Slippery Slope

One of the most familiar arguments against any type of government regulation is that if it is allowed, then it will be just the first step down the path that leads to ruinous interference, overregulation, and totalitarian control. Fairly often we encounter this mode of arguments in the public debates over handgun control and in the dispute over the censorship of pornography. The argument is called the **slippery slope argument** (or the **wedge argument,** from the way we use the thin end of a wedge to split solid things apart; it is also called, rather colorfully, "letting the camel's nose under the tent"). The fallacy here is in implying that the first step necessarily leads to the second, and so on down the slope to disaster, when in fact there is no necessary connection between the first step and the second at all. (Would handgun registration lead to a police state? Well, it hasn't in Switzerland; not yet.) Sometimes the argument takes the form of claiming that a seemingly innocent or even attractive principle that is being applied in a given case (censorship of pornography, to avoid promoting sexual violence) requires one for consistency to apply the same principle in other cases with absurd and catastrophic results (censorship of everything in print, to avoid hurting anyone's feelings).

Here's an extreme example of this fallacy in action:

> Automobiles cause more deaths than handguns do. If you oppose handguns on the ground that doing so would save lives of the innocent, you'll soon find yourself wanting to outlaw the automobile.

Does opposition to handguns logically have this consequence? Most people accept without dispute the right of society to regulate the operation of motor vehicles by requiring drivers to have a license, a greater restriction than many states impose on gun ownership. Besides, a gun is a lethal weapon designed to kill whereas an automobile or truck is a vehicle designed for transportation. Private ownership and use in both cases entail risks of death to the innocent. But there is no inconsistency in a society's refusal to tolerate this risk in the case of guns and its willingness to do so in the case of automobiles.

The Appeal to Ignorance

In the controversy over the death penalty, as the debate between Edward Koch and attorney David Bruck (pp. 392–401) shows, the issues of deterrence and executing the innocent are bound to be raised. It is tempting for the abolitionist to argue that because no one knows how many innocent persons have been convicted of murder and wrongfully executed, the death penalty is too risky. It is equally tempting for the proponent of the death penalty to argue that because no one knows how many persons have been deterred from murder by the threat of execution, we abolish it at our peril.

Each of these arguments suffers from the same flaw: namely, the **fallacy of appeal to ignorance.** Each argument invites the audience to draw an inference from a premise that is unquestionably true—but what is that premise? It is admittedly something "we don't know." But what we *don't* know cannot be *evidence* for (or against) anything. Our ignorance is no reason for believing anything, except perhaps that we ought to try to undertake an appropriate investigation in order to reduce our ignorance and replace it with reliable information.

Begging the Question

The argument we have just considered also illustrates another fallacy. From the fact that you were not murdered yesterday, we cannot infer that the death penalty was a deterrent. Yet it is tempting to do so, perhaps because the argument also commits the **fallacy of begging the question.** That is, if someone assumes from the start that the death penalty is an effective deterrent, the fact that you weren't murdered yesterday certainly looks like evidence for the truth of that belief. But it isn't, so long as there are competing but unexamined alternative explanations, as in this case. (The fallacy is called "begging the question," *petitio principii* in Latin, because the conclusion of the argument is hidden among its assumptions— and so the conclusion, not surprisingly, follows from the premises.)

Of course, the fact that you weren't murdered is *consistent* with the claim that the death penalty is an effective deterrent, just as anyone's being murdered is inconsistent with that idea). But it doesn't *imply* that, and it provides little support by way of evidence. In general, from the fact that two propositions are consistent with each other, we cannot infer that either is evidence for the other.

False Analogy

Argument by analogy, as we have pointed out in Chapter 2, and as many of the selections in this book show, is a familiar and even indispensable mode of argument. But it can be treacherous, because it runs the risk of the **fallacy of false analogy.** Unfortunately, we have no simple or foolproof way of distinguishing between the useful and legitimate analogies, and the others. The key question to ask yourself is this: Do the two things put into analogy differ in any essential and relevant respect, or are they different only in unimportant and irrelevant aspects?

In a famous example from his discussion in support of suicide, philosopher David Hume rhetorically asked: "It would be no crime in me to divert the Nile or Danube from its course, were I able to effect such purposes. Where then is the crime of turning a few ounces of blood from their natural channel?" This is a striking analogy, except that it proves the opposite of what Hume thought it proved, since it rests on a false assumption. No one has the right to divert a major international watercourse; it would be a catastrophic crime to do so, and therefore, arguing by analogy, one might well say that no one has the right to take his own life, either. But because this criticism subverts Hume's point, let us ignore the way in which his example can be turned against him. The analogy is a terrible one in any case. Isn't it patently obvious that whereas the Nile, whatever its exact course, would continue to nourish Egypt and the Sudan, the blood flowing out of someone's veins will soon leave that person dead and thus not the same. The fact that the blood is the same blood, whether in one's body or in a pool on the floor (just as the water of the Nile is the same body of water whatever path it follows to the sea) is, of course, irrelevant to the question of whether one has the right to commit suicide.

Let us look at a more complex example. During the 1960s, when the nation was convulsed over the purpose and scope of our military involvement in Southeast Asia, advocates of more vigorous United States military participation appealed to the so-called domino effect, supposedly inspired by a passing remark from President Eisenhower in the 1950s. The analogy refers to the way in which standing dominoes collapse, one after the other, if the first one is pushed. If Vietnam turns communist, according to this analogy, so too will its neighbors, Laos and Cambodia, followed by Thailand and then Burma, until the whole region is as communist as China to the north. The domino analogy (or metaphor) provided, no doubt, a vivid illustration, and effectively portrayed the worry of many anticommunists. But did it really shed any light on the likely pattern of political and military developments in the region? The history of events there during the 1970s and 1980s did not bear out the domino analogy.

Post Hoc Ergo Propter Hoc

One of the most tempting errors in reasoning is to ground a claim about causation on an observed temporal sequence; that is, to argue "after this therefore because of this" (which is what **post hoc ergo propter hoc** means in Latin). About thirty years ago, when the medical community first announced that smoking tobacco caused lung cancer, spokesmen for the tobacco industry replied that the doctors were guilty of this fallacy.

These industry spokesmen argued the medical researchers had merely noticed that in some people, lung cancer developed *after* considerable smoking, indeed, years after, but that this was not at all the same as a finding to the effect that smoking *caused* lung cancer. True enough. The claim that A causes B is not the same as the claim that B comes after A. After all, it was possible that smokers as a group had some other common trait and that this factor was the true cause of their cancer.

As the long controversy over the truth about the causation of lung cancer shows, to avoid the appearance of fallacious *post hoc* reasoning one needs to find some way to link the observed phenomena (the correlation of smoking and the onset of lung cancer). This step requires some further theory, and preferably some experimental evidence for the exact sequence, in full detail, of how ingestion of tobacco smoke is a crucial factor—and not merely an accidental or happenstance prior event—in the subsequent development of the cancer.

Protecting the Hypothesis

In Chapter 2, we contrast *reasoning* and *rationalization* (or the finding of bad reasons for what one intends to believe anyway). Rationalization can take subtle forms, as the following example indicates. Suppose you're standing with a friend on the shore or on a pier, and you watch as a ship heads out to sea. As it reaches the horizon, it slowly disappears—first the hull, then the upper decks, and finally the tip of the mast. Because the ship (you both assume) isn't sinking, it occurs to you that you have in this sequence of observations convincing evidence that the earth is curved. Nonsense, says your companion. Light waves sag, or bend down, over distances of a few miles, and so a flat surface (such as the ocean) can intercept them. Hence the ship, which appears to be going "over" the horizon, really isn't—it's just moving steadily farther and farther away in a straight line. Your friend, you discover to your amazement, is a card-carrying member of the Flat Earth Society (yes, there really is such an organization). Now most of us would regard the idea that light rays bend down in the manner required by the Flat Earther's argument as a rationalization whose sole purpose is to protect the flat-earth doctrine against counterevidence. We would be convinced it was a rationalization, and not a very good one at that, if the Flat Earther held to it despite a patient and thorough explanation from a physicist that showed modern optical theory to be quite incompatible with the view that light waves sag.

This example illustrates two important points about the *backing* of arguments. First, it is always possible to protect a hypothesis by abandoning adjacent or connected hypotheses; this is the tactic our Flat Earth friend has used. This maneuver is possible, however, only because—and this is the second point—whenever we test a hypothesis, we do so in conjunction with several other hypotheses. So the evidence for the hypothesis we think we are confirming is impossible to separate entirely from the adequacy of the connected hypotheses. As long as we have no reason to doubt that light rays travel in straight lines (at least over distances of a few miles), our Flat Earth friend's argument is unconvincing. But once that hypothesis is itself put in doubt, the idea that looked at first to be a pathetic rationalization takes on an even more troublesome character.

There are, then, not one but two fallacies exposed by this example. The first and perhaps graver is in rigging your hypothesis so that no matter what observations are brought against it, you will count nothing as falsifying it. The second and subtler is in thinking that as you test one hypothesis, everything else in your background beliefs is left safely to one side, immaculate and uninvolved. On the contrary, our beliefs form a corporate structure, intertwined and connected to each other with great complexity, and no one of them can ever be singled out for unique and isolated application, confirmation, or disconfirmation, to the world around us.

A HUMORIST'S VIEW

Max Shulman

Love Is a Fallacy

Cool was I and logical. Keen, calculating, perspicacious, acute, and astute—I was all of these. My brain was as powerful as a dynamo, as precise as a chemist's scales, as penetrating as a scalpel. And—think of it!—I was only eighteen.

Max Shulman (1919–1988) began his career as a writer when he was a journalism student at the University of Minnesota. Later he wrote humorous novels, stories, and plays. One of his novels, Barefoot Boy with Cheek *(1943), was made into a musical and another,* Rally Round the Flag, Boys! *(1957), was made into a film starring Paul Newman and Joanne Woodward.* The Tender Trap *(1954), a play which he wrote with Robert Paul Smith, still retains its popularity with theater groups.*

"Love Is a Fallacy" was first published in 1951, when demeaning stereotypes about women and minorities were widely accepted in the marketplace as well as the home. Thus, jokes about domineering mothers-in-law or about dumb blondes routinely met with no objection. After you have finished reading "Love Is a Fallacy," you may want to write an argumentative essay of 500–750 words on one of the following topics: (1) the story, rightly understood, is not anti-woman; (2) if the story is anti-woman, it is equally anti-man; (3) the story is anti-woman but nevertheless belongs in this book; or (4) the story is anti-woman and does not belong in the book.

It is not often that one so young has such a giant intellect. Take, for example, Petey Bellows, my roommate at the university. Same age, same background, but dumb as an ox. A nice enough fellow, you understand, but nothing upstairs. Emotional type. Unstable. Impressionable. Worst of all, a faddist. Fads, I submit, are the very negation of reason. To be swept up in every new craze that comes along, to surrender yourself to idiocy just because everybody else is doing it—this, to me, is the acme of mindlessness. Not, however, to Petey.

One afternoon I found Petey lying on his bed with an expression of such distress on his face that I immediately diagnosed appendicitis. "Don't move," I said. "Don't take a laxative. I'll get a doctor."

"Raccoon," he mumbled thickly.

"Raccoon?" I said, pausing in my flight.

"I want a raccoon coat," he wailed.

I perceived that his trouble was not physical, but mental. "Why do you want a raccoon coat?"

"I should have known it," he cried, pounding his temples. "I should have known they'd come back when the Charleston came back. Like a fool I spent all my money for textbooks, and now I can't get a raccoon coat."

"Can you mean," I said incredulously, "that people are actually wearing raccoon coats again?"

"All the Big Men on Campus are wearing them. Where've you been?"

"In the library," I said, naming a place not frequented by Big Men on Campus.

He leaped from the bed and paced the room. "I've got to have a raccoon coat," he said passionately. "I've got to!"

"Petey, why? Look at it rationally. Raccoon coats are unsanitary. They shed. They smell bad. They weigh too much. They're unsightly. They——"

"You don't understand," he interrupted impatiently. "It's the thing to do. Don't you want to be in the swim?"

"No," I said truthfully.

"Well, I do," he declared. "I'd give anything for a raccoon coat. Anything!"

My brain, that precision instrument, slipped into high gear. "Anything?" I asked, looking at him narrowly.

"Anything," he affirmed in ringing tones.

I stroked my chin thoughtfully. It so happened that I knew where to get my hands on a raccoon coat. My father had had one in his undergraduate days; it lay now in a trunk in the attic back home. It also happened that Petey had something I wanted. He didn't *have* it exactly, but at least he had first rights on it. I refer to his girl, Polly Espy.

I had long coveted Polly Espy. Let me emphasize that my desire for this young woman was not emotional in nature. She was, to be sure, a girl who excited the emotions, but I was not one to let my heart rule my head. I wanted Polly for a shrewdly calculated, entirely cerebral reason.

I was a freshman in law school. In a few years I would be out in practice. I was well aware of the importance of the right kind of wife in furthering a lawyer's career. The successful lawyers I had observed were, almost without exception, married to beautiful, gracious, intelligent women. With one omission, Polly fitted these specifications perfectly.

Beautiful she was. She was not yet of pin-up proportions, but I felt sure that time would supply the lack. She already had the makings.

Gracious she was. By gracious I mean full of graces. She had an erectness of carriage, an ease of bearing, a poise that clearly indicated the best of breeding. At table her manners were exquisite. I had seen her at the Kozy Kampus Korner eating the specialty of the house—a sandwich that contained scraps of pot roast, gravy, chopped nuts, and a dipper of sauerkraut—without even getting her fingers moist.

Intelligent she was not. In fact, she veered in the opposite direction. But I believed that under my guidance she would smarten up. At any rate, it was worth a try. It is, after all, easier to make a beautiful dumb girl smart than to make an ugly smart girl beautiful.

"Petey," I said, "are you in love with Polly Espy?"

"I think she's a keen kid," he replied, "but I don't know if you'd call it love. Why?"

"Do you," I asked, "have any kind of formal arrangement with her? I mean are you going steady or anything like that?"

"No. We see each other quite a bit, but we both have other dates. Why?"

"Is there," I asked, "any other man for whom she has a particular fondness?"

"Not that I know of. Why?"

I nodded with satisfaction. "In other words, if you were out of the picture, the field would be open. Is that right?"

"I guess so. What are you getting at?"

"Nothing, nothing," I said innocently, and took my suitcase out of the closet.

"Where you going?" asked Petey.

"Home for the week end." I threw a few things into the bag.

"Listen," he said, clutching my arm eagerly, "while you're home, you couldn't get some money from your old man, could you, and lend it to me so I can buy a raccoon coat?"

"I may do better than that," I said with a mysterious wink and closed my bag and left.

"Look," I said to Petey when I got back Monday morning. I threw open the suitcase and revealed the huge, hairy, gamy object that my father had worn in his Stutz Bearcat in 1925.

"Holy Toledo!" said Petey reverently. He plunged his hands into the raccoon coat and then his face. "Holy Toledo!" he repeated fifteen or twenty times.

"Would you like it?" I asked.

"Oh yes!" he cried, clutching the greasy pelt to him. Then a canny look came into his eyes. "What do you want for it?"

"Your girl," I said, mincing no words.

"Polly?" he said in a horrified whisper. "You want Polly?"

"That's right."

He flung the coat from him. "Never," he said stoutly.

I shrugged. "Okay. If you don't want to be in the swim, I guess it's your business."

I sat down in a chair and pretended to read a book, but out of the corner of my eye I kept watching Petey. He was a torn man. First he looked at the coat with the expression of a waif at a bakery window. Then he turned away and set his jaw resolutely. Then he looked back at the coat, with even more longing in his face. Then he turned away, but with not so much resolution this time. Back and forth his head swiveled, desire waxing, resolution waning. Finally he didn't turn away at all; he just stood and stared with mad lust at the coat.

"It isn't as though I was in love with Polly," he said thickly. "Or going steady or anything like that."

"That's right," I murmured.

"What's Polly to me, or me to Polly?"

"Not a thing," said I.

"It's just been a casual kick—just a few laughs, that's all."

"Try on the coat," said I.

He complied. The coat bunched high over his ears and dropped all the way down to his shoe tops. He looked like a mound of dead raccoons. "Fits fine," he said happily.

I rose from my chair. "Is it a deal?" I asked, extending my hand.

He swallowed. "It's a deal," he said and shook my hand.

I had my first date with Polly the following evening. This was in the nature of a survey; I wanted to find out just how much work I had to do to get her mind up to the standard I required. I took her first to dinner. "Gee, that was a delish dinner," she said as we left the restaurant. Then I took her to a movie. "Gee, that was a marvy movie," she said as we left the theater. And then I took her home. "Gee, I had a sensaysh time," she said as she bade me good night.

I went back to my room with a heavy heart. I had gravely underestimated the size of my task. This girl's lack of information was terrifying. Nor would it be enough merely to supply her with information. First she had to be taught to *think*. This loomed as a project of no small dimensions, and at first I was tempted to give her back to Petey. But then I got to thinking about her abundant physical charms and about the way she entered a room and the way she handled a knife and fork, and I decided to make an effort.

I went about it, as in all things, systematically. I gave her a course in logic. It happened that I, as a law student, was taking a course in logic myself, so I had all the facts at my fingertips. "Polly," I said to her when I picked her up on our next date, "tonight we are going over to the Knoll and talk."

"Oo, terrif," she replied. One thing I will say for this girl: you would go far to find another so agreeable.

We went to the Knoll, the campus trysting place, and we sat down under an old oak, and she looked at me expectantly. "What are we going to talk about?" she asked.

"Logic."

She thought this over for a minute and decided she liked it. "Magnif," she said.

"Logic," I said, clearing my throat, "is the science of thinking. Before we can think correctly, we must first learn to recognize the common fallacies of logic. These we will take up tonight."

"Wow-dow!" she cried, clapping her hands delightedly.

I winced, but went bravely on. "First let us examine the fallacy called Dicto Simpliciter."

"By all means," she urged, batting her lashes eagerly.

"Dicto Simpliciter means an argument based on an unqualified generalization. For example: Exercise is good. Therefore everybody should exercise."

"I agree," said Polly earnestly. "I mean exercise is wonderful. I mean it builds the body and everything."

"Polly," I said gently, "the argument is a fallacy. *Exercise is good* is an unqualified generalization. For instance, if you have heart disease, exercise is bad, not good. Many people are ordered by their doctors *not* to exercise. You must *qualify* the generalization. You must say exercise is *usually* good, or exercise is good *for most people.* Otherwise you have committed a Dicto Simpliciter. Do you see?"

"No," she confessed. "But this is marvy. Do more! Do more!"

"It will be better if you stop tugging at my sleeve," I told her, and when she desisted, I continued. "Next we take up a fallacy called Hasty Generalization. Listen carefully: You can't speak French. I can't speak French. Petey Bellows can't speak French. I must therefore conclude that nobody at the University of Minnesota can speak French."

"Really?" said Polly, amazed. *"Nobody?"*

I hid my exasperation. "Polly, it's a fallacy. The generalization is reached too hastily. There are too few instances to support such a conclusion."

"Know any more fallacies?" she asked breathlessly. "This is more fun than dancing even."

I fought off a wave of despair. I was getting nowhere with this girl, absolutely nowhere. Still, I am nothing if not persistent. I continued. "Next comes Post Hoc. Listen to this: Let's not take Bill on our picnic. Every time we take him out with us, it rains."

"I know somebody just like that," she exclaimed. "A girl back home— Eula Becker, her name is. It never fails. Every single time we take her on a picnic——"

"Polly," I said sharply, "it's a fallacy. Eula Becker doesn't *cause* the rain. She has no connection with the rain. You are guilty of Post Hoc if you blame Eula Becker."

"I'll never do it again," she promised contritely. "Are you mad at me?"

I sighed. "No, Polly, I'm not mad."

"Then tell me some more fallacies."

"All right. Let's try Contradictory Premises."

"Yes, let's," she chirped, blinking her eyes happily.

I frowned, but plunged ahead. "Here's an example of Contradictory Premises: If God can do anything, can He make a stone so heavy that He won't be able to lift it?"

"Of course," she replied promptly.

"But if He can do anything, He can lift the stone," I pointed out.

"Yeah," she said thoughtfully. "Well, then I guess He can't make the stone."

"But He can do anything," I reminded her.

She scratched her pretty, empty head. "I'm all confused," she admitted.

"Of course you are. Because when the premises of an argument contradict each other, there can be no argument. If there is an irresistible force, there can be no immovable object. If there is an immovable object, there can be no irresistible force. Get it?"

"Tell me some more of this keen stuff," she said eagerly.

I consulted my watch. "I think we'd better call it a night. I'll take you home now, and you go over all the things you've learned. We'll have another session tomorrow night."

I deposited her at the girl's dormitory, where she assured me that she had had a perfectly terrif evening, and I went glumly home to my room. Petey lay snoring in his bed, the raccoon coat huddled like a great hairy beast at his feet. For a moment I considered waking him and telling him that he could have his girl back. It seemed clear that my project was doomed to failure. The girl simply had a logic-proof head.

But then I reconsidered. I had wasted one evening; I might as well waste another. Who knew? Maybe somewhere in the extinct crater of her mind a few embers still smoldered. Maybe somehow I could fan them into flame. Admittedly it was not a prospect fraught with hope, but I decided to give it one more try.

Seated under the oak the next evening I said, "Our first fallacy tonight is called Ad Misericordiam."

She quivered with delight.

"Listen closely," I said. "A man applies for a job. When the boss asks him what his qualifications are, he replies that he has a wife and six children at home, the wife is a helpless cripple, the children have nothing to eat, no clothes to wear, no shoes on their feet, there are no beds in the house, no coal in the cellar, and winter is coming."

A tear rolled down each of Polly's pink cheeks. "Oh, this is awful, awful," she sobbed.

"Yes, it's awful," I agreed, "but it's no argument. The man never answered the boss's question about his qualifications. Instead he appealed to the boss's sympathy. He committed the fallacy of Ad Misericordiam. Do you understand?"

"Have you got a handkerchief?" she blubbered.

I handed her a handkerchief and tried to keep from screaming while she wiped her eyes. "Next," I said in a carefully controlled tone, "we will discuss False Analogy. Here is an example: Students should be allowed to look at their textbooks during examinations. After all, surgeons have X rays to guide them during an operation, lawyers have briefs to guide them during a trial, carpenters have blueprints to guide them when they are building a house. Why, then, shouldn't students be allowed to look at their textbooks during an examination?"

"There now," she said enthusiastically, "is the most marvy idea I've heard in years."

"Polly," I said testily, "the argument is all wrong. Doctors, lawyers, and carpenters aren't taking a test to see how much they have learned, but students are. The situations are altogether different, and you can't make an analogy between them."

"I still think it's a good idea," said Polly.

"Nuts," I muttered. Doggedly I pressed on. "Next we'll try Hypothesis Contrary to Fact."

"Sounds yummy," was Polly's reaction.

"Listen: If Madame Curie had not happened to leave a photographic plate in a drawer with a chunk of pitchblende, the world today would not know about radium."

"True, true," said Polly, nodding her head. "Did you see the movie? Oh, it just knocked me out. That Walter Pidgeon is so dreamy. I mean he fractures me."

"If you can forget Mr. Pidgeon for a moment," I said coldly, "I would like to point out that the statement is a fallacy. Maybe Madame Curie would have discovered radium at some later date. Maybe somebody else would have discovered it. Maybe any number of things would have happened. You can't start with a hypothesis that is not true and then draw any supportable conclusions from it."

"They ought to put Walter Pidgeon in more pictures," said Polly. "I hardly ever see him any more."

One more chance, I decided. But just one more. There is a limit to what flesh and blood can bear. "The next fallacy is called Poisoning the Well."

"How cute!" she gurgled.

"Two men are having a debate. The first one gets up and says, 'My opponent is a notorious liar. You can't believe a word that he is going to say.' . . . Now, Polly, think. Think hard. What's wrong?"

I watched her closely as she knit her creamy brow in concentration. Suddenly a glimmer of intelligence—the first I had seen—came into her eyes. "It's not fair," she said with indignation. "It's not a bit fair. What chance has the second man got if the first man calls him a liar before he even begins talking?"

"Right!" I cried exultantly. "One hundred percent right. It's not fair. The first man has *poisoned the well* before anybody could drink from it. He has hamstrung his opponent before he could even start. . . . Polly, I'm proud of you."

"Pshaw," she murmured, blushing with pleasure.

"You see, my dear, these things aren't so hard. All you have to do is concentrate. Think—examine—evaluate. Come now, let's review everything we have learned."

"Fire away," she said with an airy wave of her hand.

Heartened by the knowledge that Polly was not altogether a cretin, I began a long, patient review of all I had told her. Over and over and over again I cited instances, pointed out flaws, kept hammering away without letup. It was like digging a tunnel. At first everything was work, sweat, and darkness. I had no idea when I would reach the light, or even *if* I would. But I persisted. I pounded and clawed and scraped, and finally I was rewarded. I saw a chink of light. And then the chink got bigger and the sun came pouring in and all was bright.

Five grueling nights this took, but it was worth it. I had made a logician out of Polly; I had taught her to think. My job was done. She was worthy of me at last. She was a fit wife for me, a proper hostess for my many mansions, a suitable mother for my well-heeled children.

It must not be thought that I was without love for this girl. Quite the contrary. Just as Pygmalion loved the perfect woman he had fashioned, so I loved mine. I decided to acquaint her with my feelings at our very next meeting. The time had come to change our relationship from academic to romantic.

"Polly," I said when next we sat beneath our oak, "tonight we will not discuss fallacies."

"Aw, gee," she said, disappointed.

"My dear," I said, favoring her with a smile, "we have now spent five evenings together. We have gotten along splendidly. It is clear that we are well matched."

"Hasty Generalization," said Polly brightly.

"I beg your pardon," said I.

"Hasty Generalization," she repeated. "How can you say that we are well matched on the basis of only five dates?"

I chuckled with amusement. The dear child had learned her lessons well. "My dear," I said, patting her hand in a tolerant manner, "five dates is plenty. After all, you don't have to eat a whole cake to know that it's good."

"False Analogy," said Polly promptly. "I'm not a cake. I'm a girl."

I chuckled with somewhat less amusement. The dear child had learned her lesson perhaps too well. I decided to change tactics. Obviously the best approach was a simple, strong, direct declaration of love. I paused for a moment while my massive brain chose the proper words. Then I began:

"Polly, I love you. You are the whole world to me, and the moon and the stars and the constellations of outer space. Please, my darling, say that you will go steady with me, for if you will not, life will be meaningless. I will languish. I will refuse my meals. I will wander the face of the earth, a shambling, hollow-eyed hulk."

There, I thought, folding my arms, that ought to do it.

"Ad Misericordiam," said Polly.

I ground my teeth. I was not Pygmalion; I was Frankenstein, and my monster had me by the throat. Frantically I fought back the tide of panic surging through me. At all costs I had to keep cool.

"Well, Polly," I said, forcing a smile, "you certainly have learned your fallacies."

"You're darn right," she said with a vigorous nod.

"And who taught them to you, Polly?"

"You did."

"That's right. So you do owe me something, don't you, my dear? If I hadn't come along you never would have learned about fallacies."

"Hypothesis Contrary to Fact," she said instantly.

I dashed perspiration from my brow. "Polly," I croaked, "you mustn't take all these things so literally. I mean this is just classroom stuff. You know that the things you learn in school don't have anything to do with life."

"Dicto Simpliciter," she said, wagging her finger at me playfully.

That did it. I leaped to my feet, bellowing like a bull. "Will you or will you not go steady with me?"

"I will not," she replied.

"Why not?" I demanded.

"Because this afternoon I promised Petey Bellows that I would go steady with him."

I reeled back, overcome with the infamy of it. After he promised, after he made a deal, after he shook my hand! "That rat!" I shrieked, kicking up great chunks of turf. "You can't go with him, Polly. He's a liar. He's a cheat. He's a rat."

"Poisoning the Well," said Polly, "and stop shouting. I think shouting must be a fallacy too."

With an immense effort of will, I modulated my voice. "All right," I said. "You're a logician. Let's look at this thing logically. How could you choose Petey Bellows over me? Look at me—a brilliant student, a tremendous intellectual, a man with an assured future. Look at Petey—a knothead, a jitterbug, a guy who'll never know where his next meal is coming from. Can you give me one logical reason why you should go steady with Petey Bellows?"

"I certainly can," declared Polly. "He's got a raccoon coat."

A PSYCHOLOGIST'S VIEW

Carl R. Rogers

Communication: Its Blocking and Its Facilitation

It may seem curious that a person whose whole professional effort is devoted to psychotherapy should be interested in problems of communication. What relationship is there between providing therapeutic help to

---

Carl R. Rogers (1902–1987), perhaps best known for his book entitled On Becoming a Person, *was a psychotherapist, not a teacher of writing. This short essay by Rogers has, however, exerted much influence on instructors who teach argument. First, some background.*

On the surface, many arguments seem to show A arguing with B, presumably seeking to change B's mind; but A's argument is really directed not to B but to C. This attempt to persuade a nonparticipant is evident in the courtroom, where neither the prosecutor (A) nor the defense lawyer (B) is really trying to convince the opponent. Rather, both are trying to convince a third party, the jury (C). Prosecutors do not care whether they convince defense lawyers; they don't even mind infuriating defense lawyers, because their only real goal is to convince the jury. Similarly, the writer of a letter to a newspaper, taking issue with an editorial, does not expect to change the paper's policy. Rather, the writer hopes to convince a third party, the reader of the newspaper.

But suppose A really does want to bring B around to A's point of view. Suppose Mary really wants to persuade the teacher to allow her little lamb to stay in the

individuals with emotional maladjustments and the concern of this conference with obstacles to communication? Actually the relationship is very close indeed. The whole task of psychotherapy is the task of dealing with a failure in communication. The emotionally maladjusted person, the "neurotic," is in difficulty first because communication within himself has broken down, and second because as a result of this his communication with others has been damaged. If this sounds somewhat strange, then let me put it in other terms. In the "neurotic" individual, parts of himself which have been termed unconscious, or repressed, or denied to aware-

---

classroom. Rogers points out that when we engage in an argument, if we feel our integrity or our identity is threatened, we will stiffen our position. (The teacher may feel that his or her dignity is compromised by the presence of the lamb, and will scarcely attend to Mary's argument.) The sense of threat may be so great that we are unable to consider the alternative views being offered, and we therefore remain unpersuaded. Threatened, we may defend ourselves rather than our argument, and little communication takes place. Of course a third party might say that we or our opponent presented the more convincing case, but we, and perhaps the opponent, have scarcely listened to each other, and so the two of us remain apart.

Rogers suggests, therefore, that a writer who wishes to communicate with someone (as opposed to convincing a third party) needs to reduce the threat. In a sense, the participants in the argument need to become partners rather than adversaries. Rogers writes, "Mutual communication tends to be pointed toward solving a problem rather than toward attacking a person or group." Thus, an essay on whether schools should test students for use of drugs, need not—and probably should not—see the issue as black or white, either/or. Such an essay might indicate that testing is undesirable because it may have bad effects, but in some circumstances it may be acceptable. This qualification does not mean that one must compromise. Thus, the essayist might argue that the potential danger to liberty is so great that no circumstances justify testing students for drugs. But even such an essayist should recognize the merit (however limited) of the opposition, and should grant that the position being advanced itself entails great difficulties and dangers.

A writer who wishes to reduce the psychological threat to the opposition, and thus facilitate the partnership in the study of some issue, can do several things: One can show sympathetic understanding of the opposing argument; one can recognize what is valid in it; and one can recognize and demonstrate that those who take the other side are nonetheless persons of goodwill.

Thus a writer who takes Rogers seriously will, usually, in the first part of an argumentative essay
1. *State the problem,*
2. *Give the opponent's position, and*
3. *grant whatever validity the writer finds in that position—for instance, will recognize the circumstances in which the position would indeed be acceptable. Next, the writer will, if possible,*
4. *Attempt to show how the opposing position will be improved if the writer's own position is accepted.*

Sometimes, of course, the differing positions may be so far apart that no reconciliation can be proposed, in which case the writer will probably seek to show how the problem can best be solved by adopting the writer's own position. We have discussed these matters in Chapter 3, but not from the point of view of a psychotherapist, and so we reprint Rogers's essay here.

ness, become blocked off so that they no longer communicate themselves to the conscious or managing part of himself. As long as this is true, there are distortions in the way he communicates himself to others, and so he suffers both within himself, and in his interpersonal relations. The task of psychotherapy is to help the person achieve, through a special relationship with a therapist, good communication within himself. Once this is achieved he can communicate more freely and more effectively with others. We may say then that psychotherapy is good communication, within and between men. We may also turn that statement around and it will still be true. Good communication, free communication, within or between men, is always therapeutic.

It is, then, from a background of experience with communication in counseling and psychotherapy that I want to present here two ideas. I wish to state what I believe is one of the major factors in blocking or impeding communication, and then I wish to present what in our experience has proven to be a very important way of improving or facilitating communication.

I would like to propose, as an hypothesis for consideration, that the major barrier to mutual interpersonal communication is our very natural tendency to judge, to evaluate, to approve or disapprove, the statement of the other person, or the other group. Let me illustrate my meaning with some very simple examples. As you leave the meeting tonight, one of the statements you are likely to hear is, "I didn't like that man's talk." Now what do you respond? Almost invariably your reply will be either approval or disapproval of the attitude expressed. Either you respond, "I didn't either. I thought it was terrible," or else you tend to reply, "Oh, I thought it was really good." In other words, your primary reaction is to evaluate what has just been said to you, to evaluate it from *your* point of view, your own frame of reference.

Or take another example. Suppose I say with some feeling, "I think the Republicans are behaving in ways that show a lot of good sound sense these days," what is the response that arises in your mind as you listen? The overwhelming likelihood is that it will be evaluative. You will find yourself agreeing, or disagreeing, or making some judgment about me such as "He must be a conservative," or "He seems solid in his thinking." Or let us take an illustration from the international scene. Russia says vehemently, "The treaty with Japan is a war plot on the part of the United States." We rise as one person to say "That's a lie!"

This last illustration brings in another element connected with my hypothesis. Although the tendency to make evaluations is common in almost all interchange of language, it is very much heightened in those situations where feelings and emotions are deeply involved. So the stronger our feelings, the more likely it is that there will be no mutual element in the communication. There will be just two ideas, two feelings, two judgments, missing each other in psychological space. I'm sure you recognize this from your own experience. When you have not been emotionally involved yourself, and have listened to a heated discussion, you often go away thinking, "Well, they actually weren't talking about the same thing." And they were not. Each was making a judgment, an evaluation, from his own frame of reference. There was really nothing which could be called communication in any genuine sense. This tendency to react to any emotionally meaningful statement by forming an evaluation of it from our own point of view, is, I repeat, the major barrier to interpersonal communication.

But is there any way of solving this problem, of avoiding this barrier? I feel that we are making exciting progress toward this goal and I would like to present it as simply as I can. Real communication occurs, and this evaluative tendency is avoided, when we listen with understanding. What does that mean? It means *to see the expressed idea and attitude from the other person's point of view, to sense how it feels to him, to achieve his frame of reference in regard to the thing he is talking about.*

Stated so briefly, this may sound absurdly simple, but it is not. It is an approach which we have found extremely potent in the field of psychotherapy. It is the most effective agent we know for altering the basic personality structure of an individual, and improving his relationships and his communications with others. If I can listen to what he can tell me, if I can understand how it seems to him, if I can see its personal meaning for him, if I can sense the emotional flavor which it has for him, then I will be releasing potent forces of change in him. If I can really understand how he hates his father, or hates the university, or hates communists—if I can catch the flavor of his fear of insanity, or his fear of atom bombs, or of Russia—it will be of the greatest help to him in altering those very hatreds and fears, and in establishing realistic and harmonious relationships with the very people and situations toward which he has felt hatred and fear. We know from our research that such empathic understanding— understanding *with* a person, not *about* him—is such an effective approach that it can bring about major changes in personality.

Some of you may be feeling that you listen well to people, and that you have never seen such results. The chances are very great indeed that your listening has not been of the type I have described. Fortunately I can suggest a little laboratory experiment which you can try to test the quality of your understanding. The next time you get into an argument with your wife, or your friend, or with a small group of friends, just stop the discussion for a moment and for an experiment, institute this rule. "Each person can speak up for himself only *after* he has first restated the ideas and feelings of the previous speaker accurately, and to that speaker's satisfaction." You see what this would mean. It would simply mean that before presenting your own point of view, it would be necessary for you to really achieve the other speaker's frame of reference—to understand his thoughts and feelings so well that you could summarize them for him.

Sounds simple, doesn't it? But if you try it you will discover it one of the most difficult things you have ever tried to do. However, once you have been able to see the other's point of view, your own comments will have to be drastically revised. You will also find the emotion going out of the discussion, the differences being reduced, and those differences which remain being of a rational and understandable sort.

Can you imagine what this kind of an approach would mean if it were projected into larger areas? What would happen to a labor-management dispute if it was conducted in such a way that labor, without necessarily agreeing, could accurately state management's point of view in a way that management could accept; and management, without approving labor's stand, could state labor's case in a way that labor agreed was accurate? It would mean that real communication was established, and one could practically guarantee that some reasonable solution would be reached.

If then this way of approach is an effective avenue to good communication and good relationships, as I am quite sure you will agree if you try the experiment I have mentioned, why is it not more widely tried and used? I will try to list the difficulties which keep it from being utilized.

In the first place it takes courage, a quality which is not too widespread. I am indebted to Dr. S. I. Hayakawa, the semanticist, for pointing out that to carry on psychotherapy in this fashion is to take a very real risk, and that courage is required. If you really understand another person in this way, if you are willing to enter his private world and see the way life appears to him, without any attempt to make evaluative judgments, you run the risk of being changed yourself. You might see it his way, you might find yourself influenced in your attitudes or your personality. This risk of being changed is one of the most frightening prospects most of us can face. If I enter, as fully as I am able, into the private world of a neurotic or psychotic individual, isn't there a risk that I might become lost in that world? Most of us are afraid to take that risk. Or if we had a Russian communist speaker here tonight, or Senator Joe McCarthy, how many of us would dare to try to see the world from each of these points of view? The great majority of us could not *listen*; we would find ourselves compelled to *evaluate*, because listening would seem too dangerous. So the first requirement is courage, and we do not always have it.

But there is a second obstacle. It is just when emotions are strongest that it is most difficult to achieve the frame of reference of the other person or group. Yet it is the time the attitude is most needed, if communication is to be established. We have not found this to be an insuperable obstacle in our experience in psychotherapy. A third party, who is able to lay aside his own feelings and evaluations, can assist greatly by listening with understanding to each person or group and clarifying the views and attitudes each holds. We have found this very effective in small groups in which contradictory or antagonistic attitudes exist. When the parties to a dispute realize that they are being understood, that someone sees how the situation seems to them, the statements grow less exaggerated and less defensive, and it is no longer necessary to maintain the attitude, "I am 100 percent right and you are 100 percent wrong." The influence of such an understanding catalyst in the group permits the members to come closer and closer to the objective truth involved in the relationship. In this way mutual communication is established and some type of agreement becomes much more possible. So we may say that though heightened emotions make it much more difficult to understand *with* an opponent, our experience makes it clear that a neutral, understanding, catalyst type of leader or therapist can overcome this obstacle in a small group.

This last phrase, however, suggests another obstacle to utilizing the approach I have described. Thus far all our experience has been with small face-to-face groups—groups exhibiting industrial tensions, religious tensions, racial tensions, and therapy groups in which many personal tensions are present. In these small groups our experience, confirmed by a limited amount of research, shows that this basic approach leads to improved communication, to greater acceptance of others and by others, and to attitudes which are more positive and more problem-solving in nature. There is a decrease in defensiveness, in exaggerated statements, in evaluative and critical behavior. But these findings are from small groups. What about trying to achieve understanding between larger groups that are geographically remote? Or between face-to-face groups who are not speaking for themselves, but simply as representatives of others, like the delegates at Kaesong?[1] Frankly we do not know the answers to these questions. I believe the situation might be put this way. As social scientists we have a tentative test-tube solution of the problem of breakdown in communication. But to confirm the validity of this test-tube solution, and to adapt it to the enormous problems of communication breakdown between classes, groups, and nations, would involve additional funds, much more research, and creative thinking of a high order.

Even with our present limited knowledge we can see some steps which might be taken, even in large groups, to increase the amount of listening *with*, and to decrease the amount of evaluation *about*. To be imaginative for a moment, let us suppose that a therapeutically oriented international group went to the Russian leaders and said, "We want to achieve a genuine understanding of your views and even more important, of your attitudes and feelings, toward the United States. We will summarize and resummarize these views and feelings if necessary, until you agree that our description represents the situation as it seems to you." Then suppose they did the same thing with the leaders in our own country. If they then gave the widest possible distribution to these two views, with the feelings clearly described but not expressed in name-calling, might not the effect be very

[1]**Kaesong** The main contact point between North and South Korea, 1945–1951. [Editors' note]

great? It would not guarantee the type of understanding I have been describing, but it would make it much more possible. We can understand the feelings of a person who hates us much more readily when his attitudes are accurately described to us by a neutral third party, than we can when he is shaking his fist at us.

But even to describe such a first step is to suggest another obstacle to this approach of understanding. Our civilization does not yet have enough faith in the social sciences to utilize their findings. The opposite is true of the physical sciences. During the war[2] when a test-tube solution was found to the problem of synthetic rubber, millions of dollars and an army of talent was turned loose on the problem of using that finding. If synthetic rubber could be made in milligrams, it could and would be made in the thousands of tons. And it was. But in the social science realm, if a way is found of facilitating communication and mutual understanding in small groups, there is no guarantee that the finding will be utilized. It may be a generation or more before the money and the brains will be turned loose to exploit that finding.

In closing, I would like to summarize this small-scale solution to the problem of barriers in communication, and to point out certain of its characteristics.

I have said that our research and experience to date would make it appear that breakdowns in communication, and the evaluative tendency which is the major barrier to communication, can be avoided. The solution is provided by creating a situation in which each of the different parties come to understand the other from the *other's* point of view. This has been achieved, in practice, even when feelings run high, by the influence of a person who is willing to understand each point of view empathically, and who thus acts as a catalyst to precipitate further understanding.

This procedure has important characteristics. It can be initiated by one party, without waiting for the other to be ready. It can even be initiated by a neutral third person, providing he can gain a minimum of cooperation from one of the parties.

This procedure can deal with the insincerities, the defensive exaggerations, the lies, the "false fronts" which characterize almost every failure in communication. These defensive distortions drop away with astonishing speed as people find that the only intent is to understand, not judge.

This approach leads steadily and rapidly toward the discovery of the truth, toward a realistic appraisal of the objective barriers to communication. The dropping of some defensiveness by one party leads to further dropping of defensiveness by the other party, and truth is thus approached.

This procedure gradually achieves mutual communication. Mutual communication tends to be pointed toward solving a problem rather than

---

[2]**the war** World War II. [Editors' note]

toward attacking a person or group. It leads to a situation in which I see how the problem appears to you, as well as to me, and you see how it appears to me, as well as to you. Thus accurately and realistically defined, the problem is almost certain to yield to intelligent attack, or if it is in part insoluble, it will be comfortably accepted as such.

This then appears to be a test-tube solution to the breakdown of communication as it occurs in small groups. Can we take this small-scale answer, investigate it further, refine it; develop it and apply it to the tragic and well-nigh fatal failures of communication which threaten the very existence of our modern world? It seems to me that this is a possibility and a challenge which we should explore.

George Orwell, "Killing Civilians." Excerpt from *The Collected Essays, Journalism and Letters of George Orwell: As I Please, 1943–1945, III,* edited by Sonia Orwell and Ian Angus. Copyright © 1968 by Sonia Brownell Orwell and reprinted by permission of Harcourt Brace Jovanovich, Inc. and the estate of the late Sonia Brownell Orwell and Secker & Warburg Ltd.

Plato, "The Greater Part of the Stories Current Today We Shall Have to Reject." From *The Republic,* translated by Desmond Lee (Penguin Classics revised edition 1974), copyright © H. D. P. Lee, 1955, 1974, pp. 130–135, 317–325. "Crito" from *The Last Days of Socrates* by Plato, translated by Hugh Tredennick (Penguin Classics revised edition 1969), copyright © Hugh Tredennick, 1954, 1959, 1969, pp. 79–96. Reprinted by permission of Penguin Books Ltd.

Charles B. Rangel, "Legalize Drugs? Not on Your Life." Copyright © 1988 by The New York Times Company. Reprinted by permission.

William Bradford Reynolds, "Equal Opportunity, Not Equal Results." From *The Moral Foundations of Civil Rights* (Rowman & Littlefield, 1986, 39–45) edited by Robert K. Fullenwider and Claudia Mills. Reprinted by permission of Rowman & Littlefield, Savage, Maryland.

Carl R. Rogers, "Communication: Its Blocking and Its Facilitation." Reprinted by permission of Carl R. Rogers.

Jean-Jacques Rousseau, "On the Social Contract." Reprinted from *The Social Contract: Essays by Locke, Hume, and Rousseau* edited by Sir Ernest Barker (1947), by permission of Oxford University Press.

Bertrand Russell, excerpt from *Why I Am Not a Christian* by Bertrand Russell. Copyright © 1957, 1985 by Allen and Unwin. Reprinted by permission of Simon & Schuster, Inc. and Unwin Hyman Ltd.

Arthur Schlesinger, Jr., "Against a One-Term, Six-Year Presidency." *The New York Times,* January 10, 1986. Copyright © 1986 by The New York Times Company. Reprinted by permission.

Stanley S. Scott, "Smokers Get a Raw Deal." *The New York Times,* December 29, 1984. Copyright © 1984 by The New York Times Company. Reprinted by permission.

Henry A. Selib, "The Case against More Laws." *The Boston Globe,* April 3, 1973. Reprinted by permission of Henry A. Selib.

Morris Shamos, "The Lesson Every Child Need Not Learn." Reprinted with permission of the author from *The Sciences,* July/August 1988, pp. 14–20. "Shamos Replies to His Critics," reprinted with permission of the author from *The Sciences,* January/February 1989, pp. 13–14.

Max Shulman, "Love Is a Fallacy." Copyright 1951, © renewed 1979 by Max Shulman. Reprinted by permission of Harold Matson Company, Inc.

Peter Singer, "Animal Liberation." Reprinted from *The New York Review of Books,* April 5, 1973, by permission of the author.

B. F. Skinner, "Education in *Walden Two*." Reprinted with permission of Macmillan Publishing Company from *Walden Two* by B. F. Skinner. Copyright 1948, renewed 1976 by B. F. Skinner.

Thomas B. Steel, Jr., et al., "Letters Responding to Shamos." Reprinted by permission of Thomas B. Steel, Jr., Professor of Computer Science, Hofstra University; Stewart Karp; Maurice O. Burke, Ph.D.; Bruce J. Sobol, M.D., Research Professor of Medicine, New York Medical College; Joyce R. Blueford, Math/Science Nucleus; Mark H. Shapiro; Eugene Krc; and Shane D. Mayor.

Gloria Steinem, "Sisterhood." From *Outrageous Acts and Everyday Rebellions* by Gloria Steinem. Copyright © 1983 by Gloria Steinem. Reprinted by permission of Henry Holt and Company, Inc.

Thomas B. Stoddard, "Gay Marriages: Make Them Legal." Copyright © 1989 by The New York Times Company. Reprinted by permission.

Judy Syfers, "I Want a Wife." Copyright © 1971 by Judy Syfers. Reprinted by permission of the author.

Patricia Taylor, "It's Time to Put Warning Labels on Alcohol." Copyright © 1988 by The New York Times Company. Reprinted by permission.

Judith Jarvis Thomson, "A Defense of Abortion." *Philosophy & Public Affairs* 1, no. 1 (Fall 1971). Copyright © 1971 by Princeton University Press. Reprinted by permission of Princeton University Press.

Lester C. Thurow, "U.S. Drug Policy: Colossal Ignorance." Copyright © 1988 by The New York Times Company. Reprinted by permission.

Caldwell Titcomb, "Star-Spangled Earache: What So Loudly We Wail." Reprinted by permission of *The New Republic,* © 1985, The New Republic, Inc.

Ernest van den Haag, "The Deterrent Effect of the Death Penalty." From *The Death Penalty Pro and Con: A Debate* by Ernest van den Haag and John Conrad (Plenum Press, 1983). Reprinted by permission of Plenum Press and the author.

Jacob J. Vellenga, "Christianity and the Death Penalty." Copyright © 1959 Christianity Today. Used by permission.

Gore Vidal, "Drugs." From *Homage to Daniel Shays: Collected Essays 1952–1972* by Gore Vidal. Copyright © 1972 by Gore Vidal. Reprinted by permission of Random House, Inc.

Michael Walzer, "Hiroshima: An Act of Terrorism." *The New Republic,* September 23, 1981. Reprinted by permission of *The New Republic,* © 1981, The New Republic, Inc.

Ellen Willis, "Putting Women Back into the Abortion Debate." Copyright © 1985 by VV Publishing Corporation. Reprinted by permission of the author and *The Village Voice.*

Virginia Woolf, "Professions for Women." From *The Death of the Moth and Other Essays* by Virginia Woolf, copyright © 1942 by Harcourt Brace Jovanovich, Inc. and renewed 1970 by Marjorie T. Parsons, Executrix. Reprinted by permission of the publisher and The Hogarth Press.

Index of Authors and Titles

Index of Terms